William Petersen

POPULATION

The Macmillan Company / New York

Library of Congress catalog card number: 61–6163

The Macmillan Company, New York
Brett-Macmillan Ltd., Galt, Ontario

Printed in the United States of America

ACKNOWLEDGEMENTS

During the several years that I have worked on this book, I have submitted drafts of chapters for criticism to a number of colleagues and specialists. This was particularly important since some sections of the manuscript presume a greater competence in history, anthropology, and economics than I, as a sociologist and demographer, can pretend to from my own background. Those from whom I requested assistance responded with detailed and often extremely helpful comments While they cannot of course be held responsible for the final product, they did help to improve it considerably. I offer my sincere appreciation to the following, listed in noninvidious alphabetical order:

Reinhard Bendix, Department of Sociology, University of California, Berkeley

William S. Bernard, Co-Director, American Council for Nationalities Service, New York

Otis Dudley Duncan, Department of Sociology, University of Chicago

Ronald Freedman, Department of Sociology, University of Michigan

D. V. Glass, London School of Economics and Political Science

Gregory Grossman, Department of Economics, University of California, Berkeley

Philip M. Hauser, Department of Sociology, University of Chicago

Gordon Hewes, Department of Anthropology, University of Colorado

John T. Krause, Department of History, Ohio State University

David S. Landes, Departments of Economics and History, University of California, Berkeley

Josiah Cox Russell, Department of History, University of New Mexico

Mortimer Spiegelman, Associate Statistician, Metropolitan Life Insurance Company, New York

Neil J. Smelser, Department of Sociology, University of California, Berkeley

P. K. Whelpton, Scripps Foundation for Research in Population Problems, Oxford, Ohio.

I would like to thank especially three fellow demographers—

Robert Gutman, Department of Sociology, Rutgers University
Kurt B. Mayer, Department of Sociology, Brown University
Vincent H. Whitney, then associated with the Population Council, New York.

They were kind enough to read the whole of an earlier draft carefully, sympathetically, and critically, and to give me both guidance and encouragement.

WILLIAM PETERSEN

Berkeley, Calif.

CONTENTS

LIST OF TABLES

LIST OF FIGURES

LIST OF PHOTOGRAPHS

1. POPULATION AS A
FIELD OF STUDY

If the reader of this book was born in the United States or in another country of Western European culture, almost certainly his birth was entered in official statistics. As he moves through life, other major events in it will be similarly recorded: his marriage, the birth of his children, his divorce (should he get one), and, finally, his death. And once every ten years during his life, he will have been included in a general count of the entire population and classified according to the size of his place of residence, his occupation, his marital status, and so on.

These two collections of data, known respectively as vital statistics and the census, denote phenomena that intrude on our everyday life in a variety of ways; but most people are ill equipped to understand their significance. We read in the newspaper that the marriage rate has gone up: what is a marriage rate, and how adequate a measure is it of the formation of new families? The United States is becoming increasingly urban: what is the minimum population of an "urban" settlement, and what difference does living in towns make in the way that people behave? We go to an insurance broker and find that the cost of insuring our life is not the same as it would have been a year before: premiums depend on a "life table," which gives the probability that a person of one or another age will die during the next year. The decision of our church to erect a new building across town from our home was based on an expert's prognosis that the population of that presently rather barren area would grow very fast and would, moreover, include a large proportion of the social class from which our church membership is drawn: how accurate are such projections likely to be?

The first reason, then, for trying to learn about population developments is that this will give us an appreciably better understanding of the

1

world in which we live. Just as a person who spends much of his life putting electric plugs into sockets might do well to know something about electricity, even though he will never become an engineer or even his own do-it-yourself repairman, so an educated person ought also to be aware of the fundamentals of his own culture. One essential part of a liberal education can conveniently be attained by focusing one's attention on what are very aptly termed the vital processes.

Supplementing this most general reason for studying population, a second, more specific one applies to those particularly interested in the analysis of society. Social life is an especially difficult object of scientific investigation. One cannot put a society under a microscope; one cannot take an institution into a laboratory; one cannot photograph a social role. The most important techniques that have made possible the rapid advance in physical and natural sciences, that is to say, are ruled out of sociology. Many of the central issues in methodology relate to the dilemma that this contrast poses. How is it possible to structure social data so that the analyst can try to imitate the procedures of other sciences? Or, in one specific version of this question, how can one quantify social findings? During the past several decades, American social scientists have tried to develop a number of new techniques for measuring the responses to questionnaires. Public-opinion analysts who try to find out why consumers buy a particular toilet soap, or why they hold one opinion rather than another on more important matters, often find it difficult to express the replies in numerical form. Sociologists who attempt to discover the correlates of "happy" and "unhappy" marriages sometimes find that neither the respondent couples themselves nor their close friends have been wholly frank in revealing the intimacies of their family life.

Demographic facts, on the contrary, need not be converted into figures; they are most naturally expressed numerically. Whether we speak of births or of deaths or of migrants, the obvious beginning to an analysis is to count the units and divide them into subgroups by some sort of classification. These data, moreover, are assembled by the government, which at least in the West means that they constitute the most complete and the longest series available on almost any subject. It means also that the collection of the data has the authority of the state behind it; and —while no questionnaire is ever answered completely accurately by all respondents—where vital statistics and the census have been in existence for a long time and have thus attained an almost automatic acceptance, this established legitimacy is as good a guarantee of reliability as one can hope for. Population statistics form an appropriate basis for probing into the subtlest nuances of social life. The process by which parents decide whether to have a third child, for example, is as fascinating to explore as any problem in social psychology could be. At the same time, these statistics relate to the most significant events in each person's life, literally life-and-death matters.

In spite of such excursions into attitudinal research, demography is mainly a social science—that is, one concerned with the characteristics of whole populations, or of sections of populations, rather than with individuals. It deals with three types of questions:

1. The level of performance of the whole population in one particular unit of time—e.g., the number of births, deaths, industrial accidents, etc., that occurred in one day, or year, or century.

2. The comparative performance of various populations, or sectors of one population, in one particular unit of time—e.g., the number of births in city centers vs. that in suburbs, the number of Negro deaths vs. white, the number of accidents in large vs. small factories, etc.

3. The performance of the whole population, or sectors of it, in one unit of time as compared with earlier periods.

Like most fields that require some competence in mathematics, demography is more or less divided into two parts. The gathering, collating, statistical analysis, and presentation of population data demand technical skills, in some cases of a rather high order. No attempt is made in this book to teach **formal demography**, which concentrates on such techniques. The intent rather is to introduce the reader to what can be termed, for contrast, **population analysis**, or the systematic study of population phenomena in relation to their social setting. Technical details and demographic tools are discussed only when they are deemed useful in the skillful *interpretation* of population trends. For instance, the full description of the life table in Chapter 10 is designed to teach the use of this indispensable tool, but anyone who wants to construct one must seek additional guidance elsewhere. Or, as another example, the analysis of forecasts in Chapter 11 does not equip the reader to calculate projections himself, but it should enable him to understand better the meaning and probable accuracy of those prepared by others. This limitation holds even for the Appendix, which concerns elementary techniques of statistical analysis.

The principal differences between formal demography and population analysis are the range of data included and the types of skill that are consequently relevant. Population growth can be analyzed with three different models:

1. It is a self-contained process; for example, a high (or low) fertility tends to generate an age structure with a large (or small) proportion of potential parents in the following generation. This is the particular province of formal demography, though many interrelations of this type will be discussed at length in the following chapters.

2. Such self-propelled population processes, however, are controlled in their rate and especially in their ultimate limit by such other factors as natural resources, economic growth, social mobility, and family norms.

3. And, on the other hand, population growth acts also as a cause of change in the economy or in society; for instance, as a stimulus to business activity or a "social problem." Thus, when we pass from describing population trends to trying to understand them in their total setting, almost every element of a culture or a social structure may have a significant effect on population trends; and, vice versa, a change in population size or composition may influence almost every element of culture or society.

While the disjunction between formal demography and population analysis is in some respects unfortunate, within limits it is also unavoidable. Most of the professional practitioners of the former are employees of government bureaus or insurance companies, and the pressure from such official or commercial positions is to minimize any broad interpretations of the figures they compile and—in a statistical sense—analyze. On the other hand, social scientists who recognize the importance of population trends, and include them among the social, economic, and historical processes they study, typically do this without first acquiring the skills of, say, an actuary. There is a legitimate division of labor here, but also the necessity for communication. For example, a census director must be able to judge which of several possible questions would ultimately yield the most significant results in subsequent interpretations, and a sociologist must know something of how population data are collected and analyzed if he is to use them well.

To be an intelligent consumer of population analysis demands a limited competence, but a rare one. Just as a person barely able to read accepts as gospel anything in print, so the average product of the American school system, only just literate in mathematics, tends to be insufficiently critical of any numerical datum. A large portion of this work—not only all of Chapter 3, but the introductory sections of several others—is designed to instill a discriminating appreciation of demographic statistics, the ability to see them for what they are, neither more nor less.

BIOLOGY VS. CULTURE

Man is born, he lives, and he dies. These are the natural dimensions of human life, as they are of all life. The immutable facts of birth and death designate man as part of nature, one animal species among the others. Like all other living things, man must meet certain physical needs to live, and he must reproduce his kind if the species is not to die out.

But while man is one with the biological world, he is also set off from other species by a fundamental difference. The relation of all other living things to their physical environment is mainly passive. When it changes, they adapt to it at the ponderous rate of evolutionary change; and once such an adaptation has been completed, the new body-form that has evolved may prove to be overspecialized, leading to a limited life-sphere or even to the extinction of the species, as of the great reptiles of an earlier geologic era. Man, on the contrary, takes a more active part than any other species in shaping his environment to suit his needs. Instead of growing hooves for walking, he has made shoes of animal hides; instead of talons for grasping, he has iron pliers. Instead of the specialized parts of the body evolved by other animals for certain narrow functions, man has developed tools. In contradistinction to all other living beings, that is to say, mankind has culture—"that complex whole which includes knowledge, belief, art, morals, law, customs, and any other capabilities and habits acquired by man as a member of society." [1]

The boundary line between man as an animal and man as a member of a social group—that is to say, between the influence of biology and that of culture—is not easy to draw. Indeed, the definition of the two areas has been a vexatious and recurrent problem in all of the social sciences. For example, psychologists who use the results of experiments on lower animals to increase our knowledge of "human nature" can be contrasted with social psychologists who study "personality" as it has developed in various specific cultural settings. Similarly, the sharpest split in anthropology, "the study of man and his works," has always been between the two terms of this definition, between the physical anthropologists who study man as an animal and the cultural or social anthropologists who study him in the context of his works. Analysts of population have also had to cope with this distinction. The birth and death of an individual are biological events, but they take place in a social milieu. Are

[1] Edward B. Tylor, *Primitive Culture* (6th ed.; London: Murray, 1920), 1, 1.

Man's culture alters the biological balance with his environment. Land is reclaimed
from the sea, in Holland . . . (Netherlands Information Service)

population phenomena the consequence of natural laws or of cultural
conditions; and if both are operative, where does one leave off and the
other begin?

Consider the interpretation of fertility trends, for example. During the
nineteenth century, in one Western country after another, the birth rate
began a long-term decline. The many analysts who attempted to explain
this new behavior pattern can be divided into two broad schools—those
who held that the *physiological* ability of women to bear children was
being impaired by the urban-industrial way of life and those who held
that this new *cultural* setting was creating the desire for smaller families
and the means to satisfy it. It was many years before this dispute was
settled to the satisfaction of all the leading demographers.

A population law that represents man as one animal species, with no
more significant differentiation among subgroups than in any other
species, is certainly valid at the biological level. On the other hand, if
we were to analyze separately all the myriad cultures and subcultures
that manifest distinctive demographic traits—that is, not merely nations
but social classes and ethnic groups within nations—the result would be
encyclopedic but not theoretically enlightening. Biologically man is one;
culturally he is many. By what principle can a compromise be found between this unity and this diversity?

. . . and from the desert, in Israel. (Jerry Cooke)

THE INCREASE IN THE HUMAN SPECIES

If we consider the growth of the world's population over the whole of the time that man has inhabited it, this will suggest one answer to our dilemma. The first higher primates evolved from an apelike predecessor about a million years ago, and the first specimens of *Homo sapiens,* our own species, appeared about 100,000 years ago. Whether we discuss the human genus (which includes several extinct species, like Neanderthal man) or the present human species is a matter of indifference. In either case, we can assume that the number started from zero and that it grew more or less steadily (ignoring short-term fluctuations) up to the date for which we have the earliest reliable estimate of the population of the world. That date is 1650, and at that time mankind totaled about 500 million. Three hundred years later the figure was more than 2,500 million, and in 1960 it was over 2,900 million.

The significance of these data can be seen more easily in Figure 1-1.[2]

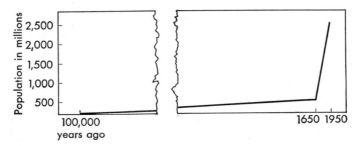

Figure 1-1. A Schematic Representation of the Increase in Numbers of the Human Species.

It must be emphasized that this is a *schematic* representation. What little we know about the growth of particular countries up to the modern era suggests a very irregular pattern, in which periods of rapid increase alternated with stagnation or decline, but there is no way of deriving a precise sum. We have good reason to believe that the population of the world in 1650 was about 500 million, and that it had never been larger than that at any earlier date; but there are no data to round out these statements.

For perhaps 99 per cent of the time since the human species first evolved, it grew slowly, fitfully. Then, during the remaining 1 per cent, it increased fivefold, and the increase is continuing at an accelerating rate. In the physical sciences such a sudden acceleration is called an explosion, and several demographers have adopted this metaphor to describe what is happening during our era. The generalizing principle we are looking for is thrust at us by this contrast. With respect to their popula-

2 See PEP (Political and Economic Planning), *World Population and Resources* (London, 1955), pp. 4–5.

tion type, all of the myriad cultures of the preindustrial era can be grouped together into one class, as contrasted with the urban-industrial culture that began to develop in Western Europe around the year 1650.

The population *of the world* can vary only by what is termed a **natural increase** (or decrease)—that is, by the algebraic difference between the number of births and the number of deaths. The fivefold growth during the past three centuries could take place only because of a change in this relation: either fertility went up or mortality went down, or both. One need know only a little social history to see that, in the main, this population explosion has been due to the decline in mortality. So long as the average number of births per woman remained more or less constant, the successive conquests of the main causes of early death effected an almost geometric increase in the population.

This growth did not, of course, take place evenly all over the world, at the same rate in all countries. On the contrary, it began in Western Europe, where the most spectacular means of death control were discovered, and spread from there to overseas countries with a Western culture (the United States and the British dominions) and finally to the rest of the world (the presently underdeveloped areas). Today the most startling population increase is to be observed in various non-Western countries, where the full application of scientific agriculture and modern medicine has hardly begun. In the West, on the other hand, the rate of increase reached a peak during the nineteenth century and then gradually fell off.

Let us illustrate this last point by using the United States as an example. Before the Declaration of Independence was signed, the population of the northern colonies more or less doubled each 25 years, and this rate continued for some time after the founding of the Republic. This "rapidity of increase almost without parallel in history," as Malthus termed it,[3] has often been taken as a standard to define very rapid growth. In Table 1-1 and Figure 1-2,[4] the actual census figures of the United States are compared with such a "Malthusian projection." For the first century of national life, from 1790 to 1890, the population of the United States

---

[3] T. R. Malthus, *An Essay on the Principle of Population* (7th ed.; London: Reeves and Turner, 1872), p. 253.

[4] Any population increasing at an equal *rate*, such as one doubling every 25 years, is represented by a straight line on semilogarithmic paper. For a detailed discussion of the use of logarithmic graphs to represent population data, see James Alfred Field, *Essays on Population and Other Papers* (Chicago: University of Chicago Press, 1931), pp. 344–386.

**TABLE 1-1. Population of the United States, 1790 to 1960,
Compared with a "Malthusian Projection"**

	Census Population	Per cent Intercensal Increase	Population Doubling Each 25 Years
1790	3,929,214	—	3,929,214 (1790)
1800	5,308,483	35.1	
1810	7,239,881	36.4	
			7,858,428 (1815)
1820	9,638,453	33.1	
1830	12,866,020	33.5	
1840	17,069,453	32.7	15,716,856 (1840)
1850	23,191,876	35.9	
1860	31,443,321	35.6	
			31,433,712 (1865)
1870	39,818,449	26.6	
1880	50,155,783	26.0	
1890	62,947,714	25.5	62,867,424 (1890)
1900	75,994,575	20.7	
1910	91,972,266	21.0	
			125,734,848 (1915)
1920	105,710,620	14.9	
1930	122,775,046	16.1	
1940	131,669,275	7.2	251,469,696 (1940)
1950	150,697,361	14.5	
1960	179,323,175 [a]	18.5 [a]	
			502,939,392 (1965)

[a] Does not include armed forces, their dependents, and other persons living abroad.

more than doubled every 25 years. In 1890 the actual and the projected figures were both approximately 62.9 million. From 1890 to date the growth curve has fallen well below the Malthusian projection.

This decline in the rate of increase could have been the effect of only four possible causes: changes in the rates of fertility, mortality, immigration, and emigration. Certainly there was not a disastrous rise in the American death rate from 1890 on. Nor was there a net emigration following that date. Immigration did fall off after 1920, but from the 1840's to 1914 it tended to increase from decade to decade until it finally averaged almost a million persons a year. Its principal effect on the relation between the two curves was to keep the actual population growth above the straight-line projection for longer than would have been the case by natural increase alone.

The reason that the rate of growth fell off after 1890 was that fertility began to decline faster than mortality. In this pattern, which has its counterpart in the population history of every Western country, we find the second generalizing principle.

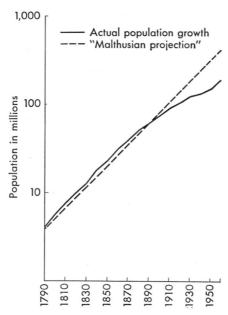

Figure 1-2. Population of the United States, 1790 to 1960, compared with a "Malthusian Projection."

THEORY OF THE DEMOGRAPHIC TRANSITION

The problem, it will be recalled, was to cut through the dilemma posed by the biological unity of man and his cultural multiplicity. By means of the two generalizing principles, the fall in mortality and the fall in fertility, we can establish three population types, which we designate as preindustrial, early Western, and modern Western.

In the **preindustrial** type are included all cultures with little or no contact with modern Western technology and science—thus, all cultures before that great transformation that we call the Industrial Revolution and, also, those contemporary nonindustrial societies that have not been significantly influenced by the West. Seemingly, this is a catchall category, with subclasses as diverse as prehistoric peoples, contemporary primitives, and 20 of the 21 civilizations defined by Arnold Toynbee in his *Study of History*. But, however varied in other respects, these cultures are similar at least in those features that shape their populations. In all of them life is precarious: on the average, people live no more than 35 years. As many die in infancy and childhood as grow to maturity; and cultural values typically favor a high birth rate, without which the very existence of the society is threatened.

The **early Western** population type is characterized by a gradual conquest of hunger and disease, while the norms favoring large families still remain more or less unchanged. Population growth, therefore, is rapid. This very increase in numbers helps shatter the prior, relatively static social structure. In any case, the village society of an agrarian economy cannot survive the new forces introduced by industrialization and urbanization, but what replaces it may vary from one historic era to another.

One of the important ways that industrialization affected Western population growth was to shift so large a proportion of the village-born people to towns that the way of life of the urban middle class eventually became the norm of all. Rational [5] death control was followed, after a considerable interim, by rational birth control. In **modern Western** society, as a goal if not yet in actuality, babies are born only to parents who want them, and persons die, at least in peacetime, only of old age or accidents.

The sequence of these three population types, which is summarized in Table 1-2, is commonly termed the demographic transition or cycle. When this theoretical reconstruction of history was first proposed, it was believed to be predictive in two senses:

TABLE 1-2. Demographic and Social Characteristics of Three
Conceptual Types of Society

Type	Fertility	Mortality	Population Growth	Economy
I. Preindustrial	High	Fluctuating and High	Static to Low	Primitive or Agricultural
II. Early Western	High	Falling	High	Mixed
III. Modern Western	Controlled	Low	Static to High	Urban-industrial

1. The decline in fertility, according to this prognosis, would continue, and the population of Western societies would soon be "stationary" or even in "incipient decline." [6] The rise in Western birth rates after 1945, the famous "baby boom," was thus a total surprise to most demographers. Actually, we know very little of the social determinants of *rational* fer-

[5] The word *rational* is used in its sociological sense; it is opposed not to *irrational* but to *traditional*. See pages 182–183.
[6] These are the designations, respectively, of Warren S. Thompson, *Plenty of People* (Rev. ed.; New York: Ronald, 1948), pp. 107–114; and Frank W. Notestein, "Population—The Long View," in Theodore W. Schultz, ed., *Food for the World* (Chicago: University of Chicago Press, 1945), pp. 35–57.

tility. As we shall see, some of the most interesting research is related to this new problem: if parents are able, both physically and morally, to decide on the number and spacing of their children, what social forces influence their decisions? The most that we can say at the present time is that fertility is controlled, but not whether it will be high or low. One can only hope that fertility will be "rationally balanced" [7] with the low mortality.

2. It was assumed, also, that the demographic transition would be followed in its essentials by the countries of the world currently undergoing industrialization. However, the differences between the past in the West and the present in underdeveloped areas are great, both in the traditional way of life and especially in the rate at which this is being transformed. It is an open question whether the historic sequence will indeed be followed some decades later in Asia, Africa, and Latin America.[8] In the West mortality declined relatively gradually, as one death-control measure after another was perfected; but such a step-by-step development is not being duplicated, of course, in the rest of the world today. Whenever an effort is made to reduce the death rate anywhere, the latest instruments of Western science are used; malaria is combatted, for instance, by spraying DDT from airplanes. As a consequence, mortality has fallen with startling rapidity in some countries, and in technical terms at least this improvement in death control is now available to every people. If fertility remains constant, or even declines no faster than it did in the West, the population of such countries increases very quickly; and some of them were already more densely populated at the beginning of their cycle of rapid growth than Europe is even today. It may be that this stupendous increase in numbers will overtake even the potentialities of twentieth-century science and that the cycle will end in widespread famines and epidemics. Or it may be that the average size of the family will fall fast enough to avoid such a catastrophe. Which will take place we do not yet know, but we can be certain that India, to take one example, will not continue to grow indefinitely by some six million persons or more a year.

One reason that the predictions implied in the theory of the demographic transition failed is that policy decisions now have a greater impor-

[7] Stephen W. Reed, "World Population Trends," in Ralph Linton, ed., *Most of the World: The Peoples of Africa, Latin America, and the East Today* (New York: Columbia University Press, 1949), pp. 94–155.

[8] Cf. Irene B. Taeuber, "The Future of Transitional Areas," in Paul K. Hatt, ed., *World Population and Future Resources* (New York: American Book Company, 1952), pp. 25–38; Kingsley Davis, "The Unpredicted Pattern of Population Change," *Annals of the American Academy of Political and Social Science,* 305 (May, 1956), 53–59.

tance in demographic trends than ever before in history. This new orientation has had a significant effect on the framework of theory: population, studied as a fact of nature in Malthus's day, is now seen as a social datum. The question now is not only what is but also what ought to be —the optimum population—and how to achieve it. In contrast to the laissez-faire West of the nineteenth century, states today intervene in various ways in trying to achieve such goals—with respect to fertility (family subsidies, state birth-control or abortion centers); with respect to mortality (state support of medical and agricultural research, health insurance, genocide); with respect to migration (immigration, or emigration, restrictions; immigration, or emigration, subsidies; forced migration). Simply to relate population to the natural resources and economy can hardly be an adequate analysis today, particularly of totalitarian states.

We are not even certain, moreover, whether the theory of the demographic transition really sums up the historical past of the West with sufficient accuracy. If it is true that the population of the Western world has increased continuously from 1650 on, then the decline in mortality that is used to explain this growth is itself something of a puzzle. The presumed fall in the death rate can neither be proved from statistics nor even, in most of the countries concerned for a substantial portion of the period, be plausibly related to known institutional changes. Thus, it is probable that the significant increase in numbers before, say, 1850 was in most cases the consequence of both a fall in mortality and a rise in fertility.[9]

For these several reasons, then, the demographic transition is no longer usually regarded as an adequate theoretical framework for anything beyond the roughest, most preliminary generalization of population trends. The dilemma posed by the biological unity of man and his cultural multiplicity is still not wholly resolved.

AN OUTLINE OF THIS BOOK

We can evade the dilemma, of course, by limiting our analysis to a single culture, and this has been done in Part I of this volume, which is entirely on the population of the United States. In these ten chapters the emphasis is on introducing the reader to demographic concepts and de-

[9] For one statement of this argument, see William Petersen, "The Demographic Transition in the Netherlands," *American Sociological Review*, 25:3 (June, 1960), 334–347. And for a more general discussion of the issue, see Leighton van Nort, "On Values in Population Theory," *Milbank Memorial Fund Quarterly*, 38:4 (October, 1960), 387–395.

scribing the population phenomena of this country. The implicit cultural background will be largely taken for granted—partly because it is native to most of those who will read this book and thus quite familiar, partly because during the historical development of the United States in some respects its culture has remained more or less constant. But those significant changes that have taken place, most of which are related to the transformation of an agricultural-rural society into an industrial-urban one, are considered in some detail.

In Part II the population of societal types different from those in the United States is analyzed. Each one of these chapters, thus, is parallel to the whole of Part I, though the discussion is necessarily much less detailed. The ordering follows the "stages" in man's cultural evolution, beginning with a discussion of the population of primitive societies and continuing with that of preindustrial civilizations. An early Western society is exemplified by England, the birthplace of modern industry and of the Malthusian theory, as well as the purest case of a free-market economy.

The other two chapters deal with types of contemporary societies that differ significantly from the United States—namely, totalitarian states and underdeveloped countries. The Soviet Union, which successfully grafted Western technology on a quite different political base, illustrates what may happen to areas currently undergoing industralization. This example suggests that neither the general cultural development nor specifically the demographic transition will necessarily be imitated wherever Western technology is adopted. In the brief survey of the populations of Asia and Latin America, the emphasis is on the interrelation between the rapid population growth there and the attempts to modernize their economies and societies.

The fact that man is distinguished from all other animals by his culture means that one cannot formulate a population law for mankind in the same sense as for other species, but it does not mean that no generalizations are possible. Man is still an animal, and at one level of analysis the facts of birth and death are the same for all members of the human species. There are general (that is, not culture-bound) determinants of fertility, mortality, and migration, and thus of population growth; and these are analyzed in the four chapters of Part III.

SUGGESTIONS FOR FURTHER READING

Dennis H. Wrong, *Population* (New York: Random House, 1956).
　　Within the limited compass of a paperback pocket book, a good preliminary survey of the whole discipline.

United Nations, Department of Social Affairs, Population Division, *The Determinants and Consequences of Population Trends* (Population Studies, no. 17; New York, 1953).

A significant effort to bring together all that is known or surmised on the subject. It has the virtues but also the faults of an anonymous work by an international agency.

Joseph J. Spengler and Otis Dudley Duncan, eds., *Population Theory and Policy; Demographic Analysis* (Glencoe, Ill.: Free Press, 1956).

Two collections of articles from a variety of journals, ranging over the whole subject matter of demography.

Clyde V. Kiser, "Population Research," in Joseph B. Gittler, ed., *Review of Sociology: Analysis of a Decade* (New York: Wiley, 1957), pp. 56–86.

Kingsley Davis, "The Sociology of Demographic Behavior," in Robert K. Merton, Leonard Broom, and Leonard S. Cottrell, Jr., eds., *Sociology Today: Problems and Prospects* (New York: Basic Books, 1959), pp. 309–333.

A review of the most recent work in population analysis and an appraisal of the results; a stimulating attempt to bring demographic theory up to date.

Population Index, published quarterly by the Office of Population Research, Princeton University.

Hope T. Eldridge, *The Materials of Demography: A Selected and Annotated Bibliography* (International Union for the Scientific Study of Population, and Population Association of America; New York: Columbia University Press, 1959).

Respectively, for general and for introductory or systematic bibliographic guidance.

PART I

The Population of
the United States

2. THE GROWTH OF THE NATION: AN OVERVIEW

In Chapter 1 the population of the United States was discussed as a prime example of extremely rapid growth. In 1790 the number of persons inhabiting the new country was not quite four million, or slightly more than the present population of Chicago. Sixty years later, at mid-century, the size of the country had grown from the original 13 states to virtually its present area, and the population had increased to more than 23 million, or about the same as the present population of Egypt or Korea. In 1900 the population was 76 million, or somewhat less than the present number of Pakistanis or Indonesians. In 1950 the count was something over 150 million, or almost three times the population of the United Kingdom. And in 1960 the population of the United States was almost 180 million. Only three countries are more populous: mainland China, with 583 million supposedly counted in the "census" of 1953; India, with an estimated 384 million in 1956; and the Soviet Union, with almost 209 million in 1959.

From four million to 180 million—this growth in the population of the United States over the roughly 175 years of its national history is closely related, as both cause and effect, to virtually every element of the country's social and political history. How to describe this interrelation is a problem. Data for the beginning of the nineteenth century, if they exist at all, are of dubious quality. Many of the most significant facts, such as how long people lived on the average, or what the level and distribution of their real income were, can only be guessed at. Garnering such facts, in any case, is far less important than understanding how great a role population change has played in the transformation of American civilization. This chapter is intended to give the reader a broad review. If he does not fully understand some of the technical terms, that does not matter, for they will be precisely defined later in the book.

19

Even for the earliest period of American history, there is some statistical base, however inadequate by present standards, to give substance to an impressionistic survey. Such numerical facts of all kinds have been collected by the Census Bureau in *Historical Statistics of the United States, Colonial Times to 1957;* [1] and these tables, read with imagination, give a fascinating picture of the development of many features of American life.

Consider the data in Table 2-1. What do they signify? What does it mean to say, for example, that the percentage of the population residing in towns increased almost ten times, that the median age almost doubled, that the amount of pig iron produced was a thousand times larger? Per-

TABLE 2-1. Some Key Demographic and Economic Statistics for the United States at 1800, 1850, 1900, and 1950

	1800	*1850*	*1900*	*1950*
1. Population (millions)	5.3	23.3	76.1	151.7
2. Population density (persons per sq. mi.)	6.1	7.9	25.6	50.7
3. Urban population (per cent)	6.1	15.3	39.7	59.0 a
4. No. of urban places	33	236	1,737	4,023 a
5. Occupied persons engaged in agriculture (per cent)	71.8 b	63.6	36.8	11.8
6. Births per 1,000 population	55.2 b	44.3 c	32.3	24.1
7. No. of children under 5 per 1,000 women aged 20 to 44 (whites only)	1,342	892	666	587
8. Deaths per 1,000 population	n.a.	n.a.	17.2	9.6
9. Median age (years)	16.0 d	18.9	22.9	30.2
10. Foreign-born population (per cent)	n.a.	9.7	13.6	6.7 d
11. Negro population (per cent)	18.8	15.7	11.6	10.0
12. Gross national product (billions of 1929 dollars)	n.a.	9.11 e	37.1 f	187.1
13. Pig iron produced (thousands of short tons)	60 g	631	15,444	64,626 h
14. Total energy produced from mineral fuels (trillions of British thermal units)	3	216	7,643	32,937

n.a. Not available.

a By the old definition of "urban." By the new, noncomparable definition, the percentage in 1950 was 64.0 and the number of urban places 4,741.

b 1820.

c 1860.

d Whites only.

e Average 1869–1873.

f Average 1897–1901.

g 1810.

h Shipment rather than production.

[1] Washington: U.S. Government Printing Office, 1960. See also Conrad Taeuber and Irene B. Taeuber, *The Changing Population of the United States* (New York: Wiley, 1958). Copyright © 1958 by The Social Science Research Council.

sons unaccustomed to reading tables very often find them difficult to interpret and therefore dull, but such figures are really a most concise statement of how the American culture was transformed.

The growth of the population (line 1) within a fixed area has meant that since 1850 the density has also gone up (2). The proportion of the population designated as urban (3) increased together with the number of places so defined (4), as well as with those engaged in urban occupations (5). Since direct data on the birth rate (6) are not reliable before about 1900, it is well to supplement them with an approximate measure of average family size—the ratio of children to women able to bear them (7). Death rates are also lacking for the early period (8); and while the median age is only a very approximate substitute—since it reflects fertility and migration as well as mortality—it is the best index available (9). The population grew in part by immigration, as indicated by the proportion of foreign-born (10). Negroes constituted almost one-fifth of the total in 1800, only about half that in 1950 (11).[2]

Economic data for the early period are even scarcer than those on the population. "Gross national product," or the total market value of goods and services produced by the nation's economy, is one of the most common measures of over-all economic power. Note that the very marked increase (12) has been converted into 1929 dollars, so that the inflation over this period is not reflected in the figures. The rise in the production of pig iron (13) and the greater amounts of energy expended (14) are two good indices of the transformation of an agrarian into an industrial society.

To appreciate the significance of data of this kind, they must be interpreted against their whole cultural context. To put flesh on these statistical bones, however, would require a full social history of the United States—a book, that is, at least as thick as this. Here we must make do with four brief cross sections within such a chronicle, at the dates suggested in the tables: 1800, 1850, 1900, and 1950.

1800 [3]

In the year 1800, when France had more than 27 million inhabitants and the British Isles more than 15 million, there were only 5.3 million

---

[2] Since many of the early data pertain to whites only, and since even at the present time statistical information about Negroes is often less accurate, it is sometimes preferable to analyze the two races separately even when the differentiation does not seem to be relevant.

[3] The principal supplementary source for this period is Henry Adams's exhaustive nine-volume survey of the administrations of Jefferson and Madison, *History of the*

persons in the new transatlantic Republic. The territory of the original
13 states extended west to the Mississippi, but more than two-thirds of
the population huddled within 50 miles of the Atlantic coast. Perhaps
as many as half a million had trickled beyond the great barrier of the
Alleghanies, where they lived, in Adams's words, "in an isolation like
that of the Jutes or Angles in the 5th century." The hundred miles of
mountainous wilderness that separated this frontier region from the more
settled area was breached only by three wagon roads, two in Pennsylvania
and one in Virginia.

The isolation of each settlement along the coast, though relatively less,
was also great. From Maine to Georgia mail took 20 days; between
Philadelphia and Nashville, 22 days. On the average, adults wrote one
letter a year. On roads between Bangor and Baltimore four miles an
hour was the usual coach speed, and in the South the difficulties imposed
on travel sometimes became insuperable. Of the eight rivers he had to
cross between Washington and Monticello, Jefferson wrote to his Attorney General in 1801, five had neither bridges nor boats; and when such
streams were swollen by spring freshets, in many cases they could not be
safely forded. The main paths of traffic were the rivers, but travel by
them also was neither safe nor comfortable. From New York it was easier
to sail to Europe than to Albany. No regular passenger service was available up the Hudson; when a sloop advertised its sailing date, prospective
passengers applied for space, then supplied their own bedding and supplies, and spent as much as a week on the 150-mile trip.

Such difficulties in communication combined with surviving local patriotism to form the beginnings of distinct regions. The democratic principles
on which the Republic had been founded were reflected most clearly,
perhaps, in the social relations among the small, relatively prosperous
farmers of Pennsylvania. Elsewhere, the upper class persisted from prerevolutionary days, with great even if diminished power over the mass.
The old families of New York State, many with Dutch names, ran their
enormous holdings almost like ducal fiefs. In Massachusetts "the cordial
union between the clergy, the magistracy, the bench and the bar, and
respectable society" constituted a situation that in Adams's opinion was
"unknown beyond New England—an organized social system, capable
of acting at command either for offence or defence."

The sharpest class distinction existed, of course, in the South, which

---

United States of America. The first six chapters of Volume I, which constitute one
of the best social surveys ever written of any period of American history, have been
reprinted separately under the title *The United States in 1800* (Ithaca, N.Y.: Cornell
University Press, 1955).

was already set off by its "peculiar institution." Of the country's 5.3 million inhabitants, just over one million were Negroes, nine-tenths of them slaves and almost all residents of the southern states. The props on which the colonial aristocracy rested had all been pulled out from under them— all but slavery. Their relation with England had been destroyed by the revolution, their integration with the top clergy by the separation of church and state, and primogeniture by laws passed in the egalitarian momentum from the Declaration of Independence. The old plantation society was in decay: even in Virginia, the wealthiest state of this region and the most populous and powerful member of the Union, the plantation oligarchy was land-poor. But out of the decay a new prosperity was being born. The invention of the cotton gin and the steam engines in English cotton mills gave a double impetus to the region. Everywhere new lands were being plowed, new slaves bought, in a frenzied effort to profit from the growing demand for cotton fiber.

The class structure of early American society is indicated also by its educational system. It was recognized in the abstract that a democracy, even one with property qualifications to voting, must have an electorate able to read and write; but in fact literacy was not a standard characteristic of the population. "In 1795," Adams tells us, "at the suggestion of Governor Clinton, an attempt had been made by the New York legislature to create a common-school system, and a sum of fifty thousand dollars was for five years annually applied to that object; but in 1800 the appropriation was exhausted, and the thirteen hundred schools which had been opened were declining." The educated class was small—and not well educated. Fewer than 40 young men graduated each year from Harvard, 30 from Yale, 15 or 20 from Columbia; and even in the subjects they had been taught—theology, Latin, mathematics, perhaps a bit of biology and medicine—they were not learned by European standards of that day. It was impossible, for example, to find a native architect capable of designing the capitol in Washington. When George Ticknor became excited by Madame de Staël's account of German universities, in all Boston and Cambridge—including the Harvard library—he could not find a single work in that alien tongue. In the characteristically sarcastic opinion of Noah Webster, "As to libraries, we have no such things."

Cutting across regional and class differences was a unity of provincial poverty. According to Samuel Blodget's contemporary estimate, in the entire country the total value of all real and personal property in 1805 was $2.5 billion. (For contrast, the estimated 1952 value of just the land and buildings on Manhattan Island was exactly five times as great.) In the census of 1800 almost 95 per cent of the population was classified as rural; 20 years later (no earlier data are available) 72 per cent of the gainfully occupied were engaged in agriculture. Even in New England, relatively the most prosperous section, "the ordinary farmhouse was hardly so well built, so spacious, or so warm as"—in Adams's striking simile— "that of a well-to-do contemporary of Charlemagne." There was manufacturing in the North: how much is indicated by the production of the key commodity of pig iron, which in 1810 was less than one-tenth of one per cent of what it would be in 1950. But manufactures were for commerce. To supply their needs, the country people had their own household industry. Clothes were made at home of homespun cloth. Agricultural instruments were as primitive as farming methods. Only the best husbandmen drained their land, spread manure, or rotated crops. "The flail was unchanged since the Aryan exodus." This backwoods society was the moral as well as the statistical norm. The spokesmen for the new political philosophy, first of all Jefferson himself, had a deep distrust of the town and believed that democracy could flourish only in the breasts of countrymen. "He perceived good even in the yellow-fever epidemic as a means of discouraging the growth of great cities." [4]

The 33 places classified as urban in the census of 1800 had a total population of 322,371, or an average of just under 10,000 each. The largest city was Philadelphia, until 1800 the seat of the national government, a metropolis of some 70,000. At a time when London had 800,000 inhabitants and Paris more than 500,000, New York's population was about 60,000, and Boston's about 25,000. In terms of health or comfort, these towns had hardly advanced beyond the standards of medieval Europe. Their taxation systems were totally inadequate, their governments an extension of the eighteenth-century village. Police were all but nonexistent. Garbage was collected by foraging pigs. Philadelphia was notable by the fact that its streets were lit at night; only Philadelphia and New York had sidewalks. The filth disfiguring every urban center was an invitation to epidemics, an invitation often accepted. Every few years, as in 1798 and 1803 in New York, yellow fever killed off a portion of the town population and frightened many of the rest off into the highlands. During the 1790's Philadelphia installed the first municipal water system, and ten years later New York began to lay down a similar network of wooden pipes.

---

[4] Arthur M. Schlesinger, "The City in American History," *Mississippi Valley Historical Review*, 27:1 (June, 1940), 43–66. Copyright, 1940, by the Mississippi Valley Historical Association. (This article has been reprinted in Paul K. Hatt and Albert J. Reiss, Jr., eds., *Reader in Urban Sociology*, Glencoe, Ill.: Free Press, 1951, pp. 103–120.)

No European traveler failed to remark on the poor American diet. In the emphatic words of Volney, a Frenchman who traveled about the United States in this period, "If a prize were proposed for the scheme of a regimen most calculated to injure the stomach, the teeth, and the health in general, no better could be invented than that of the Americans." Except for game, fresh meat was ordinarily eaten only by the rich. The pig, which cost the family nothing to keep, appeared at all three meals in the form of salt pork, supplemented by poorly baked doughs, greasy potatoes or turnips, and inordinate amounts of hard liquor.

The family, both the nuclear group of parents and children and the extended "kin folk," was still the key institution. Divorce was wellnigh nonexistent. For every thousand white women aged 20 to 44 years (that is, physiologically capable of bearing children), there were 1,342 children under five years—as compared with only 587 in 1950. More precise data on family size are lacking, but according to one estimate each married woman in 1790 bore an average of almost eight children.[5] With many children and few who lived to old age, it was a young population. The median age of whites was only 16 years, just over half of what it would be in 1950.

Little in the economy or social conditions of the United States in 1800 would have warranted a prediction of rapid change. After a hundred years of scratching New England's rocky soil, farmers were just beginning to move into the Mohawk valley; and if they needed a century to seek out the Mohawk, how long would they take to cross the mountains and reach the Mississippi? The stability seemingly dictated by circumstances was reinforced, moreover, by a deep conservatism among the respectable classes that governed the country. Many would have echoed the words of Jedediah Morse, pastor in a Massachusetts church and "the father of American geography": "Let us guard against the insidious encroachments of *innovation*, that evil and beguiling spirit which is now stalking to and fro through the earth, seeking whom he may destroy." Even Jefferson in his first Inaugural Address—delivered before the Louisiana Purchase almost doubled the country's area—told his countrymen that the United States had "room enough for our descendants to the hundredth and thousandth generation."

1850

Fifty years later, mainly as a consequence of the war with Mexico just completed, the area of the continental United States had been increased

[5] See below, pp. 211–212.

almost to what it would remain until Alaska became the forty-ninth state. "Texas" (meaning a major portion of the present state of that name plus parts of Louisiana, New Mexico, and Colorado) had been annexed in 1845; title to the Oregon Territory (Washington, Oregon, Idaho, and portions of Montana and Wyoming) had been established in 1846; and the vast Southwest (California, Nevada, Utah, plus portions of Arizona, New Mexico, Colorado, and Wyoming) had been ceded by Mexico in 1848. The Gadsden Purchase in 1853 completed the territorial expansion. Great as this was, the population growth had been still greater: in the United States of 1800 there had been 6.1 persons per square mile, and in 1850 there were 7.9.

A Jefferson of 1850 might have hesitated longer in forecasting a virtually infinite succession of generations to fill up the country. For during these fifty years several factors influencing the growth in numbers and particularly their possible future trend had become more evident. Most obviously, the traditional balance between births and deaths was changing. A prognosis in 1800 that the population would grow slowly expressed the conventional wisdom of the past centuries. The classic statement of the contrary point of view, Malthus's *Essay on the Principle of Population,* had been published in its first edition only two years earlier. And before Malthus drove home the long-run implications of a geometrical progression, one would be likely to view instances of sizable growth— as in the American colonies in the eighteenth century—as exceptions to the rule. By 1850, however, the rule had become rapid increase, not only in the United States but in all of the Western world. The greatly improved statistics had established this growth as an indisputable fact, which had penetrated the consciousness of those who used them.

The American population, 23.3 million in 1850, had been augmented by some 18 million over the preceding 50 years. What were the components of this fourfold increase? The recorded immigrants totaled something under 2.5 million. True, migration statistics were quite inaccurate (and for the first decade nonexistent), but even if we assume that the number of immigrants was as much as double that recorded—probably an overgenerous estimate—a growth by about 13 million is still to be accounted for. A portion of this was an indirect consequence of migration: immigrants, because they are predominantly young adults, typically have a higher fertility and a lower mortality than the receiving population, which also includes large numbers of children and aged. However, even if we include these indirect effects in the contribution that immigration made, a portion of the 13 million must have resulted from a change in the balance between the native fertility and mortality.

The presumption from approximate data is that the birth rate fell from 55.2 in 1820 to 44.3 in 1850. In the 1850 census of the white population only 892 children under five years were enumerated for every 1,000 women aged 20 to 44, as compared with 1,342 in 1800. The decline in mortality must therefore have been still faster, though this could be demonstrated only indirectly: mortality statistics on a national scale began only in 1933, and for the nineteenth century the best figures are little more than informed guesses.

The impact of immigration cannot be adequately expressed by the total for the whole half-century. Almost two-thirds of those who entered the country during this period came in the 1840's, and at the end of this decade the curve was still rising sharply. During the 1850's some 2.6 million aliens poured in, constituting what one scholar has termed "the Great Migration." [6] Subsequent immigration was sometimes larger in volume, but the influence of these midcentury newcomers on the empty West and the relatively small native population in the East was in some respects greater.

The primary cause of the overseas movement was the rapid growth of Europe's own population. Estimated at 188 million in 1800, this increased to 266 million by 1850, and to 401 million at the end of the century.[7] Some of the enormous rise was absorbed into Europe's cities, which multiplied in number and size during the nineteenth century; and millions more Europeans left their homes and sailed to new countries—especially, in this period, to the United States. According to American statistics, the total number of immigrants, most of whom came from Europe, swelled from a total of less than a million for the period 1790–1840 to almost 10 million for 1840–1880, and to 23.5 million from 1880 to 1920, when restrictive legislation transformed both the size and the pattern of immigration. These statistics can be accepted only as rough approximations, but in any case, by the standards of all prior history, the movement they record was of an awesome magnitude.

The exodus from Europe reflected economic conditions on both sides of the Atlantic— both, for example, the push of the Irish famine of the 1840's and the periodic pull of employment opportunities associated with economic booms in America. It reflected the contrast between a Europe getting crowded and the empty lands of the American West. It reflected

---

[6] Marcus Lee Hansen, *The Atlantic Migration 1607–1860: A History of the Continuing Settlement of the United States* (Cambridge: Harvard University Press, 1951), Ch. 13.

[7] Estimate of Walter F. Willcox, cited in United Nations, Department of Social Affairs, Population Division, *The Determinants and Consequences of Population Trends* (Population Studies, no. 17; New York, 1953), pp. 10–11.

both the political restrictions by, for example, Austria-Hungary or Tsarist Russia during the nineteenth century, and encouragement to emigration by, for example, the British government in the same period. It reflected, finally, the attraction of American democracy, "the common man's utopia," in Hansen's apt phrase. Such impediments to the democratic system as had existed when the Republic was founded were gradually sloughed off. Twelve of the thirteen original states had property qualifications for voting, but by 1850 universal male suffrage was everywhere the rule for the white population. Free primary education, which in principle and partly in practice had been established in New England since colonial days, also became general throughout the country; and by 1850 less than 10 per cent of the native whites aged 20 and over were listed as illiterate.

The one important flaw in this broadening democratic vista was the chattel slavery flourishing in the South. Over the half-century, the number of Negroes increased from one million to 3.6 million, or at a somewhat slower rate than the whites. Separating natural increase from that due to immigration, which is difficult for the white population, is impossible with respect to Negroes. The importation of slaves from Africa, prohibited in 1808, continued illegally until about 1840, but one can hardly guess how many were smuggled into the country. Only one white family in every four in the South owned slaves, but except for a small minority the whole region accepted the institution and in the Civil War would fight to defend it. In the rest of the country national norms were gradually obliterating the regional differences that had survived from the original colonies, but slavery and its direct consequences increasingly differentiated the South. Immigrants avoided a region where hard manual work was not the road to economic independence but the mark of bondage or poor-white status. While in the North and later in the West commerce, urbanism, and industry flourished, the South remained predominantly agricultural. "Historians might well give greater attention to the question of the extent to which southern secession was a revolt against the urban imperialism of Yankeedom." [8]

Not that the rest of the country had become predominantly urban. In 1850, 85 per cent of the population was still classified as rural, and 64 per cent of the occupied persons were engaged in agriculture. The urban economy, moreover, was still in a mercantile stage. The businessman was primarily a merchant, who intermittently took on subsidiary functions as manufacturer, banker, and speculator. Except for textiles, which were woven in New England factories, "manufacturing" was still largely cot-

[8] Schlesinger, "The City," *op. cit.*

tage industry, with no great change from the inefficiency and poverty of half a century earlier.

The major innovations in the economic system were in transportation, and here there had been a revolution. In 1800 settlements along the Atlantic coast had been linked by a few navigable rivers and rutted wagon roads; in 1869, a memorable year, the first transcontinental railroad and the Suez Canal were both completed. Between these dates canals and railroads were built at a rate beyond the most extravagant imagination of an eighteenth-century engineer. The Erie Canal, completed in 1825, was sensationally successful; it established New York's commercial pre-eminence on the seaboard and eventually in the whole country, and it set a precedent for canal-building throughout the Northeast. Then followed the railroads. By midcentury, a very large number of small, overlapping rail companies, with a total complex capitalization of almost a third of a billion dollars, were operating more than 9,000 miles of road.

In 1850 the 236 places classified as urban had a total population of 3.5 million. There were six cities of more than 100,000. New York (including Brooklyn, then a separate city) had a population of almost 700,-000 and was rapidly growing into one of the metropolitan centers of the Western world. Characteristic urban problems arose, not only uncollected garbage and fire hazards but increasing crime and unscrupulous political machines. On the other hand, most of the humanitarian impulses that mitigated the hardships of pre-Civil War America issued from these same urban populations.

From the cities came the effective energies behind the establishment of free public education, the more humane treatment of the insane, penal reform, the beginning of free public libraries, and the woman rights' movement. Such places also exerted an important influence on the struggle for manhood suffrage, the effort to abolish war, and the antislavery cause.[9]

1900

The population at the turn of the century, 76 million, was well over three times that 50 years earlier. This rapid growth had taken place in spite of the continuing decline in fertility. Among whites the 1900 census listed only 666 children under five for every 1,000 women aged 20 to 44 (as compared with 1,342 in 1800 and 892 in 1850). Family size varied considerably from one social class to another. Differential fertility, as in

[9] *Ibid.*

Building the St. Paul, Minneapolis, & Manitoba Railway westward through Montana Territory, 1887. (Great Northern Railway photo)

St. Paul, Minnesota, in 1857. (Minnesota Historical Society)

An illustration in Albert D. Richardson, *Beyond the Mississippi*. (Hartford, Conn., 1867)

every other country of the modern West, was inversely correlated with social class: paradoxically, the wealthier parents were—the better able they were to care for children—the fewer children they had on the average.

As in the previous half-century, the decline in mortality was much greater than in fertility, and again the evidence for this is indirect. The total recorded immigration from 1850 to 1900 was less than 17 million, and even if the unknown number that returned to Europe is ignored and the presumed undercount is corrected by upping the figure to, say, 20 million, this is still less than half of 53 million, the total increase over this period. That is to say, a large part of the population growth was again the consequence of a change in the balance between births and deaths; and since fertility had declined, mortality must have fallen off much more.

The pattern of immigration changed in a number of ways. First of all in size: before 1850 the largest number of immigrants in any one year was well under a third of a million, while in many years during the following decades it was considerably over a million, and even the average for 1901–1910 was more than 800,000. Secondly, the dominant area of emigration shifted in the 1880's from Northwest Europe to Southern and Eastern Europe. A large section of native public opinion reacted negatively to the unprecedented inflow of Italians, Poles, East European Jews, and other "undesirable types." The new immigrants, moreover, remained visible in the public eye, for most of them did not settle on isolated western farms but congregated in the slums of eastern cities.

Migration within the country also increased enormously, especially the movement to the West. In 1850, only two years after the area had been ceded to the United States, California reported 93,000 inhabitants, most of whom had just arrived as part of the fabulous gold rush. By 1900 its population had grown to 1.5 million, and by 1950 to 10.6 million, second in population only to New York among the 48 states. California has been the most spectacular instance, but only one example, of the general westward movement that is still continuing. The 1900 census reported 4.5 million persons who had been born east of the Mississippi River and were living west of it, as well as half a million that had crossed the river in the other direction. There was a similar interchange of smaller dimensions between the North and the South, with the dominant movement northward.

Overriding these interregional migrations, urbanization was so great during this period as to establish the city as indubitably the dominant force in American culture. While only 40 per cent of the population lived in urban centers in 1900, these were no longer mostly overgrown villages and small provincial towns. Metropolitan centers spread their influence over the whole country and well beyond its borders.

By 1890 New York-Brooklyn with nearly two and a half million people rivaled Paris, and Chicago and Philadelphia with more than a million each ranked as the sixth and seventh cities of the Occident. Hardly less significant was the rise of cities in the Far West and the New South. If most of them seemed small by the new yardsticks of urban magnitude, their rate of growth was spectacular, and even their size would earlier have gained them respect. Thus, Los Angeles jumped from less than 5000 in 1860 to more than 100,000 in 1900, and Denver from nothing at all to 134,000, while Memphis with 23,000 in the earlier year exceeded 100,000 in the later. In the nation as a whole, the proportion of people living in towns of eight thousand or more grew from one out of every six persons in 1860 to about one out of four in 1880 and by 1900 to one in every three. Moreover, of this increasing horde of urban dwellers, considerably more than half resided in places of twenty-five thousand or more.[10]

The growing rift between town and country was often half disguised as regional rivalry, as antagonism between the rural South and West and the urban East. But in the speeches of populist leaders like William Jennings Bryan, several times the Democratic candidate for president around the turn of the century, the farmers' envy and distrust of the big city came frankly to the surface.

Growth of the towns was still a concomitant of the economic transformation under way. Until 1880, when for the first time fewer than half of the occupied persons were engaged in agriculture, the United States was what present-day analysts would term an underdeveloped area.[11] By 1900 the proportion was down to three-eighths. There had been a remarkable advance in agricultural equipment and techniques, particularly in the West, and the products of the prairie states, shipped by the newly built railroads, became important export commodities. As increasing mechanization freed men from work on the land, they were drawn into the rapidly expanding class of factory workers.

The decisive shift from a mercantile to an industrial economy began in the Civil War. Partly in order to create the new revenue made neces-

[10] *Ibid.*

[11] Kingsley Davis, for example, has used this convenient index to denote the "peasant agricultural stage" of a country's development. See his "Population and the Further Spread of Industrial Society," *Proceedings of the American Philosophical Society,* 95:1 (February, 1951), 8–19. (This article has been reprinted in Joseph J. Spengler and Otis Dudley Duncan, eds., *Population Theory and Policy,* Glencoe, Ill.: Free Press, 1956, pp. 317–333.)

sary by that struggle, tariffs on all dutiable imports were greatly increased (from an average of 19 per cent in 1861 to 48 per cent in 1865); and behind this protective wall northern industrialists began to meet the extraordinary wartime demand for woolen goods, copper, coal, and iron and steel, virtually all of which had previously been imported. Continued industrial growth was facilitated by a new institution, the corporation, headed by such new types of men as Andrew Carnegie or John D. Rockefeller. These "captains of industry" built an industrial society overnight, amassing vast personal fortunes in the process. The railroad boom, just getting under way in 1850, also developed at an extraordinary rate once the West was opened up. Over the next half-century, rail mileage was multiplied from 9,000 to 193,000. Railroads were built with the federal government's generous assistance in land grants and money loans, often considerably augmented by fraud.

During this period of unexampled expansion, the country's national income rose from $2,380 millions in 1850 to $19,360 millions in 1900. At the same time, the real income per head of the occupied population almost doubled, that is, from $787 to $1,388.[12]

It is often assumed that this increase in the average real income was all absorbed into the swollen bank balances of the "robber barons," that it did not benefit the mass of the population. There is no evidence to support this contention, and the only empirical study of income distribution in the nineteenth century indicates that, on the contrary, it became wider after the Civil War.[13]

The living conditions of the urban working class, whatever they were in contrast to the earlier period, were certainly deplorable by the standards of the present day. The American Federation of Labor had been founded in 1886, but its membership at the end of the century was still less than one million skilled craftsmen out of the roughly 15 million wage-earners. No one could fail to be disturbed by working-class neigh-

[12] Louis M. Hacker, *American Capitalism: Its Promise and Accomplishment* (Princeton, N.J.: Van Nostrand, 1957), p. 57.

[13] Rufus S. Tucker, "The Distribution of Income Among Income Taxpayers in the United States, 1863–1935," *Quarterly Journal of Economics,* 52:4 (August, 1938), 547–587. Tucker based his study on government statistics of income-tax payments, which are available, with interruptions, from 1863 on. He converted the designated incomes into 1929 dollars, and calculated the percentage of the population that fell into various income groups in each of the years for which data were available. While the method was too rough to delineate any but gross differences, the general conclusions seem to be well based.

borhoods in the industrial towns, but the solution offered to such eyesores depended mainly on each spokesman's social philosophy. Native-born Americans, or some of them, thought they might clean out the slums by damming off the source of new slum dwellers; and they began to agitate for laws restricting immigration. Populist leaders in the Middle West cited urban evils to support their demand for greater political power for rural states. Urban intellectuals, the so-called muckrakers, wrote some of the best journalism in American history without getting far below the surface of corrupt political machines or conniving industrial tycoons. All saw the growing pains, but none really appreciated the magnitude of the growth the national economy was undergoing.

In spite of these various dissenting voices, the turn of the century was in general a period of optimism. The material progress had been so great and so rapid that, in the perspective of most persons, little else could be seen. For the millions of immigrants and their children, America was really the "land of opportunity," and it was no less so for the native-born who opened new frontiers in the West, or those who in eastern cities led in the formation of a new civilization. Nor was the progress only material. Universal education, the panacea of every democratic philosopher, was helping to fashion a composite culture out of the Anglo-Saxon base and the many and diverse immigrant strains. Some of the new wealth was spent in developing new art forms—particularly architecture—which, however, gaudy to modern taste, contemporaries found impressive. The end-of-century buoyancy was perfectly expressed in the war with Spain, by which the United States made its brash entry as a world power. The conflict did not last long enough to dampen this spirit: from the sinking of the *Maine* in February to the fall of Manila in August was only six months. With Roosevelt's dashing cavalry charge to discuss, the public hardly noticed the thousands who, in unheroic misery, died of tropical fevers.

The main reason for recalling these moods from another age is to point up their irrelevance to the complexities of the twentieth century. The most sanguine optimist might have hoped that the progress through the nineteenth century would continue at the same rate, but hardly that this would be accelerated. And the gloomiest prophet would not have forecast a whole series of wars or the novel horrors of modern totalitarianism. In several respects, adult Americans have lived, though few of them realize it, through a period of change momentous enough to be termed a social revolution.

1950

In 1950 the population of the United States was almost 152 million. From the earliest colonial days until 1900 it had grown to 76 million, and in the next 50 years it increased by virtually the same number. And in 1960 the country's population reached almost 180 million; the intercensal increase was more than three times that in any previous decade.

This considerable growth would have been greater had it not been for a number of factors that cut it down. From roughly 1900 until 1914 immigrants poured into the country at a prodigious rate. This flow was cut off during the two wars, reduced substantially by the laws both of several European countries and of the United States, and even reversed during the great depression. From 1932 to 1935, for the first time in American history, there was a net *emigration* of about 138,000. During this period, also, the birth rate fell off markedly. For a time most demographers believed that the era of rapid population growth had definitely come to an end and even that a decline was incipient. This prognosis we now know to have been wrong, but we do not quite understand the baby boom just after World War II or the continued style of moderately large families. During the past 10 or 15 years there has also been a notable success in combatting several important causes of death.

The remarkable improvement in agricultural technology that occurred during this period reduced still further the proportion of the working force required to feed the growing population. In 1900, with industrialization well under way, 37 per cent of gainfully occupied workers were still in agriculture. Fifty years later this figure was less than 12 per cent. At the turn of the century six Americans out of ten lived in rural areas; in 1950 64 per cent lived in towns and 57 per cent in the country's 168 metropolitan areas. The dominance of urban influences that these figures suggest, while apparent in some respects, is not the whole picture. It is more to the point that differences between "urban" and "rural" have been diminishing. Suburbs, which in many ways are intermediate between town and country, are growing much faster than city centers, and what were once urban amenities have become available to a larger and larger proportion of the remaining rural population. A farmer's son who, drawn by the bright lights, seeks his fortune in the Big City, where his speech and clothes mark him as a hick: this is a story out of another age. The transformation of American farm life in one or two generations,[14] while

[14] For a well rounded analysis of this transformation, see Lowry Nelson, *American Farm Life* (Cambridge: Harvard University Press, 1954), Ch. 5.

it encompasses much more than these two technical innovations, can be summed up with statistics on automobiles and rural electrification. At the beginning of the century the automobile was hardly more than a rich man's plaything; in 1950 there were more than 48 million motor vehicles registered, as compared with the fewer than 40 million families. In 1952, 88 per cent of farms had electricity, as compared with 7 per cent as recently as 1920.

While the change over the past half-century has been most dramatic in the countryside, it has pervaded the whole American society. The substitution of mechanical and electric energy for human continued, but at a greatly accelerated rate. The production of electric energy increased during this period from 6 billion to 389 billion kilowatt hours, while the average workweek of production workers in manufacturing fell from more than 50 to about 40 hours. Over the whole of the past century the average workweek in all occupations fell off from 69.8 hours in 1850 to 40 hours in 1950, or from six 12-hour days to five 8-hour days per week.

In spite of the rapidly growing population and the steady reduction of the average workweek, productivity increased fast enough to provide a steady, substantial rise in living standards. The annual average gross national product, expressed in billions of 1929 dollars to eliminate the effect of the inflation over the period, jumped from 37.1 for 1897–1901 to 187.1 for 1950. The vast increase in wealth that these figures suggest, moreover, has been distributed over the population more nearly equally than ever before.

A free public school system had been established throughout the country during the nineteenth century, but at its end education beyond grammar school was still limited to a very small minority. Of those aged 14 through 17 years, the proportion enrolled in high school has increased from 7 per cent in 1890 to 89.5 per cent in 1957; or, more significantly perhaps, the proportion of this age-group that was graduated increased over the same period from 4 to more than 60 per cent. In two generations, thus, the American high school has changed from a preparatory school for a small elite to an institution almost as universally accessible as elementary school; and this trend is continuing. Over roughly the same period college enrollment increased by more than ten times, or from about 238,000 in 1900 to about 2.6 million in 1956, or from 4 to about 30 per cent of the 18–21 age-group.

One important function of the demographer is to classify the population he studies into meaningful categories. For the American population of the present day, this task is exceedingly difficult, for neither the rural-urban dichotomy, nor that between rich and poor, nor that between manual workers and white-collar employees, is any longer sufficient. With respect to all such characteristics, today's American society presents not a two-class opposition but a continuum or a still more complex pattern. Similarly, except for the South and the Mountain West, the several regions have all but completed the adaptation to national norms that was begun when the Union was formed.

> The . . . development of the economy, the advance of education, the absorption of the immigrants, and increasing mobility contributed to convergences in rates of population growth. . . . Something of the old ways remains, particularly among the Negroes, the Spanish-speaking people in the Southwest, the Indians, and the Puerto Ricans. With the possible exception of the Indians, though, change is occurring in all these groups. There is movement out of the rural areas where conditions have encouraged backwardness. Educational advance is rapid for youth, especially for those in urban areas. Death rates have declined sharply, and birth rates are reduced.
>
> The convergences that have occurred were produced mainly by the upward movement of the groups at the bottom.[15]

Never before in history have so many of man's basic needs been filled so completely. Social problems today are often the effects of the country's economic and cultural abundance, paradoxical as this still sounds.[16] Overeating is a far greater threat to health than malnutrition. Infant mortality has all but disappeared, but the number of aged grows steadily; over the half-century average expectation of life at birth increased from 50 to 70 years. At the same time, with the rapid population growth, some of what economists term "free goods" have become, or are likely to become, commodities: water in the semiarid West, air in smog-ridden Los Angeles, space in any city to park a car.

Apart from such anomalous exceptions, *the* problem of economic theory—how to allocate scarce goods among alternative uses—seems to be in the process of becoming obsolete. With productivity as efficient as it has become, it is often not necessary to choose one or the other commodity, but rather possible to have both. In World War II, for example, the classic example of the economic problem, the distribution of productive factors between military and civilian needs, had a brand new solution in the United States—guns *and* butter. To some degree, this unique affluence is disguised by a reversal in the traditional relation between supply and demand. In any nonindustrial society, demand comes first—the need

---

15 Taeuber and Taeuber, *op. cit.,* pp. 314–315.

16 For a full exposition of this theme, see Jessie S. Bernard, *Social Problems at Mid-Century: Role, Status, and Stress in a Context of Abundance* (New York: Dryden, 1957).

for food, clothing, housing, or something almost as fundamental; and production is stimulated in an effort to meet this demand. In the United States today, on the contrary, supply often comes first, and the demand for the goods produced is then stimulated by advertising and other more subtle means of exciting social emulation. Galbraith terms this relation the Dependence Effect: "The production of goods creates the wants that the goods are presumed to satisfy." [17] With this kind of squirrel cage in operation, the economic system can never achieve satiation in consumers goods, for with greater and greater production more and more economic "wants"—in this new sense—remain unsatisfied.

The Dependence Effect operates, however, only with commodities sold on the market, not with social services. It is now far less important to increase industrial production than to find means of redressing the balance between opulence in consumers goods and public poverty. Any American city shows a marked contrast between rising retail sales and, on the other hand, crowded schools, understaffed police forces, dirty streets, and overworked transportation systems.

Moreover, one can challenge the reality of America's seeming escape from the hard confines of economics. The industrial system that so often has made it possible to choose both alternatives, rather than either one, is using up the country's natural resources at a stupendous rate. What will happen, for example, when the deposits of petroleum are exhausted? Some foresee disaster; others predict that before that date gasoline will have been made obsolete by the development of atomic power. By 1980, according to estimates of the U. S. Office of Saline Water, the consumption of water will exceed that "readily available," and the country will then have to depend in part on converted salt water.[18] It may well be that both the optimist and the pessimist of 1950, like their counterparts of 1900, are not so much wrong in their predictions as irrelevant to the world of 2000.

SUGGESTIONS FOR FURTHER READING

Conrad Taeuber and Irene B. Taeuber, *The Changing Population of the United States* (New York: Wiley, 1958).

Donald J. Bogue, *The Population of the United States* (Glencoe, Ill.: Free Press, 1959).

---

[17] John Kenneth Galbraith, *The Affluent Society* (Boston: Houghton Mifflin, 1958), p. 155 and Ch. 11 *passim*.

[18] *New York Times,* February 12, 1961.

The most general of a recently published series of monographs based mainly, though not exclusively, on census data. Bogue's considerably longer work is a valuable supplement.

J. Frederic Dewhurst and Associates, *America's Needs and Resources: A New Survey* (New York: Twentieth Century Fund, 1955).

An encyclopedic analysis of America's economic system and its productive capacity. A popularized shorter version has been written by Thomas R. Carskadon and George Soule, *U.S.A. in New Dimensions: The Measure and Promise of America's Resources* (New York: Macmillan, 1957).

National Resources Committee, Committee on Population Problems, *The Problems of a Changing Population* (Washington: U.S. Government Printing Office, 1938).

A prewar survey, written against the background of economic depression and an incipient decline in population. Interesting just because it is so thoroughly out of date.

Kingsley Davis, ed., "A Crowding Hemisphere: Population Change in the Americas," *Annals of the American Academy of Political and Social Science*, vol. 316 (March, 1958).

Emphasis is on recent population trends and the future potential. Half of the issue is concerned with Latin America.

3. SOURCES OF DEMOGRAPHIC DATA

In the early period of population statistics, each city or country began to compile the record of its own people by simply starting to count them. Enumerating the inhabitants of a designated area and registering its vital events are such straightforward procedures that no theoretical framework would seem to be necessary. It soon became evident, however, that the understanding of "obvious" terms and "simple" procedures varied greatly from one person to another, and even more from one country to another. Each statistical office had to standardize its own terminology; and, beginning in the later decades of the nineteenth century, a continuous effort has been made to increase the international comparability of population data by introducing the same definitions and procedures throughout the world. While there has been much progress in this direction, many statistics are still collected under conditions that make them only partly commensurable. In the United States, as in other countries, definitions have often been changed from one decade to the next, so that comparisons over time must also be made with care.

In one sense, however, the battle has been won. It is now universally recognized that a precise **definition of concepts** must come before any attempt is made to count. Nothing can be taken for granted. The meanings that have been given to even the most basic terms, such as *family* or *live birth*, have varied a good bit from one time or place to another; and the problem of delineating more complex concepts, like the *cause of death* or *internal migration,* can become highly technical. In the following chapters, such terms will be defined as we come to them; but it may be useful to illustrate the general point here by discussing the definition of one concept that, to a layman, would seem not to need defining—*age.*

Persons brought up in a literate urban culture might assume that everyone anywhere would know how old he is. Indeed, life roles in every society are different for children, youth, adults, and the aged, but in primitive agrarian cultures the divisions between these groups are not ordinarily made in terms of chronological age. A native of such a society would know, for example, whether he had yet undergone puberty rites, but he might not understand the question if an enumerator asked him how old he was. Age can be defined in grosser units than single years. If in years, it can be measured to the last birthday or to the nearest one. Or, most precisely, the date of birth can be asked for. Practice varies considerably from one country to another, and in any country from one type of demographic data to another.

In recapitulations of the early population growth of the United States, the breakdown by age and sex is often estimated, but the data actually collected were as follows: [1]

Free Whites
1790: Males divided into two age-groups only, under 16 years, and 16 years and over; females not classified by age.
1800–1820: Males and females each classified as follows: under 10, 10–16, 16–26, 26–45, 45 and over.
1830–1840: Males and females each classified as follows: under 5, 5–10, 10–15, 15–20, 20–30, 30–40, 40–50, 50–60, 60–70, 70–80, 80–90, 90–100, 100 and over.
Colored (except Indians not taxed)
1790–1810: Divided into slave and free; not classified by sex or age.
1820: Divided into slave and free and by sex, and each subgroup classified by age as follows: under 14, 14–26, 26–45, 45 and over.
1830–1840: Divided into slave and free and by sex, and each subgroup classified by age as follows: under 10, 10–24, 24–36, 36–55, 55–100, 100 and over.

Beginning in 1850 enumerators were instructed to ask for the exact age. Since that date it has been defined as that on the last birthday—except in 1890, when the question called for age at the nearest birthday. In other population data age is still often undefined. The standard birth-certificate form recommended by the Public Health Service, for example, merely calls for the age of the parents "at time of this birth"—and this in spite of the fact that the precise age of the mother in particular is a useful datum in demographic analysis. Most counts of whatever type include some persons whose age is reported as unknown.

It is usually especially difficult to define the groups and subgroups of a **classification**. In ordinary usage we do not find it necessary to set precise

[1] Carroll D. Wright, *The History and Growth of the United States Censuses, Prepared for the Senate Committee on the Censuses* (Washington: Government Printing Office, 1900), p. 91.

limits to most classes. We know what we mean by a tall man or a short man without specifying his height in feet and inches. But in a statistical study of height we must arbitrarily decide that "tall" means, say, six feet and over; a man one-sixteenth of an inch under six feet, then, is not "tall." The pattern of distribution of some data suggests a dividing point or occasionally forces it (as between male and female), but the statistical expression of most demographic concepts forms a continuum, with or without recognizable clusters. The real and significant differences, for example, between rural and urban, between Negro and white, or between those engaged and not engaged in a gainful occupation, make some classification appropriate. But are these simple dichotomies fine enough, or are more complex classifications called for? And in either case, what shall be done with the inevitable intermediate cases?

The problem of dividing a continuum into classes can be exemplified, again, in terms of age. Women are physiologically able to reproduce between puberty and menopause or, roughly, between the ages of 15 and 45. The general fertility rate, defined as the number of births per 1,000 women in the childbearing age-group, varies widely according to where the age limits of fecundity are put. As another example, the author of a well known work on aging decided to set 60 years as the lower limit of future research, in spite of the fact that 65 years is the usual dividing point in retirement, social-security benefits, and similar institutional frameworks.[2] Or, as a correlative example, in 1940 the Census Bureau revised the concept of the working population,[3] which from that date on was understood to be part of the age-group 14 years and over, rather than 10 years and over. Certainly the age at which persons ordinarily begin to work had risen: was this new definition the best possible reflection of the actual trend? In setting such a dividing point, there is no one correct decision. In most cases any of several more or less arbitrary classifications is equally acceptable, and the major fault with any revision is that international comparability is lost until one classification is accepted universally and that, even then, time series must be adjusted to each change.

Once it is decided precisely how to define each demographic category that is to be measured and classified, a count is made. Population data are available primarily in three sources: the census, which corresponds in business practice to a periodic inventory of stock; vital statistics, which are like a record of domestic purchases and sales; and international migration statistics, which are comparable to a list of imports and exports.

---

[2] Otto Pollak, *Social Adjustment in Old Age: A Research Planning Report* (Bulletin 59; New York: Social Science Research Council, 1948).

[3] See page 194.

THE CENSUS

In the effort to form a federal government, one of the principal impediments that had to be overcome was the jealousy between large states and small ones. Power was balanced between them by establishing a bicameral Congress: in the Senate, with equal representation from each member of the Union, the less populous states had relatively greater power; and in the House, with representation proportionate to the population, the larger ones dominated. If this balance was to be maintained, it would have to be adjusted periodically to the current size of the population; and the Constitution itself provided for the requisite census:

> Representatives shall be apportioned among the several States according to their respective numbers, counting the whole number of persons in each State excluding Indians not taxed. The actual enumeration shall be made within three years after the first meeting of the Congress of the United States, and within every subsequent term of ten years, in such a manner as they shall by law direct.[4]

The census thus established was not the first in the world; there had been prior counts of the whole population in Virginia, New France (later Quebec), and Sweden. But the census of the United States nevertheless set an important precedent.

> Until the 19th century the statistical data gathered by countries of continental Europe were usually treated as secrets of state. The modern census began in the United States in close association with democratic forms of government, and even at the start the results were immediately made public. . . . There can be no doubt that the periodic censuses of the United States have been preeminently responsible for introducing the practise into other countries.[5]

From its very beginning, the United States census included more than the minimum information required for its original purpose. And over the decades, in response to the needs of an increasingly complex civilization and sometimes even anticipating these needs, many new questions have been added to the original schedule and a constant effort has been made to improve accuracy. The unit for most of the data collected, which until 1850 was the family, was changed in that year's count to the individual; and in Willcox's opinion, this change in procedure was "perhaps the most important in the whole history of the census." [6] From 1890 on, data

---

[4] *Constitution of the United States,* Art. I, Sec. 2, Par. 3, as modified by the Fourteenth Amendment.

[5] Walter F. Willcox, "Census," *Encyclopedia of the Social Sciences,* 3 (New York: Macmillan, 1930), 295–300.

[6] *Ibid.*

were entered on Hollerith cards. With these cards it is possible by a simple adjustment to sum up involved cross tabulations (for example, the number of Italian-born stonemasons who have five or more children, or the income of college-educated Negroes north and south of the Mason-Dixon line); and the usefulness of census materials for social research was thus greatly increased.

In the relevant United Nations publication a **census** is defined as "the simultaneous recording of demographic data by the government, at a particular time, pertaining to all the persons who live in a particular territory." [7] Note also the difference in terminology: **enumeration**, the periodic count of the whole population and its characteristics made in a census, is contrasted with **registration**, a continuous notation of vital events recorded usually at the time of their occurrence. While the term *census* is often used to denote population counts of all kinds, and even other enumerations by a government (like the U.S. Census of Manufactures), it is preferable to restrict its meaning to those that more or less comply with the United Nations definition, whose terms are elucidated in the following paragraphs:

1. A census is **made by the government.** No other institution can provide the legitimate authority, and thus the presumption of objectivity, or the elaborate and expensive organization required to make a full and accurate enumeration.

2. A census is of the population of a **strictly defined territory**. One of the major difficulties in using the so-called censuses of ancient China, for example, is that "China" varied considerably from one period to another, depending on the military successes of the central government, and it is often not known how much of the outlying regions was included in population counts. In the United States geographic boundaries have ordinarily been well established in the area included in the census, but there is another difficulty related to territorial classification. This country uses a so-called *de jure* enumeration, meaning that persons are listed under their "usual place of residence." In England, as an example of a *de facto* enumeration, persons are classified according to where they happen to be on the day of the census count. [8]

---

[7] United Nations, Department of Economic Affairs, Statistical Office, *Handbook of Population Census Methods* (Studies in Methods, series F, no. 5; New York, 1954), p. 1.

[8] In a relatively static population the difference between the two systems is of little consequence; but today roughly one person out of every five in the American population moves to a different residence every year. For a discussion of the relative advantages and disadvantages of *de jure* and *de facto* enumerations, see Mortimer Spiegelman, *Introduction to Demography* (Chicago: Society of Actuaries, 1955), pp. 9–10.

3. The census enumeration is **universal**, including every person in the designated area without omission or duplication. Apart from the numerically insignificant group of untaxed Indians (who have been included only since 1890), the American census has been in principle universal from the beginning. Many so-called censuses of the ancient world, however, were established only to administer such state functions as taxation or military conscription, and thus omitted whole classes of the population—for example, females, minors, slaves, commoners, and aliens.

4. Ideally, a census consists of a **personal enumeration** of each individual in the area covered. In practice, in the United States census enumerators try to reach at least one adult in every household, but if they are unable to do so after several attempts, they fill in the schedule from information given them by neighbors. In some population counts a personal enumeration is not attempted. So-called censuses of Negro Africa, for example, have often consisted of compilations of data furnished by village chieftains; and the so-called census of religious bodies in the United States, similarly, was based on information given by the various denominations.

5. The enumeration of the entire population should be **simultaneous**, made on a single day. In the small nations of the Western world this ideal is approached, but in so large a country as the United States the census ordinarily takes three or four weeks. In more primitive areas it may take months or even years. One day is nevertheless set as the date of the census, and demographic events occurring after this are in principle excluded from the count.

6. Censuses furnish not only information about the population at a given time but, in combination, no less significant data about its development over a period. Censuses are most useful, therefore, if a **regular interval** is maintained between them. The director of a census, moreover, must weigh the advantages to be derived from any new procedure that is proposed against the disadvantage that comparability with previous data will be lost.

The preparation for any census includes as a very important part the recruitment and training of an army of enumerators. In the United States in 1960 there were about 160,000 of these basic data-gatherers, or some 890 per million population (the world average is about 2,000). Most were women, who are more often able and willing to take on a full-time job for two weeks or so. They were given nine hours of classroom training designed to explain both their specific duties and the importance of taking an accurate census, and then had to pass an examination. Paid on a

Census Bureau cartographers laying out block-identification maps in preparation for the 1960 census. (Remington Rand—Curt Gunther)

piece-work basis, they received about $13 a day (in many countries enumerators get only a token remuneration or even no payment at all). The census was taken in two stages, the first covering the items asked of all households and the second a more detailed schedule asked of only a sample of the population. Only about a third of the enumerators were retained for stage two, and the possibility of this additional income provided another incentive to careful and accurate work. The field work of the enumerators was directly controlled by about 10,000 crew leaders and, at a greater distance, by about 400 district supervisors.

Assembled at the Jeffersonville office of the Bureau of the Census, the enumeration books were counted, classified by district, provided with numbers, and microfilmed. Then the data went through the FOSDIC (Film Optical Sensing Device for Input to Computers), which translated the enumerators' entries into pulses on magnetic tape. The computer

A roll of microfilm, on to which 1,500 form sheets of the 1960 census have been transferred. (Remington Rand—Curt Gunther)

A FOSDIC (Film Optical Sensing Device for Input to Computers), which transfers data from microfilms to a magnetic tape, for input to an electronic computer. (U. S. Bureau of the Census)

performed the following tasks with great accuracy: editing and control of records, evaluation of their quality, determination of sample weights, and tabulation. The population could be divided into some 5,000 categories at the rate of 3,000 persons a minute. As a final step, the computer presented a completed table, ready for photo-offset reproduction. Because of the greater use of improved machines, it was anticipated that final reports of the 1960 census would be available much faster than had ever been possible before.

VITAL STATISTICS

The second type of population data, **vital statistics**, consists of a compilation of local records made of each person's birth, changes in civil status throughout his lifetime, and his death. In almost every culture there is a religious ritual to mark births, marriages, deaths, and so on. In the Western world the registration of these vital events was for centuries the responsibility of the church. Apart from the ancient Inca empire in Peru,

A Univac printer, which turns out 10 tabular lines per second. Robert W. Burgess, then Census Director, observes the operation. (Remington Rand—Curt Gunther)

the first secular authority to collect vital statistics was a New England colony in the seventeenth century: "Massachusetts became the first state in the Christian world to record the actual events and the dates thereof, rather than the occurrence and date of the subsequent ecclesiastical ceremonies, and the first to place this registration function under the civil authorities rather than under the clergy." [9]

In spite of this early beginning, the development of vital statistics in the United States has been slow. In most West European countries the national government took over from the churches the responsibility for collecting these data. In this country, however, vital statistics are still collected by local, though secular, authorities, so that their completeness and reliability have varied greatly from one region to another. In the censuses of 1850 to 1900 attempts were made to find a substitute for national vital statistics by asking how many births or deaths had taken place during a designated period before the enumeration date. The responses were quite inadequate, however. In the census reports themselves it is stated that as many as 100,000 infants were omitted from the 1870 enumeration, and as many as half the deaths from the 1900 count. [10]

As a result of such fiascos, the federal government undertook to guide the registration procedures of local authorities and to collate vital statistics collected in those states where, on the basis of sample counts, it was judged that the registration was at least 90 per cent complete. Model registration laws were written, and the states were urged to enact them. First, in 1880, a Death-Registration Area was established and then, in 1915, a Birth-Registration Area. They comprised those states where the count of these vital statistics was adjudged to be up to the standards Washington had set, and as the procedures in other states improved, they were gradually admitted. In 1933, with the admission of Texas to the Death-Registration Area, they both became coextensive with the continental United States. [11]

American birth and death statistics on a national scale thus really go back only about 25 years. Even today the system rests on voluntary co-

---

[9] United Nations, Department of Economic and Social Affairs, Statistical Office, *Handbook of Vital Statistics Methods* (Studies in Methods, series F, no. 7; New York, 1955), p. 4.

[10] See T. Lynn Smith, *Population Analysis* (New York: McGraw-Hill, 1948), pp. 204–205, 242–245.

[11] The contrast between more advanced and backward regions of a country and the reflection of this difference in the quality of the vital statistics collected are fairly common. In various countries of the world today a distinction is made analogous to that in the United States before 1933. In India, for example, the parts known before 1947 as the British Provinces are now denoted the "registration area," for which a more elaborate statistical coverage is attempted than for the rest of the country.

operation between the various states and the federal government, and the accuracy and completeness of registration still varies from one region to another, though now ordinarily above the Area minimum.[12] In recent years much progress has been made in setting uniform, high standards for the whole country in the registration of births and deaths. Sporadic and thus far unsuccessful efforts have been made to improve the statistics on marriage and divorce by establishing new registration areas in a similar fashion.[13]

MIGRATION STATISTICS

If we define **migration** as the permanent movement of persons or groups over a significant distance, some of the key terms of this definition ("permanent," "significant") are ambiguous and in practice have to be delimited by an arbitrary criterion. We know whether someone has been born or has died, but who shall say whether a person has migrated? A farmer who goes to the nearest town on a Saturday to buy a suit, we feel, is not a migrant. A person who leaves his home and goes to another country and settles there for the rest of his life, on the other hand, is a migrant. But between these two extremes lies a bewildering array of intermediate instances; and such criteria as distance, duration of stay, and importance of purpose do not clarify the concept entirely. Since "no objective, natural criterion exists on the basis of which migrants distinguish themselves from travellers, . . . one should not expect to arrive at a unique criterion or definition of migration." [14]

The basic distinction in migration statistics is that between **international migration**, in which the migrant crosses the boundary between one country and another, and **internal migration,** in which he does not. A difference is made also in the terms designating the two types of persons: international migrants are called **emigrants** when they leave and

[12] See page 64.

[13] Cf. Hugh Carter, "The Federal Program for Statistics on Family Formation and Dissolution," *Marriage and Family Living,* 20:3 (August, 1958), 257–261; Samuel C. Newman, "The Development and Status of Vital Statistics on Marriage and Divorce," *American Sociological Review,* 15:3 (June, 1950), 426–429; Kingsley Davis, "Statistical Perspective on Marriage and Divorce," *Annals of the American Academy of Political and Social Science,* 272 (November, 1950), 9–21 (this article has been reprinted in Joseph J. Spengler and Otis Dudley Duncan, eds., *Demographic Analysis,* Glencoe, Ill.: Free Press, 1956, pp. 243–255). The best book on the subject is Paul H. Jacobson, *American Marriage and Divorce* (New York: Rinehart, 1959).

[14] Max Lacroix, "Problems of Collection and Comparison of Migration Statistics," in Milbank Memorial Fund, *Problems in the Collection and Comparability of International Statistics* (New York, 1949), pp. 71–105 at p. 73.

immigrants when they arrive, while internal migrants are called **out-migrants** when they leave and **in-migrants** when they arrive.

The distinction between internal and international migration is not always clear-cut, for territories often have some but not all of the characteristics of independent states. Thus, according to the purpose for which the statistics are gathered, one might designate as either internal or international the movement among the occupied zones of postwar Germany; or between Puerto Rico and the United States; or between Britain and the British dominions, colonies, or mandated territories; and so on through scores of examples of ambiguous sovereignty. Each such case is decided on the basis of particular circumstances, and there are many strange anomalies. To cite but one: in the migration statistics of the United Kingdom, citizens of the Republic of Ireland are treated throughout as British subjects!

Another limitation to the internal-international dichotomy is that it tends to obscure processes that cut across it. We usually think of labor mobility or of urbanization, for example, as intranational phenomena, forgetting that much of the movement of workers or to cities has been across national boundaries. We speak of the assimilation of immigrants, but usually not of in-migrants. The implication that the difference between national cultures is *always* greater than that between rural and urban is certainly not in accord with the facts: a native of Toronto who moves to Detroit would ordinarily be, in any but a legal sense, less of an alien than an in-migrant from rural Alabama; and this contrast might even hold, for example, for a Viennese and a French peasant who go to live in Paris.

These comments are not meant to imply, of course, that whether or not a migrant crosses an international border is not important with respect to any demographic study. On the contrary, this is usually a significant variable. The point is rather that, even when an analyst deems this distinction to be irrelevant to the problem he is concerned with, he must use the two sets of statistics as they have been separately collected, and to combine data on international and internal migration is often hardly feasible.

International Migration

The statistics of international migration, as collected by the various national governments, are not ordinarily accurate, complete, or comparable. There are three main reasons for this:

1. The statistics collected are an adjunct to a border patrol that many try to evade. The neutral character of modern Western censuses and vital statistics—the fact that they are data collected for their own sake rather than as a step preparatory to unpopular state controls—is lacking in the statistics of international migration. While this deficiency might be more apparent in the records of receiving countries, it sometimes applies just as much to those of sending countries. The nineteenth-century figures on emigration from Britain, for example, are deficient for just this reason:

> Before granting clearance papers, the Customs officials were to receive lists of passengers from masters of ships and make certain that the law was being observed. The statistics were thus a by-product of legislation introduced to cope with the appalling conditions then prevalent in the vessels carrying emigrants overseas. These controls proved ineffective, as it was easy for vessels to evade inspection by sailing from out-of-the-way parts of the coast: thus in the early years the figures underestimate the number of persons who actually sailed from the United Kingdom.[15]

Distinctions made for legal or political reasons, moreover, are seldom relevant to a demographic study: for example, the difference in the United States between quota and nonquota immigrants relates only to American law and has no counterpart in the statistics of other countries. Each such specific regulation reduces the international comparability of the statistics based on it.

2. Even apart from variations in migration law, migrants are not classified by a uniform system in different countries. Among the totals entering and leaving a country, designated as **arrivals** and **departures**, the first subclassification is usually between **nationals** and **aliens,** who are both further subdivided between **visitors** and **permanent migrants**. All of these terms are ambivalent to some degree. Between "national" and "alien" there are persons of dual nationality, permanent stateless residents, and others who exemplify the complexities of international law. The distinction between "visitor" and "migrant," similarly, is hard to draw precisely. The recommendation of the United Nations, which is now followed by a number of countries, is to define removal for one year or more as "permanent." This arbitrary distinction, however, does not satisfactorily classify persons who remain abroad for more than a year but who intend to return. In the United States, for example, travelers in transit, tourists, businessmen, students, and others may get a visa for a

[15] Brinley Thomas, *Migration and Economic Growth: A Study of Great Britain and the Atlantic Economy* (National Institute of Economic and Social Research, Economic and Social Study 12; Cambridge: Cambridge University Press, 1954), p. 36.

year's stay and still remain "nonimmigrant aliens." It might be better to distinguish between **permanent migrants,** who intend to settle in a new country for the rest of their lives, and **quasi-permanent migrants,** who intend to leave for a year or more but to return at some time after that.[16] In any case, the "permanence" is based on the migrants' stated intentions at the time of their removal, and some may not tell the truth while others may change their mind.

Several classes of international migrants do not fit into this scheme. Refugees, deportees, displaced persons, transferred populations, etc., are often, but not always, admitted under special conditions and outside the legal and statistical framework of normal movements. Also, persons who live on one side of an international border and work or shop or perform similar routine activities on the other side ordinarily carry frontier cards, with which they can short-circuit the usual control of passports and visas; and their movement back and forth is usually also segregated in the statistics.

3. The relevance of the data available varies with the problem being studied. An analysis of a country's labor force would obviously have to include seasonal workers and daily commuters, though these would not have to be included in a study, say, of housing. For an analysis of future population growth, including the children to be born to immigrants, age would be more relevant than citizenship. And for some purposes the total *de facto* population, including even one-day tourists, would be the most useful figure. But migration statistics are not ordinarily compiled so that one can take out just those data that are pertinent.

American migration statistics began in 1819, when a law was passed requiring masters of arriving ships to declare the number of their passengers, as well as their age, sex, occupation, and the country "of which it is their intention to become inhabitants." Had these manifests been filled in accurately, they would have furnished a reasonable source of immigration statistics, but actually the records are neither complete nor consistent. In particular, immigrants were not distinguished from visitors in the annual totals, and naturalized citizens returning from abroad were not differentiated from aliens.

The Act of 1819 specified that the passenger lists include information on "the country to which [the passengers] belong." If unambiguous at the time, it is not now

---

[16] This is the suggestion of Julius Isaac in *British Post-War Migration* (National Institute of Economic and Social Research, Occasional Paper 17; Cambridge: Cambridge University Press, 1954), p. 2.

clear whether this is to be interpreted to mean country of citizenship, country of last permanent residence, or country of birth. Bromwell, who was in the Department of State and whose report of the Department of State immigration statistics is presumably authoritative, gives the information as "country where born." Later, tables published by the Bureau of Statistics in summary of the Department of State immigration data are entitled "Arrivals, by nationality," but indicate in the body of the table that the classification is according to country of last permanent residence.[17]

The current series of statistics began in 1892, when the Bureau of Immigration (the predecessor of the present Immigration and Naturalization Service) was established. The quality of the data did not improve markedly. For a number of years the cabin passengers were excluded from the list of immigrants, and steerage passengers included, regardless of the duration of their intended stay in the United States. Until 1903, when this arbitrary definition was abolished, immigrants could evade the legal restrictions on entry that existed simply by paying the difference in the cost of passage. It was not until 1908 that the present distinction was made between "immigrant alien," or one intending (and permitted) to remain permanently, and "nonimmigrant alien," meaning either a visitor or a prior immigrant alien returning from a trip abroad. In the first decade of the twentieth century registration at points of entry along the land borders was introduced and a number of other improvements was made, so that by 1914 essentially the same system of controls as presently exists was instituted. That is to say, reasonably accurate and complete statistics were established about the same time that restrictive legislation cut down immigration to a fraction of the pre-1914 flow.

Internal Migration

Statistics on internal migration [18] are quite limited in both the United States and most other countries. If there are no direct data, it is possible to calculate internal migration as a residue. The difference between births and deaths gives one the natural increase, which when compared with the total intercensal increase yields the presumed net movement into or out of the area. With this method, however, it can happen that the errors in all the other data are added up as part of the assumed migration.

[17] E. P. Hutchinson, "Notes on Immigration Statistics of the United States," *Journal of the American Statistical Association,* 53:284 (December, 1958), 963–1025, at p. 973.

[18] See Everett S. Lee and Anne S. Lee, "Internal Migration Statistics for the United States," *Journal of the American Statistical Association,* 55:292 (December, 1960), 664–697.

Beginning with the 1850 census, native-born persons have been asked to name their state of birth. This information, when compared with their state of residence at the time of the census, is a gauge of internal migration, but only a rough one: the migration could have taken place at any time during the respondent's whole life, and intermediate stopovers, if any, are not given. Even so, the data are sufficient to indicate both the tremendous magnitude of the movement (according to each of the censuses, only about three persons out of every four lived in their native states) and the general directions of the streams (that is, East to West, South to North, and countryside to cities).

In more recent censuses additional questions on internal mobility have been added. In 1950, thus, each fifth person was asked where he had been living one year earlier. The **mobile population,** defined as those who were living in different houses within the United States on the two dates, was divided first of all into **intracounty movers** and **intercounty migrants.** The latter category was further divided according to whether the migration had been within the same state, to a contiguous state, or to a noncontiguous state.[19] To supplement such information, the Census Bureau now also makes an annual survey of about 25,000 dwelling units and reports the results in its *Current Population Reports.*

According to the data from the census and from these sample surveys, one person out of five moves each year to another house. The annual growth of the country's population from both natural increase and net international migration has amounted to about three million persons in recent years. Annual migration across county lines is more than three times this figure, and that between states more than one and a half times. In many parts of the country, therefore, particularly in the West, internal migration is by far the most important determinant of population size and composition, but it is still the demographic factor we know least about.

OTHER DATA ON POPULATION

The census, birth and death registrations, immigration records, and whatever data exist on internal migration, can be considered the basic statistics on the population on the United States. Other figures are often available, however, and sometimes in sources that in their original purpose have little or nothing to do with population. In any analysis of the labor force, for example, the census would have to be supplemented by

---

[19] U.S. Bureau of the Census, *U.S. Census of Population: 1950,* vol. 4, *Special Reports,* part 4, Ch. B, Population Mobility—States and State Economic Areas (Washington: U.S. Government Printing Office, 1956).

the much more detailed information available from the Bureau of Labor Statistics. The fact that the application form for marriage licenses in many counties asks the prospective groom to give his father's as well as his own occupation was used as the basis for one of the better studies of inter-generational social mobility.[20] The health records maintained by the armed forces, as another example, represent a virtually total sample of a selected group of males in the prime ages of life, and such data can be used in the study of morbidity, mortality, and public health.[21] The very careful statistics maintained by the large life insurance companies are a mine of information about a wide range of subjects.[22] Estimates of im-migrants to particular areas since the last census are often made from the records of public schools, utility companies, etc. These examples, obvi-ously, merely indicate the uses to which various types of data have been or can be put.

One important method of collecting population data is not used in the United States—the continuous **population register**. Such a system has been set up by a number of European nations: the three Scandinavian countries, Finland, the Netherlands, and Belgium.[23] In each of these, local registration bureaus maintain a separate card for each individual from the time of his birth (or immigration) to his death (or emigration), and on this are entered both changes in his civil status and other demographic data. With a population register, it is thus possible at any time to have the information ordinarily derived from a census and, in addition, to know what part migration has played in bringing about population changes. Disadvantages are that it is quite expensive to set up and main-tain, that to work properly it requires a high cultural level in the general population, and that conceivably so complete a record might constitute an infringement on individual liberty.

ERRORS IN DEMOGRAPHIC DATA

Someone unpracticed in the use of statistical data is likely to regard them in the same way an illiterate does any printed material, as *ipso facto*

[20] Natalie Rogoff, *Recent Trends in Occupational Mobility* (Glencoe, Ill.: Free Press, 1953).

[21] Cf. Spiegelman, *op. cit.*, p. 126.

[22] See in particular the *Statistical Bulletin* published by the Metropolitan Life Insurance Company.

[23] For an interesting account of the establishment of the system in Europe, see Dorothy Swaine Thomas, "The Continuous Register System of Population Account-ing," in National Resources Committee, Committee on Population Problems, *The Problems of a Changing Population* (Washington: U.S. Government Printing Office, 1938), Appendix C.

true. For such a person the discovery that every census is full of errors may come as a rude disillusionment. An experienced social scientist, on the contrary, is well aware that modern demographic data, though they constitute a unique reservoir of reliable statistical information, are no more perfect than any other human creation. Indeed, some of the most important elements of formal demography deal with how to detect the errors and devise methods for reducing them.

Sources of Error

Demographic data, as has been noted with respect to censuses, ought to be universal; that is, every instance of the phenomenon being measured ought to be counted once and only once. But except under optimum conditions, this dictum is difficult to follow in practice. **Errors in coverage** are of two types, deliberate and accidental. A priori, one might say that in a totalitarian state there would be more reasons than in the democratic West for evading a population count of any type, but less opportunity to do so. There is, however, little evidence to substantiate such a judgment, and in the comparative works of international bodies like the United Nations, which includes member-nations of every political type, the contrast itself is of course never made.

In a country like the United States, where the gathering of population data has not usually been supplementary to other administrative practices, and where in general the people have no reason to fear the power of the state, the intentional evasion of a census enumeration or of registration is exceptional. As we have noted above, this is much less true of immigration records. Surreptitious crossings take place along the borders of every country, and the number entering the United States without benefit of an official welcome has in some periods been quite large. For example, the past movement from Canada, both of Canadians and of transmigrant aliens, is largely unrecorded. According to the author of the best study of the subject, his reconstruction of it "has a status intermediate between pure fact and pure speculation." [24] As late as 1954 more than a million Mexicans entered the United States illegally by its southern border.[25]

Accidental errors in coverage may consist in missing someone who ought to be included, in counting him twice, or in misclassifying him.

[24] Nathan Keyfitz, "The Growth of Canadian Population," *Population Studies,* 4:1 (June, 1950), 47–63.

[25] Estimate of Eleanor M. Hadley, in "A Critical Analysis of the Wetback Problem," *Law and Contemporary Problems,* 21:2 (Spring, 1956), 334–357.

Duplicate registration of vital events is negligible. Duplicate counts in a census, while they exist, ordinarily cause far less error than passing over some of those who should have been counted. In migration statistics too high a count is sometimes made as a result of careless classification, as when a native returning from abroad is treated in the statistics as an immigrant. With respect to all types of population data, however, an undercount is more frequent and larger than an overcount.

Either over- or undercounts can be significant even if not very large, since they are typically concentrated in particular sectors of the population, particular areas, or particular time periods. It is not merely that at one time every tenth birth in the United States as a whole, for instance, escaped registration, but rather—to take an extreme hypothetical example—every second birth to a Negro in the rural South. An interregional or interracial comparison of fertility would be seriously off if this differential pattern in underregistration were not corrected. As another example, the census of 1870 (the first after the Civil War) was marked by an especially large underenumeration in the South; if not corrected, this nonrandom error would seriously affect any analysis of the pattern of national growth during the nineteenth century. Similarly, there is no reason to suppose that immigrants from various European countries were randomly distributed between steerage, where they were counted, and first and second class, where for most of the period of heavy immigration they were not.

Errors of classification can be illustrated by perhaps the most egregious example in American statistics, the nationality statistics of the immigration records. The officials who compiled the original data were unbelievably harried. According to the Commissioner of Immigration in New York during the 1890's:

The few registry clerks in the office were supposed . . . to take a statement from the immigrants about their nationality, destination and ages, [but] as a matter of fact whole pages did not contain any reply to any of these points. They were nothing more than an index of names of people arriving at the port. It was, as a matter of fact, physically impossible for these people—the port officers—to do more. There were but a few of them who had to register sometimes 4000 or 5000 in a day. Now, under no circumstances could it be expected from them that they could examine the immigrants as to all these specific points, and put them down, and then expect that when through with the day's work they would make up the statistics.[26]

[26] *Reports of the Industrial Commission,* 15 (Washington, 1901), 179; quoted in Brinley Thomas, *op. cit.,* p. 45.

Apparently immigrants were often listed as natives of the country from which they had sailed, though many more than English left from Liverpool, or Germans from Hamburg. This confusion was particularly likely when the language spoken by the immigrants was not the one associated with their native country; thus, Flemish-speaking Belgians arriving on Dutch boats were often counted as Dutch. And what the immigration officers did with the complex ethnic structures of the empires of Austria-Hungary and Russia, no one really knows. Certainly there is no consistency in the records: Ukrainian immigrants, for instance, were sometimes so listed, and sometimes as Russians, Austrians, Galicians, and Ruthenians; eventually each of these several categories was solemnly totaled.[27]

Another type of misclassification can be exemplified by one instance out of the past statistical record concerning Negroes. The 1840 census, in which the population was classified as "insane" or not, was criticized at the time by the American Statistical Association and a number of other organizations and individuals for its gross deficiencies. According to one of the memorials submitted to Congress, "In many towns all the colored population are stated to be insane; in very many others, two-thirds, one-third, one-quarter, or one-tenth of this ill-starred race are reported to be thus afflicted." The congressional committee to which these criticisms were referred admitted that this and a number of similar errors had been made, but took no steps to correct them or to remove the official sanction from the published census volumes.[28]

The person furnishing the information that goes into population statistics may not know the proper answer or, knowing it, may not tell the exact truth. Such **errors of response** are often difficult to detect, not to say to correct. An enumerator unable to find someone at home will seek information concerning him from his neighbors, who may not know the answer to even the basic questions asked in the census. When questions are put directly to the person concerned, either in a census or on any kind of form, any answer that implies a difference in status is in principle suspect. A person may state his income and education to be higher than his actual

---

[27] This ignorance is not limited to Eastern Europe or to the past. In 1958 the Passport Office of the United States Department of State issued some statistics on the number of American tourists that had visited various European countries during the first three quarters of that year. "Holland," with 17,621 visitors, was eighth on the list, and "Netherlands" was eighteenth with 5,110. A few weeks later, the somewhat embarrassed passport authorities issued a revised list, pointing out that these two countries were, of course, the same (*Nieuwe Rotterdamse Courant,* November 1, 1958).

[28] Wright, *op. cit.,* p. 38.

earnings or schooling; he may describe himself as single rather than divorced; and so on. With respect to illegal acts, it is of course pointless to try to collect data directly by asking the participants; and the primary difficulty in studying, for example, abortions, illegitimate births, or—as we have noted—clandestine migration, is collecting reasonably accurate data.

Those responsible for assembling demographic statistics, of course, are well aware of such tendencies, and whenever possible questions that invite an emotional response are avoided. On the other hand, some data are too important not to be collected if it is at all feasible to do so. Thus, the 1940 census finally included a question on income in spite of the very vigorous opposition to it, but the Census Bureau has acceded to the probably weaker agitation against asking the respondents' religious affiliation. Whether opposition to such questions is well considered is not the main point; strong feeling against one question, even if quite irrational, may spread and damage the accuracy of the whole census.

It is convenient to discuss the reasons for errors of response in terms, again, of those with respect to age as this has been reported in United States censuses. It might be supposed that most Americans both could furnish this datum and would be willing to do so, and it is possible to check this supposition by comparing the age structure in successive censuses. As we have noted above, even in a country like the United States some report that they do not know their age. Others give it only approximately, either because they do not know it precisely or because they do not recognize the importance of accuracy. They round off their stated age to an even number, to a number ending in five, or particularly to one ending in zero.[29] How old a person is might be regarded as a relatively neutral characteristic; but whenever some prestige is clearly associated with a particular age, this fact is reflected in the record. Thus, respondents tend to heap ages at majority (that is, 21 years for males and both 18 and 21 for females), understating or overstating the correct figure as the case may be. The age of infants and young children is often overstated, and that is one reason for their usual underenumeration. Persons just below 65 years and the very old also often exaggerate their longevity. At least by popular legend, although this has seldom been validated in an empirical study,[30] middle-aged persons and particularly women tend to understate their age, or refuse to give it out.

[29] See Roberto Bachi, "Measurement of the Tendency to Round Off Age Returns," *Bulletin de l'Institut International de Statistique,* 34:3 (1954), 129–138.
[30] But see T. Lynn Smith and Homer L. Hitt, "The Misstatement of Women's Ages and the Vital Indexes," *Metron,* 13 (1939), 95–108; cited in Smith, *op. cit.,* p. 116.

There are, finally, errors committed by the official personnel collecting and processing demographic statistics. The **collection of the original data,** since it cannot be mechanized, is the stage hardest to control. The fact that physicians often make errors on the birth or death certificates they fill in suggests that even a high level of intelligence and professional competence does not in itself guarantee accuracy. Yet there is no substitute for such accuracy: "The quality of the census results is wholly dependent on the enumeration, and no country can afford to have a poor enumeration in the hope that office work subsequently will improve it." [31] This dictum applies no less, it need hardly be said, to vital statistics and migration data. In the context in which it was written, the sentence was intended to emphasize the importance of improving future censuses. In this context, we can interpret it to mean also that our analysis of the past, and sometimes of the very recent past, can be no more definite than the quality of the original statistics permits.

The responsibility for collecting immigration data in the United States has been shifted a number of times—from the Department of State (1820–1874) to the Bureau of Statistics of the Treasury Department (1867–1895), to the Bureau of Immigration (1892–1932), to the Immigration and Naturalization Service, first in the Department of Labor (1933–1940) and then in the Department of Justice (1940–). For some periods, it will be noted, duplicate sets of statistics were taken, but until the 1920's none was satisfactory. Some of the complexity of immigration statistics is the result of this frequent change in the responsible agency, and of the patent fact that the purposes these records were supposed to serve were neither clear nor constant.

Generally speaking, the greatest improvements in demographic data have been the consequence of **better administration and processing.** During the nineteenth century the staff for each census was assembled fresh every ten years. When a permanent Bureau of the Census was established shortly after the turn of the century, this act had a salutary effect on professional standards, both in the census itself and in the collection of vital statistics. Several technical inventions, particularly the Hollerith card and its various analogues, have made it possible virtually to eliminate some types of errors. Similarly, as we have noted, the guidance given by the Census Bureau and, since 1946, by the newly established National Office of Vital Statistics has been largely responsible for the improvement in the local registration of vital statistics. In general, it is worth stressing,

31 United Nations, *Handbook of Population Census Methods,* p. 21.

we can expect figures to be better if they are collected by a specific statistical bureau, rather than as an adjunct to other administrative functions.

Correction of Errors

Any single set of data can be checked for its internal consistency. There cannot be, as an extreme example, more mothers or more housewives than there are women. In current American censuses, the first check of this kind is made right in the field. Crew leaders look for contradictory statements in the schedule (for example, a respondent reported as born in the United States and also as naturalized) and for incomplete answers (for example, a person born in "Ireland" rather than Eire or Northern Ireland); and when they find one, they send the enumerator back to the original respondent to complete the form correctly.

There must also be a temporal consistency in any statistical series. Some characteristics, once acquired, are permanent—for example, literacy or legal majority; and a decline in the proportion able to read or to vote, if not due to emigration or a change in age structure or whatever, would make one suspect the accuracy of the data. Age does not remain constant but changes at a regular rate, and an unexplained variation from this pattern would also make one check the figures again.

It is often possible to compare data collected in different ways on the same facts, such as country-of-birth returns in the census with immigration records. Or the latter can be contrasted with the statistics maintained by some emigration countries. In general, the records of the receiving countries are better: for the entire period from the first colonization to the present day, overseas emigration totaled over 60 million by the statistics of the receiving countries, but about 10 per cent less by those of the sending countries.[32] For specific countries or periods, however, the discrepancy is much greater. For example, "for the years 1916 to 1920, Italian passport statistics indicate 633,000 emigrants to the United States; but the statistics of that country registered only 171,000 Italian immigrants." [33] Similarly, Dutch statistics show a total of 130,222 departures to *all* countries during 1882–1924, while for this period American statistics alone record 179,258 arrivals from the Netherlands.[34]

[32] Dudley Kirk, *Europe's Population in the Interwar Years* (League of Nations; Princeton: Princeton University Press, 1946), pp. 72–73 and n. 2.

[33] Lacroix, "Problems," *op. cit.*, p. 85.

[34] Imre Ferenczi, *International Migrations,* 1: *Statistics* (Publication 14; New York: National Bureau of Economic Research, 1929), 125, 737–746.

As a particular kind of such comparisons, it is always possible to check a census against birth registrations—though, as we have noted above, such a check is largely vitiated by the typical underenumeration of infants. In the 1940 census an especially careful cross-check of this kind was made. Enumerators filled in a separate card for each infant under four months old on April 1, the official date of the census, and these cards were compared with the registrations of births and infant deaths in each area. The results were appalling. For the entire country only 92.5 per cent of births had been registered. In 16 states the complete figure was below 90 per cent, the standard that had been used to admit them to the Birth-Registration Area; in six states it was under 85 per cent. In South Carolina and Arkansas hardly more than three births in every four were registered. Partly as a consequence of renewed efforts to improve registration procedures, and partly because of the larger proportion of hospital confinements, a similar check ten years later showed that there had been a considerable increase in the proportion of births registered. In 1950 this was almost 98 per cent over the whole nation, and for the South it was 96 per cent. Only two states still remained below the standard of 90 per cent.[35] Thus, when one imperfect instrument is used to gauge the accuracy of another, the over-all improvement attained can be great, even though it is not possible by such a comparison to detect parallel errors.

The final method of correcting errors is by an especially careful recount of a small portion of the population. With a properly drawn sample, it is possible with modern mathematics to calculate the maximum error the results represent with respect to the whole population. For example, after the 1950 census a **Post-Enumeration Survey** was made using carefully selected and specially trained interviewers. About 3,500 small areas were recanvassed in order to gauge the number of households omitted in the original census, and 22,000 households were revisited in order to see how many persons had been miscounted. On this basis, it was estimated that there had been an underenumeration of 3,400,000 persons and an over-enumeration of 1,309,000 in the census, or a net undercount equal to 1.4 per cent of the total enumerated population. Errors were relatively more frequent in the South, in rural areas, and among nonwhites.

If a sample survey can be more accurate than a complete count, the reader may ask, then why bother to have a census? A census is needed to give information about small populations, both the number of inhabitants of villages and the small residual numbers in a multiple cross classification.

[35] Sam Shapiro, "Recent Testing of Birth Registration Completeness in the United States," *Population Studies,* 8:1 (July, 1954), 3–21.

That lawyers in Philadelphia have more children than those in Denver (if they do), that among the foreign-born in Boston the Greeks have the highest average income (if this is the case)—this kind of fact can come only from a census, and one type of social research is based on such cross tabulations. But if censuses can be made more accurate by using better qualified personnel, why not do so? The answer to this is that accuracy, particularly extreme accuracy, is expensive; and it may be more useful to census users to maintain "reasonable" completeness and correctness and use the funds so saved to obtain additional data.

The objective of "optimum design" in sampling is coming to be the objective in census taking. Instead of striving for perfection, we view the task as that of balancing the costs of producing statistics against the losses from errors in the statistics.[36]

Sampling has many more uses than checking accuracy. In the 1960 census itself many questions were asked only of one person out of each four. It was possible thus to expand considerably the information gathered with a minimum increase in the cost. In its so-called Current Population Survey, the Census Bureau now counts a national sample every month, and more complete intercensal surveys are made of particular states or other areas that have experienced especially rapid growth. Other surveys, like the one on internal migration mentioned above, are used to gather data on various specific subjects.

SUMMARY

Population data are of four main types: the census, vital statistics, international migration records, and those on internal migration. Although partial precursors were found in previous historical eras, in a strict sense all four types are a product of modern Western culture. The standards of accuracy associated with the best demographic statistics did not exist anywhere in even the recent past, and they exist today only in countries with a well established statistical tradition.

The United States census, held every ten years without interruption since 1790, has gradually become more accurate and broader in the range of questions covered. Today it is an indispensable tool for—among

---

[36] Morris H. Hansen, William N. Hurwitz, and Leon Pritzker, "The Accuracy of Census Results," *American Sociological Review*, 18:4 (August, 1953), 416–423. See also Joseph Steinberg, Leon Pritzker, and Walter Perkins, "Methods of Evaluating the Coverage of the 1960 Census of Population," *Population Index*, 26:3 (July, 1960), 203.

others—statesmen, social scientists, and businessmen. Vital statistics, because of the historical accident that they are gathered by local authorities rather than by the federal government, have developed more slowly. During the past several decades, however, progress has been rapid, and reasonably accurate compilations of births and deaths are now available for the whole country. The immigration records, inadequate in a number of ways during the nineteenth century, were brought up to a reasonable standard of accuracy and completeness by about 1914. The United States statistics of many demographic phenomena are still quite poor—for example, marriage and divorce, morbidity, and, particularly, internal migration.

To avoid errors in demographic statistics, the following conditions must be met: (a) All categories to be measured must be precisely defined. (b) Each instance of the phenomenon being measured must be counted once and only once. (c) Respondents must be induced to answer truthfully the questions put to them. (d) Answers must be classified in the appropriate subcategories. (e) Errors must not be introduced in the compiling, processing, and publication of the data.

As even this list suggests, perfect accuracy is not attainable. Indeed, it is not sought: the aim in modern demographic statistics is to reduce the error to a small proportion of known size rather than to try to eliminate it altogether. The errors that are made can be detected and in part corrected by checking (a) any form for collecting information, such as a census schedule or a birth certificate, for internal consistency; (b) data of the same series, such as successive censuses, for serial consistency; (c) data of different types, such as vital statistics and the census, or the census and immigration records, for external consistency; (d) with an especially carefully drawn sample, to be compared for over-all accuracy with the grosser count.

For the past 90 years or so, several international congresses and organizations have tried in various ways to establish worldwide statistical standards. These efforts are wholly laudable, and it is particularly useful that the underdeveloped countries presently beginning their statistical records will be able, at least in some respects, to start from the highest level of the procedures so painfully attained in Western countries. It must be emphasized, however, that variation in statistical methods is in part accidental—and with sufficient effort and good will this part can be removed—and in part a reflection of differences in national culture. International migration statistics, for example, so long as they are collected as an adjunct to the political control of national borders, will be noncomparable mainly because of the great differences in various countries' migration laws. Or, as another example, what are termed common-law marriages in the United States are very frequent in Latin America, where, however, they are often not recognized either in law or in the statistics, so that thousands of mothers or even grandmothers are classified as single. Or, as an example of a contrast between the regions of one country, the common underenumeration and underregistration of Negroes in the South of the United States in part reflect the white officials' sentiment that what happens to Negroes is not important enough to be recorded. In short, while some standardization of population data is both possible and desirable, so long as national cultures are not homogenized into a worldwide uniformity, the international comparability of statistics will not be fully achieved.

SUGGESTIONS FOR FURTHER READING

United Nations, Department of Economic Affairs, Statistical Office, *Handbook of Population Census Methods* (Studies in Methods, series F, no. 5; New York, 1954).

―――, Department of Economic and Social Affairs, *Handbook of Vital Statistics Methods* (Studies in Methods, series F, no. 7; New York, 1955).

―――, Department of Social Affairs, *Problems of Migration Statistics* (Population Studies, no. 5; New York, 1949).

Recommended procedures contrasted with actual practices. Basic.

U.S. Bureau of the Census, *The 1950 Censuses—How They Were Taken: Population, Housing, Agriculture, Irrigation, Drainage* (Procedural Studies of the 1950 Censuses, no. 2; Washington: U.S. Government Printing Office, 1955).

―――, *Fact Finder for the Nation* (Washington: U.S. Government Printing Office, 1957).

Both volumes pertain to the entire work of the Census Bureau. The second is more popular.

U.S. National Office of Vital Statistics, *Vital Statistics of the United States, 1950* (Washington: U.S. Government Printing Office, 1954), 3 vols.

Includes chapters on the history and organization of vital statistics, as well as analyses and tables.

Milbank Memorial Fund, *Problems in the Collection and Comparability of International Statistics* (New York, 1949).

    A series of essays on how various demographic concepts are interpreted in different countries. Interesting.

Walter F. Willcox and Imre Ferenczi, eds., *International Migrations,* vol. 1: *Statistics;* vol. 2: *Interpretations* (Publications 14 and 18; New York: National Bureau of Economic Research, 1929, 1931).

E. P. Hutchinson, "Notes on Immigration Statistics of the United States," *Journal of the American Statistical Association,* 53:284 (December, 1958), 963–1025.

International Labour Office, *International Migration: 1945–1957* (Studies and Reports, new series, no. 54; Geneva, 1959).

    International Migrations, while out of date in some respects, is still the best general discussion of historical migration statistics. See in particular the essay by Marian Rubins Davis, "Critique of Official United States Immigration Statistics," vol. 2, pp. 645–658, which is brought up to date in Hutchinson's paper.

Mortimer Spiegelman, *Introduction to Demography* (Chicago: Society of Actuaries, 1955).

George W. Barclay, *Techniques of Population Analysis* (New York: Wiley, 1958).

    Narrowly technical but excellent over the range that they cover. Spiegelman is the official textbook of the Society of Actuaries; Barclay is perhaps more useful for a novice in formal demography.

A. J. Jaffe, *Handbook of Statistical Methods for Demographers: Selected Problems in the Analysis of Census Data* (U.S. Bureau of the Census; Washington: U.S. Government Printing Office, 1951).

    A book of readings on demographic techniques with introductions to the several chapters.

Robert Gutman, *Birth and Death Registration in Massachusetts, 1639–1900* (New York: Milbank Memorial Fund, 1959).

    A definitive study of America's earliest registration system.

4. AGE AND SEX STRUCTURE

What characteristics of the population ought to be included in a discussion of its composition? The number of possible systems of classification is all but infinite. One might, for example, divide a population into blonds, brunets, and redheads and then try to relate hair color to other variables; but, except for a physical anthropologist, the results would not be very illuminating. On the other hand, it is standard to classify the population by skin color—which intrinsically is of no greater significance than hair color—because the fertility and mortality of Negroes and whites, for example, as well as their distribution by region, occupation, education, and so on, are markedly different. For a demographic analysis, that is to say, a relevant characteristic of a population can be defined as one that exhibits a significant differential pattern with respect to demographic rates.

On this basis, the most important characteristics of the American population are the following, arranged into five broad classes:

Biological	Age, sex
Ethnic	Race
	National stock, language, citizenship
Geographic	Region, state, county, etc.
	Residence: rural, urban, metropolitan
Socio-economic	Occupation
	Income
	Social class
Cultural	Education
	Religion
	Marital status

The five classes are not rigidly separated, for the social effect designated by any one of them pervades them all. The contrast between male and female, for example, or between young and old, is fundamentally biological; but behavior varies also according to how the particular culture defines the roles appropriate to the two sexes and the various age-groups. Races or national stocks or marital status are also to some degree biological, but here the fundamental differentiation is by the culturally determined behavior patterns. In the United States, with its short history and a population built up in large part by immigration, the ethnic variation is usually more important than a regional one, which would be its counterpart in most European countries; and differences among states or other geographical units are, of course, even smaller.

The rural-urban contrast, in spite of the urbanization of almost the whole country in recent decades, is for most purposes the most significant classification in any long-term analysis of the American population. Many other characteristics are closely related to residence—not only occupation, education, and income, but also, for example, ethnic group. That in the United States the Jews and the Irish have always been urban while the Swedes settled on the land, that the Negroes are moving from rural to metropolitan areas—such facts have an obvious relation to ethnic differences. Similarly, the distinction between town and countryside denotes, especially for the past, important divergences in religious denomination and other cultural characteristics important in an analysis of population.

THE IMPORTANCE OF POPULATION STRUCTURE

This chapter is concerned with the two biological factors of sex and age and their effect on demographic processes. Persons are born into a society, some of them later move away and perhaps are replaced by others moving in, and eventually all that remain die. These processes of fertility, migration, and mortality together determine not only the current size of the population of any area, but also its **structure,** or the distribution by sex and age. Conversely, to the degree that other factors remain unchanged, the population structure sets the future rates of fertility, migration, and mortality.

Data on age, available in almost all types of population records, are relatively accurate and complete, though some care must be exercised in interpreting them.[1] Statistics on sex are even better. There is no ambiguity

[1] See pages 41–43, 61.

about the meaning of *male* and *female,* and seldom any motivation for misrepresentation. The historical record has only two significant gaps: the sex of Negroes before 1820 and the sex of immigrants before about 1850. The recorded age and sex of the whole population, however, may be a good deal more accurate than figures for the various subgroups.[2]

The reason that almost every public document asks for one's sex and age is that they are relevant to almost every circumstance. The average capabilities of a man and a woman, or even more of a child, a youth, an adult, and an old person, vary considerably in a number of ways. For example, the dominant characteristic of an army unit or of a frontier town is its maleness, the absence of women and children. What is termed a **young population**—that is, one in which young persons are relatively more numerous—is more fecund, more vigorous, and perhaps more venturesome, than an **old population.**

How important the structure of a population is in influencing fertility and mortality can be illustrated by the following historical examples.[3] In a special Massachusetts state census in 1905 it was pointed out that the average number of children ever born to mothers then living was only 2.77. This figure was compared with that in the previous generation by asking the respondents how many children *their* mothers had borne— namely, 6.47 on the average. The contrast was interpreted as evidence of a very sharp decline in average family size. Actually, of course, the number of children to the respondent mothers—aged, let us say, 15 to 44 —was compared in this census with the *completed* fertility of a group virtually all of whom had reached the end of their fecund years.

Similarly, if the influence of age structure is ignored in an analysis of mortality, the consequence can be a gross distortion of reality. During the Spanish-American War there was great public concern over the large number of soldiers dying in the Philippines. In his annual report for 1899 the Secretary of War replied to the criticism by pointing out that the death rate among the troops was almost identical with that of the civilian population of Washington or Boston. In order to make a polemical point, he overlooked the fact that soldiers are all young adults while the general population includes also infants and old persons, who generally have a higher death rate.

[2] See, for example, the discussion of the sex ratios of Negroes and whites in T. Lynn Smith, *Population Analysis* (New York: McGraw-Hill, 1948), Ch. 5.

[3] Both are given by Robert E. Chaddock in "Age and Sex in Population Analysis," *Annals of the American Academy of Political and Social Science,* 188 (November, 1936), 185–193. (This article has been reprinted in Joseph J. Spengler and Otis Dudley Duncan, eds., *Demographic Analysis,* Glencoe, Ill.: Free Press, 1956, pp. 443–451.)

THE SEX RATIO

The simplest measure of population structure is the sex ratio, defined as the number of males per 1,000 females. Thus, for the United States in 1957:

$$\text{Sex ratio} = \frac{\text{Number of males}}{\text{Number of females}} \times 1,000$$

$$= \frac{84,858,000}{86,371,000} \times 1,000 = 982 \; [4]$$

The sex ratio of any population is affected by past fertility, mortality, and migration. Although the evidence is ambiguous, it is probable that many more males are conceived than females; and while more fail to survive the nine-month gestation period, the ratio at birth is still usually about 1,060 males to 1,000 females.[5] This higher mortality rate of males continues throughout life, for not only are they generally more susceptible to disease but their occupations are usually more dangerous. Since males and females are seldom balanced in migration, whether internal or international, this also can have an important effect on the sex ratios of both the sending and the receiving areas.

One reason for studying the sex ratio is its relevance to family formation. The number of marriages possible—and thus also the number of legitimate births—depend in part on whether there are as many men as women. The sex ratio of the entire population, however, hardly indicates the number of potential new families. The pertinent figure is rather the sex ratio of that portion able to wed. This class is delimited, first of all, by age (it is usual to include that sector of the population aged 14 and over) and, secondly, by marital status (in a monogamous society, those with one spouse may not take another).[6] If marriageable persons are defined as

[4] Until about ten years ago—and thus in all books except the most recently published—the sex ratio was usually defined as the number of males per *100* females, in which case it is 98.2 for the United States in 1957. But the trend has been to eliminate the pointless decimal. Note that in Europe the convention is to define the ratio as the number of females per 1,000 (or 100) males.

[5] In a number of specific populations the sex ratio at birth has varied from a high of 1,132 (Greece) to a low of 1,011 (Cuba, colored). See Philip S. Lawrence, "The Sex Ratio, Fertility, and Ancestral Longevity," *Quarterly Review of Biology,* 16:1 (March, 1941), 35–79.

[6] Whether to include widowed and divorced persons is a moot point. Legally they are marriageable, but actually in the United States a large proportion of the persons so designated in any census will never marry; and of those that do, many will be too old to bear children.

those denoted as "single" in the census classification—that is, those aged 14 years or over and never married—for the United States in 1950 their sex ratio was 1,267. Thus, in spite of the slight female surplus in the population as a whole, among single persons there were more than five males to every four females.[7]

This marriageable class, however, cannot be considered as homogeneous. One of the prerequisites to romantic love is that most prosaic characteristic, spatial propinquity, and the availability of partners varies widely from one section of the country to another.[8] The more recently settled the region, the higher was the 1950 sex ratio of the marriageable class:

New England	1,062
Middle Atlantic	1,126
South	1,328
North Central	1,279
Mountain	1,551
Pacific	1,565
Alaska	1,897

Horace Greeley's advice has been too well heeded; his present-day counterpart might better say, "Go west, young woman!"

While perhaps the most obvious factor, distance by far is not the only one that influences marriage rates. Intermarriage is atypical across lines set by race, religion, and social class—to name only the most important— and the sex ratio of each of the essentially endogamous subgroups formed by the composite effect of all of these factors is thus the most relevant to the probability of family formation. From Table 4-1, which gives the sex ratios of subgroups divided according to only two of these variables, it can be seen that the degree of disproportion is rather high. In a more detailed analysis, it would be necessary to study the effect of all of these variables simultaneously; for, say, a white Catholic physician, aged 32, living in New York City, is more likely to marry if he finds a woman whose background is similar in every respect.

---

[7] There is good reason to believe, moreover, that young males, who make up a major portion of migratory workers and other transients, are therefore more often underenumerated.

[8] The relevant distance is actually measured not in thousands of miles but in tens of city blocks. See James H. S. Bossard, "Residential Propinquity as a Factor in Marriage Selection," *American Journal of Sociology*, 38:2 (September, 1932), 219–224, and many subsequent studies that have validated the findings of this pioneer work.

TABLE 4-1. Males per 1,000 Females among Single Persons
Aged 14 Years and Over, by Race and Residence,
United States, 1950

	White	*Nonwhite*
Urban	1,107	1,210
Rural nonfarm	1,552	1,546
Rural farm	1,763	1,344

Source: U.S. Bureau of the Census, *U.S. Census of Population: 1950,* vol. 2, *Characteristics of the Population,* part 1, U.S. Summary (Washington: U.S. Government Printing Office, 1953), p. 1–97.

THE POPULATION PYRAMID

The distribution of a population by age and sex together is usually represented by a special type of bar graph, called a population pyramid. Figure 4-1 is a population pyramid for the United States in 1950. The various bars represent successive age-groups, from the lowest age at the bottom to the highest at the top,[9] each divided between the males at the left and the females at the right. The length of all the bars together, as

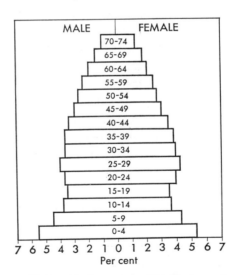

Figure 4-1. Percentage Distribution of the Population of the United States by Age and Sex, 1950

Source: U.S. Bureau of the Census, *U.S. Census of Population: 1950,* vol. 2, *Characteristics of the Population,* part 1, U.S. Summary (Washington: U.S. Government Printing Office, 1953), pp. 37–38.

[9] The ages above 74 years, which are often unreliably reported, are omitted.

denoted by the scale along the horizontal axis, represents 100 per cent (or the total population in absolute figures). Each bar thus designates what proportion that age-group is of the total. Whether fertility is high or low, therefore, is shown by the relative length of the bottom bar. The reason for the basic shape of a pyramid is that among those born, say, in 1875, some have died in each year since then, gradually reducing the length of the bars representing successively higher ages. The shape is not ordinarily a perfect pyramid, however, because mortality varies from year to year, and because fertility and migration also affect the population structure.

The depletion caused by a past famine, epidemic, or war, or by a period of particularly low fertility or large emigration, is represented by an indentation from a smooth pyramid; and, on the contrary, a past period of high fertility or of large immigration is represented by a corresponding protuberance. These irregularities remain on population pyramids of successive dates, gradually moving up to the top of the graph and disappearing only when the persons affected finally die off. Such a group of persons all born during the same year (or some other unit of time), who are analyzed as a unit through their lifetime, is called a **cohort**.

In Figure 4-2 the population pyramid for 1950 is superimposed on one for 1940. The pertinence of the contrast can be illustrated with respect

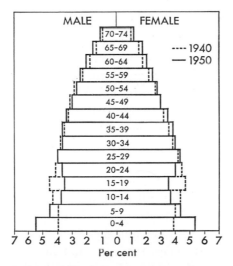

Figure 4-2. Percentage Distribution of the Population of the United States by Age and Sex, 1940 and 1950

Source: U.S. Bureau of the Census, *U.S. Census of Population: 1950,* vol. 2, *Characteristics of the Population,* part 1, U.S. Summary (Washington: U.S. Government Printing Office, 1953), pp. 37–38.

to the fertility trends the two pyramids indicate. In the 1940 graph the bars of those aged 0 to 9 years are comparatively short, reflecting the low fertility during the depression of the 1930's. Ten years later this cohort was aged 10 to 19 years, and in the 1950 graph the bars for this age-group are relatively short. The two lowest bars in the 1950 graph, however, are much longer, for they indicate the baby boom during and immediately after the war. If we wanted to know what a population pyramid for 1960 would look like, we could get a preliminary idea by shifting the bars up another ten years. The small cohorts born during the 1930's would then be in their 20's; and this means that the age-group out of which the labor force, the army, and parents are mainly recruited will be, in proportion to the total population, the smallest in American history. From 1965 on the very much larger cohorts born in the years immediately after the war will reach the age of 20, and this reversal of the trend will affect many aspects of American life.

THE THREE MAIN AGE-GROUPS

The population pyramid is a wonderfully useful tool. It tells at a glance both the structure at a given date and the accumulated effect of past fertility, mortality, and migration. For some purposes, however, a summary figure is more enlightening than this wealth of information. In order to summarize the effect of structure on society, we can divide the population into three main age-groups: dependent children, under 15 years; the active population, 15 to 64 years; and dependent aged, 65 years and over. This distribution is shown in Table 4-2 for the period since 1880, the date at which America's transformation from an agrarian to an industrial society passed its preliminary stage.

Dependent Children

From the censuses of 1790 and 1800, when half of the white population was under 16 years, until 1940, there was a steady decline in the proportion of children, at first slow and then more rapid. In 1850 two-fifths of the population was under 15 years, and in 1910 almost one-third. After the depression of the 1930's, the proportion fell to one-fourth. Then the trend was reversed.

The most obvious reason for these changes in the proportion of children, of course, was the long-term decline in fertility and its revival after 1945. The decline in the death rate, since it was concentrated in infant and child

TABLE 4-2. Distribution by Per Cent among Three
Main Age-Groups, United States, 1880–1955

Year	*Total*	*Dependent Children (under 15 years)*	*The Active Population (15–64 years)*	*Dependent Aged (65 years and over)*	*Index of Aging* $\frac{(5)}{(3)} \times 100$
(1)	(2)	(3)	(4)	(5)	(6)
1880	100	38.1	58.5	3.4	8.9
1890	100	35.5	60.4	3.9	11.0
1900	100	34.4	61.3	4.1	11.9
1910	100	32.1	63.4	4.3	13.4
1920	100	31.7	63.4	4.7	14.8
1930	100	29.3	65.1	5.4	18.4
1940	100	25.0	68.1	6.8	27.2
1950	100	26.8	65.3	8.2	30.6
1955	100	29.6	61.8	8.5	28.7

Sources: Conrad Taeuber and Irene B. Taeuber, *The Changing Population of the United States* (New York: Wiley, 1958), p. 31; U.S. Bureau of the Census, *Current Population Reports,* series P-25, no. 121 (September 27, 1955).

mortality, was in demographic terms equivalent to a rise in the birth rate. That is to say, the fall in the proportion of children up to 1940 was less, and the rise since 1940 was greater, because of declining mortality. The effect of immigration was complex. Since most immigrants were young adults, the immediate consequence of their entry was to decrease the proportion of children in the population; but in the somewhat longer run this effect was countered by their higher than average fertility.

The gradual reduction in the proportion of children, a concomitant of the country's urbanization, varied according to regional differences in fertility, mortality, and immigration. In 1880, when 38 per cent of the whole population was under 15, among the various states this percentage ranged from 24 in Montana to 46 in Mississippi. "In general, proportions of youth in the southern States in 1880 were as high as those in the national population in the colonial period, while the proportions in the northeastern industrial States were as low as those in many modern industrial nations." [10] Today these regional differences are much smaller.

The proportion aged 5 to 14 years, which more or less defines the school population through junior high school, also decreased steadily, from 24.3 per cent in 1880 to 20.1 per cent in 1930 and, more sharply, to 16.2 per cent in 1950. Although the proportion in school ages fell off, the allocations for education increased greatly, partly because of the larger per-

[10] Conrad Taeuber and Irene B. Taeuber, *The Changing Population of the United States* (New York: Wiley, 1958), p. 29.

centage of these cohorts that attended schools and even more because of the spectacular rise in the per capita cost.[11] Even so, during the depression of the 1930's and the war of the 1940's minimum amounts of money and attention were allocated to keeping the school plant and personnel up to par, so that in any case a determined postwar effort was necessary to make up deficiencies. The problem was considerably aggravated by the baby boom. During the first postwar decade more than 36 million infants were born to American parents, and as these children move up into adult life, they disrupt one after another institutions built to accommodate more modest numbers. By 1955, when the percentage of the population aged 5 to 14 years had increased to 18.6, greatly swollen student bodies had burst the grammar schools, and administrators of high schools and colleges were well aware that their turn was coming. Under these conditions, it will be particularly difficult to improve, or even to maintain, the quality of instruction over the next decades. In the public debate over the low standards in American education, the very statement of the issue, to be complete, must refer to the reversal of the secular trend in population structure: the percentage of dependent children increased from 25 in 1940 to almost 30 in 1955.

The Active Population

The definition of adulthood, while it has a biological base, varies greatly from one culture to another, and in the United States from one period or region to another. Children on a farm are assigned their chores; in today's cities child labor is prohibited. Any delimitation of active adulthood in terms of chronological ages rather than functions, therefore, must be approximate and to some degree arbitrary. The definition used here, the group aged 15 to 64, has the advantage of conforming with statistical and legal conventions, but in several respects it overstates the actual size of the active population. Few outside this age-group perform adult roles, and many in it do not.

If we define the active population in economic terms, then the principal deviations result from education beyond the high school and from early retirement. Among white males only 38.8 per cent of the 14–19 age-group were in the labor force in 1950 and, at the other end, less than 80

---

[11] The expenditure per pupil in elementary and secondary schools jumped from $20 in 1900 (or $62 in 1949–1950 dollars) to $259 in 1950, and even this increase has not kept pace with the rising costs. J. Frederic Dewhurst and Associates, *America's Needs and Resources: A New Survey* (New York: Twentieth Century Fund, 1955), p. 384.

per cent of the 60–64 group.[12] In 1950 more than nine-tenths of 15-year-old boys were in school, and more than one-fifth of those aged 20. And if we define the active population also by noneconomic roles, the same deviations can be noted. The median age at marriage, though it has been going down, is still nearer 20 than 15; and women's childbearing period ends between 45 and 50. The age at which young men are conscripted has usually been around 18; and meaningful military service ends long before 65. In most states legal maturity is set at 18 or 21 years. Voting usually begins at 21 and gradually sloughs off in the advanced ages.

As the proportion of the active population becomes larger, "the burden of dependency" declines.[13] From 1880 to 1940, as can be seen from Table 4-2, the proportion of children decreased faster than that of the aged increased, so that the percentage in the active sector rose from 58.5 to 68.1. After 1940, however, this adult sector fell off sharply, so that by 1955 it constituted almost the same proportion as in 1900. Why should the burden of dependency, which had been getting less for the whole of the nation's history, have become heavier in the last decades? No single answer can be given to this question. It is decidedly relevant, for example, that the massive pre-1914 immigration, which used to supplement the native-born adults, has been very much smaller since that date. The youngest cohorts in the active population in 1955, those aged 15 to 25, had been born during the 1930's, when the nation's birth rate was at the lowest point in its history; and these very small cohorts will remain as part of the active population for almost half a century. In the postwar years, as we have seen, the baby boom increased the proportion of dependent children, and the percentage of dependent aged continued to rise, though more slowly.

The burden of dependency will continue to get heavier, at least for a period. If we were to take age 20 rather than 15 to define the beginning of adulthood (and, as we have seen, in many respects this would be a realistic choice), then the full effect of the low fertility during the depression would appear only in 1960. Meanwhile, the proportionately much larger cohorts born in the early years of the century will successively reach 65 and add to the number of dependents at that end of the scale. This trend will be partly balanced by the larger cohorts born from 1945 on, who will begin to enter the active sector in the early 1960's. Whether the burden of dependency will continue to rise once the boom

<hr>

[12] Taeuber and Taeuber, *op. cit.,* p. 217.
[13] Cf. United Kingdom, Royal Commission on Population, *Report* (London: H. M. Stationery Office, 1949), p. 111.

babies have all assumed adult roles will depend on two unknown factors —the size of future families and the future control of death at advanced ages.

Dependent Aged

The proportion of the population aged 65 and over increased from 3.4 per cent in 1880 to 8.6 per cent in 1955. In absolute numbers the growth was from 3.1 million in 1900 to about 16 million in 1960; the population as a whole increased by 2.4 times and the aged by 5.3 times. Few demographic developments have received wider public attention than this "problem." Newspaper readers have had to learn the meaning of **gerontology** (from the Greek _gerōn,_ old man), the study of the aged, and **geriatrics** (from the Greek _gēras,_ old age), the healing of the aged. Much that has been written on the subject, however, is distinguished more by the authors' noble sentiments, not to say sentimentality, than by their knowledge and acuity. "Viewed as a whole the 'problem of aging' is no problem at all. It is only the pessimistic way of looking at a great triumph of civilization." [14]

What caused the increase in the proportion of the aged in the population of the United States and of all other Western countries? The common-sense answer to this question might be that it was the combined effect of falling mortality and falling fertility, but such an answer would be misleading. The increase in the _number_ of old people was indeed the consequence of improvements in death control. However, declines in mortality have been greater among infants and children, and the larger proportion who remained alive retarded the aging of the population. "In most Western countries the fraction over 65 would be _larger_ than it is if mortality rates had remained at their 1900 level. The average age of the population would be _greater_ if [control over] mortality had _not_ improved." [15]

The increase in the _proportion_ of old people, thus, was due to the fall

[14] Frank W. Notestein, "Some Demographic Aspects of Aging," _Proceedings of the American Philosophical Society,_ 98:1 (February 15, 1954), 38–45. (This article has been reprinted in Spengler and Duncan, _op. cit.,_ pp. 464–470.)

[15] Ansley J. Coale, "The Effect of Declines in Mortality on Age Distribution," in Milbank Memorial Fund, _Trends and Differentials in Mortality_ (New York, 1956), pp. 125–132 (italics in the original). See also Vasilios G. Valaoras, "Patterns of Aging of Human Populations," in Eastern States Health Education Conference, _The Social and Biological Challenge of Our Aging Population_ (New York: Columbia University Press, 1950), pp. 67–85; and Alfred Sauvy, "Le vieillissement des populations et l'allongement de la vie," _Population,_ 9:4 (October–December, 1954), 675–682.

in fertility, and this means that prognoses must take into account the postwar revival in the birth rate. As we can see from Column 5 of Table 4-2, the growth in the proportion of dependent aged has been slowed down by the baby boom. The two influences can be combined into a single figure,[16] as follows:

$$\text{Index of aging} = \frac{\text{Persons 65 years and over}}{\text{Children under 15 years}} \times 100$$

According to this index, shown in Column 6, the increase has not only slowed down but actually been reversed from 1950 to 1955. Most writers are still discussing the aging of Western populations when actually—unless the death rates at older ages are reduced considerably—a new "younging" may be in prospect.[17]

The problem of aging may well have been overstated also in other senses. In a preindustrial familistic culture, like America of circa 1850 or traditional China, the old were no "problem."

> The social status given them was of the best. They did not fear to grow old; for the old were not pitied or shoved aside, and were not treated as objects of charity and special worry. This situation (ideal from the standpoint of the aged) was made possible by the social and economic structure of the society in two ways. First, the structure was of the static, agricultural, and familistic type in which the old could perform useful functions. Second, it produced such high mortality that there were relatively few old people in the population.[18]

In a dynamic industrial society, the aged can play fewer useful roles. The family ties of young Americans are to their children more than to their parents;[19] and the more extended kin, who have an important place in traditional rural cultures, in an urban society are often less meaningful than friends. Even if the proportion of aged had remained constant, it would have been more difficult to accommodate them in the city apart-

[16] This index is suggested in Valaoras, "Patterns," *op. cit.,* except that he defines the aged as those 60 years and over.

[17] See Frank G. Dickinson, "The 'Younging' of Electorates," *Journal of the American Medical Association,* 166 (March 1, 1958), 1051–1057. If we consider electorates rather than whole populations, the prognosis can be made over the next 21 years without having to forecast the future trend in fertility, since these future voters are already born. Assuming that no revolutionary changes in mortality take place, the proportion of older voters, which in the United States and other Western countries has been rising rapidly in this century, will reach a peak in the next decades and then decline. According to Dickinson, such a "younging" population will probably be less interested in security than in other, quite different, social and political questions.

[18] Kingsley Davis and J. W. Combs, Jr., "The Sociology of an Aging Population," in Eastern States Health Education Conference, *op. cit.,* pp. 146–170.

[19] But see page 234.

ments, say, of their married children; and the actual much larger proportion could be given the same deference and care as once had been standard only by sacrificing some other significant values.

If we correct the sentimentality and other false perspectives that have often been used to define the problem of aging, this does not, of course, dispose of it. While the proportion of elderly persons is increasing more slowly, their absolute number is great and is going up together with that of the growing population. Sociologists and social psychologists have barely begun to analyze the characteristics of aging possibly susceptible to amelioration by changes in the social environment beyond the secure provision for basic physical needs. In 1960, though persons 65 and over earned only $1,576 on the average, they laid out more than twice as much in medical expenditures, and spent almost three times as many days in hospitals, as those under 65.

In the United States the percentage of aged varies among subgroups by a complex interrelation of several factors. The aged group carries in itself, as it were, the history of the past and changes over time are reflected in present differences between it and the rest of the population. When today's very old were children, for example, about a quarter of the population were given no more than four years of schooling, an amount now considered so inadequate that it is used to define the upper limit of the "functionally illiterate." In 1950, thus, the proportion functionally illiterate among whites ranged from 18 per cent of the 65–69 age-group down to only 3 per cent of those aged 25 through 29.[20] Similarly, since immigration was sharply curtailed after 1914, the proportion of aged among foreign-born is much higher than in the native population. The out-migration of young adults left disproportionate numbers of older persons on the farms, and in eastern cities the earlier decline in fertility also resulted in a more rapid aging. These differential patterns have been altered also by a substantial postretirement migration to states with a pleasant climate, particularly Florida and California.[21]

Perhaps the most significant difference among subgroups of the aged is that between males and females. In the United States today females live on the average more than five years longer than males. Thus, unless her husband is five years younger than she, the probability is that the

20 Taeuber and Taeuber, *op. cit.,* p. 196.

21 See Homer L. Hitt, "The Role of Migration in Population Change among the Aged," *American Sociological Review,* 19:2 (April, 1954), 194–200; "The Demography of America's Aged: A Current Appraisal," in Irving L. Webber, ed., *Aging: A Current Appraisal* (Institute of Gerontology Series, vol. 6; Gainesville: University of Florida Press, 1956), pp. 12–41.

wife will survive him. Since, on the contrary, men generally marry women younger than themselves, widows outnumber widowers by a considerable proportion. Moreover, whenever a marriage is dissolved by either death or divorce, the man is more likely to remarry than the woman.[22] For all these reasons, the sex ratio of widowed and divorced persons is very low; for the United States in 1950 it was only 420.

SUMMARY

The structure of a population, or the distribution by age and sex, is ordinarily described primarily with the sex ratio and the population pyramid. But other demographic tools have been devised to help analyze population structure and its influence. For some purposes, it is particularly useful to compare the three main age-groups of dependent children, the active population, and the dependent aged.

At the most elementary level, the reason for the population growth of any area can be stated simply by noting the contributions to it of the natural increase (births less deaths) and the net migration (immigration less emigration). In such a preliminary analysis, however, the interdependence of fertility, migration, and mortality has yet to be included. The reason that population structure is relevant to every demographic study is that birth, death, and migration rates affect the proportions of the various ages and the two sexes, and in turn are affected by them. For example, migrants are predominantly young adults, who constitute the majority of parents and have very low age-specific death rates; in an area of significant emigration, therefore, other things being equal, the birth rate will tend to go down and the death rate up. Correlatively, the area of immigration will experience a rise in the birth rate and a fall in the death rate. To analyze the shift of population resulting from migration thus means not merely counting the heads of migrants but classifying them by sex and age and relating the consequent changes in population structure to fertility and mortality.

For one who has accustomed himself to think in terms of population structure, many of the generalizations made about all kinds of social behavior are incomplete, if not actually false. Supposing we read, for example, that in Detroit during the past ten years proportionately three times as many Negroes as whites were convicted of robbery. Even if we are satisfied that the statistics are accurate and that they do not reflect a

---

[22] "Widowhood and Its Duration," in Metropolitan Life Insurance Company, *Statistical Bulletin,* September, 1953, pp. 1–3.

bias in the rates of arrest and conviction, the implications of the datum may be false. Robbery is a behavior pattern predominantly of young males; and many Negroes in Detroit, recent in-migrants from other areas, are young adults. Thus, the rate of the whites—but not of the Negroes— is calculated as a proportion of a population that includes the usual number of infants and grandmothers, who seldom commit robbery no matter what their color. Such examples, both hypothetical and actual, could easily be multiplied; [23] but the point rather is that all social statistics, no matter what their specific subject matter, must be interpreted with the possible relevance of population structure in mind.

The proportion of children and aged combined measures the burden of dependency that has to be carried by the active population. In the United States this burden decreased over the whole of the national history up to 1940, and since that date it has been increasing. The percentage aged 65 and over went up from 3.4 in 1880 to 8.6 in 1955; and when in the last decade of this rise it was combined with the baby boom, the joint proportion of all dependents began to increase. It is very easy, however, to overstate the problem of the aging, for the rise in fertility has brought about, at least potentially, a "younging" of the population. By one index, the aging of the American population was reversed in 1950.

SUGGESTIONS FOR FURTHER READING

Eleanor H. Bernert, *America's Children* (New York: Wiley, 1958).

Henry D. Sheldon and Clark Tibbitts, *The Older Population of the United States* (New York: Wiley, 1958).

> The two volumes in the series of census monographs on the subject of this chapter.

T. Lynn Smith, *Population Analysis* (New York: McGraw-Hill, 1948), Chs. 4 and 5.

> An interesting introduction to population structure. See in particular the discussion of the index numbers of age (pp. 102 ff.), a useful device introduced in this book.

United Nations, Department of Social Affairs, Population Division, *The Determinants and Consequences of Population Trends* (Population Studies, no. 17; New York, 1953), Ch. 7.

> An excellent summary of actual trends in the interrelation of population growth and structure, and of theories concerning them.

---

[23] For another example, see pages 94–95, 251.

Robert E. Chaddock, "Age and Sex in Population Analysis," *Annals of the American Academy of Political and Social Science,* 188 (November, 1936), 185–193. (This article has been reprinted in Joseph J. Spengler and Otis Dudley Duncan, eds., *Demographic Analysis,* Glencoe, Ill.: Free Press, 1956, pp. 443–451.)

Ansley J. Coale, "The Effect of Declines in Mortality on Age Distribution," in Milbank Memorial Fund, *Trends and Differentials in Mortality* (New York, 1956), pp. 125–132.

    Two outstanding articles.

Eastern States Health Education Conference, *The Social and Biological Challenge of Our Aging Population* (New York: Columbia University Press, 1950).

    One of a large number of reports of conferences on aging. See in particular the papers by Kiser, Valaoras, and Davis and Combs.

U.S. Department of Health, Education, and Welfare, Committee on Aging, *Selected References on Aging: An Annotated Bibliography, 1955* (Washington: U.S. Government Printing Office, 1955).

Federal Council on Aging, *Publications on Aging: Selected Reports of Federal Agencies* (Washington: U.S. Government Printing Office, 1956).

Irving L. Webber and Gordon F. Streib, *A Syllabus and Annotated Bibliography on the Sociology of Aging and the Aged* (Institute for Social Gerontology; Ann Arbor: University of Michigan, 1959).

Aging, monthly publication of the U.S. Department of Health, Education, and Welfare.

Journal of Gerontology.

    The literature on aging is so large that the reader may find some bibliographic assistance welcome, as in the first three items and regularly in the two periodicals cited. Among the several learned journals concerned with the aged, the *Journal of Gerontology* is the most likely to include articles with a demographic or sociological frame of reference, rather than only a medical or psychological one.

5. AMERICAN IMMIGRATION POLICY

The modern era has seen sizable movements of peoples in various parts of the world—for instance, the migration of Chinese into Southeast Asia, of Indians to Eastern and Southern Africa, or of Africans to the Americas. The most significant, however, in terms both of numbers and of the diffusion of culture patterns, was the emigration of Europeans. In the great awakening of Western civilization that we term the Renaissance, European man began to explore not only the Greek and Roman foundations of his civilization and the physical and biological laws of nature, but also the world beyond the Mediterranean basin and the eastern Atlantic. The ships of Spain and Portugal, of England and Holland, worked their way down the coast of Africa and by the middle of the fifteenth century found a sea route to Asia; at the end of the century, 3,000 miles to the west, they found a veritable New World, vast, rich in every natural resource, and virtually unpeopled. During the next 200 years tiny bands of explorers sought gold, glory, or salvation, establishing dominion over a million square miles by the planting of a flag.

The age of discovery and colonization was followed by the Great Migration. The mass movement from Europe in the nineteenth century was on a scale new in human history. Of the 67 million persons who crossed an ocean from 1800 to 1950, some 60 million were Europeans, and of these two out of every three went to the United States.[1] This chapter, therefore, is of more general significance than the others in this section, which are general only in that they introduce demographic concepts and tools but specific in applying these to the population of the United States. Any study of international migration would have to deal

[1] The figures obviously are only rough approximations. These estimates are cited from W. S. and E. S. Woytinsky, *World Population and Production: Trends and Outlook* (New York: Twentieth Century Fund, 1953), p. 72.

at length with this country, for with respect to this subject America is much more than one instance used as a case study.

The fact that immigration statistics are remarkably incomplete and inaccurate has been exemplified in a number of ways in Chapter 3, and here it is necessary only to recall it. From the historical data available the total number of immigrants during any period can be approximated, but the classification of subgroups within that total must often be based on little more than informed guesswork. For the first half of the nineteenth century we are not even sure of the immigrants' sex—a striking illustration of the nature of the record. Data on less fundamental characteristics, such as nationality or social background, are inadequate for any period except the most recent.

One reason immigration records are so bad, it will be recalled, is that they have been compiled as part of a government control that many try to evade. And, vice versa, the poor quality of these statistics is particularly unfortunate because the control of immigration has been based, at least in part, on the data available. The influence of government policy has been decisive: the most important watershed in the secular trend is formed by the laws of the 1920's, which both cut down the numbers and changed the national composition of the immigrants. In this chapter, therefore, the main emphasis will not be on analyzing the inadequate data but on discussing the background and effect of immigration laws.

THE DEVELOPMENT OF AN IMMIGRATION POLICY

One of the principles established by the American and French revolutions was that—as the French constitution of 1791 put it—"the liberty of all to move about, to remain, or to leave" is a "natural and civil right." Among the founders of the United States, this tenet was axiomatic. In the Declaration of Independence itself one of the complaints voiced against George III was that, in his endeavor "to prevent the population of these States," he had obstructed the naturalization of foreigners and refused "to encourage their migrations hither." Jefferson enunciated "the natural right which all men have of relinquishing the country in which birth or other accident may have thrown them, and seeking subsistence and happiness wheresoever they may be able, or may hope to find them." [2] Or, in the words of Washington, "The bosom of America is open to receive not only the Opulent and Respectable Stranger, but the oppressed

[2] Quoted in John Higham, "American Immigration Policy in Historical Perspective," *Law and Contemporary Problems*, 21:2 (Spring, 1956), 213–235.

and persecuted of all Nations And Religions, whom we shall wellcome to a participation of all our rights and privileges, if by decency and propriety of conduct they appear to merit the enjoyment." [3] This country was ordained as a haven for "the wretched refuse of [Europe's] teeming shores"—to quota Emma Lazarus's words as inscribed on the base of the Statue of Liberty.

There was, of course, also a dissident minority that challenged this basic value system, but the strength of xenophobia in American life has very often been exaggerated. If the Alien and Sedition Acts were enacted under Adams, it is no less significant that they were repealed under Jefferson, and in the aftermath were an important reason for the eclipse of the Federalist party that had made them law. The nativist movement of the 1830's, the Know-Nothing Party of the 1850's, the American Protective Association of the early 1890's, the Ku Klux Klan reborn in 1915 —all these movements, while indicating the persistence of antiforeigner sentiment in America, also reflect the fact that it has usually been limited to noisy groups of merely local importance. Until the 1920's the ideas that such groups propagated were not reflected in any federal legislation except that excluding Asians.

The series of laws in the last quarter of the nineteenth century limiting and finally prohibiting Chinese immigration, however, were a special case. Almost all the Chinese in the United States lived on the West Coast, and the rest of the country had no reliable information either about the exotic land from which they had come or about the migrants themselves. Twice the Supreme Court threw out Chinese exclusion laws as unconstitutional, and it finally accepted the arguments of one member of that court—Justice Stephen J. Field, a native of California—because prohibiting the influx of Chinese was not interpreted as a violation of the general principle of free immigration. [4]

Though the exclusion of Chinese was seen as an anomalous solution to a peripheral problem, it soon became an important precedent. In the following decades the immigration of Japanese laborers to the West Coast was opposed by the same type of racist demagogy, and state laws were passed excluding the Japanese. The federal government sought a solution that would satisfy local sentiment in California without offending Japan. In 1907 President Roosevelt arranged the so-called Gentlemen's Agreement by which Japan itself undertook to refuse to permit

[3] Quoted in President's Commission on Immigration and Naturalization, *Whom We Shall Welcome* (Washington: U.S. Government Printing Office, 1953).

[4] For an extended discussion, see Milton R. Konvitz, *The Alien and the Asiatic in American Law* (Ithaca, N.Y.: Cornell University Press, 1946).

its nationals to emigrate to the United States as laborers. Japan continued to issue passports, however, to women going to the United States to become the wives of Japanese residents, and these both worked in the fields as laborers and brought about a sharp rise in Japanese-American fertility. After some 38,000 women had immigrated, brides also were excluded, and in the law of 1924 all Japanese except temporary migrants like students or merchants were barred.

The "yellow peril" that the peoples of Asia allegedly represented thus formed a background to the debate on immigration policy, but never became its main theme. Much more striking is the fact that for a full century the federal government interpreted the ideal of free migration so literally that it refused to permit any immigration policy whatever to be instituted. Even the government's right to deny entry to persons universally defined as undesirable—such as criminals or prostitutes, the feeble-minded or insane—was established only slowly. Congress refused to enact such regulatory laws, and in a series of decisions federal courts denied the states the power to limit immigration in any sense. The seaboard states, particularly New York and Massachusetts, bore the brunt of dealing with antisocial aliens and charity cases, and their legislatures continually attempted to find a way through the legal impasse. In 1875, when the Supreme Court found that the latest state law to discourage pauper immigration infringed on the national government's exclusive power over foreign commerce,[5] welfare agencies begged Congress to assume the responsibility denied to the states. Seven years later, in 1882, Congress passed both the first of the Chinese exclusion acts, "suspending" the immigration of Chinese laborers for ten years, and the first federal law regulating general immigration. Under the latter, admission was denied to convicts, "lunatics," "idiots," and persons likely to become a public charge; and in a series of bills over the next decade the following classes were also excluded: contract laborers, anarchists, polygamists, and "persons suffering from a loathsome or dangerous contagious disease."

The groups that supported or opposed these first controls were not at all those that one would expect from present political alignments. In the middle of the nineteenth century, immigration was seen mainly in economic terms, as a supply of labor; and regulation by either the states or Congress was opposed first of all by the Chamber of Commerce and the National Association of Manufacturers, which defended laissez faire in migration as in all other economic matters. The South, which in recent decades has been the most vigorous proponent of immigration restriction,

[5] Henderson v. Mayor of the City of New York, 92 U.S. 259 (1875).

voted solidly against it in Congress as late as the 1890's.[6] The demand *for* regulation came from reformers of all types—ministers of the Social Gospel, trade-union leaders, eastern intellectuals. Their stand derived also from their economic interest, as they saw it, but more from an effort to redefine immigration as a social process. Immigrants became not only workers but also parents, citizens, members of their new communities. The economic theory that demanded a free flow of labor was inadequate, they believed, because it ignored these other roles, and particularly the deficiencies of some immigrants in fulfilling them. That is to say, the first reformers wanted only to subject immigrants to the same type of social control that was already exercised among the native population.

In retrospect, in order to understand better what happened, it is necessary to make some distinctions that were not obvious at the time. In a number of standard works on American immigration policy the absolute freedom of migration upheld in the American Creed has been used to gauge nineteenth-century legislation. By this criterion, "free immigration" ended around 1830, when eastern states set the first ineffective controls, or before the massive flow from Europe even got under way.[7] However, just as a society can be meaningfully free though it has prisons, so to deny admission to obviously antisocial elements is not inconsistent with the principle of free migration.[8] The exclusion of individuals with specific objectionable personal characteristics we will denote as the **regulation** of migration, which is to be distinguished from restriction. The latter can be of two types: **numerical restriction,** by which a certain maximum immigration is set for each year, and **qualitative restriction,** by which entry is denied to specified broad classes.

By the time that the federal government began to recognize that regulation of immigration was legitimate, a demand was developing for restriction. From the figures shown in Table 5-1, it would appear that immigration rose sharply after 1880, both in absolute terms and as a proportion of the resident population. While the number of immigrants fell off during the depression of the 1890's, after the turn of the century new records were set. In the fiscal year ending June 30, 1907, the high point of 1,285,349 was reached, and in each of five other prewar years more than a million immigrants were recorded. To some degree these figures are deceptive. Even at the peak of this immigration wave, the proportion of

6 See Higham, "American Immigration Policy," *op. cit.*

7 See, for example, Roy L. Garis, *Immigration Restriction: A Study of the Opposition to and Regulation of Immigration into the United States* (New York: Macmillan, 1927).

8 See Julius Isaac, *Economics of Migration* (London: Kegan Paul, Trench, Trubner, 1947), p. 104.

TABLE 5-1. Average Annual Recorded Immigration by Decades,
United States, 1819–1959

	Average Annual Immigration (thousands)	Annual Immigration per Thousand of Total Population at End of Decade
1819–1830	15	1.2
1831–1840	60	3.5
1841–1850	171	7.4
1851–1860	260	8.3
1861–1870	231	5.8
1871–1880	281	5.6
1881–1890	525	8.3
1891–1900	369	4.9
1901–1910	780	8.5
1911–1920	674	6.4
1921–1930	411	3.4
1931–1940	53	0.4
1941–1950	104	0.7
1951–1959	225	1.3

Source: U.S. Immigration and Naturalization Service, *Reports,* summarized in U.S. Bureau of the Census, *Statistical Abstract of the United States, 1960* (Washington: U.S. Government Printing Office, 1960), p. 92. For some periods the data are for fiscal rather than calendar years, but this makes no significant difference in the decennial totals, given the general level of accuracy of the records.

newcomers to the resident population—a much more meaningful index than the absolute number—did not rise much above that in the 1840's and 1850's. But the immigration of more than a million in one year was a fact that stayed in one's mind. And it was not only, not even principally, a question of numbers. Until the 1880's the "Old" Immigrants had come from Northwestern Europe, and from that date on an increasing proportion of "New" Immigrants came from Southern and Eastern Europe. Arguments for restriction narrowed down to emphasizing, or exaggerating, the difference between Old and New Immigrants.

OLD IMMIGRATION VS. NEW

The effect of immigration on employment remained an important consideration, but in the long discussion that led finally to restrictive legislation, economic arguments were gradually supplemented by broader social and especially biological theses. In the nineteenth century the word *race* had ordinarily been understood to mean color. But the development of modern genetics around the turn of the century seemed to reveal much more precise hereditary influences entirely independent of environment. Geneticists classified European peoples into the Nordic, the Alpine, and the Mediterranean "races"; and this tripartite division, which was more or less equivalent to that between Old and New Immigration, was conveyed to American readers in William Z. Ripley's *The Races of Europe* (1899). The most extreme conclusions of the new eugenics movement of Francis Galton were developed into a racist theory of history in Madison Grant's *The Passing of the Great Race* (1916). The "races" of Southern and Eastern Europe were innately inferior, it was maintained, and immigration from these areas perverted the "blood stream" of Anglo-Saxon America.

"The racial attack on the new immigration emerged as the most powerful ideological weapon of the restriction movement." [9] The new doctrine was expounded everywhere, not only in the pamphlets of the Immigration Restriction League and by trade-union demagogues, but in the more effective articles and books of serious scholars. Francis Walker, a former superintendent of the census, wrote a number of articles to prove that immigration did not even add to the population growth.[10] Sociologists like E. A. Ross or Henry Pratt Fairchild analyzed the "social problem" of immigration in a biological framework. Historians found a blood affinity between the ancient Teutons and the American way of life.[11] And the racist doctrine was brought directly into the governmental process through two important documents, the 42-volume *Report* of the Senate Immigration Commission of 1907–1910 and Laughlin's report to the House Committee on Immigration and Naturalization.

The Immigration Commission's *Report* facilitated the transition from the prior economic interpretation of international migration to the new biological one. It compared in great detail the New Immigrants with an idealized picture of the Old Immigrants, stressing the different effects on the American economy of the various "races" of Europe.[12]

9 Higham, "American Immigration Policy," *op. cit.*

10 Francis A. Walker, "Restriction of Immigration," *Atlantic Monthly,* 77:464 (June, 1896), 822–829; "Immigration and Degradation," *Forum,* 11 (August, 1891), 634–644; "Immigration," *Yale Review,* 1:2 (August, 1892), 125–145. Walker was "probably the most influential writer on population" among the post-Civil War Malthusians, who molded a dozen or more important economists and demographers. See Joseph J. Spengler, "Population Doctrines in the United States, 2: Malthusianism," *Journal of Political Economy,* 41:5 (October, 1933), 639–672.

11 For a fascinating account, see Edward N. Saveth, *American Historians and European Immigrants, 1875–1925* (Studies in History, Economics, and Public Law, no. 540; New York: Columbia University Press, 1948).

12 One of the 42 volumes prepared by the Immigration Commission was a *Dictionary of Races or Peoples* that classified immigrants to the United States into 45 ethnic groups in accordance with the current practice of the Bureau of Immigration. These groups were defined in various ways—by physical differences (for example, Negroes); by language (Germans, including German-speaking Swiss, Austrians, etc.); by nationality, even when not associated with a state (Ruthenians); by geographic region (Scandinavians, West Indians). Almost all of the data that the Commission collected

The old and the new immigration differ in many essentials. The former was, from the beginning, largely a movement of settlers who came from the most progressive sections of Europe for the purpose of making for themselves homes in the New World. They entered practically every line of activity in nearly every part of the country. Coming during a period of agricultural development, many of them entered agricultural pursuits, sometimes as independent farmers, but more often as farm laborers, who, nevertheless, as a rule soon became landowners. They formed an important part of the great movement toward the West during the last century, and as pioneers were most potent factors in the development of the territory between the Allegheny Mountains and the Pacific coast. They mingled freely with the native Americans and were quickly assimilated. . . .

The new immigration has been largely a movement of unskilled laboring men who have come, in large part temporarily, from the less progressive and advanced countries of Europe in response to the call for industrial workers in the eastern and middle western States. They have almost entirely avoided agricultural pursuits, and in cities and industrial communities have congregated together in sections apart from native Americans and the older immigrants to such an extent that assimilation has been slow as compared to that of the earlier non-English speaking races.[13]

The impact of the *Report* can hardly be overstated. The sheer mass of data contained in this document, much of it based on first-hand surveys, tended to overwhelm opposing views: no one person or organization could stand up against four years of investigation and 42 volumes of evidence and interpretation.[14] The Commission presented its views in abridged form in two volumes; and a more popular version by Jenks (one of the Commission's members) and Lauck long remained a standard college text on immigration.[15] The even more popular volumes by Fairchild were based on the *Report* as one of their main sources of information.[16]

---

on the different peoples of the world were broken down according to the "races" defined in this volume. See U.S. Senate, Immigration Commission, *Report*, vol. 5: *Dictionary of Races or Peoples* (61st Congress, 3rd Session, Document 662; Washington: U.S. Government Printing Office, 1911).

[13] U.S. Senate, Immigration Commission, *Report*, 1 (61st Congress, 3rd Session, Document 747; Washington: U.S. Government Printing Office, 1911), 13–14.

[14] In the most significant contemporary rejoinder to the *Report*, Hourwich's *Immigration and Labor*, the author concentrated on answering the thesis that immigrants took jobs away from native workers. The correlation between immigration and unemployment, he pointed out, was negative, not positive. Natives in low-status jobs were not "displaced" by unemployment but attracted to better-paying, higher-status jobs. See Isaac A. Hourwich, *Immigration and Labor: The Economic Aspects of European Immigration to the United States* (New York: Putnam, 1912).

[15] Jeremiah W. Jenks and W. Jett Lauck, *The Immigration Problem: A Study of American Immigration Conditions and Needs* (3rd rev. ed.; New York: Funk and Wagnalls, 1913).

[16] See in particular Henry Pratt Fairchild, *Immigration: A World Movement and its American Significance* (Rev. ed.; New York: Macmillan, 1925).

The most direct connection between racist doctrine and American immigration law was established by the influence of Dr. Harry H. Laughlin of the Eugenics Record Office of the Carnegie Institution of Washington. As "expert eugenics agent" to the House Committee on Immigration and Naturalization, he submitted a report entitled "Expert Analysis of the Metal and the Dross in America's Modern Melting Pot." [17] This so impressed Congress that, according to one authority, "it is often considered the principal basis of the Act of 1924." [18] In order to show that social ills are not randomly distributed among the various nationalities in the United States, Laughlin compared for each ethnic group its proportion in the total population with that in prisons, asylums, and similar institutions. For example, in 1910 persons of Italian birth made up 1.46 per cent of the total population, and if proportionally represented in the 93 insane asylums that Laughlin surveyed, they would have constituted 1.46 per cent of the total number of inmates, or 1,228. Since there were actually 1,938 Italian-born persons in these institutions, the incidence of insanity among Italians was concluded to be more than one and a half times higher than that of the general population. Moreover, the "first and primary factor" causing such a nonrandom ethnic representation in various institutions was, he asserted, the "difference in constitutional susceptibility of specific races and nativity groups in the United States to certain definite types of social inadequacy." That is to say, such "degeneracies" as "criminality" were "inherited in the blood." The implications of such an analysis for policy were clear:

> We in this country have been so imbued with the idea of democracy, or the equality of all men, that we have left out of consideration the matter of blood or natural inborn hereditary mental and moral differences. . . . There has, thus far, been no suggestion in our laws of any requirement except personal value in our sorting of would-be immigrants. [However,] the surest biological power, which the Federal Government now possesses, to direct the future of America along safe and sound racial channels is to control the hereditary quality of the immigration stream.

The many flaws in Laughlin's very influential analysis were fundamental. He assumed that such social ills as "criminality," poverty, and insanity were inherited through the genes and, moreover, were therefore differentially represented in such "races" as "American Southerner" or "Middle-West American." His data in any case were incomplete. He made no allowance for the differences in age structure and sex ratio of the various

---

[17] U.S. House of Representatives, *Hearings before the Committee on Immigration and Naturalization,* November 21, 1922 (67th Congress, 3rd Session, Serial 7-C; Washington: U.S. Government Printing Office, 1923).

[18] Garis, *op. cit.,* pp. 239–240.

nationalities, or for the regional variation in communal care.[19]

The present immigration policy of the United States can hardly be evaluated without reexamining the differentiation that was made between Old and New Immigrants. We today have no better statistical record than the Immigration Commission and Laughlin had, but we do have a better understanding of how little biological inheritance ordinarily influences cultural behavior. Some basic facts about nineteenth-century immigration will never be known, but certain of the egregious misconceptions can be corrected.

1. It will be recalled that federal regulation of immigration began in 1882, just at the time when New Immigrants were becoming dominant. The subsequent control, ineffective as it was, must have cut down the proportion of social misfits from the days of intermittent, haphazard regulation by only a few of the states. That is to say, lacking any adequate statistical base for such a comparison, one can reasonably assume that the level of health was higher, and the proportion of criminals or prostitutes was lower, among the New Immigrants than among the earlier Old Immigrants.

2. The shift, moreover, was neither so great nor so abrupt as the official immigration figures indicate.[20] Statistics on gross migration, as shown in Table 5-1, considerably overstate the proportion of New Immigrants who remained in this country permanently. For the period 1908 to 1923 —that is, from the beginning of the record on emigration of aliens to shortly after the establishment of the national-quota system—the average remigration amounted to 35.2 per cent of the immigration. But for the different nationalities this percentage varied as follows: [21]

Chinese	130	Lithuanian	25
Bulgarian, Serbian, and		Syrian	24
Montenegrin	89	Scandinavian	22
Turkish	86	African	22
Korean	73	French	21
Rumanian	66	English	21
Hungarian	66	Mexican	19
Southern Italian	60	Dutch and Flemish	18
Cuban	58	Armenian	15
Slovak	57	Scotch and Welsh	13
Russian	52	Irish	11
Finnish	29	Jewish	5

[19] For a more complete analysis of Laughlin's report, see William Petersen, "The 'Scientific' Basis of Our Immigration Policy," *Commentary,* July, 1955, pp. 77–86.

[20] The data from 1820 on are broken down by country of origin in U.S. Bureau of the Census, *Historical Statistics of the United States, Colonial Times to 1957* (Washington: U.S. Government Printing Office, 1960), series C 88–100.

[21] Imre Ferenczi, *International Migrations,* 1: *Statistics* (Publication 14; New York: National Bureau of Economic Research, 1929), 206–207.

From this list it is evident that a much larger percentage of New Immigrants returned home than of Old Immigrants.[22] There is no reason to suppose that this is not true also of the period before 1908, for which direct data are not available.[23] Indeed, one of the arguments by the advocates of restriction was that immigrants at the end of the century were not so likely to settle permanently as those 50 years earlier.

Using gross rather than net figures falsifies much more than the proportion of the various nationalities immigrating. The sex ratio of immigrants, as another example, varies considerably from one set of figures to the other. One of the standard complaints against the New Immigrants was their high proportion of males; thus, the summary of the Immigration Commission's *Report* quoted above contrasts the earlier "settlers" with the later "laboring men." It is usual that more males than females migrate to a frontier area, or to the unknown hazards of a foreign city, and that the sex ratio goes down as the new area becomes more settled, whether with people in general or, in the latter case, with compatriots. But the sex ratio of remigrants, if we judge again by the period for which data are available, is still higher; and what is true of gross immigration must again be corrected to apply to the more meaningful group of those who came to stay. Because of the several legal provisions favoring female immigrants,[24] they became the predominant sex in the 1930's, but even in this period the sex ratio of remigrants remained well above 1,000.

That the nationality and sex ratio of remigrants are so atypical of the immigrant population as a whole suggests that gross and net immigration may differ significantly in all respects. We know that the emigration of aliens increased during economic depressions, and it is a plausible deduction to suppose that remigration at any time during the business cycle was greater among those unable to get a job[25] or, more generally, among

22 Of course, special factors influenced the remigration rate of certain of the nationalities. This was particularly true of the two extremes, the Chinese (of whom more departed than arrived) and the Jews.

23 A recent study by Kuznets and Rubin has confirmed this impression. In terms of net rather than gross immigration, they found that "the really sizable influx" began before the Civil War, between 1835 and 1860. See Simon Kuznets and Ernest Rubin, *Immigration and the Foreign Born* (Occasional Paper 46; New York: National Bureau of Economic Research, 1954), pp. 22–26 and *passim*.

24 See page 106.

25 Economic motives can very easily be exaggerated, however, in seeking to explain migration in either direction. According to one of the very few detailed studies of remigration, that among Greek-Americans, their motives were varied. At the time of the crisis of 1907 many Greeks left the United States because of economic hardship, but remigration reached its lowest level during the depression of the 1930's. Greek nationalism seems to have been more significant than economic factors: many thousands of volunteers returned in order to fight in the war of independence against Turkey. Family relations were also important: migrants returned in order to visit

those unable for any reason to adapt to the new environment. This possibility must be kept in mind in judging the worth of all of the Immigration Commission's comparisons of gross immigration figures.

3. The ostensible contrast between Old and New Immigrants was to a large degree rather a comparison between two stages in emigration. The demographic transition began in Northwestern Europe, where as the death rate went down and the natural increase went up, a good portion of the rapidly growing population sought new homes overseas. In the latter decades of the nineteenth century, with the decline in the fertility of Northwestern Europe, the rates of population growth and emigration also fell off. By this time the demographic transition was under way in Southern and Eastern Europe: the transfer there of modern methods of death control resulted in a rapid increase in population and a large number of potential emigrants. Comparing Old and New Immigrants during any ten years, as the Immigration Commission did throughout its long *Report,* indeed reveals many differences; but these were due, at least in part, to the fact that an early phase of the New Immigration was being contrasted with a late phase of the Old. If we compare today the offspring of Southern and Eastern Europeans who arrived during the first decade of the twentieth century with those of Northwestern Europeans who had come 30 years earlier, most of the differences disappear—and with them the conclusion that they reflected innate characteristics of the two types of "races."

For example, according to the findings of the Immigration Commission, during the decade 1899–1909 Northwest European immigrants included proportionately more than twice as many skilled laborers as those from Southern and Eastern Europe, excluding "Hebrews." [26] During these years, indeed, 45 per cent of the immigrants from the United Kingdom, for example, were skilled workers, but only 15 per cent of those in 1880–1900. Conversely, the percentage of laborers and servants among United

---

elderly parents or to find a Greek wife, and then remained; or they wanted to bring up their children in a Greek environment. See Theodore Saloutos, *They Remember America: The Story of the Repatriated Greek-Americans* (Berkeley: University of California Press, 1956), Ch. 2 and *passim.*

[26] Jenks and Lauck, *op. cit.,* p. 32. As in many such contrasts between Old and New Immigrants, this one was sharpened by omitting Jews from the calculation. As the most urban of European peoples, Jews included a large, possibly even the largest, proportion of skilled workers. If the restrictionists had been really interested in cutting down the proportion of unskilled among the immigrants, they might have suggested—though no one ever did—that the immigration of East European Jews be facilitated. Or, still more simply, they might have proposed that the immigration of skilled workers be facilitated. These economic arguments, one must remember, were mainly a roundabout route to achieving the exclusion of certain "races."

Kingdom immigrants fell off from 60–80 in 1880–1900 to about 25 in 1900–1910.[27]

> Throughout the period of unrestricted immigration, . . . the great majority of the migrants were people without acceptable economic opportunities in their own countries who came here relatively untrained and socially disadvantaged to secure jobs at the bottom of the hierarchy of urban occupations and incomes.[28]

Other typical contrasts between Old and New Immigrants are, similarly, rather a denotation of different phases of the migration process. Thus, in the summary statement of the Immigration Commission's *Report*, the point was made that Old Immigrants "mingled freely with the native Americans and were quickly assimilated," while among New Immigrants "assimilation has been slow." But assimilation is a process that takes time. To compare the two groups, one of which had been in the country about a generation longer, stacked the cards so heavily that it was hardly necessary to collect evidence in order to reach the desired conclusion. From the American population today, in the middle of the twentieth century, one would conclude that acculturation has proceeded remarkably well among all nationalities, and that perceptible remnants of old-country culture are as evident among the Irish in Massachusetts, the Germans in Wisconsin, the Swedes in Minnesota—among the descendants of the Old Immigrants in general, that is to say—as among any of those whose forebears came from Southern and Eastern Europe.[29]

4. The shift in the main source of immigration from Northwestern to Southern and Eastern Europe also coincided with a transformation of the American economy. The German or Swedish peasant who immigrated during the years right after the Civil War took advantage of the Homestead Act and became a farmer; but when the Italian or Polish peasant arrived, this entry into the economy was closed, and burgeoning American industry was calling for more and more unskilled labor. When the Immigration Commission complained that the New Immigrants "have almost entirely avoided agricultural pursuits," one might suppose that they had a choice in making this decision. They arrived at a time when the proportion in the labor force engaged in agriculture was declining, when native-born farmers were migrating to the cities; and to have at-

---

[27] Brinley Thomas, *Migration and Economic Growth: A Study of Great Britain and the Atlantic Economy* (National Institute of Economic and Social Research, Economic and Social Study 12; Cambridge: Cambridge University Press, 1954), p. 153.

[28] Conrad Taeuber and Irene B. Taeuber, *The Changing Population of the United States* (New York: Wiley, 1958), p. 67.

[29] See Ch. 6, and especially pages 139–141.

tempted to force their way into this sector of the economy would not have benefited either themselves or their new country.

The New Immigrants, therefore, had simultaneously to undergo two processes of adjustment: from their native cultures to the American one and from a rural to an urban way of life. In many respects, the second adaptation was the more difficult. The social ills attributed to the innate inadequacies of the New Immigrants were the result basically of the extremely rapid, haphazard development of an urban-industrial society, a process of which the New Immigrants were the most conspicuous victims. Not only did city slums, for example, develop much faster after large numbers of Poles, for example, began to arrive, but it was the Poles who lived in the slums and thus developed the characteristics typical of slum dwellers. Given the level of social sciences at that time, the authors of the *Report,* among others, drew the "obvious" conclusion that Poles had caused slums.

The fact that the New Immigrants were settled mainly in the cities of the Northeast—"in response to the call for industrial workers," in the words of the Immigration Commission—meant that they were much more susceptible to the business cycle. An immigrant of the earlier period who had settled on the land could survive some years of falling prices by living off his own produce; and the return journey, should he have contemplated it, would in any case have been too difficult. But before the days of social legislation, unemployed workers in a city had no such staying power; and remigration to their homeland had also become less difficult with the great improvement in ocean transport. Such immigrants came, in the words of the Immigration Commission, "in large part temporarily"; but, as we have seen, its members did not draw the conclusion that the relevant data to be analyzed were therefore the *net* immigration figures.

Since the Old Immigrants were farmers, they were also, according to the Immigration Commission, "pioneers," "potent factors in the development of the territory between the Allegheny Mountains and the Pacific coast." New Immigrants, "from the less progressive and advanced countries of Europe," were not pioneers—except, perhaps, in contrast to the populations they had left.[30] The dean of immigration historians, Marcus Lee Hansen, has examined this popular picture of the early immigrant as

---

[30] Though the New Immigrants were, by American standards as interpreted in the *Report,* undesirable types, they nevertheless constituted "the stronger and better element" of the European population they had left, for to journey so far from home required "a degree of courage and resourcefulness not possessed by weaklings of any class" (U.S. Senate, Immigration Commission, *op. cit.,* 1, 169–170).

a pioneer, radical, and innovator—and found it faulty. Throughout the
nineteenth century most immigrants stayed in the settled areas, following
the advice of those few who had left them and generally returned: "Let
the Americans start the clearing; they alone possess the specialized technique." Thus, "the first white man to pioneer in any township was not a
Schultz or a Meyer, a Johnson or an Olson. He was a Robinson, a
McLeod or a Boone. He was a descendant of that old Americanized stock
which had learned frontiering in the difficult school that was in session
from 1600 to 1800." [31] The typical immigrant of any postcolonial period
was a pioneer only in the sense that he braved the hardships of the journey,
which indeed were greater in the days of sailing ships, and had to make his
way in a new country.

Many of the supposed differences noted between Old and New Immigrants, then, were spurious, the consequence of (a) an excessive belief in
biological continuity; (b) a failure to distinguish between gross and net
immigration; and (c) interpretation of two phases in the migration-
assimilation process, and of two stages in the economic development of
the United States, as innate variation among the persons involved. Some
of the differences may have been the consequence of the early regulation
of immigration by the United States government. If these spurious and
accidental contrasts are discarded, what are left? What are the genuine
differences between Old and New Immigrants?

Northwest Europe is a specific culture area, distinguished from Italy or
Central Europe or the Balkans by a number of real characteristics. While
Walker was engaging in hyperbole when he described the latter as "every
foul and stagnant pool of population in Europe, which no breath of intellectual or industrial life has stirred for ages," a more moderately worded
contrast would have a historical base.

From the point of view of the American restrictionists, one of the most
important characteristics of Northwest Europe may have been its religion.
Millions of Old Immigrants—from Germany, Switzerland, France, Belgium, and particularly Ireland—were Catholic, but in their vast majority
they were Protestant. The New Immigrants, coming from countries hardly
touched by the Reformation, were almost all either Catholic or Jewish.
In restrictionist pamphlets much was made of this point, but religious
bias contradicted the American value system too blatantly to be allowed
to rise above the surface in scholarly works or official documents.

Northwest Europe was also the birthplace of industrialism, the region

---

[31] Marcus Lee Hansen, *The Immigrant in American History* (Cambridge: Harvard University Press, 1948), pp. 66–67.

where modern urban patterns of life first developed. The relevance of this point to American immigration policy, however, is not so obvious as one might assume. Emigrants from Northwest Europe were also often rural. In Germany, for instance, emigrants from the cities were few in number, but in "the peaceful country districts the departing throngs threatened to depopulate the land." [32] Ireland, the emigration country par excellence, is still today not an industrial country. Moreover, the principal manpower requirements of the rapidly expanding American economy were not skilled workers, who came in sufficient number from the native population, but a fluid pool of unskilled labor, able and willing to do the work that neither Americans nor their Northwest European urban counterparts would ordinarily undertake. This work—building railroads, digging in the mines, unskilled and semiskilled labor in the factories—was done by transformed European peasants.

Northwest Europe was also the prime example, apart from its overseas extensions, of modern democracy. The point was often made that New Immigrants, coming from countries with no democratic tradition, could not understand American political life. Like other disputes of that period, this one can be settled with subsequent evidence. The quality of present political participation does not vary between the descendants of Old and New Immigrants. And the notion that Germanic blood makes for a superior political system, a theory generally accepted by American historians of fifty years ago, became one of the ideological underpinnings of Nazism.

THE NATIONAL-QUOTA SYSTEM

The goal that both the Immigration Commission *Report* and Laughlin recommended, the exclusion of Southern and Eastern Europeans, was first sought indirectly, by proposing that admission should be denied to all adults not able to read and write some language. Of the two dozen such literacy bills introduced in Congress, four were passed, to be vetoed successively by Cleveland, by Taft, and twice by Wilson. In their veto messages, President Taft pointed out that the United States needed the immigrants' labor and could itself furnish their literacy, and the more idealistic President Wilson argued that illiteracy was a measure not of man's small innate ability but of his limited opportunities, which were not a legitimate reason for denying him entry to a country that pro-

[32] *Ibid.,* p. 80.

claimed itself the land of opportunity. A law stipulating a literacy test was finally passed in 1917 over Wilson's second veto.[33] However, it soon became evident that this test, though it kept out some Southern and Eastern Europeans, was not nearly so restrictive as it had been supposed it would be: many had learned to read since the fight to impose the ban began.

Everything in postwar America favored the move to extend the restrictions. Congress was determined to isolate the country from European troubles, and from Europeans; the hysterical fear of revolution—manifested, for example, in the Palmer raids—reinforced the xenophobia; a depression added weight to economic arguments against immigration. The restrictionist bloc in Congress did not wait even to write an acceptable bill. The law of 1921 was enacted as a stopgap measure until the problem could be studied and permanent legislation written. It limited European immigration to 3 per cent of the number of foreign-born of each nationality residing in the United States at the time of the last available census figures, those of 1910.

The new law, passed in 1924, set up a second temporary system, more restrictive in two respects than its predecessor. The 3 per cent quota was reduced to 2 per cent, and the base population was changed from the foreign-born enumerated in the 1910 census to those in the 1890 census, when the proportion from Southern and Eastern Europe was smaller. In the discussion of the bill, both in Congress and in the country at large, it had been suggested that quotas ought to reflect not merely the countries of origin of the foreign-born in 1910 or 1890 or any other date, but rather the "national origins" of the entire population in 1920. By counting everyone's ancestors, one could claim to offer complete justice to each ethnic stock in the entire white population. Accordingly, the 1924 law contained a clause that from 1927 on each quota would be determined by the following formula:

$$\text{Annual quota} = \frac{150{,}000 \times \text{population of designated "national origin" in 1920}}{\text{Total population in 1920}}$$

The national-origins scheme was something of a mystery even to its advocates. It was first proposed by Senator David A. Reed of Pennsylvania and

---

[33] For a detailed discussion of the literacy test in its various legislative forms, see Jenks and Lauck, *op. cit.,* pp. 332 ff. The 1917 law not only required that all immigrant aliens aged 16 and over be literate, but also set two other important precedents. It excluded all immigration from the "barred zone" of Asia; together with the special laws excluding Chinese and sharply limiting the immigration of Japanese, the new law all but eliminated movement from that continent to the United States. Secondly, the law extended the power to exclude or deport aliens for their political beliefs.

John B. Trevor, "a patrician New Yorker who belonged to the circle of Madison Grant." [34] On the floor of Congress it excited much less discussion than clauses in the bill establishing the provisional system.[35] The bill did not define in adequate detail the process by which the national origins were to be determined; and, instead of the three years allowed, it took five years, or until 1929, to set them up.

The task was undertaken by the Bureau of the Census, assisted by two experts paid by the Council of Learned Societies. The law required that they determine "the number of inhabitants in continental United States in 1920 whose origin by birth or ancestry is attributable to [each] geographical area" treated in the immigration statistics as a separate country. Because of the frequent and untraceable intermarriages across ethnic lines, however, it was impossible to divide the American population into distinct ethnic groups.

That being the case [the committee reported], it was assumed that the "number of inhabitants" was meant to be used as a measure of the relative size or amount of the various national stocks composing the white population of the United States. So the problem was to determine what proportion or percentage of the white blood in the population of the United States was derived from each country of origin and express the result in terms of an equivalent number of inhabitants.[36]

The very language—"the percentage of white blood"—reflects the biological theory behind the law. The notion that each country of Europe has a separate type of blood, and that in the hybrid American population one can calculate percentages of these bloods, is not one to which any present-day anthropologist would subscribe.

Even if the idea of national origins had not been silly in itself, it was preposterous to suppose that these could be determined from the data available. In order to find the proportionate contribution of various national stocks to the American population, it would have been necessary to divide the whites in 1790 into ethnic classes and calculate the successive additions to each from both net immigration and natural increase. Fertility and mortality differed markedly, of course, from one ethnic group to

---

[34] Higham, "American Immigration Policy," *op. cit.*

[35] "Of the some 500 pages of the Congressional Record devoted to the debate on the Immigration Act of 1924, a total of approximately 14 pages were given over in both the House and the Senate to the consideration of the national origins system. Only a small minority of the Senators and Congressmen participated in the discussion" (President's Commission on Immigration and Naturalization, *op. cit.*, pp. 87–88).

[36] U.S. Senate, "Immigration Quotas on the Basis of National Origin," *Miscellaneous Documents 8870*, vol. 1, no. 65 (70th Congress, 1st Session; Washington: U.S. Government Printing Office, 1928).

another. Even given adequate statistics, the task would have been stupendous. In a sense it was made easier because these were more or less lacking. For the base population the principal source was the family names as enumerated in the 1790 census, but, as the committee pointed out, there was a "considerable element of uncertainty" in the classification. Many family names are common to two or more countries, and many others were undoubtedly changed to their English equivalents. "It was to be expected that whatever error there might be in this classification would be in the direction of an overstatement of the English element in the population," which was therefore reduced by slightly over one-tenth from the calculated figure. Some scholars contended, however, that even so the English element was greatly overstated, and this assertion was given some weight when the census figures were compared with army musters of the same period. Even small discrepancies in 1790, when increased by geometrical proportions from that date until 1920, made a substantial difference in the size of the eventual quota each country was allowed. To this base were added immigration figures, such as they were, and—for lack of a breakdown by ethnic groups—an over-all rate of natural increase.[37]

The Immigration and Nationality Act of 1952, ordinarily known as the McCarran-Walter Act, continued the national-origins scheme. Under it each of 85 countries is given an annual quota equal to one-sixth of 1 per cent of the number of persons in the 1920 population of that national origin, as calculated by the procedure we have described, except that the minimum quota is 100.

The success of the immigration legislation in achieving the restrictionists' purpose is indicated in Table 5-2. The total immigration from Europe—7.8 million in 1901–1910 and 6.7 million in 1911–1920 (the latter was at a higher rate if we take into account that immigration was suspended during the war)—was cut down to an annual quota of about 150,000. And the Old Immigration, which made up only about 25 per cent of the *gross* movement during these last 25 years of unrestricted immigration, was assigned quotas that added up to about 85 per cent of those for Europe, or about the same proportion as in the immigration around 1880. The two purposes of numerical and qualitative restriction had thus been achieved.

[37] *Ibid.* In submitting this report, Secretary of State Kellogg, Secretary of Commerce Hoover, and Secretary of Labor Davis, noted: "We wish it clear that neither we individually nor collectively are expressing any opinion on the merits or demerits of this system of arriving at the quotas. We are simply transmitting the calculations made by the departmental committee in accordance with the act" (p. 2).

**TABLE 5-2. Immigration Quotas under Successive Laws,
United States, 1921–1952**

	1921	1924	1929	1952
Northwest Europe [a]	197,630	140,999	127,266	126,131
Southern and Eastern Europe	159,322	20,423	23,225	23,536
Asia	492	1,424	1,423	2,990
Africa and Oceania	359	1,821	1,800	2,000
Total	357,803	164,667	153,714	154,657
	Per cent			
Northwest Europe [a]	55.2	85.6	82.8	81.6
Southern and Eastern Europe	44.5	12.4	15.1	15.2
Asia	0.1	0.9	0.9	1.9
Africa and Oceania	0.1	1.1	1.2	1.3
Total	99.9	100.0	100.0	100.0

[a] British Isles, Scandinavia, Germany, Low Countries, France, Switzerland.
Source: President's Commission on Immigration and Naturalization, *Whom We Shall Welcome* (Washington: U.S. Government Printing Office, 1953), pp. 76–77.

AMERICA'S IMMIGRATION POLICY TODAY

The McCarran-Walter Act is currently the basic immigration law of the United States, and under it the main criterion by which aspirant immigrants are judged is their country of birth. The whole immigration policy of the United States, however, is a good deal more complex than this summary statement would suggest.

Persons entering the country are classified first of all into immigrants and nonimmigrants. Immigrants are those who intend to reside permanently in the United States; all other arrivals are called nonimmigrants.[38] To be granted an immigration visa, one must be of good moral character and in good physical and mental health, and have received an affidavit from an American resident that one will not become a public charge.[39] Immigrants are either quota or nonquota, depending on whether they come in under the national-origins classification. Within each quota a preference is assigned to specified categories; and among the nonprefer-

[38] The use of the negative term "nonimmigrant," rather than the positive "visitor" used in the statistics of some other countries, may be confusing to anyone not accustomed to the language. An alien visitor is denoted a nonimmigrant when he enters the country, and a nonemigrant when he leaves it.

[39] In their first court test these affidavits of support were ruled unenforceable. In discussing the suit, the judge held that affidavits are "merely a device used by the State Department to satisfy the legal requirement that aliens could not be admitted if they were likely to become public charges" (*New York Times,* October 12, 1957).

ence quota immigrants certain ad hoc priorities have been established from time to time.

The categories granted an easier entry, either outside the quota or with preferential status within it, are the following:

1. Persons who will follow certain specified occupations, such as farming, the ministry, college teaching.[40] Preference can also be given to those with any skill that the Attorney General states to be "needed urgently," or "substantially beneficial prospectively to the national economy, cultural interests, or welfare of the United States." Occupational preferences are not very much used. In 1957, a typical year in this respect, fewer than 5 per cent of the persons eligible to enter under this special provision actually did so.[41] For "the economic functions of immigration are today marginal and relatively unimportant, and . . . almost any conceivable immigration policy likely to be adopted must be justified in noneconomic terms." [42]

2. Members of the immediate family of an American resident. The strong humanitarian appeal implicit in families separated by the immigration laws of various countries is increased by the fact that the number of persons affected is relatively small. The policy established in this respect has thus been continually liberalized. In the 1957 and 1960 revisions of the McCarran-Walter Act, for example, priorities were granted also both to illegitimate children and to orphans who had been or would be adopted by American citizens, and to 36,000 relatives of prior immigrants who could not be included previously because the quotas for their nationalities had been filled.

3. Immigrants from other countries of the Western Hemisphere, who come in outside the quota system. Why this should be so is not quite clear. At least one of the bills offered in the 1920's restricted all immigration, and the congressional committee did not explain why it adopted the version finally enacted in 1924. The logic that defines Latins as inferior in Europe would, one might think, apply doubly to Spanish Americans, who by and large are on a lower cultural level than, say, Italians. One can suggest three possible reasons why the difference was made: a sense of unity with the rest of the Americas; the economic benefits that Mexican immigrant laborers brought the Southwest, generally one of the most

<hr/>

[40] In the 1924 act, ministers and teachers could immigrate outside the quota, together with their wives and children under 18. The 1952 revision continued this exemption but for ministers only.

[41] *New York Times,* January 1, 1958.

[42] Louis L. Jaffe, "The Philosophy of Our Immigration Law," *Law and Contemporary Problems,* 21:2 (Spring, 1956), 358–375, at p. 369.

restrictionist regions; and the numerical unimportance of immigration from the Western Hemisphere.[43]

4. Refugees, who have come in under a number of ad hoc laws. The ruthless policies of totalitarian countries, first Nazi Germany and presently the Soviet Union and its satellites, have created more refugees than probably had been known in all of prior human history. The United States, by far the wealthiest country of the world and the strongest nation among democratic peoples, could not refuse to accept its share of the victims of totalitarianism, even when these were defined as unacceptable by the national-origins system.

The Displaced Persons Act of 1948, the first of several laws designed to offer special opportunities for refugee immigration, provided for the admission of a total of 400,000 persons who had been displaced by the war or forced migrations under the Nazis. Since many of the DP's had been born in countries with low quotas, the law represented a substantial policy revision with respect to both the number of immigrants and their national composition. Under the act, half of the regular quotas were mortgaged until these surplus admissions had been worked off, or in some cases for several centuries into the future. Neither supporters nor opponents of the national-origins system considered this ruling a happy compromise: persons of nationalities declared in the law to be relatively unassimilable were admitted in large numbers, but the designation of inferiority remained in the law. In the 1957 revision of the McCarran-Walter Act these mortgages of future quotas were cancelled.

The second important piece of ad hoc legislation, the Refugee Relief Act of 1953, was designed primarily to assist those who had fled from Communist countries. Some 214,000 "expellees," "escapees," and "refugees" were to be permitted to enter the United States as immigrants. These categories were defined so rigidly, however, and the security and other restrictive provisions were so unwieldy, that few applicants could qualify. (For example, no one could be issued a visa "unless complete information shall be available regarding the history of such person covering the period

[43] For a short period, it seemd as though this last point would be negated. When the European source of unskilled labor was cut off by the restrictionist laws, a substitute supply was furnished by the immigration of Canadians (including French Canadians) to New England and the North Central States, and of Mexicans to the Southwest (as well as that of Puerto Ricans to the New York area). During the 1920's the total immigration from Canada increased to almost a million, and that from the rest of the Americas to well over half a million; but in spite of the free immigration policy, this high point was never reached again. Cf. Kingsley Davis and Clarence Senior, "Immigration from the Western Hemisphere," *Annals of the American Academy of Political and Social Science*, 262 (March, 1949), 70–81. However, see below, pages 285–286.

of at least two years immediately preceding his application.") As a consequence, many of those who fled to the West returned to their Communist homeland, which with all its faults they found better than life in a
DP camp or, outside it, with no chance of establishing permanent roots.[44]

Within the framework of American immigration law it is difficult to
find a way of helping refugees from Communist oppression. The problem was especially dramatically posed after the Hungarian revolt of 1956.
Of the more than 170,000 who had fled across the border into Austria
after the Soviet Union re-established control in Hungary, some 38,000
were permitted to immigrate to the United States. This was the largest
number in absolute terms, but in proportion to its population the United
States admitted far fewer than Switzerland and somewhat fewer than
Israel, Canada, Luxemburg, Australia, Great Britain, or France.[45]

5. "Refugees" from overpopulation. The restrictive policy of the
McCarran-Walter Act, it was found by those who opposed it, could be
circumvented to some degree if the issue was whether asylum would be
offered to refugees. Given this political framework, proponents of less
restrictive legislation have succeeded in having the term *refugee* very
broadly defined. In the Refugee Relief Act of 1953 (as amended) preference quotas were given to Italians, Greeks, and Dutch—presumably,
though not ostensibly, in an effort to help relieve the population pressure
in those countries.

American immigration law, as these last examples suggest, is so complex
principally because it is the composite of two unresolved political stands.
The advocates of restriction on the principle of national origins succeeded in having the McCarran-Walter Act passed. But the bill was
vetoed by President Truman; and after Congress enacted it over his veto,
he appointed a commission to re-examine the whole issue. According to its
findings: "The dominant theme of those who appeared to testify or file
statements was criticism of the act of 1952. Some objected to specific
aspects, but most witnesses opposed the basic theories of the new law." [46]

What are the objections to the McCarran-Walter Act? They vary from

---

[44] See James Rorty, "Our Broken Promises to the Refugees," *Commentary,* October, 1955, pp. 301–309; Edward Corsi, "My Ninety Days in Washington," *The
Reporter,* May 5, 1955, pp. 10–17; Frank R. Barnett, "America's Strategic Weakness—Redefection," *Russian Review,* 15:1 (January, 1956), 29–36.

[45] American Federation of International Institutes, *Newsletter,* April, 1957; February, 1958.

[46] President's Commission on Immigration and Naturalization, *op. cit.,* p. 7. For an
attempt to gauge the attitude of political parties, organized pressure groups, and
the general public, see Harry N. Rosenfield, "The Prospects for Immigration Amend-
ments," *Law and Contemporary Problems,* 21:2 (Spring, 1956), 401–426.

one person or group to another, but the following are the most important. (a) The bill is too long and detailed, inordinately complex, so poorly written that even professors of law have found it difficult to understand.[47] (b) There is no clear division between the prosecuting and adjudicating functions of officers administering the immigration act, and this contradiction of the usual principles of Anglo-Saxon law has effected many injustices and personal tragedies.[48] (c) The immigration law of the United States and the way it has been administered have hampered American efforts to maintain friendly relations with other nations.[49] (d) Under the McCarran-Walter Act, a partial difference is made between native and naturalized citizens, so that the latter are reduced in effect to second-class citizenship.[50] (e) The total quota immigration of 155,000 is believed to be smaller than American interests demand. (f) The national-origins system is wrong in principle and should be abandoned.

Immigration policy is thus still in flux. New bills are submitted at virtually every session of Congress, and, as we have seen, enough have passed to alter considerably the original provisions—though not the basic philosophy—of what its supporters in 1952 believed was a more or less final codification of immigration law. The inadequacy of the McCarran-Walter Act is greatest in terms of American foreign policy: a nation aspiring to political and moral leadership of the democratic West cannot evade the responsibility of accepting a fair share—that is, the largest —of those who have fled from totalitarian countries seeking political asylum. Nor can it safely continue to designate some of its actual or potential allies as biologically inferior.

SUMMARY

The dominant influence on the size and national composition of immigration to the United States during the past quarter-century has been the

[47] President's Commission on Immigration and Naturalization, *op. cit.,* pp. 18, 175 ff.

[48] Many case histories are given in J. Campbell Bruce, *The Golden Door: The Irony of Our Immigration Policy* (New York: Random House, 1954). For a well argued case for a new interpretation of immigration law, see Milton R. Konvitz, *Civil Rights in Immigration* (Ithaca, N.Y.: Cornell University Press, 1953).

[49] See, for example, Walter Van Kirk, "The Immigration and Nationality Act of 1952 (McCarran-Walter Act): What It Means in Terms of our Foreign Policy," reprinted in the *Congressional Record,* 83rd Congress, 2nd Session, 100:19 (June 1, 1954), A-4032–4034.

[50] See President's Commission on Immigration and Naturalization, *op. cit.,* Ch. 16.

limitations imposed by American law. Great as was the economic and demographic impact of immigration before the restrictionist laws of the 1920's, since then the number of immigrants has been too small relative to the size of the American population to make much difference one way or the other. In the depth of the depression there was a net emigration from this country, and during the rest of the 1930's and the subsequent war years the movement was negligible. In the postwar period the quota of about 155,000, though supplemented by nonquota and refugee immigration, was the principal determinant of the total number. Thus, while the natural increase has been something like three million per year, the net immigration was one-tenth of that figure.

In order to understand demographic trends, one must know something of the development of immigration policy and of the ideologies behind it. Much of the debate over policy has been, unfortunately, between two extreme positions. Free immigration, which was firmly established in the first years of the Republic and which Congress and the federal courts maintained in an exaggerated form for a full century, is still in the abstract an ideal for many liberals, who often pay symbolic deference to the principle, as in the title *Whom We Shall Welcome,* quoted from a speech by Washington.[51] On the other side, the national-origins quotas are defended no less vigorously now that the racism implicit in them gets support from neither natural nor social sciences.

Regulation of immigration in the nineteenth century started slowly, with a few of the states making intermittent and largely ineffectual attempts to deny entry to persons with specified individual deficiencies. The first federal laws were enacted in 1882, and over the next decades two principles were established: the exclusion of Asians and the regulation of European immigration so as to admit only those in good physical and mental health, of good moral character, and able to support themselves.

Beginning in the 1880's and continuing to the present day, there has been a debate over whether and how to restrict European immigration more stringently. The "whether" and the "how" are two issues, but they were decided together. Today no one advocates a return to free immigration; the number of immigrants that the United States ought to admit annually is one relatively minor issue in the debate, but not whether there should be a numerical restriction at all. In the laws of the 1920's, as codified in the McCarran-Walter Act of 1952, the principal basis on

---

51 For a statement of the liberal position entirely free of such residues from a past age, see Jaffe, "The Philosophy," *op. cit.*

which admission is granted or denied to an aspirant immigrant is his country of birth. The "national origins" of the United States population in 1920 were established by a statistical juggling of very inadequate data, and quotas were set to maintain in subsequent immigration the ratios already established among the various national stocks. This policy meant that the quota granted to Great Britain, for example, is much larger than the number there who want to emigrate to the United States, while visas under the quotas assigned to the countries of Southern and Eastern Europe are in constant and extremely heavy demand. This differentiation between Old and New Immigrants has been retained, though racist arguments for it—as by the Senate Immigration Commission of 1907–1910 or Harry Laughlin—are no longer voiced.

Differences over immigration law, it would seem, are being resolved by the needs of American foreign policy. Aliens feel affronted if their exclusion from the United States is based on racist or other arbitrary principles, or if the administration of reasonable limitations is such as to effect unnecessary hardships. A number of countries—among others, Canada, the United Kingdom, the Philippine Republic—have used their diplomatic channels to call attention to "certain irritating inequities and administrative complexities" in American immigration law.[52] The restrictionist argument that the United States, like any other sovereign nation, has the right to enact its own immigration laws as it sees fit, is not so good a point as it was in the isolationist 1920's. The American government cannot afford to ignore entirely the opinion of other countries, for in its own national interest it must try to establish the maximum degree of friendly cooperation among all nontotalitarian powers. As the various refugee relief acts suggest, the moral and political pressure on the United States to accept a fair share of the migration within the Western world is becoming the decisive determinant of its immigration policy.

SUGGESTIONS FOR FURTHER READING

Marcus Lee Hansen, *The Atlantic Migration 1607–1860: A History of the Continuing Settlement of the United States* (Cambridge: Harvard University Press, 1951).

Oscar Handlin, *The Uprooted: The Epic Story of the Great Migrations that Made the American People* (New York: Grosset & Dunlap, 1951).

[52] President's Commission on Immigration and Naturalization, *op. cit.*, p. 50.

Sympathetic histories of the immigrants to the United States. Written by two Harvard professors of history, they both read like good novels.

Jeremiah W. Jenks and W. Jett Lauck, *The Immigration Problem: A Study of Immigration Conditions and Needs* (3rd rev. ed.; New York: Funk and Wagnalls, 1913).

Harry H. Laughlin, "Expert Analysis of the Metal and the Dross in America's Modern Melting Pot," in U.S. House of Representatives, *Hearings before the Committee on Immigration and Naturalization,* November 21, 1922 (67th Congress, 3rd Session, serial 7-C; Washington: U.S. Government Printing Office, 1923).

Two important historical documents on American immigration policy. The first is a summary of the 42-volume *Report* of the Senate Immigration Commission of 1907–1910, the second the most important of the several works introducing racist concepts into American immigration law.

President's Commission on Immigration and Naturalization, *Whom We Shall Welcome* (Washington: U.S. Government Printing Office, 1953).

William S. Bernard *et al.,* eds., *American Immigration Policy: A Reappraisal* (New York: Harper, 1950).

Two well argued statements calling for a change in immigration law.

Simon Kuznets and Ernest Rubin, *Immigration and the Foreign Born* (Occasional Paper 46; New York: National Bureau of Economic Research, 1954).

An outstanding attempt to correct raw immigration data and the interpretations drawn from them.

Benjamin Munn Ziegler, ed., *Immigration: An American Dilemma* (Boston: Heath, 1953).

Melvin G. Shimm, ed., "Immigration," *Law and Contemporary Problems,* vol. 21, no. 2, Spring, 1956.

Excellent collections of articles from various points of view. The first stresses the historical background, the second the contemporary setting.

Milbank Memorial Fund, *Postwar Problems of Migration* (New York, 1947).

———, *Selected Studies of Migration Since World War II* (New York, 1958).

The level of discussion is consistently high. Only some of the papers deal with migration to the United States.

Dudley Kirk, *Europe's Population in the Interwar Years* (League of Nations; Princeton: Princeton University Press, 1946); especially Ch. 5.

————, and Earl Huyck, "Overseas Migration from Europe Since World War II," *American Sociological Review*, 19:4 (August, 1954), 447–456. (This article has been reprinted in Joseph J. Spengler and Otis Dudley Duncan, eds., *Demographic Analysis*, Glencoe, Ill.: Free Press, 1956, pp. 297–306.)

European migration analyzed in the context of the sending countries' population and social-economic trends.

William Petersen, "The 'Scientific' Basis of Our Immigration Policy," *Commentary*, July, 1955, pp. 77–86.

Overlaps in part with this chapter.

Joseph L. Lichten, ed., *Immigration and Citizenship: A Selected Bibliography* (New York: Anti-Defamation League, 1956).

Stanley J. Tracy *et al., A Report on World Population Migrations* (Washington: George Washington University, 1956).

Harry N. Rosenfield, "Historical Research as a Tool for Immigration Policy," *Publications of the American Jewish Historical Society,* vol. 46, no. 3, March, 1957. (This article has been reprinted in Research Group for European Migration Problems, *Bulletin,* 5:4, October–December, 1957, 98–116.)

American Immigration Conference, 509 Madison Avenue, New York 22, N.Y.

For bibliographic assistance. The Conference will furnish on request up-to-date bibliographies and summaries of current and pending legislation.

6. THE DEVELOPMENT

OF A NATIONAL POPULATION

A hundred years ago three ships left the port of Hamburg. One went to New Orleans, and its passengers proceeded up the Mississippi to Missouri; the second went to Rio de Janeiro, and its passengers settled the southern provinces of Brazil; the third went to Adelaide, and its passengers founded a community in New South Wales. The migrants on all three ships were from the same region of Germany and the same social class; they were led by men of the same character. However, the immigrants' descendants in Missouri, if they know German today, learned it at school. Those in New South Wales retained much more of the home-country language and culture. Those in South America constitute "a Teutonic state in the Brazilian federation." [1] The fate of the passengers of these three ships constitutes, in capsule form, the story of what happened to the migrants to these three overseas countries. Why was the process of acculturation in the United States so much more complete than elsewhere?

The first thing to be noted is that the merging of the immigrant cultures was not inevitable, the automatic consequence of the immigration. During the first decades of the twentieth century, when the large numbers entering this country made it a subject of great interest, acculturation was usually seen as an all-or-none process. America was a "melting pot"; the phrase comes from the title of a play by Israel Zangwill, himself an immi-

[1] Marcus Lee Hansen, *The Immigrant in American History* (Cambridge: Harvard University Press, 1948), pp. 24–25. For a detailed study of the Germans in Australia, see W. D. Borrie, *Italians and Germans in Australia: A Study of Assimilation* (Melbourne: Cheshire, 1954).

114

grant.[2] Native Americans also adopted the metaphor of the melting pot; they urged immigrants to be "hundred per cent" Americans, not Swedish-Americans or Italian-Americans or other "hyphenated" Americans. Even sociologists generally interpreted acculturation in this total sense. Thus we are told in one work that "assimilation . . . goes on wherever contact and communication exist between groups. . . . It is as inevitable as it is desirable. The process may be hastened or delayed; it cannot be stopped." [3] In some instances of culture contact, on the contrary, a pattern of limited interaction has remained stable for centuries.

In American society today, one can find ample basis for emphasizing either point of view—either the millions of immigrants, more diverse in their cultural background than those who went to any other important receiving country, who came to speak the same language and share the same major institutions, or, on the other hand, the minority problem, the frequent denial to one or another ethnic or religious group of some of the rights guaranteed by the American Creed. The difficult task is to see both elements together, to see the composition of the American population in its full dynamic complexity.

ETHNIC COMPOSITION OF THE POPULATION

In some respects, the European additions to the Anglo-Saxon base have really melted down into one homogeneous people. In other respects, persistent differences can be noted if we take the trouble to look below the surface. The dichotomy between Old and New Immigrants, for instance, though as such no longer nearly so salient an issue as a quarter of a century ago, has survived to some degree in the differentiation between Protestants and Catholics or Jews. Or, as another example, the racism behind the enactment of the restrictive legislation in the 1920's is no longer an important factor in separating ethnic groups among the whites, but members of other races are still sharply distinguished from the rest of the population. To analyze acculturation in the United States, thus, it is necessary to consider three types of interrelation: (a) between natives and foreign-born, (b) among the several religious denominations, and (c) among the several races.

[2] The message of the play is that all the European strains would disappear entirely, blending into a nobler American compound. Its hero, a Russian Jewish immigrant, marries the immigrant daughter of the tsarist official responsible for the pogrom in which his own parents were killed. See Israel Zangwill, *The Melting-Pot* (Rev. ed.; New York: Macmillan, 1920).

[3] Maurice R. Davie, *World Immigration, with Special Reference to the United States* (New York: Macmillan, 1949), pp. 498–499.

Nativity of the White Population

It is possible with census data to differentiate the foreign-born and their native-born offspring (who together are termed the **foreign stock**). Native-born of native-born parents merge into the general population; for the third and higher generations, therefore, no reliable data on European background are available.

The proportion of foreign-born whites, as shown in Table 6-1, has fallen off rapidly since the restrictionist laws of the 1920's. Native-born have increased from 83.4 per cent in 1890 to 92.5 per cent in 1950, and

TABLE 6-1. Percentage Distribution of the White Population, by Nativity, United States, 1890–1950

	Total White Population	Native-born				Foreign-born
		Total	Of Native-born Parents	Of Mixed Parents	Of Foreign-born Parents	
1890	100	83.4	62.6	6.2	14.7	16.6
1900	100	84.7	61.3	7.5	15.9	15.3
1910	100	83.7	60.5	7.3	15.8	16.3
1920	100	85.5	61.6	7.4	16.6	14.5
1930	100	87.3	63.8	7.7	15.8	12.7
1940	100	90.4	70.9	6.7	12.8	9.6
1950	100	92.5	75.0	6.5	11.0	7.5

Source: U.S. Bureau of the Census, *U.S. Census of Population: 1950,* vol. 4, *Special Reports,* part 3, Ch. A, Nativity and Parentage (Washington: U.S. Government Printing Office, 1954), Table 1.

those with native-born parents from 62.6 to 75.0 per cent over the same period. Unless there is a radical revision of immigration legislation, this relative decline in the foreign stock will continue—how fast is indicated in Table 6-2. The median age of the white population, because of the decline in fertility, has risen considerably over the past half-century; but the trend is quite different for the various nativity groups. At the height of the immigration, the median age of the foreign-born was high. Most newcomers were young adults: they were born into American society, so to speak, at the age of 20 and ranged upward from this figure. Because of this age structure (as well as old-country family patterns), they had many children on the average; and in 1890 the youngest group was native-born of foreign-born or mixed parentage. Since the 1920's the

TABLE 6-2. Median Age of the White Population, by Nativity,
United States, 1890–1950

	Total White Population	Native-born		Foreign-born
		Of Native-born Parents	*Of Foreign-born or Mixed Parents*	
1890	22.5	21.0	16.2	37.1
1900	23.4	21.2	18.2	38.5
1910	24.4	22.0	20.0	37.2
1920	25.6	22.7	21.6	40.0
1930	26.9	23.4	24.7	43.9
1940	29.5	26.1	29.4	51.0
1950	30.6	26.1	36.8	56.1

Source: E. P. Hutchinson, *Immigrants and Their Children, 1850–1950* (New York: Wiley, 1956), p. 15. Copyright © 1956 by The Social Science Research Council.

number of immigrants has been reduced and their median age has gone up. Today the average foreign-born American is on the verge of retirement, and his average son is approaching middle age.

The foreign stock constitutes only a small proportion of the population, and is rapidly getting smaller still. It includes relatively few recent arrivals. Differences do persist to some degree, though perhaps less among ethnic groups per se than among religions. As we have noted, one consequence of the New Immigration—and in the long run perhaps the most important—was to add significant Catholic and Jewish minorities to the then predominantly Protestant population.

Religion

There are no satisfactory data on the religious distribution of the American population.[4] As was noted in Chapter 3, the Census Bureau has resisted the considerable, and in recent years growing, pressure to include a question on religion in the census schedule. For some of the census years during the second half of the nineteenth century, some "social statistics" were collected from county officials, including detailed data on church membership. Then, in this century four "censuses of religious bodies" were taken each ten years from 1906 to 1936. It had been planned to continue these, but in 1946 and 1956 Congress failed to

[4] For annotated bibliographies of the statistical sources available, see Dorothy Good, "Questions on Religion in the United States Census," *Population Index,* 25:1 (January, 1959), 3–16; Benson Y. Landis, "A Guide to the Literature on Statistics of Religious Affiliation with References to Related Social Studies," *Journal of the American Statistical Association,* 54:286 (June, 1959), 335–357.

appropriate the necessary funds. For the most recent period, partial data are available from three sources: public-opinion research firms and institutes, which have included questions on religion in national polls several dozen times; the membership figures of various churches, as reported in the yearbook of the National Council of Churches of Christ; and the one nationwide sample survey made by the Census Bureau.

Table 6-3 lists the number of members claimed by the various denominations as of 1956 or 1957. One can reasonably assume that these figures

TABLE 6-3. Distribution of the Population by Claimed Church Membership, United States, 1956 or 1957

	Church Members (thousands)		Percentage of Total Population	
Protestants	60,149		35.4	
Of whom: [a]				
Baptist		19,934		11.7
Methodist		11,946		7.0
Lutheran		7,401		4.4
Presbyterian		3,963		2.3
Protestant Episcopal		2,853		1.7
United Church of Christ [b]		2,179		1.3
Disciples of Christ		1,922		1.1
Churches of Christ		1,800		1.1
Christ Unity Science		1,581		0.9
Latter-Day Saints		1,438		0.9
All others		5,132		3.0
Catholics	37,272		22.0	
Of whom:				
Roman Catholic		34,564		20.4
Eastern Orthodox		2,595		1.5
Old Catholic		101		0.1
All others		12		c
Jews	5,200		3.1	
Buddhists	63		c	
Moslems [d]	20		c	
Not members of any church	67,096 [e]		39.5 [e]	
Total	169,800 [f]		100.0	

[a] All denominations with an aggregate membership of more than a million.

[b] Formed in 1957 by the union of the Congregational Christian Churches and the Evangelical and Reformed Church.

[c] Less than 0.05 per cent.

[d] Unofficial estimate.

[e] Calculated as the difference between the estimated population and the total membership of all churches.

[f] Official estimate as of January 1, 1957; see U.S. Bureau of the Census, *Current Population Reports*, series P-25, no. 153 (March 28, 1957).

Source: *World Almanac and Book of Facts for 1958* (New York: New York World-Telegram, 1958), pp. 711–712; based on National Council of Churches of Christ in the U.S.A., *Yearbook of American Churches, 1958*, supplemented by a private questionnaire. See also *New York Times*, September 3, 1957.

represent maxima, though even in that sense they are not wholly comparable. The Roman Catholic Church reports as members all persons who have been baptized, including infants and those who have drifted away. Most Protestant churches report only those who have attained full membership by confirmation or a similar ritual, thus omitting infants and children under about 13 years. One Protestant denomination, the Church of Christ Scientist, has a regulation forbidding "the numbering of people and such statistics for publication." Most of the major denominations, moreover, cannot be interpreted as altogether meaningful units. There are 27 subdenominations among the Baptists, 21 among the Methodists, 18 among the Lutherans, 9 among the Presbyterians, 19 among the Eastern Orthodox Church. The divisions are based on differences in doctrine (which are important enough to have caused schisms, however petty they sometimes appear to outsiders), in social class or region (particularly the North-South and the Negro-white dichotomies), and in language. The largest single denomination by a considerable margin is the Roman Catholic Church, though here too ethnic differences exist between the New England and Middle Atlantic states (Irish, Italian, Polish, French Canadian), Louisiana (French), and the Southwest (Mexican).

Even after the much discussed postwar revival of religion, almost 40 per cent of the population (including children and infants) is not claimed as a member of any church. To what degree this percentage denotes the irreligious cannot be said, however, for it was obtained by subtracting the sum of the inexact and incomparable membership figures from the total population.

In Table 6-4 these membership figures are compared with the results of the sample survey made by the Census Bureau in March, 1957. While these latter figures are subject to sampling variability, undoubtedly the principal reasons for the considerable differences between the two sets of data are that the Census Bureau queried only persons 14 years and over, and that it merely asked the single question, "What is your religion?" This exerts a certain pressure to answer with some religion,[5] and it is likely that nominal adherents to any faith in general replied by naming it. In any case, the sum of these personal preferences for any denomination would certainly be greater than the number of formal members, as they are for Protestant denominations. That the number of persons who reported themselves as Roman Catholics or as Jews was less by a considerable margin than the claimed membership of these churches suggests that the latter figures are very much too large.

[5] A more objective manner of putting the question would have been: "Have you a religion?" and then, if the reply was affirmative, "What is it?"

**TABLE 6-4. Distribution of the Population by Stated Religious
Preference and Claimed Church Membership,
United States, 1956 or 1957**

	Sample Survey of Civilians 14 Years and Over			Church Members		
	Thousands	*Per Cent*		*Thousands*	*Per Cent*	
Protestant	78,952	66.2		60,149	58.6	
Baptist	23,525		19.7	19,934		19.4
Methodist	16,676		14.0	11,946		11.6
Lutheran	8,417		7.1	7,401		7.2
Presbyterian	6,656		5.6	3,963		3.9
Other Protestant	23,678		19.8	16,905		16.5
Roman Catholic	30,669	25.7		34,564	33.7	
Jewish	3,868	3.2		5,200	5.1	
Other religion	1,545	1.3		2,791	2.7	
No religion	3,195	2.7		—	—	
Religion not reported	1,104	0.9		—	—	
Totals Civilian population 14 years and over	119,333	100.0				
Church membership				102,704	100.0	

Sources: U.S. Bureau of the Census, *Current Population Reports,* series P-20, no. 79 (February 2, 1958), plus the sources listed for Table 6-3.

What are the social effects of religious faith? The official supposition is that there are none of great importance: immigrants urged to acculturate in every other sense were guaranteed the right to religious freedom by the Constitution itself. This sharp contrast has in all likelihood encouraged as wide an interpretation as feasible of what constitutes "religion." In the nineteenth century, for example, Protestant ministers often confused orthodoxy with persistence of the old-country language, and among Lutherans the dispute between proponents of English and German "provoked riots and bloodshed." [6] About the time of the First World War, the Calvinist ministers of the Michigan Dutch community attempted to establish what they termed a "Christian society," with a Calvinist political party, a Calvinist newspaper, Calvinist trade unions, a Calvinist school system (of which Calvin College still exists). [7] The Irish Catholic Benevolent Society had even broader plans: separate banks, steamship companies, hotels, labor unions—"in fact almost a complete Irish Catholic economic system" [8] but these fanciful aspirations were never realized.

[6] Marcus Lee Hansen, *The Atlantic Migration 1607–1860: A History of the Continuing Settlement of the United States* (Cambridge: Harvard University Press, 1951), p. 75.

[7] See William Petersen, *Planned Migration: The Social Determinants of the Dutch-Canadian Movement* (Berkeley: University of California Press, 1955), p. 49.

[8] John J. Kane, "Protestant-Catholic Tensions," *American Sociological Review,* 16:5 (October, 1951), 663–672.

These examples from the past suggest that it is necessary to define rather precisely the freedom of religion that is granted by the Bill of Rights. Some at least of the rising tension between Protestants and Catholics [9] is the consequence of the Catholic Church's effort to have the entire population—rather than only its constituents—governed in accordance with its specific norms on birth control, divorce, censorship, and the like. Similarly, Fundamentalist Protestants have tried to make Prohibition the law of the land, and Zionists have tried to influence American foreign policy in the Middle East.

Religion *does* have an effect on behavior patterns (and in population matters, especially on fertility), but it is difficult to specify. The adherents of most faiths are congregated in one social class and often in one region as well, and to distinguish one possible influence from another sometimes requires a very subtle analysis. For instance, until a substantial number of Catholics were established in the middle class, their higher average fertility could have been ascribed with equal probability to their religion, their class position in American society, vestiges of old-country peasant cultures, or a combination of all three. Moreover, most studies of the social correlates of religious faith do not allow for the considerable variation in what people mean when they say they are religious. A "Jew" may be an atheist, and a "Protestant" or "Catholic" may subscribe to a faith too nominal to affect his behavior.

Race

While in some respects the data on races may seem to be better than those on religion, in actuality this is not the case. More figures have been collected and over a longer period, but it is difficult to say what some of them mean. The primary difficulty is in defining the key term. As Boyd has put it, a race is "a population which differs significantly from other human populations in regard to the frequency of one or more of the genes it possesses. It is an arbitrary matter which, and how many, gene loci we choose to consider as a significant 'constellation.' " [10] Thus, some physical anthropologists have found it useful to divide mankind only into the three "major" races of Caucasoid, Mongoloid, and Negroid. Dividing races according to their serological characteristics, Boyd arrived at a total of six. A recent classification based on the somatic traits used in traditional

[9] For evidence that it is rising, see *ibid.*
[10] William C. Boyd, *Genetics and the Races of Man: An Introduction to Modern Physical Anthropology* (Boston: Heath, 1950), p. 207.

nineteenth-century anthropology ended with 30 races, but the authors warned the reader that the line of distinction was arbitrary in many cases, so that the list might almost as well have been 10 or 50.[11]

If race is difficult to define conceptually, it is even more so in a statistical context. Yet all the data are markedly influenced by how one delimits each race. It is well known that American Negroes, for example, are genetically mixed.[12] Indeed, whether so composite a group should be included with their African ancestors is perhaps doubtful, and some physical anthropologists now classify American Negroes as a new race, or at least as one in the making.[13] According to state laws and local customs, which are followed also in the census classification, a known trace of Negro genes, however slight, defines one as a Negro in the United States. Only a small proportion of especially light hybrids "pass" as whites.

The number of Negroes enumerated in the successive censuses is given in Table 6-5. From 0.75 million in 1790, the Negro population grew to something more than 15 million in 1950. During the first 50 years of the Republic almost one person in every five was a Negro, or one in every three in the South. From almost the beginning of the record to 1930 the national proportion decreased steadily, rising again slightly in the last 30 years. According to preliminary reports of the 1960 census, Negroes numbered 18.9 million, or 10.5 per cent of the total. The main reason for this differential growth of the two races has been migration, which was cut off from Africa just as it was beginning to surge from Europe.

The various estimates of Negro immigration are little better than guesses. From 1619, when the first slaves were brought to Virginia, to 1808, when the slave trade was outlawed, a total of some 370,000 to 400,-000 was recorded.[14] These figures must be taken as a minimum, since some of the importation during this period, and all of the subsequent surrepti-

---

[11] Carleton S. Coon, Stanley M. Garn, and Joseph B. Birdsell, *Races: A Study of the Problems of Race Formation in Man* (Springfield, Ill.: Thomas, 1950), p. 140.

[12] Of a presumably representative sample of 1,551 Negroes that Herskovits questioned on their ancestry, 71.7 per cent *knew* of some white and 27.2 per cent of some Indian forebears. See Melville J. Herskovits, *The Anthropometry of the American Negro* (New York: Columbia University Press, 1930); cited in Arnold Rose, *The Negro in America* (Boston: Beacon, 1948), p. 46. Virtually all of the Negro-white mixture was, of course, the consequence of extramarital contacts between white males and Negro females.

[13] See in particular Coon, Garn, and Birdsell, *op. cit.,* p. 131.

[14] William S. Rossiter, *A Century of Population Growth from the First Census of the United States to the Twelfth, 1790–1900* (U.S. Bureau of the Census; Washington: U.S. Government Printing Office, 1909), p. 36. The number of slaves imported to all of the British colonies has been estimated as over two million. While both figures are approximations, it was certainly the case that many more Africans were taken to the Caribbean area than to what became the South of the United States.

TABLE 6-5. Negro Population of the United States, 1790–1950

	Number (thousands)		Per Cent of
	Slave	Free	Total Population
1790	698	60	19.3
1800	894	108	18.9
1810	1,191	186	19.0
1820	1,538	234	18.4
1830	2,009	320	18.1
1840	2,487	386	16.8
1850	3,204	434	15.7
1860	3,954	488	14.1
1870	4,880		13.5
1880	6,581		13.1
1890	7,489		12.3
1900	8,834		11.6
1910	9,828		10.7
1920	10,463		9.9
1930	11,891		9.7
1940	12,866		9.8
1950	15,042		10.0

Source: U.S. Bureau of the Census, *Historical Statistics of the United States, Colonial Times to 1957* (Washington: U.S. Government Printing Office, 1960), Series A 59–60, 65 66.

tious slave trade, went unrecorded. Little is known, also, of the fertility and mortality of the slave population.[15]

Many statistical series are broken down into only two racial groups, whites and "nonwhites." The latter is a residual catchall that makes no sense in either physiological or cultural terms except as a rough synonym for Negroes, who constitute more than 95 per cent of the "nonwhites." [16] Smaller racial minorities are numerically insignificant; in 1950 they totaled all together only 713,047 persons, or less than half of 1 per cent of the population. They are pertinent to a general discussion, thus, only for the special features associated with them; and some of these are of considerable interest.

[15] See Conrad Taeuber and Irene B. Taeuber, *The Changing Population of the United States* (New York: Wiley, 1958), pp. 252–253.

[16] For example, U.S. Bureau of Labor Statistics, *The Economic Situation of Negroes in the United States* (Bulletin S-3; Washington: U.S. Government Printing Office, 1960), is a convenient summary of statistics on "non-whites." Why the Census Bureau persists in using the classification "nonwhites" is something of a puzzle. No information is added concerning the smaller racial groups, but the delineation of Negroes is muddied by including such totally unrelated groups as Asians and Indians. For analyses of particular areas—for example, the Pacific states with their relatively high proportion of Chinese and Japanese, or the Southwest with its Indians—the data compiled about "nonwhites" are all but useless.

American Indians, for example, number only a few hundred thousand; but they present several challenging problems to the demographer and the sociologist. We know that the Indians migrated to the Americas probably by way of a land-bridge at what is now the Bering Strait, and that this trek took place some 10,000 or 25,000—possibly even 100,000— years ago.[17] Whatever the date and the route, enough came eventually to form the base of the entire aboriginal population of North and South America. No one knows, of course, what the pre-Columbian population was. Estimates for the entire hemisphere range from 8.5 to 48.5 million, and for America north of Mexico from 1.0 to 3.5 million. The usually accepted figure for the number in the present area of the United States circa 1492 is 750,000 (or somewhat less than that now inhabiting the nation's capital). From approximately this same number in 1800, the aboriginal population was reduced to about 250,000 over the next 50 years by war and disease, particularly smallpox [18] and tuberculosis; whiskey and the consequent personal disorganization; and removals of tribes to unfamiliar areas, with subsequent hardships and starvation. For the next 75 years the population seems to have remained more or less static. During the past several decades there has been a fairly rapid increase: the initial adjustment to reservation life was past, health conditions improved, the Indian wars were over.

As we have noted, untaxed Indians were the only group excluded from the census when it was prescribed in the Constitution, and those living in Indian Territories or on reservations were not counted until 1890. In subsequent censuses, policy varied on how an "Indian" should be defined.

In 1910, a special effort was made to secure a complete enumeration of persons with any perceptible amount of Indian ancestry. This probably resulted in the enumeration as Indian of a considerable number of persons who would have been reported as white in earlier censuses. There were no special efforts in 1920, and the returns showed a much smaller number of Indians than in 1910. Again in 1930

[17] The migration can be approximately timed using the relatively new process of carbon-dating. A minute but fixed proportion of the carbon contained in every living organism is radioactive, and after its death this radioactive portion, called Carbon 14, decomposes at a very slow, constant rate. Any artifacts associated with early man, if they are of organic material, can thus be tested for radioactivity and dated more accurately than by any prior method. See Robert F. Heizer, "Long-Range Dating in Archeology," in A. L. Kroeber, ed., *Anthropology Today: An Encyclopedic Inventory* (Chicago: University of Chicago Press, 1953), pp. 3–42; H. M. Wormington, *Ancient Man in North America* (3rd rev. ed.; Denver: Denver Museum of Natural History, 1949).

[18] Cf. E. Wagner Stearn and Allen E. Stearn, *The Effect of Smallpox on the Destiny of the Amerindian* (Boston: Bruce Humphries, 1945).

emphasis was placed on securing a complete count of Indians, with the results that the returns probably overstated the decennial increase in the number of Indians.[19]

The Indian population fluctuated together with census policy: from 248,000 in 1890 down to 237,000 in 1900, up to 266,000 in 1910, down to 244,000 in 1920, up to 332,000 in 1930.[20] In the 1950 census about 343,000 Indians were enumerated. This figure, however, includes neither an estimated 75,000 persons who would normally report themselves as Indians on public documents (of whom about 30,000 hybrids were enumerated as whites), nor an additional 25,000 persons entitled to legal recognition as tribe members who would not usually report themselves as Indians.[21] It is apparent that "Indian" does not mean one single thing, and that the various gradations between "Indian" and "white" denote degrees of acculturation more than of racial mixture. By any definition of Indians, their natural increase is now considerably higher than that of the white population, and recently a number of tribes have grown rapidly. To repeat, the Indians are no longer a "vanishing race." [22]

While the most striking variation in the official definition of a race has been in the changing meaning of "Indian," usage has varied also with respect to other racial or quasi-racial groups. Thus, "Mexicans" were classified in the 1930 census among "other races"—that is, "those that did not represent a homogeneous biological stock," while in 1940 and 1950 persons of Mexican birth or ancestry "who were not definitely Indian or of other nonwhite race" were classified as white.[23] Similarly, Puerto Ricans in the New York area range from white to Negro, but the fact that they also constitute a compact Spanish-American culture group makes the racial classification particularly difficult to apply and somewhat irrelevant.

The Asians in the United States are perhaps the least ambiguous racial groups. The numbers of Chinese and Japanese enumerated since the

19 U.S. Bureau of the Census, *Historical Statistics of the United States, Colonial Times to 1957* (Washington: U.S. Government Printing Office, 1960), p. 3.

20 *Ibid.*, Series A-61, 67.

21 J. Nixon Hadley, "The Demography of the American Indians," *Annals of the American Academy of Political and Social Science,* 311 (May, 1957), 23–30.

22 For example, "an impressive 'Memorial to the American Indian' is shortly to be built on the outskirts of Gallup, New Mexico—at the edge of the Navaho Indian country where the Navaho population has increased from 15,000 (at most) in 1868 to almost 80,000 in 1956 and where Navaho culture persists with great vigor!" (Evon Z. Vogt, "The Acculturation of American Indians," *ibid.,* pp. 137–146).

23 See U.S. Bureau of the Census, *U.S. Census of Population: 1950,* vol. 4, *Special Reports,* part 3, Ch. A, Nativity and Parentage (Washington: U.S. Government Printing Office, 1954), p. 3A-6.

census of 1860 are given in Table 6-6. As we have seen in the last chapter, the discriminatory practices in California and other western states, culminating in federal exclusion acts, were applied against first the

TABLE 6-6. The Chinese and Japanese in the United States, 1860–1950

	Chinese		Japanese	
	Census Count	Per cent Intercensal Increase	Census Count	Per cent Intercensal Increase
1860	34,933	—	—	—
1870	63,199	80.9	55	—
1880	105,465	66.9	148	169.1
1890	107,488	1.9	2,039	1,277.7
1900	89,863	−16.4	24,326	1,093.0
1910	71,531	−20.4	72,157	196.6
1920	61,639	−13.8	111,010	53.8
1930	74,954	21.6	138,834	25.1
1940	77,504	3.4	126,947	−8.6
1950	117,629	51.8	141,768	11.7

Source: U.S. Bureau of the Census, *Historical Statistics of the United States, Colonial Times to 1957* (Washington: U.S. Government Printing Office, 1960), Series A62, 63, 68, and 69.

Chinese and then the Japanese. The return movement of Chinese was great: the census count fell off from a high point of 107,000 in 1890 to 62,000 in 1920. From the latter date on, their number has risen again, particularly since the prior ban on immigration was somewhat relaxed in the McCarran-Walter Act. The Japanese came later but grew faster: their number increased from 55 persons in 1870 to 142,000 in 1950.

Note that the largest influx of Chinese took place before 1880, or during the height of the mining and railroad boom in the West.[24] The Japanese began to arrive only in the 1890's, when mining and railway construction were declining, and many became small agriculturists. This original differentiation, the consequence largely of the economic opportunities available during the two periods of heavy immigration, greatly influenced the subsequent history of the two groups. In the frontier coun-

[24] The following discussion is based in part on Stanford M. Lyman, "Factors Affecting the Location of Chinese and Japanese in the United States," an unpublished manuscript. See also H. Yuan T'ien, "Changing Trends in the Chinese-American Population," *Human Biology*, 30:3 (September, 1958), 201–209; Rose Hum Lee, *The Chinese in the United States of America* (New York: Oxford University Press, 1960).

try, the Chinese had undertaken "women's work" as cooks and laundry-men, and when the camps shut down, they established restaurants and laundries in towns throughout the country. Once committed to agriculture, the Japanese, on the other hand, were tied to the land. Thus, while both groups have been concentrated in the Far West, until 1940 this was much more true of the Japanese than of the Chinese. Similarly, the percentage of the Chinese living in towns had risen to more than 90 by 1940, while for the Japanese it was only slightly over half.

After Pearl Harbor the 113,000 Japanese on the West Coast— whether recent arrivals or native-born citizens, whether in sympathy with Japan or with America, or simply apolitical—were evacuated and placed in camps.[25] At the time opinion was divided, but in retrospect it is clear that this gross violation of their civil rights had no legitimate justification, either military or any other. This forced migration has effected an ultimate greater dispersion of Japanese over the whole country, and by 1950 the percentage urban among them had risen to more than 70.

ACCULTURATION VS. NATIVISM

As this survey of some of the minorities in American society may suggest in itself, acculturation is a complex process, affected by a great number of variables. It can be defined as the process of interpenetration of two cultures by the continuous personal contact of their representatives. If it is hindered only by the accidental impediments consequent from mutual misunderstanding or feelings of strangeness, then over a sufficient period of time it is indeed likely that two or more culture groups in continuous contact will merge. But this drift together may be blocked by what is termed **nativism,** or the conscious, organized effort on the part of a society's members to perpetuate selected aspects of its culture.[26] Nativism includes both attempts by the dominant group to maintain its culture pure, undefiled by immigrant infiltration (such as the Know-Nothing movement in the United States in the middle of the nineteenth century), and a minority's resistance to its disappearance into the dominant culture

---

[25] See Dorothy Swaine Thomas and Richard S. Nishimoto, *The Spoilage;* Thomas, *The Salvage* (Berkeley: University of California Press, 1946 and 1952).

[26] See Ralph Linton, "Nativistic Movements," *American Anthropologist,* 45:2 (April–June, 1943), 230–240. The usual passive, unorganized attempt by the members of any society to resist the disappearance of their own culture, it should be noted, is not included in this definition, whose crux lies in the phrase "conscious, organized effort."

(as with the Ghost Dance of the Paiute Indians or, among literate peoples, the revival of Celtic as an element of Irish nationalism). A nativist movement may seek to perpetuate elements of its culture or to revive extinct or moribund elements. While almost all nativism is unrealistic to one degree or another, one can distinguish between wholly irrational flights from reality and movements that at least by contrast can be termed rational.

Acculturation, then, denotes a continuum, with total **assimilation** at one end and total nonassimilation at the other, and various degrees of partial adaptation between. This distinction between assimilation and adaptation, moreover, is not merely one between stages—that is, between total integration in process and completed. A frequent form of adaptation is an example of what ecologists term **symbiosis,** or the interdependence of different peoples, as, for instance, in trade relations. And if a deliberate attempt to keep the two groups separate in other respects acquires ideological legitimacy and institutional forms, then such a symbiotic relation may be stable. An obvious example of such a pattern is the Jewish minority in Gentile societies. Ever since the diaspora, Jews have generally been in continuous commercial relations with the peoples among whom they lived. While the degree of integration varied considerably from one country or era to another, the complete amalgamation of Jews has been atypical. Their merging with the larger society was generally prevented by the anti-Semitism of Gentiles and the pro-Semitism of Jews, and the ghettos and similar institutions that both reflected these attitudes and helped perpetuate them.[27]

Under what conditions is nativism, the conscious, deliberate attempt to frustrate acculturation, likely to arise? We have no satisfactory answer to this important question. If a group is deprived of what the culture has defined as the ordinary satisfactions of life, the reaction may be to stress its other, nonmaterial attainments. But it is easy to exaggerate the relevance of economic factors to nativism. Participants in the effort to restrict immigration typically included, as we have seen, both self-conscious representatives of Old American families and labor-union demagogues; simi-

---

[27] Other instances can be cited from ethnographic studies. For example: over many generations, four adjacent native tribes of India exchanged the products of their specialized skills—buffalo-rearing, agriculture, metalwork, and sorcery. But this continuous contact did not blur the linguistic and other cultural differences among them. "Social intercourse was confined to a fixed number of narrowly defined activities. Any intimate contact, of a kind which would allow members of one group to mingle freely with another, was stringently tabooed." See David G. Mandelbaum, "Culture Change among the Nilgiri Tribes," *American Anthropologist,* 43:1 (January–March, 1941), 19–26.

larly, anti-Negro movements have generally been made up of both upper middle-class and poor whites. Nativism among minorities also has typically included the two extremes—the pastor of a community, say, and the poorest farmers.

How the two groups define their comparative cultural levels is probably more important in influencing nativist tendencies. If both immigrants and natives regard the culture of the receiving country as superior to that of the sending country, then the immigrants' effort to move "up" into the former pays the natives implicit deference; and all are, or can be, happy. However, when one group is dominant in numbers or power and the other regards itself, in spite of its minority status, as superior in cultural level, then acculturation is impeded. This point can be illustrated by Reynolds's interesting study of acculturation of British migrants to Canada, which challenges the implicit—and certainly often valid—assumption in the immigration laws of both Canada and the United States that newcomers will be most fully assimilated if they are from the most similar countries. But even though one could characterize the movement almost as an internal migration, few Britons ever became completely Canadian in their habits and outlook. For them Canada was only a place of residence and England was always home:

> The British immigrant . . . views himself as going out from "the mother country" to "one of the colonies"; he is obviously a superior person, having been born in Britain, and the "colonials" should welcome him gladly. . . . Canadian methods of schooling and government can scarcely be expected to compare favourably with British methods. . . . It need scarcely be added that . . . the native Canadian, both French and English, . . . endeavours to "take the 'bloke' down a notch," or else to avoid contact with him.[28]

With such attitudes, Britons failed to be integrated even by the grossest of indexes: a disproportionately large number was unable to hold their jobs and thus became dependent on public support.

The definition of one culture as "superior" and the other as "inferior" need not be, of course, a realistic view of the actual relation between the interacting groups. A distinction must be made between real differences and those seen as such by the participants. Since by definition acculturation involves contact with cultures of which all concerned are more or less ignorant, it is typically an interrelation between groups in terms of two stereotypes:

[28] Lloyd G. Reynolds, *The British Immigrant: His Social and Economic Adjustment in Canada* (Toronto: Oxford University Press, 1935), pp. 210–211.

For the most part we do not first see, and then define, we define first and then see. . . . Americanization, for example, is superficially at least the substitution of American for European stereotypes.[29]

The picture that the typical immigrant had of America was a composite of the fables circulating in his home country with generalizations drawn from an extremely limited experience after he had arrived. And, on the other side, even American immigration officials were puzzled by the complex multiplicity of European peoples, as we have seen from the records that they collected.

The mass of the American public, which was certainly no less ignorant, simplified matters by classifying newcomers into a small number of easy categories; and very often the first stage of acculturation was an immigrant's redefinition of himself in accordance with this classification. In the nineteenth century, the Germans and Irish came from self-conscious groups that had not yet achieved legal unity; they were nations but not yet states. The Norwegians and Swedes, on the contrary, came from states that were not yet nations; only the upper classes were self-conscious bearers of the national culture.[30] This variation was to be found also among the later immigrants. An East European, for example, as he saw himself when he first arrived in the United States, had four identities. He was a subject of a particular state—say, Russia; he spoke a particular language —say, Lithuanian; he was an adherent of one or another religion; and he regarded a certain village or province as "home." Typically the peasant emigrants had no special feeling of identification with Russia or "Lithuania." This was often true even of emigrants from a nation that had achieved political unity: an "Italian," for instance, was much more likely to look on himself as a Sicilian or Calabrian.

In many cases it was only after they had left it that migrants learned to identify themselves with "their" country. They were taught this first of all by the native Americans, who demanded a simple, understandable answer to the question, "What are you?" Having learned that they belonged to a nation, some of the immigrants became nationalists. They submerged their provincialisms into a broader patriotism, their local dialects into languages. The first Lithuanian newspaper was published in the United States; the Erse revival began in Boston; the Czechoslovak

[29] Walter Lippmann, *Public Opinion* (New York: Macmillan, 1947), pp. 81, 85. *Stereotype* in this sense was introduced into the language in 1922 by the first printing of this book.

[30] See Nathan Glazer, "America's Ethnic Pattern," *Commentary,* April, 1953, pp. 401–408.

nation was launched at a meeting in Pittsburgh. The nativism of such groups was often one facet of their acculturation, paradoxical as this may seem.

The paradox is even more striking in the phenomenon known as third-generation nativism, which is based on the psychological certainty that in all essential respects one's integration into American society has been completed. While immigrants to the United States were linked to their native countries by childhood memories and nostalgia, as well as by immigrant-aid societies, national churches, and other ethnic organizations, their acculturation was not ordinarily impeded by a conscious reluctance to give up these old-country remnants. On the contrary, most immigrants tried to be more American than a Mayflower descendant; and this aspiration to be more royalist than the king was taken over—a little more realistically—by the second generation, which typically attempted to learn nothing of the language and other culture traits of its European forebears.[31] The third generation, however, has often tried to organize a revival of old-country cultures. Thus, the procession of ethnic groups that came to the United States was followed two generations later by a succession of amateur historical societies, folklore associations, and other organized efforts to keep alive specific elements of the various overseas cultures. In Hansen's words, it is an "almost universal phenomenon that what the son wishes to forget the grandson wishes to remember." [32]

To sum up, we must repeat that we know rather little about what factors tend to generate a nativist movement. According to Linton, "The most that we can say is that nativistic movements are unlikely to arise in situations where both societies are satisfied with their current relationship, or where societies which find themselves at a disadvantage can see that their condition is improving." [33] Great insecurity, whether economic or psychological, or on the contrary, an unusual degree of security, has sometimes resulted in nativism—but not inevitably. Often the decisive factor seems to have been the presence of a charismatic leader who galvanized vague sentiments into a social movement. It is at least suggestive

---

[31] Many of the specific features of the American family may derive from the fact that the immigrant father has an ambivalent authority over his native-born son, who speaks English without an accent and in other respects is likely to be more successful in American society. See, among other works that discuss this hypothesis, Oscar Handlin, *The Uprooted: The Epic Story of the Great Migrations that Made the American People* (New York: Grosset & Dunlap, 1951).

[32] See Marcus Lee Hansen, *The Problem of the Third Generation Immigrant* (Rock Island, Ill.: Augustana Historical Society, 1938); reprinted in *Commentary,* November, 1952, pp. 492–500.

[33] Linton, "Nativistic Movements," *op. cit.*

that nativism is typically the reaction of upper or lower extremes rather than the middle social class, as measured in any of several ways.

INDEXES OF ACCULTURATION

To the question, has an immigrant group assimilated, a simple yes-or-no answer is ordinarily too simple. A better reply can be made by discussing separately the roles each member of a society plays. Linton divided these into three categories—"universals," "specialties," and "alternatives" [34] — and his typology is a useful tool in breaking down acculturation into more meaningful parts.

Total assimilation is expected of immigrants only with respect to those ideas and behavior patterns to which natives must also conform. These are the **universals** of the society in question. In the United States at least three things have been demanded of all immigrants—that they support themselves, learn English, and pledge political allegiance to their new country.

Linton's second type of social role pertains to the kind of work a man does. **Specialties** divide any population into subgroups, both at the occupational level (stockbrokers, stenographers, automobile workers) and at the more inclusive level of social class (businessmen, employees, wage workers). That is to say, the division of labor sets people apart not merely according to their economic function, but also, to some degree, according to their average income, political attitudes, tastes, and so on. Even in egalitarian countries a lawyer and a mechanic, say, differ greatly in their style of life.

Apart from the class structure, every culture includes a legitimate diversity of ideas, attitudes, and tastes. In the United States today those who prefer Bach to jazz, or hiking to baseball, or bow ties to cravats, have chosen certain **alternatives** over others. In the abstract, immigrants are free to make similar choices; and if they retain old-country ways, they are sometimes commended for enriching the culture of their new homeland. In practice, however, exotic tastes in such things as food have sometimes been taken as a sign of unreliability in more fundamental respects. In the 1920's, thus, the head of a ladies' Americanization society asked her audience, with poorly restrained impatience, "What kind of American consciousness can grow in the atmosphere of sauerkraut and Limburger cheese, or in that of garlic?" The influence of the alternative roles of immigrant groups on American institutions, though subtle, has

[34] Ralph Linton, *The Study of Man* (New York: Appleton-Century, 1936), Ch. 16.

sometimes been significant. To what degree is the self-conscious bon-hommie of American politics derived from Irish social relations, or its liberalism from Jewish defense organizations, or the consumption of wine among the urban middle class from the Italian example and Italian-owned California vineyards? To attempt to discuss such questions would lead us too far afield. As we will see from the following discussion of specialties and universals, even for these the data are sparse and the analysis difficult.

Economic Roles of Ethnic Groups

The major theme of nineteenth-century European history, like that of twentieth-century world history, was the conflict between traditional aristocratic institutions and the democratic principles enunciated in the American and French revolutions. The established social classes gave way gradually to an extension of the suffrage and other basic political reforms, but usually managed to retain other advantages for a longer period—for example, their monopoly in higher education or government service. Some of this conflict was transferred to Latin America and the British Dominions, but in the United States (at least in the North) the trend toward a democratic state proceeded almost unimpeded. Alexis de Tocqueville, the young French nobleman who visited America in the 1830's and wrote a classic analysis of its political system, saw the difference clearly:

In Europe two conflicting principles exist, and we do not know what to attribute to the principles themselves, and what to refer to the passions which they bring into collision. Such, however, is not the case in America; there the people reigns without any obstacle, and it has no perils to dread and no injuries to avenge. In America, democracy is swayed by its own free propensities; its course is natural and its activity is unrestrained.[35]

To Europeans of every nationality, the democratic system of the overseas Republic was an attraction of enormous strength, and particularly the fact that the democracy extended also to social and economic relations. It was necessary to work hard in the new country, but what a man produced was his own to enjoy.

The per-capita expense of government was only one fourth that of the Netherlands and less than a tenth that of England. No percentage was deducted as tithes for the clergy or as rates for the poor. Though the United States had about the

[35] Alexis de Tocqueville, *Democracy in America,* Henry Steele Commager, ed. (New York: Oxford University Press, 1947), p. 116.

same population as Prussia, the standing army of the latter was fifty times as large. It was amazing that a farm that kept eight horses paid a tax in America of only twelve dollars.[36]

Immigrants themselves strongly reinforced this established trend toward egalitarian social relations. Of humble birth in overwhelming majority, ignorant of one another's background, they were impatient with class distinctions that rested on family pedigree or even on what Tocqueville terms "the natural aristocracy of knowledge and virtue." [37] There was a country to be built, and when it was built it would be theirs. This sense of participation in a joint venture, founded in American law and tradition but more subtle than either, is the key to the successful acculturation of millions of Europeans of such diverse backgrounds.

The part that each immigrant group played in building the American economy, however, was specific to it.[38] In a few cases, skills developed in Europe were transferred to the United States (Jewish furriers and tailors, as an example), but in general the young immigrant found work in an occupation that was new to him. Employment opportunities in the United States varied considerably from one period or region to another, and each nationality tended to be shunted into a particular type of occupation. We have already noted that the shift from the Old to the New Immigration more or less coincided with the beginning of modern industry in the United States, so that, by and large, Old Immigrants became farmers, New Immigrants became miners and factory workers. There was thus a good deal of overlap in occupation among nationalities arriving during the same decades, but sometimes also marked differences. The Irish, for instance, who immigrated in great numbers from the 1840's on, did not become farm laborers or farmers but stayed in the towns in spite of their peasant background. Such a trend, once started, tended to continue. Each immigrant found work alongside men who could speak his language, drawn there both by that fact and by directives from immigrant-aid groups, clergymen, or employment agents of his nationality. Thus, for example, a National Society for German Emigration was in operation by the early 1850's; and "after his arrival the [German] immi-

[36] Hansen, *The Atlantic Migration*, p. 158.

[37] Tocqueville, *op. cit.*, p. 44.

[38] Or, better, this was the case to the degree that inadequate sources permit us to judge. For two of the best efforts to transcend the statistics on national origins and occupations and to trace the relation between them, see E. P. Hutchinson, *Immigrants and Their Children, 1850–1950* (New York: Wiley, 1956); Brinley Thomas, *Migration and Economic Growth: A Study of Great Britain and the Atlantic Economy* (National Institute of Economic and Social Research, Economic and Social Study 12; Cambridge: Cambridge University Press, 1954).

grant could proceed from city to city, receiving advice at each stage"
from compatriots who had already established themselves.[39] A similar
network, either formally organized or not, existed for each of the immigrant nationalities.

The resultant differences are suggested in Table 6-7, in which only
the Scotch and the Irish are compared for only two years and a few occupations. The index numbers for each nationality express the proportion
engaged in the given occupation as a percentage of the proportion of all
native whites in that occupation. Thus, in 1890 there were relatively 7.39

TABLE 6-7. Index Numbers of Relative Participation of Scotch and
Irish Males in Certain Occupations, United States, 1890–1900

	Total Native White	Scotch			Irish		
		1890	*1900*	Native-born of Scotch Parents, 1900	*1890*	*1900*	Native-born of Irish Parents, 1900
Miners	100	739	441	329	232	188	153
Cotton-mill workers	100	417	140	80	263	140	100
Servants	100	212	200	120	358	340	180
Clerks	100	92	105	155	44	55	160
Teachers	100	27	33	83	17	17	50
Physicians	100	53	86	114	19	29	57

Source: Brinley Thomas, *Migration and Economic Growth: A Study of Great
Britain and the Atlantic Economy* (National Institute of Economic and Social Research, Economic and Social Study 12; Cambridge: Cambridge University Press,
1954), p. 145; data from U.S. censuses.

times as many miners among those born in Scotland as among native
white males, but only 2.32 times as many among the Irish-born. Among
those born in Scotland, work in the mines or cotton mills was relatively
most frequent, but the highest proportion among the Irish-born was
servants.

Immigration helped keep the American class structure loose, and this
was probably even truer of the New than of the Old Immigration. Most
of the millions who came to this country after 1880 became industrial
workers. With few skills, often knowing little or no English, they inevitably entered the labor market at the bottom, pushing native-born
workers up at least one rung. Then, with the next wave of immigrants,

[39] Hansen, *The Atlantic Migration,* p. 302.

they themselves were "displaced" from mines or unskilled factory jobs. Such a fluid labor supply, as contrasted with the permanent caste system in the South, significantly affected both economic efficiency and social democracy.[40] This pattern of social mobility is also illustrated by the data in Table 6-7. From 1890 to 1900 the relative proportion of Scotch working as miners fell by almost half, and those working in cotton mills by two-thirds. The miners were replaced by Central Europeans, and the textile workers by Jews or Italians, while the Scotch became clerks or even physicians. This upward movement was more pronounced in the second generation. In 1900 there were proportionately more doctors among sons of Scotch immigrants than in the native white population generally! The Irish moved up too, but by a different route: here the next higher rung for most of the second generation was a job as a clerk.

If this table could be expanded to include all of the major nationalities and occupations and the whole of the nineteenth century projected to 1920, then we would have a good picture of the interrelation between country of birth and occupation in the United States. Lack of data precludes so complete a study. For the most recent period, Hutchinson sums up his work on this subject as follows:

In 1910 the foreign-born white male workers were most heavily concentrated in some branches of the clothing industry . . . , among bakers, and in several semi-skilled or unskilled employments. . . . Relatively few were found in clerical work and the learned professions; but they were well represented in the artistic professions and among welfare and religious workers. In 1950 they are much less identified with unskilled labor, and more concentrated than formerly in the clothing industry . . . and have become relatively numerous in a wider variety of occupations than before. . . . Although still underrepresented in the learned professions and clerical work as a whole they have made considerable progress in these fields of employment.[41]

More generally put, all immigrants were congregated at the bottom of the social scale on their arrival, but in different occupations. And all of them, or their children, moved up from these several starting points, but along different routes. The hypothesis can be exemplified by a number of additional instances. East European Jews, with an old-country experi-

---

[40] See Elbridge Sibley, "Some Demographic Clues to Stratification," *American Sociological Review,* 7:3 (June, 1942), 322–330; William Petersen, "Is America Still the Land of Opportunity?" *Commentary,* November, 1953, pp. 477–486; Brinley Thomas, *op. cit.,* Ch. 9. See also above, pages 38, 93 n.

[41] Hutchinson, *op. cit.,* p. 216.

ence as tailors, were in large part employed in the needle trades. These were transformed from sweatshop work to one of the highest paid manual skills, and it was possible to move up into a "middle-class" pattern of life while remaining a worker. More often the rise in status, particularly of the second generation, has been by a change of occupation. The son of an Irish servant became a clerk; the son of a Hungarian miner became a salesman; the son of an Italian laborer became a barber or possibly a dentist. The place of the second generation on the second rung, like that of the immigrants on the first rung, varied to some degree from one nationality to another.

This hypothesis—which the data available merely suggest—marks one important limitation to the melting-pot thesis. Total assimilation by ethnic background is possible only if nationalities are randomly distributed among all occupations; for to the degree that the contrary is the case, variation by ethnic background tends to persist in the form of class differences.

The effect of a narrow choice of occupations on general acculturation can be seen most clearly in the extreme case of the Negroes, who have barely begun to climb out of the lowest social classes. At one time it was generally believed that they were incapable of work at a higher level. But the supposedly innate low intelligence of the southern Negro, when he was stimulated by the better schools and greater incentives of the North, proved to be remarkably flexible: as early as the army tests of 1914–1918, New York Negroes and Alabama whites proved to be on a par in intelligence.[42] The *belief* that most or all of the differences between Negroes and whites are hereditary, however, has had tremendous effects. As Myrdal pointed out, the interdependence of racial theory and the Negroes' social-economic condition can work in either direction. Faith in the innate inferiority of the Negro race led to the establishment of special institutions adapted to their presumed smaller ability (first of all, schools, but also, for instance, segregated occupations and neighborhoods); and such institutions created the postulated inferiority and thus reinforced the belief. The change in environment in cities outside the South has destroyed the basis for the racist myth, but popular attitudes and some of the legal restrictions have persisted.

[42] For a short summary of several such tests as given to various ethnic groups, see A. L. Kroeber, *Anthropology* (Rev. ed.; New York: Harcourt, Brace, 1948), pp. 192 ff. See also William M. McCord and Nicholas J. Demerath, "Negro versus White Intelligence: A Continuing Controversy," *Harvard Educational Review*, 28:2 (Spring, 1958), 120–135.

Acculturation in Universals

The early immigrants' appreciation of America's democratic principles was countered by their certainty that they were carrying the
superior culture of the Old World to a benighted backwoods area (and,
indeed, there was more than a little substance to this sentiment). The
Germans who settled in Missouri or Wisconsin, the Scandinavians who
settled in Minnesota, did not come with the idea of giving up their
native language and way of life. From its side, the American government
did little more to foster the acculturation of early immigrants than to prohibit their formal segregation by nationalities. In 1818, when Irish immigrant-aid societies requested Congress for a land grant on which to settle
some of the charitable cases they were attempting to help, this petition
was denied on the ground that it would be undesirable to concentrate
alien peoples geographically. "Probably no decision in the history of
American immigration policy possesses more profound significance." [43]
By the natural cohesion of their common background, the immigrants
from each country tended in any case to congregate in the same region
of the Middle West, or later in the same quarters of eastern cities; but
the fact that there was no formal boundary greatly facilitated contacts
with the native culture.

Acculturation did not proceed, however, in an altogether laissez-faire
framework. Policy decisions on other matters often resulted in the dissemination of the native culture. The public school system, gradually set
up during the first half of the nineteenth century, was based on the general principle that democracy, to be viable, must rest on a literate electorate. But the influence of public schools was also decisive in establishing English as the native language of all immigrant groups, at the latest
among the second generation.

Already in 1850 less than 10 per cent of the native whites aged 20 and
over were illiterate. By 1900 the percentage illiterate among native whites
10 years old and over had fallen to 4.6, as compared with 12.9 among
foreign-born whites and 44.4 among Negroes. In the whole population
roughly one-tenth was illiterate; in the South almost one-quarter. Virtually no immigrants went to the South; and by the second generation
the foreign stock were far more literate than natives in this backward
region. Even for the whole country in 1900 native whites of native

[43] Hansen, *The Immigrant in American History,* p. 132.

parentage were 5.7 per cent illiterate and those of foreign or mixed parentage only 1.6 per cent.[44]

The portion of the foreign-born reported in any census as unable to understand English varied according to age, ethnic origin, and place of residence in this country.[45] Another index of acculturation is the foreign-language press, which measures the actual use of different languages. The circulation of non-English newspapers and magazines has always been small, and their mortality great. At the high point, during World War I, there were 1,350 foreign-language publications in 36 different languages. The subsequent sharp decline was followed by a slight revival in some languages, reflecting the refugee immigration. If for each nationality one compares the circulation of foreign-language dailies with the number of foreign-born, the ratio in 1950 varied considerably. For the Chinese, it was almost unity (that is, the two figures were almost equal); and for the Japanese, Lithuanians, Czechs, Poles, and Spanish, it was successively smaller.[46] It must be noted, however, that the principal role of these papers has not been to retain foreign languages in the United States population—they all but disappear anyway by the second generation—but to facilitate acculturation. In their political ideas, their advertising of American goods, and their use of cartoons and similar features, these newspapers and magazines have often imitated their larger English-language counterparts.[47]

The rate of naturalization of a national group, another common index of acculturation, is also ambiguous. Of the slightly more than 10 million foreign-born whites in the United States in 1950, almost 7.5 million were citizens. The proportion naturalized varied considerably from one nationality to another, but also by sex and urban-rural residence.[48] The latter difference was even sharper in the past, when farmers were more isolated

[44] Taeuber and Taeuber, *op. cit.,* pp. 186–187.

[45] *Ibid.,* pp. 188–189.

[46] Donald R. Taft and Richard Robbins, *International Migrations: The Immigrant in the Modern World* (New York: Ronald, 1955), pp. 532–535. The list suggests that the relative size of the foreign-language press, if used as an index of acculturation, ought to be controlled for the literacy of the group. It is possible, for example, that on the average Mexican-born immigrants read fewer newspapers than the other groups listed, rather than that they read relatively fewer written in Spanish.

[47] Now that the issue is dead and we know that the nativist fear of a polyglot America had no substance, we can wonder whether the victory of English was not too great. The national interest of the United States is not served by the fact that so few Americans can speak even one other language.

[48] See U.S. Bureau of the Census, *U.S. Census of Population: 1950,* vol. 4, *Special Reports,* part 3, Ch. A, Nativity and Parentage (Washington: U.S. Government Printing Office, 1954), Table 17.

from national or state politics. Old Immigrants, thus, were often slower in becoming citizens than New Immigrants; and at the turn of the century a frequent complaint against the latter was that they were being naturalized too readily and feeding their votes too quickly to the political machines of the eastern cities. In any case, acquiring citizenship may mean that the shift in allegiance has been completed, or that the allegiance is a critical public issue. Before World War II, for instance, German and Italian immigrants found it expedient to declare themselves American, and the same is true today of those of Russian birth.

Another indication of political integration is the voting record of the various ethnic groups. This is a subject that still retains emotional overtones from the beginning of the century, when the New Immigrants were accused of being hyphenated Americans if they permitted their vote to be influenced by their national origin. At that time they were too insecure to reply with anything except a resounding denial of the charge, and it became a prime shibboleth of liberal politics that a person's ethnic or religious affiliation has no possible effect on the way he votes. We now know, however, that "the Jewish vote" or "the Irish vote" is not a reactionary stereotype but a fact of American politics.

This new point of view has been presented most fully and provocatively by Samuel Lubell in *The Future of American Politics,* which offers not only an analysis of recent public-opinion polls and elections but also a reinterpretation of much of American history. As the successive waves of immigrants arrived in the United States, fitting in at the bottom of the economic scale, they were opposed in social-class terms to their Anglo-American employers. Whenever social conflict was expressed in political terms, thus, it tended also to result in a confrontation of ethnic groups. For example, in the middle of the nineteenth century most of the eastern cities were governed by Republican machines led by men of English stock. The Irish immigrants joined the Democratic opposition, and by their success built a link between Catholic and Democratic that to a large degree persists to the present day. In national politics, by Lubell's analysis, the vestigial link of the various ethnic groups to Europe has had an important influence on American foreign policy. The isolationism of the Middle West, for instance, he interprets not as a withdrawal from European politics but as the contrary. The descendants of German and Scandinavian immigrants tended to be pro-German, and the Irish to be anti-English. But as it was patently impossible to involve the United States in either war on the side of Germany, this sympathy was expressed by the demand that

America stay out of all foreign wars, and remain at home minding its own business.

To some degree, thus, Lubell and others have validated the earlier charge of hyphenated Americanism, but the differences are as important as the similarities. Recent analyses of voting records are within the framework of social science; their purpose has been to understand the workings of society rather than to condemn this or that particular group. Moreover, the interest in foreign policy from the point of view of one's forebears is not, as was once charged, a trait peculiar to recent immigrants. "Does the influence of ethnic and religious background on voting ever really disappear?" Lubell asks, and his reply is, in effect, No. Even the Yankee descendants of the original settlers vote to assist England when her need is great enough.[49]

It must be emphasized, however, that ethnic and religious affiliation is one factor, but only one among others, in determining one's political attitudes. Every group is required to rationalize its demands in terms of the national interest of the United States. English, Polish, or Jewish interventionists, German or Irish isolationists, debated America's attitude toward World War II in the name of multinational parties or other similarly broad institutions. The Irish associate anonymously, as it were, in the Roman Catholic Church, in the Democratic Party, in trade unions and professional societies, but specifically as Irish only in an unimportant organization like the Ancient Order of Hibernians; and the same is true of every other national group. Moreover, the melting pot has worked to some degree. Many Americans are the products of intermarriage; others have moved to a different social class and geographic area and thus lost touch altogether with their European background. And the national interest of the United States is more than a catchword. It is seen by all ethnic groups as self-interest and defended as such.

The foregoing discussion of acculturation in universals applies to the white population and to Asians, but less so to other colored nonwhites. With Americans of European stock, the base line of serious historical analysis must be the home-country culture. With Negroes, on the con-

[49] In 1936, when the issue in the election was the domestic policies of the New Deal, Roosevelt won in every state but Maine and Vermont. In 1940, the more important issue had become America's relation to World War II, and Roosevelt was for maximum assistance to Britain short of war. In the latter year, despite the decline in the country as a whole, Roosevelt's vote increased in the rockribbed Republican states of New England, especially in those areas with the highest proportion of English-Americans. See Samuel Lubell, *The Future of American Politics* (2nd rev. ed.; New York: Doubleday-Anchor, 1956), p. 141.

trary, it almost always is their status as slaves. A priori, one can make a good case for ignoring the African background. The tribes of those portions of West Africa from which most of the slaves apparently came speak a very large number of mutually incomprehensible languages,[50] and many slaves in all likelihood had no one to talk to until they learned some English. This sharp break with their native culture was completed, or all but completed, by slavery itself.[51] Unlike Americans of European or Asian stock, thus, Negroes have no natural ties to the homeland of their forebears. Their interest in Africa, such as it is, is principally a reflection of their general concern with color-determined castes, in part— especially among Negro intellectuals—a special case of third-generation nativism. In spite of their full acculturation in terms of universals, Negroes form a separate ethnic group because of their segregation at the bottom of the social scale. Their voting record reflects their concern with civil rights and social welfare. Traditionally Republican ever since the Civil War, Negroes shifted their major allegiance to the Democratic Party in response to the New Deal.

The Special Case of the Indians

The axiom that all ethnic groups are expected to acculturate in universals is not wholly valid with respect to Indians. In its first contacts with the various tribes, the federal government gave them the standing of foreign states and signed a series of separate treaties with them. Indians were gradually settled on the remaining portions of their lands, the "reservations," whose aggregate area in the 1870's was about 150 million acres. In 1887 Congress passed the General Allotment (or Dawes) Act, which represented the most important effort to dissolve tribal organizations and integrate Indians into the population as individuals. Under it, the President was authorized to divide reservations into personal holdings, assigning 80 acres of agricultural land, or twice as much grazing

---

50 See Kroeber, *Anthropology*, pp. 214–215.

51 In one of the most interesting scholarly disputes of recent years, the issue was whether the family type of Negroes (in which the father is transitory and the mother and children form the real nuclear unit) derived in part from a similar pattern in Africa or only from the conditions of slavery. See E. Franklin Frazier, *The Negro Family in the United States* (Chicago: University of Chicago Press, 1947); Melville J. Herskovits, *The Myth of the Negro Past* (Boston: Beacon, 1948). For more general discussions of the relation of American Negroes to Africa, see Herskovits, "The Ahistorical Approach to Afroamerican Studies: A Critique," *American Anthropologist*, 62:4 (August, 1960), 559–568, together with the appended bibliography; Harold R. Isaacs, "The American Negro and Africa: Some Notes," *Phylon*, 20:3 (Fall, 1959), 219–233; Harry S. Ashmore, *The Other Side of Jordan* (New York: Norton, 1960), Ch. 3.

land, to each family head (and smaller amounts to other individuals).[52]

The policy embodied in the Dawes Act was reversed by the Indian Reorganization Act (or IRA), passed in 1934.

The IRA sought to reinvigorate and stabilize the powers and organization of Indian tribes. It . . . vested . . . in tribes . . . the following new powers: approval or veto over the disposition of all tribal assets; the right to spend certain funds; to negotiate with the federal, state, and local governments.[53]

Giving such extensive powers to the tribes, which are ordinarily run by the older and more conservative men, inhibited the movement of younger people into the white culture. The Act rejuvenated Indians' dual nationality, with rights and privileges deriving from both United States citizenship and their membership in a particular ethnic group. Proponents of the policy argue either that such re-established tribal authority constitutes a transitional phase of acculturation, or that—in effect—the preliterate culture of the Indians, unlike that of any other minority, ought to be preserved.

The most recent trend is to terminate the government's responsibility for tribes seriatim. The two most important groups affected by this program to date are the Klamath of Oregon and the Menominees of Wisconsin, who after a short period will become full citizens with no special disabilities and no special privileges. Under the best of conditions, such a transition from wardship to equal status under the law would be difficult. As it is, a contrary trend is represented by the Indian Claims Commission Act, under which an "identifiable group of American Indians" can sue for damages based on past infringements of Indian title to land or the violation of past treaties.

The periodic "reinvigoration" of the Indians' social organization is probably the most important reason for their slow acculturation. If Negroes as a group could sue the government for the indignities and material losses imposed on them when they were forced into slavery, indi-

---

[52] The land declared surplus was to be sold to homesteaders, the proceeds being set aside to pay for the education of the tribe members. Over the following period, Indians lost some 90 million acres to whites, in part by force or quasilegal deals, in greater part by this well meant but ineffectual attempt to make farmers of hunting tribes. With no agricultural training or capital or credit, the Indians generally sold their land as soon as the 25-year government trusteeship was past and they had acquired full title to it.

[53] Theodore H. Haas, "The Legal Aspects of Indian Affairs from 1887 to 1957," *Annals of the American Academy of Political and Social Science*, 311 (May, 1957), 12–22. This issue contains a number of other interesting articles on Indian acculturation. For a sympathetic view of the IRA, see John Collier, *Indians of the Americas: The Long Hope* (New York: New American Library, 1947); Mr. Collier was U.S. Commissioner for Indian Affairs during the New Deal period.

vidual Negroes might hesitate long before trying to make their own way in white society. Or if the government had dealt with, say, the Michigan Dutch community as a group, signing agreements with the Calvinist ministers who led it, these conservative leaders would also have used the power thus granted them to maintain the tradition that, among other things, gave them their status. The effects of federal policy in the case of the Indians have been reinforced, moreover, by several other factors impeding rapid acculturation.[54] (a) The distance between Indian and American cultures was greater than that to be traversed by any immigrant group except, perhaps, the Negroes. (b) The Indians did not immigrate; they did not come, that is to say, expecting to adapt to American life, leaving behind the social structure in which their native cultures were imbedded. (c) Attempts to force acculturation have often resulted in the rise of Indian nativism.

Whether the wealth that oil and uranium deposits have brought to some tribes in the Southwest will facilitate their acculturation is not certain. The very fact that the tribe has something to defend more valuable than semi-arid grazing land may pull it together into closer cohesion. The Navaho are using their sovereign status, established by signing a treaty with General Sherman in 1868, to maintain full control of their relations with state and federal governments. During 1958 the Navaho issued a statement that they do not recognize the authority of the Utah Oil and Gas Conservation Commission; prohibited the tribe's members from joining labor unions, contrary to the Wagner Labor Relations Act; passed their own right-to-work law; and challenged the employment of Hopi Indians at a uranium mill on Navaho land, contrary to the anti-discrimination policy of the Atomic Energy Commission.[55]

Intermarriage

The ultimate acculturation, according to most analysts, is achieved when the diverse physical types merge into a new one through successive generations of intermarriage. This was the original meaning of "melting pot." "Celt and Latin, Slav and Teuton, Greek and Syrian—black and yellow—. . . . East and West, and North and South— . . . how the great Alchemist melts and fuses them with his purging flame!"[56] In this physiological sense the melting pot has been quite inefficient. Marriage

---

[54] See the stimulating article by Vogt, "The Acculturation of American Indians," *op. cit.*

[55] *Time,* November 10, 1958.

[56] Zangwill, *op. cit.*, pp. 184–185.

is still atypical across lines set by racial, religious, nationality, or class differentiation.

There is some indication that Negroes, far from merging physiologically into the general population, are becoming more sharply distinguished. Interracial marriages are quite rare; in 1958, they were prohibited by law in 28 states and discouraged in the others.[57] Extramarital relations between white males and Negro females, often declared to be less common than they once were, at any rate less often result now in conception. Persons who range in physical type between Negro and white are more likely than some decades ago to move into one group or the other, rather than building a bridge between them. Light hybrids, who in the rural South would be defined as Negro, can more easily gain anonymity by moving to a city and thus pass into the white sector of the population. "Internal miscegenation" within the Negro group, with a light complexion favored in the marriage partner, seems to be effecting a gradual stabilization of the American Negro type, with all individuals having more or less the same proportion of Negroid and Caucasoid genes.[58]

The marriage of Asians with other groups is also uncommon on the mainland of the United States. Indeed, on the basis of the general record in the Pacific states, one might conclude that the Chinese, with their own ancient and resilient culture, do not integrate easily in a Western society, and that the Japanese, though in their own country the most adaptable of non-Western peoples, cannot assimilate either. This conclusion can be checked in the new state of Hawaii; and there the evidence suggests, on the contrary, that Asians can readily adjust to American culture if they are given a chance to make the choice.

The sugar companies in Hawaii successively imported field laborers from China, Japan, Portugal, the Philippines, and Puerto Rico. Initially no different from coolies in any plantation system, they developed from this status by an all but unique process. This transformation began, but did not end, with a rise in economic level. As plantation agriculture became mechanized, its labor requirements gradually changed from a host of unskilled to a much smaller number of skilled and semiskilled.

> The rise from coolie to millionaire, if not an everyday experience in Hawaii, has occurred. . . . The much more frequent experience . . . has been a relatively slow and laborious movement on the part of the immigrants and their children from one field of labor to another, in the entire course of which a clear rise in status

[57] For a short but recent survey, see Joseph Golden, "Social Control of Negro-White Intermarriage," *Social Forces,* 36:3 (March, 1958), 267–269.

[58] See Rose, *op. cit.,* pp. 47–48.

occurs. . . . In general . . . Hawaii has provided all ethnic groups a considerable degree of opportunity to move up the social and economic scale.[59]

In spite of the continued commercial importance of sugar and pineapples, Hawaii today is highly urbanized, with more than half of the total population living in Honolulu. Many more work in servicing tourists or the armed forces than in agriculture. This shift in the social structure was made possible by democratic mores. In particular, the free public school system furnished the first step by which in each generation children of coolies were able to climb out of their parents' occupation; and this step could be followed by others much more easily than on the mainland.

The social mobility was facilitated also by the complexity of the population's ethnic composition. Whites have always constituted a relatively small proportion, and there was no poor white class that sought to maintain its higher status in terms of color. Persons of all stocks intermarried freely, so that it is difficult today even to classify the population by race:

> The ludicrous extremes to which an excessive interest in race, biologically defined, can force one in Hawaii is reflected in the report of one agency which a few years ago listed 169 different racial groups in its constituency, including such combinations as Portuguese-Caucasian-Negro-Puerto Rican, Chinese-Hawaiian-Japanese-Norwegian, Filipino-Puerto Rican-Spanish, and Filipino-Hawaiian-Japanese-Puerto Rican-Portuguese.[60]

Anthropologists now speak of this amalgamation as the neo-Hawaiian race in process of formation.

Marriage across religious lines is generally opposed by clergymen of all denominations, and this attitude is often reflected also in the advice given by secular marriage counselors.[61] How frequent interfaith marriages are in America is not known. According to one study often cited, while intermarriage across nationality lines is relatively common, the divisions between Protestant, Catholic, and Jew have remained stable.[62] Other

---

[59] Andrew W. Lind, quoted in *New York Times,* April 7, 1957.

[60] Andrew W. Lind, *Hawaii's People* (Honolulu: University of Hawaii Press, 1955), p. 23. See also Romanzo C. Adams, *Interracial Marriage in Hawaii: A Study of the Mutually Conditioned Process of Acculturation and Amalgamation* (New York: Macmillan, 1937) and, for the most recent trends, C. K. Cheng and Douglas S. Yamamura, "Interracial Marriage and Divorce in Hawaii," *Social Forces,* 36:1 (October, 1957), 77–84.

[61] See James H. S. Bossard and Eleanor Stoker, *One Marriage, Two Faiths: Guidance on Interfaith Marriage* (New York: Ronald, 1957).

[62] Ruby Jo Reeves Kennedy, "Single or Triple Melting Pot? Intermarriage Trends in New Haven, 1870–1940," *American Journal of Sociology,* 49:4 (January, 1944), 331–339; "1870–1950," *ibid.,* 58:1 (July, 1952), 56–59. See also a book developing this theme at greater length: Will Herberg, *Protestant, Catholic, Jew: An Essay in American Religious Sociology* (New York: Doubleday, 1955).

studies have indicated, on the contrary, that interfaith marriages are far more numerous than is generally recognized.[63] One reason for such differences, in all likelihood, is that studies of local data reflect local peculiarities.

Marriages across nationality lines, though more common than interracial or interfaith marriages, are also atypical. Perhaps three out of four marriages are within the same group, and the fourth is between two of closely related cultures.[64]

It is difficult to judge to what degree the opposition to interracial, interreligious, or internationality marriage is specific, and to what degree rather it is an index of an all but unexpressed opposition to interclass marriage. Most American marriages are class-endogamous. In such interclass marriages as do occur, the man usually marries down and the woman up.[65] Interclass marriage, however, is much less analyzed than any other type, and the statistics on it are even poorer.

Intermarriage is atypical by definition, for if there is no sentiment against blonds marrying brunets, for instance, then one does not characterize such a union as intermarriage. The inadequate data are sufficient to permit the statement that American marriages are generally most endogamous by race and successively less so by religion and nationality group. Class endogamy is more difficult to characterize, in part because the widely accepted ideology of romantic love proclaims it to be non-existent. The question whether a trend is discernible toward more frequent exogamy is debatable.[66]

SUMMARY

Acculturation is not an all-or-none process. It is rather a continuum from total assimilation to total nonassimilation, with various degrees and

---

[63] See, for example, John L. Thomas, "The Factor of Religion in the Selection of Marriage Mates," *American Sociological Review*, 16:4 (August, 1951), 487–491; Loren E. Chancellor and Thomas R. Monahan, "Religious Preference and Interreligious Mixtures in Marriages and Divorces in Iowa," *American Journal of Sociology*, 61:3 (November, 1955), 233–239. See also the discussion of Catholic fertility below, page 224.

[64] James H. S. Bossard, "Nationality and Nativity as Factors in Marriage," *American Sociological Review*, 4:6 (December, 1939), 792–798.

[65] August B. Hollingshead, "Class Differences in Family Stability," *Annals of the American Academy of Political and Social Science*, 272 (November, 1950), 39–46.

[66] For excellent discussions of the inadequacy of the theory of intermarriage, see Kingsley Davis, "Intermarriage in Caste Societies," *American Anthropologist*, vol. 43, no. 3, part 1 (July–September, 1941), pp. 376–395; Robert K. Merton, "Intermarriage and the Social Structure: Fact and Theory," *Psychiatry*, 4:3 (August, 1941), 361–374.

types of adaptation in between. It is convenient to break down these types of adaptation into three categories, corresponding to the three major types of social roles. In universals conformity is expected of everyone, whether immigrant or native-born. In specialties the division of labor in a complex industrial society enforces occupational differentiation and thus some divergence by social class. In alternatives the idiosyncracies of the person or group are permitted full expression without social censure, at least in theory.

Acculturation may be impeded by nativism—a conscious, organized effort on the part of the society's members to revive or perpetuate certain aspects of its culture. As used by sociologists, nativism usually means the dominant group's exclusion of minorities; as used by anthropologists, it means the minority's effort to prevent its culture from disappearing into the dominant one. This more or less fortuitous distinction is not useful in this context, and here a movement of either type has been termed nativist.

The use of English as the first language (or, with a large majority, as the only language), or citizenship, or military service—in the United States these are all automatic by the second generation at the latest. In estimating the acculturation of the white population, therefore, such gross measures are useless for a long-term analysis. Occupational differentiation by ethnic background is still evident among whites, but it seems to be disappearing rather rapidly. Endogamy is standard, but by some analysts' interpretation of the inadequate data, marriage across religious and nationality lines is also increasing. Divergence in voting behavior exists, and, particularly when the issue is policy toward the homeland of the minority, the ethnic differentiation apparently persists. By and large, especially when compared with other major immigration countries, the diverse national strains of America's population have been integrated into a new national culture, with perceptible but relatively insignificant remnants from the European backgrounds.

Acculturation can be facilitated by a number of factors, of which the most important seem to be the following: (a) A small difference between the interacting cultures, either actual or as defined by the participants. In particular, if differences are defined as immutable, then acculturation is ruled out as impossible. (b) Agreement between the interacting groups that one of the cultures, the same one, is superior. A minority finds it rankling to be dominated by a group whose culture it sees as inferior to its own. (c) The relative size of the minority. For maximum acculturation, it should be large enough to furnish psychological security to its members, but small enough to be integrated without difficulty. (d) A long period of interaction between the groups. The generalization that the longer the contact, the more acculturation is not, however, invariably true. In some instances symbiotic patterns of partial interrelation have remained constant over centuries.

Most of these generalizations about acculturation, while tentative enough with respect to whites, often are completely invalid when applied to nonwhites. Negroes have been in America longer even than most of the Old Immigrants, and Indians still longer. Among whites Daughters of the American Revolution are a rare phenomenon, but a substantial majority of Negroes are descended from Africans brought here during the colonial period. More significantly still, American Negroes have no vestigial tie to their "homeland"; their world is defined almost wholly in American terms. From their side, that is to say, acculturation has long since been completed. Asians and the other smaller minorities are so tiny that one might have expected them to sink into the white sea. Obviously neither the size of a minority, nor its period of residence, nor the strength of its ties to other cultures, determines its relative integration in American society—if the minority is not white.

That such minorities have not been assimilated in American culture is sometimes explained by their greater "visibility." One suspects, however, that the visibility of an ethnic group is less a cause than a symptom of its nonassimilation. It is easy to distinguish a Jew, for example, by his "hooked nose, oily skin, thick lips"; the only difficulty is that these features typify not real Jews but the abstraction attacked by anti-Semites. And to recognize as Negro such a man, for example, as Walter White, a blue-eyed blond who was a leader of the National Association for the Advancement of Colored People, was something of a feat. On the other hand, an American is quite likely not to recall, say, the color of the eyes of a person he met casually a week or so ago. Skin color is more "visible" than eye color because one is, and the other is not, a symbol of social differentiation.

Racial minorities remain separate groups in American society mainly —or, in the case of Negroes, only—because of the laws, behavior patterns, and attitudes that force them to be so. Any analysis of these minority races must consist in large part of an examination of the special means by which their differences from the white population are maintained and accentuated. The purpose of such laws and institutions is usually to discriminate against the minority, but sometimes (for example, Indian reservations or Negro colleges) it is the opposite. In either case, the distinctive behavior due to these special institutions is often confused with biological variation.

SUGGESTIONS FOR FURTHER READING

U.S. Bureau of the Census, *U.S. Census of Population: 1950,* vol. 4, *Special Reports,* part 3, Ch. A, Nativity and Parentage; Ch. B, Nonwhite Population by Race; Ch. C, Persons of Spanish Surname (Washington: U.S. Government Printing Office, 1953 and 1954).
  Basic census data on population composition.

Ralph Beals, "Acculturation," in A. L. Kroeber, ed., *Anthropology Today: An Encyclopedic Inventory* (Chicago: University of Chicago Press, 1953), pp. 621–641.

Nathan Glazer, "America's Ethnic Pattern," *Commentary,* April, 1953, pp. 401–408; "The Integration of American Immigrants," *Law and Contemporary Problems,* 21:2 (Spring, 1956), 256–269.

Marcus Lee Hansen, *The Problem of the Third Generation Immigrant* (Rock Island, Ill.: Augustana Historical Society, 1938); reprinted in *Commentary,* November, 1952, pp. 492–500.

Clyde V. Kiser, " Cultural Pluralism," *Annals of the American Academy of Political and Social Science,* 262 (March, 1949), 117–130. (This article has been reprinted in Joseph J. Spengler and Otis Dudley Duncan, eds., *Demographic Analysis,* Glencoe, Ill.: Free Press, 1956, pp. 307–320.)

Ralph Linton, "Nativistic Movements," *American Anthropologist,* 45:2 (April–June, 1943), 230–240.

William Petersen, "Immigration and Acculturation," *Commentary,* November, 1956, pp. 463–470; "Prejudice in American Society," *Commentary,* October, 1958, pp. 342–348.

Jerzy Zubrzycki, "The Rôle of the Foreign-Language Press in Migrant Integration," *Population Studies,* 12:1 (July, 1958), 73–82.
  Informative and often provocative articles from several points of view.

E. P. Hutchinson, *Immigrants and Their Children, 1850–1950* (New York: Wiley, 1956).

Robert C. Cook, "The American Melting Pot: 1850–1950," *Population Bulletin,* 13:7 (November, 1957), 113–130.
  Hutchinson's census monograph is the most thorough and painstaking attempt to relate ethnic background and occupation over so long a period as the last century. Its conclusions are summarized in this issue of *Population Bulletin.*

William I. Thomas and Florian Znaniecki, *The Polish Peasant in Europe and America* (2nd ed.; New York: Dover, 1958), 2 vols.

No more ambitious research of acculturation has ever been attempted. Based largely on letters and other personal documents; rather pessimistic in its general conclusions.

William F. Adams, *Ireland and Irish Emigration to the New World from 1815 to the Famine* (New Haven: Yale University Press, 1932).

Oscar Handlin, *Boston's Immigrants: A Study in Acculturation* (Rev. ed.; Cambridge: Harvard University Press, 1959).

Manuel Gamio, *Mexican Immigration to the United States: A Study of Human Migration and Adjustment* (Chicago: University of Chicago Press, 1930).

Nathan Glazer, *American Judaism* (Chicago: University of Chicago Press, 1957).

John A. Hawgood, *The Tragedy of German-America: The Germans in the United States of America During the Nineteenth Century—and After* (New York: Putnam, 1940).

Lloyd G. Reynolds, *The British Immigrant: His Social and Economic Adjustment in Canada* (Toronto: Oxford University Press, 1935).

Gunnar Myrdal et al., *An American Dilemma: The Negro Problem and Modern Democracy* (New York: Harper, 1944), 2 vols.

George E. Simpson and J. Milton Yinger, eds., "American Indians and American Life," *Annals of the American Academy of Political and Social Science,* vol. 311 (May, 1957).

C. Wright Mills, Clarence Senior, and Rose Kohn Goldsen, *The Puerto Rican Journey: New York's Newest Migrants* (New York: Harper, 1950).

Romanzo C. Adams, *Interracial Marriage in Hawaii: A Study of the Mutually Conditioned Process of Acculturation and Amalgamation* (New York: Macmillan, 1937).

Better-than-average case studies.

Julian Huxley, *Evolution: The Modern Synthesis* (New York: Harper, 1943).

John L. Fuller, *Nature and Nurture: A Modern Synthesis* (New York: Doubleday, 1954).

The first is a book, the second a booklet; both present a similar point of view that avoids the excesses of both racists and those who deny the existence of human races.

Donald R. Taft and Richard Robbins, *International Migrations: The Immigrant in the Modern World* (New York: Ronald, 1955).

A. L. Kroeber, *Anthropology* (Rev. ed.; New York: Harcourt, Brace, 1948).

Textbooks with correlative material.

7. INTERNAL MIGRATION

As we have noted earlier, migration differs fundamentally from fertility and mortality. A birth or death is a natural event that almost defines itself, but a migrant can be distinguished from travelers only by a number of more or less arbitrary criteria: the distance covered, the duration of his stay, his purpose in moving, and so on. Since a nation is almost always culturally distinct, international migrants move from one culture area to another, but it is much more difficult to find out whether and when this is so of internal migrants. We must first designate the significant subculture areas within the nation, and then try to determine from the available statistics the amount and direction of movement among them.

In the tabulation of each census the population is broken down by state, by county, and by minor civil subdivisions (such as townships, precincts, school districts, wards, etc., depending on which is the most stable in the particular state). In the 1960 census the 50 states were divided into 3,072 counties, plus 33 county equivalents;[1] and the counties in turn were subdivided into almost 50,000 of the smaller units.

An administrative entity like a state or one of its subdivisions is not, of course, a meaningless abstraction. In the East the states have histories going back to colonial days, and anywhere in the country a particularly energetic or capable governor or senator may have altered the conditions of life in his state. Sometimes contiguous states differ in what to potential migrants may be significant respects: New York has an income tax, Pennsylvania has none; North Carolina has a much better school system than South Carolina; the whole political climate in North Dakota is different from that in South Dakota. In an extreme case like Utah, where

---

[1] The latter were 27 cities in Virginia that are independent of county organization, Baltimore City, St. Louis City, the District of Columbia, and the parts of Yellowstone National Park in Wyoming, Montana, and Idaho. In Louisiana, the county is termed a "parish."

a particular group dominates both culture and politics, the state stands out from its neighbors in almost all respects. Usually, however, administrative units are not satisfactory for demographic analysis. In order to set up more homogeneous areas, one must either combine them into larger regions or divide them into smaller ones.

REGIONS AND REGIONALISM

The concept of region is used in a number of disciplines, and defined somewhat differently by each.[2] The basic element of most of these definitions (or sometimes, particularly among plant and animal ecologists and some geographers, the only element) is the **natural area,** or a physiographic unit delineated by its topography, soil type, climate, and similar features.[3] The natural environment formed by a mountain range, for instance, or a river valley, or a seacoast, can have a considerable influence on the lives of its inhabitants. As another example, one of the most important determinants of settlement patterns in the United States has been rainfall. An invisible boundary line, running from eastern North Dakota to western Texas divides an area to the east with an annual rainfall of more than 20 inches from one to the west with less than this amount. To this day the semi-arid Rocky Mountain region between this isogram and the coastal area is the most sparsely populated in the whole country.

A second meaning of region, the **culture area,** has been developed by anthropologists, in particular by Wissler and Kroeber. They divided the pre-Columbian population of North America into groups of contiguous tribes with similar patterns of life:

A culture area is delineated by listing the tribes with similar cultures and plotting their habitats on a map. The geographical shapes of the culture areas appear to vary according to the topography and other physical features that enter into the environmental complex.[4]

---

[2] Odum and Moore begin their book on regionalism by quoting 28 different definitions of regions; see Howard W. Odum and Harry Estill Moore, *American Regionalism: A Cultural-Historical Approach to National Integration* (New York: Holt, 1938), p. 2. They do not accept any of these but offer a twenty-ninth of their own.

[3] Unfortunately, ecologists have also used the term *natural area* to designate a homogeneous neighborhood of a city, even though most of its characteristics, of course, are culturally determined. In this usage, "natural" means developing outside of policy decisions rather than from the forces of nature. This confusing double meaning of a key term is probably too well established to be eliminated, but it will not be used in this book.

[4] Clark Wissler, *The American Indian,* p. 346; quoted in Odum and Moore, *op. cit.,* p. 308. See also A. L. Kroeber, *Cultural and Natural Areas of Native North America* (Berkeley: University of California Press, 1939).

From the high correlation between physical and cultural elements, it could be assumed that the history of each culture area had been essentially self-contained and more or less determined by the natural environment. There was not, however, a perfect correlation between natural and culture areas: eastern tribes living in the same type of habitat varied considerably; and the Navaho and Hopi, although occupying the same natural area in Arizona, had markedly different native cultures.

Geography, in other words, determines the limits of a group's development, but within these limits a considerable variation in culture is possible. Some overlap between natural and culture areas is thus usual, particularly among primitive peoples, but the greater the control over its natural environment a society has, the smaller this correlation will generally be, and the less can one regard it as an inescapable cause-effect relation. With respect to the population of the United States, the point can be illustrated by the history of the South. This area had a climate suited to plantation agriculture, and it imported a large number of Negro slaves to work as fieldhands, fought a war to defend its "peculiar institution," and has since been set off from the rest of the country in large part by the caste system and its effects on the rest of the society. To say that slavery and its present remnants are the consequences of the South's climate, however, would be nonsensical.

Are there regional subcultures in the United States that more or less correspond to its natural areas? Do the terms *New England, the South, the Great Plains,* and so on, designate real culture areas, with significant differences that have persisted in spite of the unifying effect of the single language, the frequent interregional migration, the school system, the national press and other mass media, the standardized consumers goods, and all the other traits and artifacts of American culture? Such questions can be answered empirically, but the answers will vary greatly according to where the limits of the various regions are drawn. These tend to merge into one another, but for a statistical analysis the lines between them must be sharp. And if the regional division is to have any practical use, the boundaries must correspond to those of the states, which define the administrative units by which census data are segregated.[5]

The concept of a region is thus impaired by a double compromise, that between natural and culture area, and that between the combination of

[5] The distortion is less, of course, if we combine not states but counties. The Census Bureau has divided the country into 501 State Economic Areas, each of which consists of one or more whole counties. These Areas are more homogeneous in their economic and social characteristics than either states or regions. See Donald J. Bogue, *State Economic Areas* (U.S. Bureau of the Census; Washington: U.S. Government Printing Office, 1951).

these and the administrative unit. That is to say, like many other tools of
social science, this one is somewhat imprecise but nevertheless useful. In
line with these compromises, a **region** of the United States can be defined as a relatively homogeneous culture area composed of a number of
whole states which in their aggregate are distinguished from other regions
in as many different ways as possible.

The four regions used by the Bureau of the Census are shown in Figure 7-1.[6] On the whole, they represent accurately the major geographic
areas in American history: the Northeast (equivalent to "the North" of
the nineteenth century), the South, the North Central region (equivalent
to "the Middle West"), and the West. Each region is broken down further into **divisions**—the Northeast between the two historic areas of
New England and the Middle Atlantic states, the North Central region
between an eastern division of five industrial-agricultural states and a western one of seven grain-producing states, and the West between the three
Pacific states and the semi-arid Mountain division. The breakdown of the
South, however, is less satisfactory. The subculture areas defined by most
indexes would seem to be the intermediate region between the South and
the Southwest, which is adequately represented by the West South Central
division; the Deep South, from the Carolinas west to Mississippi or farther;
and the border states, from Delaware west to Missouri. Odum and Moore
even assign Delaware, Maryland, West Virginia, and the District of
Columbia to the North. The line between the South Atlantic and the
East South Central divisions, on the contrary, groups these states with the
Carolinas and Georgia, and Kentucky with Mississippi and Alabama.

Of the three major migratory streams in American history, two can be
analyzed as interregional movements—from East to West and from South
to North. The third, the migration from countryside to cities, involves a
spatial pattern of a completely different type, which will be discussed in
Chapter 8.

THE WESTWARD MIGRATION
AND THE MOVING FRONTIER

Few issues in American history have generated more interest, and less
agreement, than the effect of the westward movement on the nation's
culture. In 1893 Frederick Jackson Turner, then a young man recently
out of graduate school, read a paper before his colleagues entitled "The
Significance of the Frontier in American History." Over the rest of his

---

[6] The two new states of Alaska and Hawaii, not shown in the figure, are now part of
the West.

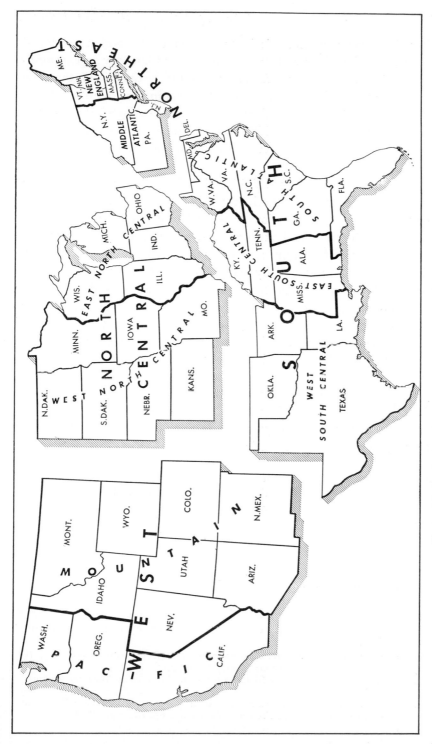

Figure 7-1. Regions and Geographic Divisions of the United States
Source: Bureau of the Census

157

lifetime, he developed its thesis in two dozen essays, which combined careful historical analysis with exuberant poetic vision into an extraordinarily convincing argument. According to the testimony of those he taught, he was one of the most effective teachers in the country's universities; and for a period his students, grand-students, associates, and followers all but monopolized the historical scholarship of the United States. Then in the early 1930's the "Turner thesis" began to be challenged and rejected, and defended anew.[7]

The frontier, by Turner's definition, is "the meeting place between savagery and civilization," "the hither edge of free land." "The West" began to evolve as a self-conscious section when it was still to the east of the Appalachians. By the first quarter of the nineteenth century, the frontier was at the Mississippi; by the middle of the century, at the Missouri and in California; and by the end of the century, in the Rocky Mountains. This east-to-west social evolution "has worked a political transformation." The frontier "promoted the formation of a composite nationality," in part by decreasing America's dependence on England. "In the crucible of the frontier the immigrants were Americanized, liberated, and fused into a mixed race, English in neither nationality nor characteristics." This fusion was the dominant theme of nineteenth-century American history, compared with which "the slavery question is an incident." The Middle West was "the typically American region," "democratic and nonsectional," where frontier individualism had most successfully developed into American democracy.[8]

American democracy was born of no theorist's dream; it was not carried in the *Susan Constant* to Virginia nor in the *Mayflower* to Plymouth. It came out of the American forest, and it gained new strength each time it touched a new frontier. Not the constitution, but free land and an abundance of natural resources open to a fit people, made the democratic type of society in America for three centuries while it occupied its empire.[9]

Or, more succinctly put:

The existence of an area of free land, its continuous recession, and the advance of American settlement westward, explain American development. . . . The true

---

[7] See George Rogers Taylor, ed., *The Turner Thesis Concerning the Role of the Frontier in American History* (Boston: Heath, 1949), pp. v–vii.

[8] Frederick Jackson Turner, "The Significance of the Frontier in American History," in *ibid.*, pp. 1–18.

[9] Turner, *The Frontier in American History*, p. 293; quoted in Benjamin F. Wright, Jr., "Political Institutions and the Frontier," in Taylor, *op. cit.*, pp. 42–50.

point of view in the history of this nation is not the Atlantic coast, it is the Great West.[10]

The main criticisms of Turner's thesis are the following: (a) His key concept is so loosely defined that it is difficult to test his assertions. The frontier "is defined and used as area, as population, as process." Sometimes it covers soil and mineral resources as well, "at times everything Western or pre-industrial or non-European."[11] (b) The European element of American culture, as transmitted by the East, is persistently minimized. The state universities of the Middle West, said to derive from frontier conditions, are in their essentials replicas of their European and eastern predecessors. The key factor of democracy, at least as measured by the provisions of state constitutions, varies very little from one region of the country to the other.[12] (c) The availability of free land in other parts of the world had no appreciable effect on social institutions; nor did it necessarily even in the Americas. "What about the Spaniards, who had the run of the whole hemisphere? Did the Mississippi Valley make them democratic, prosperous, and numerous? In a word, do not the level of culture, and the 'fitness' of a society for the wilderness, matter more than the wilderness?"[13] (d) Turner's praise of the composite American, "English in neither nationality nor characterisics," was—paradoxically— part of an attack on the amalgamation of New Immigrants. Much as the young Turner differed on other matters with the older historians of that period, he joined with them in propounding dubious theses about Southern and Eastern Europeans: immigrants from southern Italy were "of doubtful value judged from the ethical point of view"; the Jews were a "people of exceptionally stunted stature and of deficient lung capacity"; and so on.[14] (e) In the context of this chapter, the most interesting criticism of the Turner thesis concerns the so-called safety-valve theory—the proposition that the availability of free land on the frontier had served to cut down economic discontent in the eastern cities by drawing off surplus population to the farms. Turner emphasized this less than some of his followers, but for him no less than the others it was an important corollary.

---

[10] Turner, quoted in *ibid.*, p. x.

[11] George Wilson Pierson, "The Frontier and American Institutions," in *ibid.*, pp. 65–83.

[12] Wright, "Political Institutions," *op. cit.*

[13] Pierson, "The Frontier," *op. cit.*

[14] Quoted from Edward N. Saveth, *American Historians and European Immigrants, 1875–1925* (Studies in History, Economics, and Public Law, no. 540; New York: Columbia University Press, 1948), p. 129.

OUR WESTERN EMPIRE:

OR THE

NEW WEST

BEYOND THE MISSISSIPPI:

THE LATEST AND MOST COMPREHENSIVE WORK ON THE

States and Territories West of the Mississippi.

CONTAINING

THE FULLEST AND MOST COMPLETE DESCRIPTION, FROM OFFICIAL AND OTHER AUTHENTIC
SOURCES, OF THE GEOGRAPHY, GEOLOGY, AND NATURAL HISTORY, (WITH ABUNDANT
INCIDENTS AND ADVENTURES,) THE CLIMATE, SOIL, AGRICULTURE, THE MINERAL
AND MINING PRODUCTS, THE CROPS, AND HERDS AND FLOCKS, THE
SOCIAL CONDITION, EDUCATIONAL AND RELIGIOUS PROGRESS, AND
FUTURE PROSPECTS OF THE WHOLE REGION LYING BE-
TWEEN THE MISSISSIPPI AND THE PACIFIC OCEAN.

TO WHICH IS ADDED

THE VARIOUS ROUTES, AND PRICES OF PASSAGE AND TRANSPORTATION FOR EMIGRANTS
THITHER; THE LAWS, REGULATIONS AND PROVISIONS FOR OBTAINING LANDS FROM
THE NATIONAL OR STATE GOVERNMENTS OR RAILROADS; COUNSEL AS TO
LOCATIONS AND PROCURING LANDS, CROPS MOST PROFITABLE FOR
CULTURE, MINING OPERATIONS, AND THE LATEST PROCESSES
FOR THE REDUCTION OF GOLD AND SILVER, THE EXER-
CISE OF TRADES OR PROFESSIONS; AND DETAILED
DESCRIPTIONS OF EACH STATE AND TERRITORY;
WITH FULL INFORMATION CONCERNING MANITOBA, BRITISH COLUMBIA, AND THOSE REGIONS
IN THE ATLANTIC STATES ADAPTED TO SETTLEMENT, BY THOSE WHO DO NOT WISH
TO GO WEST; AND STATISTICS OF CROPS, AREAS, RAINFALL, ETC.

BY L. P. BROCKETT, A. M., M. D.

ONE OF THE EDITORS OF THE " NEW AMERICAN ENCYCLOPÆDIA," " APPLETON'S ANNUAL," AND
" JOHNSON'S UNIVERSAL ILLUSTRATED CYCLOPÆDIA," ETC., ETC., ETC.

With Numerous Illustrations and Maps

BY THE MOST DISTINGUISHED ARTISTS.

BRADLEY, GARRETSON & CO.,
PHILADELPHIA, 66 NORTH FOURTH STREET;
BRANTFORD, ONT.

WILLIAM GARRETSON & CO.
COLUMBUS, O.; CHICAGO, ILLS.; NASHVILLE, TENN.; ST, LOUIS, MO.;
SAN FRANCISCO, CAL.

1881.

Shannon has written what he calls a post mortem to the theory.[15] He points out, first of all, that the safety valve was no more effective than "a whistle on a peanut roaster": the class conflict it was supposed to mitigate was actually extremely sharp just during the decades when free

[15] Fred A. Shannon, "A Post Mortem on the Labor-Safety-Valve Theory," *Agricultural History*, 19 (January, 1945), 31–37; reprinted in Taylor, *op. cit.*, pp. 51–60.

land was available. One reason may have been that the dominant migration was in the other direction. For each industrial laborer who moved to the land, at least 20 farmers moved to the city. The free land did not even absorb the rural natural increase: for each farmer's son who became a farm owner, ten moved to the city. Of the population living west of the Mississippi, slightly over half were engaged in agriculture in 1870, and over the following decades this proportion fell off to something under half. If there was a safety valve in operation, it relieved the population pressure on the land by furnishing some members of the very large rural families a chance to make their way in urban jobs.

This dual movement can be suggested by comparing for various dates the number of persons born east of the Mississippi River and living west of it with the number who had crossed it in the other direction. In the 1880 census almost all of those enumerated as born on one side and living on the other had gone west—94.3 per cent of the total of 3.7 million. The comparable figures in 1900 were 89.7 per cent of 5.0 million, in 1930 75.7 per cent of 6.8 million, and in 1950 only 68.3 per cent of 8.5 million.[16] The westward movement, dominant as it has been in American history, was ultimately met by an eastward counter stream half as strong. Moreover, the westward migration is now also in large part a movement to the cities.

In the most recent period, after the lull in internal migration during the depression decade, the move to the West was greatly stimulated by the government's policy of subsidizing war plants on the Pacific Coast. The boom thus started has continued without serious interruption and has been an important concomitant of the extremely rapid population growth. The change during the intercensal decade 1950–1960 is indicated in Figure 7-2. In these ten years the population of California grew by 5.1 million, or 48.5 per cent,[17] as compared with a national average of 18.5 per cent. As is obvious from the size of this difference, it was due primarily to migration. The Census Bureau expects that this trend will continue at least until 1970, when it is believed that almost 12 per cent of the United States population will live in the three Pacific Coast states.[18]

---

[16] Conrad Taeuber and Irene B. Taeuber, *The Changing Population of the United States* (New York: Wiley, 1958), p. 97.

[17] For a more detailed discussion of California's postwar growth, see Warren S. Thompson, *Growth and Changes in California's Population* (Los Angeles: Haynes Foundation, 1955); Margaret S. Gordon, *Employment Expansion and Population Growth: The California Experience, 1900–1950* (Berkeley: University of California Press, 1954).

[18] U.S. Bureau of the Census, *Current Population Reports*, series P-25, no. 160 (August 9, 1957).

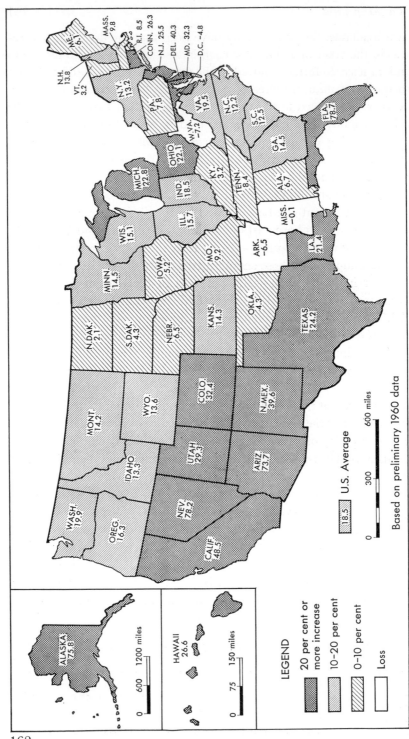

Figure 7-2. Percentage Change in Population, United States, 1950–1960
Source: U.S. Bureau of the Census, *1960 Census of Population,* Advance Reports,
Final Population Counts, series PC (A1)-1 (November 15, 1960).

LEGEND

20 per cent or more increase

10–20 per cent

0–10 per cent

Loss

18.5 U.S. Average

Based on preliminary 1960 data

ME. 6.1
N.H. 13.8
VT. 3.2
MASS. 9.8
R.I. 8.5
CONN. 25.5
N.J. 25.3
DEL. 40.3
MD. 32.3
D.C. -4.8
N.Y. 13.2
PA. 7.8
W.VA. -7.2
VA. 19.5
N.C. 12.2
S.C. 12.5
GA. 14.5
FLA. 78.7
OHIO 22.1
KY. 3.2
TENN. 8.4
ALA. 6.7
MISS. -0.1
MICH. 22.8
IND. 18.5
ILL. 15.7
WIS. 15.1
MINN. 14.5
IOWA 5.2
MO. 9.2
ARK. -6.5
LA. 21.4
N.DAK. 2.1
S.DAK. 4.3
NEBR. 6.5
KANS. 14.3
OKLA. 4.3
TEXAS 24.2
MONT. 14.2
WYO. 13.6
COLO. 32.4
N.MEX. 39.6
IDAHO 13.3
UTAH 29.3
ARIZ. 73.7
WASH. 19.9
OREG. 16.3
NEV. 78.2
CALIF. 48.5

ALASKA 75.8

HAWAII 26.6

0 300 600 miles

0 600 1200 miles

0 75 150 miles

162

"America's new frontier" [19] is the Mountain division, the desert and semi-arid mountains and plains that the earlier westward migrants had hurried through on their way to the Pacific. In large parts of the Mountains West low population density is still the dominant influence on social life. Most of Nevada and large portions of eastern Oregon, Idaho, Montana, Wyoming, Utah, western Colorado, northern Arizona, New Mexico, and western Texas had a density of under two persons per square mile as recently as 1950. The Mountain states might be called hyperrural. One of the most significant features of rural life is the relative isolation it imposes, and this in turn is a function of the distance to the nearest town, and thus of population density. In the Northeast and Middle West the farmer is in this respect almost a suburbanite, traveling a shorter distance to his market town than many commuters go each day to their place of work. "Outside the Great Plains, the Mountain states, and some areas of the South, there are few farm families that are not within ten miles of a physician and twenty miles of a hospital." [20] This example, which can be taken as *pars pro toto* for the transformation of rural life in the Northeast and Middle West, does not apply to the Mountain states. "The sparse rural population in the [Great] Plains always has been, and certainly is now, . . . too small to support certain institutional patterns, unless there is a far reaching change in the organization of those institutions and the manner and type of service rendered." [21]

Or unless the population grows to something like the rural density in other regions. One of the most striking features of postwar migration to the West is that the prior dependence of the number of people on the natural water supply has been markedly reduced. (And one of the first effects of atomic power, should it become commercially available, will be to eliminate this dependence altogether.) Between 1940 and 1950 the population of the Mountain West grew by 22.3 per cent (compared with the national average of 14.5 per cent), and for the 1950–1960 period the comparable percentages were 35.1 and 18.5. Indeed, the percentage growth of the Mountain division has been calculated on a small base: in 1960 the total population of all eight states was still only 6,855,060. The trend is nevertheless a significant new departure.[22]

[19] Morris E. Garnsey, *America's New Frontier: The Mountain West* (New York: Knopf, 1950).

[20] Lowry Nelson, *American Farm Life* (Cambridge: Harvard University Press, 1954), p. 172.

[21] Carl Frederick Kraenzel, *The Great Plains in Transition* (Norman: University of Oklahoma Press, 1955), p. 161.

[22] For a more extended discussion, see William Petersen, *A Critical Survey of Several Forecasts of the Population of Colorado* (Colorado Department of Natural Resources, Technical Paper no. 1; Denver, July, 1957).

The demographic features characteristic of a frontier region are even more clearly discernible in Alaska, the forty-ninth state. With an area of 571,000 square miles, almost one-fifth that of the continental United States, in 1960 it had a population of only 226,167, or less than any other state. This figure, however, represented a gain by three-quarters since 1950. Because of the very high proportion of young people (more than half aged 20 to 44), Alaska had the highest fertility and the lowest mortality of all the states. In 1958 its birth rate of 35 per thousand population was ten points higher than the national average, its death rate of 5.8 almost four points lower. Its natural increase has been by about 5,500 persons per year, or more than double the net civilian in-migration.[23]

The relation between the population growth of the West and its economic development is a complex matter. Until World War II the West imported a substantial portion of the goods it consumed; and the cost of the long haul from the centers of manufacturing, aggravated by discriminatory freight rates, created the equivalent of a protective tariff wall behind which even marginal manufacturing plants could be set up. With the increase of population, the number of consumers is no longer too small to attract industries; and once new enterprises are established, the employees who come into the area to work in one factory or office form an attractive market for other new business. By such an interaction, the growth of manufacturing and of population can become cumulative, and under favorable conditions (in effect, with enough water) it is appropriate to posit an analogy to the multiplier effect of economic theory.[24]

The West now has an industrial structure ranging from the several large steel plants established during the war, through such major industries as the mammoth Ford assembly plant recently constructed in California, to the literally hundreds of smaller factories established every year. California is not only the nation's leading agricultural state—with more than 200 commercial farm products—but the first state in construction and in the generation of electric power, and the third state in the value of its mineral products. In manufacturing California stands first in the value of processed foods, second in transportation equipment and in

[23] Irene B. Taeuber, "The Population of the Forty-Ninth State," *Population Index*, 25:2 (April, 1959), 93–114; Population Reference Bureau, "Alaska: A Population Profile," June 26, 1958; "The Population of Alaska," in Metropolitan Life Insurance Company, *Statistical Bulletin*, October, 1958, pp. 4–6.

[24] "The word 'multiplier' . . . is used for the numerical coefficient showing how great an increase in income results from each increase in investment. . . . [For example,] if an increase of investment of 5 billion dollars causes an increase of income of 15 billion dollars, then the multiplier is 3" (Paul A. Samuelson, *Economics: An Introductory Analysis*, New York: McGraw-Hill, 1955, p. 233).

wood products, third in petroleum, fourth in fabricated textiles, fifth in printing and publishing. This list comprises both a more impressive and a more diversified economy than that of the West as a whole, but the same forces that have engendered California's remarkable growth are apparent throughout the region.

NORTHWARD OUT OF THE SOUTH

If "the West" has been defined, and successively redefined, by the contrast between a newly settled region and the more civilized and prosperous East, this kind of process had nothing to do with distinguishing the South from the rest of the country. Virginia and the Carolinas have as long a history as Massachusetts and Pennsylvania, and in the nineteenth century the South no less than the North had its own frontier area. What has set the South apart and made it a distinct region is slavery and its aftermath.

The relations between the races is the axis upon which southern life has turned for a hundred years or more. . . . In the midst of wide diversity of economic interests and social backgrounds there is still just one South because of the Negro problem. More than anything else it has defined the section.[25]

So long as the antebellum society was intact, the ruling class saw their future entirely within the compass of the plantation system. This formed the industrial and social framework of government, and slavery was an important part of its legal code.[26] After the 1860's when rapid industrialization got under way in the North, not only was the South devastated by the effects of the war and harassed by the occupation forces, but it lacked any substantial industrial base and, for decades, the incentive to establish one. Until recently a relatively small proportion of its population has lived in cities and worked in modern industry, while a significant percentage existed in rural poverty. The specific demographic features of the South, whether its high fertility and mortality or the low accuracy of its

[25] Edgar T. Thompson, "Sociology and Sociological Research in the South," in Howard W. Odum and Katharine Jocher, eds., *In Search of the Regional Balance of America* (Chapel Hill: University of North Carolina Press, 1945), pp. 114–123. Thompson's main point, that the relations between the races have also dominated sociology in the South, is well exemplified by the career of Howard Odum, perhaps the most distinguished analyst of regionalism and particularly of the South. See Howard W. Odum, "From Community Studies to Regionalism," in *ibid.*, pp. 3–16.

[26] See Rupert B. Vance, *Human Factors in Cotton Culture: A Study in the Social Geography of the American South* (Chapel Hill: University of North Carolina Press, 1929).

statistics, have been in the main an expression of its inefficient agrarian economy.

Efforts to raise the South to the national average have repeatedly foundered on the crucial racial question. The extraordinary progress Negroes made in the two decades following their emancipation was reversed in the early 1880's, partly by a vast terror (the number of recorded lynchings of Negroes rose to a high point of 134 in 1894); partly by the enactment of a series of laws that deprived Negroes of the right to vote, of equal protection under the law, and of equal economic and educational opportunity; and partly by the establishment, or re-establishment, of a whole host of social discriminations to symbolize their redegradation.[27] With caste again the fundament of its social system, the South seemed to be coming to terms with the rest of the nation. After 1914–1918 a reference to "the War" no longer harked back to 1865. Roosevelt's Democratic administration raised southern leaders into national prominence, and New Deal programs brought some relief to the poorest of the regions. And then, in the words of Howard Odum:

> A strange thing happened. . . . a sudden revivification of the old sectional conflict and the recrudescence of the terms "North" and "South." It would have been unbelievable, if it had not actually happened, that this together with special and intensified revival of the old race conflict would bring the South to its greatest crisis and the Nation again to one of its chief domestic dilemmas since the Civil War.[28]

In the 1950's, following the Supreme Court's decision outlawing segregated public schools, the resurgence of sectional feeling was even sharper. The conflict is fundamental. The white South, at least as represented by its dominant political leadership, is unwilling to admit the Negro to the full political and social equality that is his right under American law. On the other side, a portion of northern public opinion, white as well as Negro, is no more willing to accept the caste system as a permanent feature of American life, a permanent anomaly in American democracy.

The South, with the highest rate of natural increase and the fewest economic opportunities, has been a region of out-migration for as long as statistics are available. As with the westward movement, so also with the northward one, the dominant stream of migration has been countered

---

[27] For a fascinating account of this partial reversal of Negroes' emancipation, see C. Vann Woodward, *The Strange Career of Jim Crow* (Rev. ed., New York: Galaxy-Oxford University Press, 1957).

[28] Odum, "The Way of the South," in Odum and Jocher, *op. cit.*, pp. 16–26.

by a smaller one in the opposite direction. If we compare for various dates the number of persons born in the South and living in the North with those born in the North and living in the South, these census data give us a rough idea of the dimensions of the two migrations. Of the 1.6 million that had moved in either direction according to the 1880 census, 70.1 per cent had gone to the North. After that the total migration increased, but the proportion of those going north fell off. The comparable figures in 1900 were 55.9 per cent of 2.3 million; in 1930, 63.7 per cent of 5.2 million; and in 1950, 61.8 per cent of 8.1 million.[29]

It is not wholly realistic, however, to discuss the out-migration of the two races together. A most interesting question concerning the migration of Negroes—and one to which historians have given us no satisfactory answer—is why it took so long to get under way.[30] From the 1880's on, while in the South Negroes were being reduced again to a subordinate status, the rapidly growing factories and mines of the North were giving work to unprecedented numbers of transformed European peasants, and in the West opportunities for Negroes would seem to have been even greater. Why, under these circumstances, with the strongest imaginable push and pull, should Negroes have nevertheless remained where they were for so long?

The movement of Negroes out of the southern states began very slowly in the first decade of the twentieth century. During World War I northern manufacturers, faced by a shortage of unskilled labor when the immigration from Europe was cut off, sent recruiting agents into the South to seek replacements. At that time more than nine Negroes out of every ten lived in the South, and three out of four were rural. From that time on, however, the northward movement has developed to dramatic proportions. Even during the depression, when there was a net migration of whites *to* the South, the flow of Negroes northward continued though at a lower rate.[31] Then, in the 1940's, with jobs again available in war industry, the net out-migration reached new proportions: almost 260,000 from Mississippi, or a quarter of the state's Negro population in 1940; almost 200,000 from Georgia; more than 150,000 each from South Caro-

[29] Taeuber and Taeuber, *op. cit.*, p. 98.

[30] See Gunnar Myrdal *et al.*, *An American Dilemma: The Negro Problem and Modern Democracy* (New York: Harper, 1944), vol. 1, Ch. 8.

[31] For the period 1935–1940, 96 per cent of the rural-farm migrants from South Carolina to Philadelphia were Negroes, and 94 per cent of those to New York City; of rural-farm migrants from Mississippi, 93 per cent of those that went to Chicago were Negroes, and 85 per cent of those that went to Detroit. See Henry S. Shryock, Jr., and Hope Tisdale Eldridge, "Internal Migration in Peace and War," *American Sociological Review*, 12:1 (February, 1947), 27–39.

lina and Alabama; well over 100,000 each from North Carolina, Arkansas, and Louisiana.[32] Since most migrants, particularly Negroes, are young adults,[33] the loss of workers to these states was almost as large as these total figures.

Virtually all Negro migration, whether within the South or out of it, has been to cities, and particularly to metropolitan areas. The continuing shift of Negroes into the centers of American civilization will be the basis for a stupendous change in their status over the next generation. Even their slum houses are markedly better than most available to Negroes in the South, and with respect to other conditions of life—schools, employment opportunities and wages, politics—the contrast is much sharper. This internal migration of Negroes has been analogous to the pre-1914 immigration of Southern and Eastern Europeans. In both cases the adjustment to city life was especially difficult for transplanted peasants. Just as in an earlier period the various immigrant-aid societies had helped Europeans make this transition, so the Urban League was established to assist Negro "greenhorns." In both cases, the adaptation was successful, but not complete. By any index of social or economic well-being, whether occupational distribution or family income, whether education or average length of life, Negroes are still congregated at the bottom of the scale. But a new type of Negro had begun to develop in the northern cities even before 1914. As early as the turn of the century, a small group of Negro and white intellectuals met in Niagara Falls, Canada (they had been unable to get accommodations on American soil) and laid the basis for the National Association for the Advancement of Colored People. Over the years this organization has been able to enlist the power of the federal and state courts in its effort to re-establish the principle of equality in public institutions. If this effort is wholly successful, the significance of the Negro-white differentiation in demographic statistics will disappear; for the American Negro, unlike other ethnic minorities, is—or was until very recently—wholly assimilationist.

In the South, too, Negro out-migration could have an important effect on race relations. By 1940 no southern state any longer had a majority of Negroes in its population, and in 1950 Negroes constituted more than 40 per cent in only one state (Mississippi) and between 30 and 40 per cent in only four others (Louisiana, Alabama, Georgia, and South

[32] Everett S. Lee *et al.*, *Population Redistribution and Economic Growth, United States, 1870–1950*, 1: *Methodological Considerations and Reference Tables* (Philadelphia: American Philosophical Society, 1957), 90.

[33] Daniel O. Price, "Nonwhite Migrants to and from Selected Cities," *American Journal of Sociology*, 54:3 (November, 1948), 196–201.

Carolina). If race relations were governed by reason, the large reduction in the proportion of Negroes should have eased the southern whites' fear of being dominated by the descendants of their one-time slaves; and one can hope that it will still do so.

OTHER INTERNAL MIGRATION

The two examples of internal migration that have been discussed, the westward and the northward movements, are the most important migratory streams in American history but obviously not the only ones. The secular decline in New England's economy and culture has been related, as both cause and effect, to the large out-migration from that region. The cultures of Canada and the United States are so similar, and the impediment posed by the international border between them is so slight, that one might reasonably analyze the whole of English-speaking northern America as a single labor market and the movement of Canadians to American cities as another example of internal migration. Other streams could be identified by analyzing separately specific sectors of the population in addition to Negroes— such as the aged,[34] for example, or migratory workers.[35]

No matter how many such streams were identified and analyzed, however, they would not comprise a full picture. The most significant feature of internal migration is its prevalence—not where people move to, but that they move in such large numbers. An American who lives in the same house all his life is atypical. This fact can be exemplified with both types of mobility data collected by the Census Bureau. In each of the recent censuses and periodically also between them, a sample has been asked where they were living one year previously.[36] The results from the 1950 Census are summarized in Table 7-1. The mobile population, defined as those who had moved to a different house during that one year, amounted to almost 25 million persons, or one-sixth of the population. The proportion has usually been closer to one-fifth, and for the West alone over one-quarter. Of this mobile population, a substantial majority has always moved within one county. But between 1949 and 1950, 5.6 per cent of the total population crossed a county line and were classified by

[34] See page 82.
[35] See President's Commission on Migratory Labor, *Migratory Labor in American Agriculture* (Washington: U.S. Government Printing Office, 1951); Lloyd H. Fisher, *The Harvest Labor Market in California* (Cambridge: Harvard University Press, 1953).
[36] See page 56.

Moving day in a Los Angeles housing development. (J. R. Eyerman—courtesy LIFE © 1953 Time, Inc.)

the Census Bureau as "migrants" rather than "movers." Each five or six years, thus, the average person in the United States moves to a different house and each 20 years to a different county or state. On the average, then, every American moves more than ten times during his lifetime, and more than three of these moves are into the next county at least.[37]

---

[37] It should perhaps be emphasized, however, that we do not know how evenly the propensity to migrate is distributed throughout the population. According to one study,

**TABLE 7-1. Mobility of Population One Year Old and Over,
United States, 1949–1950**

	Thousands		*Per cent*	
Mobile population	24,757		16.8	
Intracounty movers		16,508		11.2
Migrants:				
Within a state		4,380		3.0
Between contiguous states		1,590		1.1
Between noncontiguous states		2,280		1.5
Nonmobile population	119,737		81.1	
Abroad in 1949 or mobility not				
reported	3,056		2.0	
Total	147,550		99.9	

Source: U.S. Bureau of the Census, *U.S. Census of Population: 1950*, vol. 4, *Special Reports*, part 4, Ch. B, Population Mobility—States and State Economic Areas (Washington: U.S. Government Printing Office, 1956), Table 1.

The year-by-year mobility figures are summarized, as it were, by state-of-birth data, which indicate in a different way the dimensions of the process. That many persons move to California, for example, is a commonplace, but few would guess that of the 10.6 million living there in 1950 only 3.9 million were native to the state. The in-migrants came, as indicated in Figure 7-3, from all over the United States; and others, represented in Figure 7-4, left California and settled in every other state in the Union.[38] Even for this single state these two figures denote something of a simplification of the facts, for the various routes and inter-

in which census data on Norristown, Pa., were compared with city directories, vital statistics, and school records, high migration rates were the consequence in part of repeated moves of a relatively small number of persons. Out of every 100 in-migrants during 1930–1940, 52 left during the following decade, compared with only 23 out of every 100 persons resident in Norristown during the whole 1930–1940 decade. See Sidney Goldstein, *Patterns of Mobility, 1910–1950: The Norristown Study* (Philadelphia: University of Pennsylvania Press, 1958); also "Repeated Migration as a Factor in High Mobility Rates," *American Sociological Review*, 19:5 (October, 1954), 536–541; together with comment by Rudolf Heberle and rejoinder, *American Sociological Review*, 20:2 (April, 1955), 225–227. On the other hand, according to a sample survey only 1.5 per cent of those aged 18 and over had never moved (*Current Population Reports*, series P-20, no. 104, September 30, 1960).

[38] One can guess why people migrated to California from North Dakota, for example, where the recorded temperatures range from a high of 124° to a low of —60°. In fact, the population of North Dakota declined from 681,000 in 1930 to 620,000 in 1950 (but then rose again to 632,000 in 1960). Local boosters have played with the idea of changing the state's name to just "Dakota" or "South Manitoba" or even "Miami" or "Dixie"—or "anything, in fact, that would make North Dakota sound gay, cheerful as a bottle of champagne" (*Time*, January 28, 1957). Yet in 1950, even without this reform, there were 1,940 persons living in the state who had been born in California; no generalization concerning internal migration lacks its inexplicable exception.

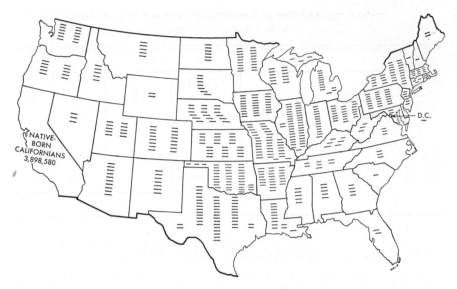

Figure 7-3. Natives of Other States Living in California, Ten Thousands, 1950

Source: U.S. Bureau of the Census, *U.S. Census of Population: 1950,* vol. 4, *Special Reports,* part 4, Ch. A, State of Birth (Washington: U.S. Government Printing Office, 1953).

Figure 7-4. Native Californians Living in Other States, Thousands, 1950

Source: U.S. Bureau of the Census, *U.S. Census of Population: 1950,* vol. 4, *Special Reports,* part 4, Ch. A, State of Birth (Washington: U.S Government Printing Office, 1953).

mediate places of residence are ignored, as are also intrastate movements. In *each* of the 48 states of the country shown, similarly, there reside persons who were born in all of the other 47 states. The congeries of accidents and personal motives that results in such utter dispersion has never been studied.

Figures 7-5 and 7-6 summarize the state-of-birth statistics recorded in

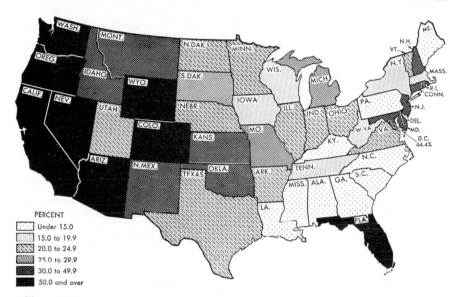

PERCENT
- Under 15.0
- 15.0 to 19.9
- 20.0 to 24.9
- 25.0 to 29.9
- 30.0 to 49.9
- 50.0 and over

Figure 7-5. Natives of Other States Living in Specified States, Per Cent, 1950.

Source: Conrad Taeuber and Irene B. Taeuber, *The Changing Population of the United States* (New York: Wiley, 1958), Figure 27, p. 96; based on U.S. Bureau of the Census, *U.S. Census of Population: 1950*, vol. 4, *Special Reports,* part 4, Ch. A, State of Birth (Washington: U.S. Government Printing Office, 1953). Copyright © 1958 by The Social Science Research Council.

the 1950 census. To some degree, but to some degree only, the two maps are complementary. The high percentage of in-migrants to California is balanced by a low percentage of out-migrants from that state, but Nevada and Arizona, for example, show the highest proportion of migration in both directions. That is to say, the pair of figures reflects the fact that the total migration between any two points is almost always very much larger than the net migration between them.

The motivation of migrants, except to the degree that it is implicit in the timing and direction of their movements, is a subject on which we have very little information. In the only sample survey on the subject ever conducted by the U.S. Bureau of the Census,[39] respondents were asked

[39] U. S. Bureau of the Census, *Current Population Reports,* series P-20, no. 4 (October 7, 1947).

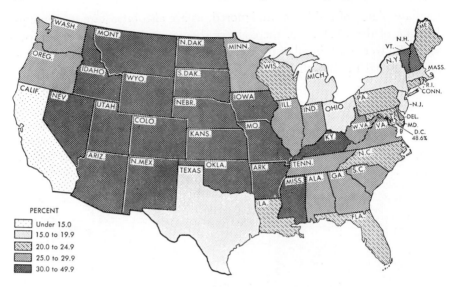

Figure 7-6. Natives of Specified States Living in Other States, Per Cent, 1950

Source: Conrad Taeuber and Irene B. Taeuber, *The Changing Population of the United States* (New York: Wiley, 1958), Figure 26, p. 95; based on U.S. Bureau of the Census, *U.S. Census of Population: 1950,* vol. 4, *Special Reports,* part 4, Ch. A, State of Birth (Washington: U.S. Government Printing Office, 1953). Copyright © 1958 by The Social Science Research Council.

their motives for having moved during the year 1945/1946, and their reasons were grouped into the following classes: (a) to take a job, (b) to look for work, (c) housing problems, (d) change in marital status, (e) to join the head of the family, (f) to move with the head of the family, (g) health, and (h) "other" (of which the most frequent instances were to attend school or live in a different climate).

These reasons are obviously not all of the same order. Many studies of migratory selection are based on the assumption, usually left implicit, that all migrants choose whether or not to move and that they make their choice in response to social-economic forces. Let us designate those of whom this assumption is valid **resultant migrants,** who make up only the first three classes in the list of motives. Those with no choice in whether to move (for example, children taken by their parents) and those who decide to move for reasons not associated with social-economic forces (but rather, for example, because of their health or the climate) are termed **epiphenomenal migrants.**[40] How important this differentiation

40 The terms for the two types are from Albert Hoyt Hobbs, *Differentials in Internal Migration* (Philadelphia: University of Pennsylvania Press, 1942), pp. 43–44.

can be is indicated in Table 7-2. The maxim that migration is primarily in response to economic and social circumstances is obviously not true in a direct sense; more than 70 per cent of the migrants were epiphenomenal. Of course, one can interpret this to mean that if a

TABLE 7-2. **Percentage Distribution of Internal Migrants**
by Motive, United States, 1945–1946

	Total	*Male*	*Female*
Resultant migrants			
Change of job (a + b)	22.6	41.1	6.2
Housing problems (c)	6.4	9.8	3.3
Epiphenomenal migrants			
Family migration (d + e + f)	61.7	38.1	82.7
Health (g)	1.2	1.8	0.8
Other reasons (h)	8.9	10.3	7.6

Source: U.S. Bureau of the Census, *Current Population Reports,* series P-20, no. 4 (October 7, 1947), p. 9.

man moves to take a different job, then the migration of his wife and minor children is also economically motivated; but this is very evidently not quite the same thing. The sex ratio of the two types of migrants varies considerably, as indicated in the table. The age structure varies even more sharply: virtually all children under 14 and persons over 65 are epiphenomenal migrants. The many generalizations concerning migratory selection based on the (sometimes tacit) assumption that all migrants are resultant, thus, can be valid only when family migration is insignificant.

SUMMARY

The freedom to move anywhere within the large area of the United States (or, in effect, within all of Northern America) has made a significant difference in the development of the American economy and culture. The national labor market operates with discernible frictions, but that it should work at all across 3,000 miles with a complete absence of forced moves is the anomaly to be explained. The weakness of tradition in the United States derives not only from the diversity of immigrant backgrounds and the frontier tradition, but also from Americans' continuing nomadic tendency.

An operational definition of migration such as that used by the Bureau of the Census—namely, a move across at least one county line—is a rough measure of distance, and thus of the significance of the move only to the degree that this is correlated with distance. In order to differentiate significant migration by any other criterion, one must delineate the culture areas within the United States. It is not possible to define these precisely, for regional subcultures, to the degree that they exist at all within the all-pervasive national culture, blend into one another gradually. The four regions used by the Bureau of the Census, and to a smaller degree the divisions within them, probably represent the most homogeneous groups of whole states that could be selected.

Interregional migration was discussed in terms of the two principal examples in American history. The westward movement began before the establishment of the Republic and is still continuing. The northward movement, smaller in absolute size, is important in part because of the probable long-run effects of Negro dispersion on race relations. Identifying such main streams of migration and analyzing them separately, however, neglects the random movements of millions of persons—"random" because we lack the data and skill to order them into meaningful patterns. In concentrating on particular migratory streams, however, we can easily lose sight of the fact that the United States is a society in motion, that each year one-sixth to one-fifth of the population moves to another house.

Some of the interregional migratory streams—for example, the northward movement of southern Negroes—are also instances of urbanization. And if at first the migration to the West was primarily one into a relatively empty countryside, it was soon met by a countermigration of persons moving to eastern cities. In order to appreciate the significance of internal migration, that is to say, one must keep in mind both types of areal classification—the delineation of regions discussed in this chapter, and rural-urban residence patterns, which will be analyzed in Chapter 8.

SUGGESTIONS FOR FURTHER READING

U.S. Bureau of the Census, *U.S. Census of Population: 1950,* vol. 4, *Special Reports,* part 4, Ch. A, State of Birth; Ch. B, Population Mobility—States and State Economic Areas (Washington: U.S. Government Printing Office, 1953 and 1956).

Basic data on mobility according to the two measures used by the Census Bureau.

Everett S. Lee, Ann Ratner Miller, Carol P. Brainerd, and Richard A.

Easterlin, *Population Redistribution and Economic Growth, United States, 1870–1950*, vol. 1: *Methodological Considerations and Reference Tables;* Simon Kuznets, Anne Ratner Miller, and Richard A. Easterlin, vol. 2: *Analyses of Economic Change* (Philadelphia: American Philosophical Society, 1957 and 1960).

Simon Kuznets and Dorothy Swaine Thomas, "Internal Migration and Economic Growth," in Milbank Memorial Fund, *Selected Studies of Migration Since World War II* (New York: 1958), pp. 196–221.

The first two volumes of what will be, when it is completed, the most comprehensive analysis of internal migration in the United States and its economic effects; and an article summarizing some of the data by Kuznets and Thomas, under whose direction the main study was made.

Howard W. Odum and Harry Estill Moore, *American Regionalism: A Cultural-Historical Approach to National Integration* (New York: Holt, 1938).

George Rogers Taylor, ed., *The Turner Thesis Concerning the Role of the Frontier in American History* (Boston: Heath, 1949).

The Odum-Moore volume is the most ambitious attempt to integrate the concept of region as it is used in a half dozen different disciplines. *The Turner Thesis,* one of the "Problems in American Civilization" series, has excerpts from Turner, his supporters, and his critics; see in particular the paper by Shannon on the safety-valve theory.

Howard W. Odum, *Southern Regions of the United States* (Chapel Hill: University of North Carolina Press, 1936).

Clyde V. Kiser, *Sea Island to City: A Study of St. Helena Islanders in Harlem and Other Urban Centers* (Columbia University Studies in History, Economics, and Public Law, no. 368; New York: Columbia University Press, 1932).

W. J. Cash, *The Mind of the South* (New York: Doubleday-Anchor, 1954).

V. O. Key, Jr., *Southern Politics in State and Nation* (New York: Knopf, 1949).

Four excellent books on the South, its population, and its institutions. Obviously, the works on Negroes recommended at the end of the previous chapter are also in large part about this region.

Warren S. Thompson, *Growth and Changes in California's Population* (Los Angeles: Haynes Foundation, 1955).

Morris E. Garnsey, *America's New Frontier: The Mountain West* (New York: Knopf, 1950).

Carl Frederick Kraenzel, *The Great Plains in Transition* (Norman: University of Oklahoma Press, 1955).

Three recent works on the West, chosen out of the great number in print.

8. URBANISM AND URBANIZATION

The reader will recall that Chapter 2, which sketched out "the growth of the nation," was concerned in large part with the transition of the United States from a rural to an urban society. No theme in national history is more important. The development of cities has been both the cause and the effect of the momentous population increase, the shift from an agrarian to an industrial economy, and America's rise from a minor appendage of Western Europe to a world power. Still other factors have been interpreted as at least partly a reflection of the country's urbanization. As we have noted, in the view of so eminent a historian as Arthur Schlesinger, most regional rivalries have merely expressed the classic opposition between town and countryside. Similarly, although perhaps with greater reservations, one might interpret a part of the differentiation among various ethnic groups as a function of their residence patterns.

The distance between rural and urban, fundamental and seemingly obvious as it is, is extraordinarily hard to pin down except in the simplest case, what Hawley terms a **community area**:

The community is comprised of two generalized unit parts, the center and the adjoining outlying area. In the one are performed the processing and service functions, and in the other are carried on the raw-material-producing functions. The two develop together, each presupposing the other.[1]

Such a relation, as between a market town and the farms it served, was once standard in the United States, but today the patterning is much more complex. The food eaten in any city can include not only milk from the local area but also (if we restrict the list to domestic products) California fruits, Wisconsin cheese, Idaho potatoes, Kansas corn and pork, and so on through all the specialized commodities of America's rationalized agri-

---

[1] Amos H. Hawley, *Human Ecology: A Theory of Community Structure* (New York: Ronald, 1950), p. 245.

179

culture. On the other hand, the urban influences impinging on rural regions, while they may be transmitted through the nearest town (in the form, say, of the local newspaper or television station), are as likely as not to have originated in New York or Washington or Hollywood. The boundaries of the modern community area, as Hawley points out, are "blurred, if not indeterminate," for "each index yields a different description of a community's margins." [2]

When all the residents of the countryside were farmers, who were all "hicks" in the view of "city slickers," it would have mattered little where one began an analysis; for in occupation, in residence, and in life style town and country were opposed. Today, a careful distinction must be made between urbanism and urbanization. **Urbanism,** the culture of cities, is the way of life of city dwellers; **urbanization** is the process of city formation, or the state of being a city. The correlation between the two, which once could be assumed, must now be a subject of empirical investigation.

"RURAL" AND "URBAN" AS IDEAL TYPES

The essential differences between rural and urban subcultures can be recaptured in the form of "ideal" or "constructed" types. These are deliberate deviations from present empirical reality, abstractions formed by accentuating those elements that are relevant to a particular research purpose. They are *ideal* types in the sense of being mental constructs, logical expedients, tools to be used in the analysis of the *real* world. No actual society is either wholly rural or wholly urban in this sense, but we can measure the degree of urbanism of any by comparing it with these pure types to see in what ways, and to what degree, it approximates one or the other.

In terms of such ideal types, the city is "a state of mind, a body of customs and traditions, and of the organized attitudes and sentiments that inhere in these customs and are transmitted with this tradition." [3] Urbanism is "a way of life." [4] Sometimes the contrast with a nonurban way of life is not left implicit, as in these examples, but rather expressed

[2] *Ibid.,* p. 249.

[3] Robert E. Park, "The City: Suggestions for the Investigation of Human Behavior in the Urban Environment," in Park and E. W. Burgess, eds., *The City* (Chicago: University of Chicago Press, 1925), pp. 1–46. (This article has been reprinted in Paul K. Hatt and Albert J. Reiss, Jr., eds., *Reader in Urban Sociology,* Glencoe, Ill.: Free Press, 1951, pp. 2–32.)

[4] Louis Wirth, "Urbanism as a Way of Life," *American Journal of Sociology,* 44:1 (July, 1938), 1–24. (This article has been reprinted in Paul K. Hatt and Albert J. Reiss, Jr., eds. *Cities and Society,* Glencoe, Ill.: Free Press, 1957, pp. 46–63.)

as the opposition of two polar types. Indeed, this is one of the most familiar conceptual frameworks in sociology. A list of only some of the most important examples would include Henry Maine's society of status vs. society of contract, Max Weber's traditional vs. rational authority, Emile Durkheim's mechanical vs. organic solidarity, Ferdinand Tönnies's *Gemeinschaft* vs. *Gesellschaft* (sometimes translated as Community vs. Society), Robert M. MacIver's culture vs. civilization, Howard Becker's sacred vs. secular society, Robert Redfield's folk vs. urban society, David Riesman's tradition-directed vs. other-directed character. Often Tönnies's terms, **Gemeinschaft** and **Gesellschaft**, are used to designate the two culture types not only as defined by him but also, more generally and approximately, as drawn by other social analysts.[5] While the variety of terminology reflects some differences in meaning and especially in emphasis, there is also a large overlap among all of these pairs, as well as with the dichotomy rural vs. urban in its most general sense.[6]

What the two terms mean can be illustrated by several quotations. According to Redfield, a folk society can be defined as follows:

Such a society is small, isolated, nonliterate, and homogeneous, with a strong sense of group solidarity. The ways of living are conventionalized into that coherent system which we call "a culture." Behavior is traditional, spontaneous, uncritical, and personal; there is no legislation or habit of experiment and reflection for intellectual ends. Kinship, its relationships and institutions, are the type categories of experience and the familiar group is the unit of action. The sacred prevails over the secular; the economy is one of status rather than of the market.[7]

An urban society, in contrast, is characterized by Wirth as follows:

The larger, the more densely populated, and the more heterogeneous a community, the more accentuated the characteristics associated with urbanism will be.

[5] In spite of the distinguished list of persons who have formulated this polarity, it has been subjected to a good deal of criticism. The dispute goes far beyond the subject matter of this chapter, and it is not feasible to do more than mention it here. It must be noted, however, that the meaning assigned to the two culture types varies somewhat. Durkheim, for instance, hardly advocated what he termed the "mechanical" community of the village, yet from his works we derive an important concept, *anomie*, together with the belief that it flourishes in towns. Weber was consciously neutral in his analysis of the development of modern society, but his early approbation of urban rationality changed in his later years to a deep pessimism. The reader interested in a more detailed discussion would do well to begin with Robert Redfield, *Tepoztlán, A Mexican Village: A Study of Folk Life* (Chicago: University of Chicago Press, 1949), and Oscar Lewis, *Life in a Mexican Village: Tepoztlán Restudied* (Urbana: University of Illinois Press, 1951). The fact that two studies of the same village are available, one exemplifying the folk-urban dichotomy and the other criticizing it, makes this pair of works a very convenient focus of any discussion of the polarity.

[6] See also the discussion of developed vs. underdeveloped countries, pages 458–459, 463–467.

[7] Robert Redfield, "The Folk Society," *American Journal of Sociology,* 52:4 (January, 1947), 293–308.

. . . The bonds of kinship, of neighborliness, and the sentiments arising out of living together for generations under a common folk tradition are likely to be absent or, at best, relatively weak. . . . Competition and formal control mechanisms furnish the substitutes for the bonds of solidarity that are relied upon to hold a folk society together. . . . The city is characterized by secondary rather than primary contacts. The contacts of the city may indeed be face to face, but they are nevertheless impersonal, superficial, transitory, and segmental. . . . Whereas, therefore, the individual gains, on the one hand, a certain degree of emancipation or freedom from the personal and emotional controls of intimate groups, he loses, on the other hand, the spontaneous self-expression, the morale, and the sense of participation that comes with living in an integrated society.[8]

In a population analysis the most interesting element of the polarity is perhaps that discussed in detail by Weber in his contrast between traditionalist and rational. In his words, **traditionalism** is "the belief in the everyday routine as an inviolable norm of conduct." "Domination that rests upon this basis, that is, upon piety for what actually, allegedly, or presumably has always existed," he termed "traditionalist authority." [9] A **rational** pattern, on the other hand, denotes "the methodical attainment of a definitely given and practical end by means of an increasingly precise calculation of adequate means," or, on an abstract level, the "increasing theoretical mastery of reality by means of increasingly precise and abstract concepts." [10] The rational sector of culture, in short, includes any area of social life in which a realizable end is consciously sought by nonmystical means. In Tylor's classical definition of culture,[11] "belief, art, morals, custom, and habits" are mainly nonrational in Weber's sense. These have functions but not purposes; they are not adaptations consciously contrived in order to meet definite needs. Even "knowledge" and "capabilities," which can be taken as the rational elements in this definition of culture, are often also in part nonrational.

The development of advanced civilizations from primitive societies has in large measure consisted in the extension of the area of rational action. In the modern West in particular, the calculated choice between alternative acts on the basis of their probable consequences is a usual behavior pattern. In technology and commerce, two broad areas of life whose rational element is strong in many cultures, Western man has reached the ultimate point—scientific method and bookkeeping. And, what is more important in this context, this view has spread from these institutions to

8 Wirth, "Urbanism as a Way of Life," *op. cit.*
9 Max Weber, *Essays in Sociology,* H. H. Gerth and C. Wright Mills, trans. and eds. (New York: Oxford University Press, 1946), p. 296.
10 *Ibid.,* p. 293.
11 As quoted above, page 5.

others, such as childbearing, which in other cultures are typically regulated according to traditionalist norms.

Until a situation is seen in rational terms no instrument is relevant, however effective it may be. The point can be illustrated by citing a health survey of an Iraqi village made by the inhabitants themselves. According to this self-estimate the state of health in the village was rather good: the incidence of many diseases was so high that they were not seen as abnormalities. All persons have two eyes, and most of them have trachoma; the difference was seen as one in degree, not in kind. Both two-eyedness and trachoma are part of "nature," and a person who "knows" this would not attempt either to create a third eye or to remove the inflammation from the two that are there. That such a community lacks scientific medicine is obvious, but this cannot be supplied in the portable form of Western know-how. For as the villagers define their situation, there is no problem to be solved, no sickness to be cured.

This distinction between the efficiency of an instrument and its relevance is often more to the point with respect to fertility. To analyze the causes of the secular decline in Western birth rates, it is necessary to consider not only the instrument (the invention of effective contraceptives) and the social environment (the conversion of an agrarian civilization into an urban-industrial one), but also the shift in typical attitudes that made these other factors operative. Children were no longer seen as facts of nature, as gifts of God, but rather as the consequence of acts that could be regulated, within limits, in order to bring about families of a larger or a smaller size. Once childbearing came to be so defined, in rational rather than natural terms, other factors could vary without affecting the fertility trend decisively—at least until the very recent past.

"RURAL" AND "URBAN" AS STATISTICAL INDEXES

The degree of urbanism, then, is ordinarily judged by comparing an actual place with the scale set by two polar ideal types. Urbanization is measured, on the other hand, by three kinds of index used in various combinations. (a) Economic: for example, the difference in the typical occupations of town and countryside. We designate a nation as urban if, say, less than half of the occupied males are engaged in agriculture. (b) Political: the settlement's administrative status. In the United States until 1874, thus, the only definition of urban was an incorporated area— that is, an aggregate that a state government had recognized as a "town." (c) Demographic: the number of persons living in a town or, more

realistically, in a population conglomeration irrespective of the administrative boundaries. This is an indirect measure of population density,
which is itself also an index. Using one criterion rather than another can
change the effective meaning of *rural* and *urban* by a wide margin. As
we shall see, the definition of the Census Bureau has been modified
repeatedly over the past 75 years, in a persistent effort to delimit categories that would reflect a society undergoing a fundamental transformation.

The number of urban places increased from 24 in 1790 to almost
4,300 in 1950. In 1790 the population of the largest city was less than
50,000; in 1960 it was more than ten million. One person out of every
12 in the United States lives in the conglomeration in and around New
York City.

Over the whole of the nation's history, the urban sector of the population has increased faster than the rural. The dramatic proportions of
this growth are indicated in Table 8-1—which still understates the trans-

**TABLE 8-1. Cumulative Percentage of the Total Population,
by Size of Place, United States, 1790–1950**

Size of place	1790	1850	1900	1930	1950 [a]
1,000,000 or more	...	...	8.5	12.3	11.5
500,000 or more	...	2.2	10.6	17.0	17.6
250,000 or more	...	2.2	14.4	23.4	23.1
100,000 or more	...	5.1	18.7	29.6	29.4
50,000 or more	...	6.3	22.3	34.9	35.3
25,000 or more	1.6	8.9	25.9	40.1	41.2
10,000 or more	2.8	11.3	31.7	47.5	49.0
5,000 or more	4.0	13.9	35.9	52.3	54.5
2,500 or more	5.1	15.3	39.7	56.2	58.8

[a] Old definition of urban; see below, p. 186.

Source: Census figures, as given in Conrad Taeuber and Irene B. Taeuber, *The
Changing Population of the United States* (New York: Wiley, 1958), p. 114.

formation that has taken place. If the definition adopted in 1950 is used
to delimit the sector, the percentage urban in that year was 64 rather
than the 58.8 shown in the table. And "while the 1790 figures understated the proportion of the population living under rural conditions, the
1950 reports tend to show that the proportion of the population living
under urban conditions is greater than the officially reported 64 percent." [12]

Obviously, the mere statement that the country is urban in such-and-

[12] Conrad Taeuber and Irene B. Taeuber, *The Changing Population of the United
States* (New York: Wiley, 1958), pp. 117–118.

such proportion is ambiguous. We must know what index or indexes were used to define the term. There is no better way of delineating the complex meanings assigned to "rural" and "urban" as statistical indexes than by tracing the gradual development of the Census Bureau's definitions.[13] Until 1874, as we have noted, incorporated towns were considered urban and everything else rural. In that year a *Statistical Atlas* was published showing the population density of each county in the country, and in the analysis of the data towns of 8,000 inhabitants or more were defined as urban and the rest of the population as rural. In 1880 the division that had been established almost by accident in this atlas was projected back to 1790, and eventually the series was continued until 1920. In the same census of 1880, however, a new definition was established: urban = an aggregate of 4,000 or more, rural = the balance. Even with this simple dichotomy, the division between rural and urban was complicated by the existence, particularly in New England, of townships with large populations of low density, and in almost all censuses some special provision has had to be made to adjust these to the national definition. In 1900 a three-way division was made between "urban" (population of 4,000 or more), "semi-urban" (incorporated places of less than 4,000), and "rural" (unincorporated places). This census, thus, introduced two novelties—a departure from the rural-urban dichotomy and the simultaneous use of two indexes.

In Willcox's supplementary analysis of the 1900 census a population of 2,500 or more was taken as the basic definition of "urban," and this has remained standard to this day. In the same analysis "cities" were defined as aggregates of 25,000 or more, and this was the first step toward the later separation of metropolitan units. In 1910 many more data were broken down by residence than in previous censuses. In a special 1920 monograph both the urban and the rural sectors were divided into farm and nonfarm, and this differentiation has been maintained for the rural one in subsequent censuses (except that in 1930 the criterion by which the "farm" population was defined was changed from occupation to residence). In 1930 the same classification was maintained with the following addition: aggregates of 10,000 or more persons with a density of 1,000 or more per square mile were defined as urban even if not so by other criteria. This provision added some 285,000 to the urban population. In 1940 the urban category was subdivided by breaking off "metropolitan districts," defined as cities of 50,000 or more together

---

[13] See Leon E. Truesdell, "The Development of the Urban-Rural Classification in the United States, 1874 to 1949," in U.S. Bureau of the Census, *Current Population Reports,* series P-23, no. 1 (August 5, 1949).

with contiguous administrative units having a population density of 150 or more per square mile.

A number of new concepts and procedures were introduced in the 1950 census. The size-of-place classification was extended to segregate two classes of villages, those of 1,000 to 2,500 inhabitants (whether incorporated or not), and those of fewer than 1,000. A new definition of "urban" was adopted, by which this population comprises all persons living in (a) incorporated places of 2,500 or more (except in New England and other states where "towns" are subdivisions of counties); (b) the urban fringe,[14] whether incorporated or not, around cities of 50,000 or more; and (c) unincorporated places of 2,500 or more outside an urban fringe. The remaining population is classified as "rural."

Two new metropolitan units were also established in 1950, the Urbanized Area and the Standard Metropolitan Area. An **Urbanized Area** is made up of at least one city (or a pair of contiguous twin cities) of 50,000 or more, plus the surrounding densely settled, closely spaced, urban fringe. A **Standard Metropolitan Statistical Area** (or SMSA), as it is now termed, is defined as one or more contiguous nonagricultural counties containing at least one city of 50,000 or more (or, again, a pair of contiguous twin cities of at least this joint size), and having a generally metropolitan character based on the counties' social and economic integration with the central city.[15]

Whether Urbanized Area or SMSA is the preferable unit depends on the use to which it is put. The first measures primarily the residence pattern in a city and its immediately adjoining area, the second the broader economic and social integration of whole counties.[16] By the definition of both metropolitan units, a city's effective population is no longer counted as the number of persons who happen to live within its corporate limits. What is commonly termed the "greater" city is a much more realistic measure of the actual social aggregate, and these new census

---

[14] For a discussion of the meaning of this term, see Otis Dudley Duncan and Albert J. Reiss, Jr., *Social Characteristics of Urban and Rural Communities, 1950* (New York: Wiley, 1956), pp. 117–118.

[15] For the full, detailed definition, see U.S. Bureau of the Budget, *Standard Metropolitan Statistical Areas* (Washington: U.S. Government Printing Office, 1961), pp. 3–5. In New England, towns rather than counties are the units used, but the criteria of integration are the same.

[16] The 157 Urbanized Areas and 168 SMA's listed in 1950 did not overlap completely, principally because the latter were based on the 1950 Census and the former on the last count prior to that. For a more extended comparison, see Taeuber and Taeuber, *op. cit.*, Chs. 6 and 7; Donald J. Bogue, *Population Growth in Standard Metropolitan Areas, 1900–1950* (U.S. Housing and Home Finance Agency; Washington: U.S. Government Printing Office, 1953), Ch. 3.

A four-layer crossover in Los Angeles. (J. R. Eyerman—courtesy LIFE © 1953 Time, Inc.)

definitions approximate it in different ways. In both, formal administrative borders are ignored also in other respects: Urbanized Areas include either incorporated or unincorporated places; both they and SMSA's extend over state lines.

Only minor revisions were made in the 1960 classification. As we have noted, the name and the precise definition of the SMSA were changed slightly. A new megalopolitan unit was set, the **Standard Consolidated Area,** and two such areas were delimited. The New York-Northeastern New Jersey SCA constitutes the New York, Newark, Jersey City, and Paterson-Clifton-Passaic SMSA's, plus Middlesex and Somerset Counties in New Jersey—with a total population of 14.8 million. The Chicago-Northwestern Indiana SCA is made up of the Chicago and Gary-Hammond-East Chicago SMSA's, and has a total population of 6.8 million.[17]

The development of the rural-urban differentiation is recapitulated in Table 8-2. At the beginning of the nineteenth century, residents of the *countryside* were *farmers* living in *unincorporated* places; and any one of these three elements could be taken as a sufficiently accurate measure

[17] U.S. Bureau of the Budget, *op. cit.,* p. 40.

TABLE 8-2. The Definition of "Urban" and "Rural" in Successive Census Documents, United States, 1874–1960

Date of Definition	Period for Which Used	"Urban"		"Rural"	
1874	1790–1920		8,000+	Residue	
1880	1880–1900		4,000+	Residue	
1890	a				< 1,000
1900	1900	4,000+		"Semi-urban": incorporated and < 4,000	Unincorporated and < 4,000
1906	1900–1910	"Cities" 25,000+	"Urban" 2,500+	"Country districts" residue	
1910	1880–1910		2,500+ and incorporated	< 2,500 or unincorporated	
1920	1920–1960			Rural nonfarm	Rural farm
1930	1930–1950	Additional classification: population of 10,000, plus density of 1,000/sq. mi.			
1940	1940	"Metropolitan district": city of 50,000+ with contiguous areas			
1950	1950–1960	Urbanized Area b SMA b	New definition of urban b	1,000– 2,500	< 1,000
1960	1960	Standard Consolidated Area b SMSA b			

a In 1890 the rural population was subdivided into "compact bodies" of 1,000 or more and the remainder, but this division was not included in the census, apparently inadvertently.

b For definition, see text.

Principal source: Leon E. Truesdell, "The Development of the Urban-Rural Classification in the United States, 1874 to 1949," in U.S. Bureau of the Census, *Current Population Reports,* series P-23, no. 1 (August 5, 1949).

of the composite status. Today, the "rural" isolation of that period and its concomitant social characteristics have all but disappeared; in some senses the entire population is "urban." In its continuing attempts to measure this transformation, the Census Bureau has experimented with a number of indexes, of which the most important were political status (e.g., incorporated or unincorporated), occupation (e.g. rural-farm), population density (e.g., the classification added in 1930), population size (with 2,500 becoming the dividing point between urban and rural), and social and economic integration (e.g., the number of telephone calls between the central city and the metropolitan ring, one of the criteria by which counties are included in an SMSA).

For any except the roughest indication of differences, then, the simple rural-urban dichotomy is now inadequate. It is usual to break down each into at least two parts—urban into "metropolitan" and "other urban," and rural into "farm" and "nonfarm."

Bogue recalculated the data back to 1900,[18] when the number of "principal" SMSA's (that is, those with a population of at least 100,000) was 52, compared with 192 in 1960. As shown in Table 8-3, over the same period the metropolitan population, so defined, increased from 24.1 to 111.1 million, or from 31.7 to 62.0 per cent of the national total. That is, while the population living in these areas increased by 3.6 times, that living outside them grew by less than a third.

TABLE 8-3. Growth of Population in the Principal[a] Standard Metropolitan Statistical Areas, United States, 1900–1960

	No. of Areas	Population in SMSA'S		Population of United States	
		Millions	Per cent Increase	Millions	Per cent in SMSA's
1900	52	24.1	—	76.0	31.7
1910	71	34.5	43.2	92.0	37.5
1920	94	46.1	33.6	105.7	43.6
1930	115	61.0	32.3	122.8	49.7
1940	125	67.1	10.0	131.7	50.9
1950	147	84.3	25.6	150.7	55.9
1960 [b]	192	111.1	75.9	179.3	62.0

[a] That is, those with a minimum population of 100,000.

[b] Excluding three SMSA's in Puerto Rico.

Sources: Donald J. Bogue, *Population Growth in Standard Metropolitan Areas, 1900–1950* (U.S. Housing and Home Finance Agency; Washington: U.S. Government Printing Office, 1953); U.S. Bureau of the Budget, *Standard Metropolitan Statistical Areas* (Washington: U.S. Government Printing Office, 1961).

[18] Bogue, *op. cit.*

SOCIAL CHARACTERISTICS BY SIZE OF PLACE

In their census monograph Duncan and Reiss have divided the urban-rural continuum into 11 size-classes, which are shown here in Table 8-4.[19] So detailed a breakdown proves its utility in their analysis, in part by differentiating those characteristics that increase (or decrease) regularly through the continuum from those whose relation with size of place is more complex.

The correlation between size of place and personal income is the most striking. The median income of males (Columns 7 and 8) ranged from $3,078 to $1,379 among whites and from $2,213 to $569 among non-whites. The considerably lower incomes of females, whether considered as a unit or divided by race, were also directly correlated with size of place. For either sex the progression was in part a reflection of regional differences (the South, in particular, had the lowest median income as well as the least urbanization), but within each region income still varied together with size of place, even when educational level and type of occupation were held constant. Since the money a person earns is an important determinant of a wide variety of social characteristics, one would expect to find, were the data available, a gradient in style of life by size of place.

When the effect of the age structure was eliminated, the proportion of the whites married was correlated with the size of place, especially among females (Columns 3 and 4). The data suggest that the age at first marriage was higher in larger places, and that the proportion of marriages dissolved was greater. Partly as a consequence of these differences in family formation, there is also the expected correlation between size of place and fertility, as measured by the number of children under 5 years per 1,000 women aged 20 to 44 (Column 5). The median age (Column 2), which in part reflects the fertility, varies as one would anticipate except that villages, especially small ones, deviate from the gradient.

The sex ratio (Column 1), on the other hand, has a different pattern altogether: the whole population was more or less the same except "other rural," which was 10 to 15 points higher. That is to say, except in the West, the excess of females obtained in all sizes of urban places.

The relation between internal migration and size of place was different again. The percentage of the population living in the same house in 1949 and 1950 (Column 6) showed a U-shaped curve. While there was a considerable variation among the four regions (the percentages non-

[19] In some of their more detailed discussions, they used an even finer breakdown.

TABLE 8-4. Selected Social Characteristics by Size of Place, United States, 1950

| Size of Place | Sex Ratio | Median Age | Married [a] | | Fertility Ratio [b] | Per Cent Non-mobile [c] | Median Income [d] | |
			White Male	White Female			White	Nonwhite
	(1)	(2)	(3)	(4)	(5)	(6)	(7)	(8)
Urbanized Areas:								
3,000,000 or more	940	33.7	−2.5	−4.2	433	85.1	3,078	2,213
1,000,000 to 3,000,000	943	32.0	−2.4	−4.1	478	83.4	3,026	2,226
250,000 to 1,000,000	940	31.5	0.5	−2.6	503	78.9	2,779	1,695
Under 250,000	935	30.9	1.0	−1.8	510	79.9	2,692	1,543
Places outside Urbanized Areas:								
25,000 or more	937	30.4	0.7	−1.8	522	77.5	2,554	1,407
10,000 to 25,000	930	30.3	1.9	−0.7	525	77.8	2,484	1,275
2,500 to 10,000	931	29.9	2.6	1.3	570	79.0	2,354	1,134
1,000 to 2,500	943	30.2	3.1	3.2	609	81.0	2,268	1,092
Under 1,000 (incorporated)	938	32.3	2.7	4.9	629	82.1	1,935	807
Other rural:								
Nonfarm	1,057	26.5	0.5	6.2	717	76.5	2,029	974
Farm	1,095	26.1	−0.2	8.4	766	85.2	1,379	569
Total United States	976	30.2	0	0	587	81.1	2,572	1,341

[a] Deviation from per cent expected on the basis of age structure.
[b] Children under 5 years per 1,000 women aged 20 to 44.
[c] Per cent of population one year and over living in same house in 1949 and 1950.
[d] Median income in dollars of males 14 years and over with an income, 1949.

Source: Otis Dudley Duncan and Albert J. Reiss, Jr., *Social Characteristics of Urban and Rural Communities, 1950* (New York: Wiley, 1956), Tables 3, 4, 6, 15, 21, and 38. Copyright © 1956 by The Social Science Research Council.

mobile were: Northeast, 87; North Central, 83; South, 77; and West, 73), within each region the same relation with size of place held.

Several general conclusions can be drawn from the data reported in this table. (a) The conventional division between rural and urban, a population of 2,500 and over, does not mark an important break in any of the series. Nor is any alternative dividing point any better. The social world is too complicated to be analyzed any longer by a simple dichotomy, as the Census Bureau itself has in effect recognized in the growing complexity of its statistical indexes. Perhaps it would be better to interpret "rural" and "urban," at least with respect to contemporary United States, only as generalized designations of contrasting poles. (b) The "rural nonfarm" category does not fit into the size-of-place continuum. The reason, as one might suspect from its very name, is undoubtedly that it is too composite a grouping. (c) Some social characteristics vary with size of place (for example, income, marriage patterns, fertility), but this is not true of all (for example, sex ratio, mobility). It may be that, just as a sharp dividing point between rural and urban is no longer discernible, so the entire differentiation between town and countryside will eventually disappear into a kind of intermediate suburbia. This trend is strengthened both by the dispersion of the urban style of life throughout the nation and, on the other hand, the efforts of city planners to convert every center into a "garden city." For the present, however, the rural-urban continuum helps us order some of the most significant social variations in American society.

Regional differences reflect many factors, but it has often been suggested that one of the most important is the degree of urbanization. In particular, the South has long been anomalous in this respect: in 1950, it was the only region lacking an urbanized area of three million or more and with as much as a quarter of the population still on the farm.[20] According to Bogue's estimate, of the 52 SMSA's in 1900, 22 were in the Northeast, 16 in the North Central region, nine in the South, and only five in the West. The rate of growth by regions has been in the reverse order—partly, indeed, because of the different bases on which the percentages are calculated, but partly as an expression of the fact that the whole country is becoming metropolitan. The West has shown consistently the highest proportionate increase, about double the national average, and in recent decades the rate of metropolitan growth has also been high in the South.[21]

Table 8-5 shows the distribution of metropolitan areas by geographic

[20] Duncan and Reiss, *op. cit.*, p. 30.
[21] Bogue, *op. cit.*, pp. 25–28.

division in 1960. By that date there were only three states without at least one SMSA—Idaho, Wyoming, and Alaska. The increase in the South was most marked in Texas, whose 21 SMSA's had a total population of 9.1 million. In the West, California's 10 SMSA's had a total population of 13.6 million. The major metropolitan concentration, however, was still in the East and Middle West. From Boston south to Washington, from the Jersey coast west to Chicago, the trend seems to be toward the formation of one enormous, more or less integrated, urban strip, including—with their 1960 populations in millions—the following SMSA's: New York (10.7), Chicago (6.2), Philadelphia (4.3), Detroit (3.8), Boston (2.6), Pittsburgh (2.4), Washington (2.0), Cleveland (1.8), Baltimore (1.7), Newark (1.7), Buffalo (1.3), Paterson-Clifton-Passaic (1.2), and Cincinnati (1.1).

TABLE 8-5. Metropolitan Population, by Region, United States, 1960

	Number of SMSA's	Total Population in SMSA's
The Northeast:		
New England	23	7,392,934
Middle Atlantic	25 a	27,953,571 a
The North Central Region:		
East North Central	47 b	24,294,164 b
West North Central	17 c	6,546,730c
The South:		
South Atlantic	35 d	13,086,991 d
East South Central	16 e	4,297,580 e
West South Central	32	9,065,524
The West:		
Mountain	13	3,348,164
Pacific	15	16,282,744
Hawaii	1	500,409
Puerto Rico	3	802,219 g
United States	215 f	113,589,030

a Including the portion of the Wilmington SMSA in New Jersey.

b Including the portions of the Cincinnati, Huntington-Ashland, Steubenville-Weirton, and Wheeling SMSA's in Ohio; those of the Evansville and Louisville SMSA's in Indiana; and those of the Davenport-Rock Island-Moline, Duluth-Superior, and St. Louis SMSA's in Illinois.

c Including the portion of the Duluth-Superior SMSA in Minnesota, that of the Davenport-Rock Island-Moline SMSA in Iowa, and that of the St. Louis SMSA in Missouri.

d Including the portion of the Wilmington SMSA in Delaware; the portions of the Huntington-Ashland, Steubenville-Weirton, and Wheeling SMSA's in West Virginia; and the portion of the Chattanooga SMSA in Georgia.

e Including the portions of the Cincinnati, Evansville, Huntington-Ashland, and Louisville SMSA's in Kentucky, and the portion of the Chattanooga SMSA in Tennessee.

f Counting each SMSA only once.

g Preliminary.

Source: U.S. Bureau of the Budget, *Standard Metropolitan Statistical Areas* (Washington: U.S. Government Printing Office, 1961).

OCCUPATIONS AND SOCIAL-ECONOMIC GROUPS

As we have noted, the rural and urban sectors can also be delimited by an economic index—the proportion of the population employed in occupations typical of one or the other. Such a classification, however, entails a number of difficulties, both conceptual and statistical.

The **labor force**, as defined by the Bureau of the Census, constitutes all persons 14 years and over gainfully occupied during a specific week when the count is made. "Occupied" does not mean "employed"; persons who are temporarily unemployed and looking for work are also included. Unpaid work in such family enterprises as farms and retail stores (if at least 15 hours were spent on it during the week) is included, but not housework in one's own home.[22] The line between persons in and out of the labor force often is not sharp. Many have more than one role—for example, students or homemakers with part-time jobs. Moreover, the concept of the labor force has been developed only recently, and data for 1930 and before are not wholly comparable with those for 1940 and after. Between these dates the change of definition reduced the enumeration of gainfully occupied persons by an estimated 1.2 million, and there have been other breaks of similar magnitude in the time series. The size of the total labor force in terms congruous with the present definition, therefore, cannot be estimated farther back than 1890.[23]

At that date roughly 35 per cent of the population was in the labor force. Over the following half-century, child labor was virtually eliminated (and the minimum age of the gainfully occupied was accordingly raised in the new definition of labor force from 10 to 14), a trend developed toward earlier retirement, and many more married women held jobs outside the home. These changes in style of life affected the size of the labor force more than increases in the population, as can be seen from Table 8-6.

If even the total labor force is more or less indeterminable before this century, then its classification into occupational groups must certainly be highly approximate. In the 1820 census the population was broken down into persons employed in agriculture, manufacturing (which included "artificers, handicraftsmen, and mechanics"—that is, all hand-workers not in agriculture), and commerce. Even at this early date difficulties in classifying the working force were anticipated. The instructions to the

---

[22] Gertrude Bancroft, *The American Labor Force: Its Growth and Changing Composition* (New York: Wiley, 1958), Ch. 1. See also John D. Durand, *The Labor Force in the United States, 1890–1960* (New York: Social Science Research Council, 1948).

[23] *Ibid.*, Ch. 2 and Appendix A.

**TABLE 8-6. Percentage Intercensal Increase in Population
and in Labor Force, United States, 1920–1950**

	Males		Females	
	Aged 14 and Over	*In Labor Force* [a]	*Aged 14 and Over*	*In Labor Force* [a]
1920–1930	18.8	15.6	21.6	26.7
1930–1940	12.1	5.4	14.9	20.3
1940–1950	9.4	9.0	12.8	28.5

[a] Or gainfully occupied aged 14 and over.

Source: Conrad Taeuber and Irene B. Taeuber, *The Changing Population of the United States* (New York: Wiley, 1958), p. 215.

enumerators remarked that "no inconsiderable portion of the population will probably be found, the individuals of which being asked, to which of these classes they belong, will answer, to all three." [24] Indeed, such replies were not only made but apparently, in spite of the warning, accepted. In several states of the South more white males aged 16 and over than the total number in this class were enumerated as gainfully employed.

Even if the classification by occupation in the nineteenth century is taken to be only a rough estimate, the decline in the proportion in farming marks the urbanization of American society as clearly as any other single series. The percentage of the occupied persons employed in agriculture, approximately 83 in 1820,[25] fell to 53 in 1870, and to only a little more than 30 per cent in 1910; and from the last date on the decline continued not only proportionately but also in absolute numbers. In 1960 the farm population was only about 15.6 million, or about the same as at the time of the Civil War.

It can be argued that the decline in the farm population, great as it has been, has still not been large enough to catch up with the remarkable improvement in agricultural production. A large proportion of today's farmers are marginal, growing barely enough to keep themselves and their families alive and certainly very little for the market; and if they migrated to the cities and got even unskilled jobs, both they and the economy would benefit from this change. Less than half of all farms produce nine-tenths of the agricultural commodities marketed.[26] The farmer-businessmen who

[24] Quoted in Taeuber and Taeuber, *op. cit.*, p. 202. See also P. K. Whelpton, "Occupational Groups in the United States, 1820–1920," *Journal of the American Statistical Association,* 21:155 (September, 1926), 335–343.

[25] Taeuber and Taeuber, *op. cit.*, p. 202. The authors note that the data from the 1820 census, including this figure, were "quite defective." In other Census Bureau publications, the estimated percentage for this date is 71.8; see above, page 20.

[26] Committee for Economic Development, *Toward a Realistic Farm Program* (New York, December, 1957), p. 13.

Harvesting the 1957 bumper wheat crop, Washington State. (Bill Lilley)

run these more efficient enterprises are, if anything, too successful; for—even after home consumption in generous amounts, heavy exports, and gifts to this or that underdeveloped country—the Department of Agriculture calls for "crash programs to limit production." A partial solution to these two quite dissimilar problems, rural poverty and agricultural

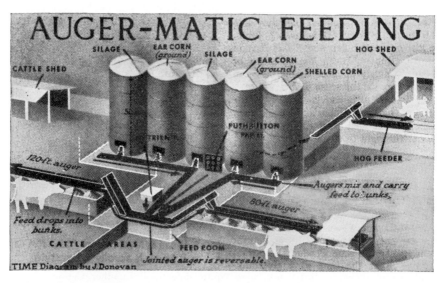

Livestock farm, Indiana. With ten minutes at the pushbutton panel, one man can feed 400 cattle and 500 hogs, a job that would have taken five men half a day working with pitchforks and buckets. (Copyright Time, Inc., 1959)

Hens laying eggs on production line, Georgia. They eat and drink from automatically refilling troughs. Another conveyor belt takes away the droppings. One man
can care for 7,000 chickens with a daily production of 4,000 eggs. (Burk Uzzle,
Leviton-Atlanta)

surpluses, would seem to be to facilitate the movement from farms to
urban occupations.

The fact that so many have made this shift, or have moved from one
type of urban occupation to another, can be analyzed in terms of internal
migration, of economic development, or of social mobility. Actually all
three are very often facets of the same process. Thus, the relative decline
of agriculture and the rise of manufacturing and services, the shift of
population from countryside to towns, and the improvement in income
and status of a substantial portion of the American people, are all the
same basic transformation of this country—as seen, respectively, by an
economist, a demographer, and a sociologist. The stupendous task of
combining those three facets into a single analytical framework and fitting
historical data into it has not yet been accomplished. In particular, there
is still a good deal of disagreement about the social implications of the
economic-demographic process. Have social classes in the United States
become more rigid than they once were; or is it now easier to move out
of the class into which one was born? If "social class" is defined as occupational group, an approximate answer at least can be given to these
questions.

The work a man does is one of the important determinants of his
relative standing in society. If it were possible to rank occupations, or

groups of occupations, from the highest to the lowest status, then changes in the proportion engaged in each could be taken as indications of the relative movement up or down the social ladder. Alba M. Edwards, for several decades an analyst at the Bureau of the Census, arranged what he called the "social-economic groups" in such a scale, from professionals at the top to servants at the bottom.[27] The distribution according to the Edwards scale in 1910 and 1950 is shown in Table 8-7. Here again, as one would expect from the proportionate decline in agriculture, the percentage of farmers and of farm laborers fell off by more than half. Apart from the small increase in servants, there was also a sharp decline in urban unskilled work. The percentage engaged in clerical work more than doubled, reflecting in part the increased employment of females. The percentage of proprietors in trade—small businessmen in the main— remained constant; but the other classes at the top and middle of the scale grew by substantial proportions. Approximate as these figures are, the trend is marked enough to warrant an unambiguous statement that upward social mobility has been an important and continuing feature of American society.[28]

TABLE 8-7. **Percentage Distribution of the Labor Force by Social-Economic Groups, United States, 1910, 1950**

	1910 [a]	*1950* [b]	*Per cent Change 1910–1950*
Professionals	4.4	7.4	68.2
Proprietors, managers, and officials:			
Farmers (owners and tenants)	16.5	7.5	−54.5
Trade	3.3	3.9	1.8
Other	3.2	5.0	56.3
Clerks and kindred workers	10.2	21.3	108.8
Skilled workers and foremen	11.7	14.0	19.7
Semiskilled workers	14.7	21.3	44.9
Unskilled workers	36.0	19.6	−45.6
Farm laborers	14.5	4.6	−68.3
Nonagricultural laborers	14.7	7.7	−47.6
Servants	6.8	7.4	8.8

[a] Gainful workers 14 years and over.

[b] Persons 14 years and over in the experienced civilian labor force.

Source: Conrad Taeuber and Irene B. Taeuber, *The Changing Population of the United States* (New York: Wiley, 1958), p. 211.

[27] For an appreciative description of the development of the Edwards scale, see Brinley Thomas, *Migration and Economic Growth: A Study of Great Britain and the Atlantic Economy* (National Institute of Economic and Social Research, Economic and Social Study 12; Cambridge: Cambridge University Press, 1954), pp. 139–141. The scale has often been criticized, but no one has yet both devised a better one and calculated the proportionate distribution of the labor force at various dates.

[28] For a discussion of this point, see William Petersen, "Is America Still the Land of Opportunity?" *Commentary*, November, 1953, pp. 477–486.

Since migration has been mostly to the largest cities, and since size of place and personal income are correlated, one might anticipate that the distribution of income has been broadened. There is, indeed, some evidence to support this expectation. Tucker's study, it will be recalled, suggested an egalitarian trend in the nineteenth and early twentieth centuries; [29] and in the most recent period this has apparently continued, although opinions among experts differ on some points. Kuznets has indicated the wider distribution by tracing the percentage of the country's income that went, respectively, to the top 1 and 5 per cent. The top 1 per cent included, for example, families of three with an income of more than $6,300 in 1933, or $12,600 in 1929, or $16,800 in 1946, while the minimum income of the top 5 per cent ranged from $1,250 to $2,000 in 1919–1938 to somewhat over $2,300 in 1946. During the interwar period the proportion of the total nonfarm income that these upper groups received varied little from year to year, but recently it has fallen sharply: [30]

	Top 1 Per Cent	*Top 5 Per Cent*
Average, 1919–1938	13	25
Average, 1947–1948	8.5	18

Income taxes, the successful efforts of trade unions and farm organizations to raise the earnings of the groups they represent, lower interest rates, and the more conservative investment habits of the very wealthy—the combined effect of these factors has been to continue the egalitarian trend in income redistribution implicit in the political principles on which the nation was founded.

SPATIAL PATTERNS IN AN URBAN COMMUNITY

By any one of its several definitions, "metropolitan" implies not only a larger size than "urban" but also a more complex structure. In neither respect, however, is the difference absolute. Just as the size range of metropolitan areas overlaps with that of single cities, so the multiplicity of functions of the metropolis is also characteristic of all but a few smaller urban aggregates—college towns, mining towns, and the like.[31]

A farmhouse is both the center of agricultural production and the home of the farmer's family, but in an urban setting the residential

---

[29] See page 34.

[30] Simon Kuznets, *Shares of Upper Income Groups in Income and Savings* (Publication no. 55; New York: National Bureau of Economic Research, 1953), pp. xxxv–xxxvi. See also Herman P. Miller, *Income of the American People* (New York: Wiley, 1955).

[31] For this reason, a functional classification of cities is a difficult and largely arbitrary process. Duncan and Reiss attempt not only to divide cities according to their functions but to correlate these with demographic variables; see *op. cit.*, Chs. 16–20.

neighborhood (or suburb) is separated from the business quarter. Within each type, moreover, a finer division is ordinarily discernible. Residential areas are lower or middle or upper class; they may have so high a proportion of a particular ethnic group as to become, for example, a "Little Italy" or a Harlem. Commercial enterprises, similarly, tend to be grouped into, say, a financial district, an amusement area, an industrial zone, a downtown business section, and so on. What factors influence this kind of patterning? Do they apply only to particular cities, neighborhoods, or industries, or are there also general determinants?

One of the first serious attempts in the United States to answer questions of this kind was made in the 1920's by Ernest W. Burgess of the University of Chicago. According to his theory, all modern American cities (in the first statement he had spoken of "any town or city") are spatially divided into five concentric zones: (a) a central business district; (b) a "transitional" zone of deteriorating real property used as boarding houses; and three residential areas: (c) working-class, (d) middle-class, and (e) upper middle-class.[32] For a number of years, this hypothesis dominated both theory and research in urban sociology, particularly at Chicago. Monographs were written on the spatial distribution of crime and delinquency, family patterns, mental disorders, and other social characteristics; and all tended to validate the theory. Then, some ten or fifteen years after its initial formulation, the hypothesis of concentric-circular zones was subjected to a good deal of criticism, both theoretically and empirically based. While the empirical studies of some cities in addition to Chicago tended to confirm the hypothesis (St. Louis, Rochester), other cities apparently had more complex and altogether different spatial patterns (New Haven, Boston, Pittsburgh, New York, Flint).[33] According to even a sympathetic critic, "The hypothesis of concentric zones as formulated by Burgess needs to be seriously modified if, indeed, it can be defended at all." [34]

In some respects, however, the theory was perceptive. The long-run trend of American urbanization was toward greater and greater concentration up until about 1920. From that date on, the rural-urban migra-

[32] The theory was first offered in a paper read before the American Sociological Society in 1923. Its most mature statement is in Ernest W. Burgess, "Urban Areas," in T. V. Smith and Leonard D. White, eds., *Chicago: An Experiment in Social Science Research* (Chicago: University of Chicago Press, 1929), pp. 113–138.

[33] See, for example, Homer Hoyt, *The Structure and Growth of Residential Neighborhoods in American Cities* (U.S. Federal Housing Administration; Washington: U.S. Government Printing Office, 1939).

[34] James A. Quinn, *Human Ecology* (New York: Prentice-Hall, 1950), p. 135. The adverse judgment by other analysts is both broader and harsher; see in particular Milla A. Alihan, *Social Ecology: A Critical Analysis* (New York: Columbia University Press, 1938).

tion was countered by an out-migration from central cities to their suburbs,[35] which has accelerated in the most recent period. About 80 per cent of the national increase between 1950 and 1960, according to preliminary reports, took place in 180 SMSA's (nine lost in population). The combined population of all the central cities, however, grew by only 8.2 per cent, and 72 actually declined in numbers, including four out of the five cities with more than a million inhabitants (New York, Chicago, Philadelphia, and Detroit, but not Los Angeles). During these ten years the population of the metropolitan rings, on the other hand, went up by 47.2 per cent.

In the metropolitan areas of the United States, there is generally a high positive correlation between distance from the center and family income. Such a pattern, familiar as it has become, is not the only conceivable one. The commutation between home and place of work is the more onerous, the greater the daily journey between them. On the basis of this factor alone, one might have expected the well-to-do to live in convenient proximity to their offices, while the poor had to add perhaps two hours' unpaid traveling time to their work-day. Indeed, something like this relation seems to have developed in some other countries, particularly where a strong family feeling made it important to retain the same dwelling from one generation to the next. In the United States, however, with its highly mobile population, the traditional family home ordinarily counts for much less than a brand new house in a "nice neighborhood," as far away as possible from the dirt and noise of the business district.[36] In a growing city, thus, where the most recently established area is likely to be at the periphery, one could expect, moving out from the center, a series of rings made up of residential zones of successively higher average family incomes. That is to say, the concentric-zone hypothesis would seem, at least in the abstract, to have some plausibility.

The main reason it breaks down is that the nonresidential portion of a city is ordinarily not so unified, either functionally or spatially, as Burgess's "central business district." Remarkably, Burgess had no place in his schema for industry,[37] nor even for differentiation among several types

---

[35] See Amos H. Hawley, *The Changing Shape of Metropolitan America: Deconcentration Since 1920* (Glencoe, Ill.: Free Press, 1956).

[36] See, however, Walter Firey, *Land Use in Central Boston* (Cambridge: Harvard University Press, 1947).

[37] This is one of the principal criticisms made by Maurice R. Davie in "The Pattern of Urban Growth," in George Peter Murdock, ed., *Studies in the Science of Society* (New Haven: Yale University Press, 1937), pp. 133–161. (This article has been reprinted in Hatt and Reiss, *Reader in Urban Sociology,* pp. 244–259.) Davie's article combined a study of New Haven's ecology with a penetrating theoretical analysis.

of commercial ventures. If residential areas vary according to the distance from nonresidential centers, as is posited in the concentric-zone hypothesis, then one must first investigate the factors that determine the location of commercial and industrial areas. Once the unrealistic assumption is abandoned that these are necessarily combined into a single all-encompassing unit, then the concentric circles spreading out from each one of a number of business or industrial districts overlap into the complex structure usually to be seen in American cities.

Location theory is a branch of economics. It would not be feasible or appropriate to do more here than indicate its subject matter.[38] Each entrepreneur, when he decides where to establish a new factory or office, ideally weighs the relative advantages and disadvantages of alternative locations in terms of a large number of factors, all of which, moreover, are constantly changing.

Since the size of the market for any firm was circumscribed by high overland transport costs, our early factories and foundries had to make the best of local sources of supply and had to market their goods close to where they were made. But in the middle of the nineteenth century transport costs declined dramatically; at the same time, mass production methods gave a heavy edge in production costs to the larger firms over their smaller competitors. For a time, then, a new balance was struck. The new large-scale firms could afford to take advantage of superior materials, wherever they might be, and to ship their products for longer distances to their markets.

Then came the third stage: The relative fall of transportation costs which was so dramatic in the nineteenth century was arrested and finally reversed in the first half of the twentieth century. At the same time, many local markets grew sufficiently large to accommodate plants with most or all of the cost advantages associated with mass production. As a result, the pattern of expansion of the large firms tended more and more toward the establishment of plants closer to their local markets.[39]

The trend in the location of residential areas has had a parallel development. With the growing population density in city centers, an impetus to move to the periphery developed perhaps as early as 1900, but it could not be realized by appreciable numbers, as we have noted, until

[38] For more detailed treatments, see August Lösch, *The Economics of Location* (New Haven: Yale University Press, 1954); Walter Isard, *Location and Space-Economy: A General Theory Relating to Industrial Location, Market Areas, Land Use, Trade, and Urban Structure* (Massachusetts Institute of Technology; New York: Wiley, 1956).

[39] Raymond Vernon, "Production and Distribution in the Large Metropolis," *Annals of the American Academy of Political and Social Science,* 314 (November, 1957), 15–29. Copyright, 1957, by the American Academy of Political and Social Science.

some 20 years later. Suburban life became feasible for a sizable percentage of urban residents only after the full development of automobiles and good roads, electric railroads, and a telephone network. In McKenzie's words, the metropolitan community is "the direct result of motor transportation and its revolutionary effect upon local spatial relations." [40] In the 1920's the same system enabled the husband to commute daily and the wife to make periodic shopping trips to the center. Better roads and faster trains did not cut down the hours spent in travel, but only increased the distance covered. The suburb was a residential quarter pure and simple.

The suggestion that it should be anything else had, as recently as 10 or 15 years ago, something of a utopian ring.[41] City planners were unable to reintegrate home and place of work, but a trend in this direction has been effected by the pressure of metropolitan life. Today the extra floor space needed by a growing corporation, not to be bought at a reasonable cost in the downtown area, is available at the periphery. At the same time, with crowded trains and clogged roads, suburbanites pay heavily in time and nervous energy for every trip to the center. A department store, a lawyer's office, or even a business firm, gets a competitive advantage by moving out to the consumer market.[42] And, from the other side, the metropolitan rings typically increase so fast as to outgrow the existent public services, including especially the school system. The extra taxes that new business and industry bring are so welcome that suburban communities, far from barring them, have on occasion sought them out.

By this decentralization of commercial and industrial enterprises, metropolitan areas have in some respects become more homogeneous. The differentiation between center and ring in terms of social class persists, however, and may even be increasing.[43] The business firms that established themselves in middle-class suburbs obviously were first of all those that

[40] R. D. McKenzie, *The Metropolitan Community* (New York: McGraw-Hill, 1933), p. 69.

[41] See, for example, Percival and Paul Goodman, *Communitas: Means of Livelihood and Ways of Life* (Chicago: University of Chicago Press, 1947); Peter F. Drucker, *The New Society: The Anatomy of the Industrial Order* (New York: Harper, 1950).

[42] See Evelyn M. Kitagawa and Donald J. Bogue, *Suburbanization of Manufacturing Activity within Standard Metropolitan Areas;* Raymond P. Cuzzort, *Suburbanization of Service Industries within Standard Metropolitan Areas* (Studies in Population Distribution, nos. 9 and 10; Oxford, Ohio: Scripps Foundation for Research in Population Problems, 1955).

[43] But see Berger's important study, which challenges this generalization: Bennett M. Berger, *Working-Class Suburb: A Study of Auto Workers in Suburbia* (Berkeley: University of California Press, 1960).

had middle-class customers; and as more and more of the amenities of middle-class life became available outside the central cities, the out-migration of the middle class increased. They were replaced by unskilled in-migrants moving from rural areas or small towns to working-class jobs in the big city. The process can be seen especially clearly when social class is linked to color, as indicated in Table 8-8 for the particular case

TABLE 8-8. Net Migration in the Chicago Metropolitan Area, by Color, 1930–1956

	Central City	*Ring*	*Chicago Metropolitan Area*
1930–1940			
Whites	−18,100	6,700	−11,400
Nonwhites	4,900	700	5,600
Total	−13,200	7,400	−5,800
1940–1950			
Whites	−28,000	24,000	−4,000
Nonwhites	18,000	3,000	21,000
Total	−10,000	27,000	17,000
1950–1956			
Whites	−40,000	36,000	−4,000
Nonwhites	18,000	3,000	21,000
Total	−22,000	39,000	17,000

Source: Donald J. Bogue, "Economic and Social Implications of Population Changes in the Chicago Metropolitan Area: A Case Study," in Milbank Memorial Fund, *Selected Studies of Migration Since World War II* (New York, 1958), pp. 125–140.

of Chicago. In each of the three periods shown there was a substantial out-migration of whites from the central city and an almost equivalent in-migration (in large part certainly the same persons) to the metropolitan ring. And in each period the dominant movement of Negroes was to the central city, with a negligible but increasing migration to the suburbs.[44]

On balance, the redistribution of the population and business firms within metropolitan areas has benefited all concerned. The density in the central cities had often become a problem in itself; and a slower rate of growth, or even a net loss, has its advantages. As we noted in the last chapter, the Negroes who moved to northern metropolitan areas from the rural or even the urban South made an enormous advance in every

[44] For a more detailed analysis of this process in Chicago, see Otis Dudley Duncan and Beverly Duncan, *The Negro Population of Chicago: A Study of Residential Succession* (Chicago: University of Chicago Press, 1957). The *New York Times* of November 19, 1957, has an account of a similar pattern in New York.

respect. And for the white middle class, the trend toward reintegration of residential and business functions in the suburbs represented a smaller but nonetheless significant gain. That even so the population redistribution is generally seen as a "social problem" is partly the consequence of an archaic tax system. Within the limits of a single city the differentiation between well-to-do and poor neighborhoods, though it is sometimes reinforced by zoning laws, is also mitigated by the more or less equal distribution of public services through the whole community. In a metropolitan area made up of a number of different administrative units, on the contrary, the tax structure reinforces the difference between upper- and lower-class communities. Just because of its dominance, the central city is called upon to serve not only its own inhabitants but also a large part of those of the whole metropolitan area. With the removal of its middle-class residents and business firms, however, the center loses its major source of municipal taxes. The delapidated real estate and slum residents left behind often require more services than they pay for. This imbalance is a particularly acute instance of a general problem in modern American society: local taxes are altogether insufficient to pay for adequate education, transportation, street cleaning, or indeed any of the public services provided at a municipal level.[45]

SUMMARY

What is loosely called "urbanization" is really a combination of two phenomena—the development of large concentrated aggregates of human beings, and the rise of new culture patterns, new ways of thinking and behaving, characteristic of these cities. In order to discuss the relation between the two, it is necessary to keep the concepts separate—urbanization, the process or state of population concentration, and urbanism, the way of life of city dwellers. The effect of density on culture patterns is important, but not absolute; that is, the correlation between urbanization and urbanism is high, but not perfect. For example, one difference between the Asian peasant and the American farmer is that the latter, though an agriculturist by vocation, is "urban" in many respects. He is literate, and he reads city newspapers. He ordinarily runs not a family subsistence farm, but a business enterprise, with specialized crops grown

[45] Several interesting papers on this theme are included in Martin Meyerson *et al.*, eds., "Metropolis in Ferment," *Annals of the American Academy of Political and Social Science,* vol. 314 (November, 1957). For a more general discussion of the contrast between affluence in private consumption and poverty in public welfare, see John Kenneth Galbraith, *The Affluent Society* (Boston: Houghton Mifflin, 1958).

for the urban market. His way of life and thinking is closer to the *Gesell-schaft,* that of Asian villagers to the *Gemeinschaft.*

More generally, "urban" patterns of living have been spreading to "rural" areas so rapidly, particularly in the last few decades, that in terms of what these words once denoted the whole of the United States is urban. The establishment of one national culture, overriding regional and town-countryside differences, was due in part to the direct diffusion consequent from the incessant migration. The merging of urban and rural subcultures, however, has not by far made the distinction meaningless in American society. The rural-urban continuum constitutes both a useful conceptual tool and a measure of how a number of important social characteristics are graded—among others, income and fertility.

Paradoxically, internal migration is an important medium not only of culture diffusion but also of culture differentiation. The farmers' sons who go to the cities are not just any farmers' sons, but those who for various reasons are especially attracted to urban occupations and ways of life; and migration in the other direction, to the extent that it exists, is selective in the contrary sense.[46] The redistribution of the population in each generation, with "urban" types going to cities and "rural" types staying in the country (or moving there), helped maintain and even reinforced the original distinction between rural and urban subcultures.

The rise of a city or metropolis is not by the simple addition of more people to the rural nucleus. No urban place is spatially homogeneous, and its growth can be studied by analyzing the changing relationship of its several parts. Since about 1920 the suburban rings of metropolitan areas have been increasing much faster than the central cities; and in the most recent period there has also been a decentralization of business and light industry.

SUGGESTIONS FOR FURTHER READING

Arthur Salomon, "Max Weber's Methodology," *Social Research,* 1:2 (May, 1934), 147–168.
John C. McKinney, "The Polar Variables of Type Construction," *Social Forces,* 35:4 (May, 1957), 300–306.
Reinhard Bendix and Bennett Berger, "Images of Society and Problems of Concept Formation in Sociology," in Llewellyn Gross, ed., *Symposium on Sociological Theory* (Evanston, Ill.: Row, Peterson, 1959), pp. 92–118.

[46] Most migration, of course, is similarly nonrandom; see pages 592–603.

Three interesting discussions of the ideal type and especially of polarities.

Robert Redfield, *Tepoztlán, A Mexican Village: A Study of Folk Life* (Chicago: University of Chicago Press, 1949).

Oscar Lewis, *Life in a Mexican Village: Tepoztlán Restudied* (Urbana: University of Illinois Press, 1951).

Horace Miner, "The Folk-Urban Continuum," *American Sociological Review,* 17:5 (October, 1952), 529–537. (This article has been reprinted in Paul K. Hatt and Albert J. Reiss, Jr., *Cities and Society,* Glencoe, Ill.: Free Press, 1957, pp. 22–34.)

The books by Redfield and Lewis, both about the same locale, present together the sharpest confrontation of views concerning the utility of the *Gemeinschaft-Gesellschaft* polarity. The article by Miner attempts to draw a balance between them.

Otis Dudley Duncan and Albert J. Reiss, Jr., *Social Characteristics of Urban and Rural Communities, 1950* (New York: Wiley, 1956).

Gertrude Bancroft, *The American Labor Force: Its Growth and Changing Composition* (New York: Wiley, 1958).

Ronald L. Mighell, *American Agriculture: Its Structure and Place in the Economy* (New York: Wiley, 1955).

Herman P. Miller, *Income of the American People* (New York: Wiley, 1955).

Four volumes of the census monograph series, of which the first two arc particularly relevant to this chapter.

Arthur M. Schlesinger, *The Rise of the City, 1878–1898* (New York: Macmillan, 1933).

Adna Ferrin Weber, *The Growth of Cities in the Nineteenth Century: A Study in Statistics* (Columbia University Studies in History, Economics, and Public Law, vol. 11; New York: Macmillan, 1899).

Two of the best historical studies.

R. D. McKenzie, *The Metropolitan Community* (New York: McGraw-Hill, 1933).

Amos H. Hawley, *The Changing Shape of Metropolitan America: Deconcentration Since 1920* (Glencoe, Ill.: Free Press, 1956).

Donald J. Bogue, *Population Growth in Standard Metropolitan Areas, 1900–1950* (U.S. Housing and Home Finance Agency; Washington: U.S. Government Printing Office, December, 1953).

Edgar M. Hoover and Raymond Vernon, *Anatomy of a Metropolis: The*

Changing Distribution of People and Jobs within the New York Metropolitan Region (Cambridge: Harvard University Press, 1959).

Otis Dudley Duncan, W. Richard Scott, Stanley Lieberson, Beverly Duncan, and Hal H. Winsborough, *Metropolis and Region* (Resources for the Future; Baltimore: Johns Hopkins Press, 1960).

Bennett M. Berger, *Working-Class Suburb: A Study of Auto Workers in Suburbia* (Berkeley: University of California Press, 1960).
    Several excellent works on the metropolis.

Donald L. Foley, "Census Tracts and Urban Research," *Journal of the American Statistical Association,* 48:264 (December, 1953), 733–742.

Gideon Sjoberg, "Urban Community Theory and Research: A Partial Evaluation," *American Journal of Economics and Sociology,* 14:2 (January, 1955), 199–206.

Martin Meyerson, Barbara Terrett, and Paul N. Ylvisaker, eds., "Metropolis in Ferment," *Annals of the American Academy of Political and Social Science,* vol. 314 (November, 1957).

American Sociological Review, vol. 21, no. 1 (February, 1956), "featuring a group of papers on urban populations."

Paul K. Hatt and Albert J. Reiss, Jr., eds., *Cities and Society* (Glencoe, Ill.: Free Press, 1957).
    Some of the hundreds of journal articles on urban populations.

Amos H. Hawley, *Human Ecology: A Theory of Community Structure* (New York: Ronald, 1950).

James A. Quinn, *Human Ecology* (New York: Prentice-Hall, 1950).
    Two textbooks complementing this chapter. Hawley's is aimed at the more mature student; Quinn's is more detailed on a number of specific topics—for example, Burgess's concentric-zone hypothesis.

9. *FAMILY AND FERTILITY*

The two principal themes in any discussion of fertility in the United States, or in any other country of the modern West, are the secular decline in average family size and the postwar reversal of this decline. Merely establishing when the birth rate started to fall off and how rapidly it did so is something of a problem, since the necessary statistics are a new development. For a historical study, therefore, we must make do with various approximate measures, none of which is really satisfactory. And for the most recent period the meaning of the data, which have become relatively full and reliable, depends in part on the index chosen and on the interpretation of the analyst.[1] In particular, what the baby boom implies for the long run is the subject of lively dispute.

Many of the elements of the transformation from a rural-agrarian to an urban-industrial society can be cited, somewhat plausibly, as causes of the small-family system. In particular, the rising status of women made it more likely for a wife to find satisfying and rewarding employment in other roles than as housewife and mother; the many new occupations in the more complex industrial society necessitated much more social mobility than there had been in the relatively static agrarian economy, and parents felt encouraged to reproduce in smaller numbers in order that both they and their offspring might be better able to take advantage of opportunities offered; the small apartments of large cities, the child-labor laws, the middle-class style of life, all meant that each child cost more in money and trouble than on a farm. The decline in family size, however, cannot be ascribed solely to urbanism, with all ancillary factors subsumed under it. The postwar rise in fertility, which also accompanied a continuing increase in the proportion of the population resident in cities, in itself indicates that a more complex hypothesis is needed.

---

[1] Demographic rates and their various uses and limitations are discussed below, pp. 622–626. The comparison of fertility measures made in this chapter is intended only to exemplify some of the general methodological points.

In demographic terms, fertility can be interpreted as a function of structural features like the sex ratio and the proportion of the population consisting of women in the childbearing ages. For example, on the western frontier, in spite of the large number of children per wife, the rate of natural increase was low because of the extremely high sex ratio; or the high birth rate of immigrants at the beginning of the twentieth century was partly a consequence of the fact that most were young adults. In a population with no migration, however, the effect of its structure on fertility, though it may be important, merely accentuates the influence of other factors. A society with large families will typically have a structure favoring rapid growth, and one with small families will develop one reinforcing this contrary growth trend.[2] Thus, an attempt to discover the first causes, the reasons for the beginning of the decline in the birth rate, must be concentrated on social-economic determinants.

THE SECULAR DECLINE IN FERTILITY

In both the crude birth rate and its various refinements, the number of births, which is derived from vital statistics, is compared with the total population count of the census. As was noted in Chapter 3, however, reasonably satisfactory standards of enumeration were developed in the nineteenth century, while the underregistration of births and deaths continued to be a serious problem until some 20 years ago. For any analysis of long-term trends, therefore, a measure using census data only is needed. The usual one is the **fertility ratio,** defined as the number of children under 5 per 1,000 women in the childbearing period, however this is specified.

It is well known that underenumeration is particularly large in the youngest age-groups, not so much apparently because infants and children are passed over altogether as because their ages are often given as of their next rather than their last birthday.[3] If mothers were consistent in this respect, there would be no infants counted under one year; in any case the error is less for the first five years than for the first year. The fertility ratio, moreover, measures what might be termed effective fertility—not the number of births per se but that figure reduced by the substantial mortality during infancy. It has been estimated that about 78 per cent of white infants born around 1800 survived to the age of 2.5

2 See pages 627–628.
3 See Wilson H. Grabill, Clyde V. Kiser, and Pascal K. Whelpton, *The Fertility of American Women* (New York: Wiley, 1958), pp. 406–413.

years, the midpoint of "under 5." For 1900 the comparable figure is 84 per cent; for 1950, 97 per cent. Corresponding estimates for Negro infants are 72 per cent in 1900, 95 per cent in 1950.[4] As these last figures suggest, both underenumeration and infant mortality have always varied considerably from one social group to another. This means that the fertility ratio is more satisfactory to indicate changes in the whole population than to compare sectors within it, although for lack of any substitute it is used—sometimes with suitable adjustments—for both purposes. In Table 9-1, thus, the number of white children has been increased by 5 per cent and that of Negro children by 13 per cent, these factors representing one estimate of the underenumeration for each race.

TABLE 9-1. Adjusted [a] Number of Children under 5 per 1,000
Women Aged 20 to 44, by Race, United States, 1800–1950

	White	Negro
1800	1,342	n.a.
1810	1,358	n.a.
1820	1,295	n.a.
1830	1,145	n.a.
1840	1,085	n.a.
1850	892	1,087
1860	905	1,072
1870	814	997
1880	780	1,090
1890	685	930
1900	666	845
1910	631	736
1920	604	608
1930	506	554
1940	419	513
1950	587	706

a The number of white children enumerated in each census has been increased by 5 per cent, that of Negro children by 13 per cent, "these being factors obtained from a study of data for 1925 to 1930." All data from 1830 to date have been standardized indirectly to the age distribution of American women in 1930.

n.a. Data not available.

Source: Wilson H. Grabill, Clyde V. Kiser, and Pascal K. Whelpton, *The Fertility of American Women* (New York: Wiley, 1958), Table 6. Copyright © 1958 by The Social Science Research Council.

With all their imperfections, the data shown in Table 9-1 nevertheless indicate a trend that can be accepted as substantially correct. The American colonies in the eighteenth century had a very high fertility. This was remarked by a number of contemporaries—Malthus (as was

[4] *Ibid.*, p. 13.

noted in Chapter 1), Benjamin Franklin, and Jefferson, among others; and it is also the conclusion of modern analysts using several techniques to manipulate various inadequate data. According to the consensus of these estimates, both contemporary and modern, around the end of the eighteenth century each married woman bore almost eight children on the average.[5] The decline in white fertility began in 1810 and continued steadily until 1940. During this period the fertility ratio fell off by 939 units—about one-third by 1850, about three-quarters by 1900, and the remainder in the twentieth century. The rates for Negroes began at a higher point in 1850 but decreased more rapidly, reaching parity with the whites in 1920.

In the 1910 census, and also in 1940 and in 1950, women were asked how many children they had ever borne. For a female aged 45 or over this figure is known as the **completed family size,** a remarkably simple and direct measure of natality. When women who have passed their childbearing ages are divided into successively older groups, the number of children they report gives an approximate indication of the decline in family size over a considerable period, as shown in Table 9-2.[6]

In any analysis of fertility, it is important to include marriage trends. We know virtually nothing about the age at marriage in the nineteenth century even for the whole population, not to speak of its various sectors. The proportion of the females who never married, as shown in Column 5 of Table 9-2, forms a U-shaped curve, with low points among cohorts having their children in the third quarter of the nineteenth century and the second quarter of the twentieth century, and an intermediate high point among those having their children just before World War I. The downward trend has continued: in 1959 only 6.1 per cent of women aged 35 to 44 were single.[7] According to these data, however, at least nine out of ten married during all periods in the past century, so that the loss to fertility by nonmarriage could never have been greater than one-tenth.

[5] For one such estimate, see Alfred J. Lotka, "The Size of American Families in the Eighteenth Century," *Journal of the American Statistical Association,* 22:158 (June, 1927), 154–170.

[6] The main sources of error of such a measure derive from the facts that under-reporting probably increases with age, particularly for the higher ages, and that there is some relation (though not a simple one) between longevity and completed family size. See Grabill, Kiser, and Whelpton, *op. cit.,* pp. 400–404. In Table 9-2, the row for women aged 45–49 in 1940 and 55–59 in 1950 indicates that the discrepancy to be found in these age-groups is not serious. On the other hand, the jump over only five years between two successive rows, women aged 45–49 in 1910 and those aged 70–74 in 1940, is probably based in part on the fact that the latter—that is, very much older—age-group is less representative of their complete cohort.

[7] U.S. Bureau of the Census, *Current Population Reports,* series P-20, no. 96 (November 23, 1959).

TABLE 9-2. Completed Family Size, United States, 1910-1950

Age of Women at Given Date			Main Child-bearing Period [b]	Per cent Never Married	Of Ever Married, Per cent Childless	Children Ever Born		
1910	1940 [a]	1950 [a]				Per Woman	Per Wife	Per Mother
(1)	(2)	(3)	(4)	(5)	(6)	(7)	(8)	(9)
70-74			1858-1882	6.5	7.7	5.0	5.4	5.8
65-69			1863-1887	6.5	7.9	5.0	5.4	5.8
60-64			1868-1892	7.3	8.2	4.8	5.3	5.7
55-59			1873-1897	7.2	8.3	4.8	5.2	5.7
50-54			1878-1902	8.4	8.9	4.5	5.0	5.5
45-49			1883-1907	9.0	9.5	4.3	4.7	5.2
	70-74		1888-1912	10.0	12.5	3.4	3.8	4.4
	65-69		1893-1917	10.0	14.0	3.2	3.6	4.2
	60-64		1898-1922	9.5	15.0	3.0	3.4	4.0
	55-59		1903-1927	9.0	16.5 [c]	3.0 [c]	3.3 [c]	3.9 [c]
	50-54		1908-1932	9.1	16.3 [c]	2.8 [c]	3.1 [c]	3.7 [c]
	45-49	55-59	1913-1937	8.9-8.0	16.1 [c]-16.9	2.7 [c]-2.7	3.0 [c]-2.9	3.5 [c]-3.5
		50-54	1918-1942	8.0	18.0	2.5	2.7	3.3
		45-49	1923-1947	8.4	19.5	2.3	2.5	3.1

[a] Whites only.

[b] Dates over which the middle cohort (aged 72 in 1910, etc.) was 20 to 44 years old.

[c] Revised estimates as of 1950, which increased the earlier per cent childless by about 1.3 points and the completed family size by less than 2 per cent.

Source: Wilson H. Grabill, Clyde V. Kiser, and Pascal K. Whelpton, *The Fertility of American Women* (New York: Wiley, 1958), Tables 9 and 16.

Childless couples, equivalent so far as fertility trends are concerned to persons who remain single, are a class particularly difficult to analyze, since they are made up of two quite different groups—sterile marriages and those in which the forces toward smaller families have reached the ultimate point. Some authorities hold that on the average one marriage in ten is naturally sterile. The figures at the top of Column 6 suggest both that this estimate is too high and that deliberate childlessness was all but nonexistent in the middle of the nineteenth century.[8] A large part of the decline in fertility can be accounted for by the rise in the number of childless couples, which constituted one out of every five in the period just preceding World War II. Still in 1957, 17.7 per cent of ever married women aged 45 to 49 were childless, but only 11.3 per cent of those aged 30 to 34.[9]

Note that there was also a steady but gradual decline in the completed size of families with at least one child (Column 9). The average number of children per mother, estimated at more than eight in 1800, was less than six in the third quarter of the century, just four in the first quarter of the twentieth century, and barely more than three in the second quarter. Even ignoring the women who remained single and the increasing proportion of married women who were childless, the completed family size decreased by almost one child per generation.

The date when this transformation started is worth emphasizing. The decline began when the United States was a relatively empty country with a wide open frontier, when it was still overwhelmingly rural and agricultural (although the rural sector was becoming increasingly involved in the town-oriented market economy), when the very term *birth control* had not yet been coined and contraceptive means were more or less limited to coitus interruptus—when, that is to say, almost all of the factors cited in later studies as causes of the decline were still in the future.

DIFFERENTIAL FERTILITY

The decline in fertility did not take place, of course, homogeneously throughout the society. If we note which social groups led the parade toward the small-family system and which lagged, the characteristics of the first groups, particularly if they contrast sharply with those of the last, can be provisionally described as causes of the decline. How shall

---

[8] But see pages 649–650.

[9] U.S. Bureau of the Census, *Current Population Reports*, series P-20, no. 84 (August 8, 1958).

these groups be defined? In a society that has changed as rapidly as that of the United States, with so much movement from one region to another and from one social class to another, no boundary lines are definite. The most accurate breakdowns (as is generally true of all demographic data) are by geographical units, but since the states and even the divisions and regions are quite heterogeneous, they are usually the least meaningful ones.

Even for more homogeneous social groups, it is ordinarily very difficult to determine which of their characteristics help determine their typical fertility patterns. In 1910, for instance, among women aged 45 to 49 years who had ever been married, foreign-born women had had 5.3 children on the average and native-born women of native parents only 4.4. Unlike the comparisons of birth rates often made at the time, in this example the age of the women is held constant, so that the difference in population structures of the foreign- and native-born is not a factor. But the datum still raises as many questions as it answers. Is the higher completed family size a reflection of residual patterns held over from the old country; or of a specific element of the European and American cultures, such as Catholicism; or of acculturation to the lower class in the American social structure, with its relatively high fertility? The way to answer such questions, of course, is to analyze each subgroup separately, but the data are generally not good enough to permit this.

Moreover, in analyzing differential fertility, one must keep in mind that the accuracy of demographic data about social groups varies markedly. As in Table 9-1, in most racial comparisons the empirical evidence for the higher Negro natality is obtained by compensating for the greater undercnumeration or underregistration with a larger correction factor. While this is the most common case, there are also significant differences in completeness of reporting, particularly for the past, by region, by rural-urban residence, by occupation, and by most of the other categories into which fertility data are classified.

Nevertheless, differential analysis is the only method we have of getting at the causes of the secular decline in an empirical context. The following paragraphs briefly summarize the contrasts to be noted according to the most important classifications used to study differential fertility.

Regions

Table 9-3 shows the fertility ratio for five dates by geographic divisions. As early as 1800, a considerable difference existed between the older regions and the frontier; and this contrast has persisted throughout the nation's history, with the Mountain Division showing the highest fertility in 1950. In general, the South has been intermediate between the frontier area and the urban Northeast (together with, at later dates, the West

TABLE 9-3. Adjusted [a] Number of Children under 5 per 1,000 Women Aged 20 to 44, White Population, by Geographic Divisions, 1800–1950

	1800	1850	1900	1940	1950
The Northeast:					
New England	1,164	636	497	365	552
Middle Atlantic	1,334	776	567	337	507
The North Central Region:					
East North Central	1,918	1,037	620	407	586
West North Central	n. a.	1,122	731	452	642
The South:					
South Atlantic	1,402	957	802	480	601
East South Central	1,875	1,115	855	556	666
West South Central	n. a.	1,061	942	492	644
The West:					
Mountain	n. a.	875	742	546	699
Pacific	n. a.	896	532	358	576
United States [b]	1,342	892	666	419	587
Ratio of smallest to largest	1:1.65	1:1.76	1:1.90	1:1.65	1:1.38

[a] See note to Table 9-1, page 211.
[b] Total population.
n. a. Not available.
Source: Wilson H. Grabill, Clyde V. Kiser, and Pascal K. Whelpton, *The Fertility of American Women* (New York: Wiley, 1958), Table 6.

North Central Division). The postwar revival in fertility, as indicated by the figures for 1940 and 1950, reduced the regional differences substantially, since the largest increases were generally in the areas that previously had shown the greatest declines. Note the last row of the table, where for each date the smallest fertility ratio is compared with the largest; this gives a rough indication of the range over the whole country. During the nineteenth century the gap between extremes steadily widened, but it was narrower in 1950 than at any other time.

Whether any portion of the regional differences in fertility is due to variation among the regions per se is a moot point. The greater part, certainly, must be interpreted as reflections of other factors, especially rural-urban residence. The initially low and rapidly decreasing fertility in the Northeast, for example, follows from the family patterns of the oldest and densest urban areas. The decline would have been even greater but for such counter factors as, for instance, the settlement of large numbers of immigrants in this region.

Rural-Urban Residence

The difference in fertility between rural and urban residents has been one of the most marked, most persistent, and most significant in the nation's history. Fertility ratios for the first halves of the nineteenth and twentieth centuries are shown in Table 9-4. That the divergence was so

TABLE 9-4. Children under 5 per 1,000 Women Aged 20 to 44, White Population, by Residence, United States, 1800–1950

	U.S. Total	Rural [a]	Urban [a]	Urban as Per cent of Rural
1800	1,281	1,319	845	64.1
1810	1,290	1,329	900	67.7
1820	1,236	1,276	831	65.1
1830	1,134	1,189	708	59.5
1840	1,070	1,134	701	61.8
1910	609	782	469	60.0
1920	581	744	471	63.3
1930	485	658	388	59.0
1940	400	551	311	56.1
1950	551	673	479	71.2

[a] By the 1940 census classification.

Source: Wilson H. Grabill, Clyde V. Kiser, and Pascal K. Whelpton, *The Fertility of American Women* (New York: Wiley, 1958), Table 7.

great in 1800 may mean that fertility in the towns had been going down during a portion of the eighteenth century. And, as was noted in the previous chapter,[10] in 1950 fertility was still inversely correlated with size of place.

What is the meaning of this rural-urban contrast? As has often been pointed out, urban living conditions favor smaller families in a number of ways. City apartments permit expansion less comfortably than the one-family houses typical of villages and farms. Children are more expensive to rear when everything has to be bought than when at least a portion of the food is home-produced. On a farm minors help earn their keep by doing chores from a very young age on, while under urban conditions parents get no financial return, as it were, on their investment in off-

[10] See Table 8-3, page 191.

spring. In towns women are more likely to find alternative roles to being a housewife, and thus to postpone procreation or even to put it off altogether. In judging the probable weight of these factors—most of them economic—it must be remembered that in both urban and rural areas the usual correlation between wealth and size of family is negative, not positive.

Since at the beginning of the nineteenth century more than 90 per cent of the white women aged 20 to 44 were residents of the countryside, the rates shown in Table 9-4 for the United States as a whole and for its rural sector do not differ by very much in this period. The major importance of the smaller urban family was in the example it set. From 1810, when the decline in fertility ratios began, to 1940, when it ended, the national ratio fell off by 890 units. Of this total decline, 24 per cent can be ascribed to the further decrease in the size of town families, 20 per cent to the rural-urban shift of population, and 56 per cent to the decreased fertility in the countryside.[11] That is to say, the small-family system spread much more by the diffusion of urban ideas to rural areas than by the migration of rural persons to urban places, much more by urbanism than by urbanization. An explanation of the decline, then, cannot reasonably be limited to hypothesizing about the influences of the actual habitats in town and countryside. Differences in the way people live, though they might be posited as reasons for the size of the family in the two places, can hardly explain the decline in the rural fertility ratio. The relation between the two ratios, shown in the last column of Table 9-4, suggests a complex pattern. Note that the trend toward convergence up to 1920 was reversed during the next two decades, when urban fertility fell off very sharply, but was then re-established in the postwar period, including the years after 1950.[12]

Social Class

The influence of social class on family size can be measured by any one of a number of indexes—among others, occupation, income or wealth, and education. While the details differ according to the index used, the general conclusion is always more or less the same as far back as our information will take us. Using whatever data were available for the first

[11] Grabill, Kiser, and Whelpton, *op. cit.,* Table 8. For a similar conclusion from somewhat different data, see Bernard Okun, *Trends in Birth Rates in the United States since 1870* (Baltimore: Johns Hopkins Press, 1958), pp. 99–101.

[12] See U.S. Bureau of the Census, *Current Population Reports,* series P-20, no. 84 (August 8, 1958), Table 4.

**TABLE 9-5. Completed Family Size,[a] White Population, by
Major Occupation Group of Husband and Residence,
United States, 1910, 1940, 1950**

	1910		1940		1950	
	Urban	Rural Farm	Urban	Rural Farm	Urban	Rural Farm
Professional, technical, and kindred workers	2.8	4.3	2.0	2.9	1.7	3.0
Managers, officials, and proprietors, except farm	3.3	4.8	2.1	3.4	1.9	2.7
Clerical, sales, and kindred workers	3.1	4.7	2.0	3.0	1.9	2.8
Craftsmen, foremen, and kindred workers	4.0	5.2	2.6	4.0	2.3	3.5
Operatives and kindred workers	4.1	5.6	2.7	4.4	2.5	4.2
Service workers, including private household	3.9	—	2.5	—	2.3	3.5
Laborers, except farm and mine	4.8	5.5	3.2	4.4	3.1	4.4
Farmers and farm managers	4.2	5.6	2.7	4.1	3.1	3.6
Farm laborers and foremen	4.4	5.1	—	4.4	3.6	4.2

[a] Children ever born to women aged 45–49 years, married once, whose husbands were still living with them at the time of the census. Data are for white women in 1950, for native white women in 1910 and 1940. Rates are not shown when there were fewer than 1,200 women in 1910 or 3,000 in 1940.

Source: Wilson H. Grabill, Clyde V. Kiser, and Pascal K. Whelpton, *The Fertility of American Women* (New York: Wiley, 1958), Table 54.

several decades of the nineteenth century, Jaffe divided the urban populations of New York, Boston, and Providence by the taxes they paid; the rural counties of New York State by the per capita ownership of agricultural property; and the counties of several southern states by the number of slaves owned. In each case he found an inverse relation between wealth and family size, largest in the cities but significant also in the rural areas.[13] For each census from 1800 to 1920 Whelpton found that the higher the proportion of a state's population employed in industry, the lower its fertility ratio.[14]

Table 9-5 shows the completed family size of women aged 45 to 49 years according to the major occupation group of their husbands. It should be kept in mind that the women had had most of their children when they were in their twenties and early thirties—thus, 10 to 20 years

[13] A. J. Jaffe, "Differential Fertility in the White Population in Early America," *Journal of Heredity*, 31:9 (September, 1940), 407–411.
[14] P. K. Whelpton, "Industrial Development and Population Growth," *Social Forces*, 6:3 (March, 1928), 458–467.

before the census dates given. The contrast between urban and rural is sharp for each occupation group at all three dates, especially when (as in the table) the sponge class of "rural nonfarm" is eliminated. At the end of the nineteenth century (1910 census) a tendency was discernible within each residence class toward an inverse correlation of occupation and fertility, but after World War I (1940 census) there seems to have been some convergence. During the 1930's (1950 census), however, a clear progression in family size by occupational group was re-established, especially among the urban population. More than any other datum, these figures on family-building during the 1930's rule out a simple economic interpretation of fertility. During a major depression, when economic pressures bore heavily on all groups but most oppressively on those at the bottom of the social scale, the inverse relation between social class and fertility not only did not disappear but seems to have been more firmly established than in prior decades.

Differentials by the education of the wife, as shown in Table 9-6, are parallel to those by the occupation of the husband, except that the contrasts stand out even more clearly. Education has several advantages over occupation as an index of social class. There is no question about ordering: under all circumstances, college can be ranked above high school, but the same cannot be said of a professional, for example, as compared with a managerial position. Also, comparisons by husband's occupation

TABLE 9–6. Completed Family Size,[a] White Population,
by Education of Wife and Residence,
United States, 1940 and 1950

	Per Woman				Per Wife			
	1940		*1950*		*1940*		*1950*	
	Urban	*Rural Farm*	*Urban*	*Rural Farm*	*Urban*	*Rural Farm*	*Urban*	*Rural Farm*
College:								
4 years or more	1.1	1.8	1.0	1.6	1.8	2.2	1.4	1.8
1–3 years	1.5	2.5	1.4	2.1	1.9	2.8	1.6	2.2
High School:								
4 years	1.6	2.6	1.5	2.5	1.8	2.8	1.7	2.6
1–3 years	2.0	3.4	1.9	3.1	2.2	3.6	2.1	3.3
Elementary or none	2.5	4.2	2.4	3.9	2.8	4.4	2.6	4.1

[a] Number of children ever born to women aged 45–49 years. Data are for white women in 1950, for native white women in 1940.

Source: Wilson H. Grabill, Clyde V. Kiser, and Pascal K. Whelpton, *The Fertility of American Women* (New York: Wiley, 1958), Tables 75 and 76.

often reflect the fact that young men start in low-level jobs and rise during their lifetime. Since in any one year their wives will usually have more children while they are younger, an annual rate (such as the birth rate, thought not a cumulative rate, like the completed family size) will generally exaggerate class differences in fertility. Education, however, is ordinarily completed as a unit and then becomes a fixed attribute of adults for the rest of their lives.

Another advantage of education as an index is that it applies to all women and not, like the occupation of the husband, only to those who are married. Thus, Table 9-6 indicates the significant effect of differential marriage patterns on fertility: the gradients for completed family size are somewhat steeper per woman than per wife. Among white women aged 45 to 49 years in 1950, for example, a quarter of the college graduates had never married, as compared with less than 6 per cent of those with eight years or less of schooling; [15] and such a contrast can be noted also for earlier dates.

When data are available, income as an index of social class has special advantages. Like education, but unlike occupation, there is no problem of ranking: a higher income is higher. And it can be argued that family income is a better index of style of life than either the rather gross groups into which occupations are classified or the education of the wife, who may have married up or down the social scale. In any case, the J-shaped curve that is sometimes vaguely suggested with other indices of social class often comes out clearly with a monetary criterion: among families of successively lower incomes, the number of children decreases slightly and then, from the upper-middle bracket down, increases steadily.

What is the meaning of class differentials in fertility?

The trends and patterns described above are indirect evidence strongly supporting the view that the practice of family limitation has gradually diffused from the upper to the lower socio-economic strata. . . . Alternative explanations can hardly account for the divergence of class fertility-rates followed by their convergence, the low fertility in occupations such as clerical and sales work and minor government employment, which are characterized by a combination of "bourgeois" standards of living with incomes lower than those of professional people, employers, and even some groups of manual workers.[16]

According to a corollary of this theory, the small-family system is particularly characteristic of persons rising in the social scale. A man can

[15] Grabill, Kiser, and Whelpton, *op. cit.*, Table 67.
[16] Dennis H. Wrong, "Trends in Class Fertility in Western Nations," *Canadian Journal of Economics and Political Science*, 24:2 (May, 1958), 216–229.

move farther and faster with fewer dependents. In an upwardly mobile family, moreover, the level of aspiration is typically higher than can be satisfied, whatever the income may be. By such a standard, there is never enough to go around, so that—however paradoxical it may be in simple economic terms—persons of middle incomes are often under heavier financial pressure than those who earn less. The hypothesis relating social mobility to family size is one plausible explanation of the historical trend,[17] but several recent studies indicate that it no longer holds today.[18] It would seem that in today's affluent society it is not necessary, at least for large sectors of the middle class, to choose between family growth and other values.

The class differential in fertility was, so to speak, the route by which the small-family system was gradually introduced to the whole population. This transitional phase was interrupted by the postwar revival in the birth rate, which in general has been largest in the classes that had shown the greatest prior decline, and smallest among those groups—for example, farm laborers and urban unskilled workers—that before the war had the most children. From both ends of the social-economic scale, thus, the present trend seems to be toward convergence. Indeed, some demographers have gone so far as to predict that "class fertility-differences are destined to disappear as a feature of the demographic structure of Western populations," [19] or even that "students of differential fertility some day may well be seeking explanations of a direct rather than an inverse relationship between education, occupation and fertility." [20]

Religion

Most of what information we have on the fertility of various denominations is based on detailed investigations of one particular community or of a sample of its population. A good example of such a local survey is the one made in Indianapolis in 1941. If the Protestants there are taken as

[17] For an especially detailed and convincing study of the process in nineteenth-century Britain, see J. A. Banks, *Prosperity and Parenthood: A Study of Family Planning among the Victorian Middle Class* (London: Routledge & Kegan Paul, 1954).

[18] See, for example, Charles F. Westoff *et al., Family Growth in Metropolitan America* (announced by Princeton University Press for publication in 1961); Seymour Yellin, "Social Mobility and Familism," unpublished doctoral dissertation, Northwestern University, 1955. In his especially careful analysis of a sample of white urban salesmen, engineers, and bankers, Yellin found that intergenerational mobility had no discernible influence on "familism," as measured by the number of children among other factors.

[19] Wrong, "Trends in Class Fertility," *op. cit.*

[20] Charles F. Westoff, "Differential Fertility in the United States: 1900 to 1952," *American Sociological Review,* 19:5 (October, 1954), 549–561.

the norm, the fertility rate standardized for age of mothers was about 18 per cent higher among Catholics, and about 25 per cent lower among Jews.[21] This contrast, similar to that found elsewhere, is difficult to interpret. The effect of religion per se on the reproductive behavior of most persons is probably close to nil. The small family size of Jews derives rather from their concentration in cities, especially in those urban occupations that are always associated with a low fertility. Similarly, family size varies among the major Protestant denominations as one would expect from the typical social class of their membership, and can be denoted a specific effect of the group's religious doctrines only in a few minor sects. The one numerically significant faith that has an important effect would seem to be Catholicism; and even here the data are not consistent.

In the 1930's the birth rate of Catholics was higher than that of non-Catholics but declining faster, and the general prognosis was that the difference would eventually disappear. "It is quite clear that the main reason why Catholic fertility is falling more rapidly arises from the fact that it has farther to fall; because there has been, in fact, a cultural lag." [22] A number of analyses, however, in particular one by Dudley Kirk, suggest that Catholic fertility is considerably higher than the national average and that the prior convergence has been reversed.[23] According to the compilation of baptisms in the *Official Catholic Directory* that Kirk cites, the trend in Catholic births as a percentage of the total number of births in the country has been as follows:

1920	21
1930–1934	23
1935–1939	22
1940–1944	22
1945–1949	24
1953	27.3

The figures are given in this form because the population base on which a birth rate would be computed—the number of Catholics in a particular year—is difficult to estimate. It is growing by natural increase, net immi-

[21] P. K. Whelpton and Clyde V. Kiser, *Social and Psychological Factors Affecting Fertility* (New York: Milbank Memorial Fund, 1946), 1, 6–8.

[22] Norman E. Himes, *Medical History of Contraception* (Baltimore: Williams & Wilkins, 1936), p. 413. Cf. Samuel A. Stouffer, "Trends in the Fertility of Catholics and Non-Catholics," *American Journal of Sociology*, 41:2 (September, 1935), 143–166; A. J. Jaffe, "Religious Differentials in the Net Reproduction Rate," *Journal of the American Statistical Association*, 34:206 (June, 1939), 335–342. For a good bibliography on the subject, see Hugh E. Brooks and Franklin J. Henry, "An Empirical Study of the Relationships of Catholic Practice and Occupational Mobility to Fertility," *Milbank Memorial Fund Quarterly*, 36:3 (July, 1958), 222–280.

[23] Dudley Kirk, "Recent Trends of Catholic Fertility in the United States," in Milbank Memorial Fund, *Current Research in Human Fertility* (New York, 1955), pp. 93–105.

gration, and net conversion; and all three of these components are more or less indeterminate. In recent years, moreover, almost a fourth of all "valid" Catholic marriages—that is, those performed by a priest in which both partners promise that any offspring shall be raised in the Church—have been mixed, so that the population contributing to Catholic baptisms apparently is somewhat larger than the number of practicing members of this denomination. If a birth rate is calculated nevertheless, in Kirk's opinion it was between 29 and 35 per thousand in 1953, or some five to ten points higher than the general one.

Such estimates seem to be much too high, however, when they are compared with the only census data we have on the matter. As can be seen from Table 9-7, the Catholic fertility rate, and especially the completed family size, are a little higher than the national average, but not by nearly so large a proportion as had been thought earlier. Both rates are still higher for Baptists.

TABLE 9-7. Fertility Rates and Completed Family Size,
by Religion, United States, 1957

	Children per 1,000 Women Aged:		
	15 to 44 Years		45 Years and Over
		a	
Protestant	2,220	2,206	2,753
Baptist	2,359	2,381	3,275
Methodist	2,155	2,115	2,638
Lutheran	2,013	1,967	2,382
Presbyterian	2,001	1,922	2,188
Other Protestant	2,237	2,234	2,702
Roman Catholic	2,282	2,210	3,056
Jewish	1,749	b	2,218
Other, none, or not reported	2,069	2,075	2,674
Total population	2,218	2,188	2,798

a Standardized for age.

b Not computed because there were fewer than 150,000 in several of the 5-year age groups.

Source: U.S. Bureau of the Census, *Statistical Abstract of the United States, 1958* (Washington: U.S. Government Printing Office, 1958), Table 40, based on a survey in March 1957.

These census data are in line with a survey of 2,713 white married women aged 18 through 39 and living with their husbands, chosen as a probability sample of the approximately 17 million women with these characteristics. As shown in Table 9-8, the number of children already

**TABLE 9-8. Average Number of Actual and Total Expected
Births per Wife, by Age of Woman and Religion,
United States, 1955**

Age of Cohort	Religion			Total
	Protestant	*Catholic*	*Other*	
	Births by 1955			
35–39	2.6	2.6	1.7	2.6
30–34	2.3	2.3	2.2	2.3
25–29	2.0	1.9	1.3	1.9
18–24	1.1	1.1	a	1.1
18–39	2.1	2.1	1.6	2.1
	Most Likely Completed Family Size			
35–39	2.8	3.1	2.0	2.9
30–34	2.9	3.3	2.6	3.0
25–29	3.0	3.5	2.5	3.1
18–24	2.9	3.8	a	3.2
18–39	2.9	3.4	2.4	3.0

a Fewer than 20 couples in base group.
Source: Ronald Freedman, Pascal K. Whelpton, and Arthur A. Campbell, *Family
Planning, Sterility, and Population Growth* (New York: McGraw-Hill, 1959), Table
9-1. By permission. Copyright, 1959, McGraw-Hill Book Company, Inc.

born to Catholic mothers was almost precisely the same in each age-group
as the average for Protestants. The Catholic women had married when
they were an average of 1.5 years older than the Protestant, and during
the shorter period of exposure had procreated at a higher rate. This more
intensive childbearing is reflected in the contrast between the expected
completed families, 3.4 children to Catholic parents as against 2.9 children to Protestant.

There is a certain underlying agreement in these somewhat inconsistent data—namely, that Catholicism per se tends to induce a high
fertility. This would be so even if there were no difference in the average
family size; for Catholics, like Jews, are predominantly urban, so that if
the weight of other factors were equal their fertility ought to be lower
than that of Protestants, who are distributed between the rural and urban
sectors. The Catholic Church prohibits its members from practicing any
mode of birth control except the so-called rhythm method, which is less
efficient than the best mechanical and chemical contraceptives; and even
this method is sanctioned, strictly speaking, only for serious reasons. The
inconsistency among various data may be due, at least in part, to a com-

plex change going on, the composite effect of the rise of a higher proportion of American Catholics to the middle class; a probable consequent
increase in the number practicing some method of birth control, whether
sanctioned or not; and changes in the Church's position on family planning.[24]

Race

The birth rate of free Negroes has always been higher than that of
whites. The data are not good enough to elaborate this statement, particularly for the early period, but the contrast itself is certainly a fact.
The reason for the difference is obvious enough: as we have noted
earlier, until World War I Negroes were heavily concentrated in the
rural South, the economic sector and the region that in general show
the highest fertility. As they began to migrate in large numbers to northern cities, their over-all fertility went down, establishing a very sharp
rural-urban difference in size of Negro families. Thus, in the 1930's it
was anticipated that their birth rate would gradually converge with the
national average.

In fact, however, this has not happened. As shown in Figure 9-1, the
white birth rate reached a peak in 1947 and then leveled off at a somewhat lower number, while that of the Negroes continued to increase over
the whole postwar period. During this same decade, as the figure indicates, the death rates of the two races have continued to converge, so
that the Negroes' natural increase has gone up even faster. The divergence
is not due to a difference in the age structure: it is about the same when
general fertility rates (the number of births per 1,000 women in the childbearing age-group) are compared.[25]

The reversal in the prior decline in Negro fertility is, on the face of it,
much more startling than the similar trend noted by Kirk among Catholics. Negroes have no culture trait that affects natality independently
of their occupation or education. Race is not a cause of family size but
an index of social class. What is there about the social situation of Negroes
that has led to this recent rise?

American Negroes are divided between the two poles of American
civilization, the depth of the rural South and the metropolitan areas of
the rest of the country. Many individuals were born and brought up at

---

[24] These matters are discussed at greater length below, pages 556–559.
[25] See Clyde V. Kiser, "Fertility Trends and Differentials among Nonwhites in the
United States," *Milbank Memorial Fund Quarterly*, 36:2 (April, 1958), 149–197.

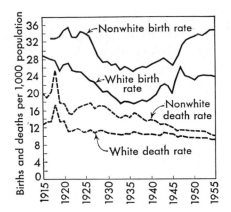

Figure 9-1. Births and Deaths per 1,000 Population by Color, United States, 1915–1955.ᵃ

ᵃ Birth rates were—and death rates were not—adjusted for underregistration and for the states not included in the respective registration area. The two series, therefore, are not wholly comparable, especially for the period before 1933.

Source: Compilations by the National Office of Vital Statistics, in Clyde V. Kiser, "Fertility Trends and Differentials among Nonwhites in the United States," *Milbank Memorial Fund Quarterly,* 36:2 (April, 1958), 149–197, Figure 1.

one and then moved to the other to live. The contrast in life-styles is reflected in, among other things, the size of the family. Note the figures in Table 9-9. Well over half of the nonwhite women are distributed between the two extremes, with either no children at all or more than four. The *general* decline in fertility, as we noted above, was more the con-

TABLE 9-9. Per Cent Distribution of Completed Family Size,ᵃ by Color, United States, 1950

Number of Children	White	Nonwhite
None	18.2	27.3
1	19.1	13.8
2	23.6	12.6
3	14.8	10.5
4	9.0	7.6
5 or more	15.4	28.1
Total	100	100

ᵃ Children ever born to women aged 45–49 years, married once, whose husbands were still living with them at the time of the census.

Source: U.S. Bureau of the Census, reported in Clyde V. Kiser, "Fertility Trends and Differentials among Nonwhites in the United States," *Milbank Memorial Fund Quarterly,* 36:2 (April, 1958), 149–197, Table 8.

sequence of the diffusion of urban culture to the countryside than of the migration of rural persons to towns; but among poorly educated rural Negroes natality tended to remain high, while in the cities Negro couples often had no children at all. The recent rise is largely the consequence of the sharp reduction in the proportion of these childless families, particularly among younger cohorts. One reason may be greater fecundity. According to various incomplete data, the incidence of gonorrhea and syphilis, and thus also of sterility and fetal deaths, used to be much higher among Negroes; [26] and in the postwar period venereal diseases were brought under better control through the use of antibiotics and improved community education. It is probable also that there has been a sufficient change in the social climate of urban communities to have influenced family size. If childlessness is seen as a symptom of social disorganization, a concomitant of the rapid urbanization of country-born Negroes, then a trend toward a family size approximating the white urban norm might have been anticipated with the development of established Negro populations in the northern cities.

In other words, in spite of the postwar reversal, there is good reason to expect that the differential birth rates by race will begin to converge again in the near future. As can be seen in Figure 9-2, among the urban populations with comparable education the fertility of whites is higher, while only Negroes in the rural-farm class have larger families. Both the continuing rural-urban migration and whatever upward social mobility this entails will presumably re-establish the downward trend in the Negro birth rate.[27]

PSYCHOLOGICAL FACTORS AFFECTING FERTILITY

Fertility varies not only from one social group to another, but also, within each, according to the personality and temperament of the individual. Of the various analyses that have concentrated on the psyche, the largest and most significant is the Indianapolis study, "Social and Psychological Factors Affecting Fertility." This was published in 33 articles in the *Milbank Memorial Fund Quarterly*, and later bound in five volumes.[28] It was in many respects a pioneer effort, with the virtues and also

26 For some evidence on this point, see *ibid.*, pp. 190–195.
27 See Anne and Everett S. Lee, "The Future Fertility of the American Negro," *Social Forces,* 37:3 (March, 1959), 228–231.
28 See in particular the final article, Clyde V. Kiser and P. K. Whelpton, "Summary of Chief Findings and Implications for Future Studies," *Milbank Memorial Fund Quarterly,* 36:3 (July, 1958), 282–329. This includes references to previous articles in the series and to various discussions of the study.

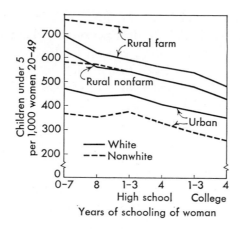

Figure 9-2. Fertility Rates Standardized for Age, by Color, Education, and Rural-Urban Residence, United States, 1950.

Source: Anne and Everett S. Lee, "The Future Fertility of the American Negro," *Population Index,* 24:3 (July, 1958), 215.

the faults one might expect from any attempt to break new ground; and it also shows the advantages and the limitations of any analysis of psychological rather than social variables.

After a preliminary household survey of most of Indianapolis (from which it was possible, as we have noted, to compare the fertility of religious denominations), couples were divided into "relatively fecund" and "relatively sterile" classes, depending on whether there had been any considerable periods during which intercourse without birth control had not resulted in conception. A more detailed analysis was restricted to a sample of 1,444 relatively fecund native white Protestant couples, who had been married during 1927–1929 and had lived in a large city most of the time since then. Of this group, 98 per cent reported some experience with contraception; 14 per cent had planned the number, and an additional 28 per cent both the number and spacing of all pregnancies. Information was also gathered on the type of contraceptive used and its relative efficiency.

The main body of the study, however, related not to such behavior patterns but rather to the more difficult problem of psychological motivation. A rather miscellaneous list of 23 hypotheses on the factors possibly affecting either planned or actual family size were tested. Of these, three pertained to the effect of economic security, five to the family background and health of the potential parents, five to their expressed interest in children and their home, eight to their personality characteristics (feelings of inadequacy, fear of pregnancy, general tendency to plan, conformity to group patterns, etc.), and two to the relations between husband and wife. Of course, some such psychological variables are implicitly assumed in a standard differential analysis: if urban families are smaller than rural, it is because the life conditions of each city dweller, his aspirations, his possibilities, and so on, combine to make this so. An attempt to analyze motives directly, however, encounters special difficulties, some of which can be exemplified from this study.

One of the hypotheses, for instance, was the following: "The greater the difference between the actual level of living and the standard of living desired, the higher the proportion of couples practicing contraception effectively and the smaller the planned families." To test this, respondents were asked what they would like in order to live in a satisfactory manner, and their reply was compared with their actual mode of living. Very often a person with a second-hand car, for instance, expressed the desire for a new one, while someone who owned a new Cadillac, say, indicated his satisfaction with it. Economic tension decreased with greater incomes, rather than the contrary, as it should have to validate the hypothesis. Yet probably no demographer doubts the at least partial validity of the thesis as stated; indeed, when it was negated, the analysts rejected their own findings. They still held that one important reason for the inverse relation between social class and family size is that the tension consequent from aspiring to more than one can afford is usually the greater the higher the income. In short, we cannot measure attitudes like levels of aspiration nearly so accurately as the behavior patterns associated with them, so that if respondents say one thing but do another, we accept the latter as the more meaningful. In this case the usual difficulty was aggravated by the fact that the verbal responses referred to motives for behavior as much as 15 years before the interviews took place.

Another of the hypotheses tested in the Indianapolis study was the following: "The stronger the interest in and liking for children, the lower the proportion of couples practicing contraception effectively and the larger the planned family." If one grants that it is possible to measure "liking" for children with reasonable accuracy from what people say, and if this proves to be positively correlated with the size of the family, then it would seem to be just as likely (as the analysts themselves point out) that couples who have children have learned to like them as vice versa. Indeed, it is difficult in most social analysis, once a correlation has been established, to distinguish between cause and effect; but it is particularly so in social psychology.

A still more probable cause-effect relation, both in this instance and generally, is that the independent variables cited in the 23 hypotheses and the supposed effects of planned and actual family size were both consequences of the relatively undifferentiated culture pattern of this white Protestant sample of a midwestern city. As the authors put it: "Our measures of psychological characteristics probably were too crude to afford precise differentiations, [and] it may be little wonder that the Study failed to indicate strong and consistent relations of fertility behavior to psychological characteristics" among so homogeneous a sample.[29] "The chief lesson" to be learned from the Indianapolis study, according to the men who directed it, is that fertility is generally more closely related to "broad social factors (including the economic)" than to psychological. Both family planning and actual fertility were clearly correlated with social-economic status; but when this variable was held constant, "the observed relation of fertility behavior to most of the psychological characteristics considered was generally much less pronounced or less regular."[30]

The main value of the Indianapolis study, perhaps, is that it demonstrated certain procedures to be unsuitable, and that such a wide range of unrelated hypotheses cannot be fruitfully tested by any method. In particular, the post factum analysis of psychological variables almost invites systematic error, which cannot be checked against other data. If a couple is asked what size family they planned some 15 years earlier, what measures they took to carry out their plan, and what the results were, the vagaries of human memory are such that many respondents will work back from the actual size of their family to the conclusion that this is what they had intended. Only a longitudinal or panel study, following a sample of couples from their marriage through their entire child-bearing period, can overcome the limitations inherent in such retrospective data.[31] And longitudinal studies have their own disadvantages—first of all, that they are inordinately expensive. Several analyses of the psychological factors in fertility have been made or are in process, and in these the lessons

[29] *Ibid.,* p. 323.
[30] *Ibid.,* pp. 318–319.
[31] *Ibid.,* pp. 323–324.

learned from the errors made in the Indianapolis study have been put to good use.[32]

TRENDS IN FAMILY FORMATION

The word *family* has a wide range of meaning—those actually or putatively descended from a common ancestor; more or less closely related kin; or what is termed the **nuclear family**, the biological unit of husband, wife, and their children. The word is used in the last sense when we speak of "family size" in studies of fertility. The Census Bureau, however, uses still another definition of **family:** two or more persons living together who are related by blood, marriage, or adoption. In addition to the wife and children of the head of the family, thus, the census definition includes other relatives of his living in the same house, but excludes grown children or an estranged spouse living elsewhere. For studies of living arrangements, dependency, and family income, the census definition is the preferable one; but it means that census data are less useful than they otherwise might be for the analysis of fertility.[33]

The age at which people marry on the average, and the proportion of the population that eventually gets married, are obviously important determinants of fertility. These figures are given in Table 9-10, but it must be emphasized that the median ages are approximate only, sufficiently accurate to indicate no more than the general trend.[34] For females they fluctuated between 1890 and 1940 and then in the following two decades fell off by 1.2 years. For males, similarly, there was a decline by 3.3 years from 1890 to 1960. In part as a reflection of this lower age, the proportion married of those aged 14 and over increased from somewhat more than half in 1890 to over two-thirds in 1960.

Table 9-11 shows the mean (*not* the median) age at marriage according to education. The numerically insignificant group with less than four years of schooling (for which data are in any case quite unsatisfactory) can be ignored. Among all classes the age was lower in 1950, and more

[32] For a list of some of these studies, see *ibid.,* pp. 324–326. In his presidential address to the Population Association of America, however, Dudley Kirk offered a contrary opinion: "I predict that the 1960's will see a growing disenchantment with intensive studies of individual attitudes in relation to family size. I suspect that greater emphasis in the future will be placed on studies of what people do rather than on what they say they think." See "Some Reflections on American Demography in the Nineteen Sixties," *Population Index,* 26:4 (October, 1960), 305–310.

[33] See Paul C. Glick, *American Families* (New York: Wiley, 1957), pp. 210–216.

[34] *Ibid.,* p. 54, n. 2. See also the exchange between Thomas P. Monahan and A. Ross Eckler in *American Journal of Sociology,* 56:2 (September, 1950), 180–187; 56:3 (November, 1950), 268–270.

**TABLE 9-10. Age at Marriage and Proportion Married,
United States, 1890–1960**

Years	Median Age at First Marriage		Percentage Married of Persons Aged 14 and Over	
	Males	Females	Males	Females
1890	26.1	22.0	52.1	54.8
1900	25.9	21.9	52.8	55.2
1910	25.1	21.6	54.2	57.1
1920	24.6	21.2	57.6	58.9
1930	24.3	21.3	58.4	59.5
1940	24.3	21.5	59.7	59.5
1950	22.8	20.1	68.2	66.1
1960	22.8	20.3	69.3	68.0

Sources: U.S. Bureau of the Census, *U.S. Census of Population: 1950*, vol. 2, *Characteristics of the Population,* part 1, U.S. Summary (Washington: U.S. Government Printing Office, 1953), p. 1–97; *Current Population Reports*, series P-20, no. 105 (November 2, 1960). U.S. National Office of Vital Statistics, *Vital Statistics of the United States, 1953* (Washington: U.S. Government Printing Office, 1955), 1, xxxiii.

**TABLE 9-11. Mean Age at Marriage, White Population,
by Education, United States, 1940 and 1950**

Education Completed	Males		Females		Decrease	
	1940	1950	1940	1950	Males	Females
College:						
4 years or more	27.7	25.7	25.4	23.2	2.0	2.2
1–3 years	26.7	25.4	24.3	22.5	1.3	1.8
High school:						
4 years	26.5	24.3	23.6	21.4	2.2	2.1
1–3 years	25.1	23.3	21.5	20.1	1.8	1.4
Grammar school:						
5–8 years	25.3	23.5	21.4	19.9	1.7	1.5
1–4 years	24.7	24.0	21.5	21.0	0.7	0.5
No schooling	27.5	27.1	25.3	23.9	0.4	1.4

Source: Christopher Tietze and Patience Lauriat, "Age at Marriage and Educational Attainment in the United States," *Population Studies,* 9:2 (November, 1955), 159–166.

so for high-school and college graduates than for those with less education. The convergence was especially marked among females: the difference between grammar-school and college graduates fell off from 4.0 to 3.3 years in one decade.

The trend toward earlier marriage is surprising, since over the same period the amount of preparatory training needed to begin remunerative work has certainly increased on the average, and in particular the proportion of adolescents attending college has gone up sharply. But the pattern of social maturation has changed. Sons of the middle class, who used to make up the larger part of the college population, had a regular progression prescribed for them: earn a degree, find a job and get established in it, marry, then—and not before—have children. This postponement of family formation until his late twenties or early thirties was the price a young man paid to start in a good position. Whether the pattern would have survived the spread of college education to greater numbers and different social classes can perhaps be questioned. In any case, it was shattered by the war. Veterans going to college were four or five years older than the standard student body, and in other respects still more mature. They could live, single or married, on their income under the so-called G.I. Bill. In 1947, thus, an estimated 200,000 college students were married; and once the pattern was set, it continued without the impetus of veterans' benefits. In the fall of 1956, one out of every four college students was married; among students in the typical college age, 18 to 24, one out of every six.[35] Age for age, the proportion married was higher among those not in school; but these latter were generally self-supporting.

How do married college students manage economically? There are no precise data on this point. One important factor has been the increasing opportunities for employment open to young women, particularly those with above-average education. But if some girls support their student-husbands, others become mothers; and in that case the couple must usually depend on their parents to help provide for the grandchild.[36] By prewar norms, such behavior is unbelievably irresponsible. That it is accepted today may mean that the isolation of the nuclear family, presumably one of the concomitants of the previous low fertility in this country, has been reduced, or was exaggerated in earlier analyses.

Not only among college students but generally, it would seem that

---

[35] Paul C. Glick and Hugh Carter, "Marriage Patterns and Educational Level," *American Sociological Review*, 23:3 (June, 1958), 294–300.

[36] Cf. Marvin B. Sussman, "The Help Pattern in the Middle Class Family," *American Sociological Review*, 18:2 (February, 1953), 22–28; "The Isolated Nuclear Family: Fact or Fiction," *Social Problems*, 6:4 (Spring, 1959), 333–340. For an especially stimulating discussion of the implications of this trend, see Elbridge Sibley, "Higher Education and Earlier Parenthood: A Changing Cycle of Family Life," *Antioch Review*, Spring, 1957, pp. 45–59.

The pattern seems to be moving down into the high schools. In Dallas in 1958, for example, there were 480 married pupils (including nine in grade schools), who had a total of 72 children. The Parent-Teacher Association was alarmed but could not decide on remedial measures. See *Time*, May 25, 1959.

many now get married on a shoestring. In the early 1950's one out of every five couples postponed for a year setting up a home of their own, one out of every eight for three years. Even so, there is a tendency to start having children early. No precise data are available on the average interval from marriage to the birth of the first child. For those women aged 30 to 34 years in 1950 who had had three children, the median interval was 1.7 years; and half of all their first births occurred before the couples had been married 30 months. "These figures are probably about the same as those which would be obtained if a wider age range and all orders of births were covered." [37] And "more young wives than formerly are having their second child relatively soon after their first, and their third relatively soon after their second." [38]

Women who just reached the end of their childbearing period (aged 45–49 years) in 1952 had borne on the average 2.35 children, and the median age at which they bore their last child was 26.1 years. It must be emphasized, however, that this is not the same group of women as those marrying and having their first children in the postwar period. A 20-year-old girl who married in 1950 had been born in 1930; but the women who just completed their fecund period in 1950 had been born in 1901–1905, and they gave birth to their last child, on the average, in 1927–1931. *If* the young women of today follow this same pattern, they will complete their childbearing some five to six years earlier than their grandmothers in 1890. Their children presumably will also marry early; if so, the last one will leave home when the mother is still in her late forties. The trend toward the earlier retirement of men, it has often been pointed out, has aggravated the problems associated with aging; but if we regard the bearing and rearing of children as the main task of women, then under present conditions they are "retired" some 10 to 15 years earlier than their husbands, and for a substantial portion of this period many of them are widows.

All of these figures, however, are based on the—probably invalid—assumption that the young women of today will follow the family cycle of the previous generation. In many respects, these two groups of women are quite different. The fact that the age at marriage fell so drastically should warn us against assuming that any other factor will remain stable. That is one reason why any measure of fertility based on the number of births during a single year is inadequate, whether an unpretentious one like the crude birth rate or an elaborate one like the net reproduction

[37] Glick, *American Families*, pp. 64–65.
[38] Grabill, Kiser, and Whelpton, *op. cit.*, p. 330.

rate.[39] For a long-term analysis, the only adequate index is completed family size—the number of children on the average that women bear during the whole of their lifetime—but it has the obvious disadvantage that it cannot be used to measure current trends. Many of the women who took part in the unprecedented rise in fertility in the mid-1940's were relatively young; let us say that they were aged 20 to 24 years in 1945. This means that they will reach the end of their childbearing period only around 1970, and until that date it is impossible to be sure whether the baby boom represented an increase in average family size or merely a rearrangement of some of its components.

An approach to this question can be made by cohort analysis.[40] A birth cohort is a group of persons all born at the same time, who are analyzed as a unit through their lifetime. For example, those born during the twelve months centering on January 1, 1900, constitute the cohort of 1900.[41] Table 9-12 illustrates how useful this method is in breaking down the several factors in any fertility rate.[42] The first row concerns girls who were born during 1936–1940 and were aged 15 to 19 years at the beginning of 1955; that is, on January 1, 1955, the average age of the girls in the cohort of 1940 was exactly 15 years, for those in the cohort of 1939 it was exactly 16 years, and so on. The next column gives the cumulative birth rate; this means that the five cohorts had had a total of 77 births per 1,000, of which 65 were first births, and so on.

It is evident that a large part of the baby boom was due to the higher fertility of young women. In Table 9-12, the cumulative birth rate of cohorts aged 15–19 years increased from 50 in 1910 to 77 in 1955, that of those aged 20–24 from 568 to 789, that of those aged 25–29 from 1,453 to 1,642. Note that the percentage increase declines for higher ages. The 1955 cumulative birth rates for cohorts aged 30–34 years, while higher than for the immediately preceding period, are lower than for 1910; and those for cohorts aged 45 and over are lower in 1955 than at any preceding date.

What of the order of births? Of course, most of the teen-age girls giving

---

[39] For the definitions of these terms, see pages 622, 625.

[40] The following discussion is based on Grabill, Kiser, and Whelpton, *op. cit.,* Ch. 9.

[41] One can also analyze fertility using "marriage cohorts," groups of women who all married in the same year. For the United States, however, data are not available for the latter analysis, and for convenience "birth cohorts" are called simply cohorts in this chapter.

[42] A similar table for all women (rather than only native white women) and brought up to 1958 is given in U.S. National Office of Vital Statistics, "Fertility Tables for Birth Cohorts of American Women, Part 1," *Vital Statistics—Special Reports,* vol. 51, no. 1 (Washington; U.S. Government Printing Office, 1960).

birth were having their first baby; but in 1955, 11 per 1,000 births to mothers aged 15–19 were second births, and one per 1,000 was a third one. Compare the women aged 20–24 in 1955 with those aged 20–24 in 1940, the last group before the baby boom started. That there should have

TABLE 9-12. Cumulative Birth Rates, by Order of Birth, for Cohorts of Native White Women, United States, 1910–1955

Cohorts of—	Jan. 1 of—	All Births	Order of Birth							
			First	Second	Third	Fourth	Fifth	Sixth	Seventh	Eighth and Higher
Exact ages 15 to 19[a]										
1936–1940	1955	77	65	11	1	(b)	...	...	...	...
1931–1935	1950	67	57	9	1	(b)	...	...	...	...
1926–1930	1945	44	39	5	1	(b)	...	...	...	...
1921–1925	1940	44	39	5	(b)	(b)	...	...	...	...
1916–1920	1935	41	36	4	(b)	(b)	...	...	...	...
1911–1915	1930	49	43	5	(b)	(b)	...	...	...	...
1906–1910	1925	51	45	5	(b)	(b)	...	...	...	...
1901–1905	1920	43	38	5	(b)	(b)	...	...	...	...
1896–1900[c]	...1915	49	43	5	(b)	(b)	...	...	...	...
1891–1895[c]	...1910	50	44	6	(b)	(b)	...	...	...	...
Exact ages 20 to 24[a]										
1931–1935	1955	789	479	222	67	17	4	1	(b)	(b)
1926–1930	1950	636	427	159	39	9	2	(b)	(b)	(b)
1921–1925	1945	520	348	125	36	9	2	(b)	(b)	(b)
1916–1920	1940	453	308	108	29	7	1	(b)	(b)	(b)
1911–1915	1935	454	300	112	32	8	2	(b)	(b)	(b)
1906–1910	1930	526	340	133	40	10	2	1	(b)	(b)
1901–1905	1925	560	358	144	44	11	2	1	(b)	(b)
1896–1900[c]	...1920	533	339	138	44	10	2	(b)	(b)	(b)
1891–1895[c]	...1915	557	349	146	48	12	2	(b)	(b)	(b)
1886–1890[c]	...1910	568	349	151	50	14	3	(b)	(b)	(b)
Exact ages 25 to 29[a]										
1926–1930	1955	1,642	757	519	233	87	30	10	3	2
1921–1925	1950	1,389	715	415	163	60	22	8	3	1
1916–1920	1945	1,188	621	337	140	57	22	8	3	1
1911–1915	1940	1,064	555	293	127	55	22	8	3	1
1906–1910	1935	1,149	567	320	151	69	28	10	3	2
1901–1905	1930	1,275	604	357	178	83	34	13	4	2
1896–1900[c]	...1925	1,331	618	373	191	91	37	14	5	2
1891–1895[c]	...1920	1,335	619	372	194	91	37	15	5	2
1886–1890[c]	...1915	1,417	629	389	220	109	46	17	5	2
1881–1885[c]	...1910	1,453	632	394	228	119	52	19	6	3
Exact ages 30 to 34[a]										
1921–1925	1955	2,126	845	648	346	158	69	32	15	12
1916–1920	1950	1,857	789	554	274	126	60	29	14	11
1911–1915	1945	1,638	715	462	230	115	59	30	15	12
1906–1910	1940	1,639	689	445	238	129	69	37	18	14
1901–1905	1935	1,795	704	478	277	159	88	48	23	17
1896–1900[c]	...1930	1,938	724	510	310	183	105	57	29	20
1891–1895[c]	...1925	2,016	742	521	326	198	113	62	31	23
1886–1890[c]	...1920	2,076	747	533	340	209	118	68	35	26
1881–1885[c]	...1915	2,175	757	544	362	230	136	76	40	30
1876–1880[c]	...1910	2,282	759	545	380	256	163	95	48	36

TABLE 9-12. (Continued)

		Exact ages 35 to 39[a]								
1916–1920	1955	2,278	839	653	376	195	99	53	29	35
1911–1915	1950	2,046	782	567	316	168	91	53	30	38
1906–1910	1945	1,987	748	524	299	172	100	61	36	46
1901–1905	1940	2,112	745	533	327	201	123	78	47	58
1896–1900[c]	...1935	2,300	760	563	366	234	149	97	60	71
1891–1895[c]	...1930	2,448	780	581	393	260	168	111	69	86
1886–1890[c]	...1925	2,567	791	597	414	280	184	125	79	98
1881–1885[c]	...1920	2,707	802	615	438	305	204	140	90	112
1876–1880[c]	...1915	2,873	809	630	464	335	235	162	103	135
1871–1875[c]	...1910	3,051	812	632	486	367	270	192	125	167

		Exact ages 40 to 44[a]								
1911–1915	1955	2,224	799	597	350	196	111	66	40	64
1906–1910	1950	2,174	770	557	331	196	118	75	47	79
1901–1905	1945	2,274	761	554	348	219	140	93	60	100
1896–1900[c]	...1940	2,473	770	579	384	254	168	115	76	125
1891–1895[c]	...1935	2,656	791	597	414	283	191	133	91	156
1886–1890[c]	...1930	2,828	803	616	440	309	213	154	106	186
1881–1885[c]	...1925	3,010	816	636	467	337	238	174	123	218
1876–1880[c]	...1920	3,206	824	654	494	367	265	199	144	260
1871–1875[c]	...1915	3,424	828	662	521	399	300	231	171	312

		Exact ages 45 to 49[a]								
1906–1910	1955	2,209	773	561	335	200	122	78	50	89
1901–1905	1950	2,313	764	557	352	223	143	96	63	114
1896–1900[c]	...1945	2,510	772	581	387	257	172	119	81	143
1891–1895[c]	...1940	2,703	792	599	417	286	195	138	96	180
1886–1890[c]	...1935	2,887	805	618	443	313	218	159	113	217
1881–1885[c]	...1930	3,084	817	639	471	342	244	182	131	258
1876–1880[c]	...1925	3,292	826	657	498	372	273	207	153	307
1871–1875[c]	...1920	3,515	830	666	526	405	308	239	181	360

		Exact ages 50 to 54[a]								
1901–1905	1955	2,315	764	557	352	224	144	96	63	115
1896–1900[c]	...1950	2,512	772	581	387	257	172	119	81	144
1891–1895[c]	...1945	2,705	792	599	417	286	195	138	96	182
1886–1890[c]	...1940	2,891	805	618	443	313	218	160	113	221
1881–1885[c]	...1935	3,088	817	639	471	342	244	182	132	261
1876–1880[c]	...1930	3,299	826	657	498	372	273	207	153	312
1871–1875[c]	...1925	3,521	830	666	526	405	308	240	181	365

[a] The year in which these ages were reached is given in the second column from the left. For example, the cohorts of 1936–1940 reached ages 15 to 19 at the beginning of 1955; i.e., on January 1, 1955, the average age of the women in the cohort of 1940 was exactly 15 years; for those in the cohort of 1939 it was exactly 16 years; etc.

[b] 0.5 or less.

[c] The rates for the cohorts of 1896–1900 and earlier are preliminary estimates, subject to minor changes.

Source: Scripps Foundation for Research in Population Problems, cited in Wilson H. Grabill, Clyde V. Kiser, and Pascal K. Whelpton, *The Fertility of American Women* (New York: Wiley, 1958), Table 114.

been more first and second births one expects, but the rate went up from 29 to 67 for third births (an increase of 130 per cent in 15 years), from 7 to 17 for fourth births (140 per cent), from 1 to 4 for fifth births (300 per cent), from less than 0.5 to 1 for sixth births (at least 100 per cent). Of course, these increases are calculated from the period of lowest fertility, but note that for the women aged 20–24 the cumulative birth rates in 1955 are also higher than those in 1910 for every order of births up to the sixth!

Another reason for the baby boom was that women who postponed having children during the depression of the 1930's often had them after 1945, relatively late in their fecund period. This can also be illustrated from Table 9-12. Note the cohorts born in 1911–1915 in the third deck: their cumulative birth rate at ages 25–29 was 1,064 per thousand, or the lowest of any group of cohorts of this age. In 1955, when the 1911–1915 cohorts were aged 40–44, their cumulative birth rate was 2,224. Of the increase, 244 (799 − 555) units represented first births to women aged 30–44 years.

The annual average number of births to native white women increased from 1.90 million in 1930–1939 to 3.01 million in 1945–1954, or by 58.7 per cent. These are the dimensions of the baby boom. What caused this unprecedented and wholly unanticipated rise in natality? Four factors are relevant: (a) The population increased, so that there were more people to have children. (b) The age at marriage went down, and a larger proportion married. (c) Of those who married, a larger proportion had children. (d) The average number of children per family increased. By an ingenious calculation, Whelpton has shown that the relative importance of these four factors in producing the postwar rise in the number of births was as follows: [43]

Larger number of women	24.3%
More women marrying	30.1%
More wives bearing the first child	33.5%
More births per mother	12.1%

Whelpton emphasizes that the fourth variable—the increased size of the family per mother—"is by far the least important." The low figure of 12 per cent, it must be noted, was arrived at by averaging the increased family size among young cohorts with the *decreased* family size among older ones. This is a sound procedure for establishing the reasons for the postwar rise in the number of births—which was the purpose of the analysis. The reader must not assume, however, that any indication of future trends was intended. The greatest increase in the number of children per family was for mothers aged 15–28, who are physically capable of having many more children. Whether indeed they will have more, and if so how many on the average, is a question of a different order.[44]

[43] Grabill, Kiser, and Whelpton, *op. cit.*, pp. 365–371. Dr. Whelpton has informed me that he alone was responsible for this passage.

[44] For a further discussion of this matter, see below, Ch. 11.

SUMMARY

Fertility in the United States declined steadily from almost the beginning of the nation's history to the mid-1940's. Among whites the number of children under 5 per 1,000 women aged 20–44 fell off from 1,358 in 1810 to 419 in 1940. That the decrease began so early is worth emphasizing. In the first half of the nineteenth century the United States was a relatively empty country with a wide open frontier; it was still overwhelmingly rural and agricultural; contraceptive means were more or less limited to coitus interruptus. In other words, almost all of the factors later denoted as the causes of the small-family system were still in the future when this social transformation got under way.

According to the limited data available, the secular decline in fertility began in the urban middle classes, and from them spread to the urban working classes and to the rural population. The small-family system became established much more by the diffusion of urban ideas to rural areas than by the migration of rural persons to urban places. It is necessary to look for causes, thus, not so much in the living conditions in cities as in the ideas and aspirations associated with the urban population. The greater rationality (in Max Weber's sense of the word) of town life presumably induced a larger and larger proportion of the population to weigh the advantages and disadvantages to be derived from each child and to adjust the size of the family accordingly. In the 1930's almost every demographer thought in terms of such a stylized picture of Rational Man and believed that the downward trend in fertility would continue. Once it became general to adjust family size according to the loss in money and convenience incurred from having children, many couples, perhaps eventually most, would have none at all.

In the postwar decade, however, there has been a wholly unexpected revival of births. In general, this has been most marked among the social classes that previously had shown the greatest decline. Apart from a few groups, in particular Negroes and perhaps Catholics, the present trend seems to be toward a greater convergence in fertility, with both social-economic extremes moving toward a central norm of a middle-sized family.

Much of the baby boom was the reflection of the new family-building habits of young women. In 1950 their median age at marriage was 20 years—or a year and a half younger than in 1940. And from the inadequate data available, it appears that more postwar brides had a child within a year, and that the intervals between the first and the second, and the second and the third births, were shorter than they used to be. For every birth order up to and including the sixth, the cumulative birth rates of women aged 20 to 24 in 1955 were higher than those of comparable cohorts in 1910. The meaning of the baby boom for future fertility and population growth (which will be discussed more fully in Chapter 11) depends on what the young women who married in the postwar decade will do during the rest of their lives. Their age-specific birth rates are probably the highest in the nation's history, and if they continue producing children in anything like these numbers during the rest of their fecund period, their completed family size will be tremendously larger than that of the interwar generation. On the other hand, one can surmise that these women have all but completed their childbearing, getting it over during their twenties, and that we can more or less equate their cumulative birth rates up to the age of 30 with their eventual completed family size. Where between these two extremes the actual trend of American fertility will fall cannot be definitely answered until the 1970's, when these cohorts will come to the end of their fecund period.

SUGGESTIONS FOR FURTHER READING

Wilson H. Grabill, Clyde V. Kiser, and Pascal K. Whelpton, *The Fertility of American Women* (New York: Wiley, 1958).

Paul C. Glick, *American Families* (New York: Wiley, 1957).
> Two volumes in the census monograph series, of which the first in particular is relevant to the subject matter of this chapter.

Ronald Freedman, Pascal K. Whelpton, and Arthur A. Campbell, *Family Planning, Sterility, and Population Growth* (New York: McGraw-Hill, 1959).
> An analysis based on a nationwide sample.

A. M. Carr-Saunders, *World Population: Past Growth and Present Trends* (Oxford: Clarendon, 1936).

Norman E. Himes, *Medical History of Contraception* (Baltimore: Williams & Wilkins, 1936).

Frank Lorimer and Frederick Osborn, *Dynamics of Population: Social and Biological Significance of Changing Birth Rates in the United States* (New York: Macmillan, 1934).

Warren S. Thompson and P. K. Whelpton, *Population Trends in the United States* (New York: McGraw-Hill, 1933).

Some of the best of the prewar books on fertility trends, both in the United States and in Western countries generally.

Bernard Okun, *Trends in Birth Rates in the United States since 1870* (Baltimore: Johns Hopkins Press, 1958).

P. K. Whelpton, *Cohort Fertility: Native White Women in the United States* (Princeton: Princeton University Press, 1954).
Two long-range analyses, emphasizing technical problems in measuring fertility trends.

Robert C. Cook, "Baby Boom Decade, 1946–1955," *Population Bulletin,* 13:3 (May, 1957), 41–59; "Recession in Births?" *Population Bulletin,* 14:6 (October, 1958), 109–123.

Lincoln H. Day, "Age of Women at Completion of Childbearing," *Public Health Reports,* 73:6 (June, 1958), 525–531.

John Hajnal, "The Marriage Boom," *Population Index,* 19:2 (April, 1953), 80–101. (This article has been reprinted in Joseph J. Spengler and Otis Dudley Duncan, eds., *Demographic Analysis,* Glencoe, Ill.: Free Press, 1956, pp. 220–242.) "Age at Marriage and Proportions Marrying," *Population Studies,* 7:2 (November, 1953), 111–136.

Everett S. and Anne S. Lee, "The Differential Fertility of the American Negro," *American Sociological Review,* 17:4 (August, 1952), 437–447.

William Petersen, "The New American Family," *Commentary,* January, 1956, pp. 1–6.

Norman B. Ryder, "The Reproductive Renaissance North of the Rio Grande," *Annals of the American Academy of Political and Social Science,* 316 (March, 1958), 18–24.

Christopher Tietze, "Statistical Contributions to the Study of Human Fertility," *Fertility and Sterility,* 7:1 (January–February, 1956), 88–94.

Charles F. Westoff, Elliot G. Mishler, and E. Lowell Kelly, "Preferences in Size of Family and Eventual Fertility Twenty Years After," *American Journal of Sociology,* 62:5 (March, 1957), 491–497.
The baby boom has effected a boom also in analyses of fertility. These articles, some of the best postwar contributions, are in addition to those already cited in the chapter.

10. *MORBIDITY AND MORTALITY*

The spare statistics on fertility in the nineteenth century can be supplemented, as we have seen, by comparing the number of children with the number of women in the childbearing ages. Data on mortality are just as fragmentary,[1] but unfortunately there is no counterpart to the fertility ratio. Indirect evidence suggests that the death rate must have begun to fall no later than the birth rate, since the population growth was considerably greater than the probable size of the immigration. Direct information on mortality before 1900, however, is limited to surmises from local figures.[2] These indicate that expectation of life at birth at the beginning of the nineteenth century was probably not much higher than 35 years, or about half of what it is today. In the cities during an epidemic year perhaps as many as one person out of 20 died; but what their death rates were in other periods we do not know. According to contemporary opinion, not only was urban mortality higher than rural, but it was increasing. There are some data to support the reasonable supposition that the mortality of slaves was considerably higher than that of the white population.

During the second half of the century, it will be recalled, attempts were made to collect statistics on mortality through the censuses, but the results were so deficient that they were sometimes denoted as worthless even in the reports themselves. During this period, vital statistics were collected systematically in Massachusetts, where the expectation of life at birth went up from 38.3 years in 1850 to 46.1 in 1900–1902 for males, and from 40.5 to 49.4 for females.[3] To what degree this progress can be generalized

---

[1] See pages 50–51.

[2] For a brief summary, see Conrad Taeuber and Irene B. Taeuber, *The Changing Population of the United States* (New York: Wiley, 1958), pp. 269–272.

[3] Louis I. Dublin, Alfred J. Lotka, and Mortimer Spiegelman, *Length of Life: A Study of the Life Table* (Rev. ed.; New York: Ronald, 1949), p. 48.

to the United States is difficult to guess; Massachusetts was hardly a typical state in any respect. Nevertheless, the inadequate evidence from the censuses, particularly when supplemented by what is known concerning the advance in medicine and public health, permits the inference that mortality over the whole country declined during the second half of the century.

Data on mortality on a national scale go back really only to 1933, when the last state was admitted to the Death-Registration Area. If we begin a table of death rates in 1900, it must be on the assumption that the death-registration states were typical. Since there is every reason to believe, on the contrary, that greater control over death developed together with better statistics concerning it, such a series probably understates the decline in mortality that has taken place in the twentieth century, great as this has been according to the record.

CAUSES OF DEATH [4]

The causes of death as specified by physicians are compiled in the nation's vital statistics, ideally in accordance with the International Statistical Classification of Diseases, Injuries, and Causes of Death. This schedule has evolved gradually over the past century—from 1853, when the First Statistical Congress commissioned two of its leading members to work up an improvement of the alphabetical list of causes of death then in general use, to 1955, when the seventh revision went into effect. The categories in this latest edition include 612 diseases and morbid conditions, 153 types of injury, and 189 types of lesion.[5]

While the International Classification is an enormously valuable instrument, to which the best demographers from William Farr to the present generation have devoted much thought, in analytical terms it is inelegant. As a practical statistical tool, it reflects compromises made with the current state of medical knowledge, international differences in usage, and the greater or lesser relevance, with respect to any category, of medicine, anatomy, or law. The physician—and, following him, the vital statistician—is primarily interested in the immediate cause of death, what MacIver has termed the *precipitant*.[6] The doctor's job is to prevent death, and his attention is typically fixed on the proximate factor involved in it—in the words of a death certificate, the "disease or condition

---

[4] See also pages 587–590.

[5] World Health Organization, *Manual of the International Statistical Classification of Diseases, Injuries, and Causes of Death* (7th ed.; Geneva, 1957), 2 vols.

[6] Cf. R. M. MacIver, *Social Causation* (Boston: Ginn, 1942), Ch. 6.

directly leading to death." The standard form specifically instructs him *not* to designate "the mode of dying, e.g. heart failure"; and if he ever lists as the cause of death simply the breakdown of an organ, without specifying the external agent or the type of malfunctioning responsible, this is only because the limits either of medical knowledge or of his examination do not permit him to do more.

It is, of course, the improved control over certain specific causes of death, especially infectious diseases, that has effected the decline in mortality. This fact is illustrated by Table 10-1, which compares death

TABLE 10-1. Death Rates per 100,000 Population by Selected Causes, Death-Registration Area of the United States, 1900 and 1950

Cause of Death	Average 1900–1904	1950
Scarlet fever	11.8	>0.05
Typhoid fever	26.8	0.1
Measles	10.0	0.3
Diphtheria	32.8	0.3
Whooping cough	10.7	0.7
Appendicitis	9.3	2.2
Influenza	22.9	3.5
Diarrhea and enteritis	115.6	5.0
Syphilis	12.9	6.8
Tuberculosis	184.8	23.4
Pneumonia	161.5	31.6
Chronic nephritis	84.2	46.9
Cerebral hemorrhage	106.3	92.0
Motor vehicle accidents	—	23.1
Diabetes mellitus	12.2	28.4
Cancer	67.6	138.4
Diseases of the heart	147.7	326.1
All causes	1,622.3	963.8

Source: Various reports of the National Office of Vital Statistics, compiled in Mortimer Spiegelman, *Introduction to Demography* (Chicago: Society of Actuaries, 1955), p. 65. Copyright 1955 The Society of Actuaries.

rates by some of the principal causes at the beginning and middle of the twentieth century, arranged from low to high incidence in 1950. Almost all in the first group, most of which were reduced to insignificant figures by this date, are communicable diseases, particularly those to which children are susceptible. The second group, where the incidence, though substantially reduced, still remained significant in 1950, comprises both communicable diseases more difficult to control (tuberculosis and pneumonia) and certain morbid conditions. The third group, where the rate has increased over the half-century, includes no infectious diseases but only morbid conditions and some types of nonbiological death.

That morbid conditions are now more important than infectious diseases as causes of death in advanced countries can be interpreted in two ways. In one sense, the statement is simply a tautology, meaning no more than that medical science can control what it understands. At one time, for instance, the condition of the body called "fever" was regarded as the cause of many deaths; today it is interpreted as a symptom associated with the action of many different germs. What we term "heart disease" is a current example of such a composite term; and, similarly, "cancer is not a single clear-cut disease entity" but "a group of diseases, involving a multitude of possible causative factors." [7] That is to say, some "morbid conditions" are simply those diseases about which we know too little either to effect cures or to classify, except in such a composite grouping.

Or, to make the same point in a different way, the category of diseases known as "chronic" is usually defined operationally simply in terms of their duration, either as a morbid condition lasting for three months or more (U. S. National Health Survey) or as one that is permanent, nonreversible, or requiring a long period of care (Commission on Chronic Illness).[8] Once it is known what causes a morbid condition, in many cases it is no longer chronic in this sense; and this is so, within limits, whether the cause is genetic (hyperthyroidism) or environmental (pellagra). In the recent past a considerable number of both types of chronic diseases have been brought under control, either wholly or in part.[9]

The greater importance of morbid conditions as causes of death may be due, however, not merely to ignorance but to inherent, irremovable weaknesses in the human body. As more and more of the controllable causes of death are brought under control, the residual group acquires a greater and greater relative importance. "Ironically, the increases in recent years in the number of deaths from cancer and heart disease is a measure of medical progress." [10] Mortality from cancer went up by almost two and a half times from 1900 to 1954, but only by about 70 per cent if allowance is made for the larger number of elderly persons in the

[7] U.S. Public Health Service, *Meeting the Challenge of Cancer* (Publication no. 419; Washington: U.S. Government Printing Office, 1955), p. 17.

[8] Cited in Mortimer Spiegelman, *Introduction to Demography* (Chicago: Society of Actuaries, 1955), pp. 109–110. See below, page 250.

[9] Cf. David Seegal, "On Longevity and the Control of Chronic Disease," in Eastern States Health Education Conference, *The Social and Biological Challenge of Our Aging Population* (New York: Columbia University Press, 1950), pp. 96–111.

[10] Frank G. Dickinson, "The Medical Care Team," *Annals of the American Academy of Political and Social Science*, 273 (January, 1951), 25–33.

population.[11] The rise in mental illness, which in impressionistic writings has often been ascribed to the hectic life of modern times, seems also to be a consequence of the aging of the population. The larger number of admissions of elderly persons to mental hospitals can be explained by the longer average life expectancy, the greater tendency today to hospitalize persons afflicted with senility, and possibly a higher incidence of arteriosclerosis. However, according to a careful long-term analysis, for ages under 50 the rate of age-specific first admissions is the same today as it was a century ago. When age is held constant, the virtually complete urbanization of American society has not brought about any increase in the incidence of mental illness.[12]

The revolution in medical science that has taken place during the lifetime of today's adults is hard to see in its true dimensions. "It can be strongly argued that greater progress has been made in medical science in the past fifty years than in the previous five thousand." [13] If *all* mortality before the age of 40 were eliminated and age-specific death rates for 41 years and over remained the same as they were in 1948, the average expectation of life at birth would be 70.7 years for white males and 75.0 for white females.[14] The actual figures for whites in 1958 were, respectively, 67.2 and 73.7 years. That is to say, any appreciable decline in

[11] Harold F. Dorn, "Ecological Factors in Morbidity and Mortality from Cancer," in Milbank Memorial Fund, *Trends and Differentials in Mortality* (New York, 1956), pp. 74–97. This should not be interpreted as a statement that only the aged are susceptible to cancer. With the decline in child mortality from other causes, cancer (including leukemia) has become responsible for about 20 per cent of all deaths between the ages of 5 and 20, or more than any other cause except accidents.

[12] Herbert Goldhamer and Andrew W. Marshall, *Psychosis and Civilization* (Glencoe, Ill.: Free Press, 1953). This conclusion, which contradicts the preconceptions derived from previous theory, has had a certain confirmation in a study of the Hutterites, a relatively isolated, highly homogeneous religious sect with the reputation of being entirely free of mental disorders. It is a closely knit *Gemeinschaft,* whose members seldom have to face life's uncertainties unaided and without normative guidance. Though none were under treatment by a psychiatrist, according to this survey a small but significant percentage suffered from mental disorders, especially depressive symptoms, feeble-mindedness, and epilepsy. By the authors' hypothesis, the reasons were both the large amount of inbreeding and the fact that the same social system and religion that give them great personal security engender strong guilt feelings. The existence of psychoses and other forms of mental disorder in so secure and stable a way of life suggests that "there are genetic, organic, and constitutional elements which predispose a few individuals to mental breakdown in any social system, no matter how protective and well integrated it may be." Joseph W. Eaton and Robert J. Weil, *Culture and Mental Disorders: A Comparative Study of the Hutterites and Other Populations* (Glencoe, Ill.: Free Press, 1955), pp. 209–210.

[13] Raymond B. Allen, "Professional Education in the Service of Health," *Annals of the American Academy of Political and Social Science,* 273 (January, 1951), 11–18.

[14] Harold F. Dorn, "Prospects of Further Decline in Mortality Rates," *Human Biology,* 24:4 (December, 1952), 235–261. Cf. Barnes Woodhall and Seymour Jablon, "Prospects for Further Increase in Average Longevity," *Geriatrics,* 12:10 (October, 1957), 586–591.

mortality from its present level will be attained, if at all, less by a simple extension of past improvements than by the introduction of new factors, especially control over senescence.

HEALTH AND MORBIDITY

With the reduction in early death has come a tendency to conceptualize "health" not merely in negative terms, as the physical condition that inhibits mortality, but also positively. The World Health Organization, for example, has made the distinction explicit: "health is a state of complete physical, mental, and social well-being and not merely the absence of disease or infirmity." Such a positive definition, however attractive it may be as an ethical norm, involves logical and statistical puzzles that are yet to be solved.

The death rate (or the average life expectancy) is certainly a meaningful index of a population's level of health, and until the 1930's these were almost the only ones ever used. It is true, of course, that there can be a wide discrepancy between either of these and morbidity. Some diseases with virtually no effect on mortality may bring about a considerable decline in efficiency, a high degree of discomfort, or similar impairments. The common cold, for instance, is not a direct cause of death, but it is a leading reason for absenteeism among school children and industrial workers. Trachoma, an infection of the eye prevalent in the Near East, is another example; those afflicted with it eventually become blind, but they do not die appreciably earlier than their uninfected neighbors. Blindness is one example of what is called a "permanent total disability"; the very term emphasizes that life can continue for a period with well-being markedly below the optimum level.

It would be useful, then, to devise other measures of health, in order to supplement mortality statistics. Any such alternative would be difficult to apply with the grossly inadequate morbidity data presently available, but this deficiency could be remedied in the future. A more significant obstacle is to define "health" in terms that make it possible to collect meaningful statistics. Death is a precise event, occurring only once for each person and at a time that can be specified fairly exactly. It is hard, on the other hand, even for the person affected or for a trained physician always to distinguish a morbid condition precisely from acceptable good health.

Our thoughts with regard to this may perhaps be sharpened up if we for the moment imagine that we are grading health and illness along a single axis. . . .

We might well take one specific point on this axis and label it "death." We would think of the points to the right of this point and adjacent to it as points representing degrees of serious illness. If we proceed still farther to the right, we would have points representing a lesser degree of illness, and continuing still farther on this axis, we would come into a state that we would call a state of "positive health." However, . . . there is no definite end-point to the axis as was represented by death at the other end, . . . no definite point that represents a fixed position indicating a state of ideal positive health; rather the axis seems to proceed off indefinitely to the right, as we consider improvement of the state of health of the individual or, similarly, of the population. . . . We do not have the classification of states of positive health that we need for a scientific approach to this question.[15]

Cross-cultural comparisons in level of health are still more precarious. Illness or disability is typically penalized by the loss of one's function, income, prestige, and so on, but the severity of the penalty varies greatly from one society to another. Moreover, each individual's state of health depends in part on his personality: he may imagine he has diseases and produce real symptoms, or he may ignore actual impairments and function efficiently in spite of them.

It is possible to compile morbidity data from existent medical records, as collected by physicians, clinics and hospitals, or health-insurance plans of one type or another. However, any such data have an obvious flaw. The incidence of disease as measured in medical records depends on the existence of the physicians who compiled them; and in this sense the more medical facilities that are available, the higher is the incidence and thus the lower the level of health. This is a special example of the recurrent difficulty in interpreting the statistical record of any social deficiency: typically measures taken to control it and the quality of the data improve together, so that we are likely to interpret the trend as a decline from an idyllic past when everything was perfect—in the sense that nothing imperfect was recorded.

If the state of health is to be measured independently of the differential access to medical care, the index cannot be a by-product of existent records. It was not until very recently, however, that special health surveys were made. In 1949, in an effort to improve the morbidity statistics then available, a National Committee on Vital and Health Statistics was established, and a number of important local studies of health conditions followed. In 1956 Congress passed an act under which the Surgeon General of the United States is authorized to gather data regularly on

[15] Lowell J. Reed, "Principles Applying to the Collection of Information on Health as Related to Socio-Environmental Factors," in Milbank Memorial Fund, *Backgrounds of Social Medicine* (New York: 1949), pp. 24–32.

the health of the whole country's population. In this continuing Health Household-Interview Survey, the concept of morbidity is defined as "a departure from a state of physical or mental well-being, resulting from disease or injury, of which the affected individual is aware." Similarly, "illness" is defined as a period when a person considers himself to be "sick" or "injured." [16] However inaccurate these subjective reports may be in one sense, they undoubtedly reflect fairly precisely the behavior of the respondents. A man must be quite sick or disabled before he is deprived completely of choice of action, and, short of that state, the way he himself defines his health is an important determinant of what he does.

These subjective reports are supplemented, moreover, by a periodic Health Examination Survey made by physicians of a sample of the population. Its purpose is not to prescribe therapy, but only to provide comparable national estimates of the incidence of important diseases for which accurate and simple diagnostic criteria exist. Because of its high cost, it must be limited to a relatively small sample, which is further restricted by the fairly large number of refusals.

During the few years that the National Health Survey has been in existence, it has only begun to grapple with the difficult conceptual and methodological problems inherent in its work. As the third element of its function, the service conducts its own methodological studies. To measure precisely and for the whole country the economic cost of illness and disability, for instance, requires a new combination of several types of incomparable data—gross national product, attitude surveys, physicians' diagnoses, census classifications, and concepts specific to the survey itself. As such problems are overcome, the United States will gradually acquire an improved measure of its state of health, one important component of the well-being of its citizenry as well as of its industrial and military efficiency.

DIFFERENTIALS IN MORTALITY BY AGE

In any society a person's age and sex are important factors in the probability that he will die within that year; and with the convergence of other differentials, these physiological determinants have become rela-

---

[16] U.S. Public Health Service, *Origin and Program of the U.S. National Health Survey* and *Concepts and Definitions in the Health Household-Interview Survey* (Series A-1 and A-3, Health Statistics from the U.S. National Health Survey; Publications 584-A1 and 584-A3; Washington: U.S. Department of Health, Education, and Welfare, 1958).

tively more significant in the United States in recent years. Figure 10-1 shows the age-specific death rates for 1900 and 1950. The U-shaped curve representing the mortality at the turn of the century is the char-

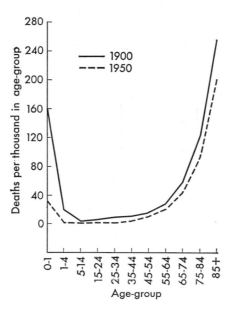

Figure 10-1. Age-Specific Death Rates, Death-Registration Area of the United States, 1900 and 1950

acteristic one wherever modern death control has not been fully established. Under such conditions, infancy and early childhood are dangerous periods; but for those who survive them the death rate is relatively low until senescence becomes a significant factor, at the age of 40 or 50. Since the greatest advance over the half-century was in the control of infectious diseases, especially those to which babies are particularly susceptible, the sharpest drop was in the mortality of infants and young children. Even so, the probability of dying during infancy is still greater than during childhood or early adulthood. That is to say, some sort of U-shaped curve describes the age-specific death rates of all cultures, no matter how primitive or advanced. If one imagines superimposed on such a curve another one representing age-specific fecundity—that is, a U-shape upside down—one can see why age structure can have so great an effect on population growth: the young adults who are most likely to have children are also the persons least likely to die.

The improvement in death control by age-group is shown in greater detail in Figure 10-2. By far the steepest slope is in the curve for the 1–4

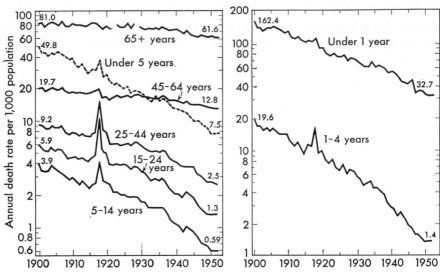

Figure 10-2. Death Rates by Age-Groups, Death-Registration Area of the United States, 1900–1952
Source: U.S. Public Health Service, *Health and Demography* (Washington: U.S. Government Printing Office, 1956), Chart 9.

age-group, whose death rate fell from 19.6 to 1.4 per thousand. Significant though smaller decreases are evident also for infants under one year and for persons aged 5–44. For those aged 45 and over, however, the declines have been much slower and smaller.

Infant and Fetal Rates

In any analysis of general mortality, it obviously makes good statistical sense to segregate so important a class of deaths as those of the very young and consider it separately. This is done in the **infant mortality rate,** or the number of deaths between birth and age one year per 1,000 live births.[17] For the United States in 1958, for example, it was:

[17] Since both the numerator and the denominator designate these groups during any one calendar year, the ratio does not really indicate the risk of dying before one's first birthday, for some of the children born in any calendar year die the following year but still before they are one year old. That is to say, the infant mortality rate assumes a constant fertility, and a large and rapid change in the number born will introduce a significant error (see Iwao M. Moriyama and Thomas E. N. Greville, "Effect of Changing Birth Rates upon Infant Mortality Rates," *Vital Statistics— Special Reports,* vol. 19, no. 21, November 10, 1944). In most cases, however, the rate as conventionally calculated is satisfactory without adjustment. An age-specific death rate for those aged one year and under would be still less accurate, because the census count of young babies is generally less complete than the registration of births.

$$\text{Infant mortality rate} = \frac{\text{Deaths at age one year or under}}{\text{Live births}} \times 1,000$$

$$= \frac{113,789}{4,198,856} \times 1,000 = 27.1$$

Infant mortality is high relative to that at other ages for two reasons—because a baby, if barely born alive, may not be able to remain so very long, and because any baby, even if born healthy, is especially susceptible to disease. These two causes of infant mortality have been termed **endogenous,** referring to what might be considered a postponed fetal death, and **exogenous,** referring to a death that differs from general mortality only in the age of the person affected.[18] The differentiation is important in that it separates causes of death difficult or impossible to control at the present level of medical knowledge (inherent weakness of the mother or fetus, extraordinary difficulty in delivery, etc.) from those that can be prevented by modern medicine and public-health measures. The same distinction can be made in statistical terms, though only approximately, by separating deaths during the first lunar month (that is, 28 days) from those during the rest of the first year. The first class, **neonatal mortality,** represents that part of infants' deaths that until a few years ago was regarded as the irreducible minimum. More recently, however, marked improvements in obstetrics have cut down the critical period to the seven days after birth. One demographer has suggested a new term, **semanatal mortality** (from *semana,* week), to designate that during the first week.[19]

The marked decline in infant mortality since 1900, both in the United States and in other countries of the Western world, was stimulated considerably by vital statisticians. In the United States the American Association for the Prevention of Infant Mortality, organized in 1909, devoted its main effort during the first years to campaigning for the extension and improvement of birth and death registrations. As more accurate statistics on infant mortality became available, these denoted both the seriousness of the problem and the causes of death that most urgently required medical attention. Various authorities have pointed out the striking paral-

---

[18] See Jean Bourgeois-Pichat, "De la mesure de la mortalité infantile," *Population,* 1:1 (January–March, 1946), 53–68; 6:2 (April–June, 1951), 233–248; 6:3 (July–September, 1951), 459–480.

[19] Sigismund Peller, "Mortality, Past and Future," *Population Studies,* 1:4 (March, 1948), 405–456.

lel between this attack on infant mortality a half-century ago and the present situation with respect to fetal mortality.[20]

According to the definition recommended by the World Health Organization, **fetal mortality** is "death prior to the complete expulsion or extraction from its mother of a product of conception, irrespective of the duration of pregnancy; the death is indicated by the fact that after such separation the foetus does not breathe or show any other evidence of life." The WHO also suggested that fetal mortality be classified into four groups according to the duration of the gestation period, as follows: early fetal deaths, 20 weeks or less; intermediate fetal deaths, 20 to 28 weeks; late fetal deaths, 28 weeks or over; and group 4, gestation period not classifiable. The term *stillbirth*, according to this recommendation, would be abandoned, and stillbirths would be classified either as late fetal deaths or neonatal deaths, according to whether any sign of life was evident after the complete expulsion of the fetus.

Stillbirths have been registered for some time in the United States, but New York City is the only political unit in this country that has required the registration of *all* fetal deaths for a considerable period. As one might expect, statistics are still grossly inadequate in all respects. In contrast to about 80,000 fetal deaths reported nationally, Yerushalmy and Bierman estimate an annual incidence of about 500,000. Moreover, since in many cases the cause can be determined only by a post mortem examination, which is seldom made, we know even less about how to classify fetal mortality than about its incidence. Even in New York City, which has the best statistics, more than 70 per cent of all fetal deaths (or more than 80 per cent of early fetal deaths) are reported with an unknown or ill defined cause.

As is implied in the distinction between endogenous and exogenous infant mortality, deaths shortly before and shortly after birth may not be different in principle. The two types are grouped together as **perinatal mortality,** meaning deaths between the time when the fetus becomes viable to the time after birth when prenatal causes of death are no longer significantly operative. While usage differs, perhaps the best definition of perinatal mortality includes that between the twentieth week of gestation and the first week after birth, or the sum of intermediate and late fetal deaths and semanatal deaths.[21]

[20] See the review of the subject by J. Yerushalmy and Jessie M. Bierman, "Major Problems in Fetal Mortality," *Obstetrical and Gynecological Survey,* 7:1 (February, 1952), 1–34.

[21] Unfortunately, there are also two ways of calculating the perinatal mortality *rate.* The usual method is to relate the appropriate sum of prenatal and postnatal deaths to

Since the reader may have found this multiplicity of definitions confusing, it will be well to review the principles underlying them, for on these there is more agreement. An effort is being made to refine the natural notion, which has been the basis of most demographic rates, that human life begins with birth. Actually, of course, life begins with conception, and from that point on one can designate several stages of development: (a) a viable fetus, (b) birth, and (c) a time after birth when endogenous causes of death are no longer significant. The precise definition of these three stages must be somewhat arbitrary, and conventions have not yet been universally accepted. Even "birth," which may seem to be less vague than the other two, must be very precisely defined to avoid confusion; there used to be a considerable variation in the definition of "stillbirth," and this has made international comparisons more difficult.

Another reason for the differences noted in definitions is that all rates represent something of a compromise between an abstract ideal and the measure most useful with the data actually available. If five out of six fetal deaths still go unreported, then it can be questioned whether it is worth while using a refined rate incorporating these data; but some analysts nevertheless prefer to do so.

The Life Table

The various rates used to measure the mortality of the very young can be duplicated for other age-groups. It is possible, for example, to calculate what might be termed a "senile mortality rate," or the number of persons aged 65 and over who died as a proportion of the total in that age-group. Indeed, this rate was shown in Figure 10-2.

Information of this kind can be better presented in the form of a **life table** (or, as it is sometimes called, a mortality table), which shows what the probability is of surviving from any age to any subsequent age, according to the age-specific death rates prevailing at any particular time and place. It is assumed, as a convention, that 100,000 babies are all

---

the number of live births, as in calculating an infant mortality rate. It makes better sense, however, to calculate perinatal mortality as a proportion of the total number of viable fetuses conceived, whether or not they survive till after birth. In that case, the rate is equal to the following ratio:

$$\frac{\text{Fetal deaths after the 20th week of gestation} + \text{Semanatal deaths}}{\text{Fetal deaths after the 20th week of gestation} + \text{Live births}}$$

See Harold F. Dorn, "Some Problems for Research in Mortality and Morbidity," *Public Health Reports*, 71:1 (January, 1956), 1–5; "Perinatal Mortality," in Metropolitan Life Insurance Company, *Statistical Bulletin*, April, 1956, pp. 1–4.

born on the same day, and the experience of this cohort is followed until its last surviving member finally dies. The life table does not show what will happen, but what *would* happen if the age-specific death rates remained constant. When the control of death is rapidly improving, as generally in the modern period, life tables have to be revised frequently, and they are typically calculated for a period of several years in order to eliminate the effect of short-term fluctuations.

A life table for the United States population in 1949–1951 is given in Table 10-2,[22] beginning on page 258. These particular figures will be used to exemplify a brief explanation of each of the columns.

The figures in Column 1, the year of age, are precise; that is, 0 is the date of birth, 1 is the date of the first birthday, and so on. The first of the two figures (which sometimes is the only one given) is denoted in subsequent column headings by x. The figures given in Column 2 are *not* the usual age-specific death rates but the probability of not surviving from one birthday to the next one. (The highest probability, absolute certainty, is conventionally denoted by unity; but in order to avoid a long series of decimals, the figures in Column 2 are sometimes, though not in this example, multiplied by 1,000.)

Given these probabilities of dying (Column 2) and an original cohort, called a **radix,** of 100,000 (Column 3), the number of persons dying (d_x, Column 4) is found by multiplying the rate by the number of persons living (l_x), thus:

$$.02976 \times 100,000 = 2,976$$
$$.00230 \times 97,024 = 223$$
$$.00139 \times 96,801 = 134$$

and so on. Given the number who die each year, the number who survive can be calculated by subtraction, thus:

$$100,000 - 2,976 = 97,024$$
$$97,024 - 223 = 96,801$$
$$96,801 - 134 = 96,667$$

and so on, for the whole of Column 3.

Columns 5 and 6 both refer to what is called a **stationary** (or life-

22 Monroe G. Sirken and Gustav A. Carlson, "United States Life Tables, 1949–51," *Vital Statistics—Special Reports,* 41:1 (November 23, 1954), 8–9. The methods of constructing a life table, a subject beyond the scope of this book, are discussed briefly in Dublin, Lotka, and Spiegelman, *op. cit.,* Ch. 15, and more thoroughly in Spiegelman, *op. cit.,* Ch. 5; or George W. Barclay, *Techniques of Population Analysis* (New York: Wiley, 1958), Ch. 4 and Appendix.

table) **population**—that is, one that does not change in either its age composition or its size.[23] While the assumptions underlying a life table are unrealistic (no immigration or emigration, the birth each year of a new cohort of 100,000, and no change in the age-specific death rates), the concept of a stationary population is often useful as a model. Much can be learned by comparing this hypothetical population with a real one that shares some of its characteristics.

Column 5 gives the number of years lived (L_x) during the designated year by the whole of the surviving cohorts of this stationary population. All of those who survive until the next year have lived one year each, while those who die before their next birthday have each lived a portion of a year. For the first years of life and advanced ages this portion must be calculated exactly, but for ages with a lower death rate it is sufficiently accurate to assume that those who died during the year lived six months on the average. Thus, Column 5, beginning with age 15–16, is calculated as follows:

$$95,801 + \frac{84}{2} = 95,843$$

$$95,706 + \frac{95}{2} = 95,754$$

$$95,601 + \frac{105}{2} = 95,653$$

and so on. Column 6 gives the total (T_x) number of years lived by the survivors in the year x and all subsequent years. It is derived from Column 5 by calculating a cumulative total, beginning with the highest age. For age 109–110, thus, the two columns have the same figure, and successive figures are calculated as follows:

$$1 + 1 = 2$$
$$1 + 1 + 3 = 5$$
$$1 + 1 + 3 + 4 = 9$$

and so on.

Column 6 (T_x) gives the total number of years to be lived by the cohort survivors, and Column 3 (l_x) gives the number of survivors in the cohort at each age. To calculate Column 7 of the life table, the aver-

---

[23] Compare the definition of stable population, page 625.

TABLE 10-2. Life Table for the Total Population, United States, 1949–1951

YEAR OF AGE	PROPORTION DYING	OF 100,000 BORN ALIVE		STATIONARY POPULATION		AVERAGE REMAINING LIFETIME
Period of life between two exact ages stated	Proportion of persons alive at beginning of year of age dying during year	Number living at beginning of year of age	Number dying during year of age	In year of age	In this year of age and all subsequent years	Average number of years of life remaining at beginning of year of age
(1)	(2)	(3)	(4)	(5)	(6)	(7)
x to $x+1$	q_x	l_x	d_x	L_x	T_x	$\overset{\circ}{e}_x$
0–1	0.02976	100,000	2,976	97,429	6,807,222	68.07
1–2	.00230	97,024	223	96,913	6,709,793	69.16
2–3	.00139	96,801	134	96,734	6,612,880	68.31
3–4	.00105	96,667	102	96,616	6,516,146	67.41
4–5	.00086	96,565	83	96,523	6,419,530	66.48
5–6	.00076	96,482	74	96,445	6,323,007	65.54
6–7	.00068	96,408	66	96,375	6,226,562	64.59
7–8	.00061	96,342	59	96,313	6,130,187	63.63
8–9	.00056	96,283	54	96,256	6,033,874	62.67
9–10	.00054	96,229	52	96,203	5,937,618	61.70
10–11	.00053	96,177	50	96,152	5,841,415	60.74
11–12	.00054	96,127	52	96,100	5,745,263	59.77
12–13	.00058	96,075	56	96,047	5,649,163	58.80
13–14	.00065	96,019	62	95,989	5,553,116	57.83
14–15	.00075	95,957	72	95,921	5,457,127	56.87
15–16	.00087	95,885	84	95,843	5,361,206	55.91
16–17	.00100	95,801	95	95,754	5,265,363	54.96
17–18	.00110	95,706	105	95,653	5,169,609	54.02
18–19	.00119	95,601	114	95,544	5,073,956	53.07
19–20	.00127	95,487	121	95,427	4,978,412	52.14

Age	q_x	l_x	d_x	L_x	T_x	e_x
20–21	.00135	95,366	128	95,302	4,882,985	51.20
21–22	.00141	95,238	135	95,170	4,787,683	50.27
22–23	.00147	95,103	140	95,033	4,692,513	49.34
23–24	.00150	94,963	143	94,892	4,597,480	48.41
24–25	.00152	94,820	144	94,748	4,502,588	47.49
25–26	.00153	94,676	145	94,603	4,407,840	46.56
26–27	.00155	94,531	147	94,458	4,313,237	45.63
27–28	.00159	94,384	150	94,309	4,218,779	44.70
28–29	.00164	94,234	155	94,157	4,124,470	43.77
29–30	.00171	94,079	160	93,999	4,030,313	42.84
30–31	.00179	93,919	168	93,835	3,936,314	41.91
31–32	.00188	93,751	177	93,662	3,842,479	40.99
32–33	.00200	93,574	187	93,480	3,748,817	40.06
33–34	.00213	93,387	199	93,288	3,655,337	39.14
34–35	.00227	93,188	212	93,082	3,562,049	38.22
35–36	.00243	92,976	226	92,863	3,468,967	37.31
36–37	.00262	92,750	243	92,629	3,376,104	36.40
37–38	.00284	92,507	263	92,375	3,283,475	35.49
38–39	.00309	92,244	286	92,101	3,191,100	34.59
39–40	.00337	91,958	310	91,803	3,098,999	33.70
40–41	.00368	91,648	337	91,480	3,007,196	32.81
41–42	.00402	91,311	367	91,128	2,915,716	31.93
42–43	.00440	90,944	400	90,744	2,824,588	31.06
43–44	.00481	90,544	436	90,326	2,733,844	30.19
44–45	.00527	90,108	474	89,871	2,643,518	29.34
45–46	.00575	89,634	516	89,377	2,553,647	28.49
46–47	.00628	89,118	559	88,838	2,464,270	27.65
47–48	.00685	88,559	607	88,255	2,375,432	26.82
48–49	.00745	87,952	656	87,624	2,287,177	26.00
49–50	.00808	87,296	705	86,944	2,199,553	25.20

TABLE 10-2. Life Table for the Total Population, United States, 1949–1951 (Continued)

YEAR OF AGE	PROPORTION DYING	OF 100,000 BORN ALIVE		STATIONARY POPULATION		AVERAGE REMAINING LIFETIME
Period of life between two exact ages stated	Proportion of persons alive at beginning of year of age dying during year	Number living at beginning of year of age	Number dying during year of age	In year of age	In this year of age and all subsequent years	Average number of years of life remaining at beginning of year of age
(1)	(2)	(3)	(4)	(5)	(6)	(7)
x to $x+1$	q_x	l_x	d_x	L_x	T_x	$\overset{\circ}{e}_x$
50–51	0.00876	86,591	759	86,212	2,112,609	24.40
51–52	.00950	85,832	815	85,424	2,026,397	23.61
52–53	.01033	85,017	878	84,578	1,940,973	22.83
53–54	.01124	84,139	946	83,666	1,856,395	22.06
54–55	.01222	83,193	1,017	82,684	1,772,729	21.31
55–56	.01327	82,176	1,090	81,631	1,690,045	20.57
56–57	.01441	81,086	1,168	80,502	1,608,414	19.84
57–58	.01563	79,918	1,249	79,293	1,527,912	19.12
58–59	.01693	78,669	1,332	78,003	1,448,619	18.41
59–60	.01830	77,337	1,416	76,629	1,370,616	17.72
60–61	.01977	75,921	1,500	75,171	1,293,987	17.04
61–62	.02133	74,421	1,588	73,627	1,218,816	16.38
62–63	.02302	72,833	1,676	71,995	1,145,189	15.72
63–64	.02475	71,157	1,761	70,276	1,073,194	15.08
64–65	.02652	69,396	1,841	68,476	1,002,918	14.45
65–66	.02843	67,555	1,921	66,595	934,442	13.83
66–67	.03060	65,634	2,008	64,630	867,847	13.22
67–68	.03313	63,626	2,108	62,572	803,217	12.62
68–69	.03598	61,518	2,213	60,411	740,645	12.04
69–70	.03908	59,305	2,318	58,146	680,234	11.47

Age					
70–71	.04249	56,987	2,422	55,777	622,088	10.92
71–72	.04626	54,565	2,524	53,303	566,311	10.38
72–73	.05044	52,041	2,625	50,729	513,008	9.86
73–74	.05499	49,416	2,717	48,057	462,279	9.35
74–75	.05988	46,699	2,796	45,301	414,222	8.87
75–76	.06516	43,903	2,861	42,472	368,921	8.40
76–77	.07089	41,042	2,909	39,588	326,449	7.95
77–78	.07713	38,133	2,942	36,661	286,861	7.52
78–79	.08380	35,191	2,949	33,717	250,200	7.11
79–80	.09085	32,242	2,929	30,778	216,483	6.71
80–81	.09841	29,313	2,884	27,871	185,705	6.34
81–82	.10661	26,429	2,818	25,020	157,834	5.97
82–83	.11558	23,611	2,729	22,246	132,814	5.63
83–84	.12533	20,882	2,617	19,574	110,568	5.29
84–85	.13576	18,265	2,480	17,025	90,994	4.98
85–86	.14688	15,785	2,318	14,626	73,969	4.69
86–87	.15867	13,467	2,137	12,398	59,343	4.41
87–88[a]	.17112	11,330	1,939	10,361	46,945	4.14
88–89[a]	.18424	9,391	1,730	8,526	36,584	3.90
89–90[a]	.19803	7,661	1,517	6,902	28,058	3.66
90–91[a]	.21249	6,144	1,306	5,491	21,156	3.44
91–92[a]	.22762	4,838	1,101	4,288	15,665	3.24
92–93[a]	.24343	3,737	910	3,282	11,377	3.04
93–94[a]	.26012	2,827	735	2,459	8,095	2.86
94–95[a]	.27768	2,092	581	1,802	5,636	2.69
95–96[a]	.29582	1,511	447	1,287	3,834	2.54
96–97[a]	.31423	1,064	334	897	2,547	2.39
97–98[a]	.33260	730	243	608	1,650	2.26
98–99[a]	.35115	487	171	402	1,042	2.14
99–100[a]	.37006	316	117	257	640	2.03

TABLE 10-2. Life Table for the Total Population, United States, 1949–1951 (Continued)

YEAR OF AGE	PROPORTION DYING	OF 100,000 BORN ALIVE		STATIONARY POPULATION		AVERAGE REMAINING LIFETIME
Period of life between two exact ages stated	Proportion of persons alive at beginning of year of age dying during year	Number living at beginning of year of age	Number dying during year of age	In year of age	In this year of age and all subsequent years	Average number of years of life remaining at beginning of year of age
(1)	(2)	(3)	(4)	(5)	(6)	(7)
x to $x+1$	q_x	l_x	d_x	L_x	T_x	$\overset{\circ}{e}_x$
100–101[a]	0.38904	199	77	161	383	1.92
101–102[a]	.40779	122	50	97	222	1.83
102–103[a]	.42600	72	31	56	125	1.74
103–104[a]	.44354	41	18	32	69	1.66
104–105[a]	.46060	23	11	18	37	1.59
105–106[a]	.47740	12	6	10	19	1.53
106–107[a]	.49413	6	3	4	9	1.46
107–108[a]	.51100	3	1	3	5	1.40
108–109[a]	.52810	2	1	1	2	1.34
109–110[a]	.54529	1	1	1	1	1.29

[a] Proportions dying at ages above 87 are not based on actual statistics at these ages. Therefore, proportions dying and other life table functions based on them at these ages may not necessarily represent actual conditions.

Source: Monroe G. Sirken and Gustav A. Carlson, "United States Life Tables, 1949–51," *Vital Statistics—Special Reports*, 41:1 (November 23, 1954), 8–9.

age **expection of life** from year x $(\overset{o}{e_x})$,[24] thus, one must merely divide the total years by the number of persons, as follows:

$$6{,}807{,}222 \div 100{,}000 = 68.07$$
$$6{,}709{,}793 \div 97{,}024 = 69.16$$
$$6{,}612{,}880 \div 96{,}801 = 68.31$$

and so on. This, the most important column in the life table, measures mortality conditions independent of the effect of age structure. The first figure in the column, the expectation of life at birth (68.07 years in this case), is for many purposes the best index of mortality whenever a crude death rate is not sufficiently accurate.

Since the average life expectancy at birth is based in part on the considerable number who die during the first year, it is always the smallest of the yearly totals. Indeed, the subsequent figures in general are smaller, but they indicate in each case the expectation of life from the year x, which increases by one for each row. Obviously, the total years lived is the sum of each figure in Column 7 and the appropriate value for x; thus:

$$68.07 + 0 = 68.07 \text{ total years lived}$$
$$69.16 + 1 = 70.16$$
$$68.31 + 2 = 70.31$$

and so on. The **median expectation of life** (or what is sometimes called the "probable lifetime") is always greater than the average. It is the age to which a person has a 50–50 chance of living or, from birth, the age at which the original cohort of 100,000 will be reduced to 50,000. In this example the median expectation of life from birth is more than 73 years, or about five years more than the average.

DIFFERENTIALS BY SEX

Figure 10-3 and Table 10-3 show the record of improvement in death control over the first half of the twentieth century, as measured by the increase in expectation of life at birth in the United States. Note that the

---

[24] The symbol with the superscript zero refers to the complete expectation of life, as defined in the text. It is to be distinguished from the curtate expectation of life (e_x), or the average number of *whole* years to be lived from age x, which is approximately half a year less than the more usual measure.

difference between whites and Negroes has decreased substantially, reflecting the convergence in the welfare of the various social classes in the

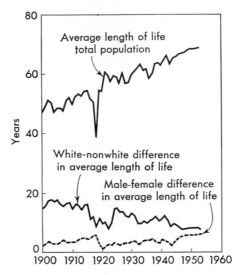

Figure 10-3. Expectation of Life at Birth, by Color and Sex, Death-Registration
Area of the United States, 1900–1953
Source: U.S. Public Health Service, *Health and Demography* (Washington: U.S.
Government Printing Office, 1956), Chart 10.

United States. The difference between the sexes, on the other hand, has
increased, particularly in the most recent period. Each year some 200,000
more men than women die in this country. By 1959 the number of
widows had gone up to an estimated 8.0 million (or 12.6 per cent of all
females aged 14 and over), and it is expected that it will continue to rise.
By 1975, according to the Census Bureau's estimate, women will outnumber men by about 3.25 million.

The principal reason [25] for this differential pattern is that as mortality
declined and the relative importance of various causes of death changed,
those affecting females fell off more. The bearing of children, for example, used to be a great hazard. During the 1920's, 66 women died from
causes related to maternity per 10,000 live births in the Death-Registration Area. This rate was almost stable, lower than during the influenza
epidemic of 1918 but slightly higher than in 1915. In 1957 the rate was
4.3! In other terms, there was one maternal death for every 165 births

[25] For a discussion of the two sexes' innate resistance to diseases, see pages 577–578.

TABLE 10-3. Expectation of Life at Birth, by Color and Sex, Death-Registration Area of the United States, 1900–1958

	1900–1902	*1929–1931*	*1958*
Total population	49.2	59.2	69.4
White males	48.2	59.1	67.2
White females	51.1	62.7	73.7
Negro males	32.5	47.6	60.6[a]
Negro females	35.0	49.5	65.5[a]

[a] Total nonwhites, including about 95 per cent Negroes.

Source: U.S. National Office of Vital Statistics, "Abridged Life Tables, United States, 1953," *Vital Statistics—Special Reports*, vol. 42, no. 10 (October 14, 1955); U.S. Bureau of the Census, *Statistical Abstract of the United States, 1960* (Washington: U.S. Government Printing Office, 1960), p. 58.

in 1915, and one per 2,300 births in 1957. This is indeed "one of the most significant achievements of modern medical science." [26]

The relative decline of infectious disease as a cause of death has also meant a marked change in sex differentials.[27] In the mid-1950's, nearly 40 per cent of all deaths were ascribed to heart disease, and for every 100 females 178 males died from this cause. The reasons for the disparity are not well understood; it has been suggested that one factor may be the greater tension associated with male occupations, particularly as contrasted with the lack of it in a housewife's life. In cancer, another cause of death that has become more important in recent years, the age-adjusted death rate for the white population was 65 per cent higher for females in 1900, about equal for the two sexes in 1947, and 20 per cent higher for males in 1955. One reason for this reversal, presumably, is that the diagnosis and cure of the most frequent cancers among females (breast and uterus) improved faster than of those most frequent among males (digestive system and lungs).[28]

By far the most important single reason for the higher mortality among males is their greater susceptibility to fatal accidents. The sex differential is smaller than it used to be (largely because of the decline in deaths from accidents at work, almost exclusively to males), but the relative impor-

[26] "Advances in Maternal Health," *Progress in Health Services*, vol. 7, no. 9 (November, 1958).

[27] "Health and the Sexes," *Progress in Health Services*, vol. 6, no. 10 (December, 1957).

[28] See Dorn, "Ecological Factors," *op. cit.*

tance of accidents as a cause of death has gone up. In 1955, 260 males died from this cause for every 100 females.

The contrast in mortality by sex is not coincidental but a direct consequence of the uneven improvement in control of various causes of death. The difference is greater in advanced than in underdeveloped countries; in the United States it is larger among whites than nonwhites. So long as further declines are by an extension of past improvements rather than by a breakthrough to cures, for example, of cardiovascular-renal diseases, the greater survival of females can be expected to increase.

DIFFERENTIALS BY RESIDENCE AND SOCIAL CLASS

The relation of urban and rural life to mortality is a complex question. A century or two ago towns were termed "the graveyard of countrymen," and this widely held folk belief has the implicit support of much sociological theory.[29] In many writings, a *Gemeinschaft* is almost by definition a better place to live than a *Gesellschaft*. A part of the recorded difference, it must be remembered, is spurious: certainly one reason for the higher death rate of the towns of the past is that a better count was made there than in the countryside. The contrast for the nineteenth century is so large, however, that in the opinion of the Taeubers it is "presumably" real.[30]

· In the twentieth century public-health measures and new medicines have cut down the importance of infectious diseases as causes of death, and eliminated altogether the epidemics that used to decimate town populations. Air pollution, traffic, overcrowding, and the stress of urban life still present special hazards, but the medical care available to city dwellers of all classes has become better than that in rural areas, which are "supplied with proportionately smaller numbers of physicians, dentists, nurses, technicians, and every other class of medical personnel except untrained midwives and possibly chiropractors."[31] The interaction of these two factors—the greater hazards of city life and the better medical care available there—has resulted in a complicated pattern, with sharper differences probably within the urban and the rural sectors than between them. Ranked by white males' expectation of life at birth in 1949–1951,

[29] According to a "census of opinions" from ancient times to the present day, 95 per cent of those who expressed a view believed that rural life is more healthful than urban; see Pitirim A. Sorokin, Carle C. Zimmerman, and Charles J. Galpin, *A Systematic Source Book in Rural Sociology,* 1 (Minneapolis: University of Minnesota Press, 1930), 143.

[30] Taeuber and Taeuber, *op. cit.,* p. 274.

[31] Milton I. Roemer, "Rural Programs of Medical Care," *Annals of the American Academy of Political and Social Science,* 273 (January, 1951), 160–168.

the five states with the lowest mortality were South Dakota, Nebraska, Minnesota, Iowa, and Kansas; and the five with the highest were West Virginia, South Carolina, New Mexico, Arizona, and Nevada.[32] All ten of these states are heavily rural. That is to say, in some regions of the United States and for some age-groups, age-specific death rates are higher in urban environments; but in other regions and for other age-groups they are lower.[33] The over-all trend, finally, has been toward convergence, particularly in the most recent years.[34] As measured by white males' expectation of life at birth, the rural advantage amounted to 10.0 years in 1900, 7.7 years in 1910, 5.4 years in 1930. By 1950, with the continuation of this trend, the contrast had disappeared.

One would expect differences in mortality by social class to show a clearly marked inverse correlation. Those at the upper level have less dangerous occupations, live under more healthful conditions, and can more easily afford medical attention whenever it is necessary. But with mass control of infectious disease, the influence of living conditions on mortality is not so great and direct as it once was; and the development of free clinics, group health insurance, and similar institutions has made adequate medical care much more widely available than it once was. The evidence from various recent studies is not wholly consistent, probably because of both the inadequacy of the primary data and marked variation from one area to another during a period of rapid change.

In one study, all American men aged 20 to 64 were divided into six broad occupational groups, and the age-adjusted mortality of each in 1950 was calculated as a percentage of that of all males in this age-group. The resultant **standardized mortality ratios** were as follows:

I. Professionals	84
II. Technicians, administrators, and managers	87
III. Proprietors, clerks, sales persons, and skilled workers	96
IV. Semi-skilled workers	100
V. Laborers, except farm and mine	165
VI. Agricultural workers	88
All U. S. males aged 20–64	100

[32] Mortimer Spiegelman, "Mortality Trends and Prospects and Their Implications," *Annals of the American Academy of Political and Social Science*, 316 (March, 1958), 25–33.

[33] For a detailed analysis of this point, see Dorothy G. Wiehl, "Mortality and Socio-Environmental Factors," *Milbank Memorial Fund Quarterly*, 26 (October, 1948), 335–365. (This article has been reprinted in Paul K. Hatt and Albert J. Reiss, Jr., eds. *Cities and Society*, Glencoe, Ill.: Free Press, 1957, pp. 335–355.)

[34] See "Improvement in Urban Health," *Progress in Health Services*, vol. 7, no. 1 (January, 1958).

Among the five urban classes there was a definite tendency for the curves of the age-specific rates of the first four to cluster and overlap. The sharpest difference at all ages was in the higher rates for laborers (V). The expected inverse correlation between social class and mortality, that is to say, is somewhat blurred for occupational groups apart from the definite contrast between unskilled workers and all others.[35] More detailed studies of separate areas—Cincinnati, Chicago, rural Ohio—have shown similar inverse relations between social class and mortality, with a substantial convergence over time.[36] Two recent studies have indicated no consistent relation between social class and morbidity.[37]

Differentials by color can be interpreted as mainly a reflection of the contrast between the lowest social-economic group and the rest of the population. The mortality of Negroes has always been higher than that of whites, but it has been falling faster, particularly in the most recent period. This trend is evident both with death rates and with expectations of life at birth;[38] that is to say, it has not been merely the effect of the different age structure of the two races. The convergence has been due principally to the smaller significance of communicable diseases as causes of death. In 1914, thus, almost half of the racial difference was the consequence of Negroes' higher rates of death from tuberculosis, influenza, and pneumonia. The more recent decline in the incidence of venereal diseases, already mentioned as a possible factor in Negroes' fertility, has also affected their death rate.

Negro mortality today, as can be seen from Figure 10-4, is above that of whites at all ages up to 75 years, but varies considerably from one age-group to another. Why this is so can be plausibly explained in some cases. One reason for the higher rates of infants and young adults, for example, is the family-building pattern. Negro women bear more children on the average; have them both earlier and later than the optimum childbearing period; enjoy less prenatal and postnatal care, apparently even when this is available at no cost; and give birth in a hospital only three-fourths as often as whites. As a consequence of such

[35] I. M. Moriyama and L. Guralnick, "Occupational and Social Class Differences in Mortality," in Milbank Memorial Fund, *Trends and Differentials in Mortality* (New York, 1956), pp. 61–73.

[36] See Taeuber and Taeuber, *op. cit.*, pp. 275–276. See also John M. Ellis, "Socio-Economic Differentials in Mortality from Chronic Diseases," *Social Problems*, 5:1 (July, 1957), 30–36, together with the studies cited in his bibliography.

[37] Saxon Graham, "Socio-Economic Status, Illness, and the Use of Medical Services," *Milbank Memorial Fund Quarterly*, 35:1 (January, 1957), 58–66; Katherine B. Laughton, Carol W. Buck, and G. E. Hobbs, "Socio-Economic Status and Illness," *Milbank Memorial Fund Quarterly*, 36:1 (January, 1958), 46–56.

[38] See pages 226–227, 264–265.

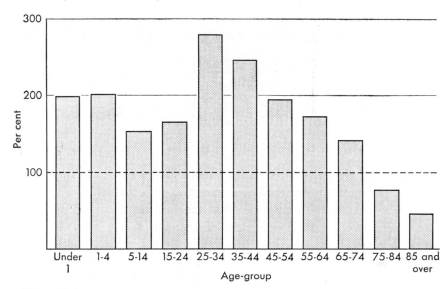

Figure 10-4. Nonwhite Mortality as a Percentage of White Mortality, by Age-Groups, United States, 1956
   Source: Various reports of the National Office of Vital Statistics, as compiled by Health Information Foundation in "The Health of the Nonwhite Population," *Progress in Health Services,* vol. 7, no. 4 (April, 1958).

social and medical factors, the fetal death rate in the mid-1950's was almost twice as high for nonwhites, the infant mortality rate twice as high, and the maternal death rate almost four times as high. Among females in the 25–34 age-group, 340 nonwhites died for every 100 whites. Other factors in the high Negro mortality are also more the consequence of a slum culture than of medical or even economic causes. Homicide, which ranked seventh among the causes of death of nonwhites, was proportionately ten times more numerous than in the white population. The rate of fatal accidents was also higher, though by a smaller margin.[39] Such differences, tied in with the way of life of the two races, will not be eliminated as easily as the earlier higher mortality from communicable diseases; but it must be emphasized that there is still a divergence also in death rates from these causes.

SUMMARY

Data on mortality for any except the most recent period are quite inadequate. There are good reasons for believing that average expecta-

[39] "The Health of the Nonwhite Population," *Progress in Health Services,* vol. 7, no. 4 (April, 1958).

tion of life at birth was about 35 years in the first half of the nineteenth century. From 1900 until the present the statistical record gradually improved.

The recent advances in death control have been so momentous that they are almost equivalent to the elimination of all mortality before the age of 40. In 1958 the average expectation of life at birth was 67.2 years for white males and 73.7 for white females, or roughly double the estimated figure a hundred years earlier. The major nineteenth-century causes were general rather than specific—public sanitation, better personal hygiene, the over-all rise in the level of living, as well as immunization. In the next period there was a great improvement in cures of most infectious diseases, a process that reached its climax in the most recent period with the development of antibiotics and other "wonder drugs" but also included progress in surgical techniques, particularly in obstetrics; in diagnosis and medicine; and in institutional forms of medical care—blood banks, medical teams, group health insurance, and so on.

The infectious diseases that used to be the major factor in mortality are now relatively unimportant, and they have been replaced by morbid conditions and nonbiological death—diseases of the heart, cancers, and fatal accidents. This shift in the causes of death has meant that differentials by age, sex, and social group have also changed markedly. The sharpest decline was in the mortality of infants and young children, while for the advanced ages improvement in control of death has been slow and moderate. The difference in death rates between the sexes is large and can be expected to increase still more. All social differentials—by urban-rural residence, by social class or occupational group, by race—are converging. The difference by residence seems to have all but disappeared. That between whites and Negroes is still significant: the mortality of Negroes today is roughly that of the whites in the mid-1930's.

If all of the improvements in death control over the past decades were made fully available to the whole population, a sizable reduction in the death rate might still be achieved, but not nearly so dramatic a one as has already taken place. Medical research is approaching a plateau. Seen from the nineteenth century, the prospective complete elimination of infectious disease as a cause of death is an all but miraculous achievement. Whether mortality at later ages will fall significantly depends on whether the considerable research on cancer and cardiovascular-renal diseases opens up new possibilities of prevention and therapy. This is a question to which even medical specialists have no firm answer, but we shall review some of the opinions in Chapter 19.

SUGGESTIONS FOR FURTHER READING

Louis I. Dublin, Alfred J. Lotka, and Mortimer Spiegelman, *Length of Life: A Study of the Life Table* (Rev. ed.; New York: Ronald, 1949).

The best general discussion of the factors that have determined the average length of life in the United States.

Mortimer Spiegelman, *Introduction to Demography* (Chicago: Society of Actuaries, 1955); *Significant Mortality and Morbidity Trends in the United States since 1900* (Philadelphia: American College of Life Underwriters, 1956).

Two works by the associate statistician of the Metropolitan Life Insurance Company, the first a rather technical text, the second a brochure summarizing twentieth-century trends in American mortality.

Milbank Memorial Fund, *Trends and Differentials in Mortality* (New York, 1956).

A number of excellent papers about recent trends, both in under-developed and advanced countries.

Franz Goldmann and Hugh R. Leavell, eds., "Medical Care for Americans," *Annals of the American Academy of Political and Social Science,* vol. 273 (January, 1951).

Institute of Life Insurance, *Life Insurance Fact Book 1958* (New York, 1958).

Two works that give some background material on the new institutional patterns affecting mortality trends.

Milbank Memorial Fund Quarterly, New York.

Health Information Foundation, *Progress in Health Services,* New York.

Metropolitan Life Insurance Company, *Statistical Bulletin,* New York.

Three excellent periodicals that devote a good deal of attention to trends in mortality and public health.

11. *POPULATION FORECASTS*

Demographers are called on not only to furnish data about the present size and composition of the population and their past development, but also to estimate their future trend. Such a prognosis, however it is made, is likely to be incorrect, but this does not mean that it is useless. It may be compared in many respects to a weather prediction by a meteorologist. In both cases, the estimate by a competent expert will generally be more accurate than a layman's guess. Moreover, much of what we know about the weather or about the determinants of population growth has been learned by comparing false predictions with the actual events and trying to understand why the error was made. In one respect, however, there is an important difference between a meteorologist's and a demographer's forecast. If the weather bureau predicts that it will rain on a certain day, this statement has no effect on the weather; but a population forecast, if it is made a basis for government policy, itself becomes one of the determinants of population change. The very predictions of incipient population decline in the 1930's, for example, may have helped reverse the trend and thus make the forecasts false. Or, on the smaller scale of urban planning, it is well known that a new road or a new school or any other new facility, constructed in accord with carefully estimated rates of in-migration and population growth, often attracts many more families to the area than had been anticipated. In the social sciences a prediction that would have been accurate if it had been kept secret may be made incorrect by the fact that people actually do know about it, and act accordingly.

The chronological account of population projections is largely a history of developing methodology. The linear extrapolations of the nineteenth century gave way to a search for a natural law of population growth and, most recently, to attempts to analyze separately changes in fertility, mortality, and migration. In some cases, however, the earlier projections were the most successful in predicting the actual growth of the population. This does not mean that the present methods represent a deterioration from the nineteenth century, but rather that one or two accurate forecasts are not enough to guarantee the worth of the theory on which they were based.

PROJECTIONS OF TOTAL POPULATION GROWTH

The simplest type of projection is an extrapolation of the past growth of the total population. The most famous, perhaps, of the several calculations of this type made early in the nation's history [1] was that by Elkanah Watson, a minor figure of the revolutionary period. He noticed that the population of the United States had increased by about a third during each of the first two decades following the 1790 census, and in a two-page article he calculated the growth if this decennial rate of increase were to continue.[2] Up until 1860 this remarkable forecast proved to be extraordinarily close to the actual population growth. For 1840 the projected figure was 17,116,526 and the census count 17,069,453, representing an error of about 0.3 per cent. For 1850 the projected figure was 23,185,368 and the census count 23,191,876, representing an error of about 0.03 per cent almost 40 years after the calculation was made! The astounding accuracy was a fluke: it so happened that until the middle of the century the gradual decline in the country's natural increase was matched almost exactly, decade by decade, by increasing immigration. Yet none of the later, technically more pretentious efforts to project population growth has been nearly so successful over so long a period.

An only slightly more elaborate extrapolation by Francis Bonynge also predicted actual growth over a considerable span. He divided the population into the three groups of whites, slaves, and free Negroes, and applied a rate of decennial increase to each. Watson's forecast was reasonably accurate for 50 years, Bonynge's for 70 years.[3]

Both Watson and Bonynge assumed that the population would grow at a constant rate up to 1900. During the following century, according

---

[1] For a good review of these early efforts, see Joseph J. Spengler, "Population Projections in Nineteenth Century America," *American Sociological Review*, 1:6 (December, 1936), 905–921. See also W. S. and E. S. Woytinsky, *World Population and Production: Trends and Outlook* (New York: Twentieth Century Fund, 1953), Ch. 7.

[2] Cf. Winslow C. Watson, ed., *Men and Times of the Revolution: or, Memoirs of Elkanah Watson . . .* (New York: Dana, 1856), pp. 455–456.

[3] Francis Bonynge, *The Future Wealth of America* (New York, 1852); cited in Woytinsky and Woytinsky, *op. cit.*, p. 245.

to Watson, the rate of increase would fall off gradually, with a total of 100 million in 1900, 133 million in 1930, 177 million in 1940, 236 million in 1970, and 300 million in 2000. These figures, though less preposterous than they must have seemed when the country had fewer than 8 million inhabitants, are still too high for the period behind us today.

TABLE 11-1. Some Nineteenth-Century Projections of the Population
of the United States (in millions)

	Census Population	Watson (1815)	Tucker (1843)	DeBow (1850)	Bonynge (1852)
1820	9.7	9.6			
1830	12.9	12.8			
1840	17.1	17.1			
1850	23.2	23.2	22.0–24.4		
1860	31.4	31.8	28.8–29.4	31.5	30.9
1870	39.8	42.3	36.5–38.3	42.8	39.9
1880	50.2	56.4	46.5–49.6	58.2	49.7
1890	62.9	77.3	59.8–63.0	79.0	61.9
1900	76.0	100.4	74.0–80.0	100.3	77.3

Sources: Various, as compiled in Joseph J. Spengler, "Population Projections in Nineteenth Century America," *American Sociological Review*, 1:6 (December, 1936), 905–921; W. S. and E. S. Woytinsky, *World Population and Production: Trends and Outlook* (New York: Twentieth Century Fund, 1953), p. 245.

In the 1840's a more thorough analysis of population growth was made by George Tucker, a professor of political economy and moral philosophy at the University of Virginia. He calculated fertility ratios from 1800 on and deduced that the family size had been decreasing since that date. This decline in fertility had begun, according to Tucker, because of "moral causes," but the decisive factor would eventually become the "difficulty of subsistence." The rate of growth would fall, therefore, unless immigration steadily increased. He predicted a population of 74 to 80 million in 1900 (compared with the census count of 76 million) and one of 200 million in 1940 (compared with the actual 132 million).[4]

J. D. B. DeBow, superintendent of the 1850 census, believed that the most likely figure in 1900 was 100 million, but that thereafter the rate of growth would fall off sharply. He predicted the 1950 population of 150 million precisely.[5]

These estimates are summarized in Table 11-1. How is it that these men, some of them wholly untrained (Bonynge was a retired China mer-

[4] George Tucker, *Progress of the United States in Population and Wealth* (New York, 1843); cited in Spengler, "Population Projections," *op. cit.*
[5] *Compendium of the Seventh Census* (Washington, 1854), pp. 130–131; cited in Spengler, "Population Projections," *op. cit.*

chant), all of them using crude methods, were able to forecast the growth of the population over many decades? Of course, most of the predictions were off by considerable amounts for later dates, but even so they are enough of a curiosity to excite any student's wonder.

As we have seen, until 1860 the population of the United States increased by a regular proportion each decade, and the formulas used by these early forecasters were not much more complex. Toward the end of the century, several efforts were made to fit the past growth to a more elaborate curve. H. S. Pritchett, who used a third-degree parabola, forecast the population of 1900 within 2 per cent and that of 1910 within less than 3 per cent; but by the year 2900, according to his series, the United States would have 40 billion inhabitants.[6]

The best known effort to find a more complex growth pattern is the Pearl-Reed logistic curve, as enunciated in several books and articles and applied to the populations of various countries and times. Raymond Pearl was a zoologist, and he developed his theory from analyzing the actual multiplication of fruit flies with a given amount of food in a closed bottle. As the adult drosophilae able to propagate increased from the original pair, their number went up at an ever accelerating rate until the limiting factor of the fixed food supply became relevant. Then the S-shaped growth curve gradually flattened out, approaching but never quite reaching a maximum level fixed by the subsistence available.

The populations of a number of countries were fitted to logistic curves of various formulas, with a good deal of success in the first period.[7] For example, a forecast that Pearl and Reed made in 1920 predicted the 1950 population of the United States with an error of only about 1 per cent.[8] In the meantime, however, since Logistic I had predicted a population in 1940 some 3.5 per cent higher than the census count in that year, Pearl and his associates calculated Logistic II, which missed the 1950

---

[6] H. S. Pritchett, *A Formula for Predicting the Population of the United States* (1890); cited in Woytinsky and Woytinsky, *op. cit.,* p. 245.

[7] It was used, for instance, by Janisch in Germany, Yule in England, and Maclean in Canada. See F. Janisch, *Das Exponentialgesetz als Grundlage einer vergleichenden Biologie* (Berlin, 1927); G. Udny Yule, "The Growth of Population and the Factors which Control It," *Journal of the Royal Statistical Society,* 88:1 (January, 1925), 1–58; M. C. Maclean, "The Growth of Population in Canada," in Canada, Dominion Bureau of Statistics, *Seventh Census of Canada, 1931,* 1: *Summary* (Ottawa, 1936), 99–132. For a critical comment on the last, see William Petersen, *Planned Migration: The Social Determinants of the Dutch-Canadian Movement* (Berkeley: University of California Press, 1955), pp. 204 ff.

[8] Raymond Pearl and Lowell J. Reed, "On the Rate of Growth of the Population of the United States since 1790 and its Mathematical Representation," *Proceedings of the National Academy of Science,* 6:6 (June 15, 1920), 275–288; see also Pearl, *The Biology of Population Growth* (New York: Knopf, 1925), p. 14.

population by 7 rather than 2 million. The figures are shown in Table 11-2.

TABLE 11-2. Projections of the Population of the United
States by the Logistic-Curve Method (in millions)

	Census Population	Population Estimates	
		Logistic I	Logistic II
1910	92.0		91.4
1920	105.7	107.4	106.1
1930	122.8	122.4	120.1
1940	131.7	136.3	132.8
1950	150.7	148.7	143.8
1960	179.3	159.2	153.0
1970	—	167.9	160.4
1980	—	174.9	166.3
1990	—	180.4	170.8
2000	—	184.7	174.3
Ultimate		197.3	184.0

Source: Various publications of Raymond Pearl and his associates, cited in Harold F. Dorn, "Pitfalls in Population Forecasts and Projections," *Journal of the American Statistical Association,* 45:251 (September, 1950), 311–334. (This article has been reprinted in Joseph J. Spengler and Otis Dudley Duncan, eds., *Demographic Analysis,* Glencoe, Ill.: Free Press, 1956, pp. 69–90.)

A decisive test of his theory was to be found, according to Pearl, in the one instance of a self-contained population of which adequate statistics had been maintained over a considerable period.

The native Algerian population . . . affords a crucial case. It is a human population which has virtually completed a cycle of growth according to the logistic curve within the period of recorded census history. One can now feel more certain that this curve is a first and tolerably close approximation to a real *law* of growth for human populations, than was possible when the completion of a cycle for a human population demanded extrapolation of the curve for many years beyond the period of the observation.[9]

When his first projected figure, 5,234,000 in 1931, was short of the actual population by some 300,000, Pearl fell back on the explanation that a law in 1919 had extended political rights to certain of the native Algerians and had thus changed the influences on growth. Since social changes of this importance are frequent occurrences in every country, it meant that the theory, even if valid on other grounds, was far less precise than he had suggested in his first statement of it. Sometimes two logistic curves of

[9] *Ibid.,* pp. 125–126.

different equations were combined into a single growth curve. In the case of Germany, for example, the shift from one equation to another was supposedly necessitated by the change from a predominantly agricultural to an industrial society; but an exactly comparable change in, for example, American society did not require a compound curve.[10]

In retrospect, the success of the logistic curve, like that of the earlier predictions, must be regarded as coincidental. What most condemns it is the biological rationale on which it is based. The relative abundance of food, which in Pearl's basic model was the only determinant of population growth, is in a country like the United States hardly even a relevant factor—except, of course, possibly in the very long run. In Pearl's extension of this model the limit was not merely food but the total physical resources as developed by the technology of the period. While this seems reasonable enough, it is actually not a very useful theory on which to base forecasts. This is so for two, seemingly contradictory, reasons: (a) In the modern period the control over the environment becomes more effective year by year. To set a maximum population (the asymptote that the logistic curve will never quite reach) in terms of present technology would be unrealistic, but to set it in terms of an extrapolation of improving technology involves a guess no less hazardous than the projection of the number of people. On the other hand, (b) the population pressure that will later develop may be felt immediately, for human decisions are made not merely in response to physical difficulties but often in anticipation of them. The ultimate limit to growth, that is to say, is not a useful guide to the future rate of increase, because that limit will change and, in any case, its effect may be significant much before the ultimate point.

The growth rate of the human population did not decline because of hunger, as with the fruit flies, but because parents decided to have fewer children. For a period mortality fell faster than fertility, and the population increased rapidly; then fertility fell faster and the curve began to flatten out. That is to say, the S-shaped curve, to the degree that it has actually described the growth of human populations, has done so because of the demographic transition, not because of the biological determinants that Pearl posited.

REPRODUCTION RATES

In the 1920's Dublin and Lotka laid the basis for what later were termed *reproduction rates,* and these were given wide publicity in the

[10] *Ibid.,* pp. 14, 21.

early 1930's, particularly following the publication of a number of works by Kuczynski.[11] A **gross reproduction rate** is the ratio of female [12] births in two successive generations, assuming no change in the age-specific birth rates and no deaths before the end of the childbearing period. A **net reproduction rate** is the ratio of female births in two successive generations, assuming no change in the age-specific birth and death rates. That is, the gross rate measures fertility only, the net rate the natural increase.

Both rates are related to the **stable population**—that is, the population of fixed age and sex distribution that would develop if the present age-specific fertility and mortality were to continue without change for a century or more. The professional demographers who developed the rates were well aware of this base, of course, but thousands became familiar with them without understanding their real meaning, in part because they were often carelessly defined.

Reproduction rates do *not* show whether the populations are increasing or decreasing. A rate of more than unity does *not* mean that a population is increasing or even that it will necessarily increase in the future. A net reproduction rate of 0.75 means not that the population *is* declining, but that it *would* decline if the current age-specific fertility and mortality continued without change for several generations. The reproduction rates, that is to say, are population projections, half-disguised as fertility rates. A projection based on wholly unrealistic assumptions—such as that the demographic rates of any one year are a permanent fixture—is often a useful device: we know this will not happen, but let us see what the consequences would be if it were to take place. But if one forgets that these assumptions were made, the tool is less helpful than misleading.[13] The average net reproduction rate of the United States during the 1930's was 0.98, or 2 per cent below the replacement level of 1.0. The annual age-specific birth rates during that one decade, however,

---

11 Louis I. Dublin and Alfred J. Lotka, "On the True Rate of Natural Increase As Exemplified by the Population of the United States, 1920," *Journal of the American Statistical Association,* 20:150 (September, 1925), 305–339. Robert R. Kuczynski, *The Balance of Births and Deaths* (Brookings Institution; New York: Macmillan, 1928, 1931), 2 vols.; *The Measurement of Population Growth: Methods and Results* (London: Sidgwick & Jackson, 1935). For instructions on constructing reproduction rates, see below, pages 624–625.

12 Reproduction rates are usually calculated for females only, though this is no more than a convention. See, for example, Robert J. Myers, "The Validity and Significance of Male Net Reproduction Rates," *Journal of the American Statistical Association,* 36:214 (June, 1941), 275–282.

13 Cf. George J. Stolnitz and Norman B. Ryder, "Recent Discussion of the Net Reproduction Rate," *Population Index,* 15 (April, 1949), 114–128. (This article has been reprinted in Joseph J. Spengler and Otis Dudley Duncan, eds., *Demographic Analysis,* Glencoe, Ill.: Free Press, 1956, pp. 147–161.)

are not a good indication of what the completed family size of any cohort would be. Older women, who had borne children in the 1920's, refrained in greater numbers from having more; and younger women put off having children until the 1940's. This temporary phenomenon was widely interpreted as the first step toward the impending decrease in population, a spelling out of Spengler's "decline of the West" in literal terms.

In 1931 Dublin presented two forecasts based on the principles underlying the net reproduction rate. According to the first, which in his opinion was "altogether too optimistic," the population of the United States with no migration would reach a maximum of 154 million between 1980 and 1990 and then decline to 140 million by 2100. By the second, "more reasonable" estimate, the maximum of 148 million would be reached by 1970, followed by a decline to 140 million by 2000 and to 76 million by 2100! As Dorn has pointed out:

> These predictions are remarkable not so much for their specific numerical values as for the fact that a prominent American demographer had stated publicly that the population of the United States almost certainly would decline in the very near future. The most pessimistic of previous forecasters had assumed merely that the rate of increase would approach zero at some distant time.[14]

The main reason that reproduction rates are inappropriate as predictive instruments, to sum up, are that (a) they are ordinarily (though not necessarily) based on the fertility and mortality of a single year and (b) they assume that these will remain constant for 100 years or so after that. As Grabill, Kiser, and Whelpton aptly put it, these measures "are analogous to the speedometer on a car in that they measure the approximate speed or force of reproduction at a given time but not necessarily the actual distance being covered or the actual time required to reach the destination. The 'speed' fluctuates too much [to be a] reliable measure of distance." [15]

COMPONENT PROJECTIONS

In virtually all projections made today the total population is not extrapolated as such but is rather divided up first into its component parts and, as it were, reassembled at successive future dates. The growth

[14] Harold F. Dorn, "Pitfalls in Population Forecasts and Projections," *Journal of the American Statistical Association*, 45:251 (September, 1950), 311–334. (This article has been reprinted in Spengler and Duncan, *op. cit.,* pp. 69–90.)

[15] Wilson H. Grabill, Clyde V. Kiser, and Pascal K. Whelpton, *The Fertility of American Women* (New York: Wiley, 1958), p. 73. See also *ibid.,* pp. 313–314, 360.

in an area during any particular period is the consequence of its natural increase and the net migration. If one analyzes separately the trend in the three components—fertility, mortality, and migration—the most important variable is the age and sex structure. Since childbearing is physiologically possible only to women between the ages, roughly, of 15 and 45, the proportion of the total population in this particular age-group of females is a relevant factor in judging its future fertility. Similarly, since the probability of dying within the next period is higher for infants and the old than it is for children or young adults, mortality will also vary according to the age structure. Migration, finally, is a behavior typical of young adults or, to some degree, of the young children or elderly persons that they may take with them. A component projection, then, is made by applying simultaneously age-specific rates of fertility, mortality, and migration to a given population in the process of gradual change in both size and structure.

The method can be illustrated by the forecasts that Warren S. Thompson and P. K. Whelpton of the Scripps Foundation for Research in Population Problems made in the 1930's for the Committee on Population Problems of the National Resources Committee.[16] This example is worth discussing both because of its intrinsic importance as a document that had a considerable impact on public opinion of the time, and because it illustrates very well the reasons why demographers in the 1930's (and also very often for a considerable period thereafter) believed that population would soon stop growing or even begin to decline.

Thompson and Whelpton tried to judge the future growth by assessing recent trends in mortality, fertility, and immigration, both in the United States and in other Western countries. Their appraisal is summarized in the following paragraphs.

Death Rates. The major advances in the past, the authors pointed out, had been made through the decline in death rates of infants and young children, especially by the greater control over infectious diseases. They believed that one important cause of death among adults, pneumonia, would decline rapidly, but others—in particular, heart disease, cancer, nephritis, and cerebral hemorrhage—were "likely to prove much more difficult to control than such former scourges as smallpox, tuberculosis, typhoid fever, and diarrhea and enteritis." They estimated, therefore, that the lowest probable mortality in 1980 could effect only a moder-

---

[16] National Resources Committee, Committee on Population Problems, *The Problems of a Changing Population* (Washington: U.S. Government Printing Office, 1938), pp. 20–24.

ate decline, with expectations of life at birth at that date of 72 years for males and 74 for females. With the highest probable mortality, these figures would be 65.6 and 68.4 years, respectively, levels close to what had already been attained by New Zealand and some other countries with a Western culture. The most likely figures, in their opinion, were based on a medium assumption—68.8 years for males and 71.2 for females; and these were the ones used in most of the projections.

Birth Rates. "It seems far easier to judge what can be done in lowering death rates in the future than to judge what people may want to do regarding the size of their families; hence the relative difference between high and low birth rate assumptions . . . is roughly four times as great as that between the high and low death rate assumptions." "In view of the past trend in the United States, and the lower rates that prevail in certain other nations," the highest future fertility trend that seemed reasonable was that the age-specific birth rates of 1930–1934 would continue unchanged until 1980. During that period the completed family size was less than 2.2 children per woman, or about 2.4 children per wife, or about 2.9 per mother. According to the probable lower limit, the decline in birth rates would continue until 1980, though at rapidly diminishing rates. In 1980, by this assumption, there would be 1.5 children per woman, or about 2 children per mother. "This is approximately the present situation in California and Washington, D.C., as well as in all of England." In the opinion of the authors, the most likely trend was a medium one, by which fertility would fall by 13 per cent over the next 50 years, ending with completed family sizes in 1980 of 1.9 children per woman, or slightly more than 2.5 per mother.

The Committee on Population Problems rejected the high estimate as too improbable to consider. In some regions of the country, it believed, fertility would continue to fall off, and "it seems extremely unlikely that this decline will be offset by increases of such magnitude, in areas where birth rates are low, as to cause fertility rates for the Nation as a whole to remain constant. Accordingly, emphasis is here placed on the estimates based on 'medium' and 'low' assumptions as regards fertility, combined with the 'medium' assumption as regards mortality."

Immigration. Under the quota laws in effect in the 1930's, 153,714 immigrants were permitted to enter each year from quota countries and an unlimited number from other countries. In an Executive Order of 1930 consular officers had been instructed to be especially careful in screening out aspirant immigrants likely to become public charges. Actually, in every year from 1931 to 1935 there had been a net emigration.

Thompson and Whelpton chose to calculate projections with two alternative assumptions concerning migration—no immigration and the net arrival of 100,000 immigrants. The Committee seemed to lean toward the first as the more probable. New permanent restrictions were likely, it believed, in particular the extension of the quota principle to the Western Hemisphere.

With three assumptions concerning mortality, three concerning fertility, and two concerning immigration, the total number of possible projections is the product of these, or 18. Of these, however, only seven were worked out at all, and three were considered by the Committee to be most probable: (a) medium fertility and mortality with 100,000 immigrants per year; (b) medium fertility and mortality with no immigration; and (c) low fertility, medium mortality, and no immigration. The projected populations in 1950 and 1980 based on these three sets of assumptions were, respectively: (a) 142 and 158 million, (b) 141 and 153 million, and (c) 137 and 134 million.

Looking back at these estimates with today's perspective, one can very easily judge them too harshly. It must be emphasized that the appraisals of future trends were made in the light of what seemed to be reasonable expectations on the basis of everything that was known in the 1930's. Unlike Pearl, Thompson and Whelpton did not attempt to develop a "natural law" of population growth. And, unlike those who became so enamored of the net reproduction rate that they assumed a priori that the age-specific birth and death rates were fixed, Thompson and Whelpton attempted to judge this question empirically, on the basis of the social and economic conditions then prevailing. So long as the depression continued the forecasts made by this method were accurate, even amazingly so. The figure for 1940 that Thompson and Whelpton had calculated in 1933 was more precise than the census count itself before this was corrected for underenumeration!

For the period after the depression, however, the forecasts made in its social-economic context were off by a wide margin. Several of the most important calculated before the census of 1950 are shown in Table 11-3 (the one dated 1935 is essentially the same as that included in the National Resources Committee, discussed in detail above). The succession of figures suggests what happened. The projection made in 1928, just before the onset of the depression, overstated the population of 1940 by 6.6 million and that of 1950 by almost a million, but understated that of 1960 by 16.6 million. The following projections, beginning with the one made in 1931, were adjusted to the expected population of 1940 with

**TABLE 11-3. Some Component Projections of the Population
of the United States (in millions)**

	1930	1940	1950	1960	1970	1980	1990	2000
Census population	122.8	131.7	150.7	179.5				
Scripps Foundation:								
1928	123.6	138.3	151.6	162.7	171.5	....	....	186.0
1931		132.5	139.8	143.9	144.6	142.9 [a]		
1933:								
High		134.5	148.5	....	....	190.0		
Low		132.5	140.5	....	146.0	145.0 [a]		
1935:								
High		132.6	146.1	159.5	172.8	185.8		
Medium		132.0	141.6	149.4	155.0	158.3 [a]		
Low		131.2	136.2	137.1	134.0	127.6 [a]		
1943:								
High			145.0	156.5	167.9	179.4	189.4	198.7
Medium			144.4	153.4	160.5	165.4	167.1	166.6 [a]
Low			143.0	147.7	148.7	145.8	138.9	129.1 [a]
1947:								
High			148.0	162.0	177.1 [b]			
Medium			146.0	155.1	162.0 [c]			
Low			144.9	149.8	151.6 [a]			
Census Bureau								
1949			149.9	160.0				

[a] Declines thereafter.
[b] Increases thereafter.
[c] Increases until about 2000, then declines.

Sources: Various, as compiled in Harold F. Dorn, "Pitfalls in Population Forecasts and Projections," *Journal of the American Statistical Association,* 45:251 (September, 1950), 311–344. (This article has been reprinted in Joseph J. Spengler and Otis Dudley Duncan, eds., *Demographic Analysis,* Glencoe, Ill.: Free Press, 1956, pp. 69–90.)

much greater accuracy, but they were much farther off in 1950 and thereafter. Note that not a single estimate for 1960—high, low, or medium—comes close to the actual population of 179.3 million, and only one series (the high estimate made in 1947) approaches this figure even by 1970.

The main reason these projections went so far off was the baby boom of the 1940's and the continuing high fertility of the 1950's. To say that this was unanticipated hardly reflects the mood of the 1930's. Most demographers would have gone along with the Committee on Population Problems in rejecting as improbable the high estimate of Thompson and Whelpton, based on the assumption that birth rates would remain static at the 1930–1934 level. The misjudgment concerning fertility was compounded, moreover, by errors in the same direction with respect to mortality and immigration. Death rates went down faster than was anticipated, and immigration went up faster.

During the 1930's demographers did not see the low birth rates of the depression as an aberration from the secular downward trend or even as its culmination, but as an indication that the long-term decline was accelerating. That is, they were too much influenced by the most recent period. During the postwar years, however, the most recent period has often been seen as least relevant to projecting future trends. The baby boom was first discounted as the consequence of postponed births, then of high marriage and first-birth rates. Both of these factors are relevant, but it is also true that something more fundamental has changed in America's family-building patterns.

For some years after 1945, therefore, most short-run projections still underestimated future fertility and population growth. For example, in 1950 the Census Bureau issued a set of "illustrative" projections for the following decade. The high-to-low range of the estimates for the population in 1960 was from 180 to 161 million, a considerable leeway for an extrapolation over only ten years. Less than two years later it was noted that the birth rate, the most important component of short-run change, was higher than had been anticipated. A new projection was made, with a range from 180 to 165 million in 1960, or a leeway of 15 million in a projection over only eight years.[17]

SOCIAL-ECONOMIC PREMISES
OF PRESENT POPULATION FORECASTS

If one follows the example of Thompson and Whelpton in their report to the National Resources Committee and attempts to appraise the relative influence of the factors that will determine population growth over the immediate future, one must admit that this cannot be done any more reliably today than in the 1930's. The one thing demographers have learned in the interim, perhaps, is how little they really know.

It is convenient to take as a starting point the assumptions underlying two series of Census Bureau projections made in 1955 and 1958.[18] The premises on which the 1955 projection was based were critically discussed

[17] U.S. Bureau of the Census, *Current Population Reports,* series P-25, no. 43 (August 10, 1950), and no. 58 (April 17, 1952). Cf. Kingsley Davis, "Future Population Trends and Their Significance," *Transactions of the Eighteenth North American Wildlife Conference* (Washington: Wildlife Management Institute, 1953), pp. 8–21.
[18] U.S. Bureau of the Census, *Current Population Reports,* series P-25, no. 123 (October 20, 1955); no. 187 (November 10, 1958).

by Whelpton and Taeuber,[19] and some of these criticisms were taken into account in the revised projection. This contrast of several points of view offers a good basis for the discussion of current practice.

Immigration

In the first of the two Census Bureau projections, it was assumed that the net arrival of 1.4 million during 1950–1955 would be duplicated during 1955–1960, and that subsequently the figure would fall off to 1.2 million per five-year period. Over the 20 years from 1955 to 1975, this would make a total of 5 million net arrivals or, assuming the same age structure and consequently the same fertility and mortality as for those who entered during 1950–1955, a total of 6.5 million persons added by immigration and the natural increase of the immigrants.

In the second projection the postulated net immigration for the entire period was 1.5 million per quinquennium, or roughly the number of net arrivals during the years 1951–1956. Assuming again that the age structure, fertility, and mortality remain the same as in this base period, up to 1980 a total of 10.2 million persons (rather than 6.5 million to 1975) will be added by immigration and the natural increase of the immigrants.

Presumably this revision in the assumed number of future immigrants was based primarily on the experience between the dates of the two projections. In 1956 and again in 1957 about 325,000 immigrants were admitted, or more by a considerable margin than in any previous postwar year. The size of the nonquota immigration from the Western Hemisphere went up especially fast. The number of immigrants from Mexico (note that these are *not* the temporary or illegal entrants) increased from about 6,000 in 1951 to almost 50,000 in 1957, that from Canada from an average of 23,000 in 1946–1955 to 29,000 in 1956 and 33,000 in 1957. (The movement of Puerto Ricans—which is not included in the immigration figures, though it amounts to the same thing in demographic and social-economic terms—also has been increasing.)

Several reasons can be given for assuming that immigration is likely to rise over the period of the projections, rather than either fall off or remain constant.

1. As we noted in Chapter 5, there is a considerable pressure on Con-

---

[19] Pascal K. Whelpton, "Census Projections: Some Areas of Doubt," *Conference Board Business Record*, 13:8 (August, 1956), 2–6. Conrad Taeuber, "The Census Bureau Projections of the Size, and the Age and Sex Composition of the Population of the United States in 1975," in Donald J. Bogue, ed., *Applications of Demography: The Population Situation in the U.S. in 1975* (Oxford, Ohio: Scripps Foundation for Research in Population Problems, 1957), pp. 53–58.

gress to modify or eliminate the national-quota system. Whether proponents of a different criterion for judging aspirant immigrants will
succeed in having their bills enacted is difficult to judge. It is worth
noting, however, that if national quotas were abolished and the total
number admissible from all quota countries remained the same, immigration might go up by as much as a third, for most visas are now reserved
for countries with, by and large, the smallest impetus to emigrate. Thus,
only about 70 per cent of the quotas have been used in the postwar
period—48 per cent of those for Northwestern Europe and (including
the "mortgaged" quotas) 187 per cent of those for Southern and Eastern
Europe.

2. As this last figure suggests, the national-quota system has already
been stretched considerably by the political necessity of admitting refugees
from the totalitarian enemies of the United States. As of 1957, 323,335
immigrants had been permitted to enter against "mortgaged" quotas;
and an act passed in that year wiped out these mortgages, freeing approximately 8,200 visas per year to countries with a high propensity to
emigrate.

3. Nearly one immigrant out of every four admitted during 1946–
1957 was a displaced person or refugee. The fact that so much of present
migration is politically motivated reduces the significance of economic
trends. If there were a depression in the United States, immigration from
many countries would fall off sharply; but the political pressure to leave
Communist-dominated areas, and that on the United States to accept
its share of refugees, would remain.

It is true, nevertheless, that immigration makes up no more than a
small part of the current population increase of roughly 3 million persons
per year, and that so long as anything like the present legislation remains
on the books this will continue to be so. As Taeuber pointed out, even so
dramatic an event as the defeat of the Hungarian revolution added only
some 38,000 refugees to the inflow. The number of immigrants fell off
from about 325,000 in 1956 and in 1957 to about 250,000 in 1958 and
260,000 in 1959.

Mortality

In the first of the two projections the Census Bureau assumed that
age-specific death rates for each sex would continue to decline at the
same rate as during the 1940's until 1955–1960, but that after that
date there would be no change up to 1970–1975. This slow decline was
postulated on the general assumption that there would be "no disastrous

war, major economic depression, epidemic, or other catastrophe" during the period of the projection. Actually, the extension of life that was anticipated over the next two decades was completed in one year!

According to the assumptions on which the 1958 projection was based, the average expectation of life at birth would increase, for males, from 66.7 years in 1955 to 69.8 in 1975–1980 and 71.3 in 2000, and, for females in the same years, from 72.9 to 76.0 and 77.1. Depending on whether fertility is high or low, the crude death rate would decline from 9.5 to 8 per thousand or slightly more. These figures are based on the assumption that there will be a continuous medium (that is, average between "high" and "low") improvement in death control throughout the period of the projection.

A more important innovation in the 1958 projection was the attempt to forecast mortality trends on the basis of what seems to be happening to specific causes of death: "Hypothetical low and high age-specific death rates, by sex, for the year 2000 were arrived at by applying assumed high and low percentages of reduction between 1953 and 2000 of death rates by age, sex, and 10 broad groups of causes of death, to the corresponding rates for 1953, and converting the results to age-sex-specific rates for all causes combined." While this method may not result immediately in greater accuracy, it is certainly a step in the right direction. The future decline in mortality, if any, depends not on the past rate of decline (except indirectly), but on future advances in the control of death. That it is admittedly difficult to predict such advances accurately is irrelevant to the logical point.

In their report to the National Resources Committee in the 1930's, it will be recalled, Thompson and Whelpton pointed out that control over the major infectious diseases had become so efficient that it would be more difficult to effect further reductions in mortality. Yet a considerable improvement was actually attained during the next quarter-century. From 1929–1931 to 1958 the average expectation of life at birth increased as follows: white males, 59.1 to 67.2 years; white females, 62.7 to 73.7 years; nonwhite males, 47.6 to 60.6 years; nonwhite females, 49.5 to 65.5 years. Existent cures had been made available to broader sectors of the population, and there had also been dramatic, unexpected innovations in every relevant field—diagnosis, medicine, surgery, and public health.

It is much truer today than it was in the 1930's that the major communicable diseases have been brought under control and that further advances depend on significant medical discoveries or innovations. A layman hardly dares suggest whether, or how soon, these will be made. Will there be a conquest of fetal mortality comparable to that of infant mortality during the past fifty years? Will the considerable amount of research on cardiovascular ailments and cancers produce substantial results over the next decade or two? Will the health insurance now enjoyed in one form or another by about 100 million Americans spread through the rest of the population? In short, will the improvement in death control consist only in the extension of known methods to more people and to peripheral areas of infectious diseases, or will there again be new types of control?

To assume that there will be no breakthrough in medical knowledge and techniques would be rash—how rash is indicated by the 1955 projection. The assumption in the second projection, that there will be a steady progress during the rest of this century, seems decidedly more plausible. And it is also possible that significant advances will be made in combatting degenerative diseases, in which case mortality might well decline faster than in the recent past. The effect of any improvement in death control on population growth will be smaller than in the past, however, since future advances will affect principally age-groups beyond the usual reproductive period. An error in forecasting such changes in mortality is not compounded from one generation to the next, as is one in forecasting fertility or mortality at younger ages.

It may be that some improvement in forecasting mortality trends could be effected by shifting the base of the analysis from age-specific to cohort rates. According to present medical opinion, the probability of survival depends not merely on age and the current efficacy of death-control measures, but also on the relevant social history that was experienced by each cohort. For example, persons born and brought up in the relative privation of the great depression of the 1930's are inherently weaker on the average, while those born after the big postwar improvement in obstetrical surgery, as a contrary example, reflect this advance in an increased average longevity. It is true that, with the present rate of medical advance, bringing this new factor to bear would not make much difference in mortality projections; but it is a possible improvement that can be made by a mere change in the method of calculation.

The Crucial Question of Fertility

As against our considerable uncertainty about the future trends in immigration and mortality, we are almost totally ignorant concerning future fertility. Compared with one hypothesis for immigration and one for mortality in each of the two projections, thus, the Census Bureau used four alternative assumptions about the trend of fertility.

From high to low, the four assumptions in the 1955 projection were as follows:

Series AA. The age-specific birth rates of 1954–1955 will remain constant over the whole 20 years.

Series A. The somewhat lower age-specific birth rates of 1950–1953 will remain constant over the whole 20 years.

Series B. The age-specific birth rates of 1950–1953 will remain constant until 1965, and then fall off linearly to the 1940–1942 rates by 1975.

Series C. The age-specific birth rates of 1950–1953 will fall off linearly to those of 1940–1942 by 1975.

On July 1, 1958, after only three years, the actual population was 360,-000 greater than the projected one with AA fertility, and almost 2 million greater than that with C fertility. As in previous postwar efforts, the major error by far was an underestimate of the fertility. In the 1958 projection, therefore, the assumed fertility was increased considerably, as follows:

Series I. The age-specific birth rates will average 10 per cent above the 1955–1957 level. This "very high" fertility "is not expected to be sustained over any length of time."

Series II. Age-specific birth rates will remain constant at the 1955–1957 level.

Series III. Age-specific birth rates will decline from the 1955–1957 level to the 1949–1951 level by 1965–1970, then remain constant.

Series IV. Age-specific birth rates will decline from the 1955–1957 level to the 1942–1944 level by 1965–1970, then remain constant.

The range in the projected populations, as well as the three Scripps-Michigan series,[20] can be suggested by citing the figures even for a single year. The various estimates of the 1975 population (in millions) are as follows:

[20] Ronald Freedman, Pascal K. Whelpton, and Arthur A. Campbell, *Family Planning, Sterility, and Population Growth* (New York: McGraw-Hill, 1959), Table 11-1. This was a collaborative effort of the Scripps Foundation for Research in Population Problems and the University of Michigan.

Census Bureau, 1955	Census Bureau, 1958	Scripps-Michigan, 1958
AA: 228.5	I: 243.9	High: 239.3
A: 221.5	II: 235.2	Medium: 222.5
B: 214.6	III: 225.6	Low: 205.4
C: 206.9	IV: 215.8	

Note the increase in the range from high to low estimates; it is 21.6 million in the 1955 projection, 28.1 million in the 1958 Census Bureau projection, and 33.9 million in the Scripps-Michigan projection. All series of all three projections, however, indicate a substantial increase from the 1955 population of 165 million. If projections are to be believed at all, the "incipient decline" in population spoken of in the 1930's is indeed a thing of the past, even as a myth.

The fertility as calculated in the three Scripps-Michigan projections is shown in Table 11-4. These figures deserve special attention, not so much because they are different from the Census Bureau projections

TABLE 11-4. Completed Family Size, Actual and Projected, by Cohorts of Ever-Married Women, United States, 1920–1985

Years of Birth	Year Aged 45–49	Completed Family Size		
1871–1875	1920	4.37		
1876–1880	1925	4.03		
1881–1885	1930	3.73		
1886–1890	1935	3.49		
1891–1895	1940	3.24		
1896–1900	1945	2.92		
1901–1905	1950	2.63		
1906–1910	1955	2.44		
		High	Medium	Low
1911–1915	1960	2.46	2.46	2.46
1916–1920	1965	2.70	2.68	2.66
1921–1925	1970	3.05	2.95	2.85
1926–1930	1975	3.15	3.00	2.85
1931–1935	1980	3.25	3.05	2.85
1936–1940	1985	3.35	3.05	2.75

Source: Ronald Freedman, Pascal K. Whelpton, and Arthur A. Campbell, *Family Planning, Sterility, and Population Growth* (New York: McGraw-Hill, 1959), Table 10-4.

The Census Clock, Washington, D.C., designed as a means of visual presentation of the principal factors bearing on the growth of the U.S. population. (U.S. Bureau of the Census)

(although this is also the case) as because the method used was superior in two important respects:

1. The calculation was based on the fertility of cohorts, which in principle (as with mortality projections, but even more so) is better than age-specific birth rates. One reason for the baby boom, it will be recalled,[21] was that many women who had postponed having children during the 1930's had them in the 1940's, relatively late in their fecund period. Once this special circumstance was no longer relevant, one could expect that the birth rates of women over 40, or perhaps even of those over 30, would fall off. That is, the age-specific birth rates of this group—and of cohorts generally—depend both on the general determinants of fertility and on the specific past experiences of each cohort.

[21] See pages 237–239.

2. The estimate of future fertility, moreover, is not simply one or another extrapolation of past trends but an interpretation of data on the expected completed family size, as gathered in a nationwide sample survey. It is true, of course, that what married women say about the number of children they expect to have is an insecure base for fertility forecasts, yet even such inaccurate and incomplete data are better than no direct contact with the presumed parents to be.

With respect to future trends, the most important component of the baby boom was the higher fertility of young women. Those aged 20–24 in 1955 had higher cumulative birth rates than any comparable set of cohorts for as far back as there are records, and probably for the whole of the nation's history. This amazing increase was the consequence of earlier marriage and earlier childbearing. Let us consider each of these factors in turn.

A decline in the age at marriage affects fertility in two ways—actual but temporary, and permanent but only potential. The first type can be illustrated by arranging the recent trend into a schematic pattern. If we assume that all girls in 1940 married when they were 21 and that by 1950 all married when they were 20, this means that one extra cohort was crowded into the regular procession, increasing the average annual number of marriages between 1940 and 1950 by one-tenth of the average size of the cohorts. It means also that the number of first and second births rose sharply and thus also the crude birth rate, but if the average number of children per family remained constant this increase would be temporary and not very significant in the long run. Conversely, if the average age rises again, there will be a fall in the annual number of marriages and in the birth rate. Is this likely to happen? The remarkable decline in the median age at marriage, which for females decreased by about a year and a half from 1940 to 1950, was in part the effect of the war; but, as was noted in Chapter 9, less temporary factors also seem to be operative.

In order to consider the long-term effect of a decline in the age at marriage on fertility, we must pose a second question: What will the typical young mother do after she has had the three children she wants? The earlier in life that marriage and the bearing of planned children takes place, the longer the interval between the birth of the last planned child and the end of the fecund period, and the greater the possibility for additional births. How many American women use contraceptives, and how effectively? How many children would they like to have, and how probable is it that they will have this number?

By far our best information on these questions comes from the Scripps-

Michigan study, based on interviews in 1955 with 2,713 married women, representing a national probability sample of all white couples with the wife aged 18 to 39 years. Of this group, almost one in ten was completely sterile, usually because of an operation performed either as a health or a contraceptive measure. About one-third of the total sample was classified as "subfecund," including the definitely and the probably sterile, those with some but less than "normal" fecundity, and those of whom the fecundity was indeterminate. Of the remaining "fecund" couples, 83 per cent had tried to space wanted pregnancies or prevent those not wanted, 5 per cent intended to do so at a later date, and an additional 6 per cent may have reduced their conception rate by having the wife douche "for cleanliness" soon after each intercourse. Only 6 per cent of the fecund couples reported that they would never use any control measure.[22] Family-planning is thus nearly universal among couples of normal fecundity.

The wives in the sample were asked how many births they thought they would have, and their answers suggest that a rise in fertility is likely. For cohorts born in 1931 to 1937, the expected number of births ranges between 2.8 and 3.4, with 3.2 the "most likely" figure.[23] All of these respondents had married before ages 18–24, which they reached by 1955. Since members of these cohorts who marry at later ages will probably have fewer children, the average number of expected births to all who will marry before middle age is lower—between 2.8 and 3.2, with 3.0 as a medium figure.[24]

It is difficult to know how accurately an offhand response to a question about expected births reflects the actual size of the family over the next several decades, even assuming that the general social-economic determinants of population growth do not change. It is significant, nevertheless, that the wives aged 18–39 in 1955 said that they expected more children than were borne by the average wife then aged 40–54. The medium and high estimates of future fertility are therefore substantially above the actual 2.4 births per ever-married white woman born in 1906–1910.[25]

How likely is the expected size of the family to be realized? The answer to this question depends principally on (1) the extent of subfecundity and (2) the effectiveness of contraceptives.

1. Subfecundity will probably reduce fertility less than it did in the

[22] Freedman, Whelpton, and Campbell, *op. cit.,* pp. 61–62.
[23] *Ibid.,* p. 228.
[24] *Ibid.,* p. 340.
[25] Grabill, Kiser, and Whelpton, *op. cit.,* p. 325.

interwar period, partly because of medical advances (for example, the better control of venereal disease, greatly improved obstetrical surgery) and partly because of the decline in the age at marriage and childbearing. The period of maximum fecundity is during the woman's twenties. The middle-class style in the 1930's, getting married when the bride was in her middle twenties and postponing having children for another several years, meant that in peripheral cases the couple would be unable to conceive. With the present pattern, involuntary childlessness is reduced substantially.

2. Women now marry at the median age of 20 and have an average of about two children over the next six or seven years. Thus, they "expect" to have only one more child on the average during the remaining 15 to 20 years of the fecund period. Only the best methods of contraception are effective for 15 years of exposure, and what little evidence there is suggests that many couples who intend to plan the size of their family use relatively inefficient means.[26]

On the average, then, the size of the actual family is likely to be larger than the expected one; and since the latter already indicates a rise in completed family size, there are two reasons for supposing that the birth rate will go up. It is possible, however, that these factors will be offset by changes in the timing of births, which contributed heavily to the high birth rates during 1947–1959. If the average size of completed family goes up in accordance with the *maximum* expectations of the wives in the 1955 sample, the crude birth rate will decline from an average of 24.8 in 1955–1960 to 23.7 in 1960–1965. And if the size of the family is lower than the maximum, the decline in the birth rate will, of course, be sharper, and last longer.[27]

Such specific variables as age at marriage and the size of the planned family are themselves the consequences of more general underlying conditions that set a pro- or antinatalist mood in the population. Obviously,

---

[26] For example, the Indianapolis study, which was restricted to couples who had been married 12 to 15 years, showed that they tend to improve their contraceptive means after a number of failures. Nevertheless, over 35 per cent of this sample were still using "ineffective" or "very ineffective" methods at the time of the survey. For all contraceptives together, there was an average pregnancy rate of 12 per 100 years of exposure, and for specific methods this ranged from four with diaphragm and jelly to 26 with Lysol douche (Charles F. Westoff, Lee F. Herrera, and P. K. Whelpton, "Social and Psychological Factors Affecting Fertility, Part 20: The Use, Effectiveness, and Acceptability of Methods of Fertility Control," *Milbank Memorial Fund Quarterly,* 31:3, July, 1953, 291–357). See also Christopher Tietze, *The Clinical Effectiveness of Contraceptive Methods* (New York: National Committee on Maternal Health [1958]).

[27] Freedman, Whelpton, and Campbell, *op. cit.,* p. 383.

these more basic factors cannot be described precisely, and particularly not today, when fertility patterns are a composite of two conflicting tendencies. The forces that impelled the decline in American fertility from the beginning of the nineteenth century on did not suddenly disappear in 1940; some of the values and styles of living in modern America still push toward a decline in the birth rate. On the other hand, the counter forces that resulted in the baby boom and the continued high postwar fertility are also a reality, not merely an aberration from the downward trend.

In an especially interesting paper, Frank Notestein has made a post factum analysis of why demographers in the 1930's, he himself included, had been mistaken in their expectations with respect to fertility. The thesis is that they had been wrong in their timing but not fundamentally.[28] Notestein cited three main reasons for the belief generally held during the interwar period that the decline in the birth rate would continue:

In the first place, the downward trend got under way in a differential fashion, spreading from the upper urban classes of the population down through the social-economic structure and outward from the city to the rural regions. By the end of the interwar period the highest rates were the ones that were declining most rapidly, the lowest were declining least rapidly, and no evidence of a real up-turn was in sight. In the second place, the differences in fertility were closely correlated with differences in the prevalence and effectiveness of contraceptive practice, and there was every indication that contraceptive materials were becoming more abundant, and that the knowledge of their use was spreading. In the third place, the middle class standards, which had been such a strong factor in the motivation for small families, appeared to be spreading throughout the mass of the population. Thus the nature of the trends, the means by which they were brought about, and the nature of the pressures and incentives motivating restrictionist practices all suggested a pattern of decline that had not run its course.

Each of these points calls for some comment.

Certainly the wider distribution of contraceptive knowledge and means facilitated the decline in fertility, but it was never decisive, even in the nineteenth century. As we have seen, the fertility ratio began to fall off in the United States from 1810 on, and its decline was substantial before a method of control more reliable than coitus interruptus became available. In the Western world generally the trend in fertility depended less

---

[28] Frank W. Notestein, "The Population of the World in the Year 2000," *Journal of the American Statistical Association,* 45:251 (September, 1950), 335–345. See also the appended note by Joseph S. Davis, "Population and Resources," pp. 346–349. (The article without the note has been reprinted in Spengler and Duncan, *op. cit.,* pp. 34–43.)

on the manner of controlling conception than on the will to control it. In Ireland, where the Catholic Church blocked the general sale of contraceptives, the demand for smaller families found alternative expression in the postponement of marriage; and in the Netherlands, which had had a fairly successful birth-control movement, fertility never fell to the general Northwestern European level. In other words, the statement that "differences in fertility were closely correlated with differences in the prevalence and effectiveness of contraceptive practices" is true only with important qualifications.

One can also question the extrapolation of a past trend to its completion. It is true that most Americans try to plan the size of their families, but even today many do so inefficiently; and the data do not tell us how fast the best contraceptive means are being adopted outside the upper middle class, where they now prevail. With the wider dissemination of some kind of contraception, some of the fervor of the pioneers of the movement evaporated. Advocates of birth control, in order to emphasize that they favored the *control* rather than the limitation of births, began using the term "planned parenthood," and their clinics started to devote a good deal of time and effort to treating sterility.

Similarly, the assertion that "no evidence of a real upturn was in sight" in the 1930's is subject to challenge. The first studies in differential fertility had shown a negative correlation between social class and size of family, but this uniform pattern was broken, possibly first in Sweden but also in other Western countries, especially if the length of marriage was held constant.[29] Particularly when one uses income as the index of social class, the typical pattern seemed to be a J-curve rather than a linear relation. The average family size of upper classes in the cities—precisely those who had led the revolt against procreation up to the physiological limit—was in some cases no longer declining in the 1930's. Middle-class standards were indeed spreading throughout the mass of the population, but they were not unambiguously "such a strong factor in the motivation for small families" as they had once been.

Finally, the point that "the highest rates were the ones that were declining most rapidly, and the lowest were declining least rapidly," could also have been offered as evidence that the downward trend was leveling off. This would seem to be especially so if the indications of the revival

[29] Cf. Frank W. Notestein, "The Relation of Social Status to the Fertility of Native-Born Married Women in the United States," in G. H. L. F. Pitt-Rivers, ed., *Problems of Population: Being the Report of the Proceedings of the Second General Assembly of the International Union for the Scientific Investigation of Population Problems, London, June 15–18, 1931* (London: Allen & Unwin, 1932), pp. 147–169.

of middle-class fertility had been taken into account. In the United States, if not in Europe, the postwar trend seems indeed to be toward stabilization at a middle-sized family, with the social classes below this fertility level moving up to it and those above it moving down.

We ought to have learned one thing from the postwar baby boom— that parents can rationally choose to have children, as against alternative ways of life. In the 1930's it was believed that the only possible choice for a couple, once contraception was made available in both physical and moral terms, was to help establish a norm of childless marriages. For all the reasons that potential parents had for preventing the conception of a fifth or sixth child seemed to apply *a fortiori* to the first child, which cost them the most in money, time, effort, and loss of freedom. The conceptual framework in which population extrapolations were made was a simple equation: middle-class rationality added to access to contraceptives ultimately will effect an average family too small to maintain the population. If a couple with no impediments to comfortable childlessness nevertheless sometimes chooses to have three or more children, what determines this choice?

The "new look" in family size, like any other change in style, has spread in part simply by contagion. But it has also been motivated by the deepest aspirations of the American middle class. With a certain exaggeration, the United States can be termed the country of upward mobility. The behavior patterns of the typical American, to the extent that such a person exists, can probably be best defined in terms of the hopes and expectations excited by the "American promise" of a happier life. In the past middle-class parents regarded it as their duty to offer the maximum advantages to a very small number of children; and this value was certainly an important reason for the spread of the small-family system. Today, however, the psychologists' dictum that the single child is more likely to be neurotic has been spread through women's magazines to become a commonplace of middle-class lore. Whether it is true or not is beside the point; the theory, even if spurious, has been widely enough accepted to affect present attitudes and behavior, as the Indianapolis study indicated. If one has children at all, one must—for their sake—have at least two, and preferably three. The fact that the new trend in family size has been based on a reinterpretation of the parents' duty, rather than on an attempt to reject it, indicates a greater likelihood of permanence.

The small family of the recent past was, one might say, built into the small city apartment, which made an additional child an expensive and bothersome undertaking. During the postwar period, it will be recalled, many middle-class families have moved to the suburbs, which combine urban amenities with a style of life that invites, almost demands, children. Hardly anyone rents a house in the suburbs; and home ownership, which increased by half between 1940 and 1950, has always been associated with large or middle-sized families. It may be less meaningful than it once was to speak of the family's loss of function, for in the suburban setting the home is apparently becoming the focus of a significant family life. If the wife works, as she often does, it is not as a rule in order to establish a career independent of her role as wife and mother, but in order to supplement her husband's salary or wage. If the man is usually away at work during the day, he spends evenings and weekends with his family; the do-it-yourself craze that has spread through American suburbia is a way of bringing the continuous extension and decoration of homes under the heading of "fun." Parents no longer educate their children directly, but they are enormously concerned with finding a "good school" or trying to establish one through a Parent-Teacher Association. When details of this kind are added up, the sum is a milieu in which a childless couple feels out of place.

The institutional setting that the three-child family now has suggests that—if the general social and economic conditions remain more or less the same [30]—a relatively high fertility is likely to be a fairly stable element of American life. This does not mean, of course, that it will be. It means that potential parents' decisions on whether to have children are determined not only by their "selfish" desire for "comfort" but also by "pride in progeny." Now that birth control is all but universal, it is the relation between these that principally determines the size of the family—and the accuracy of population projections.

PROJECTIONS VS. FORECASTS

It has become usual to distinguish two types of estimates of future population growth. When all of the independent variables are given in demographic terms—for example, certain age-specific birth and death rates and net migration at a given annual rate—the extrapolation of the past trend is termed a population **projection.** When at least some of the independent variables are given in social or economic terms, or the greater or lesser probability of demographic variables is posited in a social-economic framework, the same extrapolation is termed a population

[30] For a discussion of the interrelation of population growth and the economy, see pages 530–534.

forecast. Many extrapolations are not clearly in either one class or the other. Let us consider first those that are.

Demographers often project the future population that will result from the current rate of increase not in order to make a valid forecast but, on the contrary, to demonstrate that the present growth *cannot* continue. An extreme example can be cited from the Australian demographer George Knibbs: If a population grew from a single couple at the annual rate of 1 per cent, at the end of 10,000 years it would require 248,293,000,000,000,000,000 earths to furnish the material for the bodies of the people.[31] The actual rate of growth of the world population during the past 30 years has been at 1.2 per cent per year, and during the past five years at more than 1.5 per cent. With such a calculation as Knibbs made, one is struck by the fact that the current increase of the human species is a highly temporary phenomenon, which could not have begun very long ago and cannot continue for very much longer.

On the more modest scale of extrapolations of one country's population growth over a few decades, such projections are much less useful. It is quite likely, as we have seen, that the future trends of immigration, mortality, and fertility will all favor a rapid increase of the population of the United States. To point out that if such a process were to continue for several centuries there would be "standing room only," does not help us determine what the population will probably be in 1975. It is only in countries where the population pressure is both already great and increasing rapidly, as in India or China, that an extrapolation over even a relatively short period helps demonstrate that present growth rates cannot continue, and may encourage policy-makers to consider whether they would prefer a decreased fertility or an increased mortality.

At the other extreme from a projection that specifically does not forecast there is a forecast that is placed fully in the economic and social context of population change. There is no reason why a population analyst should be expected to know, for example, whether and when an economic depression will occur, or a war, or a cure for cancer, or any of the other hundred significant changes in the economy, technology, society, cultural patterns, that are relevant to population growth. Even a specialist in these various fields is not only generally unable to predict their future development but also often unable to summarize their past trend accurately. For instance, the crucial error of the demographers, their

---

[31] George Handley Knibbs, *The Shadow of the World's Future: Or the Earth's Population Possibilities & the Consequences of the Present Rate of Increase of the Earth's Inhabitants* (London: Benn, 1928), p. 49, n. 1.

failure to predict postwar fertility correctly, was based in large measure on the sociologists' analysis of urbanism. If it is believed that in a *Gesellschaft* all social relations are atomized, then it is reasonable to conclude that increasing urbanization would also atomize the family. In the words of the leading family sociologist of the 1930's, Ernest Burgess, the family was being transformed from an "institution" to "companionship." This was also a false prognosis.

It is within the province of the demographer to consider, however, "the determinants and consequences of population trends" (as it was put in the title of the well known United Nations publication), and these also are not ordinarily known with any precision. Most of the forecasts of the 1930's, for instance, were hedged with the condition that there would be no major war over the period of the projection; for the excess mortality resulting from it, together with the loss in fertility from the subsequent unbalanced population structure, would mean a faster decline in population growth. The war came, but for most of the belligerent countries the consequence was the opposite of what had been anticipated. Similarly, the effect of an economic depression on the birth rate is not really well understood. Indeed, family size fell off during the 1930's, but in part because the economic crisis came as a culmination to many other depressants on fertility. The fact that the well-to-do had the smallest families and the men on work-relief the largest should warn us against a simplistic economic interpretation of fertility trends. If there is to be another depression of a given severity—measured, let us say, by the proportion of the labor force unemployed—no demographer would be able to estimate how much, or even whether, the birth rate would fall as a result.

Actually, in order to forecast accurately one ought to know not only the probable effect of a war or a depression on population growth but also, vice versa, the probable effect of population growth of a given rate in helping bring on, or avoid, a war or a depression. Three analytic models can be distinguished—population growth interpreted as (a) a self-contained process, as (b) the consequence of economic and social factors, or as (c) one of the causes of the changes in other factors being investigated. All three are valid and useful for various specific purposes. Since population processes are to some degree cumulative, they can indeed be analyzed independently of other factors. And since the increase in numbers is controlled in its rate and especially in its ultimate limit by other factors, it can also be seen as the dependent variable, the consequence of natural resources, economic development, and such cultural influences as religion and family attitudes. Or it can be analyzed as the independent variable, one important cause of change in the economy or in society.

Actual forecasts, however, are usually based on the assumption that population growth is self-contained. The influence of other factors on it is always at least implied in the negative assumption that no significant change in social-economic conditions will take place over the period of the projection. Occasionally, but not very often, alternative projections are specifically linked to various possible changes in the social-economic conditions. But the effect of population growth on the society and thus back on itself has seldom or never been included except in such broad, generalized forecasts as the theory of the demographic transition: an improved efficiency in death-control measures increased the rate of population growth, which stimulated the need or desire for birth control. We do not know enough to discuss this kind of interaction in the framework of a specific short-term projection.

Both projections and forecasts, if these words are narrowly defined, are thus useful primarily for a rather loose analysis over a relatively long period. Most population extrapolations are a little of both, in form purely mathematical calculations of what would happen under certain demographic conditions, but in actuality with premises chosen because they seem reasonable in the given social and economic context. The difference, some critics have intimated, lies only in the temerity of the analyst: in the 1930's, when the accuracy of the extrapolations was sometimes uncanny, they were termed "forecasts," while the less successful efforts of the postwar period, though based on precisely the same type of calculations, are called "projections." And if the demographer tries to hold to the differentiation, he is put under pressure to abandon it.

Maintaining the distinction between population projections and population forecasts is not easily done. Once assumptions have been spelled out and the consequent arithmetic has been done, it seems difficult to remove the aura of predictions from the resulting numbers. Hard pressed planners in government and business and in all other endeavors which need indications of future developments ask simply for a number. What they seem to want is a forecast, and sometimes they express impatience with the explanation that a forecast is exactly what is not available. And when confronted with several numbers and the statement that, though they differ widely, each of these is a reasonable number, there is sometimes a tendency to pick one of the numbers and treat it as though it were a forecast.[32]

One way out of the dilemma would be to bring the implicit gradient of probabilities to the surface and estimate both the future population

[32] Taeuber, "The Census Bureau Projections," *op. cit.*

trend and the degree of uncertainty of alternative projections.[33] Unfortunately, no techniques yet exist by which the relative probability of various assumptions can be reliably judged.

SUMMARY

The need for estimates of future population growth is too great to be denied. Government agencies, federal, state, and local; both the production and the sales divisions of corporations; colleges, churches, and other cultural institutions—the list of those using population forecasts includes all who deal on a sizable scale with people and attempt to plan their operations some way into the future. The demand for extrapolations has if anything increased, in spite of the conspicuous failure of most recent projections to make an accurate forecast.

So long as a population is growing at a uniform or regularly changing rate in the same direction, one can predict its future with very simple techniques, as was done by a number of men in the nineteenth century. However, it is a useful rule of thumb in social analysis that any trend, once it goes beyond a certain point, tends to build up a resistance that eventually leads to a reversal. Merely extrapolating the decline in the rate of population growth, for example, was satisfactory for a period, but only for a period. In order to understand the increase one must divide it into its three components of fertility, mortality, and net migration; try to judge how these will be affected by the probable social and economic developments; and apply variable age-specific rates to a population changing in both size and structure.

The principal difficulty in making an accurate forecast is in judging the probable trend of the birth rate. In the 1930's demographers generally believed both that the incentives that had induced the middle class to reduce its average fertility would eventually establish a one-child or childless family as the norm in that class, and that this example would spread through the social structure to other classes. In the 1940's, however, the gradual decline in the average size of the family over the past century or more was reversed. Depending on whether the postwar baby boom and the continued high fertility are interpreted as a temporary aberration in the secular trend or as the beginning of a new style in the American family, it is reasonable to set markedly different estimates of the country's future fertility and thus of its population growth; but in any case the estimates are likely to differ from those made in the 1930's. One

---

[33] See H. V. Muhsam, "The Utilization of Alternative Population Forecasts in Planning," *Bulletin of the Research Council of Israel*, 5c:2–3 (March–June, 1956), 133–146.

can argue that the present higher level of American fertility has established an institutional base that will tend to insure its continuity. In the new suburbs, where the most rapid population growth is taking place, children form so essential a part of the social environment that a childless couple feels out of place. On the other hand, many of the influences that resulted in the long-term decline in average family size are still operative and may reassert themselves without warning. Moreover, some of the very high fertility during the postwar years has been the result of an overlap between two styles of family life, with the younger women having their children early in their life and the older women having their children later in their life.

If effective cures are found for such diseases as cancers and cardiac ailments, the age-groups that will benefit are principally those beyond the reproductive period. That is to say, the resultant population growth would not be cumulative. The major long-run determinant of population growth is fertility, and relatively small changes in marriage and family patterns can effect appreciable variation in both the size and the structure of the population. On balance, whatever evidence is available suggests that the average family size will remain moderately large. And with mortality as low as it is—and will remain, barring a catastrophe on the scale of an all-out war—a moderately large family is enough to ensure a rapid population growth.

If we do not know enough about the determinants of population growth to predict its future trend more or less accurately, might it not be better to concentrate on the prior task of learning better what has happened, and put off until a later time speculations about what will happen? The principal answer to this reasonable question is that there is not so sharp an opposition between the two as it might seem. The contrast, for example, between the forecast decline in family size and the actual baby boom stirred many demographers' especial interest in fertility and thus may increase our knowledge about this subject. New types of research have been undertaken; new methods of analysis have been developed. If more accurate estimates of future population growth will be made one day, it will be in part because of the stimulus given by recent fiascos.

SUGGESTIONS FOR FURTHER READING

Joseph J. Spengler, "Population Projections in Nineteenth Century America," *American Sociological Review*, 1:6 (December, 1936), 905–921.

Raymond Pearl, *The Biology of Population Growth* (New York: Knopf, 1925).

Robert R. Kuczynski, *The Measurement of Population Growth: Methods and Results* (London: Sidgwick & Jackson, 1935).

> On linear projections, the logistic curve, and the net reproduction rate—three methods of population forecasting now mainly of historical interest.

U.S. Bureau of the Census, *Current Population Reports,* series P-25, no. 123 (October 20, 1955); no. 187 (November 10, 1958).

Donald J. Bogue, ed., *Applications of Demography: The Population Situation in the U.S. in 1975* (Oxford, Ohio: Scripps Foundation for Research in Population Problems, 1957).

> Two of a series of forecasts by the Census Bureau, and an application of the figures of the 1955 projection to a number of fields.

Ronald Freedman, Pascal K. Whelpton, and Arthur A. Campbell, *Family Planning, Sterility, and Population Growth* (New York: McGraw-Hill, 1959).

> The best analysis to date of the future American population.

Harold F. Dorn, "Pitfalls in Population Forecasts and Projections," *Journal of the American Statistical Association,* 45:251 (September, 1950), 311–334. (This article has been reprinted in Joseph J. Spengler and Otis Dudley Duncan, eds., *Demographic Analysis,* Glencoe, Ill.: Free Press, 1956, pp. 69–90.)

Kurt Mayer, "Fertility Changes and Population Changes in the United States," *Social Research,* 26:3 (Autumn, 1959), 347–366.

Pascal K. Whelpton, "Census Projections: Some Areas of Doubt," *Conference Board Business Record,* 13:8 (August, 1956), 2–6.

Kingsley Davis, "Future Population Trends and Their Significance," *Transactions of the Eighteenth North American Wildlife Conference* (Washington: Wildlife Management Institute, 1953), pp. 8–21.

Frank W. Notestein, "The Population of the World in the Year 2000," *Journal of the American Statistical Association,* 45:251 (September, 1950), 335–345. (This article has been reprinted in Joseph J. Spengler and Otis Dudley Duncan, eds., *Demographic Analysis,* Glencoe, Ill.: Free Press, 1956, pp. 34–43).

> Interesting and provocative articles on the reasons for the failure of recent population forecasts to predict accurately, and on whether some improvement can be expected soon.

United Nations, Department of Economic and Social Affairs, *Methods for Population Projections by Sex and Age* (Population Studies, no. 25; New York, 1956).

Techniques explained in simple language, with examples drawn from many populations.

PART II

Population in Various Types of Society

Part I of this volume, it will be recalled, had a dual purpose—to introduce the reader to some of the main concepts of population analysis and to discuss specifically the past and future population growth of the United States. This country was chosen more or less arbitrarily, because it is the one most familiar to the author and presumably of greatest interest to most of the readers. There was also another reason for singling out one country, any country—namely, to postpone complicating the discussion with cross-cultural comparisons. While the United States has undergone momentous transformations during its short history, certain features of its social structure and culture have either remained constant or changed in a relatively direct fashion. This comparative simplicity is apparent once we pose the question of how to generalize from this one example. Among all the societies that exist or have existed, which ought to be included here, and why?

The first three chapters of Part II trace the cultural evolution of mankind through three major stages—preurban peoples, preindustrial civilizations, and England during the rise of modern industry. Since the very words "cultural evolution" are still almost an invitation to misunderstanding, it is important to distinguish, however briefly, the classical definition of this term from what it means today.

Anthropology in the middle of the nineteenth century was passing from an emphasis on the collection of data to their systematization. Partly as a result of the intellectual furor aroused by Darwin's *Origin of Species,* partly as a parallel expression of the *Zeitgeist* of progress, this systematization usually took the form of a theory of cultural evolution. According to Edward B. Tylor, Lewis Henry Morgan, Herbert Spencer, and dozens of lesser figures, mankind had evolved through a series of cultural stages, each one well defined by its technical culture, family type, social organization, religion, art, and so on. Morgan, for example, divided all of human history and prehistory into three main stages, which he termed Savagery, Barbarism, and Civilization. The data he collated on peoples as widely separated as ancient Greeks and Romans, the natives of Australia and America, were structured largely in terms of the Iroquois, whom he knew by personal study. Thus, because the relatively advanced Polynesians lacked the bow and arrow, they were placed in the middle status of Savagery, or below the level of all North American tribes.[1] This example is typical of the most egregious error of the nineteenth-century evolutionary theorists—their assumption that the level of technology determined directly and without exception all other cultural and social forms. The family, thus, was postulated to have begun with indiscriminate mating in a food-gathering horde, developed through matriarchy to polygyny in agricultural societies, and reached its moral apex in the monogamy of industrial Europe. Today no anthropologist outside the Soviet orbit would support either the substance or the ethical overtones of this "history" of the family; and as more and better ethnographic data were collected from various parts of the world, it became clear that the evolutionary schema was no more adequate in many of its other details.

By the beginning of the twentieth century anthropologists were attacking the doctrine of cultural evolution itself: it was necessary to start fresh, to clean out all these fanciful theories and concentrate on building a solid empirical base. The most influential person in this movement, at least in the United States, was Franz Boas, who taught a whole generation of anthropologists and stamped them with his methodological and conceptual predilections.[2] Boas had important limitations, however, as well as great merit. The "Boas school," while performing a very necessary pruning job, ended by chopping at the very tree of the theory of culture change. During the past several decades, thus, there has been a marked revival in the concept of cultural evolution.

The **unilinear** evolutionary scheme developed by Tylor, Morgan, and others was clearly wrong in many respects, but its essential outline is beyond question. The culture of the human species has indeed developed through a number of broad stages. No one doubts that hunting and gathering preceded the domestication of plants and animals, and that agriculture was a prerequisite to urban civilizations whenever these developed. Such a theory of **universal** evolution, however, is highly abstract and difficult to relate to actual cultures, rather than "culture." A third conceptual schema, **multilinear** evolution, is more empirical than

---

[1] For a convenient summary and commentary, see Robert H. Lowie, *The History of Ethnological Theory* (New York: Rinehart, 1937), Ch. 6.

[2] Representative statements on evolutionary theory include Franz Boas, *The Mind of Primitive Man* (New York: Macmillan, 1929), Ch. 7 and *passim;* Robert H. Lowie, *Primitive Society* (New York: Liveright, 1947); Alexander A. Goldenweiser, *Early Civilization: An Introduction to Anthropology* (New York: Knopf, 1922). For a sympathetic appreciation of Boas, see Melville J. Herskovits, *Franz Boas: The Science of Man in the Making* (New York: Scribner, 1953).

deductive, and variation within societal types is no less emphasized than their general features.[3] By such an approach, an attempt is made to overcome the conceptual limitations both of unilinear evolutionists (culture stages relatively bare of empirical data) and of anti-evolutionists (a large number of ethnographic studies with no over-all theory in which their interrelations can be indicated).

Multilinear evolution is a theoretical framework especially appropriate to a work on population. Whether the art or the religion or the language of advanced civilizations is "higher" than those of primitives is a moot, if not indeed a meaningless, question. That there is an enormous difference in population, however, is indisputable; and with respect to this variable, apart from short-term fluctuations, the change has been all in one direction. Even to term this consistent increase "progress" is not ethnocentric, for the death control that has been attained by modern Western society, and to a lesser degree by other high civilizations, is a universal value.

The demographic transition, like the broader theory of unilinear cultural evolution of which it is one specific application, is valuable in that it points to the most abstract stages of population change. But, as we have noted in Chapter 1, it is also too simple, too mechanistic. All of the societies in Stage III are industrial, but not all industrial societies are sufficiently similar in their population patterns to be classed together.

Chapter 15 is an analysis of the population of totalitarian societies, specifically of the Soviet Union and Nazi Germany, and thus of societies that are both industrial and totalitarian. The main thesis suggested in such a classification is that it makes a real difference whether the state intervenes in the processes of fertility, mortality, and migration. Even when the object of policies is not achieved, the insistent attempt to impose them alters the natural development assumed in the theory of the demographic cycle.

Chapter 16, on the population of underdeveloped areas, is necessary because Stage II of the Western demographic cycle, the period of falling mortality and increasing numbers, does not adequately describe present trends in non-Western countries. The decline in the death rates has been precipitous, and the rise in populations explosive. When the same processes develop so much more rapidly, they become, or may become, totally different in their social effects.

It would have been useful in a larger book to include yet another

[3] See Julian H. Steward, *Theory of Culture Change: The Methodology of Multilinear Evolution* (Urbana: University of Illinois Press, 1955), Ch. 1.

chapter on the population of present-day Western Europe. Given the limitations of space, however, the rather full discussion of the United States in Part I must be accepted, *pars pro toto,* as the main analysis also of population phenomena in the modern Western world. As one would expect, the populations of Western nations have been analyzed in great detail, and the reader interested in this subject will have no difficulty in finding supplements to this volume. The following English-language works are especially recommended:

Dudley Kirk, *Europe's Population in the Interwar Years* (League of Nations; Princeton: Princeton University Press, 1946).

D. V. Glass, *Population Policies and Movements in Europe* (Oxford: Clarendon, 1940).

United Kingdom, Royal Commission on Population, *Report* (London: H.M. Stationery Office, 1949).

Joseph J. Spengler, *France Faces Depopulation* (Durham, N. C.: Duke University Press, 1938).

Kurt B. Mayer, *The Population of Switzerland* (New York: Columbia University Press, 1952).

Alva Myrdal, *Nation and Family: The Swedish Experiment in Democratic Family and Population Policy* (London: Kegan Paul, Trench, Trubner, 1945).

William Petersen, *Planned Migration: The Social Determinants of the Dutch-Canadian Movement* (Berkeley: University of California Press, 1955).

W. D. Borrie, *Population Trends and Policies: A Study in Australian and World Demography* (Sydney: Australasian Publishing Company, 1948).

Norman Lawrence, *Israel: Jewish Population and Immigration* (U.S. Bureau of the Census, International Population Statistics Reports, series P-90, no. 2; Washington: U.S. Government Printing Office, 1952).

Hope T. Eldridge, *Population Policies: A Survey of Recent Developments* (Washington: International Union for the Scientific Study of Population, 1954).

12. *THE POPULATION*
OF PRIMITIVE SOCIETIES

Population data concerning either prehistoric or contemporary primitive societies are of a completely different order from those based on even inadequate statistics. It is not merely that population size, structure, movements, and whatever, must be inferred from indirect evidence, but also that the latter is incomplete and often biased. Our information concerning present-day primitive peoples comes mainly not from themselves but from representatives of advanced societies, who usually began to record fairly reliable observations only after a considerable period of contact. Reconstructing the true primitive culture, entirely free of influence from civilized peoples, is thus almost as difficult with contemporary as with prehistoric examples.

Since the population of a primitive society depends very directly on its economy, it is reasonable to combine data on the prehistoric period with those on contemporaries in the same "stage" of development. Peoples do not live in economic stages, of course; they possess economies, which are generally combinations of such ideal types as collecting, hunting, fishing, cultivation, and stock-raising. However, so long as we keep in mind that these are abstractions, they can be useful in analyzing the various ways that real societies at different cultural levels acquire their food. Between the physical environment and the number of people that subsist on it, there is always an intervening variable, the cultural pattern; but the less efficient the technology, the more direct the relation is between habitat and population.

Any study of primitive economics deals largely with the production and consumption of food. This is so partly because of the directness of the nutritional aim and the absence of intermediaries such as an entrepreneur and a money payment;

313

partly because of the relatively small range of objects of economic interest; and partly because of the extensive use of food for other than purely nutritive purposes.[1]

TYPES OF PRIMITIVE ECONOMY

The geologic period that runs from several hundred thousand years ago to almost the beginning of history is called the Pleistocene, or "most recent." Four times during this era enormous ice sheets expanded to cover substantial portions of Eurasia and North America. Forms of life suited to milder climates perished unless they adapted to the cold or migrated southward. At the beginning of the Pleistocene, or perhaps even earlier in the Cenozoic era, hominids began to evolve, and from these there developed the new species of *Homo sapiens*.

We know very little about the emergence of man. We cannot time it, except very approximately. It may have taken place in Asia, as was once generally believed, or in Africa, as many human paleontologists are now inclined to think. The uncertainty about whether man developed in a single line of descent or by a convergence and blending of several pre-human stocks still continues.[2] We do know, however, that the evolution from primates through hominids to man, a process that took eons to complete, produced a species qualitatively different from all that had preceded it. However "wild" the first man in the fossil record may seem to us, he was much closer to present-day humans than to his animal forebears. He used tools to hunt, he kept himself warm with fire, he almost certainly spoke a language, he even had an occasional ability to represent his world on the walls of caves. In all probability, his life was not too different from that of the most primitive of peoples alive today, and these can be used to fill in the details in our account of ancient man.

Which of the contemporary primitives is used to round out our knowledge of our earliest forebears is to some degree an arbitrary choice. It is important only that it be a food-gathering tribe, which has not domesticated either plants or animals and which has been little influenced by more advanced cultures. The Xetá of the Brazilian interior, or the Semang, a Negrito people of the Malay peninsula, live off fruit and roots and any other vegetable food that is available, hunting and fishing only

[1] Raymond Firth, *Primitive Polynesian Economy* (New York: Humanities Press, 1950), pp. 37–38.

[2] For an interesting discussion of recent data, see Pierre Teilhard de Chardin, "The Idea of Fossil Man," in A. E. Kroeber, ed., *Anthropology Today: An Encyclopedic Inventory* (Chicago: University of Chicago Press, 1953), pp. 93–100.

Members of a primitive food-gathering people, the Xetá, who number altogether about 100. They were discovered in 1958 in an isolated area of Paraná State in southern Brazil. Note the stone ax. (José Loureiro Fernandes—University of Paraná)

when in need or as the opportunity arises, and then only small animals. Because of the restricted resources of any one locality, they live in bands of no more than 20 or 30 persons, including children. Each one of such bands has a traditional territory of some 20 square miles over which it slowly wanders, gathering food on the way. Temporary shelters are made of branches and leaves, and abandoned each time a move is made. From one end of his life to the other, a Semang remains with his small group, occasionally seeing other bands of similar size but total strangers only rarely. The Xetá, even more isolated, were discovered by whites only a few years ago. "This limited range of contact and stimulus is of fundamental importance in understanding the stability and slowness of change among the simpler societies of man." [3]

The Xetá and Semang are typical of a class that has been termed Lower Hunters—"peoples who (1) live very largely by gathering fruits and nuts, digging roots, collecting shellfish, and devouring reptiles, insects, and vermin; (2) have no permanent dwelling, but erect windbreaks, live in caves, or put up very slight and temporary huts of boughs or palm leaves; (3) have no spinning and weaving except in the form of plaiting, no pottery, no metal, and very poor canoes; (4) no domestic animals except the dog and possibly a few pets." [4]

The surviving Lower Hunters are unrepresentative precisely because they have remained at this level, pushed off into an inhospitable corner by their more robust neighbors, fearful of contact with them or any stranger. Prehistoric man may well have been a more virile and enterprising type. During some periods he shared his habitat with as many large animals of various species as were to be found, say, on the African veld a generation ago; and if Carleton Coon is correct in his interesting reconstruction of ancient man's life, he subsisted mainly from the chase.[5] The hunting techniques of paleolithic man, the use of fire especially, made him a formidable opponent even of much more powerful and ferocious beasts. A band of five to ten men, armed with spears or bows and arrows and accompanied by dogs, could bring back a ton of meat from a successful hunt.

The economy of such primitive hunters is suggested by that of the Plains Indians before their whole culture was transformed by the acquisition of the horse. Until about 1750 the Blackfoot, for instance, were pedestrian hunters, carrying their scanty possessions on dog sledges or the

[3] C. Daryll Forde, *Habitat, Economy, and Society: A Geographical Introduction to Ethnology* (New York: Dutton, 1952), p. 13 and Ch. 2. Concerning the Xetá, see José Loureiro Fernandes, "The Xetá—A Dying People in Brazil," *Bulletin of the International Committee on Urgent Anthropological and Ethnological Research,* no. 2 (1959), pp. 22–26; *Time,* January 5, 1959.

[4] L. T. Hobhouse, G. C. Wheeler, and M. Ginsberg, *The Material Culture and Social Institutions of Simpler Peoples: An Essay in Correlation* (London: Chapman & Hall, 1930), p. 17.

[5] See Carleton S. Coon, *The Story of Man: From the First Human to Primitive Culture and Beyond* (New York: Knopf, 1955), Ch. 3.

backs of women. A buffalo hunt was conducted in the following fashion. Women gathered down wind from the herd and placed their sledges upright in the earth so as to form a semicircular fence. Several swift-running hunters up wind from the herd drove the buffalo into this enclosure. Shouting women and barking dogs confused the animals, and in the turmoil hunters were able to rush in and with lance or bow and arrow kill a number of the herd. With such a method of garnering food, the camp had to consist of 10 to 30 tents, for the hunt depended on the cooperation among that many persons but did not furnish enough food for more. With only primitive means of transportation, the aged, sick, and infirm were left behind to die whenever the camp moved.[6]

As this example suggests, ancient man was certainly often hungry and sometimes hungry enough to die of starvation. According to a classical example in animal ecology, when rabbits increase, the foxes that live off them also multiply; then the more numerous foxes eat most of the rabbits and themselves begin to die of starvation; and when the number of foxes has been sufficiently reduced, the rabbits again increase, starting the cycle once again. Hunting peoples depend in the same way on maintaining a balance between their numbers and their food supply; many contemporary primitives that live from the chase prohibit with strong sanctions the slaughter of more animals than can be eaten. However, when one food supply gives out, man can turn to another; for he is omnivorous and physiologically adaptable to an extraordinary degree.[7]

Among food-gatherers, fishing peoples are most likely to enjoy a regular subsistence, and they are not compelled to be on the move constantly following their food supply. Their level of culture and also their population density are typically higher than those of hunters. This observation can be exemplified by the several Indian tribes living along the Pacific coast of the United States and Canada, "whose common culture is one of the most specialized in North America and perhaps the most advanced found among any non-agricultural people." Indeed, they were on the verge of developing independently the domestication of fish and plants. If the run of salmon in a particular stream began to fall off, the Nootka

[6] John C. Ewers, *The Horse in Blackfoot Indian Culture, with Comparative Material from Other Western Tribes* (Smithsonian Institution; U.S. Bureau of American Ethnology, Bulletin 159; Washington: U.S. Government Printing Office, 1955).

[7] "He has the incisors of a rodent, the molars of a plant eater, and the canines of a canivore; . . . an added length of gut for the digestion of green food, gastric juice for the conversion of starch to sugar, pepsin for the metabolism of proteids, and pancreatic fluid for the emulsification of fats" (Audrey I. Richards, *Hunger and Work in a Savage Tribe: A Functional Study of Nutrition among the Southern Bantu,* Glencoe, Ill.: Free Press, 1948, pp. 7–8).

"re-stocked it, obtaining spawn from another river at the breeding season and carrying it back in moss-lined boxes to start a new generation in the depleted stream." And two of the tribes, the Tlingit and the Haida, cultivated a tobaccolike plant that was chewed for its narcotic effect. Some of the tribes carried on a primitive trade, exchanging fish for vegetable products gathered inland by neighboring groups. The houses were substantial, built in permanent settlements of 30 or more, with each village thus having a population of several hundred.[8]

For perhaps 98 per cent of his time on earth, man has lived from gathering food. Some 8,000 years ago, probably somewhere in the area between Afghanistan and Abyssinia, he learned to domesticate both plants and animals. This momentous innovation, it is believed, arose not from hunger but from leisure. "Famine-haunted folk lack the opportunity and incentive for the slow and continuing selection of domesticated forms." [9] That is to say, these very first steps toward civilization depended on an economic surplus, and one wonders why this should not have been absorbed into a population increase. The reason, presumably, is that the social structure even of a food-gathering band determined the distribution of food. "Nonliterate societies everywhere, producing more goods than the minimum required for the support of life, translate their economic surpluses into the social leisure which is only afforded those members of the community who are supported by this excess wealth." [10]

The step from food-gathering to food-producing marks the transition from the paleolithic to the neolithic age. The earliest domesticated breeds of both plants and animals were, of course, indistinguishable from the wild ones, and the first methods were crude. Cultivation was by what is termed hoe culture (although the usual implement is not a hoe but a digging stick) or sometimes slash-and-burn culture. As still carried on by primitive cultivators in various parts of the world, this system establishes a life only slightly less mobile than hunting. A patch of woodland is cleared and burnt, and the seeds are planted; two or three years later, when the soil is exhausted, the process is repeated elsewhere. In an interesting article, Lewis has compared the productivity of hoe culture and

---

[8] Forde, *op. cit.*, Ch. 6.

[9] Carl O. Sauer, "The Agency of Man on the Earth," in William L. Thomas *et al.*, eds., *Man's Role in Changing the Face of the Earth* (Chicago: University of Chicago Press, 1956), pp. 49–69.

[10] Melville J. Herskovits, *Economic Anthropology: A Study in Comparative Economics* (New York: Knopf, 1952), pp. 412–413. Cf. George Dalton, "A Note of Clarification on Economic Surplus," *American Anthropologist*, 62:3 (June, 1960), 483–490, together with cited references.

plow culture in the Mexican village of Tepoztlán, where both are practiced. The former takes three times as many man-hours as the latter to
raise one hectare of corn.[11] The neolithic production with a digging stick
required still more work, and the plot had to be constantly watched to
protect it against predatory animals.

Specialized agriculture or stock-raising as the sole basis of food seems
to have been a later development from the earlier domestication of plants
and animals. Many of the pastoral peoples of Asia are "denuded agriculturists," induced to abandon half of their prior economy by "unsettled
political conditions." [12] Flight to the steppe, which is difficult or impossible to cultivate, made such a specialization necessary. Nomads depend
on their animals for their food, clothing, and shelter; and their culture
must thus accommodate itself to the seasonal search for pasture. Such
a society could subsist only in small mobile units: a Mongol camp consists ordinarily of six to ten tents of five to six persons each, or a group
only about twice as large as a food-gathering band.

All the elements of the neolithic economy—hunting, hoe culture, and
nomadism—implied a migratory way of life, and by 2000 B.C. the essential pattern had spread throughout Eurasia, from Ireland to China.
Each local culture was specific, distinguished by its particular balance
between cultivation and stock-breeding, by the plants or animals raised,
by adaptations to the climate or other natural features, by accidental
variations. But overlying this diversity were not only the production of
food, the basic invention of neolithic man, but also tools of polished rather
than chipped stone, pottery, houses.

In the meantime a considerable advance over this level had been made
in the Near East, where food production had started. By 3000 B.C., in
Egypt and Mesopotamia the domesticated ox was put in front of a wooden
plow, furnishing man the first source of energy apart from his own
muscles. About the same time metallurgy was developed; and copper-
smiths became the first full-time craftsmen, added to the simple social
structure of food-producers, chief, and priest. The wheel was already in
existence, and the same harness used to pull a plow could be attached to
a cart. With this technical base, true agriculture (the word is from the
Latin *ager*, field) could supplant the tillage of small plots; but the type
of economy and society that developed was fundamentally different from
what we associate with the word.

[11] Oscar Lewis, "Plow Culture and Hoe Culture—A Study in Contrasts," *Rural
Sociology,* 14:2 (June, 1949), 116–127.
[12] Forde, *op. cit.,* pp. 404–405.

Agriculture is of two types, that based on rain and that on irrigation.[13] Rain agriculture, the usual form in all of the Western world, leads to a minimum of social cohesion among a dispersed peasantry. The picture we have of "the" peasant or "the" rural culture is associated with this type. Irrigation-agriculture, the economy of the great civilizations of the ancient Near East, India, China, and portions of pre-Columbian America, gave rise to a different kind of society. To establish and maintain vast irrigation and flood-control works required a much greater degree of social control. A leading stratum had to keep a record of available man-power, recruit it when necessary, assign it to designated jobs—both the direct construction or maintenance of dams and channels and such sub-sidiary tasks as assembling building materials or food for the workers. In a hydraulic civilization, as Wittfogel terms one based on irrigation-agriculture, those whose function it was to administer the complex task of maintaining the works were uniquely prepared to wield supreme politi-cal power. Once the institutional framework of bureaucratic control over the whole of the society was established for one purpose, it spread from this to others. Indeed, it had to be applied to military operations; a people based on rain-agriculture could flee before a stronger foe, but one that had spent generations in building irrigation works had to try to defend them. Hydraulic civilizations built Great Walls and other massive de-fenses, as well as highways and postal systems that provided, given the technical level, excellent communications across enormous empires. Corvée labor was also used to construct grandiose monuments—palaces, temples, tombs—to the glorification of the despotic ruler.

The social structure that evolved from such a system of agriculture can be delineated by contrasting it with the feudalism of medieval Europe, with which it is often confused. The keynote of feudalism is decentraliza-tion, the diffusion of power in many competing hands. The king, the titular head of the state, had a contractual relation with his vassals, who owed him so much allegiance but no more and were jealous of their own prerogatives. In certain periods the church was more powerful than the emperor, and in late feudalism the free cities were in some respects more powerful than either. The keynote of hydraulic civilizations, on the other hand, is centralization. All power derives from the bureaucratic appara-tus, and in most cases from the person of the despot. His "vassals" owe him total and immediate obedience, and symbolize their utter degrada-tion by such rituals as prostrating themselves before him. Religion is not

13 The following discussion is based on Karl A. Wittfogel, *Oriental Despotism: A Comparative Study of Total Power* (New Haven: Yale University Press, 1957).

an antagonistic or even an independent force, but is assimilated as the state's main ideology; in the most developed form of Oriental despotism the head of the state is also the god to be worshipped. In short, in a hydraulic civilization the state is stronger than society.

The great advance that irrigation-agriculture brought in the production of food, combined with the extreme difference in social prerogatives, established a leisure class of new dimensions. A sizable number of persons who do not have to grow their own food is the sine qua non of urban existence; the first towns may have been the administrative centers of hydraulic societies. By modern standards, these cities were small: the famous Ur had no more than 25,000 inhabitants, Erech about the same. Much later, around 1600 B.C., Thebes at the height of its splendor as Egypt's capital may have had as many as 225,000 by a liberal estimate.[14] Nevertheless, these urban populations in the Near East were the centers of a new level of culture and the site of a number of important inventions associated with bureaucracy (writing, accounting, censuses), religion (a solar calendar and, through astronomy, the beginnings of science), and to some degree technology (bronze and iron). These developments, and parallel ones in India and China, marked the threshold between primitive cultures and higher civilizations, and between prehistory and history. We shall return to these urban civilizations in the following chapter.

POPULATION OF PREURBAN SOCIETIES

The evolution from paleolithic bands to the first cities was, once it began, startlingly rapid relative to man's term on earth. After millenia of cultures based on a food-gathering economy, in a few thousand years stone tools gave way to iron and hunting to agriculture. The transformation in demographic variables was also great, as even the very approximate data indicate.

For any preliterate culture (that is, either prehistoric or contemporary primitive), the level of the economy suggests reasonable estimates concerning the maximum population density. Some deductions can be made about mortality from fossil skeletons and from the probable death rate of contemporary primitives. Data on fertility are nonexistent for prehistoric peoples and sparse for contemporary primitives, so that we must ordi-

[14] Kingsley Davis, "The Origin and Growth of Urbanization in the World," *American Journal of Sociology*, 60:5 (March, 1955), 429–437. Cf. Gideon Sjoberg, *The Preindustrial City: Past and Present* (Glencoe, Ill.: Free Press, 1960), pp. 36–37, Ch. 4.

narily be satisfied with the figure obtained by subtracting the presumably high mortality from the presumably low natural increase. Some tentative conclusions can be offered concerning prehistoric migrations, but nothing very satisfactory.

Natural Increase

One way of deducing prehistoric man's rate of natural increase, as we have seen,[15] is to show that it could not have been very great over the period since *Homo sapiens* evolved. Starting from a single pair, man would have had to double his numbers only 30 times in order to reach 2.1 billion, or almost the present population of the world. Under conditions most conducive to growth each doubling takes 25 years, and with such a Malthusian projection the increase from two persons to the present world's population would have taken slightly more than 750 years. Since we know that man began to evolve many hundreds of thousands of years ago, we know also that the rate of growth in the modern world is anomalous, and that during the whole of the paleolithic period man's numbers must have been close to stationary.

This conclusion is substantiated by another line of reasoning. The balance of births and deaths of hunting peoples depends a good deal on the natural environment, but under all circumstances the population densities of food-gatherers are very low. They were estimated for contemporary primitive cultures by Friedrich Ratzel, one of the great nineteenth-century pioneers of human geography, and his summary of an array of data is reproduced here in Table 12-1. Neither the peoples living in such especially unfavorable habitats as the Arctic or semi-arid regions, nor those subsisting on fish or domesticated animals, are pertinent to a general discussion. The population density of typical food-gatherers, given relatively advantageous conditions, is likely to be that of the Xetá and the Semang, or of the order of one per square mile.

The total land surface of the earth is about 57 million square miles, including Antarctica, the Arctic region, mountains, and deserts. The habitable portion, counting both optimum and marginal areas, is only slightly more than half this figure. If we assume one person per square mile as the average population density in the paleolithic era, then the *maximum* world population in that period was of the order of 30 million. If we restrict the area to that archeologists know to have been inhabited at that time, it could hardly have been more than 5 million. Assuming

[15] See pages 7–8, 299.

TABLE 12-1. The Density of Hunting Populations according
to Ratzel's Estimates

	Square Miles Per Capita	Persons per Square Mile
Hunting and fishing peoples in the Arctic	75–200	
Hunting peoples in semi-arid regions (Bushmen, Patagonians, Australians)	45–200	
Hunting peoples with some agriculture or trade with agricultural tribes	0.5–2	
Shepherd nomads		1.8–4.7
Fishing peoples (North America, Polynesia)		4.5

Source: Cited from A. B. Wolfe, "The Fecundity and Fertility of Early Man," *Human Biology*, 5:1 (February, 1933), 35–60.

that the paleolithic lasted only 100,000 years, the rate of increase of the human species during this period was about 1.5 per cent *per century*.[16]

The domestication of plants and animals, even at the neolithic level of efficiency, increased the potential population of the earth enormously. The carrying capacity per square mile, which for hunting and fishing peoples is one to five persons, for primitive agriculture is between 26 and 64, and for more advanced agriculture ranges up to 192.[17] For example, the prehistoric population of the present area of France, as estimated from a detailed survey of archeological findings, was never more than about 20,000 so long as food-gathering furnished its subsistence. During the fourth millenium B.C., when the first agricultural settlement appeared, the population grew to 500,000, and over the next thousand years to 5,000,000,[18] which is also the theoretical carrying power of an area of this size with primitive agriculture. It is a reasonable inference that the spread of domestication to the rest of Europe and the world also effected an increase, though perhaps not by so large a jump as in France.

The growth in numbers brought about by neolithic inventions was a cause as well as a result of social efficiency. Some tasks cannot even be attempted by a small group. When Robinson Crusoe was joined by Friday, the work the two could do together was much more than double what Crusoe had been able to accomplish alone; and this greater than

---

[16] Cf. John D. Durand, "World Population: Trend and Prospects," in Philip M. Hauser, ed., *Population and World Politics* (Glencoe, Ill.: Free Press, 1958), pp. 27–37.

[17] Estimate of Wiechel, cited in Amos H. Hawley, *Human Ecology: A Theory of Community Structure* (New York: Ronald, 1950), p. 151.

[18] L. R. Nougier, "Essai sur le peuplement préhistorique de la France," *Population*, 9:2 (April–June, 1954), 241–271.

proportionate increase in economic production with each new addition
to the population continues up to a certain number. Food-gathering
bands have an optimum size of about 25 to 30 persons, and one that
grows much beyond this splits into two. Similarly, peasant agriculture
can be carried on most efficiently by a village of about 500 to 1,000 persons; up to this number, the gain from new hands more than offsets the
loss to new mouths. A village does not grow into a town, but rather
founds daughter villages in the near distance. With conditions that favor
continuous increase, the ultimate pattern is like that in sections of India
or Java, with thousands and thousands of small villages making up a
dense but generally nonurban population.

The precise relation between population size and the other features of
a primitive society in part dependent on it has been formulated in a very
interesting study by Naroll.[19] As can be seen in Figure 12-1, if the popula-

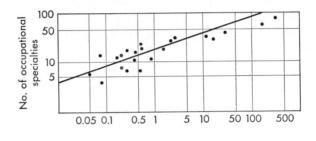

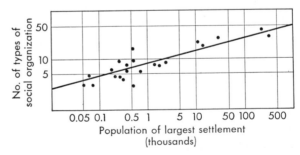

Figure 12-1. Relation Between Population Growth and Two Other Social Variables
in 22 Societies

Source: Raoul Naroll, "A Preliminary Index of Social Development," *American
Anthropologist,* 58:4 (August, 1956), 687–715.

tion of the largest settlement (P) of each of 22 peoples is plotted on a
logarithmic grid, together with the number of occupational specialties

[19] Raoul Naroll, "A Preliminary Index of Social Development," *American Anthropologist,* 58:4 (August, 1956), 687–715.

(S) or the number of types of social organization (r) in each culture, the points tend to fall along two straight lines. The two regression lines shown have the formulas:

$$P = \left(\frac{S}{2}\right)^3 \qquad \text{and} \qquad P = \left(\frac{2r}{3}\right)^4$$

This means that if the largest settlement grew from a hamlet of 500 to a town of 10,000, say, the average number of occupational specialties in the culture would increase from 16 to 42, and the number of types of social organization from 7 to 15.

Mortality and Fertility

Some information on the diseases of prehistoric man is obtainable from the archeological record. The number of skeletons that have been recovered is small, of course, and we do not know to what degree they represent a typical sample; in any case, few deductions are possible from their examination. But there is no question that even before *Homo sapiens* evolved, his forebears were suffering from disease: the femur of one specimen of Java Man has marked exostoses, or knoblike protuberances, indicating a pathological condition of great severity.

Alteration of skulls due to ulcerations; scoliosis; various hyperostoses; caries of bone and teeth; atrophy of the skull; exostoses and osteomata; and many varieties of arthritides indicate to us the variety of afflictions to which early man was subject.[20]

Perhaps disease caused the death of primordial man less often, however, than the drownings, burns, wounds, and fractures associated with his dangerous life. Judging from the number of skeletons that show marks of heavy blows or arrow and spear points, combat was also an important cause of death. Some skeletal remains show evidence of a continued life after a serious injury and of its final healing, and these indicate at least the probability of some skill in surgery. Among 18 instances of fractures in prehistoric skeletons, one paleontologist found only three

[20] Roy L. Moodie, *The Antiquity of Disease* (Chicago: University of Chicago Press, 1923), p. 89. The record from ancient Egypt, which provides mummies as well as skeletons for the examination of archeologists, is of course more complete; and it is at least probable that the diseases observable there existed also in ancient man: "Pott's disease, pneumonia, smallpox (variola?), deforming arthritides of many kinds, renal abscesses, arteriosclerosis (atheroma), many types of fractures, necroses, tumors, cirrhosis of the liver, caries, alveolar osteitis, and many other interesting lesions" (*ibid.*, p. 116).

that had healed badly, and he came to the conclusion that early man was amazingly skillful at setting broken bones.[21] One of the more spectacular operations was trepanation, or the boring or scraping of a hole into the skull. When this is performed in modern surgery, it is usually to relieve the pressure from a brain tumor; early man, like those contemporary primitives that follow this practice, probably opened the skull also in order to release an evil spirit from the body.[22]

The triple threat of disease, violent death, and starvation made life a very precarious matter for paleolithic man. Table 12-2 shows the estimated age at death of a large sample of fossil remains. There were 31 fossils for which it was impossible to determine the age; and of these,

TABLE 12-2. Estimated Age at Death of 187 Human Fossil Remains

Age-group	Neanderthal		Upper Paleolithic		Mesolithic	
	No.	*Per cent*	*No.*	*Per cent*	*No.*	*Per cent*
0–11	8	40	25	24.5	20	30.8
12–20	3	15	10	9.8	4	6.2
21–30	5	25	28	27.4	32	49.3
31–40	3	15	27	26.5	6	9.2
41–50	1	5	11	10.8	1	1.5
50+	..	...	1	1.0	2	3.0
Total	20	100	102	100.0	65	100.0

Source: Henri V. Vallois, "La durée de la vie chez l'homme fossile," *Anthropologie*, 47:5–6 (December, 1937), 499–532.

19 were not yet adult and the other 12 had almost certainly not attained old age. From these and similar data, one can say that the expectation of life at birth must have been hardly 20 years, and that anyone who managed to survive to 40 would be by this fact the Old Man of the band.[23] Only about half of those born survived to become parents. Young humans must have been as much at a premium as they are with contemporary primitive peoples with similar high rates of infant and child-

[21] *Ibid.,* p. 89.

[22] In a few prehistoric groups trepanation was practiced quite frequently. "In one burial mound in France yielding the bones of 120 individuals more than 40 showed the effects of trepanation. . . . A few ancient skulls reveal five cruel openings, which had all healed. The patient had survived them all" (*ibid.,* p. 100).

[23] For discussions of evidence on this point, see also A. B. Wolfe, "The Fecundity and Fertility of Early Man," *Human Biology,* 5:1 (February, 1933), 35–60; S. F. Cook, "Survivorship in Aboriginal Populations," *Human Biology,* 19:2 (May, 1947), 83–89.

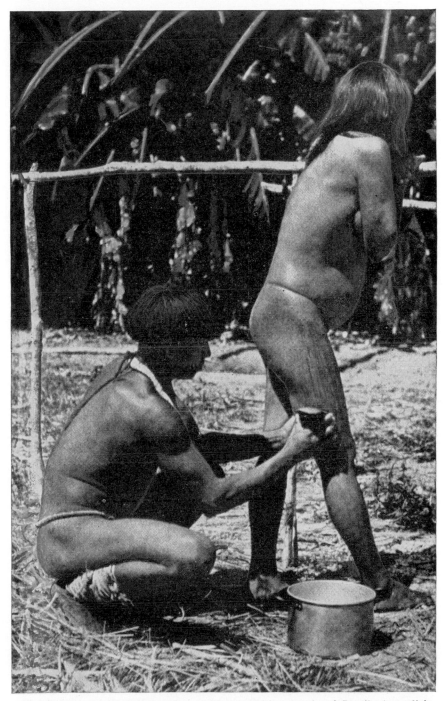

Members of the Camaiurá tribe, another primitive people of Brazil. A medicine man is scarifying the woman's leg with the teeth of a piranha fish to bleed the evil spirits from her body. (Anthony Linck—courtesy of Time, Inc.)

hood mortality. "From one end of Bantu Africa to the other, there has never, until very recent times, been an unwanted child. . . . The only dispute may be as to which man has the right to claim the infant." [24] There is no reason to hypothesize, as some writers have done, that the natural fecundity of early man was lower than that of his present-day descendants, not only because there is no evidence to support this supposition but because mortality at that time was so high that, unless fecundity and fertility were high, mankind would have died out.

Prehistoric Migrations

If, as paleontologists and anthropologists now generally agree, *Homo sapiens* evolved from some lower primate form only once, then the existence of humans over the whole of the world indicates that a series of prehistoric migrations took place from mankind's birthplace, wherever that was. How can we imagine that ancient man was able to anticipate by many eons the extraordinary feats of the Age of Discovery, when Europeans first pushed beyond the outer frontiers of the Mediterranean basin and sailed around Africa to the South Seas and across the Atlantic to the "New" World? These primeval migrations are explicable by several of their characteristics. The passage from what is now one continent to another was made possible by the fact that the succession of Pleistocene glaciations absorbed a large portion of the oceans' water into ice sheets, so that land-bridges may have been in existence across the Mediterranean, for example, and (more certainly) down through the East Indies, facilitating the movement away from the climate of the Northern Hemisphere. It must be recalled that the glaciations, which foreshortened in retrospect may seem cataclysmic, took place so slowly as to cause no perceptible fall in average temperature during the whole of a lifetime. The push to migrate, though real, was exerted so gradually as to effect a movement by stages.

Food-gatherers and hunters, because of the limitations of their economy, must be on the move; they are **rangers.** Herdsmen and primitive agriculturists, as we have seen, are hardly more sedentary. While today such people move over a limited area that is theirs by tradition, in a world relatively unpopulated by humans each band would follow wher-

---

[24] D. M. Goodfellow, *Principles of Economic Sociology: The Economics of Primitive Life as Illustrated from the Bantu Peoples of South and East Africa* (Philadelphia: Blakiston, 1939), p. 101.

ever the available subsistence led it. Most prehistoric migrations, as we can imagine them, constituted movements of groups of 20 or 30 persons, walking a few miles a day, as do the Semang, in order to collect their food supply. Similarly, Childe explains the wide distribution of the neolithic Danubian cultivators by their nomadic agriculture: "Assuming quite short shifts of territory every twelve years or so, it would take only a few centuries for a modest initial population to spread from say the Drave to the Harz." [25] In geologic time, at the rate and with the prodigious waste of a natural process, food-gathering or agricultural bands separated by thousands of miles and became nuclei of discrete populations.

It is possible, then, to state that prehistoric migrations took place, to time some of them within wide limits by carbon-dating, and to offer plausible hypotheses about routes and the rate of movement. To fill in these generalizations with details on specific migrations, however, is extraordinarily difficult. A prehistoric migration, by definition, is one of which we have no written record, and of which we must therefore reconstruct all the details from circumstantial evidence. The methodological problem to be solved—namely, to infer prior motion from static data—can be indicated by a rather farfetched analogy. Suppose that there are several species of beetles, each of which leaves a track of a different color when it walks. We have only a broken and scratched pane of glass over which various beetles, long since dead, have passed, and the task is to reconstruct their movements from the color pattern. The first step, obviously, is to classify the colors themselves: orange must be distinguished from red, green from blue, and each intermediate case must be put into one or the other category. Then all irrelevant influences must be considered and their effect taken into account: other insects may have marked the glass, portions of it may have faded in the sun, and so on. Only then, finally, can an attempt be made to reconstruct the beetles' movement over the glass.

The reconstitution of prehistoric migrations from any type of data, then, ordinarily consists of three steps: (a) classifying the data into a meaningful geographical pattern, (b) discounting the factors other than migration that might have changed the pattern, and (c) inferring migrations from the remaining systematic differences in the pattern. Whether the data have been gathered by archeologists, physical anthropologists,

[25] V. Gordon Childe, *Prehistoric Migrations in Europe* (Instituttet for Sammenlignende Kulturforskning; Oslo: Aschehoug, 1950), p. 93.

ethnologists, or linguists, the method is essentially this, and the difficulties in following it are considerable.

An attempt to reconstruct prehistoric migrations from the present distribution of human races, for example, does not lead to an unambiguous conclusion. (a) While human beings do differ in a number of physical traits, and while these tend to cluster into distinguishable races, where to divide adjacent clusters is an arbitrary matter on which there is little agreement among experts. (b) The hypothesis that these physical traits are wholly hereditary has been disproved with respect to some of them and is an unproved assumption with respect to some others. To the degree that racial characteristics respond to environmental influences, it is impossible to deduce a prior contact from present similarities. (c) And to the degree that physical traits are inherited, the decisive factor is the separation of gene pools, and this can be effected either by migration or by such a social pattern as caste endogamy. Migration, while it generally results in sexual isolation, is clearly not a necessary condition to it.[26]

An attempt to reconstruct a prehistoric migration from cultural rather than physical traits must follow the same method, and thus involves the same hazards. Scientific archeology begins with the classification of artifacts, a task of considerable difficulty. "On many points there are two or three views that are almost equally likely. Which of them any author chooses, may depend largely on *a priori* assumptions or quite subjective prejudice." [27] When a satisfactory classification has been agreed on, how shall it be interpreted? If we find two widely separated peoples with an identical or very similar item of culture, must we assume that there was a link between them at some time in the past, or can this resemblance be simply the coincidental effect of the fact that man's basic needs and the material goods with which they can be satisfied are both limited? Much of nineteenth-century anthropology was concerned with this issue. The "diffusionists" believed that invention is exceptional and that any significant similarities between two cultures indicated a prior contact between the two peoples. The "parallelists," on the other hand, postulated a natural autonomous evolution—like Morgan's progression

[26] Nevertheless, a prior migration has often been inferred from racial patterns. For instance, differences in various physical characteristics afford a certain basis for dividing the peoples of Europe into three "races"—Mediterranean, Alpine, and Nordic; and it has been deduced that the continent was peopled in three migratory waves corresponding to these three stocks. See, for example, Griffith Taylor, *European Migrations: Past, Present and Future* (Sydney: Dey, 1928), lecture 1.

[27] Childe, *op. cit.*, p. 2.

from Savagery to Barbarism to Civilization—which needed no stimulus from the outside to reach higher cultural levels. Today these extreme positions have few if any supporters, but the dilemma remains.

Even when the probability of diffusion is accepted, one cannot reasonably infer a migration from it, or no migration from a lack of it.

Migrations . . . form the crass instances of the process, easily conceived by a simple mind. That a custom travels as a people travels carrying it along is something that a child can understand. The danger is in stopping there and invoking a national migration for every important culture diffusion, whereas it is plain that most culture changes from without have occurred through subtler and more gradual or piecemeal operations.[28]

If a prior movement *is* deduced from a similarity among the surviving artifacts, one still cannot know in every case which way the prehistoric bands went. For instance, after citing four archeologists who have reconstructed a neolithic migration from the Danube basin to what is now Macedonia, Childe suggested—"reluctantly"—that the movement had been in the opposite direction.[29] An analogous state of knowledge with respect to modern migration would leave us in doubt as to whether Englishmen had populated the United States, or Americans England.

One way of cutting through the problem is by tracing culture contacts through language. That the weapons of two peoples are very similar, for example, may be the consequence only of their function; but the combination of sounds used to denote a weapon is wholly arbitrary, so that a similarity in language is a much more cogent argument that the two peoples were associated.

The classification of languages, however, is in dispute among linguists, and the difficulties are analogous to those in classifying races. In both cases, the basic problem is how to distinguish clusters in a continuum from one another.

All languages that are known to be genetically related, i.e., to be divergent forms of a single prototype, may be considered as constituting a "linguistic stock" [which we may take as analogous to race]. . . . When we set it up, we merely say, in effect, that thus far we can go and no farther. At any point in the progress of our researches an unexpected ray of light may reveal the "stock" as but a "dialect" of a larger group. The terms dialect, language, branch, stock—it goes without saying

[28] A. L. Kroeber, *Anthropology* (Rev. ed.; New York: Harcourt, Brace, 1948), p. 473.

[29] Childe, *op. cit.,* p. 50.

—are purely relative terms. They are convertible as our perspective widens or contracts.[30]

Once a classification has been agreed on, how to interpret it remains a problem, for languages long disconnected sometimes pass through strikingly similar phases by the parallel operation of phonetic laws and thus end up with forms that, in the absence of contrary evidence, would be mistakenly interpreted as divergences from an identical primitive form.[31] When two languages do come into contact, there is no uniform pattern of change. Sometimes a people lives for centuries in a larger community without losing its own language (for example, the Bretons in France or the German enclaves in Slavic Europe); sometimes the two are combined into one (Old English and Norman French into English); and sometimes one disappears altogether (the West African languages of the Negro slaves in the United States—but not in Surinam). While we can find plausible reasons for these differences, in cases where we do not know the historical background we must exercise extreme care in reconstructing past migrations from present linguistic relations.

Such a reconstruction is not generally possible even from a combination of several types of data. For one thing, experts in one field are often unwilling to accept the conclusions derived from another.[32] The interpretations from the several relevant disciplines, moreover, often diverge. An occasional ethnic group, such as the Basques, is sharply distinguished from neighboring peoples in both blood type and language. But generally the confusion of linguistic with racial stocks is an error against which

[30] Edward Sapir, *Language: An Introduction to the Study of Speech* (New York: Harcourt, Brace, 1921), pp. 163–164. Copyright, 1921, by Harcourt, Brace and Company, Inc.; renewed 1949, by Jean V. Sapir. Reprinted by permission of the publishers.

Compare Boas on the same point: "It follows from all this that for many distantly related languages the history of which is unknown, a categorical answer in regard to their genetic relationship cannot be given. In many cases historical relation must be assumed, but whether we are dealing with mixture of languages or with divergent branches of an ancient stock will remain doubtful" (Franz Boas, "Language," in Boas, ed., *General Anthropology*, New York: Heath, 1938, pp. 124–145). This caveat is especially significant since, as compared with Sapir for example, Boas is much more sanguine concerning the possibilities of prehistoric reconstruction from linguistic differences. For an interesting article that attempts to reconcile the famous dispute between them, see Morris Swadesh, "Diffusional Cumulation and Archaic Residue as Historical Explanations," *Southwestern Journal of Anthropology*, 7:1 (Spring, 1951), 1–21.

[31] "Here is an interesting example. The English type of plural represented by *foot: feet, mouse: mice* is strictly parallel to the German *Fuss: Füsse, Maus: Mäuse*. One would be inclined to surmise that these dialectic forms go back to old Germanic or West-Germanic alternations of the same type. But the documentary evidence shows conclusively that there could have been no plurals of this type in primitive Germanic" (Sapir, *op. cit.*, p. 184).

[32] In the opinion of an archeologist like Gordon Childe, thus, unless a change in physical type is accompanied by a change in culture, "anthropometry is little use in tracing prehistoric migrations" (*op. cit.*, p. 2).

responsible scholars have been struggling for several generations; to use a linguistic term like *Aryan* as a racial designation is the surest sign of an ignoramus. The English-speaking sector of the world's population is a telling example that language communities are not congruent with races. The English themselves are a combination of a large number of racial strains, and in the United States and other overseas countries, English is the natural language not only of a still broader variety of European stocks but also of a large number of Negroes and Asians.[33] But if migration had been a significant determinant of the differentiation in both races and languages, the geographical patterns of both, apart from anomalies and peripheral cases, would tend to be the same.

In view of these difficulties, it is not possible in a general work on population even to summarize the evidence on prehistoric migrations without oversimplifying it.

THE DEPOPULATION OF PRIMITIVE PEOPLES

An important limitation to the analogy that we have drawn between paleolithic populations and those of contemporary primitives results from the effect that advanced cultures have had, or may have had, on the latter. The usual contention is that food-gathering peoples, even the most isolated, have suffered a loss in numbers as compared with a prior "natural" state; but this depopulation among primitives, though much discussed, is still a subject on which there is little agreement. Thirty years ago the English anthropologist Pitt-Rivers commented on this process in the Pacific Islands, and what he wrote is still true to a large degree:

During the past fifty or sixty years the dying out of the native Pacific populations has frequently been the subject of official and unofficial inquiries, and it is remarkable that there is as little agreement on the subject now as when it was first investigated. Not only does the failure in diagnosis remain as evident as before, but

[33] "Many other, and more striking, examples of the lack of correspondence between race and language could be given if space permitted. One instance will do for many. The Malayo-Polynesian languages form a well-defined group that takes in the southern end of the Malay Peninsula and the tremendous island world to the south and east (except Australia and the greater part of New Guinea). In this vast region we find represented no less than three distinct races—the Negro-like Papuans of New Guinea and Melanesia, the Malay race of Indonesia, and the Polynesians of the outer islands. The Polynesians and Malays all speak languages of the Malayo-Polynesian group, while the languages of the Papuans belong partly to this group (Melanesian), partly to the unrelated languages ('Papuan') of New Guinea. In spite of the fact that the greatest race cleavage in this region lies between the Papuans and the Polynesians, the major linguistic division is of Malayan on the one side, Melanesian and Polynesian on the other" (Sapir, *op. cit.,* p. 227).

little or no progress has been made in methods of investigation. No satisfactory system or method has been established, and, largely in consequence of this, during the whole period few exact vital statistics are obtainable which might throw light upon the matter and establish the correctness or otherwise of diagnostic attempts.[34]

Pitt-Rivers went on to compile an amusing table, listing the "causes" of depopulation among South Sea Islanders in two columns. In the first was, for example, the allegation that the abolition of head-hunting, by depriving the natives of their chief interest in life, had brought about a despondency which eventually led to a decrease in fertility; and in the second, on the other hand, the fact that head-hunting still continued and contributed to a high mortality. In the first, again, were listed various types of European foods or clothing that had been condemned as unsuitable, and in the second various types of native foods, clothing, housing, etc., that had been condemned as unsanitary.[35] Analysts have found it all too easy to ascribe as the cause of depopulation any prior condition, either the continuation of elements of the native culture, or the change in these by acculturation, or whatever. *Post hoc, ergo propter hoc,* has seldom been applied so freely to any problem.

Where it has taken place, depopulation can be ascribed to the following types of factors:

1. In any struggle with higher cultures, primitives have invariably lost out. The establishment of control over an area has very often been through a war in which their opponents' more effective weapons proved to be a decisive advantage. Wherever it has been introduced, slavery has decreased the population of the enslaved peoples. The attacks in which slaves are taken result not only in many deaths but very often in the disorganization of the native society. The low population density of Negro Africa, for example, is at least in part the result of over a millenium of slave-raiding, first among the African tribes themselves, then by Arabs and Europeans. In the Pacific islands, slave-raiders generally carried off young males, and the females left behind were often unable to marry and have children. Even when slaves are of both sexes, their birth rate is typically low, and apparently only in part because it usually does not suit the slavemaster to have it higher.

2. Depopulation was less the consequence of violence and servitude, however, than of disease. This is always more virulent in a fresh popula-

34 G. H. L. F. Pitt-Rivers, *The Clash of Culture and the Contact of Races* (London: Routledge, 1927), p. 19. Cf. A. M. Carr-Saunders, *World Population: Past Growth and Present Trends* (Oxford: Clarendon, 1936), Ch. 20.
35 Pitt-Rivers, *op. cit.,* p. 48.

tion, for its effect is later reduced by the natural selection of those best able to resist it, as well as often by an acquired immunity from mild childhood cases in areas where it has become endemic. The transfer of diseases, moreover, has usually been from advanced to primitive peoples, since the latter are relatively isolated, almost by definition, and are thus more likely to meet any infection for the first time. Europeans have transported to other parts of the world syphilis, malaria, tuberculosis, measles, whooping cough, chicken pox, dysentery, smallpox, and even the common cold; and all of these were more often fatal among the new host than in Europe. Venereal diseases in particular spread rapidly between a dominant and a subordinate population.[36] According to one of the most careful surveys of depopulation in the Pacific islands, "the cause of native decay is largely disease." [37] "Gonorrhea alone has created enough havoc to merit a major role in the dispeoplement of the Carolines." [38] According to another study, just smallpox was responsible for cutting the populous Mexican Indians by about a third, and the smaller Indian populations north of Mexico by substantial proportions.[39]

Epidemics are of course more visible, but endemic disease may disrupt a society as much. A people infected by malaria, for example, lacks energy, and anthropologists are likely to describe it as suffering from melancholia. Endemic syphilis may kill few, but it prevents the birth of many. The full effect of disease on a society is therefore not at all easy to measure, particularly in retrospect from incomplete and inaccurate records.

3. The introduction among primitives of the elements of a more efficient culture *sometimes* has the consequence, even with no purposeful action on the part of either group, of reducing their population. It is hardly necessary to point out that steel knives and repeating rifles have made their wars more deadly. The charge has often been repeated that

[36] "Brazil would appear to have been syphilized before it was civilized. The first Europeans . . . did not bring civilization, but there is evidence to show that they did bring the venereal plague. . . . [A] 'barbarous superstition' held that those suffering from gonorrhea would be cured if they contrived to have intercourse with a [slave] girl at the age of puberty" (Gilberto Freyre, *The Masters and the Slaves: A Study in the Development of Brazilian Civilization,* 4th ed., New York: Knopf, 1946, pp. 71, 325).

[37] S. M. Lambert, *The Depopulation of Pacific Races* (Special Publication 23; Honolulu: Bishop Museum, 1934), p. 41.

[38] William A. Lessa, "Depopulation on Ulithi," *Human Biology,* 27:3 (September, 1955), 161–183.

[39] E. Wagner Stearn and Allen E. Stearn, *The Effect of Smallpox on the Destiny of the Amerindian* (Boston: Bruce Humphries, 1945). Cf. Woodrow Borah and S. F. Cook, *The Population of Central Mexico in 1548* and *The Indian Population of Central Mexico 1531–1610* (Berkeley: University of California Press, 1960).

missionaries, by forcing Pacific Islanders to wear clothing in an environment where they could not protect themselves against frequent showers, helped spread tuberculosis. Elements of a European diet, even when wholesome if consumed together, were considerably less so after a partial transfer to other peoples. This is especially so of alcohol, which has had a deleterious effect on many primitives.

4. The disruption effected by the infiltration of such alien elements can be cumulative. The social structure of a primitive people, though resilient in the face of normal difficulties, often proves to be fragile in an encounter with a higher culture. When the chief whose authority rests on his military prowess is decisively beaten, when the magic of the shaman is ridiculed and his direst spells have no effect, the whole social fabric begins to erode. If this disorganization eventually reaches the family, there is no institution in which the young can be reared. In a world that is falling apart, normal day-to-day activities like raising children may no longer seem to be worthwhile. All primitive cultures have the ability to limit the size of the family, whether by restrictions on coitus, crude contraceptives or abortions, or infanticide. Since these means exist, they can be applied at will; and when the family declines as an institution, the consequent reduction in the birth rate has on occasion been substantial. Primitive fertility regulation, however, is less elastic in the other direction. Coitus during certain periods, for instance, is often forbidden, and these taboos are not easily relaxed in response to a rational need for increasing the number of births. It is probably only in the most recent period that such traditional restrictions have been deliberately abrogated.[40]

Such a list of causes of depopulation is so impressive that it proves too much. One wonders how it was that primitives anywhere have survived. Yet while some preliterate peoples, particularly Polynesians and American Indians, have undoubtedly undergone a loss in numbers, this has not been the case universally. Where it took place, moreover, depopulation varied greatly in its severity. For example, among three peoples in the Caribbean area in the seventeenth century, the Indians of Hispaniola (Haiti) were nearly extinct within a single generation, the Omagua were reduced by half within 40 years, and the neighboring Cocama have re-

---

[40] "A rumor was current among the Yapese in 1948 that a secret meeting on the depopulation [had been] held by the chiefs and religious leaders in 1946. These men supposedly decided that most of the former taboos on coitus should be discontinued" (Edward E. Hunt, Jr., *et al.,* "The Depopulation of Yap," *Human Biology,* 26:1 February, 1954, 21–51).

tained about their original numbers to the present day.[41] Such a range, from complete extinction to an actual increase, results from a complex interplay of a no less full range of causal factors, some of which are related to the native culture. Disease, generally the most important cause, ordinarily did not effect a permanent loss of population except in conjunction with other factors. If conditions favor growth, losses from even the most calamitous epidemic can be made up in a few generations.

TABLE 12-3. Estimates of Native American Population, c. 1492
(thousands)

	Sapper (1924)	Kroeber (1939)	Rosenblat (1945)	Steward (1949)
North of Mexico	2,000– 3,500	1,001	1,000	1,001
Mexico	12,000–15,000	3,000	4,500	4,500
West Indies and Central America	8,000–10,000	200 [a]	1,100	961
South America	15,000–20,000	4,300 [a]	6,785	9,129
Total	37,000–48,500	8,501	13,385	15,591

[a] Central America included with South America.

Source: Julian H. Steward, "The Native Population of South America," in Steward, ed., *Handbook of South American Indians* (Smithsonian Institution; U.S. Bureau of American Ethnology, Bulletin 143; Washington: U.S. Government Printing Office, 1949), vol. 5, part 3, p. 656.

There is good reason to believe, moreover, that the depletion of primitive peoples has probably been exaggerated in many cases. There are several reasons why this may be so, as follows:

1. Primitives, of course, keep no record of their own population, and the later estimates by anthropologists or other Westerners are seldom securely based. The principal source concerning the number of native inhabitants of the Pacific islands, thus, is Captain Cook, who gave it as his opinion that the population of Hawaii, for example, was in excess of 300,000, that of Tahiti 204,000, "a number which at first exceeded my belief," and so on for the other islands he touched at. Table 12-3 shows, as another example, four estimates of the number living in the Americas at the time of Columbus's first voyage. The range in the total from 8.5 to 48.5 million is by almost six times.

[41] Julian H. Steward, "The Native Population of South America," in Steward, ed., *Handbook of South American Indians* (Smithsonian Institution; U.S. Bureau of American Ethnology, Bulletin 143; Washington: U.S. Government Printing Office, 1949), vol. 5, part 3, p. 657.

Estimates of the original populations not only are rough approximations, as one would expect, but tend to run too high. The first figures
for any area are likely to be set by missionaries or administrators, who
may exaggerate them for bureaucratic reasons; thus, those cited from
Kroeber in Table 12-3 had all been reduced from the Spanish sources.
There is a natural inclination, moreover, to generalize from the most
horrible examples—which are also the most striking—of population decline. The deduction that a large and prosperous people flourished before
the Europeans came is often given support by nativist accounts of the
more or less legendary past.

2. When no figures are available at all, one common method of estimating the past numbers is to calculate the maximum population of the
territory a primitive people inhabited. The figures cited from Sapper in
Table 12-3, for example, were based on the assumed carrying power of
various types of soil, given the level of technology and the type of land
use of the various Indian peoples. He assumed that the population in
each case was the greatest possible with food-gathering or primitive agriculture, and by this exclusive attention to economic factors he altogether
neglected the effect of intertribal warfare or human sacrifices, to cite
only the most obvious of the relevant social factors.[42] The population
density of what is now the eastern portion of the United States, for
instance, was certainly below what one could deduce with such a method.
That is to say, peoples at the same technical level, even if as widely
separated in time as prehistoric savages and contemporary primitives,
have a population *potential* of the same general order. Whether this is
realized, however, depends on more than ecological or technical or economic factors. An implicit assumption that the social-cultural milieu of
primitives is optimum with respect to their numbers will generally result
in an overestimate.

3. If approximations of aboriginal populations before contact with
another culture tend to run too high, those of the current numbers are
often too low. To the degree that racial mixture and acculturation take
place, non-Europeans "disappear" not in a physical but in a statistical
sense.

For example, the proportion of the population of the various Latin
American countries designated as "Indian" ranged in 1947 from a high
of 67 per cent in Guatemala to a low of 2 per cent in Argentina or

[42] See S. F. Cook, "Human Sacrifice and Warfare as Factors in the Demography of
Pre-Colonial Mexico," *Human Biology*, 18:2 (May, 1946), 81–100.

Costa Rica, with none at all in several of the countries. What these figures mean, however, is another matter.

The "racial" definitions vary. Thus "Indians" include "wild" and tribal or communal Indians, those speaking Indian language as mother tongue and also those of mixed ancestry who appear predominantly Indian in physical characteristics. . . . The classification accordingly is neither social nor physical, nor even an entirely sensible combination of these.[43]

The term *mestizo*, which ostensibly denotes a mixture of European, Indian, and in some cases Negro racial stocks, is also principally a cultural designation. An Indian is really defined as a person who "lives like an Indian," and when he lives like a European he will be reclassified either as a mestizo or, if he had some European forebears, as white. Moore constructed an index (reproduced in Table 12-4) of "Indianness" in

TABLE 12-4. Per Cent of "Indianness" according to Clothing Worn and Language, Present-Day Mexico

Footwear	Other Clothes	Language		
		Indian Only	*Bilingual*	*Spanish (or Foreign) Only*
None	Indian	100	80	60
Huaraches	Indian	80	60	40
Huaraches	European			
	or {	60	40	20
Shoes	Indian			
Shoes	European	40	20	0

Source: Wilbert E. Moore, *Industrialization and Labor: Social Aspects of Economic Development* (Ithaca, N.Y.: Cornell University Press, 1951), p. 216. Copyright 1951 by Cornell University.

Mexico by the criteria of clothing and language. Those who go barefoot and wear Indian clothing and who speak only an Indian language are Indian; those who wear shoes and European clothing and who speak only a European language are white; and the various combinations of these two cultural elements indicate the gradual acculturation from one "racial" component to the other. As Moore points out, the charge that the Indian is inferior in industrial tasks is not only true but a truism, for when this inferiority disappears he is redefined as a non-Indian.

[43] Wilbert E. Moore, *Industrialization and Labor: Social Aspects of Economic Development* (Ithaca, N.Y.: Cornell University Press, 1951), pp. 207–208, Table 1 and n.

In Brazil, to take another example, miscegenation was routine from the very first days of Portuguese colonization. Portugal, in 1500 a nation of barely more than a million persons, was able to control its vast empire because the small number of European colonists, like "unbridled stallions," multiplied themselves many times over. Indian slaves, and later the Negroes who replaced them, were divided with utter simplicity into male fieldhands and female housekeepers. Since there were few or no European women, the freedom white men had with their numerous slaves effected a very rapid race mixture.[44]

At least part of the apparent depopulation in Polynesia, similarly, has been the consequence of race mixture and the loss of some of the natives' progeny into the portion of the population defined as white. This is particularly true of Hawaii, where successive immigrations from all over the world have created an ethnic melting-pot of almost unique heterogeneity.[45] In 1853, the first complete census of the islands reported a total of 71,019 native Hawaiians. The fact that in 1950 there were only 12,206 "full-blooded Hawaiians" does not of itself indicate a depopulation, for there were also 73,885 "part-Hawaiians" plus an indeterminate number of descendants of Hawaiian stock listed in other ethnic groups.

SUMMARY

The direct evidence on paleolithic populations is so slight that it was necessary to consider ways by which it might be extended. Following the most recent trend in anthropology, certain features of the life of contemporary food-gathering primitives have been accepted as a probable close counterpart to that of preagricultural peoples. Combining archeological with anthropological data, we can conclude that the average density of paleolithic man was of the order of one person per square mile, and that therefore no more than about 30 million or, more probably, around 5 million lived in the entire world. Population was all but static, growing slowly in relatively favorable periods and being reduced sharply in time of distress. Expectation of life at birth was probably less than 20 years, and the maximum life span not much more than double that figure. Fertility must have been high in order to offset the high mortality.

The circumstantial evidence concerning prehistoric migrations, although it has been much less questioned than the analogy with con-

---

[44] Freyre, *op. cit.*, p. 85 and *passim*.
[45] See pages 145–146.

temporary primitives, we have found to be less reliable. It is assumed that mankind developed only once from lower primate forms and therefore that a series of prehistoric migrations took place. The present geographical pattern of both physical and cultural traits is undoubtedly related in a distant way to these past migrations, but so many other factors have influenced it that it is not possible to trace this relation except in the most tentative fashion.

Contact with advanced cultures has often resulted in a decline of population among primitives. The factor generally most responsible was the new diseases brought by Europeans. There is good reason to believe, however, that this depopulation has often been exaggerated.

SUGGESTIONS FOR FURTHER READING

L. T. Hobhouse, G. C. Wheeler, and M. Ginsberg, *The Material Culture and Social Institutions of the Simpler Peoples: An Essay in Correlation* (London: Chapman & Hall, 1930).

Julian H. Steward, *Theory of Culture Change: The Methodology of Multilinear Evolution* (Urbana: University of Illinois Press, 1955).

Karl A. Wittfogel, *Oriental Despotism: A Comparative Study of Total Power* (New Haven: Yale University Press, 1957).

   The Hobhouse-Wheeler-Ginsberg volume offers the most complete evidence for cultural evolution. Steward's theory of multilinear evolution has found its most significant application to date in Wittfogel's distinction between rain- and irrigation-agriculture.

Ernst Kirsten, *Raum und Bevölkerung in der Weltgeschichte,* vol. 1: *Von der Vorzeit bis zum Mittelalter* (Würzburg: Ploetz, 1956).

Carleton S. Coon, *The Story of Man: From the First Human to Primitive Culture and Beyond* (New York: Knopf, 1955).

   Kirsten gives an encyclopedic survey of archeological data, Coon a highly readable interpretation of them.

Ludwik Krzywicki, *Primitive Society and its Vital Statistics* (London: Macmillan, 1934).

T. E. Smith, "The Cocos-Keeling Islands: A Demographic Laboratory," *Population Studies,* 14:2 (November, 1960), 94–130.

   A most painstaking compilation, which has become the standard work in its field; and an interesting analysis of a primitive people with an almost unique set of population records.

Melville J. Herskovits, *Economic Anthropology: A Study in Comparative Economics* (New York: Knopf, 1952).

C. Daryll Forde, *Habitat, Economy, and Society: A Geographical Introduction to Ethnology* (New York: Dutton, 1952).

    Two excellent works on the economic institutions of primitives, with some discussion of their population.

Raymond Firth, *We, the Tikopia: A Sociological Study of Kinship in Primitive Polynesia* (London: Allen & Unwin, 1936).

W. D. Borrie, Raymond Firth, and James Spillius, "The Population of Tikopia, 1929 and 1952," *Population Studies,* 10:3 (March, 1957), 229–252.

    A classical monograph on a relatively isolated Polynesian population, and a recent discussion of population trends on the same island.

13. *THE POPULATION OF*

PREINDUSTRIAL CIVILIZATIONS

The neolithic inventions of agriculture and stockherding gave primitive food-gathering tribes a valuable supplement to their prior means of subsistence. Once it had developed, the domestication of plants and animals also became the technical base for the urban civilization that flourished in the Near East at the dawn of written history. With respect to population growth, there was no social change of comparable significance until several millenia later, when the industrial revolution transformed Western Europe in the eighteenth and nineteenth centuries. Tremendous contrasts can be noted between, say, ancient Rome and Manchu China, or Tokugawa Japan and medieval Europe. The demographic characteristics of these and similar societies also differed significantly—about as much, perhaps, as those of Low Hunters and Fishers. But several over-all factors are markedly similar, and it is therefore possible to consider the population of all preindustrial civilizations as a group.[1]

Compared with the food-gathering cultures of prehistory, these civilizations developed tremendous populations, though still rather small by present-day standards. While urban settlements were founded, they were different in many respects from cities based on industry. In peaceful, prosperous times the number of people increased, but periodically it was cut back by pestilence, famine, or the breakdown of social order. Even so, there was some over-all extension in the average life expectation, from less than 20 in the neolithic era to something between 20 and 30 years.

---

[1] The designation *preindustrial* rather than *nonindustrial* has been chosen intentionally, in order to exclude today's underdeveloped areas. The current population development and the social and economic problems of such countries as India or China, even though they have themselves not yet become industrialized, are markedly influenced by the industrial civilizations of the West and Russia.

A final common characteristic is that these societies maintained records, sometimes even had so-called censuses. The demographic statistics are usually just good enough to form the basis of an argument, but often not one that other specialists see as convincing. On many particular issues there is no consensus of scholarly opinion, in part because so few have worked in this field. Most demographers have lacked the technical training to do the kind of research needed; judging the meaning of a Roman or a Chinese census is quite a different problem from analyzing modern statistics. And most historians have also shown little interest; according to one of them, "there is no subject of the first importance in ancient scholarship in which our thoughts are vaguer, in which we almost refuse to think (because the evidence is unsatisfactory), than that of population." [2] Yet the population of the preindustrial world is too important a subject to pass over, if only because we cannot really understand industrial societies without this perspective.

SOURCES OF INFORMATION

The kinds of data compiled in various preindustrial civilizations differ considerably, and also the portion of the record that has survived from each area or period. Underlying this variation, however, there are several common features, which can be exemplified by specific instances.

The most detailed information available usually comes from the accounts of economic transactions. In this class, for instance, are the lists of grain shipments from the whole Empire to the city of Rome; but to translate these into population figures requires a rather hazardous guess as to what the per capita consumption was.

Economic and demographic data for particular localities are sometimes known in meticulous detail. In ninth-century France, for instance, abbeys maintained an estate book listing all their landed property and its production; and "we know today the name of almost every man, woman, and child who was living on these little *fiscs* [or estates] in the time of Charlemagne, and a great deal about their daily lives." [3] But one never can be certain how representative such figures are for larger areas. The most famous survey of this type, and the only one covering a considerable territory, is the Domesday Book, the inventory of his lands that William the Conqueror had made in 1086. According to the man historians know as the "Saxon chronicler," "there was not one single hide

2 A. W. Gomme, *The Population of Athens in the Fifth and Fourth Centuries B.C.* (Oxford: Blackwell, 1933), p. 1.
3 Eileen Power, *Medieval People* (New York: Doubleday-Anchor, 1954), p. 17.

nor rood of land, nor—it is shameful to tell but he thought it no shame to do—was there an ox, cow, or swine that was not set down in the writ." [4]

Most population data were collected as part of the administration of taxes, military conscription, and similar governmental functions. Whenever it was possible, of course, people evaded such counts; and they ordinarily pertained, moreover, only to certain sectors, so that it is necessary in each case to estimate the number of inhabitants from an unknown fraction. Sometimes the enumerated portion was rather large: the Roman head-tax introduced under Diocletian, for example, apparently was imposed on the entire labor force, and thus excluded only children, the aged, the infirm, and the feeble-minded. The Roman census was narrower; originally it was a count of certain adult males primarily for military conscription.

Even when statistics were not specific to particular portions of the population, such a limitation was often effected by their nature. For example, one of the better sources on mortality in Rome is the life table drawn up by Ulpian, a famous jurist of the second and third centuries A.D.; since, however, this was used by courts to settle property disputes, it was presumably based on the death rates of the well-to-do classes. The inferences to be drawn from old epitaphs concerning the range in the age at death, and thus the general mortality conditions, are similarly selective. In ancient Rome "tombstones with ages were an essentially middle-class and lower-middle-class institution. The governing classes, . . . having many more interesting things to say about themselves and their relatives, generally did not give ages; and the really poor could not afford tomb-stones." [5] And these were seldom erected for infants, who constitute a very important sector in a study of mortality.

Within the social class or classes to which any set of data pertains, moreover, the unit often was not the individual but the family. A good portion of the information we have about late medieval Europe, for example, is based on the so-called hearth taxes. In order to obtain the total population in any area, one must multiply the given figure by a number equivalent to the size of the family, including parents, children, and others living with them. What this index should be for various countries and periods is not known precisely. A parallel problem is how to judge the population of a community, given certain other data about it.

---

[4] G. M. Trevelyan, *History of England* (New York: Doubleday-Anchor, 1953), 1, 171. For a discussion of the population figures to be deduced from the Domesday Book, see J. C. Russell, *British Medieval Population* (Albuquerque: University of New Mexico Press, 1948), Ch. 3.

[5] A. R. Burn, "Hic Breve Vivitur: A Study of the Expectation of Life in the Roman Empire," *Past and Present*, no. 4 (November, 1953), pp. 2–31.

"Diis Manibus (to the ancestral spirit gods). Albia Urbica erected [this tomb] to her very sweet stepson, Marcus Octavius Aerius, who lived 10 years, 7 months, and 19 days." Marble plaque 41x35 cm., attached to the wall of a tomb in Isola Sacra, Italy. Date uncertain.

Two well preserved Roman tombstones, of the type from which demographic data are extracted. Note that the translations require a thorough knowledge not only of the language but of the conventional abbreviations and usages. (Dr. Hilding Thylander, Stockholm)

It is often possible from archeological research, for example, to calculate rather exactly the area inside the walls of ancient or medieval cities, so that with a guess as to what their average density was one can estimate the number of their inhabitants.

Even within the same political unit there was seemingly little uniformity in any of the conditions surrounding the collection of population statistics. Over such areas as the Roman Empire or ancient China, tax or conscription laws, or the stringency with which they were enforced, or the care with which records were kept, certainly varied greatly from one time or locality to another. The number enumerated in the Roman census, for instance, increased abruptly from about 900,000 in 69 B.C. to 4,063,000 in 28 B.C. A jump by four and a half times in 40 years obviously did not reflect only a growth in population, but scholars are not agreed on whether it represented a rapid extension of citizenship, or the inclusion of females in the count, or what.[6] Or, as an even more striking example, the supposed

[6] See J. C. Russell, "Late Ancient and Medieval Population," *Transactions of the American Philosophical Society,* vol. 48, part 3 (June, 1958), p. 48. Copyright © 1958 by The American Philosophical Society.

Diis Manibus (to the ancestral spirit gods). Ampliatus, slave of the emperors, has erected [this tomb] for Claudia Soteris, his wife who well deserved it. She lived 19 years. Marble plaque, 24x35 cm., Isola Sacra, Italy. Date: second half of the 2nd Century A.D.

population of China increased by 78 million from 1911 to 1912.[7] The obvious reason for so great a discrepancy, one might say, is the very large underenumeration reflected in the first figure, though this was generally accepted as substantially accurate until the new one was published.

In summary, the extant statistical data on the population of various preindustrial civilizations are almost all indirect, and require a good deal of interpretation. It is ordinarily necessary to estimate the total from the number of persons, or even of families, in one particular sector. Figures on such classes as minors and females, slaves and aliens, are usually especially poor. And when the data do relate to the total population (as on grain deliveries or the areas of cities), it is nevertheless difficult to use these statistics for demographic analyses.

The estimates by different scholars, made by manipulating these unsatisfactory sources in various ways, often have a wide range. Of 14 figures for the population of Rome at the time of Augustus, for instance, the low is 250,000 (Lot, 1927) and the high 1.6 million (Lugli, 1941–

[7] Ping-ti Ho, *Studies on the Population of China, 1368–1953* (Cambridge: Harvard University Press, 1959), p. 79.

1942).[8] The population of the Roman Empire of the same period was estimated by Beloch at 50 to 60 million, by Lot at 60 to 65 million, by Stein at 70 million. The range for the third century is even wider: Delbrück suggested 90 to 100 million, Bury 70 million, and Stein only 50 million.[9] Nor is it possible to assume that, because of improvements in method or in the sources available, later estimates are likely to be better. The serious study of the population of the ancient world, for instance, was initiated in the nineteenth century by Beloch, and it is generally agreed that "no one has really improved upon his work since then." [10]

A much greater degree of consensus, however, is to be found on other questions. While classical scholars differ concerning the population of the Roman Empire at any one date, they all agree, for example, that it fell off by a considerable proportion from roughly the third century on, that the density in Italy was higher than in any of the provinces, that slavery and plagues had an important influence on population trends, and so on. That is to say, one can examine the determinants, general trends, and possible effects of population growth in preindustrial civilizations even though certain data are approximate or lacking.

PREINDUSTRIAL CITIES

Until agriculture and stock-raising became efficient enough to provide a sizable surplus, every person had to devote himself to caring for his basic needs. In a food-gathering band everyone is a food-gatherer. And in the late neolithic period, when hunting had been supplemented by primitive agriculture, only metal-working or magic were likely to be full-time specialties. The development of the first cities meant that the division of labor was extended beyond these few examples to become a basic principle of social structure. The distinction between a village and a town or city is not primarily one of size but one of function: a village is a focal point of agriculture, a city is complementary to rural life. The very existence of a city indicates that its inhabitants live off the agricultural surplus and perform nonagricultural functions. Occupational differentiation is characteristic also within the urban sphere; there is no generalized urban "husbandry." Each urban dweller is a specialist and by this fact may also be more efficient.

[8] F. G. Maier, "Römische Bevölkerungsgeschichte und Inschriftenstatistik," *Historia*, 2:3 (1954), 318–351.
[9] Arthur E. R. Boak, *Manpower Shortage and the Fall of the Roman Empire in the West* (Ann Arbor: University of Michigan Press, 1955), pp. 5–6.
[10] Russell, "Late Ancient and Medieval Population," *op. cit.*, p. 7. See Julius Beloch, *Die Bevölkerung der griechisch-römischen Welt* (Leipzig: Duncker & Humblot, 1886).

This differentiation in occupation between rural and urban was ordinarily less sharp in preindustrial civilizations, however, than it is today. The town-country distinction is "misleading" with respect to ancient Mesopotamia. "About 400 B.C. roughly three-quarters of the Athenian burghers owned some land in Attica." [11] In fourteenth-century England, as another instance, many town dwellers cultivated their own plots just outside the walls, and grazed cattle or sheep on the common pasture.

> In 1388 it was laid down by Parliamentary Statute that in harvest time journeymen and apprentices should be called on to lay aside their crafts and should be compelled "to cut gather and bring in the corn." . . . Even London was no exception to the rule of a half rustic life. . . . No Englishman then was ignorant of all country things, as the great majority of Englishmen are today.[12]

For the modern reader, who is likely to think of any "city" as similar to those he knows personally, this osmosis between the urban and rural worlds must be stressed. However, it is no less important that, in contrast to prior ages, there were towns and some town dwellers who did not themselves cultivate the soil.

A distinctive function of the preindustrial city was to furnish a haven, a place of protection. The English word *town,* like the Russian equivalent *gorod,* originally meant enclosure; the German *Burg* (related to the French *bourgeois* and the English *burgher* and *borough* and hundreds of place names—Hamburg, Pittsburgh, etc.) means fortress. In medieval Europe one important criterion of a city, a feature that distinguished it from a village, was that it had a wall surrounding it. It was, in the common phrase, a "walled city."

Within these enclosures there lived, first of all, the political and religious bureaucracy. The chieftain and medicineman of a food-gathering band had each, as it were, grown into an urban stratum. The city of classical China, thus, was "the seat of the administration, . . . the home of officials." There were no city charter, no municipal law, no "concept of the city as an independent unit." [13] The provincial capitals of the Roman Empire had a similar status; and later, in the early medieval period, the Church based its diocesan boundaries on those of the earlier secular units. The town that was the center of a duchy or bishopric was

[11] Henri Frankfort, *The Birth of Civilization in the Near East* (New York: Doubleday-Anchor, 1956), p. 61.

[12] G. M. Trevelyan, *English Social History: A Survey of Six Centuries, Chaucer to Queen Victoria* (London: Longmans, Green, 1942), p. 28.

[13] Wolfram Eberhard, "Data on the Structure of the Chinese City in the Pre-Industrial Period," *Economic Development and Cultural Change,* 4:3 (April, 1956), 253–268.

nothing more. It included a small group of craftsmen and servants attached to the political and religious administrators. It was also often a
market town, in the sense of a distribution point for the local produce,
but this task required no urban class to carry it out.

Another important function of preindustrial cities, sometimes second
to administration and sometimes superseding it, was long-distance trade.
In medieval Europe, the first merchants were the humblest of men, of
poor peasant stock, beginning by traveling from fair to fair to hawk the
wares they carried on their backs, but in many cases ending their lives as
rich men.[14] The mercantile center, designated as the "new burg" in order
to distinguish it from the "old burg" or administrative center, was the
nucleus of the modern Western city. Its inhabitants were the "burghers,"
in contrast to those of the older quarter, who were called "castellani" or
"castrenses." [15] The merchants, merely in carrying on their trade, gradually evolved into a homogeneous and self-conscious class.

Little by little the middle class stood out as a distinct and privileged group in the
midst of the population of the country. From a simple social group given over to the
carrying on of commerce and industry, it was transformed into a legal group, recognized as such by the princely power. And out of that legal status itself was to come,
necessarily, the granting of an independent legal organization. . . . Courts whose
members [were] recruited from among the burghers, were able to render them a
justice adequate to their desires and conforming to their aspirations—a justice, in
fine, which was *their* justice.[16]

Inside the walls, whatever their differences in wealth, all men were of
equal civil status. A serf who fled to a city and lived there for a year and
a day had the freedom of the city and could not be ejected without a
court trial. As the German proverb put it, *Die Stadtluft macht frei*—the
air of the city makes one free. The middle class were not consciously
missionaries, but by their very existence they challenged, and gradually
eroded, the social structure of feudalism. Once the only alternative had
been to own land and be a lord or to till it and be a serf. It was now
possible to live in the city and be a man.

In political terms, thus, there were important differences between the
cities in medieval Europe and those in other preindustrial civilizations—
differences parallel to those already noted between European feudalism

[14] See the short biography of St. Godric of Finchale, in Henri Pirenne, *Medieval
Cities: Their Origins and the Revival of Trade* (New York: Doubleday-Anchor, 1956),
pp. 82–83. Copyright 1925, by Princeton University Press.

[15] *Ibid.*, pp. 107–108.

[16] *Ibid.*, p. 135.

and Oriental despotism.[17] In many respects, however, the cities in all
these societies were similar. The urban population was everywhere small,
in two senses: the proportion living in towns never was more than a
few per cent of the total, and the size of even the large towns was modest
by today's standards. Rome was certainly the largest city of antiquity.
The exact number of its inhabitants, as we have seen, is not known. After
a careful consideration of the evidence, Russell has suggested 350,000
as the probable maximum in the first century A.D., equivalent to a
density of about 250 persons per hectare, which would seem rather high

TABLE 13-1. Population Estimates of Some Large Medieval
European Cities

City	Date of Estimate	Population	Persons per Hectare
London	{ 1086	18,000	108
	{ 1377	35,000	121
Milan	13th century	52,000	166
Naples	1278	27,000	133
Paris	1292	59,000	157
Padua	1320	41,000	117
Bruges	1340	25,000	58
Ghent	1356	60,000	93
Venice	1363	78,000	240
Bologna	1371	32,000	76
Florence	{ 1381	55,000	107
	{ 1424	37,000	73
Nuremberg	1449	23,000	165
Bourges	1487	32,000	289
Genoa	early 16th century	38,000	129
Barcelona	1514	31,000	118
Rome	1526	55,000	40

Source: J. C. Russell, "Late Ancient and Medieval Population," *Transactions of the
American Philosophical Society*, vol. 48, part 3 (June, 1958), Tables 63, 64, 65.

for a city with many open squares and public buildings.[18] From this
figure, Rome declined to about half by the middle of the fourth century.
Of the Holy Roman Empire's approximately 3,000 "cities" (in the sense
of walled enclosures with charters) at the end of the Middle Ages, 2,800
had populations ranging between 100 and 1,000.[19] And the others also
were not large. Table 13-1 is a summary of the more detailed data that
Russell has compiled from a variety of sources. All of the cities with an
estimated population of 30,000 or more are included, together with a few
others that might be of interest—London, with 18,000 in the eleventh cen-

[17] See pages 320–321.
[18] Russell, "Late Ancient and Medieval Population," *op. cit.*, pp. 63–68.
[19] Robert E. Dickinson, *The West European City: A Geographical Interpretation*
(London: Routledge & Kegan Paul, 1951), p. 290.

tury; or Nuremberg, whose medieval aspect has survived in part to today, with only 23,000 in the fifteenth century. Even if we grant that these are rough approximations, and in an extravagant gesture double the number of inhabitants, these medieval towns would still be classified today as small.

The city of preindustrial civilizations was also different in other respects from its modern counterpart.[20] The various handicrafts were grouped together in, for example, a "street of the goldsmiths," and the in-group solidarity of such neighborhoods was strengthened by the guild, which closely regulated the conditions of work. Membership in a guild was a prerequisite to the practice of almost any urban occupation, and apprentices were ordinarily chosen on the basis of kinship rather than universalist standards. Not only the family but also religion (each guild had its patron saint) and even magic were interwoven with economic activities. In short,

In the preindustrial cities of medieval Europe and of other parts of the world, certain elements (e.g. economic, class, and family systems) are found which are common to all urban communities. But their form in the preindustrial city differs markedly from that in the industrial city. The difference can be attributed primarily to industrialization.[21]

Very few of the typically urban characteristics, as specified, for example, in Wirth's well known article,[22] apply to preindustrial cities. In other words, the dichotomy between *Gemeinschaft* and *Gesellschaft* passes over one important class, which does not really fit into either type. Preindustrial civilizations are neither "folk" societies, in the sense that primitive tribes are, nor are they "urban" in the sense that this word is ordinarily used today.[23] The following characterization of the cities of Roman Britain applies much more widely:

From the strictly economic point of view the towns were a luxury. Their function was cultural and political. They stood for the decencies and elegances of civilized life, and they provided a link between the Roman government and the mass of the

[20] The following discussion is based largely on Gideon Sjoberg, "The Preindustrial City," *American Journal of Sociology*, 60:5 (March, 1955), 438–445. (The article has been reprinted in Paul K. Hatt and Albert J. Reiss, Jr., *Cities and Society*, Glencoe, Ill.: Free Press, 1957, pp. 179–188.) See also Sjoberg, *The Preindustrial City: Past and Present* (Glencoe, Ill.: Free Press, 1960).

[21] Sjoberg, "The Preindustrial City," *op. cit.*

[22] See pages 181–182.

[23] See Gideon Sjoberg, "Folk and 'Feudal' Societies," *American Journal of Sociology*, 58:3 (November, 1952), 231–239.

people, to whom those decencies and elegances were things out of reach. Their populations, rich and poor alike, thus formed a privileged section of the people, privileged to enjoy the blessings of romanization at the expense of the country-folk. . . .

It is necessary to dwell on this conception, because to us it is a little strange. We inherit the words that once expressed it: words like politics from the Greek and words like civility and civilization and citizenship from the Roman; but for us these words are sublimated into metaphor, and we have forgotten, what the Greek and Roman never forgot, that originally they had no meaning in abstraction from the bricks and stones of the city itself.[24]

FAMILY AND FERTILITY

Preindustrial civilizations, thus, were urban in the sense that a new type and level of culture flourished in their cities, but the overwhelming majority of the people were still rural. The depopulation in the Roman Empire, for instance, cannot reasonably be ascribed to merely the decline of fertility in the city of Rome, although the implicit assumption has sometimes been made that the urban norms, about which we know much more, were general throughout the society.

One way to analyze the fertility of preindustrial civilizations is to reduce them to an ideal type—the "familistic" society, or one in which the family is the dominant institution. This is often exemplified by classical China, which remained essentially unchanged through several thousand years of invasions, wars, and social turmoil, primarily because of the enormous resilience and stability of its family system. As in China, so generally in all societies lacking the full development of a wide variety of institutions, each person was dependent on his kin for the services now rendered by employment agencies, banks, schools, trade unions, and so on. In any agrarian country, moreover, the family is likely to be an economic as well as a domestic unit, and thus a more important one. But in classical China and India these characteristics were more marked because of the influence of the **joint family.**

Under this family system, adult sons did not leave the ancestral home when they married but brought their wives into it, so that three or four or even more generations lived under one roof as a social, religious, and economic unit. The property and the income from it, along with the

[24] R. G. Collingwood and J. N. L. Myres, *Roman Britain and the English Settlements* (2nd ed.; Oxford: Clarendon, 1937), pp. 199, 186. See also Bert F. Hoselitz, "Generative and Parasitic Cities," *Economic Development and Cultural Change*, 3:3 (April, 1955), 278–294; reprinted as one chapter in his *Sociological Aspects of Economic Growth* (Glencoe, Ill.: Free Press, 1960).

earnings of all the family members, constituted a common fund out of which the needs of all were met. This joint family was administered by the oldest male, the patriarch, to whom all others owed absolute obedience. The larger the family, the greater was his realm and the more he was honored: according to legend, the head of a family of nine generations who lived during the T'ang dynasty was visited and decorated by the Emperor in person. The decision when and whom to marry did not rest with the two participants but with their elders; the Confucian classics defined marriage as "a union between two persons of different families, the dual object of which is to serve the ancestors in the temple and to propagate the coming generation." The strength of the institution, thus, was based not only on its current structure but on its intergenerational continuity, with ancestor worship reaching into the past and emphasis on a numerous progeny into the future. While this ideal of the Chinese family was realized only among the gentry, the more numerous peasantry also accepted it as their standard and strove to imitate the upper class to the degree that their poverty permitted.[25]

A joint household favors early marriage. Adolescents can undertake such roles as parenthood while they are still socially immature, for the main responsibility will not rest on them. Moreover, since the dominant motive in arranging a marriage is to perpetuate the line, many children are wanted. In classical China marriage was typically early; in India, by an aberration from the joint-family pattern, it was—and is—still earlier, often before puberty.[26] Neither postponement of marriage nor nonmarriage by a portion of the adults—two methods of controlling fertility in a society lacking efficient contraceptives—is likely to develop in familistic societies. In both China and India, there was some female infanticide—how much no one knows. But the main control over population growth was by mortality.

During the two thousand years that intervened between the ancient and the modern period India's population. . . . must have remained virtually stationary. . . . In "normal" times, . . . the customs governing fertility would provide a birth rate slightly higher than the usual death rate. This would build up a population surplus as a sort of demographic insurance against catastrophe. Inevitably, however, the

[25] See Olga Lang, *Chinese Family and Society* (Institute of Pacific Relations; New Haven: Yale University Press, 1946); Daniel Harrison Kulp, *Country Life in South China: The Sociology of Familism* (New York: Teachers College, Columbia University, 1925).

[26] see page 563.

catastrophe would come in the form of warfare, famine, or epidemic, and the increase of population would suddenly be wiped out.[27]

The same cyclical pattern can be deduced from the population data on China.[28]

In Japan, however, the country whose culture is most similar to the Chinese, family size was controlled. The population of Tokugawa Japan apparently remained virtually stationary at 26 to 27 million over the 125 years for which a reasonably satisfactory statistical record exists (1726–1852). While contraceptives and abortifacients were known, and sometimes used among the upper classes, the principal means of control was infanticide, which was practiced in all regions and by all social strata. The ideal family size seems to have been two sons and one daughter. Thus, the first two or three children born were usually retained and, in view of the high infant mortality, perhaps even the first five or six. Why should it be that a familistic culture, which in China was associated with a strong emphasis on a numerous progeny, in Japan sanctioned a small-family system? The practice of infanticide was not formally approved; most contemporary descriptions condemn it. Many children would have brought prestige to the mother and honor to the father. But with no more land available and opportunities outside agriculture scarce, familism itself, according to Irene Taeuber's interpretation, imposed a prior duty: to maintain the family line by keeping at least one male offspring alive.[29]

In ancient Europe a substantial check on family size was effected in several ways. One important evidence for this with respect to Rome is the pronatalist sentiment expressed by various writers and officials, particularly by Augustus, emperor at the beginning of the Christian era. Three famous laws—*Lex Julia de adulteriis coercendis*, *Lex Julia de maritandis ordinibus*, and *Lex Papia et Poppaea*—were intended to raise the family's prestige and thus to encourage marriage and reproduction. The unmarried and childless were penalized by various legal disabilities; fathers were given preferential treatment in the allocation of public offices; "matrons" (probably the mothers of three or more children) were given the right to wear distinctive clothes. These laws were repeatedly modified,

[27] Kingsley Davis, *The Population of India and Pakistan* (Princeton: Princeton University Press, 1951), p. 24. Copyright, 1951, by Princeton University Press.
[28] See, for example, Ho, *op. cit.*, Ch. 10.
[29] Irene B. Taeuber, *The Population of Japan* (Princeton: Princeton University Press, 1958), Ch. 2.

but in one form or another they remained in effect for a considerable period, finally to be rescinded by Justinian in the middle of the sixth century. Landry believes that they had a beneficial effect on family life and helped to raise the birth rate.[30] Their influence, however, cannot have been great; for beginning in the third century at the latest, the population of the Empire declined.

One important factor in cutting down the birth rate of antiquity was slavery.[31] The slaves themselves had few offspring, first of all because their masters wanted it that way. So long as it was possible, their owners found it more advantageous to purchase adults than to pay for the raising of children. After the price went up (in Rome about the time of Augustus), apparently the birth rate still remained low, partly because the masters did not perceive their interest immediately, partly because the slaves themselves often wanted even less to reproduce. The slave population, thus, could be maintained only by continuous recruitment; and when this lagged, it moved toward extinction. The number of slaves is unknown, but estimates for both Greece and Rome run as high as one-third of the free population—a large enough proportion to have a considerable effect on reproductive trends. The fertility of freed men was also very low. In Rome slaves were generally not manumitted unless they promised never to marry, for if they died without issue, their property reverted to their former owner.

Slavery was also a significant depressant on the birth rate of the free population. Among the upper classes a man who owned a female was not induced to marry by either his sexual drive or his need for someone to care for his household.[32] Casual unions with slaves were generally infertile, as were, of course, the frequent homosexual ones in Greece. Among the lower classes, the competition of slave labor stimulated a sizable outmigration from the centers of the Hellenistic or Roman empires to their peripheries.

[30] Adolphe Landry, *La révolution démographique: Études et essais sur les problèmes de la population* (Paris: Sirey, 1934), p. 95. Cf. D. V. Glass, *Population Policies and Movements in Europe* (Oxford: Clarendon, 1940), pp. 86–90.

[31] The following discussion is based largely on Adolphe Landry, "Quelques aperçus concernant la dépopulation dans l'antiquité gréco-romaine," *Revue Historique,* 61:177 (January–February, 1936), 1–33.

[32] According to the Greek historian Polybius (circa 140 B.C.), "the whole of Greece has been subject to a low birth-rate and a general decrease of the population," for men have fallen into "such a state of pretentiousness, avarice, and indolence that they did not wish to marry, or if they married to rear the children born to them, or at most as a rule but one or two of them." See Polybius, *The Histories,* W. R. Paton, trans., vol. 4 (London: Loeb Classical Library, 1927), book 36, para. 17.6–13.

As every Roman citizen had much better opportunities of earning a living in the provinces, Italy was constantly being drained of her best men, and the gaps were filled by slaves. When an abundant supply of slaves ceased to be available, Italy began to decay in her turn, for the process of emigration never stopped, as one land after another was opened up for settlement.[33]

Slavery was not the only factor that reduced the fertility of antiquity. Among those that married, the age was apparently low enough to make a large average family possible. The evidence from a sample of Roman epitaphs suggests that the average ages at marriage were 18 for females and 26 for males.[34] These figures, to the degree that they are representative, suggest a high marital fertility, which Rome evidently lacked. Probably some form of birth control was fairly widely practiced; coitus interruptus at least was generally known, and possibly other primitive methods as well. According to Himes, "the most brilliant and original account of contraceptive technique written prior to the nineteenth century is undoubtedly that in the *Gynaecology* of Soranos of Ephesus," who practiced in Rome during the first century A.D.[35] The means he recommended were relatively effective, but magic potions and amulets seem to have been much more common in his colleagues' prescriptions. In any case, their patients could not have included more than the urban upper class.

Among the mass of the people the functional substitute for birth control was infanticide. In many of the ancient Greek city-states, it was not only permitted but prescribed under some conditions. In Rome it was circumscribed with various legal restrictions and finally, in the fourth century, made a capital offence. The motivation for these decrees was not ethical but a practical concern about the lagging population growth. The increasing stringency of the prohibition itself suggests that the practice was not exceptional, and the high incidence continued during the following centuries.

It is true that the Christian doctrine of the inestimable worth of every human soul, no matter how humble its vehicle, led the medieval Church to condemn infanticide in the strongest terms. Five forms of controlling family size were specifically forbidden—inducing sterility by drugs or

---

[33] M. Rostovtzeff, *The Social and Economic History of the Roman Empire* (2nd rev. ed.; Oxford: Clarendon, 1957), 1, 375.

[34] Albert Granger Harkness, "Age at Marriage and at Death in the Roman Empire," *Transactions of the American Philological Association*, 27 (1896), 35–72.

[35] Norman E. Himes, *Medical History of Contraception* (Baltimore: Williams & Wilkins, 1936), pp. 88–92.

incantations, aborting the fetus by violent exercise, killing the infant at birth, refusing to nurse one's child, and accidentally sleeping on it; and they were enough stressed to permit the inference that all were common.[36] But moral injunctions apparently became effective only when they were reinforced by a new institution, the foundling hospital. The first of these was established in the early Middle Ages, but their number grew very slowly; "the strong sense always evinced in the Church of the enormity of unchastity probably rendered the ecclesiastics more cautious in this than in other forms of charity." [37] As late as the seventeenth century, when St. Vincent de Paul established the order associated with his name, one impetus to his act was the continuing high frequency of infanticide.

The most significant check to the fertility of late medieval and early modern Europe, however, was its family organization. The **stem family,** as it is termed,[38] typically consisted of the peasant, his wife and minor children, his unmarried brothers and sisters, and perhaps his aged father and mother. This kind of three-generation household once prevailed throughout most of Europe and still exists in a number of rural areas. From generation to generation the holding remains undivided in the same line, but to this important desideratum is sacrificed the procreative life of many adults. In this respect, the two types of "extended" family are poles apart: the joint household facilitates, virtually demands, universal marriage at an early age; but the stem family furnishes a function, a home, and a subordinate status to the siblings of the holder and, in some cases, of his wife. A considerable reduction in fertility was achieved by the nonmarriage, or very late marriage, of a sizable proportion of the population.

From the sparse data available, it would seem that the average age at marriage gradually went up from the early Middle Ages on.[39] This conclusion is supported by what we know of the norms and regulations governing several institutions, in all of which a principle was eventually established that a man might not marry until his living was assured.

[36] Russell, *British Medieval Population,* p. 160.

[37] W. E. H. Lecky, *History of European Morals from Augustus to Charlemagne* (New York: Braziller, 1955), 2, 33.

[38] Sometimes it is given the French name, *famille souche,* following the usage of Frédéric LePlay, who was the first to analyze the type systematically. For a brief description in English, see Conrad M. Arensberg, "The American Family in the Perspective of Other Cultures," in Golden Anniversary White House Conference on Children and Youth, *The Nation's Children* (New York: Columbia University Press, 1960), 1, 50–75.

[39] Russell, "Late Ancient and Medieval Population," *op. cit.,* pp. 18–19.

Guilds, for example, generally did not permit apprentices to take a wife until they had finished their training period and moved up to the next level.

Apprenticeship in its fully grown Elizabethan form required that those learning any trade then practised in England should serve an apprenticeship for seven years or until he was twenty-four years of age, with the possible exception of agriculture in which it was sufficient that he should attain the age of twenty-one if the parties had been unable to agree on twenty-four. It is clear that these provisions were looked upon quite as much as a check on the exuberance of youth as essential for the technical education of the country.[40]

In agriculture, numerically by far the most important sector of the medieval and early modern economies, farmhands were in some respects almost members of a farmer's family, sleeping and eating in and thus under no social pressure to marry early. In England an 1824 report on the poor laws discusses this "old system," by which men "did not marry until they were perhaps near thirty years of age, and until they had got a little money and a few goods about them." [41] The trend in rural marriage patterns is suggested also by etymology. The word *husband* derives from two words meaning "house" and "dwell," and its original meaning (still preserved in *husbandman* and *husbandry*) was a householder, a man who had a home. The Middle English word for an unmarried man was *anilepiman* ("only man"). These two terms, one referring to the management of property and the other to marital status, gradually became associated as opposites, *anilepiman* coming to mean a man who had no living and therefore could not marry, and *husband,* a man who was able to care for a family and therefore could get (or, eventually, was) married.[42]

The norm of marital responsibility lasted in Western Europe well into the modern period, until the traditional social structure was broken up by industrialization, and family limitation could be achieved with less onerous deprivations than prolonged celibacy. The effect of the medieval pattern on fertility is dramatically illustrated in the recent history of Ireland.[43]

---

[40] G. Talbot Griffith, *Population Problems of the Age of Malthus* (Cambridge: Cambridge University Press, 1926), p. 112.

[41] Quoted in *ibid.,* p. 109.

[42] Cf. George Caspar Homans, *English Villagers of the Thirteenth Century* (Cambridge: Harvard University Press, 1941), pp. 136–137.

[43] See page 564.

In summary, the data available suggest that in ancient and medieval Europe, and also in Tokugawa Japan, fertility was held substantially under the physiological maximum. In Europe this control was effected primarily by marriage patterns, to some degree by infanticide; in Japan mainly by infanticide. Enough children were born to maintain the population and provide for a small growth, but the margin was not great. In classical China or India, on the contrary, girls married at puberty or before, and there was strong social pressure on everyone to marry and have many children. It may be that the population of these civilizations therefore pressed closer on their subsistence, and this is suggested also by what is known about their mortality.

MORTALITY

Age-specific death rates *per 1,000 deaths* in three regions of Roman Italy, as calculated by Beloch from tombstone inscriptions, are shown in Table 13-2. The figures in the last column for Prussia of 1876 were

TABLE 13-2. Age-Specific Deaths per 1,000 Deaths,
Roman Italy, as Calculated from Epitaphs

Age-Group	Male	Female	Total	Prussia (1876)
0–15	315	252	289	540
16–30	331	428	370	67
31–45	171	169	170	⎱ 185
46–60	81	71	76	⎰
Over 60	102	80	95	199
Unknown				9

Source: Julius Beloch, *Die Bevölkerung der griechisch-römischen Welt* (Leipzig: Duncker & Humblot, 1886), p. 48.

included for comparison. In the latter, more than half of those aged up to 15 died each year, and the markedly lower proportion in Roman Italy certainly reflects only the fact that tombstones were seldom erected for infants or young children. Note that for the relatively small number of minors represented, the sex ratio is 1,250, while for the major reproductive period it is 841. Childbirth apparently was dangerous to mothers, and by inference also to their children.[44] Why the Roman rate for those over 60 was so low compared to that for Prussia is not clear. The number of

[44] See also Russell, "Late Ancient and Medieval Population,"*op. cit.,* Tables 3 and 4; Burn, "Hic Breve Vivitur," *op. cit.*

persons who reached this advanced age was small, and the inadequacy of the sample of epitaphs would thus have affected the rate more.[45]

Median expectations of life as calculated by Beloch are given in Table 13-3. These figures have the same limitations, of course, as the "death rates" on which they are based. In particular, it is impossible to calculate the expectation of life from birth, since we have no data on the mortality

TABLE 13-3. **Median Expectations of Life, Roman Italy,**
as Calculated from Epitaphs

From Age	Males	Females
10	17–18	15–16
20	16–17	10–11
30	15–16	11–12
40	15–16	15–16
50	10–11	10–11
60	10–11	8

Source: Julius Beloch, *Bevölkerung der griechisch-römischen Welt* (Leipzig: Duncker & Humblot, 1886), p. 51.

of infants and young children. However, if the probability was that children of 10 would live only to their late twenties, then the expectation of life from birth, which would take into account the certainly larger infant mortality, could not have been more than the early twenties.[46]

Russell calculated life tables from data on the English royal house during the medieval period. For its members born before 1348, the year that the Black Death struck England, the expectation of life at birth was generally slightly above 30 years. It fell during the plague period to

[45] In Beloch's more detailed table giving rates by single years of age, a very definite tendency is discernible to heap at ages ending in 5 and 0, exactly as in the returns from modern censuses. Even in so personal a datum as the inscription on one's tombstone, age was rounded off.

[46] See, however, John D. Durand, "Mortality Estimates from Roman Tombstone Inscriptions," *American Journal of Sociology*, 65:4 (January, 1960), 365–373, where it is inferred from the assumed population growth that the expectation of life at birth must have been higher. Both the high mortality and such specific features as the difference between the sexes are similar to conditions prevailing in modern underdeveloped areas some decades ago, and Willcox suggested that data from the latter could be used to supplement those obtained from ancient tombstone inscriptions. The expectation of life, he hypothesized, is of either an "Oriental" or an "Occidental" type. Since for mature ages Rome conformed to the former, it is plausible that it more or less did also with respect to infant mortality. In India, for example, infant mortality was over 200 per 1,000 live births during the first decades of the twentieth century, falling to about 175 during the 1920's. See Walter F. Willcox, "The Length of Life in the Roman Empire: A Methodological Note," in *Congrès international de la population, 2, Démographie historique* (Paris: Hermann, 1938), 14–22; Davis, *op. cit.*, p. 34.

17, and then rose very slowly over the next 75 years again to something over 30. Life tables for a small sample of monks, another favored group, give about the same figures.[47] These are fairly accurate estimates for the social classes from which the data were drawn, and they thus probably represent maxima for the general population, who were more susceptible to some causes of death. The difference between an expectation of life at birth of something over 20 in ancient Rome and approximately 30 in medieval Britain may indicate nothing more than imperfections in the data. If there was an advance in death control, it was not a great one compared with what has taken place since then.

The causes of this high mortality cannot, of course, be specified in terms of the modern classification. We know very little about why people died in a "normal" year; but over a longer period a large proportion died as the consequence of famines, epidemics, or the breakdown of the social order (including war). Some over-all data on these three types of catastrophe are available for the whole of the historic era.

Famine

Until recently most of the people in the world have suffered from a shortage of food, but in Europe—ancient, medieval, or modern—actual famines have been relatively rare. That grain had to be shipped over ever-growing distances to Roman Italy was a problem of increasing gravity, but so long as the state control remained intact the system never broke down. Medieval Europe suffered from severe famines, such as that in 1315–1317,[48] but they were relatively infrequent. In the last great famine of the Western world, in Ireland in the 1840's, several hundred thousand persons died of starvation, and the already large emigration was given a mighty stimulus.

Such a figure would have been insignificant in the great civilizations of Asia, whose normal death rate, as Mallory put it, "may be said to contain a constant famine factor." Between 108 B.C. and A.D. 1911, China withstood 1,828 famines, or nearly one per year in some of the provinces during these two millenia.[49] Most of them were over only a portion of the country; the worst were nationwide. But everywhere throughout China, every district experienced a famine at least several times during

---

[47] Russell, *British Medieval Population,* pp. 178–193.

[48] Henry S. Lucas, "The Great European Famine of 1315, 1316, and 1317," *Speculum,* 5 (October, 1930), 343–377.

[49] Walter H. Mallory, *China: Land of Famine* (New York: American Geographical Society, 1926), p. 1.

each person's lifetime. And even this record, according to Ho, under-states the probable catastrophic effects of crop failures, droughts, floods, and locusts and other pests. The information in general official works "often fails to indicate the scope and severity of a famine," which can be gauged more accurately from the local histories he used as sources. A good example is provided by the province of Hupei, for which Ho calculated year by year the number of counties affected by natural calamities (including also epidemics) from 1644 to 1911. Out of this period of 267 years, there were only 27 entirely free of disaster (including those for which the record is known to be incomplete). Droughts occurred in 92 of the years, floods in 190. In the average year slightly more than one-tenth of the province was hit.[50]

One of the worst famines of modern China struck four northern provinces in 1877–1878. Communications were so poor that almost a year passed before news of it reached the capital. Cannibalism was common, and local magistrates were ordered "to connive at the evasion of the laws prohibiting the sale of children, so as to enable parents to buy a few days' food." The dead were buried in what are still today called "ten-thousand-men holes." From 9 to 13 million, according to the estimate of the Foreign Relief Committee, perished from hunger, disease, or violence during these two years.[51]

Of course, it is not possible to measure the mortality from Asiatic famines directly. The registration of deaths, never very accurate at best, breaks down completely during such a period. Davis has estimated the mortality in India due to the famines during the 1890's by comparing the country's natural increase in this decade with that in the ones before and after it:

In the previous decade [the population of India] grew 9.4 per cent, and in the following decade 6.1 per cent. If the 1891–1901 decade had experienced the average rate of growth shown by these two decades, it would have grown by 7.8 per cent instead of 1 per cent. The difference is a matter of some 19 million persons, which may be taken as a rough estimate of loss due to famines. It should be borne in mind, however, that relief measures were functioning at this time and that this saved the lives of millions of persons who otherwise would have died.[52]

This contrast between the famine-ridden civilizations of China and India and those of ancient and medieval Europe, relatively free of this cause of death, cannot be explained by a difference in technical skill.

[50] Ho, *op. cit.*, pp. 228–229, 292–300.
[51] *Ibid.*, pp. 231–232.
[52] Davis, *op. cit.*, p. 39.

If anything, the Chinese peasant was a better agriculturist than his Western counterpart. (a) One reason for the difference is geographical: the uncertainty of rainfall in India has been characterized as "the biggest single factor influencing life" there,[53] and the same might be said of monsoon Asia in general. (b) In both India and China, agriculture was based to a large extent on irrigation and flood-control works, which, as we have seen, gave rise to a type of society known as Oriental despotism. The inefficiency of the bureaucracy in all matters except collecting rapacious taxes, the routine banditry and civil war, made it difficult—and even, from the point of view of the bureaucrats, unimportant—to store food against times of need.[54] (c) To this day the transportation system of either China or India is poor compared with that, for example, of the Roman Empire. Most famines are local, at least in origin. If food cannot be shipped in from other areas, however, the starving people leave their homes and steal food where they can, spreading the famine and often pestilence as they go. (d) A final reason for the difference was probably the higher fertility in Asia. While family size was controlled by means of coitus interruptus, abortion, and particularly infanticide, China and India probably had a higher fertility than other preindustrial civilizations. Their populations therefore pressed more closely on the subsistence available to them.

Pestilence

With respect to diseases, the preindustrial civilizations were more or less on a par. Their doctors did not know the cause of most ailments and usually had little success in curing them. As one would expect, the best information we have concerns the most devastating—the plague, malaria, cholera, and the other major epidemic diseases.[55]

The plague appears in three forms—pneumonic, septicemic, and bubonic. A person infected with the first type, the least important of the three, is directly contagious. The other two are spread by a complex interaction among the bacillus, its host (the flea), and the flea's hosts (the rat and man). The bubonic plague was the most terrible of the epidemics of the ancient and medieval worlds. It struck in the first half of the sixth century and then again some 800 years later.

The path of the fourteenth-century epidemic, the famous Black Death,

[53] L. Dudley Stamp, quoted in *ibid.*, p. 38.

[54] For a first-hand account of the "political causes of famine" in China, see Mallory, *op. cit.*, Ch. 3.

[55] For discussions in two different social contexts, see Russell, "Late Ancient and Medieval Population," *op. cit.*, pp. 35–45, and Davis, *op. cit.*, pp. 42–61.

is shown in Figure 13-1. The first cases were in Constantinople in 1347; and the presumption is that the infection came from China, where it may have been endemic. By the fall of 1347 it was reported in Sicily.

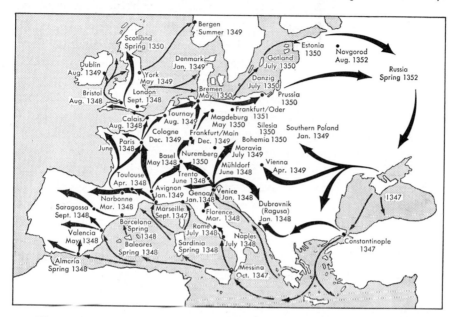

Figure 13-1. The Path of the Bubonic Plague, Fourteenth-Century Europe

Source: Ernst Kirsten, *Raum und Bevölkerung in der Weltgeschichte,* 1 (Würzburg: Ploetz, 1956), 92. © 1956 by A. G. Ploetz-Verlag Würzburg. (From material by Dr. W. Buchholz and Dr. Stikker.)

During the spring of 1348 it spread throughout the Mediterranean basin to Italy, France, and Spain, reaching Paris in June, London in September. From London it went west to Dublin (1349), north to York (1349) and Scotland (1350). From Italy and France it traveled to various German cities, reaching East Prussia in 1350 and Russia in the spring of 1352. In each place it struck in epidemic form several times—in England, for example, in 1348–1350, 1360–1361, 1369, and 1375—and continued endemic for some 80 years. The mortality throughout Europe was appalling. Contemporary figures reflect the variation from one place to another and are often exaggerated, but even the more conservative estimates of present-day scholars indicate an unparalleled loss of life. One of the most careful analyses is by Russell,[56] who believes that most European nations sustained a depletion of 20 to 25 per cent in the first attack of 1348–1350, and of 40 per cent by the end of the century.

[56] Russell, *British Medieval Population,* pp. 214–232; "Late Ancient and Medieval Population," *op. cit.,* pp. 40–45.

Urban death rates were probably higher than the average, because of the greater contagion in congested areas, and the depopulation of cities was aggravated by a mass exodus of their terror-stricken inhabitants. Since pregnant women seem to have been particularly susceptible, the stupendous loss could not be quickly repaired. "Only one disease, the plague, seems to have been lethal enough to destroy population faster than humanity could restore it in the late ancient and medieval period." [57]

The total mortality from other major diseases, however, was great. It is not possible in most cases even to suggest their rates of incidence, except to state that they were high. There is a marked difference in the relative susceptibility of various age-groups. The plague strikes heaviest at older persons, which is presumably one reason why the best known figures of fourteenth-century Europe died in such an overwhelming proportion during the first attack of the Black Death. Tuberculosis, on the contrary, typically infects young children and kills at the beginning of their adult life, thus placing the burden of support on society with no economic or demographic return. The age differential for malaria is parallel to that for general mortality, very high in infancy, low in the teens, and gradually rising with adult ages.

The Breakdown of Social Order

That famine and pestilence ordinarily appear together suggests a direct relation between them, but apparently the usual reason is that both the supply of food and public health depend on—and can affect—the maintenance of social order. People who have seen hundreds of their neighbors die of hunger or disease do not themselves continue to carry out their usual pursuits in accordance with established norms. They flee from their homes, carrying the blight with them.

The interaction of these three major factors in mortality can be illustrated by some pages from the history of the late Roman Empire. The process began as early as the reign of Trajan (A.D. 98–117), whose military successes, according to Rostovtzeff, brought "the empire to the verge of ruin."

The dread symptom of this decay was the depopulation of the peninsula and the concurrent decline of Italian agriculture. . . . Nerva endeavoured to repopulate the country by reviving the plan of distributing land to poorer citizens. . . . Trajan forbade emigration from Italy and settled Roman veterans in the immediate

[57] *Ibid.,* p. 45.

vicinity of Rome; he forced senators to acquire land in the mother country; and he helped Italian landowners in general, both large and small, to improve their situation by supplying them with cheap credit.[58]

Over the following several hundred years these remedies would be applied again and again, with less and less effect.[59] The capital's disorganization was reflected in a virtual civil war in the countryside. During a 50-year period of the third century, there were 27 official emperors in Rome, plus twice that number of aspirants. Armies broke up into antagonistic units, which successively requisitioned (or stole—the distinction was not sharp) standing crops, food stores, and livestock, leaving impoverishment and starvation in their wake. At the end of the century, barbarians invaded Italy and also ravaged the countryside. The cultivators were mostly either slaves, who took the opportunity to escape, or *coloni* (tenant farmers), who also often fled from their holdings. The brigand bands that they formed in some cases constituted veritable armies, large enough in Gaul to menace cities. In the middle of the third century Italy was infested by the plague, which was rapidly spread by the movement of troops and irregulars.

Efforts to repair the damage often increased it. Much land had gone out of cultivation, and Rome was deprived both of its produce and of taxes. In the fourth century a system evolved by which these abandoned plots were assigned to adjoining estates, so that their owners would both cultivate them and pay the land tax again. Rather than accept what was often an intolerable burden, many gave up their own properties. With land out of use and drainage systems neglected, breeding places for mosquitoes multiplied; and malaria became a greater threat to the population, killing many and sapping the strength of others. Early in the fourth century the *coloni*, who had been using their contractual right to leave their farms, were bound to the soil. They became serfs. Their status was gradually imposed also on the free agricultural workers, so that by the fifth century the prior distinction between them and *coloni* had all but disappeared.

As this brief account suggests, the barbarians did not so much cause the downfall of Rome as fit into a process of gradual disintegration well under way before they became a significant factor. Constantine (306–337) had forced a treaty on the Visigoths, who agreed to supply soldiers to the Roman army in return for yearly payments, and over the follow-

[58] Rostovtzeff, *op. cit.*, pp. 358–359.
[59] The following account derives largely from Boak, *op. cit.*, Ch. 2.

ing period the Roman army was gradually germanized. Assigned to frontier duty, German soldiers acquired land there and in many places became the dominant element of the population. After Ulfilas (or Wulfila; 311–381), a bishop of Arian convictions, translated the Bible into Gothic, a large number of Germans were converted to Christianity and thus even more subject to Roman influence than before. In the following period the distinction between "Roman" and "barbarian" became less and less distinct. The relation between the two cultures was not so often a confrontation on the field of battle as a divided loyalty of marginal men—for example, Alaric, the leader of the Visigoths who sacked Rome, a romanized German, a former officer in the Roman army, a Christian; or Stilicho, the *de facto* emperor at that time, a German by descent who had reached this high post through a successful army career.

The aim of the invaders was not to destroy the Roman Empire but to occupy and enjoy it. By and large, what they preserved far exceeded what they destroyed or what they brought that was new. . . . [The civilization of the Empire] outlived its authority. By the Church, by language, by the superiority of its institutions and law, it prevailed over the conquerors. . . . They barbarized it, but they did not consciously germanize it.[60]

The decisive break with the civilization of antiquity came not from the German infiltration or the attendant circumstances that made it possible, but much later, in the eighth and ninth centuries, when Europe was unable to repel invasion. Moslems conquered Spain and threatened Constantinople; Norsemen plundered the coasts of the North Sea and of every river that emptied into it; the Hungarians swept in from Asia. "The devastation was so complete that, in many cases indeed, the population itself disappeared." Too weak to defend its periphery, Europe turned inward. "The Empire of Charlemagne . . . was essentially an inland one, . . . a State without foreign markets, living in a condition of almost complete isolation." [61]

During most of the first millenium of the Christian era, then, the civilization of antiquity was in decline. It is not easy, and in this context not relevant, to distinguish such a general social disintegration, inevitably aggravated by combat, from formal warfare. Present-day Americans are likely to conceptualize war in terms of their own experience —a process in which young men are trained, sent overseas to fight, and

---

60 Pirenne, *op. cit.*, p. 5. For a more complete account of this complex and subtle interpenetration of the two cultures, see J. B. Bury, *The Invasion of Europe by the Barbarians* (London: Macmillan, 1928).
61 Pirenne, *op. cit.*, pp. 21, 19.

welcomed home on their victorious return. War in the country where the battles are fought, particularly when a defeated army breaks up into small marauding bands, is much less clearly distinguished from civilian life.

Another striking example is the Taiping Rebellion of 1851–1864, which Ho terms "the greatest civil war in world history." Indeed, as he writes, "in sheer brutality and destruction it has few peers." In the usual tactics against the rebels, not only were all prisoners summarily slaughtered but a scorched-earth policy was used to starve the armies into submission. In one area of some 6,000 square miles no trace of human habitation was left. The usual estimate of the number who died, 20 or 30 million, is too low in Ho's opinion. The devastation is merely suggested by the fact that in 1953 the population of three of the provinces most affected—Chekiang, Anhwei, and Kiangsi—was still 19.2 million, or 14 per cent, under the estimated number in 1850.[62]

POPULATION CYCLES

The main emphasis in the previous chapters was on population growth, and this was appropriate in either of two contexts. With respect to the term of *Homo sapiens* on earth, the dominant trend has been an increase in numbers. And in the modern world, from roughly 1650 on, this increase has been at a rapid and accelerating rate. But a closer view of preindustrial civilizations reveals a striking exception to the rule: as we have noted, their populations typically grew and declined in a cyclical pattern.

The gradual development of classical antiquity as a unit, for example, was certainly accompanied by a substantial rise in population. The depopulation of the Roman Empire as a whole probably began in the third century and continued for several hundred years. The nadir was reached, by Russell's estimate, around 600, and Europe's population remained more or less static at this low level for almost 400 years. The epidemic of the bubonic plague with which this period was opened was possibly the most devastating in history. Then there came the Moslem, Norse, and Hungarian invasions.[63]

By 950 Europe had developed enough power to protect its borders, and the ensuing four centuries constitute the "medieval increase," as Russell terms it. From the middle of the eleventh century to just before

[62] Ho, *op. cit.,* pp. 236–246, 275.
[63] Russell, "Late Ancient and Medieval Population," *op. cit.,* Ch. 8.

the Black Death, the population of England, for example, increased from
1.1 to 3.7 million, that of France (territory of 1328) from 4.0 to 13.5
million.[64] A decline started with the outbreak of the plague in 1348, and
continued for about 80 years. From 1430 to the present day, the
population of Europe has grown steadily, though at different rates at
various times.

The evidence concerning Asia also suggests a cyclical pattern, though
these data are usually harder to analyze. Ancient India had no censuses
that have survived, and the interpretation of Chinese statistics presents
extraordinary difficulties. In Ho's reconstruction of China's population
history, there has been an irregular increase—from 65 million in 1400,
to 150 million in 1600 and still in 1700, to 313 million in 1794, 430
million in 1850, and 583 million in 1953. Other scholars, while agreeing
that growth occurred over this period, have stressed its irregularity more.[65]

What is the meaning of these long cycles? In what way are they associated with trends in economic and social life? Depopulation in the late
Roman Empire coincided with the disintegration of classical society, and
the low point was during the Dark Ages; from 950 to 1350 marked a new
rise in population and the evolution of medieval culture to its high point;
the subsequent increase from 1430 on coincided with the Renaissance and
beginning of modern Europe. There certainly is a correlation here. But
in which direction is the causal relation? Is population size an effect of
the economic level or, on the contrary, a cause of a more general development or decline? Or is the cause-effect relation both more variable and
more complex than either of these alternatives? Let us consider these
questions with respect to depopulation, which is atypical in human history
and therefore the most interesting feature of preindustrial civilizations.

The decline of Europe's population in the second half of the fourteenth
century was indubitably caused by the Black Death. The unreliable rainfall of monsoon Asia is indeed the greatest influence on the life of its
inhabitants. That is to say, sometimes a single factor is so dominant that
analysts have no hesitation in designating it as the cause of demographic
processes. But even in such cases, it must be emphasized, these factors
operate within a certain cultural-social-economic context. India's de-

---

[64] *Ibid.*, Ch. 9.

[65] For one series of estimates for the population of China from the beginning of the
Christian era, see Abbott Payson Usher, "The History of Population and Settlement in
Eurasia," *Geographical Review*, 20:1 (January, 1930), 110–132. See also K. W.
Taylor, "Some Aspects of Population History," *Canadian Journal of Economics and
Political Science*, 16:3 (August, 1950), 301–313. (Both articles have been reprinted
in Joseph J. Spengler and Otis Dudley Duncan, eds., *Demographic Analysis*, Glencoe,
Ill.: Free Press, 1956, pp. 3–25, 44–51.)

pendence on rainfall, for example, was mitigated by irrigation systems, and increased by family-building norms that pushed the population always up to the subsistence available. And more often there is no such single factor on which all scholars agree, but a multiplicity of causes, each emphasized by a different writer. In explaining the depopulation of the ancient world, for instance, Landry singled out the fall in fertility.[66] Others have stressed the high mortality, sometimes even that from a single disease.[67] Still others have paid greatest attention to the gradual disintegration of the state's political control, and its eventual effect on everything from family life to agricultural produce. Such separate factors can be singled out in order to examine them more thoroughly, but the most reasonable hypothesis usually is that the decline in numbers was brought about not by any single one but by the interaction of all.

Nor is it any easier to analyze the effects of depopulation on the rest of society. The first to be noted is that on military prowess. While there is not a simple one-to-one relation, it is true that states of grossly different sizes can wield power more or less proportionate to their populations; and this was even more the case in the past, when there were not such great differences in military technology. As its title indicates, this is one principal theme of Boak's book, *Manpower Shortage and the Fall of the Roman Empire in the West*. In order to maintain the boundary of the Empire safe against incursions, Rome—as we have seen—had to recruit an increasing number of Germans into its army. A vigorous and expanding Roman population could have absorbed this barbarian element, but, as it was, the Germans not only came to dominate the ranks and officer corps but were well represented among commanding generals. Even so, the manpower shortage continued, and in the next stage treaties were signed by which nominally dependent—though actually autonomous—German tribes were paid to defend the frontiers. And the proximate cause of the fall of the city of Rome was a struggle between the Latin and German parties in the Empire.[68] Such a loss of military power, moreover, can be cumulative. One reason that Europe was unable

[66] Landry, "Quelques aperçus," *op. cit.* The establishment of Christianity and the consequent abolition of Roman family norms, he believes, reversed the downward trend. Most scholars who have studied the question, however, agree that the depopulation continued for a considerable period after all Europe was Christian. Moreover, the early Christians did not favor large families; see Boak, *op. cit.*, p. 129.

[67] See, for example, W. H. S. Jones, *Malaria: A Neglected Factor in the History of Greece and Rome* (Cambridge: Macmillan & Bowes, 1907).

[68] See Boak, *op. cit.*, pp. 115–116. Note, however, that he concludes his discussion as follows: "I should be the last person to claim that the fall of the West Roman Empire can be explained solely in terms of a problem of shortage of recruits for the army."

to defend its borders against Saracens, Norsemen, or Hungarians was its lack of manpower; and, vice versa, one reason that this low population level remained characteristic of the Dark Ages is the effects, both direct and indirect, of the continued raids that Europe had to withstand.

The broader effects of depopulaton can be suggested only very tentatively. Russell's hypothesis is that the decline in numbers during the late ancient and early medieval period brought about an economic, social, and intellectual depression, which induced a stronger religious interest.[69] The shortage of workers following the Black Death, on the contrary, led to a rise in wages and probably facilitated the shift from serfdom to free labor. Instead of an intellectual depression and stronger religious interest, Europe moved into the Renaissance. Of course, the period of the decline was much shorter, only 80 years as compared with several centuries. But the contrast indicates that it is no easier to specify the "effects" of a loss of population than its "causes."

Each of the various types of food-gathering and primitive agricultural societies, as we noted in the last chapter, has a typical population density and community size. One can hypothesize that preindustrial civilizations also had a characteristic carrying power, based on their control of the important causes of death. The maximum numbers reached under the best of temporary conditions would be larger than this long-term maximum. Cyclical growth can then be described as the composite effect of such fluctuations with a slow improvement in, for example, the supply of food available.

Ho traced not only the growth of China's population but also the rise of the country's carrying power. The Sung Emperor Chen-tsung (998–1022) introduced from Indochina a drought-resistant variety of rice, which ripened in 100 days, eventually in 60, rather than the 150 days needed by the then standard Chinese varieties. Since in the Yangtze area rice is usually a summer crop, the shorter maturation period made it possible to sow such winter crops as wheat or rape on the same land. On the basis of this double-cropping system, the number of Chinese rose to 100 million by the beginning of the twelfth century. In the ensuing centuries new varieties of rice were developed that ripened in 30 days, irrigation was extended, and significant improvements were made

---

[69] J. C. Russell, "The Ecclesiastical Age: A Demographic Interpretation of the Period 200–900 A.D.," *Review of Religion*, 5:2 (January, 1941), 137–147; "Late Ancient and Medieval Population," *op. cit.,* p. 140. For a more general statement of his theory of the interaction of population and cultural growth, see his "Demographic Pattern in History," *Population Studies,* 1:4 (March, 1948), 388–404. (This last article has been reprinted in Spengler and Duncan, *op. cit.,* pp. 52–68.)

in pumps, so that the production of rice about doubled between 1000 and 1850. In the sixteenth century, maize, sweet potatoes, Irish potatoes, and peanuts were introduced from America; and these new food plants began another agricultural revolution, which is still to run its full course. The peanut plant, with its nitrogen-fixing nodules, improves the soil where it is grown, and peanuts are now a common food in the North, even among the very poor. China is by far the world's largest producer of sweet potatoes, which rank below only rice and wheat in the country as a whole and constitute the poor man's staple. The large and continuing population increase is based in part on these new plants.[70]

SUMMARY

The term "preindustrial civilizations" has been used to designate a class of societies based on agriculture and trade but with no industry, with an urban population and a high culture but few of the characteristics associated with urbanism in the modern West. These societies, particularly ancient Rome, medieval Europe, and classical China and India, have certain important elements in common.

The populations of preindustrial civilizations typically grew to a maximum and then declined sharply, as the consequence of famines, epidemics, and the breakdown of social order. This cyclical pattern was characteristic of all of them, but differences can be noted between Asia and ancient or medieval Europe. In the former, the female age at marriage was generally puberty, and virtually all adults of both sexes were married, while in Europe postponement of marriage and nonmarriage of some adults cut the average family size to well below the physiological maximum. Because of this partial control of fertility, the European population did not press so closely on its means of subsistence, with the probable consequence that it was seldom devastated by famine. In Asia, on the contrary, starvation seems to have been more important even than disease as a cause of high mortality.

During the downswing of a cycle the population, economy, and culture have often declined together, and this correlation has given rise to a variety of theories. In the most general terms, the cause of the periodic depopulation was that much larger numbers developed during favorable periods than could be maintained permanently. On the other hand, the loss of population was often an important factor in the decline in politi-

[70] Ho, *op. cit.*, Ch. 8.

cal power, economy, and culture, but it cannot be designated as "the" cause.

SUGGESTIONS FOR FURTHER READING

Julius Beloch, *Die Bevölkerung der griechisch-römischen Welt* (Leipzig: Duncker & Humblot, 1886).

J. C. Russell, *British Medieval Population* (Albuquerque: University of New Mexico Press, 1948); "Late Ancient and Medieval Population," *Transactions of the American Philosophical Society,* vol. 48, part 3 (June, 1958).

The work by Beloch is acknowledged as the best in any language on the population of antiquity. Of the two works by Russell, the first is an excellent analysis of medieval population, the second a conscientious summary of a mass of material.

Ping-ti Ho, *Studies on the Population of China, 1368–1953* (Cambridge: Harvard University Press, 1959).

Kingsley Davis, *The Population of India and Pakistan* (Princeton: Princeton University Press, 1951).

Irene B. Taeuber, *The Population of Japan* (Princeton: Princeton University Press, 1958).

Excellent analyses of the populations of three high civilizations of Asia.

J. B. Bury, *The Invasion of Europe by the Barbarians* (London: Macmillan, 1928).

A fascinating account of a very interesting period.

Hans Zinsser, *Rats, Lice and History:* . . . *The Life History of Typhus Fever* (Boston: Little, Brown, 1935).

George Rosen, *A History of Public Health* (New York: M.D. Publications, 1958).

A highly readable work on the effects of epidemics on history, and an account of how public health developed, with unusually good coverage of the early period.

Henri Pirenne, *Medieval Cities: Their Origins and the Revival of Trade* (New York: Doubleday-Anchor, 1956).

Alfred F. Havighurst, ed., *The Pirenne Thesis: Analysis, Criticism, and Revision* (Boston: Heath, 1958).

Pirenne's provocative work has stimulated a good deal of discussion, some of which is given in the second book.

Philip M. Hauser, ed., "World Urbanism," *American Journal of Sociology,* vol. 60, no. 5 (March, 1955).

Gideon Sjoberg, *The Preindustrial City: Past and Present* (Glencoe, Ill.: Free Press, 1960).

See in particular the papers by Kingsley Davis, Gideon Sjoberg, and William Bascom. Sjoberg's book is the product of a decade of intensive work in this generally neglected subject.

C. M. Chiao, Warren S. Thompson, and D. T. Chen, *An Experiment in the Registration of Vital Statistics in China* (Oxford, Ohio: Scripps Foundation for Research in Population Problems, 1938).

Required reading for anyone inclined to accept the population data of preindustrial civilizations at face value.

14. *POPULATION DURING THE*
INDUSTRIAL REVOLUTION

The development of industrial societies must be a recurrent theme in any work on population. It has been discussed in the most general terms as the major factor in the demographic transition, and somewhat more specifically in the context of American culture. In this chapter we shall take a still closer look at the country where the industrial revolution started and where its immediate effects can best be studied—England from roughly 1760 to 1840. To say, however, that it can be studied "best" there does not mean also easily. On the contrary, there are great difficulties in interpreting the sparse, often dubious, sometimes contradictory data; and, as we shall see throughout the chapter, little consensus is to be found among the best scholars in the field.

The very phrase "industrial revolution" does not define a precise period on which all agree; and its various elements, though overlapping and interacting, are also in some senses discrete. It is important, in any case, not to interpret the term too narrowly. Many present-day readers, misled by the label, would miss the point of the story of the schoolboy who began his theme on The Industrial Revolution with the sentence, "About 1760 a wave of gadgets swept over England." One must remember that while the metamorphosis was greater in manufacturing, it was also significant in mining, transportation, and agriculture; and that while the significance of all the new machines and the technological processes together was tremendous, their impact was also "revolutionary" because they were accompanied by no less dramatic changes in the social structure. More important even than the building of factories, for instance, was the creation of a factory *system,* with the imposition of a new type of discipline and the gradual amalgamation of industrial entrepreneurs and urban workers into two new social classes.

376

Did industrialism improve the living conditions of the working classes? The controversy over this question between what have come to be known as "optimists" and "pessimists" began during the industrial revolution itself and has continued intermittently ever since. In the 1830's Andrew Ure so admired the new order that he could compare factory children to "lively elves" at play, while Thomas Carlyle saw the world of the mill-hand as "a dingy prison-house." [1] In the later decades of the century, as "the voice of the social reformer mingle[d] with that of the historian," the gloomier view came to be generally accepted, not only by liberals like Arnold Toynbee (*Lectures on the Industrial Revolution in England,* 1884), but especially by the considerable number of socialists who wrote about the period—in particular Sidney and Beatrice Webb, G. D. H. Cole, and J. L. and Barbara Hammond. Their prime inspiration was a book written by Marx's friend and collaborator, Frederick Engels; [2] and, while they did not use the whole elaborate schema developed by Marx, they, like him, explained the social history of this period principally as an opposition between "exploiting" and "exploited" classes. In the 1920's there appeared a number of works which struck a less dismal note. Several of these—by Griffith, Buer, and George—were in large part about population movements, and the most important, J. H. Clapham's *Economic History of Modern Britain* (1926), attempted to show that real wages had risen during industrialization. Even apart from the point of view expressed, this recourse to new types of statistical data opened up the dispute again.

Analysts today interpret early English industrialization in terms of an ideology somewhere along the scale from Stalin to Hayek, but typically with a more careful attention to sources than some of their nineteenth-century predecessors. Unfortunately, many of the primary data are also biased; their ambiguity reflects, at least in part, an ambivalence among the lower classes themselves toward the great changes in their life. It would be impossible in one chapter to attempt to reconcile these several points of view and thus avoid all the biases. A whole volume would be needed merely to spell out in full the variety of interpretations deriving

[1] Both are cited in A. J. Taylor, "Progress and Poverty in Britain, 1780–1850: A Reappraisal," *History,* 45:153 (February, 1960), 16–31. The following account is based in part on this useful summary.

[2] Frederick Engels, *The Condition of the Working Class in England,* W. O. Henderson and W. H. Chaloner, trans. and eds. (New York: Macmillan, 1958). The editors' footnotes and appendices throw some doubt on the author's scholarship. On the other hand, as recently as 1955 a UNESCO bibliography denoted Engels's book as a model for present-day social scientists ("Urban Sociology: Trend Reports and Bibliography," *Current Sociology,* 4:4, 1955, 30).

from different approaches or methods of analysis. While some of the polemical areas are too important to pass over altogether, the principal emphasis in the following discussion will be on factors in the population growth, using the rather thin statistical base to the degree that this is possible, and relating the demographic changes inferentially to those taking place in England's institutional structure.

No characteristic of the population remained unchanged in this transformation of the economy and society. The movement of laborers, even though retarded by legal impediments, became greater than ever before. Growth in numbers, which had been relatively slow from the beginning of the modern period, accelerated. Authorities pretty much agree in designating this a natural increase: the overseas emigration was about balanced in this period by immigration from Ireland. However, whether it was the consequence of a rise in births or a fall in deaths—or, if both, in what proportion—has also been the subject of a learned debate.

SOURCES OF INFORMATION

In the second half of the eighteenth century, no one knew whether the population was increasing or decreasing. The debate on the social and demographic effects of industrialization was in full swing, with sometimes more vehemence than logic. From the fact that fewer were dying, Richard Price, for instance, argued that there were fewer to die—that the population was decreasing.[3] Even after the first censuses were taken, the dispute continued. For William Cobbett, thus, the returns of the 1821 census were "the biggest lie ever put in print, even in romance." The huge population increase they showed was fanciful: "the size of the churches alone was sufficient to convince any man of sound judgment that there had been a prodigious decrease!"[4]

At least in contrast with this confusion one can speak of an advance in knowledge. "There is now a rough consensus of opinion among English economic historians about the broad chronology of English population history."[5] Late medieval and early modern England, excepting the period of the Black Death, had a population well under 4 million. At the end of the seventeenth century, according to the careful estimate that Gregory

[3] M. Dorothy George, *London Life in the XVIIIth Century* (New York: Knopf, 1925), p. 23. For Malthus's contribution to this debate, see below pages 514–518.

[4] Quoted in C. R. Fay, *Life and Labour in the Nineteenth Century* (Cambridge: Cambridge University Press, 1947), p. 83.

[5] H. J. Habbakuk, "The Economic History of Modern Britain," *Journal of Economic History,* 18:4 (December, 1958), 486–501.

King made from hearth-tax returns, England and Wales had some 5 million inhabitants, and 100 years later there were more than 9 million. Virtually all of this increase, moreover, was in the second half of the eighteenth century, during the first decades of quickening industrialization. This pattern of growth is summarized in Table 14-1.

TABLE 14-1. Estimated Population of England and Wales, 1086–1841

Date	Population (millions)	Source of Information
1086	1.1	Domesday Book
1348	3.7	Hearth tax times estimated family size
1377	2.2	Same, after Black Death
1545	3.2	Chantry lists
1695	4.8–5.5 a	Gregory King's estimate
1801	9.2	First census (corrected)
1811	10.2	
1821	12.0	Census returns
1831	13.9	
1841	15.9	

ᵃ The larger figure is King's. Glass has suggested the range given, with the most probable figure above its midpoint.

Sources: J. C. Russell, *British Medieval Population* (Albuquerque: University of New Mexico Press, 1948); D. V. Glass, "Gregory King's Estimate of the Population of England and Wales, 1695," *Population Studies*, 3:4 (March, 1950), 338–375; census returns.

The details to fill in this picture, however, are another matter. The first English census was taken only in 1801, and both it and its immediate successors were less accurate and less complete than those taken later in the century.[6] National vital statistics date from 1837. For much of the key period, from 1760 to 1840, we must depend on a variety of other sources.

John Rickman, the director of the first four censuses, compiled the basic data from which both he and several later analysts attempted to describe the population growth during the previous century. He had a questionnaire sent out to every "Rector, Vicar, Curate, or Officiating Minister," asking them to extract from their parish records the numbers of baptisms and burials, distinguishing between male and female, for each decade from 1700 to 1780 and for each following single year up to

---

[6] "There were fears that the census of 1801 was to be the basis for new taxes (the triple assessment and the income tax were fresh in people's minds) or for the levy of men for the unpopular and, at the same time, unsuccessful, war" (J. T. Krause, "Changes in English Fertility and Mortality, 1781–1850," *Economic History Review*, 2nd ser., 11:1, August, 1958, 52–70).

1800. How well this formidable task was performed is a question to which no definite reply can be given, though it is reasonable to suppose that there must have been great lacunae in data so collected.[7] In any case, these Anglican parish registers did not include Dissenters, some paupers, and others. To reconstruct birth and death rates, therefore, one must increase the given figures on baptisms and burials by a more or less arbitrary proportion, representing the best guess on the total size of the several deficiencies. Then, working back from the census count of 1801 (corrected for its substantial underenumeration), one can calculate the population totals and crude rates. The method depends, thus, on three assumptions: (1) that the corrected 1801 count was accurate, (2) that the underregistration in the parish records was at the proportions given, and (3) that there was no net migration.

1. We can accept the corrected 1801 census figure as substantially accurate. At the very least, it is the best datum up to that time.

2. The disparity in the ratio of births to baptisms, and in that of deaths to registered burials, was a symptom of the transformation the country was undergoing. So long as the relatively stable agrarian society persisted, one could assume that underregistration was at a constant proportion (although even then there may have been some oscillation with the business cycle, for one factor in reducing the later registration was that many Anglicans were unwilling to pay the relatively high fees for their rites). However, as the center of population moved from the South to the new industrial regions in the North, churches and clergy were left behind. The migration from villages to towns was marked by the same lag. "The London parish of Marylebone, with 40,000 inhabitants, had church accommodations for only 200." [8] The war also had its effect on the record, for while soldiers died in higher proportion than equivalent civilian cohorts, they escaped ecclesiastical registration. It is reasonably certain, then, that the birth/baptism and death/burial ratios varied considerably from one year or one locality to another; but this means that any average for the nation as a whole or for a decade or longer period can be only the roughest guess.[9]

---

[7] For an interesting discussion, see Barbara Hammond, "Urban Death-Rates in the Early Nineteenth Century," *Economic History (Supplement to the Economic Journal)*, 1:3 (January, 1928), 419–428.

[8] Krause, "Changes," *op. cit.*

[9] Griffith raised the recorded baptisms by 15 per cent and the burials by 10 per cent; see G. Talbot Griffith, *Population Problems of the Age of Malthus* (Cambridge: Cambridge University Press, 1926), p. 18. He has been criticized—correctly, I would judge —for assuming that the two ratios remained constant. "There is . . . much reason to believe that the registration of deaths deteriorated sharply between 1781 and 1821 and

3. The postulate that net migration was zero is even less well based statistically. Adequate migration data were compiled only after this transitional period was long past, and what records exist up to 1840 hardly form the basis for an informed guess. Emigrants from the United Kingdom were officially counted only from 1815 on, and the statistics were a by-product of a law, frequently evaded, introduced to compel ship masters to assign a specific minimum space to each passenger. Accuracy at a usable level begins in 1840, when the first Cunard steamships went into service and the Colonial Land and Emigration Commission was established.[10] Whether the unknown number of emigrants from England and Wales was matched, as is generally assumed, by an equal number of Irish (and Scotch) immigrants, also cannot be established. The English census of 1841, the first to include such data, recorded 419,000 residents of Irish birth; and this figure, even if it were wholly accurate, would represent only a portion of the Irish who had taken up residence in England during the previous 80 years.[11] If we accept the hypothesis that the total numbers of persons entering and leaving England were the same, the age structure of the immigrants and emigrants, and consequently their fertility and mortality, may well have differed considerably.

In short, it is impossible to build from national data a sound statistical argument concerning population growth up to 1840. These have to be supplemented by analyses of parish records, and important work is being done in this respect. It would not be appropriate here, however, to attempt to summarize such monographs, bristling with difficulties of every kind, of which the first always is to what degree the locality is representative of the nation as a whole. At some time in the future it may be possible to collate these more detailed analyses and derive a better understanding of what happened to the English population during these decades. Establishing a more accurate numerical base, if it is ever possible, would still be only the preliminary step to analyzing *why* the changes in mortality and fertility occurred.

What we propose to do here is to examine the theory of the demographic transition in the context of English social history, reinforced

---

improved thereafter. Farr's estimated death-burial ratios, 1.23 in 1801–10, 1.33 in 1811–20, 1.16 in 1821–30, and 1.12 in 1831–40, are plausible in so far as the trend is concerned" (Krause, "Changes," *op. cit.*).

[10] See Brinley Thomas, *Migration and Economic Growth: A Study of Great Britain and the Atlantic Economy* (National Institute of Economic and Social Research, Economic and Social Study 12; Cambridge: Cambridge University Press, 1954), p. 36. See above, page 53.

[11] For a good summary of such data as exist, see Arthur Redford, *Labour Migration in England, 1800–50* (Manchester: University of Manchester Press, 1926), Chs. 8–9.

with statistical data only when these are reasonably precise. According to this theory, it will be recalled, the population growth of an area undergoing modernization is divided into three stages: (a) a more or less static population at high levels of fertility and mortality, (b) a period of constant fertility and falling mortality, with a consequent rapid increase in population, and (c) a more or less static population at more efficient levels of birth as well as death control.

THE TRANSFORMATION OF ENGLISH AGRICULTURE

The first step toward understanding the population developments during the industrial revolution is to survey the momentous changes that took place in the English countryside. In the first half of the eighteenth century, the agrarian system of the Middle Ages still persisted in full force over a great portion of England. All cultivation of land, whether by proprietors or by tenants, was in accord with decisions of the village council, following the practices made impregnable by tradition. Arable land was divided into three strips, of which one was left fallow each year and two were planted in coarse grains. Pasture was ordinarily inadequate, and the animals fed from stubble and heath. Since there was little or no hay to store, most of the herd was killed in the autumn and eaten through the winter as salt meat. Available pasture was usually held in common, as well as woods (for both hunting and firewood) and water (which included fishing rights). Attached to most villages were a number of squatters, who were permitted to eke out a miserable living though they had no legal right to the use of the joint property.

Landlords and tenants were equally ignorant and sunken in routine, while mutual suspicion divided them; for the landlord feared that the farmer would exhaust the land by forcing a few richer crops out of his fields during the last years of his tenancy, and therefore refused to grant leases for a fixed period, preferring the unstable state of things known as tenure at will. As a result, any spirit of enterprise, any undertaking that involved a considerable period for its completion, were out of the question for the farmer, since he lived under the constant threat of instant dismissal and of the loss of a whole year's labours. Thus the effect of backwardness was to make for more backwardness.[12]

This whole mode of agriculture was transformed in the second half of the eighteenth century. In a series of individual acts of Parliament, the

[12] Paul Mantoux, *The Industrial Revolution in the Eighteenth Century: An Outline of the Beginnings of the Modern Factory System in England* (Rev. ed.; London: Cape, 1952), p. 162.

common land of villages was transferred to the private ownership of families with some ancient right to it. Deprived of the use of the commons, the squatters and cottagers often suffered a decline in even their modest living conditions. The more substantial cultivators, who were recompensed in land or money (the amount was set by the parliamentary commissioners, and no appeal could be made from their decision), were sometimes unable or unwilling to maintain themselves in the new circumstances, and some of them also sank into tenancy or pauperism. But if the social cost was high, it paid for an astounding advance in English agriculture. The first act of the new owner was always to enclose the open field with a hedge, in order to protect it against grazing cattle. "The age of enclosure was also the age of new methods of draining, drilling, sowing, manuring, breeding and feeding cattle, making of roads, rebuilding of farm premises and a hundred other changes, all of them requiring capital." [13] Potatoes and other root crops became staples. New breeds of farm animals were developed. Feed was grown that could be stored during the winter, and the prior custom of converting the major portion of a herd into salt meat was abandoned. The improved methods were applied also to waste land, of which about 2 million acres were brought under cultivation during the eighteenth century.

There is hardly any question, then, that the food supply improved enormously in both quantity and variety.[14] The issue, rather, is over what happened to the country people. According to the Hammonds,

Enclosure was fatal to three classes: the small farmer, the cottager, and the squatter. To all of these classes their common rights were worth more than anything they received in return.[15]

For many years it was held that these classes, ousted from the village, were the raw material out of which the industrial labor force was formed. Indeed, this "Marxist doctrine," as Chambers terms it, may have been the model that the Soviet planners followed in the 1930's.[16] In eighteenth-

---

[13] G. M. Trevelyan, *English Social History: A Survey of Six Centuries, Chaucer to Queen Victoria* (London: Longmans, Green, 1942), p. 376.

[14] Some analysts, it is true, have argued the contrary. From the increasing use of the potato, "the cheapest and one of the most efficient single foods man has as yet cultivated in the temperate zones," Salaman, for instance, concludes that the living conditions deteriorated. See Redcliffe N. Salaman, *The History and Social Influence of the Potato* (Cambridge: Cambridge University Press, 1949), Chs. 25–26.

[15] J. L. and Barbara Hammond, *The Village Labourer, 1760–1832: A Study in the Government of England before the Reform Bill* (London: Longmans, Green, 1932), p. 73.

[16] See pages 415–420.

century England, however, the main factor in supplying the developing urban industry with workers was not the displacement of villagers but rather the growth of the total population. While there was a good deal of migration to the towns, this did not result in the "rural depopulation" that Cobbett and others feared at the time. "The period 1780–1840 saw only a sporadic exodus . . . from the rural areas, . . . and side by side with it an actual filling up of empty spaces and a steady rise in the great majority of established centers of rural population." [17] If numbers were increasing in both town and country, as was certainly the case at least for the period covered by the census records, then the supposed sharp decline in rural levels of life may well have been exaggerated.

If the population grew and also the subsistence, what of the balance between them? Was the food per capita more or less plentiful, better or worse on the average? Did real wages rise or fall? Unfortunately, it is not possible to answer such questions altogether satisfactorily, and the main reason is that this was a period of rapid and all-encompassing change. At almost any time during these decades the situation of some in the lower classes was improving, and that of others deteriorating. For example, we can reasonably deduce from the data available that the real wages of cotton operatives went up steadily, and this may even have been so of factory workers generally. But the most important determinant of many workers' incomes was not their wage rate but how regularly they were employed. In Hobsbawm's words, "No discussion which overlooks the massive waves of destitution which swamped large sections of the labouring poor in every depression, can claim to be realistic." [18] But his view of "realism" is to overlook, on the contrary, the rise in wages of the employed workers.

And if the amount of money received by workers varied widely, what they could buy with their wages varied even more. The cost of all foodstuffs differed greatly from one part of the country to another, and in any one locality "the price of a loaf of bread or a pound of beef might double or halve within the course of a few months or even weeks." [19] Since this condition resulted from the primitive consumers market rather than specifically from food production, one can conclude that there was a

---

[17] J. D. Chambers, "Enclosure and Labour Supply in the Industrial Revolution," *Economic History Review,* 2nd ser., 5:3 (1953), 319–343. See also Redford, *op. cit.,* pp. 58–69.

[18] E. J. Hobsbawm, "The British Standard of Living, 1790–1850," *Economic History Review,* 2nd ser., 10:1 (August, 1957), 46–61.

[19] T. S. Ashton, "The Standard of Life of the Workers in England, 1790–1830," in F. A. Hayek, ed., *Capitalism and the Historians* (Chicago: University of Chicago Press, 1954), pp. 127–159. Copyright 1954 by the University of Chicago.

similar variation in the prices of all essential commodities. For Hobsbawm, "the discussion of food consumption . . . throws considerable doubt on the optimistic view." [20] And Habakkuk also concludes: "The scantiness of the evidence makes any judgement dangerous, but the surviving examples of labourers' diets hardly suggest that any improvement in their diet can have been substantial." [21] Ashton's tentative conclusion is that, "all in all, conditions of labor were becoming better, at least after 1820, and that the spread of the factory played a not inconsiderable part in the improvement." [22]

Perhaps the best evidence that diets improved during this period is the lower incidence of food-deficiency diseases, and especially their virtual disappearance as causes of death. Even Drummond and Wilbraham, who lean toward the pessimistic view, note that by 1830 scurvy had become so rare that a well known physician was unable to diagnose its symptoms.[23] They conclude, even if somewhat reluctantly, that the incidence of rickets also declined, possibly in part because of the beginning use of cod liver oil as a specific. This would have an important influence on fertility as well as mortality, for rickets frequently causes pelvic deformations and thus fetal and maternal deaths.

THE STANDARD OF LIVING

If objective criteria like the trend in real wages are difficult to establish in themselves, this is doubly so because the subjective meaning of such measures was also undergoing a rapid change. When we speak of "standard" rather than "level" of living, we mean to include the norms by which conditions were judged to be better or worse. For example, industrialism was frequently compared with an idyllic preindustrial society. To idealize the past was characteristic of Romanticism, which flourished during these same decades, and the mood was strong enough to cut across political lines. Revolutionary socialists like Engels wrote prose poems celebrating the Good Old Days,[24] and representatives of the landed gentry opposed the developing factory system in part because they saw it as a challenge to their social and political power. The latter point of

[20] Hobsbawm, "The British Standard," *op. cit.*

[21] H. J. Habakkuk, "English Population in the Eighteenth Century," *Economic History Review*, 2nd ser., 6:2 (December, 1953), 117–133.

[22] Ashton, "The Standard," *op. cit.*

[23] J. C. Drummond and Anne Wilbraham, *The Englishman's Food: A History of Five Centuries of English Diet* (Rev. ed.; London: Cape, 1957), p. 392.

[24] Engels, *op. cit.*, Ch. 1, particularly pp. 10–11.

view especially is well represented in the parliamentary hearings. The "too liberal use of weak tea, as extremely debilitating to the stomach," was, as Hutt points out, only the most frequent proof of moral degradation deduced from changes that to us would suggest economic and social advance.

Thackrah lamented the fact that children were no longer contented with "plain food" but must have "dainties." The Reverend G. S. Bull deplored the tendency of girls to buy pretty clothes "ready-made" from shops instead of making them themselves, as this practice unfitted them to become "the mothers of children." Gaskell saw decadence in tobacco. "Hundreds of men may be daily seen inhaling the fumes of this extraordinary plant." He also saw moral decline in the growth of workmen's combinations [that is, trade unions]. The men were no longer "respectful and attentive" to their "superiors." [25]

This last sentence suggests that the factory system was generating a new type of person, who fitted ill into the prior model of class relations. "The ideological break with traditionalism," as Bendix terms it, was based on the proposition that "the slave must be compelled to work; but the freeman should be left to his own judgement and discretion." [26] During the transition a kind of medieval paternalism was often carried over into factory management: the responsibility of the upper classes was interpreted as including the duty, and the right, to control every move the workers made. In one factory the doors were locked during working hours. It was prohibited to drink water in spite of the heat. Fines were imposed for washing oneself or for being dirty, for putting out the light too soon or not soon enough, and so on.[27] Those regarded as the best of the new employers were often the most painstaking in preserving the pre-industrial master-servant relation. Robert Owen, for example, who is usually cited as a prototype of the modern manager, gave his employees

[25] W. H. Hutt, "The Factory System of the Early Nineteenth Century," in Hayek, *op. cit.,* pp. 160–188. Copyright 1954 by the University of Chicago. If here tea-drinking and smoking were taken as signs of lower-class degeneration, for Hobsbawm the *slow* adoption of these new customs is proof, on the contrary, that consumption standards were lagging ("The British Standard," *op. cit.*). The example indicates how difficult it is to distinguish what consumers wanted and could not buy from what they did not want. How many of the imprecisely recorded shifts reflected a change merely in taste?

[26] Joseph Townsend, quoted in Reinhard Bendix, *Work and Authority in Industry: Ideologies of Management in the Course of Industrialization* (New York: Wiley, 1956), p. 74. Bendix's main theme is "the role of ideas in the management of economic enterprises," and he traces in detail the process by which the traditional master-servant relation was gradually supplanted by one between the two new urban classes, whose legitimacy evolved together with the growth in their membership.

[27] J. L. and Barbara Hammond, *The Town Labourer, 1760–1832: The New Civilisation* (2nd ed.; London: Longmans, Green, 1932), pp. 19–20.

marks for their moral conduct—bad, denoted by black; indifferent, by blue; good, by yellow; and excellent, by white—"during every day of the week, Sundays excepted, for every year they remained in my employment." [28] Workers in his model factory at New Lanark had to attend dancing lessons for the sake of their health, and some quit their jobs on that account.[29]

The reader is likely to sympathize with the worker who rebelled against constraints of this kind. The situation is more complex, however, when it was the workers who tried to preserve traditional patterns, and particularly such abhorrent ones—to the present-day person—as child labor. While the pre-factory system of spinning and weaving varied greatly, one common element was that the family constituted an economic unit. The place of manufacture (literally, "making by hand") was the countryman's cottage, and the manufacturers were the cottager, his wife, and his children. The kinship base of this domestic system, as it is termed, survived for a while the shift to the factory.

Witnesses before the parliamentary committees from 1816 through 1819 testified consistently that masters allowed the operative spinners to hire their own assistants (piecers, scavengers, etc.) and that the spinners chose their wives, children, near relatives, or relatives of the proprietors. Many children, especially the youngest, entered the mill at the express request of their parents. . . . Most of the early trade unions' rules explicitly prohibited members from recruiting assistants outside the narrowly defined classes of children, brothers, orphan nephews, etc.[30]

Parents retained, thus, their traditional authority over their children, who learned their trade while contributing to the family income. "Little wonder, then, that the conditions of child labour did not offend spinners interviewed by Factory Commissioners in 1833." [31] But both improved technology and structural changes in the factory system led to a greater differentiation of roles, and thus both broke down the economic authority of the father-spinner over his children-assistants and in many cases reduced the composite wage that he received. *Some* of the misery of the period, as seen by those who suffered it, was due to the decline of this semi-apprenticeship system based on kinship; and the "array of threats

---

[28] Cited in Bendix, *op. cit.*, p. 50.

[29] J. H. Plumb, *England in the Eighteenth Century* (Harmondsworth: Penguin, 1950), p. 145, n.

[30] Neil J. Smelser, *Social Change in the Industrial Revolution: An Application of Theory to the British Cotton Industry* (Chicago: University of Chicago Press, 1959), pp. 188–189.

[31] *Ibid.*, p. 190.

An illustration from one of the many white papers reporting governmental investigations of labor conditions in nineteenth-century England. The accompanying
text reads as follows:

" 'By far the greater number of Children and persons employed in coal-mines are
engaged in propelling and drawing tubs laden with coal, from the face to the pit-eye,
or the main-levels in those pits where they have horses. This is done by placing the
hands on the back of the waggon, and propelling it forward with as great velocity
as the inclination of the mine, the state of the road, and the strength of the waggoner
admit of. The mines in this district [Lancashire and Cheshire] are for the most part
laid with rails, and the waggon runs on wheels. . . . There are, however, mines . . .
where the old mode of drawing the baskets or wooden sledges (called in Lancashire
"sleds") is still retained. The drawer is in this case harnessed by means of a chain
attached to the "sled"; the other end of the chain passes between his legs, and fastens
in front to a belt round the waist. When thus harnessed, and moving along on his
hands and feet, the drawer drags after him the loaded basket; if he is not sufficiently
strong he has a helper rather younger than himself.' . . . [The figure] represents
three young Children hurrying or drawing a loaded waggon of coals. The Child in
front 'is harnessed by his belt or chain to the waggon; the two boys behind are assist-
ing in pushing it forward. Their heads, it will be observed, are brought down to a
level with the waggon, and the body almost in a horizontal position. This is done
partly to avoid striking the roof, and partly to gain the advantage of the muscular
action, which is greatest in that position. It will be observed the boy in front goes on
his hands and feet: in that manner the whole weight of his body is in fact supported
by the chain attached to the waggon, and consequently his power of
drawing is greater than it would be if he crawled on his knees. These boys, by constantly pushing against the waggons, occasionally rub off the hair from the crowns of
their heads so much as to make them almost bald' " (Great Britain, Children's Employment Commission, *First Report of the Commissioners: Mines;* London: H.M. Stationery Office, 1842, pp. 81–82).

to the family's traditional organization underlay much of the turmoil
among operatives and others between 1825 and 1850." [32]

In short, the way that the participants in England's early industrialization defined their situation helped determine their behavior. What the

[32] *Ibid.,* p. 199.

members of parliamentary committees, or their witnesses, or factory operatives, saw as problems became the main content of the data collected. This "bias" is especially difficult to cope with, since it was not consistent: most of the people living through that turbulent period must have been confused concerning what it was they really wanted. And we aggravate this confusion if we assume that the common people must have demanded "progress" as a present-day liberal defines it, and that their protest *for* child labor or for a *longer* workday are anomalies that can best be ignored.

We have argued, then, that it is all but impossible to find conclusive evidence on the trend in living conditions during this period, and that this difficulty has typically been compounded by the fact that most data were gathered and interpreted as part of a political dispute. Yet many of the causal links implied in this long debate are not necessary ones. As Ashton has put it,

What happened to the standard of life of the British working classes in the late decades of the eighteenth and the early decades of the nineteenth centuries? Was the introduction of the factory system beneficial or harmful in its effect on the workers? These, though related, are distinct questions. For it is possible that employment in factories conduced to an increase of real wages but that the tendency was more than offset by other influences, such as the rapid increase of population, the immigration of Irishmen, the destruction of wealth by long years of warfare, ill-devised tariffs, and misconceived measures for the relief of distress.[33]

Since England's example is still often used to argue the case for or against industrialism, or to discuss (as in this chapter) the relation between industrialization and population developments, it is important to consider how general a case this really represents.

From roughly 1790 to 1815, England was at war with France; and this was "the central economic characteristic of these years." Three to 5 per cent of the population, and, of course, a far higher proportion of the labor force, were in military service. The rise in the real cost of many commodities, especially of imports and therefore some foodstuffs, was more the consequence of the war than of any other factor.[34] As another instance, the fact that homes in the rapidly growing cities were ramshackle, and if not worse than the hovels of the rural areas then also not much better, still does not settle the question of why this was so. The state deflected requisite materials and labor to the prior demand of mili-

[33] Ashton, "The Standard," *op. cit.*
[34] W. W. Rostow, *British Economy of the Nineteenth Century* (Oxford: Clarendon, 1948), pp. 13–14.

tary necessity, and this was an important reason for the inadequacy of the rapidly constructed homes of the new industrial towns. A new word was added to English—*jerry-built*, from the nautical word *jury* (as in "jury mast"), meaning "temporary," "emergency." [35] The shortage of houses persisted, however, and these "temporary" residences were occupied for decades.

To sum up, evidence concerning the trend in living conditions is typically ambiguous enough to permit a variety of judgments; and this tendency has often been compounded because of the political implications to be drawn from the conclusion that real wages were rising, or falling. Actually, the political argument is not only scientifically unfortunate but also often unwarranted, for whatever happened to the average Englishman's living conditions was not the consequence merely of "capitalism," or the factory system, or any other single factor.

MORTALITY

There is no question that the population increased substantially from, say, 1760 to 1840. Was this growth the consequence, either wholly or mainly, of a decline in mortality, as is assumed in the model of the demographic transition? Perhaps the best answer to this question is that by two medical historians, McKeown and Brown.[36] They divided the possible causes of a reduction in mortality into three broad classes: (1) a change in the balance between virulence and resistance, (2) specific therapy, and (3) improvement in living conditions. Let us consider each of these in turn.

1. A change in the balance between the virulence of the infective organism and the resistance of the host. In specific instances—for example, the transformation of scarlet fever from a frequently fatal disease to a relatively trivial complaint—this was probably the decisive factor. The general effect of such changes on the long-term trend in the death rate, however, was probably slight.

2. Specific preventive or curative therapy. Most treatment of the various important causes of death can be discounted for the period earlier than the middle of the nineteenth century. It is a moot question whether fever hospitals, for example, helped restrict contagion by the semiquaran-

---

[35] T. S. Ashton, "The Treatment of Capitalism by Historians," in Hayek, *op. cit.*, pp. 33–63.

[36] Thomas McKeown and R. G. Brown, "Medical Evidence Related to English Population Changes in the Eighteenth Century," *Population Studies*, 9:2 (November, 1955), 119–141.

tine they imposed or, on the contrary, raised the death rate by the fact that virtually all persons who entered them would be infected. So long as bleeding was the first treatment for illness, the contribution that physicians made to their patients' health was minimal; so long as something like half of surgical patients died of infection, it can be questioned whether surgeons saved more patients than they killed. "It might safely be said," McKeown and Brown conclude, "that specific medical treatment had no useful effects at all, were it not for some doubt about the results of the use of mercury in syphilis, iron in anaemia, cinchona in malaria and inoculation against smallpox."

Of the four diseases, the last was by far the most important in England of the eighteenth century, when it is estimated that one out of every five persons died from smallpox, typically in childhood. The terror it caused can be imagined. "Men would not marry until or unless the lady had had smallpox, servants were advertised for who had had it." [37] Inoculation with a small, nonfatal amount of infected liquid, it was discovered, could establish immunity. This practice was introduced in the 1720's and used intermittently through the rest of the century, but medical historians disagree on its effect. It was dangerous to the patient if not skillfully administered, and unless he was segregated he could spread the disease to others. In 1798 Edward Jenner discovered that vaccination with cowpox germs, which causes only a minor skin irritation, also effects immunity against smallpox. In part because of the ambivalent results from inoculation, there was some opposition at first also to vaccination, and we do not know how rapidly its practice spread.[38]

3. Improvement in living conditions, by which McKeown and Brown mean "any change which would have reduced the risk of infection, or increased the survival rate among those infected: under the first are such measures as improvement in housing, water-supply or refuse disposal; under the second influences affecting the general standard of health, of which by far the most important was probably nutrition."

[37] Griffith, *op. cit.*, p. 248.

[38] Griffith argues that there was a sharp fall in the death rate from 1800 to 1810, largely the consequence of a reduced incidence of smallpox, and that the subsequent rise was partly due to the increased mortality from this disease until it was discovered that immunity must be periodically renewed. But the evidence is not clear on any of his allegations: We do not know whether the death rate fell in the century's first decade; many authorities believe it rose. We do not know whether Jenner's discovery was much used only two years after it was made; a widespread system of free vaccination was established only in the 1840's and there were serious outbreaks of smallpox still after that date. We do not know, finally, whether the effective control of one important disease, supposing that it took place, would have reduced substantially the death rate of a society with so few guards against epidemic diseases in general.

It is not likely that there could have been a very great improvement in living conditions in the first sense; on the contrary, the risk of infection almost certainly increased, assuming that the villagers' style of life remained essentially the same after they migrated to the towns, or even that it improved somewhat. Lower-class urban quarters were probably no more squalid than their rural counterpart, but the higher population density made of cities the graveyard of countrymen, to cite again that graphic aphorism. Both in England and elsewhere in the Western world urban death rates were higher than rural until the last quarter of the nineteenth century, by which time public sanitation was sufficiently established to cancel the biological effect of crowded living quarters.

There was little direct incentive to control urban filth, for the theory relating it to disease was by no means universally accepted. The understandable desire to mitigate the stink of even middle-class homes was probably more relevant. In any case, public sanitation was not much improved before 1840,[39] as can be illustrated by the fact that so important a step as the separation of sewage from drinking water was taken only very gradually. During the first half of the eighteenth century excrement was dumped out of town windows on to the street. From about 1750 on the "night soil" was gathered by scavengers in the better-class neighborhoods. The water closet, invented toward the end of the century, emptied into either large vaults under the houses or, later, into sewers that flowed into a river. Iron pipes were first used in the 1740's, iron mains in the following decade. Until 1850 one of London's drinking-water companies still had its intake within a few feet of the mouth of the Westbourne, which had become the Ranelagh common sewer! [40] The cholera epidemic of 1831–1832, which came just when urban sanitation was at its worst, is considered by some to have been almost a blessing; for it helped the physicians in their effort to establish minimum norms of public health.

A change in the environment may have brought about a fall in the death rate without anyone at the time becoming aware of the relation. For example, an important factor—perhaps the decisive one—in the earlier decline of the plague was that the black rat, which had lived in close proximity to man, was driven out of many areas by the brown rat, which prefers to live in sewers or under the docks. Similarly, the crucial reason for the sharply reduced incidence of typhus was probably the

---

[39] See, for example, E. P. Hennock, "Urban Sanitary Reform a Generation before Chadwick?" *Economic History Review*, 2nd ser., 10:1 (August, 1957), 113–119.

[40] M. C. Buer, *Health, Wealth, and Population in the Early Days of the Industrial Revolution* (London: Routledge, 1926), p. 108.

shift from woolen to cotton clothing and the improved cleanliness that this facilitated.[41]

Since other possible factors are partly eliminated, the improvement in the food supply would seem to be the major cause of any important decline in mortality before, say, 1850; and McKeown and Brown believe it to be the principal reason for the population growth of the late eighteenth and early nineteenth centuries. Paradoxically, there has been a tendency on the part of analysts to discount the effect of the factor they studied most intensively.

Surprisingly, these medical historians [McKeown and Brown] argued that . . . medical advances, with the exception of vaccination, were demographically irrelevant, and that environmental changes, mainly economic, were at work. Their view, thus, contradicts that of T. H. Marshall, the economic historian, who held that economic factors were unimportant, and that medical factors were responsible.[42]

To sum up, while it is impossible to document it statistically, there probably was a more or less continuous decline in mortality from roughly 1760 to 1840. Medical advances had little to do with this, except possibly in the single case of smallpox. The most important factor seems to have been the better food supply, and possibly the improved living conditions in other respects, enjoyed by the lower classes. Yet the evidence for this advance is at best probable, sometimes hardly that; and the pessimistic view that there was a decline in consumption and health can also be supported with plausible data, particularly for the war years. In any case, was the decline in mortality sufficient to account for the population increase —taking only the period measured by censuses—from roughly 9.2 million in 1801 to 15.9 million in 1841? Or is there not a *prima facie* case here for the probability that fertility rose while mortality declined?

FERTILITY

The population of early industrial England has been studied principally by economic historians, who, as one would expect, have tended to stress economic factors. While this emphasis can lead to a reasonably good understanding of mortality trends, the state of the economy is not the most important determinant of fertility. One economic historian, thus, finds the "sociological weakness" of his colleagues' studies to be "striking."

[41] Characteristically, Engels cited this change to cotton as one further evidence of the deterioration in the living conditions of the English working class (*op. cit.*, pp. 78–79).

[42] Krause, "Changes," *op. cit.*

Allowing for exceptions such as Marshall and Glass, British researchers have tended to slight the analysis of the social determinants of birth rates, nuptiality, and the other components of population change. They have placed most of their emphasis on material considerations—Malthusian checks and their shifting incidence—and to such proximate relations as the immediate influence of the birth and death rate on population. And they have perhaps been too quick to assume away the significance of nonmaterial factors: witness Habakkuk's statement that "within any given social group marriage habits might be expected to be stable"; or the neglect of socially determined changes in fertility as a possible factor in population growth.[43]

As was noted in the last chapter, the population growth of medieval Europe was held to well below the physiological maximum by ethical and institutional norms. The principle that a man ought to be able to support a family before he married and had children was embodied in the regulations of the major medieval institutions. In the old system, as it functioned in both town and countryside, a male assistant or apprentice, or a female domestic, generally lived in as a subordinate member of the master's family. As a consequence, the morals of adolescents were supervised: sexual dalliance meant the possible loss of one's position in a secure world. Young people were not under economic pressure to marry early, since they were meaningful members of a functioning household. At the same time, parents may have restricted the number of their children because extended kin were also included in the family economy.

Virtually all urban occupations were governed by guilds, which particularly in England prohibited their members from marrying until they had completed their apprenticeship.[44] Guild regulations apparently were still enforced in England during the first half of the eighteenth century, but pamphleteers were finding them unnecessary and onerous. By 1775 the system was in an advanced state of decay.[45] As we have seen, however, it persisted for a while even in some of the new factories, where operatives retained the prerogatives of master craftsmen. But England was still predominantly rural, and national population trends were set principally by what was happening in the countryside. Whatever effect the enclosure movement had on living conditions generally, it certainly tended to release the average countryman from traditional bonds, whether he stayed in the village or migrated to the towns, whether he retained his prior status or sank into pauperdom.

Indeed, the distinction between a worker and a pauper became tenuous

---

[43] David S. Landes, "Discussion," *Journal of Economic History,* 18:4 (December, 1958), 531–536.
[44] See page 359.
[45] Griffith, *op. cit.,* pp. 114, 116.

during this period. In 1795 the magistrates of Berkshire County met at Speenhamland, a suburb of Newbury, in order to fix and enforce a minimum wage. Instead, they drew up a scale of doles to be paid in relation to three factors—the wages earned, the price of bread, and the size of the family. This so-called Speenhamland scale, which was imitated over a large portion of England, was popular with almost everyone concerned. Workers were safe from extreme want under all market conditions. Employers could find workers at almost any wage, no matter how low, for it was supplemented up to the subsistence level out of taxes. And the general public found the system good, both because it gave charity to those in need of it and because it inhibited, it was believed, the spread of revolutionary ideas from France.

In spite of its popularity, the Speenhamland system was what Malthus termed it, "a pernicious evil." [46] It is true that the alms mitigated the distress suffered by individuals, but it is no less true that in over-all terms the Berkshire scale aggravated and prolonged the misery occasioned by the rapid social change.[47] With the massive shift taking place from agrarian to industrial occupations, when a prime economic need consequently was a mobile labor force, the new poor law restricted free movement. A man who left one parish and remained for a full year in another lost his right to relief in the first and established it in the second.

For this reason parish authorities were reluctant to receive outsiders, and employers who were large ratepayers would sometimes offer work only for a period short of a full year. If before a labourer had gained a settlement in a new parish he fell on evil days he could be moved back summarily to the parish from which he had come, and this made him think twice before leaving his native village to seek work far away.[48]

The main burden of poor relief fell on the small farmer, who paid taxes but, unlike the new gentry, got no cheap labor in return.[49] The decline

---

[46] See T. R. Malthus, *An Essay on the Principle of Population* (7th ed.; London: Reeves and Turner, 1872), Book 3, Chs. 5–7; Book 4, Ch. 8.

[47] "The right solution would have been the enforcement of a legal minimum wage in agriculture. This the labourers demanded in the 1790's, appealing to the Elizabethan Statute of Artificers (1563). But the appeal was useless, for the Wages sections were by this time inoperative, and they had never been used as a lever for raising wages beyond the prevailing competitive level" (Fay, *op. cit.*, p. 92).

[48] T. S. Ashton, *The Industrial Revolution, 1760–1830* (London: Oxford University Press, 1948), p. 110.

[49] By a wide margin, the cost of poor relief was the major item in local taxation. From 1782 to 1793, its average annual cost was £2 million, as compared with £0.2 million for all other local expenditures; in 1813 the figures were £7 and £1.5 million (Trevelyan, *op. cit.*, pp. 353, 470).

of the yeoman class was certainly quickened by the administration of the poor law, and undoubtedly at least some of those pushed down themselves became paupers.

In the long run the result was ghastly. Although it took some time till the self-respect of the common man sank to the low point where he preferred poor relief to wages, . . . little by little the people of the countryside were pauperized. . . . But for the protracted effects of the allowance system, it would be impossible to explain the human and social degradation of early capitalism.[50]

It is usual to conceptualize the dynamics of Western fertility patterns in terms of the changes that took place in the second half of the nineteenth century—the erosion of the preindustrial norms and the gradual evolution of the small-family system. We tend to think, following the logic of the demographic transition, that a breakdown of traditionalism always results in a lower fertility; but this is nonsense. The control of family size, no matter what means is used, demands *self*-control; and self-control is likely to prevail only in a society in which individuals have strong motives for imposing it. The smaller family of the urban middle class developed, that is to say, principally because in a mobile society a man with fewer children could advance farther. But in the period we are discussing, and particularly for the mass of the people, there was no question of achieving self-improvement through self-control. Here the breakdown of the ethical and institutional norms, with the limitation to procreation they had set, meant only a rise in fertility.

The dissolution of village society could result in a rise in fertility because of (1) less frequent or less effective control of conception within marriage, (2) a higher incidence of illegitimacy, (3) a lower age at marriage, together with a higher proportion marrying, and (4) a change in the age structure. Let us examine each of these factors briefly, beginning with the most hypothetical.

1. Less Effective Birth Control

The main point to be made here is that this change was *possible*. Once again, we tend to view this period in terms of irrelevant comparisons. It is true that the mechanical and chemical contraceptives developed in the last hundred years are more efficient than prior methods, but it must not be supposed that the latter cannot reduce fertility substantially. The

---

[50] Karl Polanyi, *The Great Transformation* (New York: Rinehart, 1944), p. 80.

average family size in the United States, it will be recalled, began to fall at the beginning of the nineteenth century,[51] and in France probably even earlier, in both cases presumably because of the more frequent practice of coitus interruptus. If England's marital fertility was held in check by this method in the eighteenth century, a matter on which we have no information, and if self-control was reduced during the transitional period as we have hypothesized, then—— Not a firm conclusion, but the contrary one is no firmer, and is generally believed.

2. Illegitimacy

Data on illegitimacy are poor. In 1830, by Griffith's estimate, 5 per cent of all births were outside marriage,[52] but this figure is "far too low" in Marshall's opinion: "the rate for 1851–60 was 6.5 per cent., and it had been falling." [53] If we accept this view and assume that, say, 7 to 8 per cent of the births in all regions and all social classes were illegitimate, then for the particular declassed villagers evolving into the new proletariat the rate must have been, as a guess, three times that figure.

Under the law in effect from 1808 to 1834, an unmarried mother could force support from the man she claimed to be the father. Whether she married thus made little difference to her financially. It was held that under the Speenhamland system the mother of enough illegitimate children could support herself by her breeding:

There was one thing better than to marry and have a family, and that was to marry a mother of bastards. . . . As one young woman of twenty-four with four bastard children put it: "If she had one more, she should be very comfortable." [54]

The conditions of work, particularly in the mines, afforded temptations and opportunities for extramarital intercourse, which is frequently mentioned in the reports of the period.[55] If the breakdown of village institutions meant a concomitant decline in the moral standards associated with them, as we should expect in theory, then a considerable proportion of the population must have become indifferent to the distinction between marital and illegitimate conception.

[51] See pages 210–214.

[52] Griffith, *op. cit.*, pp. 125–126.

[53] T. H. Marshall, "The Population Problem during the Industrial Revolution," *Economic History (Supplement to the Economic Journal)*, 1:4 (January, 1929), 429–456.

[54] *Report on Labourers' Wages*, 1824, quoted in Redford, *op. cit.*, p. 71.

[55] See, e.g., Smelser, *op. cit.*, pp. 283–284. Smelser believes, however, that many of these reports were exaggerated, the product of the heated polemics on industrialism.

3. Decline in the Age at Marriage

The reports of the period are full of complaints that young people were marrying irresponsibly as a consequence of the Speenhamland system. According to a Factory Report of 1833, thus, operatives often married before they were 18, and the usual age was probably not even so high in rural areas affected by enclosures. "Much of the evil [of improvident marriages] would be remedied," the *Poor Law Report* of 1831 tells us, "if the farmers would return to . . . keeping their unmarried [farm-hands] as servants in the house, boarding them and lodging them and giving them pecuniary wages." [56] Malthus shared the prevalent opinion that poor relief fostered early marriages and large families, and for this reason he advocated that public relief be abolished. The one exception he would have made was families with six or more children, whose misery could be alleviated without encouraging still more procreation. [57]

Though the alleged relation between the dole and the size of the family cannot be proved statistically, there is good circumstantial evidence to support it. Since the amount of the relief payment was based in part on the size of the pauper-worker's family, employers were able to pay lower wages to those with more children.

As the farmers have under the scale system a direct inducement to employ married men rather than single, in many villages . . . they will not employ the single men at all. In others they pay them a much lower rate of wages for the same work in the hope of driving them to seek work out of the parish.[58]

Or, as seen from the point of view of the working men,

Men who receive but a small pittance know that they have only to marry, and that pittance will be augmented in proportion to the number of their children. . . . An intelligent witness, who is much in the habit of employing labourers, states that when complaining of their allowance they frequently say to him: "We will marry, and you must maintain us." [59]

[56] Griffith, *op. cit.,* pp. 105, 109.

[57] Malthus, *op. cit.,* p. 474. As Habakkuk points out, "Malthus's views on this subject are apt to be misinterpreted. He did not argue that people had more children in order to profit from the earnings of the children in factories, or to enjoy larger poor-law benefits. His point was that the prospect of parish relief and the earning capacity of children at an early age reduced the force of the incentive to postpone marriage" ("English Population," *op. cit.*).

[58] *Reports on the Poor Laws,* 1834, quoted in Griffith, *op. cit.,* p. 263.

[59] *Report on Labourers' Wages,* 1824, quoted in Redford, *op. cit.,* p. 71.

In the four counties in which industry was most important, Krause has shown, there were 677 children under 5 per 1,000 women aged 15 to 49 in 1821, as contrasted with only 580 in the rest of England. Since there is good reason to believe that infant and child mortality was greater in the first class, the higher fertility ratio there is doubly impressive.[60]

The implied causal relation is not proved, of course; it is just as likely that the breakdown of the traditional society increased both the average relief and fertility. In fact, it is rather unfortunate that the factual question of whether the birth rate rose has so long been associated with the policy question of whether Speenhamland was a just and efficient poor law. It is always difficult to analyze the effect of such subsidies or quasi-subsidies on the size of the family.[61] Even those instituted in the twentieth century, when accurate fertility data were available, are not easy to separate from a dozen other factors that may have influenced family size.

4. Change in the Age Structure

A rise in fertility for any other reason tends to become cumulative by increasing the proportion of persons physiologically capable of parenthood. Since at this time a large proportion died in the first years of life, most of whatever decline in the death rate took place was equivalent to an additional rise in the birth rate. Even a relatively small change in each of the several factors affecting fertility or mortality, thus, could have brought about a substantial population increase over several generations.

To sum up, during this transitional period, we can hypothesize, there were three family types in existence concurrently.[62] In the **Traditional** family typical of the preindustrial period, the postponement of marriage, plus the nonmarriage of a considerable portion of the secular population,

---

[60] Krause, "Changes," *op. cit.*

[61] Blackmore and Mellonie, with what Marshall termed "a touching faith in the sanctity of even the shadiest figures" ("Population Problem," *op. cit.*), proved to their own temporary satisfaction that the Speenhamland system had effected a *decline* in the birth rate. Some months later, however, they offered "a second analysis" showing that there was no relation between the subsidy and fertility. See J. S. Blackmore and F. C. Mellonie, "Family Endowment and the Birth-Rate in the Early Nineteenth Century," I and II, *Economic History (Supplement to the Economic Journal)*, 1:2 (May, 1927), 205–213; 1:3 (January, 1928), 412–418.

[62] The following is based largely on an article by E. W. Hofstee, "Regional Differentiation in the Dutch Fertility during the Second Half of the 19th Century" (in Dutch), in Koninklijke Nederlandse Akademie van Wetenschappen, *Akademie-Dagen*, 7 (Amsterdam: Noord-Hollandsche Uitgevers, 1954), 59–106. See also William Petersen, "The Demographic Transition in the Netherlands," *American Sociological Review*, 25:3 (June, 1960), 334–347.

constituted an onerous but efficient means of reducing fertility. With the
Proletarian family, typical of the mass of either rural or urban workers
who had been released from these institutional and normative restrictions,
social control was barely strong enough to force a marriage once a child
had been conceived. Once the sexual urge developed, there was certainly
no effective bar to marriage. In the **Rational** family type, which arose
first among the middle class and during the nineteenth century spread to
the rest of the society, a sense of parental responsibility and, with it, a
limitation of family size reappeared. The average age at marriage rose
again, and the same end was also achieved with less privation by the
use of contraceptives.[63] In order to trace the change in fertility in detail,
thus, we would need the statistics on completed family size by social
class going back at least as far as 1750. While such data will never become available, we can be reasonably certain that the shifts in the over-all
crude birth rate were largely the consequence of the gradual substitution
of one of these family types for another.

SUMMARY

During the 80 years or so following 1760 England's economy and
social structure underwent a complete transformation, commonly known
as the industrial revolution. In agriculture, the medieval three-field system was supplanted by enclosed fields, resulting in both a greatly increased productivity and new social relations in the rural areas. Manufacturing, which had been scattered through the countryside, was
concentrated into factories, around which new urban centers rapidly
developed. The prior relative isolation of the countryside ended with the
construction of roads and canals, by which both men and goods could
move about more easily. These economic changes constituted the first
fundamental advance since the establishment of preindustrial cities
several millenia before.

All the authorities who have analyzed it agree that England's population grew at an unprecedented rate during these 80 years, and that this
was primarily a natural increase, since the emigration of Englishmen was
more or less balanced by the immigration of Irish and Scotch. Differences
arise over whether the increase in numbers resulted mainly from a decline
in the death rate (Griffith, McKeown and Brown, *et al.*) or from a rise

---

[63] See pages 547–552.

in the birth rate (Malthus, Habakkuk, Krause, *et al.*). It is worth stressing that there is nothing in logic against accepting each set of arguments as partly correct, and we have taken the position that there was *both* a decline in mortality and a rise in fertility. Probably the actual process was more complex than either side has pictured it. During this transitional period, in all likelihood, birth and death rates were simultaneously rising and falling in different sectors of the population. Institutional bars to early marriage still kept the birth rate low; their erosion permitted it to rise; and the small-family system, based on both the postponement of marriage and birth control, began to be established among the middle class. Death rates, similarly, certainly differed from one area or social class to another, varying with diets, styles of life, and other conditions affecting mortality. It is just this variety, compounded by the teasingly thin statistical data, that has made possible the continuous dispute over what really happened.

Even so, it is fairly clear that the theory of the demographic transition is too gross a simplification to reflect the changes during beginning industrialization. For England the theory more or less accurately sums up the period from 1850 or even 1875 to 1945— that is, from the time when medicine and public sanitation really effected a rapid decline in mortality, particularly of infants and children, to the postwar baby boom. For earlier decades, most death-control measures were too inefficient to have been so clearly the principal factor in the demonstrable population growth. During the first three-quarters of the nineteenth century, it must be emphasized, the trend in England's birth rate was upward. The secular decline in fertility that began in the year of the Bradlaugh-Besant trial,[64] that is to say, did not start from the high plateau that is assumed in the theory. In most other countries of the Western world, it would seem, there was also an increase in average family size before the downward trend set in. Two important exceptions are the United States [65] and France,[66] where the earliest reliable records suggest the beginning of the subsequent steady fall in natality. These two countries, thus, constitute another important qualification to the theory: that the trend toward a smaller family size got under way in the first decade or two of the nine-

---

[64] See pages 551–552.

[65] See pages 210–214.

[66] See Gerhard Mackenroth, *Bevölkerungslehre: Theorie, Soziologie und Statistik der Bevölkerung* (Berlin: Springer, 1953), pp. 122–134. This section is divided into two parts, the first on the general development of fertility in Northern and Central Europe, the second on the reasons for the exceptional development in France.

teenth century (United States) or even some 50 years earlier (France) means that a prior significant increase in population size is not a necessary precondition to this change in fertility patterns. The social causation of the small-family system is too complex to be adequately encompassed within a purely demographic model, with only fertility and mortality as independent variables. It is certainly relevant that France and the United States are the two countries that established revolutionary regimes in the last quarter of the eighteenth century, and that these governments were based on rationalist doctrines that, when applied to the family, challenged the traditional bases of procreation.

England is probably a better model than either of these countries to analyze population trends in a country undergoing modernization. But England is also atypical in that it was the first country to develop an industrial society. All subsequent modernization, and especially that currently under way in underdeveloped areas, has been far more rapid. And all countries that have imitated England's example have done so, to one degree or another, under the direction of the state.

SUGGESTIONS FOR FURTHER READING

Paul Mantoux, *The Industrial Revolution in the Eighteenth Century: An Outline of the Beginnings of the Modern Factory System in England* (Rev. ed.; London: Cape, 1952).

T. S. Ashton, *The Industrial Revolution, 1760–1830* (London: Oxford University Press, 1948).

Neil J. Smelser, *Social Change in the Industrial Revolution: An Application of Theory to the British Cotton Industry* (Chicago: University of Chicago Press, 1959).

Reinhard Bendix, *Work and Authority in Industry: Ideologies of Management in the Course of Industrialization* (New York: Wiley, 1956).

> Some of the best general accounts of a very interesting period. Mantoux and Ashton are economic historians, Smelser and Bendix sociologists.

J. L. and Barbara Hammond, *The Town Labourer, 1760–1832: The New Civilisation,* and *The Village Labourer, 1760–1832: A Study in the Government of England before the Reform Bill* (London: Longmans, Green, 1932).

F. A. Hayek, ed., *Capitalism and the Historians* (Chicago: University of Chicago Press, 1954).

Frederick Engels, *The Condition of the Working Class in England,* W. O. Henderson and W. H. Chaloner, trans. and eds. (New York: Macmillan, 1958).

> The once prevalent view that the mass of the people suffered as a result of the industrial revolution is dramatically presented in a number of works by the Hammonds, and convincingly answered in several essays in Hayek's book. Both points of view are represented in this edition of Engels's famous work.

G. Talbot Griffith, *Population Problems of the Age of Malthus* (Cambridge: Cambridge University Press, 1926).

Arthur Redford, *Labour Migration in England, 1800–50* (Manchester: University of Manchester Press, 1926).

J. T. Krause, "Changes in English Fertility and Mortality, 1781–1850," *Economic History Review,* 2nd ser., 11:1 (August, 1958), 52–70.

H. J. Habakkuk, "English Population in the Eighteenth Century," *Economic History Review,* 2nd ser., 6:2 (December, 1953), 117–133.

Thomas McKeown and R. G. Brown, "Medical Evidence Related to English Population Changes in the Eighteenth Century," *Population Studies,* 9:2 (November, 1955), 119–141.

J. D. Chambers, "Enclosure and Labour Supply in the Industrial Revolution," *Economic History Review,* 2nd ser., 5:3 (1953), 319–343.

T. H. Marshall, "The Population Problem during the Industrial Revolution," *Economic History (Supplement to the Economic Journal),* 1:4 (January, 1929), 429–456.

> No book-length discussion of England's population during the industrial revolution is wholly satisfactory. Though out of date in many respects, Griffith and Redford are still important. The five articles are among the best of the many on this subject that have appeared in recent years.

K. H. Connell, *The Population of Ireland, 1750–1845* (Oxford: Clarendon, 1950); "Some Unsettled Problems in English and Irish Population History, 1750–1845," *Irish Historical Studies,* 7:28 (September, 1951), 225–234.

E. F. Heckscher, "Swedish Population Trends before the Industrial Revolution," *Economic History Review,* 2nd ser., 2:3 (1950), 226–277.

William Petersen, "The Demographic Transition in the Netherlands," *American Sociological Review*, 25:3 (June, 1960), 334–347.

John T. Krause, "Some Implications of Recent Work in Historical Demography," *Comparative Studies in Society and History*, 1:2 (January, 1959), 164–188.

H. Gille, "The Demographic History of the Northern European Countries in the Eighteenth Century," *Population Studies*, 3:1 (June, 1949), 1–65.

    Some of the best analyses of the early population growth in other Western countries.

15. *THE POPULATION OF*
TOTALITARIAN SOCIETIES

The distinction between democracy and totalitarianism is the most important one of twentieth-century life. In a democracy the state is an instrument of society; the will of the people, as expressed in periodic elections, determines fundamental policies. A totalitarian state is stronger than society, which it shapes to the purposes of an elitist Party. Democratic control of institutions and individuals is, and is intended to be, partial; constraints or special inducements are used to guide society toward what are defined as good ends, but dissidents are permitted a considerable latitude. The totalitarian intent, on the contrary, is to establish and maintain total control over everything and everyone. This contrast in definitions does not, of course, fully describe actual democratic and totalitarian societies; in both cases deviations exist from the principles on which the states are founded. But such exceptions to the rule do not abrogate these principles.

How do totalitarian population phenomena differ from those in a democracy? In order to answer this question in concrete terms, we shall concentrate on the Soviet Union, which today, after the defeat of Nazi Germany and before the rise of Communist China to full economic power, is the most important totalitarian state. Like the section on the United States, that is to say, this chapter has a dual purpose—to give the reader some specific information about the population of one country, and to discuss more generally the type of controls that totalitarian states impose on fertility, mortality, migration, and population composition. To discuss Soviet population trends against their political, economic, and social background, it will be necessary to summarize relevant portions of Soviet history; but it will obviously not be possible in this brief space to do full justice to this large, complicated, and inordinately polemical subject.

405

SOURCES OF INFORMATION

Soviet statistics differ in several respects from those available for any Western country. There is, first of all, a difference in sheer quantity. A planned economy is feasible only if a record of past production can be related to future goals; and since in principle virtually everything in the society is planned, a huge, complex system of record-keeping, reporting, and accounting embraces almost every activity and every person in the country. In 1939, the last date for which this figure is available, record-keepers, tally clerks, registrars, bookkeepers, accountants, and statisticians totaled some 2 million persons, or about 7 per cent of the nonagricultural working population. Whether this army is effective in compiling even the most essential data is another question.

The Soviet government undoubtedly has more statistical data at its disposal than any other government in the world, but, nevertheless, its knowledge of what is going on in the economy and society is not absolute. For example, in 1954, every collective farm sent to statistical agencies twenty-eight different reports consisting of more than 10,000 items of data, but not a single form asked for and provided any figures on the organization, utilization, productivity, and actual remuneration of labor in the collective farms. . . . Until 1939, many small enterprises, institutions, and organizations did not report their balance-sheet accounts; until 1954, complete statistics on natural resources were lacking; as late as 1955 the government received data for the first time on the total volume of production and consumption of dairy and meat products.[1]

A second difference concerns the reliability of the primary data. Any statistical count is likely to be most accurate if it is independent of any other administrative function. One important reason that American immigration data are so poor, it will be recalled, is that they are an adjunct to immigration control. In a planned economy, however, *all* data are compiled as one element of state control. A person asked a question by the representative of a totalitarian regime may answer falsely either because of fear (a true answer, he believes, would prejudice him in the eyes of the Party) or, on the contrary, as a mild form of sabotage. As we shall see, there is good reason to suppose that both fear and resentment have been fairly characteristic attitudes, not only in the general population but also among members of the Party and the associated industrial elite. Administrators of all types are likely to advance their careers only by

[1] Vsevolod Holubnychy, "Organization of Statistical Observation in the U.S.S.R.," *American Statistician*, 12:3 (June, 1958), 13–17.

filling the unreasonably high quotas set by their superiors, and we can judge the strength of the temptation to adjust their records by the severity of the punishment imposed: "Any deliberate distortion or falsification of data is subject to penalties of from six months to eight years of confinement to prison." [2] This typical dilemma of any Soviet statistician is acute for those who compile demographic statistics, since these reflect in part the welfare that the economy affords the common man, and the discrepancy on this issue between Soviet propaganda and Soviet reality has been great. It is at least possible that the original compilations of births and deaths are often falsified by hospital clerks and registration offices. "There are many reports of such cases in the Soviet press and in the pages of *Vestnik Statistiki,* the organ of the Central Statistical Administration of the U.S.S.R." [3]

> Soviet statisticians, interestingly enough, were among the first to suffer the impact of the Stalinist assault on scientific freedom. Many of the foremost representatives of the economic and statistical sciences in the U.S.S.R. fell victim to a purge in 1929–30. . . . The regime's . . . purpose was to get rid of those whose evaluations of economic conditions and prospects were inimical to the industrialization and collectivization policies.[4]

Thus far, we have been discussing the limitations in the record accessible to Soviet officials. But some types of the most fundamental data have not been made available outside the country, and those that have been published are often of dubious quality. In 1956 the Soviet government issued an official statistical *Handbook,*[5] which was critically reviewed by Naum Jasny, an outstanding Western sovietologist.[6] His criticisms of this particular volume apply to Soviet statistics generally, and represent an excellent introduction to this difficult terrain. Many important data, which we know from other sources are collected in the Soviet Union, were omitted from the *Handbook*—for instance, all statistics on family budgets or the consumption of various goods. As in this case, the reason

[2] *Ibid.*

[3] Myron K. Gordon, "Notes on Recent Soviet Population Statistics and Research," *Population Index,* 23:1 (January, 1957), 2–16. See also John F. Kantner, "Recent Demographic Trends in the USSR," in Milbank Memorial Fund, *Population Trends in Eastern Europe, the USSR and Mainland China* (New York, 1960), pp. 35–63.

[4] Stephan E. Schattman, "Dogma vs. Science in Soviet Statistics," *Problems of Communism,* 5:1 (January–February, 1956), 30–36.

[5] See the English translation: Central Statistical Board of the U.S.S.R. Council of Ministers, *National Economy of the U.S.S.R.: Statistical Returns* (Moscow: Foreign Languages Publishing House, 1957).

[6] Naum Jasny, *The Soviet 1956 Statistical Handbook: A Commentary* (East Lansing: Michigan State University Press, 1957). Copyright © 1957 The Michigan State University Press.

for the concealment is usually patent. The published figures are also full of traps for the nonspecialist. For example, the territory of the Soviet Union is now appreciably larger than before the war, but time series have in general not been recalculated to take this difference into account. Some series are calculated as percentages of the figure for 1940, a year when several territorial changes occurred, without informing the reader which area is taken as the base. Or, as another example, the crop "yields" reported until 1954 were estimates made in the field, before harvesting; for the years 1950–1953 these "biological" crops ranged between 121 and 131 million tons, while the actual annual yields as now officially reported for these same years were between 76 and 89 million tons.[7] In short, "Soviet statistics are an amalgam of elements varying from trustworthy data (mostly pertaining to physical units or details) through ambiguities to obviously distorted estimates (mostly data for aggregates)."[8]

The most egregious manipulation is to be found, as one would expect, in the calculation of statistical answers to the most important and comprehensive questions: What has the trend been in industrial production, in national income, and so on? In a demographic analysis we typically take such economic and social series as data, but in this case it is questionable whether anything can be accepted as given, particularly for international comparisons. The meaning of statistical constructs of this type depends in large part on how the component elements are weighted, and on which mathematical formula is used. For instance, from 1928 to 1956 Soviet industrial production increased by almost 23 times according to the official claim, while according to one American calculation the increase was by only 7.7 times.[9] The difficulty is even greater with respect to the national income, for here even the basic units are incomparable: in an economy where state fiat sets prices, these tell us more about the regime's political intentions than about the relation between the demand for and the supply of various commodities.

Most of these limitations and flaws are characteristic also of demographic data. Published vital statistics are grossly incomplete.

Publishing the statistics only for favorable factors or periods, is certainly very much akin to falsification. For example, the birth rate in 1938 was made known in due time (38.3 per 1,000), but not for 1939 and 1940. Western analysts realized

---

[7] *Ibid.,* pp. 94–95.
[8] *Ibid.,* p. 14.
[9] See Gregory Grossman, "Thirty Years of Soviet Industrialisation," *Soviet Survey,* 26 (October–December, 1958), 15–21.

that, due to the change in age composition and other factors, the birth rate in 1940 must have been lower than in 1938, but nobody seems to have thought of as low a figure as 31.7 per 1,000, now, after all those years, disclosed in the *Handbook*.[10]

Our main source of Soviet population data is the censuses, but these also are not very satisfactory. The first census taken under Soviet auspices was in 1920, only three years after the Bolsheviks took power and while their rule was still being fought in parts of the country. Scores of enumerators were beaten up as representatives of the government, and 33 were murdered by the people they were attempting to count. The 1920 census is not regarded as accurate.

The next Soviet census was taken in 1926, after the country had been pacified. In order to insure an accurate return, special directives were issued to the public promising, on the one hand, to treat all information received as confidential, and, on the other hand, threatening with reprisals and indictments those who gave false information. While no enumerators were killed, the response of the people in many areas was not friendly.

A special correspondent of *Izvestia*, an official Government newspaper, reported from Piatigorsk (Caucasus) and from Rostov-on-Don, that about ten percent of householders refused to give the required information on the first day of the preliminary survey before the actual enumeration. The same report complained that rumors were circulating among the peasants that the census was conducted for the cause of Antichrist, while the others claimed that it was aimed at the increase of taxation burden.[11]

In spite of these limitations, the 1926 census is the best to date, and the only one of which the Soviet government has published full reports.

Censuses were ordered in 1933 and 1935, but they did not take place.[12]

A census was taken in 1937, but the results were suppressed in their entirety because—according to the official report—inaccuracies and ideological errors were discovered in the formulation of questions and the

[10] Jasny, *op. cit.*, p. 13. Note the comment by the French demographer Sauvy: "M. Depoid, a French statistician, using the two official [Soviet] censuses of 1926 and 1939, estimated that if natality had continued to decline it would have reached 27 per thousand population by the eve of the war. The Americans use a birth rate of 38 per thousand for the year 1938, a figure that appeared in a *Pravda* article in 1939. This is a rather fragile base. One figure may be the result only of an error, and it was never confirmed or denied" (Alfred Sauvy, "Doctrine soviétique en matière de population," *Rivista Italiana de Demografia e Statistica*, 2:4, December, 1948, 475–484).

[11] Galina V. Selegen and Victor P. Petrov, "Soviet People versus Population Census," *American Statistician*, 13:1 (February, 1959), 14–15.

[12] Holubnychy, "Organization," *op. cit.*

development of the data.[13] The actual reason, it can be surmised, is that the population figure would have suggested how many millions had been killed in the enforced collectivization.

The next attempt was made two years later, in 1939. Both "unconscientious" respondents and irresponsible enumerators were threatened with official reprisals.

Soviet citizens were invited to denounce cases, where someone was found failing to supply proper information to the census takers. They were also requested to watch enumerators, whose behavior aroused suspicion. This last measure was designed "to prevent appearance, in the role of enumerators, of some impostors, coming from the ranks of remaining criminals still at large."

The reports on the completed 1939 census have repeatedly accentuated the friendly attitude and extreme cooperation of Soviet citizens. And no wonder. It was hardly possible to expect any other report, since any error or failure to answer the questions might have been interpreted as a hostile attitude or even an attack of the "enemy of the people." [14]

Only a small portion of the data collected in the 1939 census, however, was ever published. Some of the unpublished parts were found in German-occupied areas during the war, and these have formed a basis for a new analysis of population trends during the 1930's.[15]

According to rumors, a sample survey of the population was taken shortly after World War II, but once again the returns were so low that they were suppressed.[16]

The last population census was taken in 1959, after careful preparation.[17]

Some officials of enterprises and institutions have, under one pretext or another, refused to allow their workers to take part in the census. . . . The success of the forthcoming census depends in great part on how clearly the whole population of our country grasps the political and economic importance of these measures. Party, trade union, Young Communist League and other public organizations must ex-

[13] See Frank Lorimer, *The Population of the Soviet Union: History and Prospects* (League of Nations; Princeton: Princeton University Press, 1946), p. 222, n. 3.

[14] Selegen and Petrov, "Soviet People," *op. cit.*

[15] See Basilius Martschenko, "Soviet Population Trends, 1926–1939" (in Russian) (New York: Research Program on the U.S.S.R., 1953; mimeographed).

[16] Gordon, "Notes," *op. cit.*

[17] See U.S. Bureau of the Census, *Materials on the Preparation and Conduct of the U.S.S.R. All-Union Population Census of 1959* (Working Paper no. 8; Washington, 1959); "The 1959 Census of Population of the U.S.S.R.: Methodology and Plans," *International Population Statistics Reports,* series P-90, no. 10, April 15, 1959. See also U.S.S.R., Central Statistical Administration, *The All-Union Population Census of 1959* (in Russian) (Moscow, 1960).

plain the purposes, importance, methods and schedule of the census to the working people on a broad scale.[18]

Sovietologists everywhere are waiting to see what portion of the data is to be published. Up to the time of this writing, two short preliminary reports have appeared, and even this limited information has changed our prior understanding of such important questions as, for instance, the number of persons killed during the last war.

In summary, Soviet statistics available abroad include distortions and inaccuraries of a number of types, apart from the errors that result simply from human fallibility or inefficiency. (a) The pressure to maintain production norms is so great that the response to it sometimes is to tamper with one's reports. Original data include deliberate falsifications in a literal sense; a manager of a factory or a collective farm changes 5,000 to 6,000. Whether adulteration of this kind takes place at the level of the Central Statistical Administration is a moot point among Western sovietologists. (b) A more appropriate term to describe the usual practices of the Moscow bureaus is contextual distortion. For example, two percentages are compared without informing the reader that they were calculated on different bases, or a standard word like *harvest* is used in a very special sense. The intent is to give the foreign public a false impression, but this intent can be defeated (as it cannot be with falsification of the first type) by the application of careful and informed scholarship. (c) The omission of crucial data can be considered another type of distortion. For example, figures are published for good years, none for poor years. Or statistical aggregates are calculated with no hint as to which of several alternative formulas was used.

With this meager and somewhat dubious base to work from, Western scholars interested in Soviet demography have had to devote as much effort to compiling data as to analyzing them. They have devised ingenious methods for extrapolating scraps of information into presump-

[18] *Pravda,* January 8, 1959; translated in *Current Digest of the Soviet Press,* February 11, 1959. In January, 1960, a special housing census was taken, and rumors started that this was to be the first step in the nationalization of all private homes. This slander was being spread, according to the official statement, by speculators who hoped thus to buy houses cheap and sell them at a profit. "There are not many such speculators, of course," but they are sly and clever. "Our people are well aware that the Party and the government are constantly concerned about improving the life of Soviet people. The forthcoming census of home-owning is being undertaken solely in the interests of the people and has no other purpose." See "Whispers Muddy the Waters," *Sovetskaya Rossia,* November 11, 1959; translated in *Current Digest of the Soviet Press,* December 30, 1959.

tions about population size or growth or distribution. For example, production figures are sometimes given both in total and per capita forms, and by simple calculation it is possible to estimate the number of persons they imply. From production figures cited at the Twentieth Communist Party Congress, for instance, Harrison Salisbury estimated that the Soviet population in January 1956 was between 199.4 and 203.4 million, or appreciably lower than previous estimates.[19] Indeed, the official estimate for April 1956, as published in the *Handbook* later that year, was 200.2 million. As this example suggests, demographic information derived by such indirect calculations may have been included just for that purpose. One can hardly assume that statistics could appear in an important speech by accident. The alternative hypothesis is that such indirect data serve the same purposes as a diplomatic trial balloon or a deliberate "leak" to the press: it is possible for the Soviet government to give out figures for which it is not directly responsible,[20] or to soften the impact of unfavorable data that will shortly appear in official form.

Like those concerning early English industrialization, the figures on Soviet population are just good enough to form the basis of an argument, but seldom precise enough to settle it. And far more than in the English case, it is difficult to separate Soviet statistics from the ideological message they are intended to convey.

WAR AND REVOLUTION

The tsarist regime, ruling in barbaric splendor over one-sixth of the earth's surface, offered a facade of great power still in 1914, but the impression was short-lived. In the very first month of the war, at the battle of Tannenberg, the Germans took over 100,000 Russian prisoners and the Russian general, in desperation, shot himself on the field.[21] The following spring, the Russian forces—already handicapped by a lack of rifles, artillery, ammunition, and clothing—gave way to a renewed

[19] Harrison E. Salisbury, "Population Loss Hidden by Soviet," *New York Times,* March 11, 1956.

[20] Jasny points out, for example, that per capita production figures for steel, coal, etc.—which had been a favorite component of Soviet propaganda—were missing from the 1956 *Handbook*. "Why? Perhaps because their presence would have been an acknowledgment that Malenkov (in his report to the 19th Party Congress), Baibakov, Chairman of the Gosplan, in the journal of the Party, *Communist* (1956, No. 6), and certain others deliberately used incorrect population figures in their calculations of per capita data" (*op. cit.,* p. 8).

[21] The military facts and estimates in this account are from William L. Langer, ed., *An Encyclopedia of World History* (Rev. ed.; Boston: Houghton Mifflin, 1948), pp. 913 ff.

German advance. In the spring of 1916 the Russians moved forward on a broad front against the Austrians, taking many prisoners but losing about a million men in the process. When this offensive was blocked by German reinforcements, it left the whole Russian army demoralized and ripe for revolution. Two revolutions ensued, one in March, 1917, and the second in November. An armistice followed between Russia and the Central Powers, and eventually the Treaty of Brest-Litovsk took Russia officially out of the war.

In fact, it became a civil war—principally because the Bolsheviks, though supported by only a small fraction of the population, insisted on ruling absolutely. During the eight months that it was in power, the provisional government had begun a number of basic social reforms; and when Lenin demanded that this democratic regime be overthrown, he lacked the support even of his own Party.[22]

The years 1917–1921 are known in the Party histories as the period of War Communism. The new regime's economic program extended little beyond its slogan, "Peace, bread, and land," for in 1917 socialist economics hardly existed even as a theory. The sale or purchase of commodities was prohibited, but no alternative system of distribution could be established. Industry was disorganized, the transportation system damaged and worn out, the government administration disrupted by widespread strikes. Cities could be fed only by sending armies out into the countryside to confiscate the peasants' food. The state printing presses deprived paper rubles of all value: from 1913 to 1917, prices increased by three times, but by 1921 they were some 16,800 times the 1913 figure.[23] A serious strike wave in Petrograd, which quickly developed from economic to political goals, was broken with lockouts and military force. The Kronstadt garrison outside Petrograd's harbor made a series of demands on the government. Their Left Communist pro-

---

[22] Five members of the Party's Central Committee resigned against what they termed his "disastrous policy," which was also opposed by eleven of the fifteen members of the Council of People's Commissars. The statements are quoted in Julien Steinberg, ed., *Verdict of Three Decades* (New York: Duell, Sloan and Pearce, 1950), pp. 12–13. In the election to the Constituent Assembly, which was called before but took place after the Bolshevik coup, 32 million out of the total of 36 million votes were cast for various socialist parties; and the remnants of the thoroughly discredited tsarist regime could hardly have undertaken a war against such odds. Of the 32 million socialist votes, however, only about 9 million were cast for the Bolsheviks, who forcibly disbanded the Constituent Assembly the day it met and set up what soon became a Communist Party dictatorship.

[23] George Vernadsky, *A History of Russia* (3rd rev. ed.; New Haven: Yale University Press, 1951), p. 286.

gram, "for the liberation of the toilers from the despotic power of the Communist usurpers," echoed the Bolsheviks' earlier promises, by now all abrogated: the freeing of political prisoners, free elections, a free market in food, and so on.[24] The Kronstadt rebellion was ruthlessly quashed in ten days of heavy fighting, but at the same time the Party ordered what it declared to be a "temporary retreat" to the New Economic Policy (or NEP). The food levy was abolished and supplanted by a limited grain tax, and small-scale private enterprise was again permitted in agriculture and petty trade.

The seven years of war, aggravated by tsarist and Bolshevik bureaucratic inefficiency, had a fearful impact on the population. Thousands were killed by terror and counterterror, hundreds of thousands in the civil strife; but these were by far not the major component of the extraordinary mortality. With the constant movement of hungry hordes, epidemics spread through the country. Typhus alone killed more than 1.5 million in 1919–1920. In the winter of 1921–1922, after years of food shortages and a serious drought, Russia suffered a devastating famine.[25]

The depletion in the population during this whole period is not at all easy to calculate. Tsarist Russia's only census was in 1897, and, as we have noted, the first reliable Soviet census was in 1926. Over this interval, adjusting for changes in Russia's territory, the population increased from 106 to 147 million, or by 38.6 per cent in slightly less than 30 years, in spite of the losses suffered between 1914 and 1923. These losses can be estimated [26] if we postulate that the "normal" rate of natural increase was constant from 1897 on. Actually, such an assumption would seem to be reasonable. In the 39 provinces of European Russia that remained Russian after the revolution, the average birth rate fell from 50.4 in 1899–1901 to 47.6 in 1911–1913, and the average death rate from 33.1 to 29.6. The rate of natural increase varied, thus, only between 17.3 and 18.0 per thousand. If, to be conservative, we take 17.15 as the average annual increase per thousand from 1897 on, this would have resulted in a population of 175 million in 1926. The actual census count was 28 million short of this (or 16 per cent); and this difference can be taken as the total deficit. The factors responsible for the population loss from

---

24 Robert V. Daniels, "The Kronstadt Revolt of 1921: A Study in the Dynamics of Revolution," *American Slavic and East European Review,* 10 (December, 1951), 241–254.

25 See H. H. Fisher, *The Famine in Soviet Russia, 1919–1923* (New York: Macmillan, 1927).

26 The following argument derives mainly from Lorimer, *op. cit.,* Ch. 3.

1914 to 1926, as estimated by Lorimer from various more or less satisfactory data, are as follows:

Military deaths	2 million[27]
Civilian deaths	14 million
Net emigration	2 million
Birth deficit[28]	10 million
Total	28 million

These figures are not precise, of course, but they are probably correct
to the nearest million, as shown. "During the years 1915–1923 the
Russian people underwent the most cataclysmic changes since the Mongol
invasion in the early thirteenth century." [29]

THE SECOND BOLSHEVIK REVOLUTION

The Bolshevik revolution was a *political* coup; its main purpose was to
take power. Thus, after the ineffectual attempt to plan the national
economy had broken down and the New Economic Policy was inaugu-
rated, the main social consequence of the revolution was the contrary
of what the Communists intended—the division of the landed estates
among the peasantry. Every Party leader had been taught that the
progressive momentum from the French revolution had been blocked by
the stolid immovable conservatism of the French peasantry, the class
created when the feudal estates of that country were broken up into family farms.

The Bolshevik *social* revolution began on October 1, 1928, when the
First Five-Year Plan went into effect. While the principal purpose of the
planned economy has generally been to develop heavy industry, in the
first plan the emphasis was on the collectivization of agriculture—not an
easy goal. The peasant's proverbial attachment to his land was strong in
Russia, in part because he had acquired it so recently. Serfdom had been
abolished in 1861, almost within the memory of living man, and millions

[27] The Russian casualties reported by Langer for 1914–1918 only are 1.7 million
dead, almost 5 million wounded, and 2.5 million prisoners (*op. cit.*, p. 951). These
statistics suggest that 2 million for 1914–1926 may be on the low side, but in a civil
war the distinction between "military" and "civilian" deaths is blurred.

[28] That is, the difference between the actual number of births and the number that
would have occurred if the "normal" rate of natural increase had continued during
this period.

[29] Lorimer, *op. cit.*, p. 42.

had acquired their plot in 1917–1918, only ten years before. Efforts by the state to coax peasants into collectives had failed completely: in mid-1928 only 1.7 per cent of the peasant households, and 2.3 per cent of the crop area, were collectivized.[30] Mass terror was needed to implement the program; and this momentous process not only converted the peasantry into a landless proletariat, peons of the state, but also shaped every element of Soviet society. In particular, it had a tremendous effect on the population, both directly by the millions who were killed, and indirectly by the fact that the Soviet Union has to this day not been able to establish an efficient agriculture.

The first step in the heightened effort to collectivize agriculture was, in Party language, to intensify the class struggle in the village. The Russian peasantry was essentially a single class, unified by both its miserable living conditions and the hostility of the regime. In Soviet law and in Party practice, however, the class was divided into three: the "wealthy" kulaks,[31] the "middle" peasants, and the "poor" peasants. These designations, it must be emphasized, are not to be interpreted in Western terms; in 1926 the average per capita annual income of the three groups was, respectively, $88, $46, and $39.[32] The Party's program was "dekulakization," if possible by engaging the poor and middle peasants against the kulaks. In Stalin's words,

> We have recently passed from the policy of *restricting* the exploiting proclivities of the kulaks to the policy of *eliminating the kulaks as a class*. . . . The expropriation of the kulaks is an integral part of the formation and development of the collective farms. That is why it is ridiculous and fatuous to expatiate today on the expropriation of the kulaks. You do not lament the loss of the hair of one who has been beheaded.
>
> There is another question which seems no less ridiculous: whether the kulak should be permitted to join the collective farms. Of course not, for he is a sworn enemy of the collective farm movement. Clear, one would think.[33]

As the collectivization proceeded, the legal criteria defining kulaks were changed repeatedly; the precise boundary became more and more elusive as the Party approached its goal. Eventually all those who tried to fight

[30] *Handbook,* p. 89.

[31] The word means *fists;* the implication is a greedy, grasping person who closes his hand around anything put into it.

[32] Data presented at the 15th Party Conference, cited in Vernadsky, *op. cit.,* p. 328, n.

[33] Joseph Stalin, "Problems of Agrarian Policy in the U.S.S.R." (1929), *Leninism: Selected Writings* (New York: International Publishers, 1942), pp. 145–164; italics in the original.

the Party programs were defined as kulaks or, if this was too preposterous, as kulak-followers (*podkulachniki*).[34]

By reinforcing the jealousies and hatreds in the village, by recreating the mood of the civil war, the tiny Party was able to manipulate the overwhelming majority of the population and expropriate the peasants' property *in toto* almost before they knew what was happening. At first some of the "middle" and "poor" peasants probably really believed that the Party organizer had intervened in their interest. This does not mean, however, that even they voluntarily surrendered their property to the collectives, as was claimed in official reports. Anna Louise Strong, a fervent American Communist who traveled in the Russian countryside in this period, has described how these "voluntary" votes for collectives were obtained:

> Organizers ask: "Who is for the collective?" and when the meeting fails to respond, vary the question to "Who is against the Soviet Power?" Naturally no one admits to counter-revolution, so he declares them all enrolled in the collective "which is the policy of the government."

And when even these persuasive methods were insufficient, a more direct threat often helped.

> A village which cannily decides to postpone collectivization "till we see how it works with others" is declared by the outraged organizer a "village of kulaks, every family of which needs investigation." In another village fourteen families refuse to join and are threatened with "being sent up to the white bears." [35]

All through the year 1929 collectivization was pushed forward with such quasi-legal methods—through extra tax levies, quotas, attachments, auctions, trials before special traveling courts, and so on. As a consequence, "a million families suddenly found themselves pariahs, without any rights which need be respected, and without any knowledge as to what they might do to be saved." [36] This newly created class of outcasts

---

[34] In Nazi Germany, similarly, as the campaign against Jews rose to a climax following 1938, the number of persons included in the critical category was continually extended. As Karl Lueger had put it, "*Wer Jude ist, bestimme ich!*"—*I* decide who is a Jew. Later Himmler wrote to one of his underlings: "Do not publish the decree defining Jews. Such foolish precision ties our hands." Quoted in Gerald Reitlinger, *The Final Solution: The Attempt to Exterminate the Jews of Europe, 1939–1945* (New York: Beechhurst, 1953), p. 175.

[35] Anna Louise Strong, *The Soviets Conquer Wheat: The Drama of Collective Farming* (New York: Holt, 1931), pp. 82–83. Copyright, 1931, by Henry Holt and Company, Inc.

[36] *Ibid.*, p. 81.

was expropriated of its means of subsistence, disfranchised, deprived of ration cards and of the right to purchase in the cooperative stores; their children were expelled from school, and their sick were excluded from medical treatment. By the beginning of 1930, however, still less than one-quarter of the peasant households were collectivized. The Party dropped its pretense that it was intervening to support the poor peasants against their class enemies and opened up a mass offensive against the Russian people. The world was justifiably horrified when the Nazis punished the activities of the Czech underground by completely destroying one village, Lidice; but we have no record of how many Russian Lidices were obliterated by their own state police. For example,

Sixteen villages in the Ukraine failed to produce the grain required from them, and their failure was attributed by the authorities to deliberate sabotage. A decree was published in the local papers announcing that all grain hoarded in the offending villages was to be confiscated, the coöperative stores in the villages were to be closed, and no state distributing authority was to arrange to send food to them—in other words sixteen villages were condemned to starve or secretly flee from their homes.[37]

With such methods, Stalin's "solid collectivization" developed rapidly. From January 20 to March 1, 1930, the number of peasant homesteads collectivized increased from 4.4 to 14.3 million, or from 21.6 to 55.0 per cent of the total.[38] After these 40 days of terror Stalin condemned the "feverish pursuit of inflated collectivization figures" he had previously decreed. His famous speech, "Dizziness from Success," was promptly published and distributed by the millions.

The peasants waved it in the faces of over-zealous organizers, who were often dismayed by it, some of them even protesting: "But if collectivization is voluntary, it will go to pieces." And in fact, an exodus began from the hastily organized collectives which deflated their alleged numbers by more than half in the next two months. Those that remained and actually sowed land collectively were still 24 per cent. of all the peasantry, whereas the Five-Year Plan had anticipated only 20 per cent. three years later. . . . The Bolsheviks had pursued their typical tactics—

[37] Allan Monkhouse, *Moscow, 1911–1933* (Boston: Little, Brown, 1934), p. 207. Monkhouse, a British engineer, worked in Russia during this period and witnessed the events he describes. Later, he was one of a large number of foreign engineers accused of sabotage. His account is verified by William Henry Chamberlin, then correspondent of the *Christian Science Monitor,* who also described what he himself saw: *Russia's Iron Age* (Boston: Little, Brown, 1934), pp. 85–86.

[38] *Izvestia,* March 9, 1930, cited in Alexander Baykov, *The Development of the Soviet Economic System* (Cambridge: Cambridge University Press, 1946), p. 196.

they had driven through with greater strength than needed, and could retire to consolidate position.[39]

The collectives formed by these methods were hardly model farms. Rather than deliver their property to the state, the peasants chose to destroy it. They burned the seed grain and killed the livestock. Two-fifths of the cattle disappeared, two-thirds of the sheep and goats, more than half of the swine and of the horses.[40] In 1930 all Russia had only 72,000 tractors;[41] this was the mechanical base of the collectivization. And on such a base a large farm without draft animals was a contradiction in terms. There was a comparable depletion in human labor power. After the most skillful and diligent peasants had been ousted, their place as rural leaders was taken by 25,000 city men and youths,[42] anxious only for the Party career they could establish by successfully corraling the peasant mass.

The chaos in agriculture had as its inevitable consequence an increasing food shortage, culminating in another famine.

Beginning with 1929–1930, the famine spreads over the immense country like leprosy. People learn to make bread of oilcakes, to eat herbs and bark.

Little children have swollen bellies, epidemics perpetuate themselves: typhoid, exanthematic typhus carried by lice (soap is a rare product), dysentery, cholera. Public rumour announces cases of the plague in Stavropol (Northern Caucasus) during the winter of 1932–1933. Whole regions—I have lived in them—are sapped by malaria. There is a shortage of medicaments. The nomadic populations of Central Asia are decimated by hunger and maladies.[43]

In the number of deaths it brought about, this famine was comparable to the one twelve years before, but the regime's attitude was different. In 1920–1921, the Soviet Union had appealed for and received substantial aid from abroad; in 1932–1933, the government denied the very fact of the famine. Dr. Ewald Ammende, who had worked in Russia a decade earlier as a representative of the Red Cross, in 1933 became secretary

[39] Strong, *op. cit.*, pp. 92, 93.

[40] See the official statistics tabulated by Lorimer, *op. cit.*, p. 109.

[41] Baykov, *op. cit.*, p. 331.

[42] See the report of Kaganovich to the 16th Party Congress, "Organisational Report of the Central Committee," *International Press Correspondence,* 10:34 (July 25, 1930), 638–649.

[43] Victor Serge, *Russia Twenty Years After* (New York: Pioneer, 1937), p. 178. Serge was born in Brussels, the son of liberal Russian emigres. He became a Communist and a member of the Comintern Executive Committee; and he was in Russia, as a political prisoner, during what he terms "The Great Wretchedness," the title of the chapter opening with the quoted passage.

of another international relief organization; but he was not permitted
to do more than send in a few food parcels, some of which were returned.[44]

The Soviet Government could easily have averted the famine from its own
resources if it had desired to do so. A complete cessation of the export of foodstuffs in 1932 or the diversion of a small amount of foreign currency to the purchase of grain and provisions would have achieved this end. The Soviet attitude
was pretty adequately summed up . . . to me: "To have imported grain would have
been injurious to our prestige. To have let the peasants keep their grain would have
encouraged them to go on producing little." [45]

In general, city dwellers fared better, but their life was not easy during
this period. Instead of 3,200 million paper rubles, the maximum prescribed for the First Five-Year Plan, the government presses produced
6,800 million. "Indeed, the most indubitable overfulfillment of the plan
was in the matter of printing paper money." [46] Housing was incredibly
poor, and for a period got worse. To enforce labor discipline, the government reintroduced from tsarist days the internal passport and instituted
a wide range of measures designed to quicken the country's industrialization. Food cards were abolished, and class distinctions were made in the
amount of food given out. The recurrent purges of the Party leadership
were extended to large numbers in the rank and file of the membership
and the Party's periphery.

Under such conditions the control of the population was possible only
by a considerable increase in the size and power of the terror apparatus.[47]
A few weeks after they had taken power, the Bolsheviks established the
Cheka, or the Extraordinary Commission for Combatting Counterrevolu-
tion, Sabotage, and Speculation. Over the years, the designation of the
state police has been changed repeatedly—from Cheka to GPU, to
OGPU, to NKVD, to MVD—reflecting a continual reorganization and
enlargement of its function, as well as probably an attempt to keep some
of its activities secret. As the People's Commissariat (or, later, Ministry)
of Internal Affairs—the NKVD or MVD—it has become an outlandish

---

[44] His book is the best account of the famine: Ewald Ammende, *Human Life in Russia* (London: Allen & Unwin, 1936). See also Eugene Lyons, "The Press Corps Conceals a Famine," *Assignment in Utopia* (New York: Harcourt, Brace, 1937), Book 4, Ch. 15. Lyons was the United Press correspondent in Moscow at the time.

[45] Chamberlin, *op. cit.*, p. 89, n. 6.

[46] *Ibid.*, p. 101.

[47] This account derives largely from the excellent summary of Soviet sources in Herbert McClosky and John E. Turner, *The Soviet Dictatorship* (New York: McGraw-Hill, 1960), Ch. 14.

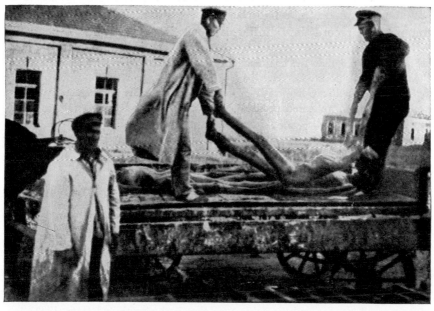

Street secenes in Kharkov, U.S.S.R., summer, 1933. (Top) Familiarity breeds indifference: pedestrians pass by several who died of hunger with hardly a glance. (Bottom) Collecting corpses for burial. (From Ewald Ammende, *Human Life in Russia*, London: Allen & Unwin, 1936.)

combination of routine civil administration and terror apparatus. Its functions have ranged from tasks like the registration of vital events or fire-fighting to the resettlement of populations and the administration of forced-labor camps and other penal institutions.[48]

In later years Western friends of the Soviet Union generally denied the very existence of the forced-labor camps, but during the First Five-Year Plan, when the penal system was being expanded into a branch of the planned economy, this development was not only admitted but even advertised. The most remarkable instance was a paean to one of the first large forced-labor projects, the construction of a canal between Leningrad and Archangel. A team of Soviet writers under the editorial guidance of Maxim Gorky wrote a book about it, *Belomor,* and this was translated into several languages and distributed everywhere through the Party bookstores.[49]

The Russian state had been considering the project since the eighteenth century, the opening chapter informs us, but to bourgeois engineers the difficulties had been insurmountable. The terrain of Karelia, through which the canal had to be dug, is a peaty, contorted mass; and its climate is harsh and treacherous—"a land where it will be difficult to pour concrete, and where unexpected thaws will be particularly dangerous" (p. 40). Nevertheless, what the tsarist regime found impossible was completed in record time during the First Five-Year Plan.

Stalin proposed that the construction of this Canal should be entrusted by the Communist Party to the G.P.U. . . . Stalin it was who started the idea of building the White Sea-Baltic Canal with prisoners, because under his leadership such a method of reform appeared possible (p. 20).

Thirty thousand [50] men—and women, most of them political prisoners and "kulaks," were shipped to this desolate region, where they attacked

---

[48] Throughout, with no matter what name, in the words of a Soviet jurist, "The activity of the Cheka was permeated with a lofty Party spirit, communist ideology and genuine humaneness"! V. S. Tikunov, "Socialist Legality is the Guiding Principle in the Activities of the State Security Agencies," *Sovetskoye gosudarstvo i pravo,* August, 1959; translated in *Current Digest of the Soviet Press,* November 11, 1959. Indeed, he admitted, certain shameless careerists had violated legality, but only under the leadership of such a political adventurer as Beria. In January, 1960, the U.S.S.R. Ministry of Internal Affairs was broken up into Union-Republic Ministries of Internal Affairs—presumably as the final step in the Party's action against Beria.

[49] Maxim Gorky et al., *Belomor: An Account of the Construction of the New Canal between the White Sea and the Baltic Sea* (New York: Smith and Haas, 1935).

[50] This figure is from the book. In *Pravda* the number of prisoners on this project was given as 72,000; see McClosky and Turner, *op. cit.,* p. 488.

the rock with pickaxes and wheelbarrows. Those who survived the two years of hardship and danger (the volume gives no intimation of how many) were encouraged to rush the work to completion by a promise of earlier liberation. But when they finished this task, the "reforged" "criminals" "volunteered" to work on another project, the Moscow-Volga canal. "Experience has almost made the Chekists [GPU-men] engineers, and has taught the engineers the Chekists' style of work" (p. 326).

For subsequent years, while we lack such official descriptions, a good deal of information on the forced-labor system has been collected from former inmates, former GPU camp administrators, and correlative economic and population data published by the Soviet state itself. Responsible estimates of the number of inmates (for example, by Walter Krivitsky) have ranged as high as 20 million. Immediately after World War II, in what is still the best general work on Soviet forced labor, Dallin and Nicolaevsky estimated the total at between 7 and 12 million. About 85 to 90 per cent of the prisoners are male, and at that time these constituted some 16 per cent of the adult male population.[51] This vast army was recruited first of all from the mass of dissident peasants, but minority ethnic groups, members of outlawed political parties and Communist factions, and urban workers were also well represented.

The forced-labor system has had a number of effects, both direct and indirect, on the Soviet population. The camp inmates themselves have, of course, fewer offspring than free laborers, and the removal of millions of males from the general population also affects its sex ratio and fertility rate. The death rate in the camps is extremely high. Many of them are situated in the far North, where even under the best conditions life is dangerous. A camp inmate works from 10 to 14 hours a day at heavy, exhausting labor—removing earth, felling and chopping trees, mining, fishing. He is driven to work hard both by the guards and by a differential food ration, which ranges from grossly inadequate for those who complete their quota of work to a starvation diet for those who do not. The clothing of prisoners is unsuitable, and when they take sick they have to depend on a poorly staffed dispensary that lacks essential equipment and drugs. According to one estimate, during a six-month period 30 per cent of the inmates of one camp died;[52] and something like this rate must be typical until the middle-aged and less sturdy portion of a new batch of prisoners

[51] David J. Dallin and Boris I. Nicolaevsky, *Forced Labor in Soviet Russia* (New Haven: Yale University Press, 1947), pp. 86–87.
[52] See McClosky and Turner, *op. cit.*, p. 493, n. 126.

are killed off. The life expectancy of all camp inmates, including the young and healthy among them, we have no way of determining precisely, but it can hardly be more than four or five years on the average.

The effect of the forced-labor system on population redistribution has also been marked. The tsarist government had repeatedly tried to entice a larger portion of the Russian population across the Urals into Siberia, but these efforts were unsuccessful—as inefficient, one might say, as its attempts to build the Belomor canal. In even the most inhospitable areas the Soviet government has been able to establish large cities—in the sense of population settlements of a certain minimum size. Between the 1926 and the 1939 censuses, net in-migration to towns and cities totaled some 23 million. Urbanization was still at a relatively low rate in 1927–1928, but from 1929 on, with deportations getting under way, it rose rapidly. 1931 marks the high point of both dekulakization and urbanization, with a net in-migration to cities of 4.1 million persons in that year.[53] The impression given by this chronology is reinforced when we look at the new urban sites. Lorimer lists 49 "boom cities"—that is, those with 50,000 or more inhabitants in 1939 that had increased by three times or more during the intercensal period. The one heading the list—which did not exist in 1926 and in 1939 had a population of 166,000—was Karaganda,[54] the center of a particularly notorious forced-labor complex. A number of other Soviet "cities" grew in the same way. Similarly, among the country's regions Karelo-Murmansk underwent the largest intercensal urban increase—by 5.6 times; and this growth was concentrated in the extreme northern districts, the site of a number of large forced-labor mining complexes. The intercensal increase in urban population in Central Siberia was by 3.1 times, in East Siberia by 3.8 times, in the Soviet Far East by 3.3 times.[55] In large part these figures reflect mining, logging, and construction camps, all peopled by forced laborers.

Lorimer attempts to estimate the total depletion in population growth during the whole of the intercensal period, using the inadequate data available.[56] By his interpretation, "the collectivization of agriculture, the

---

[53] Lorimer, *op. cit.,* p. 150.

[54] *Ibid.,* p. 148.

[55] *Ibid.,* p. 152.

[56] "The official vital statistics for 1927 were published in 1932. A preliminary survey of births and deaths in the European part of the U.S.S.R. and in the rural parts of each region in 1928 had already been published in 1930. Data transmitted in the Health Section of the League of Nations cover births and deaths for the European part of the R.S.F.S.R., Belorussia, and the Ukraine through 1928, and the series for the Ukraine extends through 1930. We have later official information about the crude birth rate in the whole U.S.S.R. in 1938; there is also official information on the ratio

settlement of the nomads, and the initial phases of the drive for the use of undeveloped resources and for rapid industrialization" resulted in a total "excess mortality" of about 5.5 million persons.[57] The figure can be taken as a probable minimum. Compared with the enumerated 1939 population, a projection made as part of the Second Five-Year Plan indicated a depletion of 13.5 million, and one by two Soviet actuaries a decline of 20.6 million.[58] A projection based in part on unpublished portions of the 1939 census concluded that "the total number of persons who died from hunger, exhaustion, and abuse during the famine of 1932–33 may have amounted to no less than eleven million." [59]

THE EVOLUTION OF SOVIET FAMILY POLICY [60]

In any society the family has three main functions: to perpetuate the population, to maintain cultural continuity from one generation to the next, and to determine the place of each newborn infant in the social structure. The family policy of totalitarian societies often reflects a conflict among these functions. On the one hand, the totalitarian state denies the legitimacy of the society it has supplanted, and it cannot tolerate the strong emotional bond between the old and the new inherent in the father-son relation. Nor can such a regime accept the principle that the son shall inherit, even as a base from which to rise, his father's place in society, for ultimately each person's status must be determined solely by his relation to the Party. On the other hand, a totalitarian regime finds the family something of a necessary evil, for its expansionist aims demand a rapidly growing population. The only way out of this contradiction would be to devise an alternative procreative institution, but all attempts to do this have failed.

The dilemma is clearly marked in Nazi institutions and policies. One avowed purpose of the *Hitlerjugend* (Hitler Youth), for instance, was

---

of deaths to births in 1938, and on changes in birth rates from 1935 through 1938. These supply by inference the death rate for 1938 and birth rates for 1935, 1936, and 1937. There is no precise official information on the movement of births and deaths in the intervening period" (*ibid.*, p. 112). It is reasonable to suppose that the vital statistics for the missing years were not published because they would have revealed too clearly the dimensions of the terror.

[57] *Ibid.*, p. 133.
[58] *Ibid.*, pp. 112–113.
[59] Martschenko, *op. cit.*, p. 1.
[60] This section is in part a summary of an article, William Petersen, "The Evolution of Soviet Family Policy," *Problems of Communism*, 5:5 (September–October, 1956), 29–35. See also Petersen, "Marx vs. Malthus: The Men and the Symbols," *Population Review* (Madras), 1:2 (July, 1957), 21–32.

to break down family influence, while on the other hand such antifeminist slogans as *Kinder, Kirche, Küche* (Children, Church, Kitchen) were given substance by decrees granting subsidies to parents of large families. One of Himmler's titles was Reich Commissar for Strengthening German Folkdom (or RKFDV), and he and his assistants proposed a number of means of improving—from the Nazi point of view—Europe's racial composition.[61] SS-men were given weekend leaves in order to impregnate women that the Party selected for their racial characteristics, and this effort to bypass the family, though not successful, is important as an indication of the regime's intent. In the words of Martin Bormann, a favored lieutenant of Himmler, "After the war, those women who have lost husbands, or who do not get husbands, should enter a marriage-like relationship with preferably one man, from which should result as many children as possible." The stipulation "after the war" was made, of course, only to prevent a drastic decline in morale: if the plan had been made public immediately, "not every soldier forthwith would desire that in event of his death his wife or his betrothed should beget children by another man." [62]

In the Soviet Union the Party has responded to the dilemma by a gradual shift of emphasis in its family policy. During the first 15 years or so of Soviet rule a generally consistent and complete policy was gradually developed.[63] All legal inequalities between the sexes were abolished. Bigamy, adultery, even incest were dropped from the statutory list of crimes. Religious marriage was no longer recognized by law, and even a civil ceremony was legally unnecessary and socially unimportant. There were perhaps a quarter-million "nonregistered marriages" by 1936, when the law was changed. Divorce could be had simply and cheaply at the wish of either partner, and at least among the small minority directly influenced by the Party line, it was frequent. That these early decrees were predominantly negative reflects their principal purpose: to hasten the

[61] See Robert L. Koehl, *RKFDV: German Resettlement and Population Policy, 1939–1945* (Cambridge: Harvard University Press, 1957).

[62] Oron J. Hale, "Adolf Hitler and the Post-War German Birthrate: An Unpublished Memorandum," *Journal of Central European Affairs,* 17:2 (July, 1957), 166–173. The whole memorandum is a remarkably interesting document, particularly for the intricate mixture of Nazi racism with such "progressive" ideas as, for instance, that the legal distinction between legitimate and illegitimate births must be abolished.

[63] See in particular the codes dated October 17, 1918, and November 19, 1926. Both are translated in Rudolf Schlesinger, *Changing Attitudes in Soviet Russia: The Family in the U.S.S.R.* (London: Routledge & Kegan Paul, 1949), pp. 33–41 and 154–168. A former member of the German Communist Party, Schlesinger is still sympathetic to the Soviet regime. In spite of its bias, the book is the best one on its subject.

disintegration of the patriarchal family of tsarist Russia. In Bukharin's words, "this formidable stronghold of all the turpitudes of the old regime" was the most pervasive and therefore, perhaps, the most powerful brake on the forward course of the revolution; it had to be removed.[64]

In spite of the assiduously propagated legend to the contrary, the right of parents to decide for themselves on the spacing and number of their children was never established as a Soviet norm. Opinion on the matter within the Party was divided, and policy therefore ambivalent, but in the dominant official view,

Birth control [was] . . . a bourgeois panacea for social ills which could have no place in a socialist society. [The Communists] interpreted the question from the point of view of a conscious limitation of the race rather than of permitting women to choose for themselves whether they wished to give birth to an endless succession of children.[65]

Since contraceptives were not generally available, even in the cities, abortion was the usual means for limiting family size. The official policy toward abortions was unambiguously hostile: they were legalized only in order to facilitate their rigid control. [66] According to the official in charge of Moscow's clinics, the Soviet Union of this period was "the country in which abortion is least practiced." [67] This was hardly the case in Moscow itself during the worst years of the dekulakization and famine. The rate in that city is not known for the early 1930's, but in 1934 there were 2.71 known abortions for every birth.[68]

While it combatted the traditional family, the state also tried to institute various alternatives to it. During the middle 1920's an attempt was made in Party circles to develop "socialist" marriage and other family ceremonies, and the regime also began to establish state-run nurseries and kindergartens as substitutes for the parents. Progress was slow, however, in translating these visions into actuality. Indeed, all these early efforts

[64] This early phase is now passed over lightly in Communist accounts. According to *Pravda* (May 10, 1959), for example, "Concern for children and mothers and for strengthening the family has always been a major task of the Soviet state" (translated in *Current Digest of the Soviet Press,* June 10, 1959).

[65] Jessica Smith, *Woman in Soviet Russia* (New York: Vanguard, 1928), p. 186.

[66] A woman desiring an operation was required to go before an official committee, which tried to convince her that it was her duty to society to give birth to her child. In cases of first pregnancy, requests were denied except when supported by urgent medical considerations. See Alice W. Field, *Protection of Women and Children in Soviet Russia* (New York: Dutton, 1932), p. 89; Mark G. Field, "The Re-Legalization of Abortion in Soviet Russia," *New England Journal of Medicine,* 255 (August 30, 1956), 421–427.

[67] Fannina W. Halle, *Woman in Soviet Russia* (London: Routledge, 1934), p. 144.

[68] Lorimer, *op. cit.,* p. 127.

to make over the family were more important as indications of future Soviet policy than for their immediate effect. The decrees of far-off Moscow were barely heard in the hamlets and certainly not rigidly enforced.

Beginning in the mid-1930's the line shifted toward tightening family bonds again. Marriages were stimulated by an official approval of romantic love of the old-fashioned bourgeois variety. Divorce was discouraged by a succession of increasingly restrictive measures, which ultimately removed all but political reasons as absolute grounds. These changes in policy culminated in a decree issued in 1944, [69] which re-established the distinction between civil and unregistered marriages, and hence between legitimate and illegitimate children. The stringent restrictions on abortion were replaced by a flat prohibition except when it was necessary to save the woman's life. Unmarried persons and parents of only one or two children were subjected to special taxes, while especially fertile mothers received progressively larger subsidies according to their procreation. A woman who had borne and raised ten or more children was entitled to the highest award—the title of "Heroine Mother," carrying a lump payment of 5,000 rubles plus 300 rubles monthly for four years.

The Soviet Union was not, of course, the only state to pay family subsidies. [70] In the 1930's the countries that had instituted such a policy included the full political range, from Sweden or Britain at one extreme to Nazi Germany or Fascist Italy at the other. This very fact suggests that various ends can be sought by this means, and it is necessary to estimate their purpose if family endowments are to be judged accurately. The most succinct way of doing this is to ask, *cui bono*—the individual, the family, or the state? In the classical liberal philosophy the stress is on the rights and duties of individuals; and liberal parties have usually opposed subsidies. Some liberals, however, have supported them in order to help equalize the distribution of income (since in general larger families are also poorer) or to improve the welfare of the indigent. In the Western world the most consistent proponents of family endowments have generally been Catholic parties. In the Catholic view the family rather than the individual is the natural unit of society, and various encyclicals have called for a "family wage" graded according to the number of dependents a breadwinner has rather than (or in addition to) his economic

---

[69] The full text is translated in Schlesinger, *op. cit.*, pp. 367 ff. See also W. Parker Mauldin, "Fertility Control in Communist Countries: Policy and Practice," in Milbank Memorial Fund, *op. cit.*, pp. 179–215.

[70] See D. V. Glass, *Population Policies and Movements in Europe* (Oxford: Clarendon, 1940); William Petersen, "Family Subsidies in the Netherlands," *Marriage and Family Living,* 17:3 (August, 1955), 260–266.

worth. A family subsidy is obviously a step in this direction. The same provision as decreed in a totalitarian country is not intended to assist either individuals or families. Its purpose is to strengthen the state, more specifically to induce its subjects to breed faster. In the Soviet Union the device of progressive premiums was, as Schlesinger has pointed out, primarily intended as "an incentive to the production of enormous numbers of children." By his estimate, a mother of six or more children could acquire an income sufficient to live modestly during her childbearing years.[71]

In the postwar period the main emphasis has been pronatalist, though with some at least apparent deviations. In 1958 the first official meeting of Soviet gynecologists in 22 years convened and discussed the advantages of birth control.[72] However, the general Party line is still hostile to neo-Malthusianism. The pronatalist state subsidies are still in effect. When abortion was once more legalized in 1955, the reason for the change was indicated in the preamble to the decree: "The repeal of the prohibition on abortions will permit the limitation of the harm caused to the health of women by abortions carried out outside of hospitals." The state's effort to glamorize marriage is suggested by Leningrad's "Palace of the Happy," where weddings are performed in blue or gold rooms with costly rugs, crystal chandeliers, and radios playing Tschaikovsky marches. Champagne is served in the restaurant; a souvenir shop is available on the premises.[73] In 1961 two similar palaces were opened in Moscow.

The usual explanation of the shift in Soviet family policy after the early 1930's has been, to borrow the words of Maurice Hindus, that "conservatism, in the sense of respect for the acceptable heritage of the past as well as for the fruitful achievements of the present, was edging radicalism out of the picture." [74] But this explanation seems somewhat wide of the mark. While it is difficult to find a single adjective to describe the Soviet society of this period, "conservative" scarcely characterizes the stupendous

---

[71] Schlesinger, *op. cit.*, pp. 368, 372, 397.

[72] Abraham Stone, of the American Planned Parenthood Association, addressed the meeting; see his report in *Planned Parenthood News,* Winter, 1958.

[73] "Palace of the Happy," *Komsomolskaya pravda,* October 24, 1959; translated in *Current Digest of the Soviet Press,* November 18, 1959. The reported crude birth rate for the first half of 1960, 26.5 as compared with 25.0 for 1959, was welcomed as an indication that the prior downward trend in fertility had been reversed; see *New York Times,* December 26, 1960.

[74] Maurice Hindus, "The Family in Russia," in Ruth Nanda Anshen, ed., *The Family, Its Function and Destiny* (New York: Harper, 1949), p. 117. This has been the dominant interpretation offered not only by Soviet apologists but also by profoundly anti-Communist writers like the Catholic sovietologist Nicholas S. Timasheff in his *The Great Retreat: The Growth and Decline of Communism in Russia* (New York: Dutton, 1946).

goals of the five-year plans, the collectivization of the peasants at the rate of 1 million a day (with 5 or 6 million discards), the Moscow show-trials, the *Gleichschaltung* of the arts and sciences, the territorial expansion in Europe and Asia.

Two factors underlay the decision to revitalize the family. The first was the huge population loss resulting from the collectivization program— which later was multiplied by World War II. The second was the need to restore stability to Soviet society, which the social revolution of 1928–1939 had broken down into a dangerously fluid mass.[75] In both phases the Soviet family was different from its Western counterpart. When the policy was ostensibly "liberal," individuals were not given the right freely to determine what size family they would have. When it became "conservative," religious and other traditional norms did not set the pattern of family life. During the whole of the Soviet regime, that is to say, the Party set family policy by what it interpreted the state's interests to be.

The effects of these policies are difficult to gauge, as they would be even with full and accurate statistics. Russia's crude birth rate has fluctuated greatly, but the general trend has been downward, from 45 or 50 in tsarist days to half that today. Would the decline have been greater without state props to natality? In all likelihood, yes; but an adequate analysis would require many more data than have ever been furnished. While the statistical thaw beginning in 1956 has released crude birth rates for the most recent years and for many areas of the Soviet Union, nothing has been given out that would permit a more refined analysis.

ETHNIC COMPOSITION OF THE U.S.S.R.

The nationality policy of the Soviet Union has undergone shifts similar to those in family policy, and the reason once again is an underlying ambivalence in the Party's general line. Three elements can be distinguished:

1. In the Marxist view class differences are basic, national differences superficial. The nonsocialist world is divided into exploiting capitalists and exploited workers, and national sentiments cutting across this "natural" dichotomy merely serve the capitalists as a class weapon. In this classic view, which predominated in socialist writings up to 1914, a worker has no fatherland, no country to which he owes allegiance. Thus,

---

[75] The trend in Soviet education policy was parallel. The first period was dominated by a calculated chaos, instituted "consciously and purposely in order to eliminate the power of the old school and undermine the domination of the pre-Revolution intellectuals." Then, when the system had been reduced to a malleable pulp, it was restructured as a prop to Soviet authority. See Fred M. Hechinger, *The Big Red Schoolhouse* (New York: Doubleday, 1959), p. 49.

when both the German and the French socialists supported their governments in World War I, Lenin used this as the pretext to split from them and set up a Russian-controlled Comintern.

2. On the other hand, an important element of socialist propaganda was to promote the nationalist aspirations of minority peoples in the Russian, Austro-Hungarian, and German empires. As early as 1896 the socialist international declared itself in favor of "national self-determination." From the beginning, the meaning given this formula, even as an expression of intent, was principally negative—that is, the absence of oppression. Lenin asserted, however, that national self-determination included the right of any minority to secede from a multinational state, and this right was guaranteed in the first Soviet constitution. Actually, during the very process of formation of the Soviet Union, its troops were used to put down the independent, sometimes socialist, regimes in Georgia, the Ukraine, and Poland. In short, the agitation for "self-determination," as Fainsod puts it, has been merely tactical, "useful in stirring up the forces of minority unrest and in winning supporters among the oppressed nationalities. . . . But . . . to the extent that it fed the flames of nationalism, it set in motion fissiparous tendencies which would ultimately have to be harnessed and bridled." [76]

3. Soviet nationality policy has been greatly influenced by the actual dominance of Great Russians in the country's important institutions. For example, while Russians constituted only slightly more than half the population of the country in the middle 1920's, they made up almost three-quarters of the Party membership.[77] This Russian paramountcy was strongly reinforced during the 1930's. Once the conflict with Germany started, the Party reacted to what it termed the "Great Patriotic War" by reviving tsarist symbols and incorporating them with those of Communism.[78] Many Western analysts, therefore, have interpreted the Russian patriotism of the Soviet Union as merely a device, an ideological weapon against Nazism; but even the premise of this argument is dubious. Many were alienated by the change, both those unable to unlearn the hatred of tsarism the Party had taught them and, more significantly, the

---

[76] Merle Fainsod, *How Russia Is Ruled* (Cambridge: Harvard University Press, 1957), pp. 58–59.

[77] McClosky and Turner, *op. cit.*, p. 253. The ethnic composition of the Party at later dates, or of such other institutions as, for instance, the NKVD, is not available.

[78] A Soviet tank brigade was awarded the title "Guards," which recalled the special bodyguard of the Tsar, once the object of Bolshevik hatred. Three new military orders were created, named after two tsarist generals, Suvorov and Kutusov, and Alexander Nevsky, a Grand Duke, member of the ruling house, revered by the Orthodox Church as one of its saints. In the new national anthem that replaced the *Internationale,* the tsarist past was also amalgamated with the Soviet present into a messianic patriotism.

ethnic minorities in the Soviet Union, who made up about half the country's population. It is difficult to imagine that the non-Russians joined in the war effort more enthusiastically once even the facade of federalism was all but abandoned.[79]

The fate of the minority peoples in the Soviet Union (and, with the extension of its influence, in Eastern Europe), thus, has been based on these three doctrines: (1) the Marxist and particularly the Bolshevik opposition to nationalism, (2) the Communist slogan of national self-determination, and (3) the growth of Russian patriotism from the First Five-Year Plan on. National self-determination has been consistently followed only at the propagandistic level of folk dancing and the like. With respect to more significant elements of minority cultures, the Party has vacillated, sometimes encouraging minority-language schools, newspapers, and theaters, sometimes banning them. Over the whole period of Soviet rule the dominant trend has been toward russification.

The relevance of Party policy is ubiquitous. Even the simplest statistical fact—how many ethnic groups exist—has marked political overtones. National self-determination of a kind has been encouraged for small minorities, in order to prevent them from coalescing into more meaningful but also more powerful units. The Bashkir Republic is one instance of this policy of divide and rule: "the task of Bashkir nationalism from the Soviet point of view was to render impossible the emergence of a Moslem State on the borders of Europe and Asia, which might have covered over 150,000 square miles with a population of over 5,000,000." [80] Some 180

---

[79] The revival of Russian nationalism included even the retrospective approbation of tsarist imperialism. Indeed, the *Literary Gazette* chastised one writer for speaking of the tsarist "conquest" of minority peoples: "Do not the author and editor know that as a result of the union (and not 'conquest') the Kirghiz people escaped from the danger of being enslaved by other states . . . far more backward than Russia?" "In spite of the negative sides of the policy of colonisation of Russian Tsarism," we are similarly informed in the Soviet historical journal, "the entry of the Kirghiz into the Russian Federation represented an advance." Soviet historians have the duty, according to the same journal, to reveal fully "the importance of the progressive Russian civilisation for the development of the civilisation of other peoples." Respectively, *Literaturnaya Gazeta*, December 7, 1947; *Voprosy Istorii*, 1950, no. 7, p. 130; *ibid.*, 1949, no. 11, pp. 3 ff. All three citations are from Klaus Mehnert, *Stalin versus Marx: The Stalinist Historical Doctrine* (London: Allen & Unwin, 1952), pp. 93–104.

[80] Walter Kolarz, *Russia and Her Colonies* (3rd ed.; New York: Praeger, 1955), p. 41. "Soviet nationalities policy, if . . . applied to. . . . Nigeria, for instance, would have consisted in creating national States for the Hausa, Yoruba, Ibo, Fulani, etc., and other states of a lower order for the smaller Nigerian nationalities. These 'States' would have no links with each other, but would be directly subordinate to a central imperial government. Every important step in the economic life of these 'national States' would be decided by this far-away central administration" (*ibid.*, p. 310).

TABLE 15-1. Census Population of the Soviet Union, by Some
of the Important Nationalities, 1926, 1939, and 1959

	Population (thousands)			Percentage Change	
	1926	1939	1959	1926 to 1939	1939 to 1959
U.S.S.R.	147,028	170,467	208,827	+16	+22
Major Nationalities a					
Russian	77,791	99,020	114,588	+27	+16
Ukrainian	31,195	28,070	36,981	—10	+32 b
Belorussian	4,739	5,267	7,829	+11	+49 b
Uzbek	3,955	4,844	6,004	+22	+24
Tatar	3,478	4,300	4,969	+24	+16
Kazakh	3,968	3,099	3,581	—22	+16
Azerbaidzhanian	1,707	2,275	2,929	+33	+29
Armenian	1,568	2,152	2,787	+37	+30
Georgian	1,821	2,249	2,650	+24	+18
Lithuanian	43	32	2,326	—24	b
Jewish	2,672	3,020	2,268	+13	—25
Moldavian	279	260	2,214	— 7	b
Displaced Nationalities					
German	1,247	1,424	1,619	+14	+14
Kirghiz	763	884	974	+16	+10
Chechen	319	408	418	+28	+ 2
Ingush	74	92	106	+24	+15
Balkar	33	43	42	+28	— 2
Karachay	55	76	81	+37	+ 7
Kalmyk	129	134	106	+ 4	—21

a Those with more than 2 million in 1959, in order of size at that date.
b Increase due to annexation of new territory.
Sources: Frank Lorimer, *The Population of the Soviet Union: History and Prospects*
(League of Nations; Princeton: Princeton University Press, 1946), Table 55; *Pravda*,
February 4, 1960, translated in *Current Digest of the Soviet Press*, March 2, 1960.

nationalities, the usual figure cited in Soviet statistics, [81] is double the
number of peoples with even a minimum cultural or linguistic self-expression; and only 30 to 45 nationalities are generally represented in formal
institutions.

The Soviet population has been classified by nationality in each of the
three major censuses, as shown in Table 15-1. These figures are difficult
to interpret, however, for a recorded intercensal growth or decline can be
the consequence of any of three factors:

[81] In the preliminary 1959 census report, only 108 nationalities were listed separately, the smallest with 400 members, and the rest combined into a miscellaneous
category.

1. *Statistical reclassification*. The counts in the three censuses, it must be emphasized, are not wholly comparable. Even the Russian word translated as "nationality" was different (*narodnost* in 1926, *natsionalnost* in 1939 and 1959), and the returns in 1939 and 1959 were far less complete than in 1926. It is reasonable to suppose that some of these adjustments were made to disguise the size of the depletion of the peoples that suffered especially from one or another policy.

2. *Assimilation*. Between 1926 and 1939, there was an absolute decrease in most of the minorities not identified with a U.S.S.R. republic or district—Poles, Estonians, Latvians, Lithuanians, Bulgarians, Kurds, Iranians, and Chinese. In most cases the presumed reason was that these scattered groups assimilated to one of the major Soviet nationalities, particularly the Russian. It is likely that a large part of the decrease in the number of Ukrainians reflected their self-identification as "Russians." From 1926 to 1959, while the total population increased by 42.0 per cent and the Russians by 47.3 per cent, the Ukrainians increased by only 18.5 per cent—in spite of the annexation of territories with large Ukrainian populations. There was a decline in the number of enumerated Ukrainians living outside the Ukraine from 8.0 million in 1926 to 5.1 million in 1959; and most of this loss was presumably through assimilation.[82]

3. *Differential growth*. The Ukraine bore the brunt of the enforced collectivization and the consequent famine, and a portion of the decline in the number of Ukrainians represents the price they paid for the social transformation. The demographic effect of the parallel policy of forcing nomads to settle on the land, similarly, can probably be measured by the figures given for some of the nomadic peoples. The reported number of Kazakhs, for instance, decreased by 869,000 between 1926 and 1939; and since this is a group whose age structure and social norms favored rapid procreation, we should have expected an increase at least at the average rate for the whole country, or by 631,000 persons. Thus, some 1.5 million disappeared during the enforced "denomadization," when Kazakh herds were depleted by about four-fifths. The virtually stationary Kalmyk population presumably reflects the somewhat less devastating effects of the policy on this nomadic people.

The nationalities subjected to special terror during the 1930's included those at both ends of the cultural spectrum—large minorities with a cultural level comparable to the Russians', such as the Ukrainians and the

---

[82] Solomon M. Schwarz, "K natsional'nomu voprosu v SSSR," *Sotsialisticheskii Vestnik,* April, 1960, pp. 63–64. See also Lorimer, *op. cit.,* p. 139.

ethnic Germans, and more primitive, usually smaller, peoples, many of which had a long and bloody history of opposition to russification. In 1941, when the Nazis broke the Friendship Pact and invaded Russia, in many places they were welcomed as liberators, especially by peoples who had undergone particularly rapid collectivization or denomadization. During and immediately following World War II the Soviet government dissolved four Autonomous Republics and expunged four major and several minor peoples from the ethnographic list. In his famous speech to the Twentieth Party Congress in 1956, Khrushchev characterized these mass deportations as "monstrous." The policy of the Soviet government, in his words, was "to make whole nations responsible for inimical activity, including women, children, old people, Communists and [members of the Young Communist League], to use mass repression against them, and to expose them to misery and suffering for the hostile acts of individual persons or groups of persons." [83]

The "unpeoples," as Bertram Wolfe terms them, include the following:

The almost 400,000 Volga Germans. In August 1941, only two months after the war started, the Volga German Autonomous Soviet Socialist Republic was dissolved and the German-speaking people were forcibly removed, part to Siberia, part to industrial areas in the Urals and the Kuznetsk Basin. "Probably many of the million and a half persons of German culture living in other parts of the Soviet Union were also affected." [84]

Perhaps as many as a million persons in the Caucasus, especially Chechen, Ingush, Balkars, and Karachay—who were all deported *in toto* —but also Osetins and others. Most seem to have been shipped to Central Asia, where, according to the estimate of a Chechen refugee scholar, about half died of typhus, starvation, and hardship.[85] The Chechen-Ingush ASSR and the Autonomous Province of Karachay were abolished,

---

[83] Nikita S. Khrushchev, "The Crimes of the Stalin Era: Special Report to the 20th Congress of the Communist Party of the Soviet Union, Closed Session, February 24–25, 1956," *New Leader*, section 2, July 16, 1956, pp. 44–45. This edition of the speech is valuable for the annotations by Boris I. Nicolaevsky. Khrushchev's denunciation should not be taken as evidence of a fundamental change in policy. As Party chief in the Ukraine, Khrushchev had been an important participant in implementing the terrorist policy he later condemned. His purpose in 1956 was to supplant the "collective leadership" in the Party by his dictatorship, and to do this he tried to win favor by attacking the safely deceased Stalin.

[84] Frederick C. Barghoorn, *Soviet Russian Nationalism* (New York: Oxford University Press, 1956), p. 80. See also R. Conquest, *The Soviet Deportation of Nationalities* (London: Macmillan, 1960), Ch. 4 and *passim*.

[85] A. Avtorkhanov, cited in Barghoorn, *op. cit.*, p. 81.

and the Kabardinian-Balkar ASSR dropped the second half of its name.

Over 100,000 Kalmyks, who were punished when a small number of this minority voluntarily withdrew with the retreating German army in 1943. At first, the population as a whole had been officially commended for its patriotic behavior, and the Soviet government never did complain of Kalmyk treachery. But the Kalmyk ASSR was absorbed into the Astrakhan Province, and the population was deported *en masse*.

About 200,000 Crimean Tatars, who were also expelled from their traditional homeland in 1944. "The equally 'unreliable' Greek and German colonists have disappeared from [Crimea] . . . The Russian-Ukrainian element which only a short time ago had a narrow majority over the combined non-Slav peoples now dominates the peninsula." [86]

According to Khrushchev, "The Ukrainians avoided meeting this fate only because there were too many of them and there was no place to which to deport them. Otherwise, [Stalin] would have deported them also." [87]

For 12 years or so, these peoples disappeared from the record. The edition of the *Great Soviet Encyclopedia* published in this period, for instance, listed no Germans, no Chechen or Ingush, no Tatars or Kalmyks. In most cases place names in the local languages were abolished and replaced by Russian ones. As happens so often in the Soviet Union, the new line was also projected back into past history. The *Great Soviet Encyclopedia,* for instance, speaks of the founding of the "Kabardine" Republic in 1936, whereas at that time its official name was actually "Kabardine-Balkar." [88] All together, the depopulated areas totaled about 60,000 square miles, or the size of South Carolina and Maine together. The deportations (except in the case of the Volga Germans) were not a preventive but a punitive measure, carried out when the war was virtually over and victory assured. The charge that the Chechen and Ingush collaborated with the Germans, as made in the official Soviet announcement, must be contrasted with the fact that the German troops, stopped short of the Chechen-Ingush Republic, never occupied it.

During World War II the Soviet Union annexed territories inhabited

---

86 Kolarz, *op. cit.,* p. 81.

87 Khrushchev, "The Crimes," *op. cit.,* pp. 44–45. According to the report, this remark was greeted by "laughter and animation in the hall."

88 Conquest, *op. cit.,* p. 61.

by over 21 million persons, principally non-Russians, as detailed in Table 15-2. A considerable number was considered to be unreliable and was also deported to Siberia. From the three Baltic countries, by Conquest's rough estimate, the deportations totaled more than a million, or about one-sixth of the population.[89]

TABLE 15-2. Territorial Changes in the U.S.S.R., 1939–1945

Date	Region	Size (sq. km.)	Population (thousands)
November, 1939	Polish provinces (excl. Vilna)	194,800	12,500 [a]
March, 1940	Finnish provinces	35,100	420 [a]
August, 1940	Rumanian provinces (Bessarabia and North Bukovina)	50,400	3,700
August, 1940	Lithuania (incl. Vilna)	59,800	2,925
August, 1940	Latvia	65,800	1,951
August, 1940	Estonia	47,500	1,122
September, 1944	Petchenga Raion (Murmansk)	10,480	5
September, 1944	Tuva Autonomous Oblast	150,000	70
October, 1944	Memel territory	2,850	150
August, 1945	Kaliningrad Oblast (Koenigsberg area)	9,000	400
August, 1945	Byalistock-Suwalki and Przemysl areas—lost to Poland	−14,200	−850
September, 1945	Transcarpathian area	12,620	800
September, 1945	Karafuto (South Sakhalin)	36,090	420
September, 1945	Kurile Islands	10,100	5
	Net gain, November, 1939– September, 1945	670,340	23,618

[a] The cited figures do not take into account concomitant losses. Following the partition of Poland, an exchange of populations between Germany and the U.S.S.R. resulted in a net loss of 260,000 persons from the Soviet-annexed Polish provinces; similarly, from the Soviet-incorporated Finnish areas some 415,000 Karelians were evacuated to Finland.

Source: Abram Bergson and Hans Heymann, Jr., *Soviet National Income and Product, 1940–48* (New York: Columbia University Press, 1954), Table 1, p. 6. Copyright 1954, The RAND Corporation.

From September 17, 1939 to June 1941 [that is, during the period of the Soviet-Nazi Friendship Pact], 1,692,000 Poles, Jews, Ukrainians, and Byelorussians were forcibly taken from their homes and deported to Russia. This number included 230,-000 soldiers and officers of the Polish Army; 990,000 civilians, who were deported because of their "nationalistic bourgeois background"; 250,000 political "class enemies"; 210,000 Poles conscripted into the Red Army and then sent deep into the

[89] *Ibid.,* p. 188. As he remarks, "Practical, theoretical and propaganda difficulties rather than any lack of ill-will seem to have been all that stood in the way of the complete dispersion of these nations too."

Soviet Union; and 12,000 other Poles gathered forcibly from the Baltic area. Among the deportees were 160,000 children and adolescents.[90]

Then, in 1957, the list of "autonomous" republics and territories was expanded to include again some of those that had been expunged, and some of the deported people—of those who had survived the 12 years of resettlement, often combined with forced labor—were permitted to return.[91] The re-established Chechen-Ingush Republic does not have the same boundaries: some of the Ingush territory was not regained, and in its place the inhabitants were compensated with an area marked "sand" on the official map.[92] Some of the deported peoples had not yet been permitted to return by the time of this writing.

Soviet policy toward the Jews deserves special attention, for from the revolution on propaganda has contrasted it with tsarist or Nazi programs. Actually, Soviet policy has never been entirely free of anti-Semitism.[93] While many Jews of tsarist Russia were socialists, few were Bolsheviks.[94] The Bolshevik victory meant that Jews were persecuted as members of a religious faith, as small businessmen, as nationalists, as socialists; but for a time the pogroms that had been endemic in tsarist Russia disappeared. Specific anti-Semitism, opposition to Jews as Jews, developed during the 1930's. According to a Communist source of 1928, "dozens" of anti-Semitic letters were received daily in the offices of the Young Communist League, and both this and the Party itself were infected.[95] A number of the main defendants in the Moscow show-trials of the mid-1930's were Jews, and they were generally denounced in the press as, for example, "Trotsky (Bronstein)," though the Party names of non-Jewish defend-

[90] Edward J. Rozek, *Allied Wartime Diplomacy: A Pattern in Poland* (New York: Wiley, 1958), p. 46. "These figures were compiled by the Polish Embassy in the U.S.S.R. during the period from August 1941 to April 1943 and are based on the testimony of over 18,000 eyewitnesses—Poles who passed through prisons, concentration camps, and forced labor camps in the Soviet Union. This collection is now in the Hoover Library on War, Revolution, and Peace in Stanford, California" (*ibid.,* p. 66, n. 27).

[91] *New York Times,* February 12 and May 5, 1957.

[92] Conquest, *op. cit.* p. 173.

[93] Reporting on the 1907 Party Congress, which he had attended as a Georgian delegate, Stalin said: "One of the Bolsheviks (Comrade Aleksinskii, I think) jokingly said that the Mensheviks were a Jewish faction, while the Bolsheviks were truly Russian, and so it might be a good idea for us Bolsheviks to start a pogrom within the party" (quoted in Solomon M. Schwarz, *The Jews in the Soviet Union,* Syracuse: Syracuse University Press, 1951, p. 260).

[94] In 1918, when the Party decided to publish a Yiddish newspaper, only one out of the three editors so much as knew the language (*ibid.,* p. 94).

[95] *Ibid.,* pp. 243 ff.

ants were not thus elucidated. Anti-Semitism was strongly reinforced by the Nazi-Soviet Friendship Pact of 1939–1941, and it survived the German invasion of Russia.[96]

In the postwar period, in both Russia and its East European satellites, the campaign against Jews developed from opposition to "cosmopolitans" or "Zionist bourgeois nationalists" to virulent, undisguised anti-Semitism.[97] In 1956 one J. B. Salzberg, a Canadian Communist, visited the Soviet Union and discussed the treatment of Jews there in a two-hour session with Khrushchev. He was so outraged by the Soviet leader's anti-Semitism that, on his return to the West, he issued a statement demanding an "open polemic" against Khrushchev in Communist parties. This was printed in the *Morgen Freiheit*, the Yiddish-language Communist newspaper published in New York, which also gave the statement indirect editorial support.[98] As Khrushchev said, the trouble with Jews is that "they do not like collective work, group discipline. . . . They are individualists. . . . Jews are interested in everything, they want to probe into everything, they discuss everything, and end up by having profoundly different opinions." [99]

A NOTE ON NAZI GENOCIDE

In this analysis of the population of totalitarian societies the Soviet Union has been used as a case study. The reasons for this choice, as indicated in the introductory paragraphs, is that (as contrasted with Communist China) there are enough data to analyze over several decades, and that (as contrasted with Nazi Germany) the Soviet system is of both historical and topical interest. Yet one must consider the question, how typical really is the Soviet Union; is not Nazism a phenomenon *sui ge-*

[96] For many details, see *ibid.*, pp. 334 ff. See also Erich Goldhagen, "Communism and Anti-Semitism," *Problems of Communism*, 9:3 (May–June, 1960), 35–43.

[97] Some of the most informative accounts appeared in *Commentary*, published by the American Jewish Committee. See, for example, Peter Meyer, "Soviet Anti-Semitism in High Gear," February, 1953, pp. 115–120; Franz Borkenau, "Was Malenkov Behind the Anti-Semitic Plot?" May, 1953, pp. 438–466; Walter Z. Laqueur, "Soviet Policy and Jewish Fate," October, 1956, pp. 303–312; A. Wiseman and O. Pick, "Soviet Jews under Khrushchev," February, 1959, pp. 127–132. A more detailed account of East European Jews is given in Peter Meyer *et al.*, *The Jews in the Soviet Satellites* (Syracuse: Syracuse University Press, 1953).

[98] *New York Times*, December 25, 1956. The British Communist Professor Hyman Levy also openly attacked Soviet anti-Semitism; see *Time*, May 5, 1958.

[99] Nikita S. Khrushchev in an interview with Serge Goussard, *Le Figaro* (Paris), April 9, 1958; cited in Goldhagen, "Communism and Anti-Semitism," *op. cit.*

neris? It is indeed, in some respects, but in others not at all. The parallels are obvious in the ubiquitous control by the Party, in the pronatal policies, the deaths imposed by the terror apparatus, the forced migrations. The main difference lies in the Nazi campaign to exterminate the Jews. In what ways was this specific, in what ways part of the general pattern? [100]

Nazi anti-Semitism, which in the 1920's had been used to rouse revolutionary passions, was rationalized very soon after the Party came to power. "There is no more beerhouse brawling and indiscriminate parading of uniforms and banners. The State Enemy must now be defined by police regulations"—namely, the Nuremberg Laws, which divided the inhabitants of Germany into two castes, "citizens" and "subjects," and established suitable relations between them.[101] Until the outbreak of the war, the denigration of Jews was by legal or quasi-legal methods—ousting them from professions or business, fining them a billion marks to pay for the damage in anti-Semitic riots, and so on.

The second step was the forcible emigration of German Jewry. There was an attempt to induce the Western powers to ransom Jews to assist in moving them, for instance, to Madagascar. When this plan failed, "the most fanatical of the racialists," as Reitlinger terms Reinhardt Heydrich, believed that small nations might be used as compulsory dumping grounds for the Jews of Germany; and this policy continued for the first year and a half of the war. Some thousands of Jews were bundled into nine freight trains and transported to the Free French Zone; many more were pushed into Poland, to join there the 2 million Jews who had fallen into the Gestapo's hands when the Nazi-Soviet Friendship Pact was signed. Subsequently thousands more were shipped still farther east, particularly to Riga and Minsk.

Preparatory to these moves, both German and Polish Jews were congregated into ghettos. In the fall of 1940 the Warsaw ghetto was enclosed, and 360,000 Jews were concentrated in an area that normally housed 160,000 people. It was left to the Jewish welfare organization to provide food, mainly a weak brew. "By the end of 1941 there were 100,000 people living on this soup which had sometimes to be made of hay." [102] The con-

---

[100] The principal source for this account is Gerald Reitlinger's *The Final Solution (op. cit.)*, which is to be commended as much for its unemotional style as for its impeccable scholarship. A briefer account is Léon Poliakov, *Harvest of Hate: The Nazi Program for the Destruction of the Jews of Europe* (Syracuse: Syracuse University Press, 1954).

[101] Reitlinger, *op. cit.*, p. 7.

[102] *Ibid.*, pp. 58–59.

ditions were murderous, and many died. But this was not yet mass murder.

"It does not seem," in Reitlinger's opinion, "that at this period systematic extermination of the Jews was considered." [103] Indeed, in 1939 two SS-men were court-martialed for murdering 50 Jews and sentenced to nine and three years of imprisonment, respectively.[104] The Nazis' *Endlösung*—final solution—of the Jewish problem meant total emigration until some time in 1941. From that date on it meant total extermination. The reasons for this shift [105] are obscure, though it seems to be related to the course of the war. In that year the Soviet Union, the United States, and Japan became belligerents; it became in fact World War II.

The main death camp was four kilometers from Auschwitz (in Polish, Oswiecim), a small town in Upper Silesia. It was adjacent to several rail lines, close to forced-labor camps, and yet in a relatively isolated site. Its director, Rudolf Hoess, a former convict, stated at the Nuremberg trial that under his administration 2.5 million persons were killed at the camp. According to Reitlinger's estimate, the actual total of those killed was less than a million.[106] Whatever figure is correct, it is significant that Hoess, the ambitious Nazi bureaucrat, chose the higher. His SS service file commended him as "a true pioneer in this field." At the railroad siding, two SS-physicians divided newcomers between able-bodied workers and victims by pointing their walking-sticks right or left. Their rule of thumb depended mostly on age and sex, and the percentage denoted fit for labor varied greatly from one shipment to another. Hoess used hydrogen cyanide crystals for killing his charges, rather than the less efficient carbon monoxide from internal-combustion engines. He initiated a routine deception that saved time and trouble: candidates for gassing were informed that they were to take a shower, so that they undressed themselves and walked into the gas chamber. The conditions of the forced laborers at Auschwitz, on the other hand, were not different from those in other Nazi camps.

[103] *Ibid.*, p. 34. Cf. Poliakov, *op. cit.*, p. 2, where the author states the same view.
[104] Reitlinger, *op. cit.*, p. 33.
[105] About the same time, an important change took place in Party line concerning the ethnic Germans outside the borders of the Reich. During the 1930's, these enclaves were regarded as advance posts of a potential expansion, German minorities that needed the protection of the "mother country." Actually some 400,000 ethnic Germans (plus another 500,000 Reich Germans) were moved either to Germany or to the portion of Poland that had been incorporated. Many ethnic Germans were unwilling to leave their ancestral homes, and during the period of the Friendship Pact, Nazis brought them into line by threatening to turn them over to the NKVD. See Koehl, *op. cit.*, pp. 34, 190, 91.
[106] Reitlinger, *op. cit.*, pp. 460–461.

Door to a gas chamber at the Dachau concentration camp. The words under the skull read: "Caution, gas. Mortal danger. Do not open." The sign above gives time when door may be opened again. (Documentation Française)

That prisoners should be cheated of their food and forced to "organise" in order to live, that they should be beaten to death at their work in order to give their guards exercise, that they should drop from exhaustion at evening *Appell* because of the inability of these guards to count, were inevitable things, given the nature of their masters.[107]

As the German armies moved east into Russia, they were followed by four *Einsatzgruppen,* or Action Groups, which operated in the field. Action Group A was assigned to the Baltic countries, up to the outskirts of Leningrad; Action Group B to the area of White Russia between Warsaw and Moscow; Action Group C to the major portion of the Ukraine, in-

[107] *Ibid.,* p. 121.

cluding Kiev and Kharkov; and Action Group D to Crimea and the Caucasus. Their function was to check the conduct of German military commanders, and to supervise the murder of Jews, Gypsies, and Communist commissars.

Basically, the procedure of "Resettlement" was the same everywhere. Jews who could produce no sort of protection certificate were collected in market places or large buildings, herded into trains, buses, lorries, or sledge carts and taken to the woods or moors, where the burial pits had been prepared. . . . A Semitic appearance or a neighbourly denunciation was enough. Thus numerous Tartars, Gipsies, and people of Oriental appearance were often included.[108]

British troops clearing the Belsen concentration camp. (Imperial War Museum, London)

How many Jews did the Nazis kill? In the Nuremberg indictment in 1945 the figure 5,721,800 was given, and in most subsequent accounts this had been rounded up to 6 million. This total was derived by subtracting the number of survivors from the prewar Jewish population, which for many countries is highly conjectural. Reitlinger has compiled a table

[108] *Ibid.,* pp. 203–204.

from SS records, which he believes are fairly accurate and err, if at all, in exaggerating the extraordinary mortality. His estimate of the total number of Jews killed is between 4,194,200 and 4,581,200.[109] More than a third of the missing European Jews, and of German Jews perhaps as many as four-fifths, died from overwork, disease, hunger, and neglect. Two-thirds, or roughly 3 million, were exterminated directly. Even these figures, monstrous as they are, understate the number of Nazi victims, since they pertain only to Jews, who constituted the major component. The total would be considerably larger if it included also other "inferior" "races" (Gypsies, Slavs, Balkan peoples), political opponents (democrats, Catholics, socialists, Communists), and bystanders.

The differences and parallels between the extraordinary mortality under Nazi and Soviet auspices can be summed up as follows:

1. The Nazis lost the war. Their own statements, their own records, were used to make a legal case against them at Nuremberg. Otherwise we would have to depend mainly on the testimony of former camp inmates, not generally an unbiased source. Until almost the end of the war, a false death certificate was in principle prepared for each person exterminated, and this fabrication might have withstood any but minute scrutiny. For even when the evidence became overwhelming, the ordinary man in the West found it difficult to believe that death-camps were part of the world he thought he knew.

2. The Nazi ideology was racist; the Communists oppose class enemies. The difference is important but not fundamental, for terror generates a momentum of its own. Both the Nazi and the Soviet terror machines used hardened criminals under the supervision of self-hardened zealots, and under these circumstances the careful discrimination between the "guilty" —however defined—and the innocent was impossible. The terror began in different sectors of the population and was concentrated there, but in both cases spread to the whole society.

3. The Soviet terror is more rational, or less rational, than the Nazi. Both points have been made by various writers, and both have an element of truth. The Soviet regime has never erected gas chambers and crematoriums, but it has not hesitated to exterminate large numbers of persons by other means. The massacre of some 14,000 Polish army officers in Katyn Woods is a well known example.[110] Moreover, large areas of the Soviet Union constitute, under the conditions of life imposed on camp dwellers, natural death-camps. Forced labor was apparently more im-

109 *Ibid.,* p. 501.
110 For a survey of the evidence, see Rozek, *op. cit.,* Chs. 4–5.

portant in Soviet than in Nazi camps.[111] The Communist rationalization of forced labor is that it "reforges" the criminal, whereas the dominant purpose of Nazi camps was to punish. Nazi prisoners were poorly fed, but until shortages developed throughout Germany, probably the food was better than in Soviet camps, where differential hunger is used as a spur to harder work.[112]

In neither system is the terror merely instrumental, and it cannot be adequately analyzed only in terms of its alleged purpose, whether punitive or economic. Totalitarian systems are too inflexible to be very efficient. In the middle of a war for its survival, the Nazi regime should not—in rational terms—have used scarce manpower, supplies, and transport to eliminate a scapegoat that would soon be needed to enable the Party to escape censure for postwar shortages. Similarly, the rationality of the forced-labor system of the Soviet Union is questionable. Many—though not all—of the tasks could have been performed more efficiently by free workers; and if police force was required to get anyone to work in the most inhospitable areas, in rational terms the prisoners should have been better fed and clothed, so that they would live longer.

In short, the principal drive in a totalitarian society is to maximize the Party's power, and this generic feature overrides the specific aspects of this or that example.

SOVIET POPULATION SINCE THE WAR

Hitler's armies invaded Russia on June 22, 1941; and they moved into Soviet territory like a hot knife through butter. Why was the advance so rapid? In 1937 the officer corps of the Soviet army had been decimated: Marshal Tukhachevsky, eight generals, and an estimated 15,000 officers were purged. In Khrushchev's words:

During these years [1937–1941] repressions were instituted against certain parts of military cadres beginning literally at the company and battalion commander level and extending to the higher military centers. . . . [Some] managed to survive, despite severe tortures to which they were subjected in the prisons. . . . However, many such commanders perished in camps and the Army saw them no more.[113]

---

[111] See, e.g., Reitlinger, *op. cit.*, p. 115; McClosky and Turner, *op. cit.*, p. 498.

[112] A number of persons who were interned in both Nazi and Soviet camps have written interesting comparative reports. See in particular Margarete Buber, *Under Two Dictators* (London: Gollancz, 1949). Mrs. Buber, a German oppositionist Communist, was arrested in Moscow in 1938 and sent to Siberia. During the Nazi-Soviet Friendship Pact, she and a number of other former German Communists were handed over to the Gestapo, and she spent another five years in the Ravensbrück camp.

[113] Khrushchev, "The Crimes," *op. cit.*, pp. 39–40.

According to Khrushchev, the Party (he said "Moscow") refused to build defensive works along the border, since the Germans might regard these as a provocation.[114]

It is also relevant that the war came after a decade of dekulakization and denomadization, of forced industrialization, of russification. A sizable portion of the population was inclined to welcome any enemy of the regime.[115] During the first four months of the war the Germans took more than 2 million Russian prisoners; by March 1, 1942, the number was 3.6 million.[116] "From the first days of the conflict thousands of ex-Soviet soldiers offered to serve in the ranks of the *Wehrmacht*," and before the war was over at least a half million, and perhaps as many as a million, did so.[117] It is true that the cheering crowds that often greeted the advance of the Nazi columns as liberators were soon disabused of their illusion. In agony, the Soviet peoples learned that the enemy of one dictatorship can be an equally ruthless dictatorship. Ernst Koch, Reich Commissioner for the Ukraine, put it succinctly: "We are a master race, which must remember that the least German laborer is racially and biologically a thousand times more valuable than the population here." [118]

The number of Soviet subjects killed in the war was as great as the record of the 1930's would lead one to expect. The Soviet Union has steadfastly refused to cooperate with the United Nations agencies that collect and publish the world's population data, and one reason certainly is that such figures would have revealed its disastrous military weakness.

One interesting attempt to estimate the war losses was made by Eason, whose results are summarized in Table 15-3.[119] Amazingly, these figures are realistic, as can be shown by analyzing the age structure. Note the

---

[114] *Ibid.*, p. 38.

[115] "When in April and May of 1940 German missions arrived in eastern Poland to register the refugees from western Poland for the return to their homes, an overwhelming majority of Jews, as well as Poles, declared their willingness to live under German occupation. . . . The Germans agreed to accept all Poles who were registered but allowed only one transport of Jews, so the latter mingled with the Poles in order to overcome the restriction. Others bribed their way by paying off German guards with money or jewelry. Still others attempted to cross the borders illegally. Most of those Jews who remained were immediately deported to Siberia and Kazakhstan" (Rozek, *op. cit.*, p. 50).

[116] George Fischer, *Soviet Opposition to Stalin: A Case Study in World War II* (Cambridge: Harvard University Press, 1952), p. 3.

[117] *Ibid.*, pp. 44–45.

[118] Quoted in *ibid.*, p. 201, n. 18.

[119] See also Galina V. Selegen, "The First Report on the Recent Population Census in the Soviet Union," *Population Studies*, 14:1 (July, 1960), 17–27; Michael K. Roof, "The Russian Population Enigma Reconsidered," *ibid.*, pp. 3–16; Y. Mironenko, "Recent Official Statistics on the Population of the USSR," *Population Review* (Madras), 4:2 (July, 1960), 37–46.

**TABLE 15-3. Estimated Changes in the Population
of the Postwar Territory of the Soviet Union,
Excluding Emigration, 1940 to 1950 (millions)**

Population, January 1, 1940			194
"Normal" ten-year increment		30	
Birth deficit and extraordinary infant mortality	20		
Extraordinary general mortality	25		
Total war losses		45	
Decrease in population			15
Population, January 1, 1950			179

Source: Warren W. Eason, "The Soviet Population Today: An Analysis of the First Results of the 1959 Census," *Foreign Affairs,* 37:4 (July, 1959), 598–606.

sex ratio of the successive age-groups in Table 15-4. Among cohorts aged 0 to 19, most of whom were born after the war, there was a sizable predominance of males, presumably reflecting the sex ratio at birth. Among cohorts aged 20 to 29, who were children during the war, there was a slight predominance of females. This discrepancy may be due to the

**TABLE 15-4. Population of the Soviet Union,
by Age and Sex, 1959**

Age-Group	Number (thousands)		Males per 1,000 Females
	Males	Females	
0–9	23,608	22,755	1,037
10–19	16,066	15,742	1,021
20–24	10,056	10,287	978
25–29	8,917	9,273	961
30–34	8,611	10,388	829
35–39	4,528	7,062	641
40–44	3,998	6,410	624
45–49	4,706	7,558	623
50–54	4,010	6,437	623
55–59	2,906	5,793	502
60–69	4,099	7,637	537
70 and over	2,541	5,431	468
Not specified	4	4	—
Total	94,050	114,777	819
0–31	62,729	62,489	1,004
32 and over	31,317	52,284	599

Source: *Pravda,* February 4, 1960; translated in *Current Digest of the Soviet Press,* March 2, 1960.

effects of the forced-labor system, which is also relevant to an analysis of the sex ratio of older cohorts. Note that almost the lowest sex ratio was for the cohorts born in 1900–1904, who bore the brunt of both the collectivization and the war. The census report divided the population into two age-groups, as shown in the last two rows of the table. In the group aged 32 years and over, the youngest cohort of which had been 14 to 18 years old during the war years, the shortage of males was just under 21 million. The number of men reported to have served in World War II was only about 20 million; and if we assume, with Eason, that half were killed, this still leaves an unexplained deficit of males of around 11 million. The reason cannot be the bombing of cities or other civilian hardships, for mortality from such causes was surely not especially differentiated by sex.

Actually, the whole of the Soviet era has been building up a male deficit, as we can see from successive census figures:

1897	700,000 males short
1926	4,900,000 males short
1939	7,200,000 males short
1959	20,800,000 males short

Not all types of extraordinary mortality are included in these statistics (famine, for example, does not generally result in an unbalanced sex ratio), but they are a rough index of a portion of the deaths from war, terror, and forced labor.

Even these approximate data permit the definite assertion that the heavy loss of life during World War II, coming immediately after the heavy loss of life during the 1930's, has markedly shaped every social trend in the postwar period. The total depletion during the whole of the Bolshevik era has been approximately 80 million—about 25 million extraordinary deaths and nonbirths during the civil war and the establishment of the Communist dictatorship, at least 10 million during the social revolution of the 1930's, and some 45 million during World War II. Since the beginning of the Five-Year Plans in 1928, nearly the whole of this impact fell on the village, as Grossman has pointed out. He thinks it likely that the economy gained a short-term advantage from the fact that rural underemployment was abolished, or at least markedly diminished.

With 50 (or 40, or 30) million more people in the village after the War, could the rate of extraction of agricultural "surplus" have been as high as it was?

If not: Could recovery in urban living standards from the postwar low in 1946 have been as fast as it was? Could there have been as large an urban population, and hence as rapid reconstruction and further economic growth, as there was in the late 'forties and the 'fifties?

It follows from the argument in this paragraph that the two demographic disasters explain a substantial part of the sharp rise in the statistical urbanisation ratio. If both the total and the rural population of the U.S.S.R. were now, say, 50 million larger than they are, the urban population would comprise not about 45 per cent of the total population as it does [48 per cent in 1959], but about 35 per cent.[120]

For more than two decades the Party used the rural population as though it were an inexhaustible natural resource. It seems now to have been exhausted. From admittedly poor data, Eason estimated the size of the Soviet labor force from 1930 through 1975. The results are given in Table 15-5. In general, young people in the Soviet Union start working at 16; and 16 years after each major disaster a shortage in the number of workers is a problem. Whether the figures are correct or not, the trend is accurate, reflecting the end of the collectivization and famine in the mid-1930's, the relative prosperity of the late 1930's, and the war beginning in 1941 and quickly developing into a national calamity.

TABLE 15-5. Soviet Labor Force, Estimated and Projected, 1900–1975

	Labor Force (thousands)						Per cent Female of Total Labor Force
	Total	Average Annual Increment	Males	Average Annual Increment	Females	Average Annual Increment	
1900	64,400	—	35,400	—	29,000	—	45.0
1930	88,500	803.3	47,400	400	41,100	403.3	46.4
1940	105,300	1,680	58,400	1,100	46,900	580	44.5
1950	105,300	—	51,900	−650	53,400	650	50.7
1955	111,600	1,260	58,000	1,220	53,600	40	48.0
1960	114,800	640	62,100	820	52,700	−180	45.9
1965	117,100	460	65,800	740	51,300	−280	43.8
1970	123,100	1,200	72,000	1,240	51,100	−40	41.5
1975	130,600	1,500	79,400	1,480	51,200	20	39.2

Source: Warren W. Eason, "Comparisons of the United States and Soviet Economies: The Labor Force," in Joint Economic Committee, Congress of the United States, *Comparisons of the United States and Soviet Economies*, part 1 (80th Congress, 1st Session; Washington: U.S. Government Printing Office, 1959), Table 1.

Undoubtedly labor shortages were an important factor in aborting the Sixth Five-Year Plan (1959–1960), and they are the most critical factor in the current Seven-Year Plan (1959–1965). During these seven years the increase in the population of working age will amount to only half

[120] Grossman, "Thirty Years," *op. cit.*

the 11.5-million rise in employed persons called for in the plan.[121] The rest will have to be squeezed out of unemployed human resources, of which, however, there is no great abundance. More than 95 per cent of males aged 16 and over have been gainfully employed in postwar years; and of females roughly two-thirds.[122] On "Women's Day"—March 8, 1960—it was announced that females constitute not only 60 per cent of the collective-farm laborers but also, for example, 70 per cent of the teachers and 75 per cent of the physicians.[123] M. Y. Sonin, a prominent Soviet economist cited by Kantner, believes that it would be useful to draw still more women, especially many housewives and domestics, into more productive work. Actually, the postwar period has been marked by a rise in the proportion of women married and, presumably as a consequence, apparently by a decline in the proportion gainfully employed.[124] As part of the current Plan, it is intended to construct enough nurseries and kindergartens to shift five to six million mothers from household duties by 1965.

One purpose of recent educational reforms, similarly, has been to augment the labor supply. The number of years of compulsory schooling was raised from seven to eight, but it became somewhat more difficult to continue in a vocational high school *(tekhnikum)*. In general, those expecting to enroll in institutions of higher learning must first work for at least two years,[125] and this ruling would seem to endanger the plan to increase the number of highly trained professionals of all types.

It will not be possible, thus, to make up the deficiency of roughly 6 million in the labor force merely by employing more females and youth. A portion must come from using the male working population more intensively (but it has also been announced that the workday in industry will be cut to seven hours) and more efficiently. The Kremlin's repeated calls for the reduction of the armed forces are not due to love of peace, or even to the needs of propaganda, but mainly to the population structure. The marked reduction in the number of forced laborers, similarly, is both one element of the post-Stalin mood and, more significantly, an attempt to utilize these workers less wastefully.

[121] See John F. Kantner, "The Population of the Soviet Union," in Joint Economic Committee, Congress of the United States, *Comparisons of the United States and Soviet Economies,* part 1 (80th Congress, 1st Session; Washington: U.S. Government Printing Office, 1959), pp. 31–71.

[122] Warren W. Eason, "Comparisons of the United States and Soviet Economies: The Labor Force," in *ibid.,* pp. 73–93, Table 2. See also Eason, "Problems of Manpower and Industrialization in the USSR," in Milbank Memorial Fund, *op. cit.,* pp. 68–88.

[123] *New York Times,* March 9, 1960.

[124] Kantner, "The Population," *op. cit.*

[125] *Izvestia,* June 4, 1958, cited in *ibid.*

The crucial issue is Soviet agriculture, which is still the prime economic problem. Immediately after Stalin's death in 1953, Khrushchev issued a report on the agrarian economy. Since just before the war the grain available per head of the urban population had decreased by a quarter; it was urgent that production be raised.[126] Even more desperate was the trend in livestock. In 1953, in spite of the sizable increase in the population during the intervening period, the number of cattle, sheep, and goats, was still smaller than in 1928, before the enforced collectivization began; [127] and the depleted herds gave low per capita yields of milk, meat, and wool.[128] In an effort to pull the economy out of its doldrums, Khrushchev proposed his famous "virgin lands" scheme, by which 32 million acres were to be added to the country's farmland, as the first installment of a continuing increase. No surplus rural population was available, however, to staff the new collectives. State employment offices and the Communist Youth League were ordered to induce urban youths to migrate to the farms. "Nominally, all migrants are volunteers, though the authorities undoubtedly exert pressure." [129] In the first few months after the summons, 150,000 are said to have moved, but in order to make the virgin-lands plan work, millions of new settlers would have been needed. This is one reason why the program was not realized.[130] Since 1956 about a quarter-million urban youth have been sent out each year to help bring in the harvest. Still in 1961, collective farms bought butter from stores to meet their delivery quotas, and killed off prize breeding bulls to fulfill their meat quotas.[130a]

[126] Leon M. Herman, "Soviet Economic Policy Since Stalin," *Problems of Communism*, 5:1 (January–February, 1956), 8–14.

[127] This was so in spite of the fact that many animals were acquired together with the conquered territories; see Jasny, *op. cit.*, p. 42.

[128] According to Khrushchev's figures, milk yields, for instance, ranged from 1,600 to 2,000 pounds per cow in 1952. This compared with 5,300 to over 6,000 pounds for the same year in the United States; see Lazar Volin, "Report on the Agricultural Front," *Problems of Communism*, 4:6 (November–December, 1955), 10–18.

[129] Gregory Grossman, "Soviet Agriculture Since Stalin," *Annals of the American Academy of Political and Social Science*, 303 (January, 1956), 62–74. This is an excellent brief summary of its subject. For a first-rate discussion of internal migration generally, see Michael K. Roof and Frederick A. Leedy, "Population Redistribution in the Soviet Union, 1939–1956," *Geographical Review*, 49:2 (April, 1959), 208–221; also Roof, "Recent Trends in Soviet Internal Migration Policies," Research Group for European Migration Problems, *Bulletin*, 8:1 (January–March, 1960), 1–18.

[130] One reason, but not the only one. At a two-day conference of new settlers, Khrushchev cited some of the others. "When the new State farms were established, some of them were set up in a hurry and not quite successfully. Land was chosen unsuitably not only because of the [inadequate] amount of rainfall, but also because of the [excessive] salt content of the soil. . . . There is little rain in Kazakhstan" (quoted in *Manchester Guardian Weekly*, January 26, 1956). See the *New York Times*, October 2, 1960, for a report of the poor harvest in Kazakhstan that year.

[130a] Report of Dmitri S. Polyansky, Premier of the Russian Republic; quoted in *New York Times*, January 12, 1961.

Sonin asserts, on the contrary, that the rural areas have a surplus labor force:

Owing to industrialization and socialist reconstruction of agriculture, unemployment and agrarian overpopulation were definitely liquidated as early as in 1930. In consequence of a high degree of mechanization and rapid increase of labor productivity in socialist agriculture, there is in the [collective farms] a surplus labor force (due to its better utilization) that can shift to employment in industry and construction or move from regions with not enough arable land to those having much land. The number of such [collective farmers] runs for the whole Soviet Union to about 5 million.[131]

In the abstract Sonin is correct: the mechanization of Soviet agriculture has proceeded at a tremendous pace, and the many tractors and other farm implements should have released a sizable portion of the agrarian labor force to other occupations. But the important fact, as Jasny points out, is that "the socialized agriculture of the U.S.S.R., equipped with all those machines, . . . does not succeed in getting the yields per acre which were obtained by the landlords and better peasants more than forty years ago." [132] In treating the peasantry as an expendable resource, the Party not only expended too much of it but also removed the rest from even the modest level of efficiency characteristic of prerevolutionary Russian agriculture.

SUMMARY

The Soviet Union is an industrial country (as was also Nazi Germany), and to the degree that industrialism influences them, population phenomena there have been similar to those characteristic of the modern West. Thus, for example, the Soviet birth rate has declined by almost half since 1900, and the reported death rate fell off to 7.2 per thousand in 1958, or somewhat lower than in most advanced nations. The reason for this extraordinarily low rate, according to the official claims, is the superiority of a planned society and, more specifically, of the country's social-welfare system; and indeed the latter is certainly relevant.[133] One must also remember, however, that the registration of deaths is probably less complete than in the West; that it is now possible to reduce mortality

---

[131] M. Y. Sonin, *Problemy Economiki,* 1940, cited in Eugene M. Kulischer, "Comment," in *The Measurement and Behavior of Unemployment* (National Bureau of Economic Research; Princeton: Princeton University Press, 1957), pp. 433–437.

[132] Jasny, *op. cit.,* p. 90.

[133] For a good analysis of Soviet medicine as a social institution, see Mark G. Field, *Doctor and Patient in Soviet Russia* (Cambridge: Harvard University Press, 1957).

significantly without improving living conditions (as we shall see in the following chapter, on underdeveloped countries) ; and that the low rate in part reflects the age structure, which is the consequence of the extraordinary mortality of the recent past. That is to say, just as the death rates of the great civilizations of Asia contain, in Mallory's words, "a constant famine factor," so the vital statistics of totalitarian states include a constant terror factor. For not only is the population depleted periodically by mass purges, but these have a marked effect on the age structure and sex ratio, and thus on the birth and death rates, during the whole of the subsequent generation. Causes of death include not only diseases, accidents, and old age, but also war and civil war, terror and forced labor, death-camps and man-made famines. These are not accidental features but reflect the essence of totalitarian systems, the "constant balance between oppression and relaxation." [134]

Demographic movements, more directly mortality and migration, and less directly, fertility, are dominated by direct government intervention on a scale far exceeding that in the West. . . . Although economic considerations are clearly significant as foundations to government policy, they are by no means exclusive explanations. . . . Certain demographic concepts such as the inevitability of slower population growth with rising urbanization may not be valid universals but be culturally limited in their scope.[135]

In the Soviet Union the total population deficiency up to 1959 from both extraordinary deaths and nonbirths is of the order of 80 million or more: 25 million during the taking of power and the wrecking of the capitalist economy; another 10 million during the collectivization, denomadization, purge of the Party, and russification of the 1930's; and 45 million during the war started by the Nazi-Soviet Friendship Pact. In this category political rather than economic or social factors have dominated.

These depletions in the population have not been randomly distributed in any sense. Among cohorts aged 32 and over in 1959, there were only six males to every ten females, and the consequences for postwar marital and fertility patterns hardly need to be spelled out. Efforts to repair the extraordinary mortality by encouraging a high fertility, though they undoubtedly have had some influence, have not been successful. One reason is the Party's initial hostility to the family, but more important

[134] Zbigniew K. Brzezinski, *The Permanent Purge: Politics in Soviet Totalitarianism* (Cambridge: Harvard University Press, 1956), p. 168.
[135] Demitri B. Shimkin, "Demographic Changes and Socio-Economic Forces within the Soviet Union, 1939–1959," Milbank Memorial Fund, *op. cit.,* pp. 224–246.

is the fact, as Bormann put it concerning Nazi Germany, that the Party "cannot order the women and girls to beget children." [136] The effort to increase Soviet fertility has been frustrated also by the necessity of bringing as many females as possible into the labor force. Males had been killed off in monstrous numbers, and the new cohorts that were to replace them were extremely small. In 1955, by Eason's estimate, more than half of the labor force was female, and more than two-thirds of women aged 16 and over were gainfully employed.

The totalitarian system has been a decisive factor also in determining the population composition by nationality, by region, by social class, by rural or urban residence. Nationality policy, though somewhat more complex than that under the tsars, has been essentially a continuation of the prior russification; and the hardships inflicted on specific minority groups are reflected in their slow growth or actual numerical decline. The regions with the most rapid growth are the inhospitable sites of forced-labor camps. The Soviet regime has been able to realize, at least in part, the traditional tsarist program of increasing the population density in the trans-Ural section of the empire. Even urbanization, which on the face of it might seem to be politically neutral, has been in part the consequence of the terror in the countryside and of the founding of forced-labor camps that were labeled "cities."

In short, the population trends of a totalitarian state, like all other social phenomena, are shaped by the Party's drive for total power. The word *shaped* is used advisedly: most social events are in response to policy decisions, but not necessarily the response that the Party planned. The specific demography of the Soviet Union has been analyzed both to illustrate generic features, as one example of all totalitarian societies, and to suggest the overlaps that exist with Nazi Germany and, even more closely, with China.[137]

SUGGESTIONS FOR FURTHER READING

Herbert McClosky and John E. Turner, *The Soviet Dictatorship* (New York: McGraw-Hill, 1960).

David J. Dallin, *The Changing World of Soviet Russia* (New Haven: Yale University Press, 1956).

Two general surveys of the U.S.S.R., excellent in terms of scholar-

---

[136] Hale, "Adolf Hitler," *op. cit.*
[137] See pages 490–499.

ship, documentation, and range of matters covered. Dallin is somewhat shorter and less detailed.

William Henry Chamberlin, *Russia's Iron Age* (Boston: Little, Brown, 1934).
A caustic, on-the-spot review of the First Five-Year Plan.

David J. Dallin and Boris I. Nicolaevsky, *Forced Labor in Soviet Russia* (New Haven: Yale University Press, 1947).

Anonymous, *The Dark Side of the Moon* (New York: Scribner, 1947).
The best general work on forced-labor camps, and one of the most moving collections of first-hand narratives.

Naum Jasny, *The Soviet 1956 Statistical Handbook: A Commentary* (East Lansing: Michigan State University Press, 1957).
Required reading for any who accept Soviet statistics at face value.

Frank Lorimer, *The Population of the Soviet Union: History and Prospects* (League of Nations; Princeton: Princeton University Press, 1946).
The standard work on the prewar population.

Milbank Memorial Fund, *Population Trends in Eastern Europe, the USSR and Mainland China* (New York, 1960).

"L'U.R.S.S. et sa population," *Population (Numéro spécial)*, 13:2-*bis* (June, 1958).
Generally excellent analyses, including some on matters not touched on in this chapter—the populations of eastern Europe and China, housing in the Soviet Union, the Soviet theory of population.

Warren W. Eason, "The Soviet Population Today: An Analysis of the First Results of the 1959 Census," *Foreign Affairs*, 37:4 (July, 1959), 598–606.

Galina V. Selegen, "The First Report on the Recent Population Census in the Soviet Union," *Population Studies*, 14:1 (July, 1960), 17–27.

Robert C. Cook, "USSR Census: A Power Myth Exposed," *Population Bulletin*, 15:4 (July, 1959), 61–65.
Analyses of the 1959 Soviet census.

Walter Kolarz, *Russia and Her Colonies* (3rd ed.; New York: Praeger, 1955).

Solomon M. Schwarz, *The Jews in the Soviet Union* (Syracuse: Syracuse University Press, 1951).

R. Conquest, *The Soviet Deportation of Nationalities* (London: Macmillan, 1960).

Interesting analyses based on a wide range of documentation.

Gerald Reitlinger, *The Final Solution: The Attempt to Exterminate the Jews of Europe, 1939–1945* (New York: Beechhurst, 1953).

Robert L. Koehl, *RKFDV: German Resettlement and Population Policy, 1939–1945* (Cambridge: Harvard University Press, 1957).

Reitlinger is the most balanced and best documented of several works on the Nazis' attempt to exterminate the Jews. Koehl discusses other elements of Nazi population policy.

16. *THE POPULATION OF*

UNDERDEVELOPED COUNTRIES

In Chapter 13 we analyzed the population of preindustrial civilizations, and in Chapter 14 that of England during the industrial revolution. How do population phenomena of underdeveloped countries, one might ask, differ from these? Are not India and Egypt going through essentially the same process that began in the Midlands some two centuries ago? It is true that industrialism implies a high incidence of several important characteristics—not only nonagricultural employment but also, for instance, urban residence, literacy, secularization, and so on—and that these will presumably also evolve in any society undergoing development today. But the rate of social change is so much higher than in the past, and the contrast between the traditional style of life and the one that is replacing it is so much sharper, that the process today is not merely a continuation of nineteenth-century European history. Any attempt to predict the non-Western future from the Western past, as in the theory of the demographic transition, is likely to be quite unsuccessful.

In Europe some of the features of modern society unfolded over a period of centuries. The most specific element of industrialism, the introduction of technical innovations, is an expression of scientific method—that is to say, of a way of perceiving and understanding the world that was already well advanced in Isaac Newton's grand synthesis. Underdeveloped countries today generally lack this long preparation for modernization. And the more unprepared any one of them is, the more likely it is to be interested in rapid development: an area that has had least association with the West and thus the smallest benefit from its more efficient institutions may for that very reason be most strongly motivated

457

to seek immediate and direct contact with industrial society.[1] The relation then is in the form of a fantastic jump, with the most backward areas absorbing the most advanced elements of modern urban culture. Eskimos who have never seen a bicycle or automobile are quite familiar with airplanes. The potions of witch-doctors are replaced by the latest antibiotic. "It is quite common to see Papuans walking along jungle trails listening to transistor radios."[2] The largest steel plant in the world is in India. Countries like Russia and China, less developed economically and thus with a smaller proportion of industrial workers, have undergone the "proletarian" revolution that Marx predicted for the West. In short, the urban-industrial civilization, the most dynamic force in the world today, does not merely gradually seep into other societies but often bursts their traditional forms asunder.

Every viable culture, almost by definition, inculcates a resistance to fundamental change; and how strong this is constitutes an important factor in determining readiness for modernization. On the other hand, the very designation "underdeveloped" suggests that "developed" countries are accepted as the standard. Indeed, "poor" and "backward" are also relative terms, but here the comparison is not necessarily invidious: preindustrial peoples generally accepted their lower level of life as their immutable fate. "Underdeveloped," like the analogous "underprivileged" as applied to individuals, implies an egalitarian norm; it includes both the fact of difference and the no less important fact that it is seen as unjust and remediable.

Our lumping together areas as diverse as those in Latin America, Central Africa, the Near East, and Asia, passing over the great variety in historical and cultural background, is permissible only because of these two overriding characteristics: the lack of modern industry and the endeavor to achieve parity with the Western nations. The probable success of this effort depends in part on the indigenous society and culture, but

---

[1] The point can be illustrated by a study that Wilbert Moore made of factory labor in Mexico. Two villages—San Baltasar, isolated in the mountains, with poor soil, where only four per cent spoke Spanish as their mother tongue; and San Juan, scarcely a kilometer off a main highway, whose fertile farms had benefited substantially from an agricultural reform, where more than half spoke Spanish as their mother tongue—were each about nine miles from the city of Atlixo. The more isolated, the more traditional San Baltasar sent a larger number of factory workers to the city. Its harsher poverty and the fewer alternative opportunities there stimulated a larger outmigration than from the village more influenced by urban behavior patterns. The residents of San Juan, partly just because their closer association with the city had resulted in a higher level of living, had a smaller incentive to leave. See Wilbert E. Moore, *Industrialization and Labor: Social Aspects of Economic Development* (Ithaca, N.Y.: Cornell University Press, 1951), Ch. 10.

[2] *New York Times,* June 3, 1960.

exactly what their influence is we do not know. Is it more relevant that India has an old and complex civilization, comparable in these respects with that of the West, or that one important element of this civilization is the pervasive caste system, which impedes any shift in the social structure? Modernization means a greater transformation in Negro Africa than in India, but the traditional society there, just because of the lower cultural level, is weaker; and is it not therefore perhaps less resistant to change? Can underdeveloped areas that have acquired a European language and religion, as in Latin America, be regarded as half-way toward full modernization?

To all such questions we have no firm answers. The one general point that can be made here—and that must be stressed—is that what is termed "industrialization" or "economic development" is never merely a change in techniques of production. It is true that an underdeveloped country can assimilate a vast amount of so-called know-how before its lack of basic scientific knowledge and ability becomes a significant factor; but if that happens, these technical innovations eventually disrupt the institutional structure of the society to which they were alien. Industrialization is possible only as part of a much deeper social change. Thus, one cannot merely cite, say, the annual yield per acre in an agricultural experiment station in Iowa and multiply this by the number of acres of arable land in the world and thus prove that hunger can be completely abolished. Such an engineering view of the world's food shortages, though it typically poses as humanitarian, is rather totalitarian; for it completely ignores the human element in the problem. There are a dozen reasons why any people may say No to such a facile solution. The means may be unacceptable: for example, adding artificial fertilizers to the "natural" soil may be regarded as blasphemous (such an attitude was common in Germany and Holland as recently as the 1890's). The end may be unacceptable: if the product—say, corn—is foreign to the diet of the country, it may be rejected even in times of general malnutrition. The agent may be unacceptable: a Western agronomist sent to train peasants may be defined as a tool of imperialism. Or the whole of industrial society may be unacceptable: Gandhi, for example, considered the Indian village so superior a way of life that he was willing to keep its lacks in order also to retain what he considered to be its advantages.

Even if an attempt to introduce an innovation does not conflict with any overt value and all concerned are anxious to cooperate in establishing the new pattern, this does not mean that technical difficulties are typically the only ones to be met. The manner of dividing land, to take

Concrete conveyors, 1957. Women workers at Durgapur, in eastern India, helping in the construction of a bridge. (Wide World Photos)

Ten thousand villagers in Vietnam recently building a dike that reclaimed 15,000 acres of arable land from the sea. (Courtesy I.C.A.)

one example, is relevant to the level of agricultural output, and this varies greatly from one part of the underdeveloped world to another. In British Africa, for instance, the interaction between communal or tribal "ownership" and the Western pattern of individual holdings has often developed into a compromise of enormous legal complexity, which most decidedly affects production. As another instance, the cow is sacred to Hindus, and attempts to increase India's food production are seriously hampered by the fact that the large number of useless cattle may not be disturbed.[3] If it is difficult to transfer superior agricultural technology and the better food supply derivative from it across cultural boundaries, this is certainly no less so of other elements of industrialism, which usually involve still greater breaks with traditional society.

To analyze specifically the population trends that accompany modernization demands a certain simplification. Abstracting this segment of the complicated and interrelated whole, the reader must bear in mind, means that we must pass over much that is important. But it is also true that population is a key question: while the success of developmental programs depends on many factors, none is more crucial than whether the increased production leads to improved living or only to an increased number of persons existing at the same substandard level.

A NOTE ON THE QUALITY OF DATA

The statistical data of underdeveloped nations are generally scanty and of poor quality, but also steadily improving. When we try to assess any of the social transformations these countries are undergoing, we must keep in mind that our measuring rods are in all probability changing as rapidly as anything else in the society. Some types of statistics are today fairly satisfactory for some countries, but in almost every case this level of accuracy is too recent to permit equally firm comparisons with those of even several decades earlier.

The best past data were collected in a number of European colonies, and we can take British India as an example of an underdeveloped country with an exceptionally good statistical record. The directors of the nineteenth-century censuses included great scholars of Indian civiliza-

---

[3] A few years ago, when peasants were being harassed by thousands of wild antelope, an Indian government decree changed the name of this animal from *neilgai* (literally, "blue cows") to *neilghora* ("blue horses"), so that Hindus could feel free to shoot them. See Samuel P. Hayes, Jr., "Personality and Culture Problems of Point IV," in Bert F. Hoselitz, ed., *The Progress of Underdeveloped Areas* (Chicago: University of Chicago Press, 1952), pp. 203–229.

tion—historians, anthropologists, and linguists as well as, later, statisticians. From 1870 on, the censuses they supervised represent, in Davis's opinion, "the most fruitful single source of information about the country, . . . an accomplishment of which India may be justly proud." [4] This judgment should not be interpreted to mean, however, that the censuses were reasonably accurate by modern Western standards. For example, when the enumerated population of British India in 1871 was corrected for underenumeration and areas not included, the count was raised from 203.4 to 236 million; and by Davis's estimate the actual population was 255.2 million.[5] Similar though smaller corrections must be made for each of the subsequent counts at least through that for 1901. These figures of gross population are, of course, only the most basic demographic data, and breakdowns by any classification are typically less rather than more accurate.

A uniform system of vital statistics was established in British India in 1864, but a reasonable level of completeness was never achieved. For the first four decades of the twentieth century, the underregistration of births and deaths certainly exceeded 30 per cent at all times and was probably nearer to half.[6] In independent India, the roughly half-million village headmen are required by law to register vital events, but the record is still very poor.[7]

A more general appreciation of the population statistics of underdeveloped areas can be had by browsing through the *Demographic Survey of the British Colonial Empire,* to which Kuczynski devoted the last ten years of his life.[8] It is hardly possible to summarize this massive work except to say that no generalization is valid, not even the obvious one that all the statistics analyzed in it are poor. British colonial officers have long been required to give basic demographic information in their

---

[4] Kingsley Davis, *The Population of India and Pakistan* (Princeton: Princeton University Press, 1951), p. 5.

[5] *Ibid.,* pp. 26–27.

[6] *Ibid.,* pp. 34, 67.

[7] See S. Chandrasekhar, "A Note on Demographic Statistics in India," *Population Review* (Madras), 4:1 (January, 1960), 40–45.

[8] Robert R. Kuczynski, *Demographic Survey of the British Colonial Empire,* vol. 1: *West Africa;* vol. 2: *South Africa High Commission Territories, East Africa, Mauritius and Seychelles;* vol. 3: *West Indian and American Territories* (New York: Oxford University Press, 1948–1953). When he died in 1947, he had completed the first two volumes, as well as drafts of two more. The third, edited by his daughter, has since appeared, and the fourth is promised. For a more recent survey of demographic data, especially of former French territories, see Robert Blanc and Gérard Théodore, "Les populations d'Afrique noire et de Madagascar," *Population,* 15:3 (June–July, 1960), 407–432.

regular reports, and when they lack statistics, they furnish the results of their limited observations and general impressions. Thus,

> Thousands of reports . . . submit as facts what are actually reasoned guesses. [The demographer] finds over and over again a consensus of opinion without any real evidence to support this opinion. . . . A considerable portion of this Survey had, therefore, to be devoted to reinterpretation of the statistical data. . . . [But] to appraise fertility, morbidity, mortality, or migration is about as difficult in most African Dependencies as to appraise the frequency of adultery in [Great Britain].[9]

Kuczynski rigorously judges "censuses," "counts," poll-tax estimates, and vital statistics, and the authority with which he dismisses many of them makes this work much livelier reading than its subject matter would suggest.

At least in quantity, and generally also in quality, the postwar period has seen a considerable improvement in the demographic statistics collected in underdeveloped areas. During the decade centering on 1950 about four-fifths of the world's population was enumerated in some kind of census, a larger proportion than had ever been counted previously. The United Nations has been pushing for an expansion of this program, as well as for an improvement in the accuracy of the data collected.[10] The statistics available are published annually by the United Nations in its *Demographic Yearbook,* a uniquely valuable compilation. Laymen must learn to use it with care, however, and to pay very close attention to the comments on the estimated adequacy of the data. In general, statistics are printed as they are received from the various national governments and coded as "C," meaning that the coverage was judged to be reasonably complete; "U," meaning that this was not so; or ". . . .," meaning that no judgment was possible. The alternative procedure, to apply different correction factors to various sets of data, would require not only detailed knowledge of each country's statistical procedures, but also the willingness to offer affront in assessing the degree to which official figures are probably incorrect. By their very nature, the anonymous teams working for international agencies do not qualify on either count.

If the statistical base is often so insecure, the reader may ask, how is it possible to discuss in great detail and with a good deal of assurance the population trends of the underdeveloped areas? The first answer to this most pertinent question is that a trained demographer, especially one

---

[9] Kuczynski, *op. cit.,* 1, v–vi.
[10] United Nations, Statistical Office, *Principles and Recommendations for National Population Censuses* (Statistical Papers, series M, no. 27; New York, 1958).

who is also familiar with a particular country, can in many cases derive reasonably accurate estimates from even quite faulty basic data. And the second is that the changes in mortality and in population size and density have been so momentous that we can discuss their effects quite realistically without bothering about the probability that our figures are some percentage points off. Similarly, the contrast between developed and underdeveloped areas by almost any statistical index remains patent even after a generous allowance is made for the probable inaccuracy of the data.

This last point is illustrated in Table 16-1. Two sets of figures for a number of countries, per capita income in 1939, and per capita net national product in 1952–1954, have been converted into dollar equivalents and compared with the United States figure for each of the two dates. There are many deficiencies incorporated in the table.[11] The most obvious one, that income and net product are not the same index, is perhaps the least important. In underdeveloped economies, a large proportion of production and consumption takes place outside the mar-

TABLE 16-1. Per Capita Income, 1939, and Per Capita Net
National Product, 1952–1954, Selected Developed and
Underdeveloped Countries

Country	Per Capita Income, 1939			Country	Per Capita Net National Product, 1952–1954		
	US $ per Year	Un-weighted Average	Index Number (US = 100)		US $ per Year	Un-weighted Average	Index Number (US = 100)
United States	$554	$554	100	United States	$1,870	$1,870	100
Germany	520			Canada	1,310		
United Kingdom	468			Switzerland	1,010		
Switzerland	445			New Zealand	1,000		
Sweden	436			Australia	950		
Australia	403			Sweden	950	903	48
New Zealand	396	402	73	Belgium	800		
Canada	389			United Kingdom	780		
Netherlands	338			Denmark	750		
Denmark	338			France	740		
France	283			Norway	740		

[11] For a good discussion of the special difficulties, see Harry T. Oshima, "National Income Statistics of Underdeveloped Countries," *Journal of the American Statistical Association,* 52:278 (June, 1957), 162–174.

TABLE 16-1 (Continued)

Norway	279			Finland	670		
Belgium	261			Venezuela	540		
Eire	248			Germany	510		
Argentina	218			Netherlands	500		
Union of				Argentina	460		
South				Eire	410	444	24
Africa	188	199	36	Austria	370		
Finland	184			Chile	360		
Chile	174			Italy	310		
Austria	166			Cuba	310		
Italy	140						
Greece	136						
Cuba	98			Union of			
Japan	93			South			
Venezuela	92			Africa	300		
Egypt	85			Colombia	250		
Colombia	76			Panama	250		
Peru	72	79	14	Brazil	230	220	12
Panama	71			Mexico	220		
Ceylon	63			Greece	220		
Mexico	61			Japan	190		
				Dominican			
				Republic	160		
				Guatemala	160		
Dominican				Ecuador	150		
Republic	51			Honduras	150		
Guatemala	48			Philippines	150		
Brazil	46			Paraguay	140		
Honduras	45			Peru	120	119	6
Ecuador	44	42	8	Egypt	120		
Paraguay	39			Ceylon	110		
India	34			Pakistan	70		
Philippines	32			India	60		

Sources: United Nations, Statistical Office, *Per Capita National Product of Fifty Five Countries: 1952–1954* (Statistical Papers, series E, no. 4; New York, 1957). United States, Department of State, *Point Four* (Rev. ed.; Washington: U.S. Government Printing Office, 1949), pp. 99–100.

ket, and to convert family enterprises into Western economic categories requires much manipulation of the data. The conversion of these figures into dollars introduces another error. The gaps in the list also represent a lack of a different kind; in particular, the Soviet Union and all other economies using the concept "net material product" have been omitted. Neither set of figures directly indicates national welfare, since this is affected not only by net product (or income) but also by climate, natural resources, tastes, and the pattern of distribution, among other factors.

Large differences in these indexes, however, certainly suggest a com-

parable range in average level of living. The United States leads both
lists, and the gap between it and the rest of the world has been increasing.
Before the war the average per capita income of the other developed
nations was about three-quarters of the American; after the war the
comparable ratio was less than half. The figures may be correct enough
to warrant the conclusion that over this period the per capita incomes
of the underdeveloped countries also declined relative to the United
States.

With the statistics usually available, an underdeveloped country is
best defined as one with more than half of the occupied males engaged
in agriculture. Even in those advanced countries whose agriculture contributes heavily to the national product (such as Holland, Denmark,
New Zealand, or Argentina), only a small proportion of the labor force
is needed to work the commercial farms. A subsistence economy, however,
is coupled typically with low productivity and high population density,
and these two variables are closely related. As much as half of the
agrarian population of Egypt,[12] and a smaller but nonetheless significant
proportion in other densely populated underdeveloped countries, is economically surplus, in the specific sense that if these workers left the land,
the amount of food produced would not be less. This "hidden unemployment," as it is called, is not corrected in a family enterprise: a peasant
does not "fire" a kinsman who is not needed to work the family plot.
The very fact that the relation is not merely a contractual one means that
it will be continued even when it is no longer economically efficient.
Under such circumstances, increasing labor productivity may not be a
meaningful improvement; heavy population density can best be eased by
building up industry and thus furnishing an alternative occupation to those
willing to accept it.

The most precise meaning of economic development, and thus the
measure to be used when data are available, is an increase in per capita
real income (or, alternatively, real product). As we have noted, this is
highly correlated with a wide variety of other social and economic indexes—literacy; the number of telephones, automobiles, physicians, and
so on; the total number and kind of calories consumed daily; the proportion of the population in cities or in various occupations. Buchanan
and Ellis [13] divide such measures of development into two types, of which

[12] Charles Issawi, *Egypt at Mid-Century: An Economic Survey* (London: Oxford
University Press, 1954), p. 242.
[13] Norman S. Buchanan and Howard S. Ellis, *Approaches to Economic Development* (New York: Twentieth Century Fund, 1955), Ch. 1.

the first expresses in various ways the fact *that* a country is poor (for example, infant or general mortality) and the second some of the reasons *why* it is poor (for example, agricultural productivity). For the most recent period, remarkably, these two types of indexes are no longer always highly correlated. Even when all of the indigenous means of controlling death remain constant, for instance, or even deteriorate, the typical postwar pattern has nevertheless been a rapid fall in mortality. The most important demographic feature of an underdeveloped country—and indeed perhaps the most decisive characteristic altogether—is that it can remain backward in every other respect and yet match the death rate of the most advanced countries.

THE DECLINING DEATH RATE

The death rate, the number of deaths per 1,000 population, requires both vital statistics and a census count. Even for those underdeveloped areas with a reasonably accurate census, therefore, it is often impossible to calculate it directly, since underregistration is still generally too great. The death rate of such countries can be estimated from the age structure in successive census years. Using this method, Davis concluded that India's death rate before 1920 fluctuated between 40 and 50 per thousand, and that after that date it fell off to an average of 36.3 in 1921–1931, and 31.2 in 1931–1941.[14] The precise reasons for this decline are difficult to establish, since any explanation must embrace medical, economic, political, and social factors. Some of the causes that Davis suggests seem to be relevant mainly to an earlier period: the elimination of war and banditry, which was completed long before the decline began; improvement of the food supply, which was undertaken on a large scale from the middle of the nineteenth century on and was efficient enough by 1900 to prevent nationwide famines. The trend in diseases is difficult to analyze: up to 1945, 60 per cent of all registered deaths in British India were ascribed simply to "fever" and over 25 per cent to catchall "other causes." Nevertheless, it is reasonable to suppose that three of the most important epidemic diseases—plague, smallpox, and cholera—became less important as causes of death.

The experience of British India is typical of a fairly large number of underdeveloped areas. At the beginning of usable records, crude death rates are generally around 45 or 50; and one can assume that still earlier,

[14] Davis, *op. cit.,* p. 36.

before the social order permitting the collection of statistics was established, even higher rates prevailed. During the several decades prior to World War II, mortality in various underdeveloped countries underwent a gradual decline, the consequence of a no less gradual improvement in the level of living.[15] Progress was often faster than in the demographic history of Western countries, for the slow development of each medical or technological improvement was of course not duplicated overseas. However, before 1940 the effective operation of most death-control measures depended on a rise in the general welfare, which, when it occurred, took place slowly.

The crucial difference in the postwar period, as we have noted, is that this prior link between a rise in the level of living and a decline in mortality has been broken.

The most startling instance of this new pattern was Ceylon, where the estimated expectation of life at birth increased from 43 years in 1946 to 52 in 1947. The gain achieved in this one year had taken half a century in most Western countries. While it was relevant that the war had ended and the food shortage was eased, this precipitous decline in mortality was based essentially on a single factor, DDT, an especially powerful insecticide developed during World War II. Sprayed over low-lying areas from airplanes, it all but eliminated malaria, the principal cause of death, by killing the mosquitoes that carry it. From 1946 to 1949 the reported malaria morbidity rate was reduced by 77.5 per cent and the mortality rate by 82.5 per cent. Since malaria debilitates those it does not kill, death rates from other causes also declined sharply. From the average for 1944–1946 to 1948 mortality from these causes declined by the following percentages: dysentery, 65.4; influenza, 43.3; pneumonia, 21.4; diarrhea and enteritis, ages 0–2, 36.3; maternal mortality, 46.1.[16]

Expectation of life at birth rose by over 2 years between 1947 and 1948, by over a year in 1949, and at an annual rate of nearly seven-tenths of a year between 1949 and 1953. These gains can be put in perspective by considering that an annual rise of only two-thirds of a year is well above the largest short-run increase found in

[15] See Jean Bourgeois-Pichat and Chia-lin Pan, "Trends and Determinants of Mortality in Underdeveloped Areas," in Milbank Memorial Fund, *Trends and Differentials in Mortality* (New York, 1956), pp. 11–25.

[16] Kingsley Davis, "The Amazing Decline of Mortality in Underdeveloped Areas," *American Economic Review*, 46:2 (May, 1956), 305–318.

Western nations. Similarly, where Ceylon's life expectancy at age 15 rose at an annual rate of about seven-tenths of a year between 1947 and 1953, the maximum known Western changes have been far below a half year.[17]

That Ceylon's death rate fell off by more than half in nine years had nothing to do specifically with Ceylon, its culture, its social structure, its economy. Inevitably, the amazing success achieved there was repeated elsewhere. In India, as one other specific example, the incidence of malaria fell from 75 million cases in 1953 to 4 million in 1959, and the decline over the same period in deaths due to this disease was from 800,000 to 10,000 annually. In 1960 the United States made a grant of slightly more than $1 million toward an effort to complete the eradication program.[18] As of that year, the World Health Organization estimated that malaria continued to threaten the lives and well-being of some 1.2 million persons in 148 countries and territories throughout the world. In 13 of these areas the incidence had been reduced to a handful of cases, but in 56 no significant effort had yet been made to combat the disease.[19]

Malaria, which before World War II had been the world's most potent single cause of sickness and death, will soon become almost an anomaly. Moreover, it is only the most important of the human diseases carried by insects, and thus subject to control by insecticides.[20] Mosquitoes also help spread yellow fever, an important cause of death in Middle Africa and portions of South America. Kala-azar, an often fatal disease in India and China, which appears sporadically in Africa and South America, is spread by a sand fly. African sleeping sickness is spread by the tsetse fly, and the related Chagas' disease of Central and South America by the kissing bug. Relapsing fevers and typhus fevers are spread by ticks or lice. Elephantiasis and other forms of filariasis are spread by mosquitoes and biting flies. The flea carries the plague. If we try to extrapolate from the successful war against malaria, it seems reasonable to suppose that the incidence of many other human ills will also be markedly reduced in the

---

[17] George J. Stolnitz, "Comparison between Some Recent Mortality Trends in Underdeveloped Areas and Historical Trends in the West," in Milbank Memorial Fund, *op. cit.,* pp. 26–34.

[18] *New York Times,* July 3, 1960.

[19] Statement by M. G. Candau, director general of the World Health Organization, quoted in *ibid.,* July 17, 1960.

[20] For a fascinating discussion of insect-transmitted diseases, see Meir Yoeli, "Animal Infections and Human Disease," *Scientific American,* 202:5 (May, 1960), 161–170.

A swarm of locusts on the Kenya-Uganda border. A recent infestation in this area destroyed £7 million worth of crops, and several hundred thousand cattle died of starvation. (British Information Services)

next decade or two. Of course, it will not be a campaign without reverses. New races of mosquitoes have evolved that are highly resistant to DDT; and the wholesale destruction of insect life inevitably disturbs the ecology of any area, often to the detriment of man. But in this war the odds are that scientific ingenuity will outwit the blind adaptations of nature. The

RAF planes spraying poison dust on a locust breeding area in Tanganyika. (British Information Services)

mass attack on human disease with insecticides is as significant an innovation as the development of Western public sanitation a century ago.

A second postwar development, potentially no less important than the antimalaria campaign, is the use of sulfa compounds and antibiotics to combat still other diseases on a mass scale. Trachoma, endemic syphilis, yaws, as well as infections better known to the West, yield to such treatment readily. Peasants all over the world who know nothing of modern medicine in any other sense have become quite familiar, as we have noted, with penicillin. These preparations are rather expensive, but the cost of both supplying and dispensing them is generally borne in large part by advanced countries, acting through the dozen international agencies helping to fight disease in underdeveloped areas.

Table 16-2 indicates the results of these new types of death-control measures. In general, progress has continued since the dates indicated. "The only major area for which there is as yet no evidence of a firm

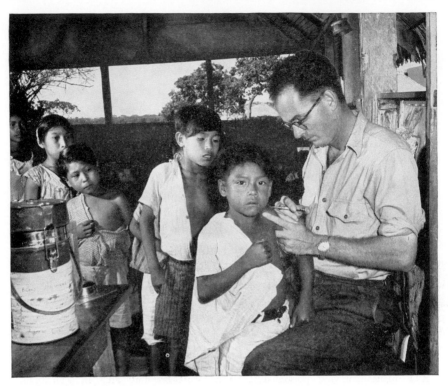

Children in British Guiana being vaccinated against tuberculosis. (British Information Services)

trend towards decreasing death risks is Middle Africa." [21] If the decline continues, it would be reasonable to estimate that in another decade or so the average expectation of life in underdeveloped countries will be more than 60 years, or only about 10 years less than the utmost that has been achieved in advanced Western nations.

Life-expectation figures are not influenced, of course, by the age structure, which means that in this case they depreciate the influence of the declining mortality on growth. Since without exception the populations of underdeveloped areas include a very high percentage of children and young adults, there are proportionately few who die of old age. Thus, once the major causes of early death have been brought under control, the death rates are extremely low, as can be seen in Table 16-3. The countries listed there include all those ordinarily regarded as under-

[21] United Nations, Department of Economic and Social Affairs, *The Future Growth of World Population* (Population Studies, no. 28; New York, 1958), p. 5.

TABLE 16-2. Expectation of Life at Birth in Selected Countries, Latest Available Date

	Date	Males	Females
Developed Countries			
United States			
Whites	1958	67.2	73.7
Nonwhites	1958	60.6	65.5
Canada	1950–52	66.33	70.83
England and Wales	1957	67.9	73.6
Netherlands	1953–55	71.0	73.9
Sweden	1951–55	70.49	73.43
Australia	1953–55	67.14	72.75
Intermediate Countries			
Italy	1950–53	63.75	67.25
Union of South Africa [a]			
Whites	1945–47	63.78	68.31
Asians	1945–47	50.70	49.75
Negroes	1945–47	41.70	44.00
Underdeveloped Countries			
Costa Rica [a]	1949–51	54.65	57.05
Trinidad and Tobago	1954–56	59.81	63.13
Chile	1952	49.84	53.89
Venezuela	1950–51	56.34	58.76
India [a]	1941–50	32.45	31.66
Thailand [a]	1947–48	48.69	51.90
Belgian Congo, African population	1950–52	37.64	40.00
Réunion	1951–55	47.50	53.40

[a] Note that the earlier date makes the figures somewhat incomparable.

Source: Compiled from various sources in *Population Index,* 25:4 (October, 1959), 365–369. No adjustment was made for deficiencies in reporting, which in some cases may be serious.

developed for which there are reasonably accurate data, as well as the Soviet Union and the United States for comparison. While the adequate statistical record may be correlated with other social characteristics, such a relation is no longer necessary. The vital rates of these countries can be conservatively interpreted as typical of most underdeveloped areas today, and all of them a decade hence. Note that the countries of Southern and Eastern Europe have in general about the same birth and death rates as the United States. In Asia and Latin America, and to some degree in Africa, however, while the death rates have fallen precipitously, the birth rates have generally remained quite high. The consequent natural increase is by 3 or even 3.5 per cent per year.

**TABLE 16-3. Birth and Death Rates of Selected Underdeveloped
Areas with Adequate Statistical Coverage, c. 1958**

	Rates per 1,000 Population		
	Birth	Death	Natural Increase
Africa			
Ghana	52.4 a	20.9 a	31.5
Réunion	45.2 b	14.1 b	31.1
Mauritius	40.8	11.8	29.0
Latin America			
Costa Rica	38.7 b	9.0	29.7
El Salvador	47.3	13.5	33.8
Guatemala	48.7	21.3	27.4
Mexico	44.5 b	12.5 b	32.0
British Honduras	46.8	9.3	37.5
Jamaica	38.1	8.8	29.3
Trinidad and Tobago	37.6	9.2	28.4
Venezuela	45.8 b	10.0 b	35.8
British Guiana	44.5 b	10.1 b	34.4
Asia			
Taiwan	41.7	7.6	34.1
Malaya	43.2	11.0	32.2
Aden Colony	39.2	13.1	26.1
Hong Kong	38.8	7.5	31.3
Singapore	42.0	7.0	35.0
Europe			
Bulgaria	17.9	7.9	10.0
Hungary	16.1	9.9	6.2
Poland	26.2 b	8.4 b	17.8
Portugal	23.7	10.2	13.5
Rumania	21.6	8.7	12.9
Spain	21.9	8.7 b	13.2
Yugoslavia	23.8 b	9.2 b	14.6
USSR	25.3	7.2	18.1
United States	24.3	9.5	14.8

a Registration area only.
b Provisional.
Source: United Nations, Statistical Office, *Population and Vital Statistics Report* (Statistical Papers, series A, vol. 12, no. 1; New York, 1960).

THE STABLE BIRTH RATE

The past trend in fertility cannot be measured with anything like the same assurance as mortality. Since changes in the birth rate, if any, have been much smaller, the inaccuracies in the data constitute a more serious disturbance. According to the best estimates of India's birth rate, for instance, it fell slowly from an average of 49 in 1881–1891 to 45 in 1931–1941 to 43.1 in 1951. The indicated decline of six units in 70 years, if indeed it took place, is certainly very slow, and the most recent information indicates that, on the contrary, there has been a steady and significant increase in the number of children per couple since the 1930's.[22]

A decline in family size, should it come about, would of course not take place evenly throughout society. As in the West in the nineteenth century, so also in underdeveloped countries today, we use a differential analysis as an indication of probable future trends. In India, however, the only differentials large enough to be significant refer to tiny segments of the population. In one study, for instance, Chandrasekaran found that completed family size ranged from more than six children for women with primary schooling or less, to five for women with a high-school education, down to two for women with a college education; but the number of women with more than primary schooling is too small to have a measurable effect on national rates.[23] In his analysis of prewar data, Davis found a sizable difference between cities and countryside; but he did not feel that this indicated a future decline in fertility. "The rural-urban differentials are certainly present, and are correlated with size of city, but they have not increased in fifty years." [24] According to a number of postwar studies, this rural-urban differential has become much smaller or has even disappeared, as can be seen in Table 16-4.[25]

The reader should not imagine that these trends are true only of India. Indeed, it is worth emphasizing the point by citing figures for an area as different from India as possible within the underdeveloped category—namely, Latin America.[26] There are substantial rural-urban differences in the fertility ratio of those countries with statistics that permit this comparison. Apart from Argentina, which is not underdeveloped by any of the usual indexes, estimated Latin American birth rates during 1950–

---

[22] Davis, *Population of India and Pakistan*, p. 69; Ansley J. Coale and Edgar M. Hoover, *Population Growth and Economic Development in Low-Income Countries: A Case Study of India's Prospects* (Princeton: Princeton University Press, 1958), p. 44; India, Ministry of Finance, Department of Economic Affairs, *The National Sample Survey*, no. 7: *Couple Fertility* (Calcutta, 1955).

[23] Cited in Coale and Hoover, *op. cit.*, p. 48.

[24] Davis, *Population of India and Pakistan*, p. 81.

[25] See also Warren C. Robinson, "Rural-Urban Fertility Differentials in India," *Population Index*, 26:3 (July, 1960), 204–205.

[26] The following discussion is based principally on Christopher Tietze, "Human Fertility in Latin America," *Annals of the American Academy of Political and Social Science*, 316 (March, 1958), 84–93. For a convenient compilation of demographic and other data, see Center of Latin American Studies, University of California, *Statistical Abstract of Latin America, 1960* (Los Angeles, 1960).

**TABLE 16-4. Completed Family Size by Rural-Urban Residence,
India, c. 1951**

	Children Ever Born to Married Women Aged 45 and Over	
	Rural	Urban
Travancore-Cochin	6.6	6.4
Madhya-Pradesh		
Eastern	6.1	6.3
Other	6.6	6.4
Mysore State	5.8	5.9

Sources: Various, as compiled in Ansley J. Coale and Edgar M. Hoover, *Population Growth and Economic Development in Low-Income Countries: A Case Study of India's Prospects* (Princeton: Princeton University Press, 1958), pp. 47–48.

1955 were about 35 per thousand in Chile, Cuba, and Puerto Rico, between 40 and 50 in all other countries. Since these last rates are close to the physiological maximum, there can hardly have been a substantial prior decline. Indeed, those countries with adequate prewar statistics often show an *increase* in the birth rate from 1938–1940 to 1953–1955 —by 7.6 per cent in El Salvador, by 6.8 in Guatemala, by 4.6 in Chile, by 4.1 in Mexico. While more nearly complete registration undoubtedly contributed to this rise, it was not the only reason. Unless the governments of Latin America undertake programs to facilitate family limitation— and, except for Puerto Rico, there are few indications that this will take place—in Tietze's estimate, birth rates there are hardly likely to decline during the next decade. The population of most Latin American countries can be expected to increase by 3 per cent per year, which means a doubling each 23 years. What Davis concluded concerning India, thus, applies much more widely:

The crucial question is therefore this: Will fertility be brought down in time to avoid either a disastrous growth of population or a calamitous rise in the death rate? The study of differential fertility . . . leads us reluctantly to a negative conclusion.[27]

That fertility has not fallen nearly so fast as mortality is what we should expect from both the population history of the West and our knowledge of social behavior. Indeed, it would be even more amazing if the decline in Ceylon's death rate by one-third within one year, to cite again this

[27] Davis, *The Population of India and Pakistan,* p. 81.

remarkable example, had been matched by a comparable decline in the birth rate. No matter how underdeveloped areas vary in their other cultural values, these include a hatred and fear of early death, and thus a generally willing acceptance of any life-saving technique that has proved its efficacy. Moreover, the acquiescence of each person is neither asked for nor required in such measures as spraying DDT from airplanes, or even mass inoculations. The control of fertility, on the contrary, must operate by influencing the personal decisions of the individual parents. Until fairly recently, nearly one infant out of every four born in these countries died in its first year, and a considerable additional proportion before maturity. If the society was to continue to exist under such circumstances, it demanded a value system and institutional structure that encouraged a large procreation.

It is very easy, however, to overestimate the influence of such a tradition. We know that the value systems of peasant societies favor high fertility, and we know that the actual birth rate is also high. The conclusion is "obvious" that families are large because parents want them so. In India, where "among the Brahmins the traditional blessing to a married girl when she bowed to her elders was 'Be the mother of eight sons and may your husband live long,' " [28] how many brides really want so many children? Until 10 or 15 years ago we had no information at all on the actual attitudes, but by now several surveys have been completed and their conclusions are impressive.

One of these studies was organized by the World Health Organization at the request of the Indian government, and conducted by Dr. Abraham Stone. He was restricted to investigating the feasibility of using the rhythm method, the only one, in the opinion of the Minister of Health at that time, that would not come into conflict with India's "traditions, culture, or mores." It would also have the great advantage of not requiring any expenditure for supplies.[29] About three-quarters of the couples

[28] N. V. Sovani, "The Problems of Fertility Control in India: Cultural Factors and Development of Policy," in Milbank Memorial Fund, *Approaches to Problems of High Fertility in Agrarian Societies* (New York: 1952), pp. 62–73.

[29] Abraham Stone, "Fertility Problems in India," *Fertility and Sterility*, 4:3 (May–June, 1953), 210–217. The difficulties of teaching the rhythm method to an illiterate population posed special problems, which Dr. Stone overcame with great ingenuity. "I constructed a special necklace containing 28 beads, one bead for each day of an average cycle. There are orange beads to indicate the days of the menstrual flow, green beads to indicate the days of the cycle which are safe from conception, and red beads for the fertile days. The beads could be strung for the individual woman on the basis of the duration of her cycles by the physician or health worker, and the woman could then be instructed to move one bead daily from one side of the string to the other, beginning with the first day of her menstrual flow. During the time that the green beads appear, she will be in her safe period; but when the red ones come around, sexual relations should be avoided."

interviewed wanted information on how to control conception, but of these only 4 per cent were still using rhythm at the end of the observation period of almost two years. The method was declared to be "scarcely favorable." [30] It was not the attitudes of illiterate peasantry that blocked the institution of an effective family-planning program in this instance, but rather the opposition of Catholic representatives to the World Health Organization and of certain leading members of the Indian government.

Table 16-5 is a compilation of several other Indian surveys. The percentages are far lower than the three-quarters noted above, but they pertain to a different question: these are the persons who would like no

TABLE 16-5. Percentage of Married Persons Desiring No More than Three Children, by Sex and Residence, India, 1950's

	Urban		*Rural*	
	Husband	*Wife*	*Husband*	*Wife*
Poona [a]	22	26	15	11
Nasik [b]	26	32	20	12
Kolaba [b]	18	16	10	8
Satara North [b]	15	17	13	12
Mysore State [c]	25	30	14	17

[a] V. M. Dandekar and Kumudini Dandekar, *Survey of Fertility and Mortality in Poona District* (Publication no. 27; Poona: Gokhale Institute of Politics and Economics, 1953), pp. 153, 168.

[b] N. V. Sovani and Kumudini Dandekar, *Fertility Survey of Nasik, Kolaba and Satara (North) Districts* (Publication no. 31; Poona: Gokhale Institute of Politics and Economics, 1955), pp. 104, 120, 166.

[c] C. Chandrasekaran, "Fertility Survey in Mysore State, India," in Milbank Memorial Fund, *Current Research in Human Fertility* (New York, 1955), pp. 11–23.

more than three children. Note that in the rural samples the female proportion is generally lower, and in the urban higher. An important task still is to convince the mass of the Indian people that it is in their interest to curb their procreation, but it would seem that this is less difficult than one would have supposed before these studies.

The attitude of the Indian government has undergone a remarkable shift. At first most national leaders were either opposed to contraception on moral grounds (especially Gandhi and his followers) or, at best, indifferent to family planning as a social program.

In the first flush of national awakening, Indian leaders became acutely conscious of the poverty of the masses and they believed that it was increasing year after year and that its main cause was economic exploitation by Britain. To this accusa-

[30] C. P. Blacker, "The Rhythm Method: Two Indian Experiments," *Eugenics Review*, 47:2 (July, 1955), 93–105; 47:3 (October, 1955), 163–172.

tion the British reply was that the growing poverty of the people of India was a result of population growth and the people of India were themselves responsible for it. This gave the cue to the nationalist leaders to argue that . . . India was a land of infinite and rich natural resources which could support a much larger population at a considerably higher standard of living than that obtaining in recent times. . . . This [dispute] prevented for a very long time an objective appraisal of the population situation.[31]

Reflecting this point of view, Nehru in 1948 termed India "an underpopulated country": "If we increase our production, agricultural and other, if this population is put to work for production, then we are not overpopulated."[32] Only three years later, the report of the Planning Commission, presided over by Nehru, reversed this stand:

Unless measures are initiated at this stage to bring down the birth rate and thereby to reduce the rate of population growth, a continuously increasing amount of effort on the part of the community will be used up only in maintaining existing standards of consumption. . . . A population policy is therefore essential to planning.[33]

One of the most outspoken leaders in formulating such a policy has been R. A. Gopalaswami, former Registrar General of India and later a prominent member of the Madras State Family-Planning Board. In an official census volume he defined all childbirths above the third order as "improvident maternity," and this designation in itself created something of a sensation. The incidence of improvident maternity, between 40 and 45 per cent in 1951, had to be reduced to under 5 per cent within fifteen years, in his opinion.

The task before the nation is first of all to bring about such a change in the climate of public opinion that every married couple will accept it as their duty (to themselves, to their family, and to that larger family—the nation) that they should avoid improvident maternity. The occurrence of improvident maternity should evoke social disapproval, as any other form of anti-social self-indulgence. This is necessary; but not enough. There should be standing arrangements for ensuring that advice is given to every married couple on the various ways open to them for discharging this duty and to make available the necessary facilities. . . . The preparation should consist of two sets of measures, of which one may be described as the creation of organisation and the other as the standardisation of technique. Both are equally important; they should proceed side by side.[34]

[31] Sovani, "The Problem," *op. cit.*
[32] *Indian Information,* July 1, 1948; quoted in *ibid.*
[33] India, Planning Commission, *Report,* July, 1951; quoted in *ibid.*
[34] R. A. Gopalaswami, *Census of India, 1951,* vol. 1, *India,* part 1-A, *Report* (New Delhi, 1953), pp. 218–219; quoted in Robert C. Cook, "Asian Population Roundup," *Population Bulletin,* 11:1 (March, 1955), 1–12.

Calcutta, 1956—people sleeping in the street. (James Burke—courtesy **LIFE** ©
1956 Time, Inc.)

In Gopalaswami's opinion, sterilization is the most suitable method of
birth control available to a country like India.[35] He gave the following
reasons:

[35] R. A. Gopalaswami, "How Japan Halved Her Birth Rate in Ten Years: The
Lessons for India," *Population Review* (Madras), 3:2 (July, 1959), 52–57. A family-
planning manual published by Madras State in 1956 discussed various modes of contraception and recommended "husband-sterilization" and "wife-sterilization," which
are performed free of charge in Madras State hospitals. See Gopalaswami, "Administrative Implementation of Family Planning Policy," *ibid.*, 3:1 (January, 1959),
43–62.

1. Contraceptives are too expensive for either most individual users or the state to purchase. Sterilization is relatively cheap, costing only an estimated Rs.150 per thousand of the total population annually, including compensation for loss of pay during hospitalization.

2. Indian homes generally lack the privacy and running water that are needed for contraceptive devices.

3. The use of contraceptives requires a sustained determination to limit families, and while government propaganda can help people to come to one decision, it is again too expensive to have to maintain this will to control conception.

4. Contraceptive devices, in any case, are rejected by many who could use them on other grounds, because they are considered unesthetic or "too much of a bother."

Effective, inexpensive and entirely harmless methods are already available, by which every married couple can stop their career of child-bearing at that stage of their married life when they decide they have had enough children. What is required to be done immediately is for the leaders of the people to acquire the conviction that this is so and to transmit that conviction to the people. The next step is for every State Government to organise the provision of necessary surgical facilities free of all expense to the people. *There is no doubt whatever that India's birth rate can be halved if such facilities are organised and used on a scale sufficient to perform 5 operations every year in every local community of one thousand people.*

The solution of the population problem of India, which seems so intractable today, is really as simple as that.[36]

In 1960 a body of experts that the Indian government constituted to study the problem of population growth issued a report recommending that family planning be given the highest priority in the Third Five-Year Plan, beginning in April, 1961. It suggested that $210 million be allocated to this purpose, as contrasted with less than $12 million in *both* the First and Second Plans. The means recommended by the committee was sterilization.[37] By the end of the Second Plan period, there were to be almost 1,800 family-planning centers established (1,121 rural and 676 urban). During the term of the Third Plan, the number would be increased by 2,000, at a cost of approximately $52.5 million.[38]

If the effort to reduce the rate of population growth is successful, what effect will this have on India's economy? In most attempts to answer such a question the authors more or less confine themselves to the single

---

[36] Gopalaswami, "How Japan," *op. cit.;* italics in the original.
[37] *New York Times,* March 7, 1960.
[38] *Population Review* (Madras), 4:2 (July, 1960), 69–70.

issue of whether people or food will increase faster. If the former, then there will be famines; if the latter, starvation will be avoided. Coale and Hoover's *Population Growth and Economic Development in Low-Income Countries*,[39] on the contrary, goes beyond the issue of mere subsistence. This interesting and important work attempts to give a specific answer to the question, how would India's over-all economic development be affected if its birth rate, instead of remaining constant, fell by half during the next generation? The population of the country was projected up to 1986, assuming that the probable sharp fall in mortality will take place, together with one of three alternative hypothetical courses in fertility: (a) no change or (b) a decline by half between 1966 and 1981 or (c) between 1956 and 1981. The population of 357 million in 1951 will increase, depending on the trend in the birth rate, to 775, 634, or 590 million in 1986, respectively, and the rate of continued growth in that year will be 2.6, 1.0, or 1.0 per cent per annum. Since growth is cumulative, the failure to control fertility now will present the next generation with the same problem of population pressure in much aggravated form.

In a country like India economic development depends on how much of the national income can be invested. A rapidly increasing population diverts income, instead, to current consumption of food, housing, education, and general "social overhead." Cutting the birth rate, the authors show, would raise total production, which would have to be divided, moreover, among a smaller number. The real income per consumer of the low-fertility population thus would be *at least* 38 per cent higher in 1986, and growing much faster than with the alternative projections. If a rise in real income is possible with a rapidly increasing population, that is to say, it would be substantially greater if births were controlled.

If a decline of fertility in underdeveloped countries would help accelerate economic growth, then it would be worthwhile for these nations to invest, as it were, in nonbirths. The American economist Stephen Enke has calculated that in India today the value of permanently preventing a birth is roughly $125, and that a considerable percentage of this sum might advantageously be offered as a bonus to young, married, fecund men who volunteer to have themselves sterilized.[40] A similar plan has been in operation for a number of years in Madras. As it was set up in mid-1958, the scheme was limited to lower civil servants in Madras

[39] Coale and Hoover, *op. cit.*

[40] Stephen Enke, "Government Bonuses for Smaller Families," *Population Review* (Madras), 4:2 (July, 1960), 47–50. See also the more detailed discussion in *Review of Economics and Statistics* of May, 1960, and *Economic Development and Cultural Change* of July, 1960.

City; fathers who underwent an operation were paid 15 rupees (about $3) and females 25 rupees (about $5). A year and a half later, the scheme was extended to include the 35 million people of Madras State, and the bonus was increased to 30 rupees (about $6). Up to the end of 1959, only 6,193 sterilizations had been performed under the plan, in part because of the restrictions in the first law, in part because some persons ignorantly confuse sterilization with castration. In the state of Maharashtra a sterilization campaign was started on "All-India Family-Planning Day," December 18, 1959; and during the next three weeks more than 7,000 men who underwent a vasectomy were each paid 20 rupees (about $4) for their loss of working time.[41]

Since there is more information about the fertility of India than that of most other nonindustrial countries, the discussion in this chapter has concentrated on this one example. In the following paragraphs we will both sum up the main points and indicate their relevance to other countries.

1. While it is true that the traditional value systems of underdeveloped countries typically encourage large families, actual attitudes deviate from this norm to a significant degree. Hatt's study of a probability sample of Puerto Rican households, which supplements the Indian surveys already mentioned, showed that not quite half of the males and slightly more than half of the females believe two children to be the ideal family size.[42] More generally, in societies undergoing basic transformations attitudes are also in flux, and where the desire for small families has not arisen spontaneously it could probably be induced by propaganda, certainly by monetary incentives.

2. This does not mean, however, that the mere stimulus of industrialism will suffice to establish the small-family pattern. The most immediate influence of modernization, it must be remembered, is to *raise* the birth rate. Improved health (particularly the disappearance of debilitating diseases like endemic malaria) results in a higher incidence of marital coitus, as well as in a sharp drop in infant and maternal mortality.

---

[41] S. Chandrasekhar, "A Comment on Dr. Enke's Article," *Population Review* (Madras), 4:2 (July, 1960), 51–54; *New York Times,* November 4, 1960; *Time,* December 5, 1960.

[42] Paul K. Hatt, *Backgrounds of Human Fertility in Puerto Rico: A Sociological Study* (Princeton: Princeton University Press, 1952), Table 37, p. 53. With a somewhat more personal form of the same query—"How many children would you like a daughter of yours to have?"—a still larger proportion of both sexes answered "two children" (Table 38, p. 55). See also J. Mayone Stycos, *Family and Fertility in Puerto Rico: A Study of the Lower Income Group* (New York: Columbia University Press, 1955), Ch. 7.

Indigenous practices that function to limit procreation are sometimes discarded as barbarous (e.g., infanticide, the prohibition of widows' remarriage) or as no longer important in a secularized community (e.g., bans on sexual intercourse during holy days). Western values have been spread through various media, but the most specific carriers have been missionaries, not the first group usually to propagate planned parenthood.

If the fertility of any country were to decline in the near future, this would be evident now in differential birth rates for various sectors of the population. The groups in India with relatively low fertility are either minuscule (e.g., college-educated women) or a carry-over from the past (e.g., high-caste Hindus, who observe the ban on widows' remarriage more strictly). The specific association that the theory of the demographic cycle suggests—that between urban residence and a lower fertility—is slight or even nonexistent in India, as also in some other underdeveloped countries.[43] While *some* town dwellers respond to their new environment by choosing other values in place of some of their potential offspring, the way of life of the urban masses is not such as to encourage sexual restraint, whether for religious reasons or to foster upward mobility.

3. In discussions of family limitation in countries like India, it is usual to reduce the issue to the alleged lack of means: "We have no known harmless, simple, or low cost method today with which we can apply fertility control." [44] This is not so. One may object to sterilization on ethical grounds, but hardly because it is not known, harmless, simple, and cheap. In Puerto Rico, "sterilization is becoming so popular among the lower class that securing bed space for it in the hospitals has become a plum dispensed by local politicians." [45] According to various studies there, 17.8 per cent of hospital deliveries are followed by salpingectomy, and as many as one-fifth of all wives have had what is termed "the operation." [46]

Moreover, the lack of a chemical contraceptive suitable for under-developed countries is perhaps more the consequence of ethical qualms than of technical difficulties. Far less money is spent on this research

[43] See, for example, M. A. El-Badry, "Some Aspects of Fertility in Egypt," *Milbank Memorial Fund Quarterly,* 34:1 (January, 1956), 22–43.

[44] Clair E. Folsome, "Progress in the Search for Methods of Family Limitation Suitable for Agrarian Societies," in Milbank Memorial Fund, *Approaches to Problems of High Fertility in Agrarian Societies* (New York, 1952), pp. 129–138.

[45] Stycos, *op. cit.,* p. 224, n. 9.

[46] *Ibid.* Even in the United States, it will be recalled, one couple in ten cannot procreate because a sterilization, either contraceptive or therapeutic, had been performed on one or the other partner. See page 293.

than on discovering cures for any one of the major diseases, and this is hardly accidental.

4. The Indian Government has come to recognize the need for a policy designed to stabilize the country's population. Its attitude today is more rational and—to quote Aldous Huxley—"less superstitious" than that of most governments, whether Western or non-Western. While it is true that the amount allocated to family planning even in the Second Five-Year Plan constituted less than 2 per cent of the total for medical and health programs, it is also true that few other nations have evinced even this much concern.

Certainly there will be no retardation soon in the momentous population increase of underdeveloped countries unless their governments attempt to reduce fertility. The issue of population policy in this sense is a crucial one, and bristling with difficulties. Because the family is the basic institution of all societies, values associated with it are strongly felt. Is it a legitimate function of the state to try to influence the country's fertility altogether? Virtually all modern states have some laws and institutions that are pronatalist either in intent or at least in effect; the prohibition of contraceptives in Massachusetts and Connecticut, and the deduction permitted in taxable income for each dependent minor, are examples from American law. In a country where the birth rate is clearly too high for the general good, then, may the government intervene in the contrary sense? If so, what should be the character of that policy? Depending on the circumstances and the willingness of the persons concerned to temper traditional values, any one or more of the following types of state activity may be considered legitimate: (a) To make contraceptives or other birth-control measures available through public agencies, either at cost or for less. (b) To conduct publicity campaigns in an effort to induce more couples to avail themselves of these clinics. (c) To offer a monetary subsidy of one kind or another to persons who refrain from reproducing or, more practically, who have themselves sterilized. (d) To impose sterilization on designated persons, as is done in many jurisdictions with those who have serious hereditary defects.

The question is not only where to draw the line but also whether the policy is carried out by an agency acting in the interest of the people. In the 1930's pronatalist measures in France and Sweden, and in Nazi Germany and the Soviet Union, were similar in themselves; and to some degree the same is true today of family-planning policies in India and in China of 1955–1958. But only a very naive observer could fail to note that in a totalitarian state everything the state does is by that fact qualitatively different.

Since family-planning policy is so important, it is worth exploring it further with respect to two other countries, Japan and China. Modern Japan is certainly not underdeveloped, but as a nation that has successfully instituted a policy to cope with its overpopulation, it is regarded by some as a mentor to other countries of Asia. Gopalaswami, it will be recalled, entitled one of his articles "How Japan Halved Her Birth Rate in Ten Years: The Lessons for India"; and this theme is a frequent one.[47] Others see Communist China as a model, not only because of its rapid development but also because of its attempts to institute family planning.

POPULATION POLICIES IN JAPAN

There are certainly lessons to be learned from the Japanese experience, but they will not necessarily be easy to apply. As the only country of Asia that has become an industrial power, Japan is anomalous in virtually every respect.

From 1873, shortly after the Meiji regime was installed, to 1918, when the initial phase of rapid industrialization was over, the population of Japan went up from 35.2 to 55.0 million.[48] The rate of increase rose gradually from 0.75 per cent per year in the 1870's and 1880's to not quite 1 per cent in the 1890's, and to almost 1.5 per cent in the first two decades of the twentieth century. This accelerating growth was the consequence primarily of the substantial decline in mortality, the result of the expanding industrial economy and the successful efforts to prevent early death. Moreover, the incidence of infanticide, which apparently had been higher in traditional Japan than in other Asian civilizations, was much reduced: children who had no place in the village economy could now migrate to industrial jobs in the cities or to posts overseas in the colonies. In the Japanese version of familism, according to Taeuber, the prime value sought was not many children but, rather, the welfare of the eldest son and heir, which under the new circumstances was enhanced by a large progeny, since relatives widely distributed both geographically and economically broadened the basis of the family's security.

In the interwar years the upward trend in the population of Japan

---

[47] Another example is "Japan's Population Miracle: An Asian Solution to Asia's Greatest Problem," *Population Bulletin,* vol. 15, no. 7 (November, 1959).

[48] The first census in Japan was taken in 1920. These figures are the estimates of Irene B. Taeuber; see her *The Population of Japan* (Princeton: Princeton University Press, 1958), p. 45. Much of the following discussion is based on this work.

Proper continued, from 56.0 million in 1920 to 73.1 million in 1940. The impact of the increase of 17 million in these two decades can hardly be described in meaningful terms. This increment alone would have peopled an empty expanse of Japan's area with 114 persons per square mile, and only 16 per cent of the actual land was cultivable. While the Empire was important as an economic base, it absorbed only a small portion of the growing population: of the world's ethnic Japanese, 97.7 per cent lived in Japan Proper in 1920 and 95.6 per cent still in 1940. Government policy in this period was to stimulate growth, for Japan's dominion over Eastern and Southeastern Asia in a "Co-Prosperity Sphere" demanded a continuing flow of soldiers and administrators. While the prohibition of contraceptives and other pronatalist regulations undoubtedly retarded the fall in fertility somewhat, it did not prevent it. The continuous but slow decline in birth rates in the interwar period, from an average of 36.7 in 1920–1925 to 29.3 in 1935–1940,[49] was the consequence principally either of postponement of marriage or the separation of couples by the husband's military service or temporary emigration.

Japan's population pressure, bearable so long as the main islands were the center of an expanding Empire, was less so after her defeat in World War II. Not only did the country lose its colonies, but 3.1 million soldiers and sailors, and 3.2 million civilian administrators and former emigrants with their families, were repatriated to Japan Proper.[50] This influx of some 6.3 million persons to the war-damaged homeland aggravated its already acute problems. There were no houses to live in, no urban jobs, no land for sale or rent. Moreover, the natural increase went up appreciably. The birth rate, which had been as low as 26.6 in 1939, was 34.3 in 1947. This was a typical postwar rise, due almost entirely to the return of millions of young men from their army service, but it electrified public opinion. The death rate, which in the prewar years had never been below 15.7, was 14.6 in 1947 and fell rapidly in the ensuing years to about half that.[51] Japan had been a stock example of population pressure for decades, but the situation had never been so desperate.

Japan's birth rate fell from 34.3 in 1947 to 17.2 in 1957, or by almost exactly half in a decade. While this decline does not, of course, solve the problems related to Japanese population, it was certainly a rational adaptation to the postwar pressure. But is it indeed an example that the other nations of Asia and the underdeveloped world can realistically emulate?

[49] *Ibid.,* p. 242.
[50] *Ibid.,* p. 346.
[51] *Ibid.,* p. 311.

If the Indian government, say, should undertake a more serious effort to reduce that country's fertility, would the postwar record in Japan indicate its probable success?

It can hardly be said that the Japanese government guided the people into adopting a program of planned parenthood. The measure under which the subsequent population policy developed did not have this overt intention. It was rather the Eugenic Protection Law of 1948, whose stated purpose was "to prevent the increase of the inferior descendants from the standpoint of eugenic protection and to protect the life and health of the mother as well." [52] Under the law, the state provided voluntary and in some cases compulsory sterilization, abortion facilities, and "practical guidance in adjustment of conception" when there were eugenic or medical reasons for preventing births. In an amendment the following year, economic factors were added; and the program quickly developed into a mass state-subsidized effort to reduce natality. While the official fees for an abortion are from 1,000 to 2,000 yen, the actual amount paid under insurance plans and health services is usually about 300 yen (or less than $1), and in at least one place the cost to the woman is only 15 yen. By 1953 there were 692 public clinics, as well as 55 private ones. In that year, the 1.1 million abortions officially reported terminated somewhat more than a third of all conceptions; and if the estimated actual number of 1.8 to 2.3 million is correct, then the proportion was about half. Or, according to another study, between 1.4 and 2.1 million more births (depending on varying estimates of fecundity) would have taken place in 1955 if there had been no abortions.[53]

In short, once the opportunity to reduce the size of their families was made available, even if almost fortuitously, the Japanese people took advantage of it. In the opinion of Dr. Muramatsu of Tokyo's Institute of Public Health,

The most significant factor . . . was the desire of the average couple to control the number of children they would have. . . . A level of birth limitation similar to that existing today would have been attained in the absence of governmental

[52] Quoted in *ibid.,* p. 269. Taeuber does not believe that the law was "a devious route by which the government could sponsor abortions as a means of 'solving' the population problem," but she does point out that "its major advocates were those who favored the diffusion of contraception" (pp. 269, 372).

[53] Minoru Muramatsu, "Effect of Induced Abortion on the Reduction of Births in Japan," *Milbank Memorial Fund Quarterly,* 38:2 (April, 1960), 153–166. See also Yoshio Koya, "Five-Year Experiment on Family Planning among Coal Miners in Joban, Japan," *Population Studies,* 13:2 (November, 1959), 157–163.

support for it, though it probably would have taken a somewhat longer period of time.[54]

There was no general reluctance to be overcome, and the reasons for this important fact distinguish Japan from such a country as India: (a) In Japan's traditional family system, the emphasis was not on mere procreation but on assuring the well-being of the heir. For centuries before the Meiji Restoration, the country's population was nearly static, in part because of its small-family pattern.[55] (b) Traditional practice also sanctioned the method used, for abortion had been an important supplement to infanticide. Neither of the country's dominant religions, Buddhism and Shintoism, is hostile to family planning. (c) Japan, in any case, is an urban-industrial country, with all of the rationalization of family life that this implies. The misery of the defeated nation in 1945 was not its routine condition, and the reaction to it was less likely to be apathy.

In an underdeveloped country with a strong pronatalist tradition, it would almost certainly not suffice merely to make family planning available. While some sentiment for birth control is generated by the conditions of life, the government's role would have to be more active if a comparable decline was hoped for. And whether this active intervention ought to be in the form of sponsoring abortions is questionable. Japan's record is the only one that affords an opportunity to test the common notion that abortions are intrinsically injurious to the women's health—that is, apart from the conditions prevailing in countries where they are illegal. In Japan trained physicians perform aseptic operations and prescribe penicillin for every patient. On the other hand, while the program was being set up, there were some unskilled practitioners, and operations were permitted up to the seventh month of pregnancy rather than only before the end of the third month, as medical opinion generally considers mandatory. While the evidence to date is not conclusive, it suggests that one or two abortions under optimum medical conditions are not typically harmful, but repeated abortions may be—as are also repeated deliveries in many cases. For this reason, some sentiment exists in Japan to shift the major emphasis in the state clinics from abortion to contraception or sterilization, or both. Dr. Muramatsu, for instance, believes that female sterilization will undoubtedly become more important in Japan. "We

[54] Minoru Muramatsu, "Family Planning Practice Among the Japanese," *Eugenics Quarterly*, 7:1 (March, 1960), 23–30.
[55] Compare page 355.

are watching with keen eyes what is happening in Puerto Rico and other parts of the World" [56]—including, one might say, India.

POPULATION POLICIES IN CHINA

China, the second Asian nation that some leaders of underdeveloped countries see as a model, has also put through a drastic reversal of population policy, which at first sight might seem parallel to the one in Japan. Indeed, it is so in some respects, but the differences are more important than the similarities.

In China, as in Russia 30 years earlier, the Communist Party came to power in part through a land reform that won support among the peasantry. In Russia this alliance lasted till after Lenin's death, from 1917 to 1928–1929; in China only from 1949 to 1953, when the distribution of land among poor peasants was replaced by a move toward collectivization. In 1953 there was also a census, the results of which induced a shift in the population policy. Both economically and demographically, thus, the first four or five years of the regime constitute a distinct period.

The tremendous resilience of Chinese civilization, which endured for several millenia without fundamental change, can be ascribed principally to the enormous strength of the traditional Chinese family; and any revolutionary regime would have had no choice about whether to hasten the disintegration of this bedrock of conservatism. A decree of May 1, 1950,[57] provides for marriage "based on free choice of partners, on monogamy, on equal rights for both sexes, and on protection of the lawful interests of women and children." It prohibits "polygamy, concubinage, child betrothal, interference with the re-marriage of widows, and the exaction of money or gifts in connection with marriage." Husband and wife should love and respect each other, "engage in [economic] production," and work "for the building up of a new society." Thus, by the decree itself, the family is directed to become a political instrument of the new regime, and this aim is implemented in various ways.

Families are urged to sign family patriotic pacts, the members pledging themselves to help one another to mold their political thinking and to engage in patriotic activities under official direction. . . . Children are encouraged to watch critically the thoughts and actions of their parents. . . . In the purges and public trials

[56] Quoted in Thomas K. Burch, "Induced Abortion in Japan Under Eugenic Protection Law of 1948," *Eugenics Quarterly,* 2:3 (September, 1955), 140–151.

[57] For an English translation of the text, see *People's China,* 1:12 (June 16, 1950), 28–30.

of 1951 it became a regular practice to ask children to testify against their parents and wives to bring charges against their husbands. . . . Filial piety is condemned as a feudal survival; antifilial piety has become a common slogan of the propagandists.[58]

One might presume that this effort to break down the family would have reduced the birth rate, and certainly the taking of power sharply increased the death rate. Estimates of the total number of "enemies of the people" who were killed in the first years range between 3 and 20 million, and various official statements suggest that the latter figure is much more realistic.

According to an official figure the number of landlords executed for "various crimes" was about 2.5 million. And in 1951 Lo Jui-ch'ing, then Minister for Public Security, claimed that his Ministry alone had "liquidated 15 million counter-revolutionaries," although it was not made clear what the term "liquidation" in this context meant. In 1952, Mr. Po I-p'o, the Minister for Finance, publicly admitted that the People's Government had liquidated 2 million "bandits" in the preceding three years. The term "bandit" was not defined though the present regime also applies the word to anyone who is against the present Communist Government.[59]

During all the years up to 1953, therefore, the policy was to encourage China's traditionally high fertility. The *South China Daily* started a campaign against infanticide, of which there had been some 2,000 known recent cases in Canton Province. Birth control was condemned as "a means of killing off the Chinese people without shedding blood." [60] In this period the Party repeatedly boasted of the high rate of population growth, which reflected, according to its claims, the improved living conditions.

To the extent that the new Chinese regime could influence it, in short, the population increase would be accelerated. The "hundreds of millions of people" were constantly referred to as China's most treasured asset. As Clement Attlee, the former British Prime Minister, said after a visit to China in 1954,

[58] Theodore Hsi-en Chen, "The Marxist Remolding of Chinese Society," *American Journal of Sociology,* 58:4 (January, 1953), 340–346.

[59] S. Chandrasekhar, *China's Population: Census and Vital Statistics* (Hong Kong: Hong Kong University Press, 1959), p. 58. According to Mao himself, the Party had killed only 800,000 between 1949 and 1954, when the terror allegedly ended (*New York Times,* June 13, 1957).

[60] *Jen-min jih-pao* (Peiping), April 25, 1952; quoted in E. Stuart Kirby, "Peiping's Growing Dilemma—Population," *Problems of Communism,* 7:2 (March–April, 1958), 36–41.

Not only is there no policy of restraint but there is actual encouragement toward intense fruitfulness. I think the real reason for this is that China, being admittedly a backward country, hopes to make up in quantity what it lacks in quality in order to achieve a position of power in the world. This is a disturbing thought.[61]

This policy was rationalized, moreover, in an extension—one might well say a *reductio ad absurdum*—of Marxist population theory. According to this view, "overpopulation is not the cause of China's impoverishment, but merely a reflection of that deterioration in Chinese society which began under the rule of the alien Manchus." With the new Communist regime, this deterioration has been reversed and all difficulties will now vanish as though by magic:

Effective administration can increase production by at least 30 per cent within 10 years and by 50 per cent within 20 years. . . . The current dearth of trained technicians and skilled labor does not pose an insoluble problem. . . . All signs indicate that before long China should have little difficulty in procuring machinery through regular trade channels. . . . Rapid industrialization, together with modernization and eventual mechanization of agriculture, will raise the standard of living and thus, after the initial period of adjustment, effect a marked decline in the birth rate.

Estimates of the Chinese birth rate ranged from 38 to 55 per thousand population, and those of the death rate from 33 to 50. "The one point on which estimates agree is that a difference of five exists between the birth and death rates," and the analysis consists in the assumption that this rate of natural increase will not change by very much. "The new China that is now emerging does not conform to any of the three demographic types defined by Notestein, but instead represents a distinct new type"— a country whose population grows at a nearly constant rate, because as mortality falls fertility will also fall just enough to maintain this comfortable near-balance.[62]

In mid-1953, according to the announced results of a census-registration, the population of Mainland China was almost 583 million, or almost one-quarter of the world's total. Understandably, the first reaction to this

[61] Quoted in Robert C. Cook, "China's Achilles Heel: Explosive Population Growth," *Population Bulletin,* 12:8 (December, 1956), 129–145.

[62] Chang Chih-yi, "China's Population Problem—A Chinese View," *Pacific Affairs,* 22:4 (December, 1949), 339–356. As Barclay commented in a reply to this article, "Dr. Chang performs his demographic analysis backwards, and in effect invents a Procrustean procedure to estimate a birth rate which will suit his purposes under all possible conditions" (George W. Barclay, "China's Population Problem: A Closer View," *ibid.,* 23:2, June, 1950, 184–192).

stupendous figure was disbelief.[63] Previously even the Communists themselves had generally estimated the population of the country at about 100 million less than this. The jubilant tone of the announcement, the fact that it was used to make political capital, also argued against accepting it. Pai Chien-hua of the Chinese Census Bureau declared that the over 600 million people (that is, including the Chinese in Taiwan and overseas) constitute "the source of wealth of our great country and the basis of its socialist reconstruction."

After the liberation, the rate of natural increase rose considerably owing to the restoration and development of production, the improvement of the people's material conditions, and progress in medicine and hygiene. . . . Children living in the age of Mao Tse-tung are carefully looked after and benefit from favorable conditions of life. The era of poverty, sickness and ignorance is no more. The time when girls were maltreated or drowned is gone. . . .[64]

Western scholars, however, soon began to accept as a fact the claim that China represents one-quarter of the human race. While the enumeration was faulty, the adminstrators had expert Soviet advisors. There is even some reason to believe that the claimed total reflected a considerable undercount.[65] But there is no reason also to accept the 1954 vital rates, supposedly based on a survey among 30 million persons, as even approximately true. Both the birth rate of 37 per thousand and the death rate of 17 are too low, but the natural increase may nevertheless be of the order of the 2 per cent a year that is indicated. For instance, as Taeuber has pointed out, a birth rate of 47 and a death rate of 27 are rather plausible, and this would result in a population increase of 12 million Chinese per year.[66]

[63] See, for example, U.S. Bureau of the Census, "The Population of Communist China: 1953," *International Population Reports*, series P-90, no. 6, March 4, 1955. The results of the census were characterized as "dubious" even by Ta Chen, one of Mainland China's best known demographers; see Choh-ming Li, *Economic Development of Communist China: An Appraisal of the First Five Years of Industrialization* (Berkeley: University of California Press, 1959), p. 198.

[64] Quoted in Kirby, "Peiping's Growing Dilemma," *op. cit.*

[65] Lawrence Krader and John Aird, "Sources of Demographic Data on Mainland China," *American Sociological Review*, 24:5 (October, 1959), 623–630. See also Irene B. Taeuber and Leo A. Orleans, "A Note on the Population Statistics of Communist China," *Population Index*, 22:4 (October, 1956), 274–276. But see also Taeuber and Nai-chi Wang, "Questions on Population Growth in China," in Milbank Memorial Fund, *Population Trends in Eastern Europe, the USSR and Mainland China* (New York, 1960), pp. 263–302, where the authors conclude that, in effect, China is a "country without statistics."

[66] Irene B. Taeuber, "China's Population: Riddle of the Past, Enigma of the Future," *Antioch Review*, Spring, 1957, pp. 7–18.

The most convincing argument for the probable correctness of the 1953 census is that the Chinese Communists themselves reacted to it. Since 1954 the naive approbation of large numbers has disappeared, to be replaced by what might be called a "soft" and a "hard" population policy. The soft line has been to reduce fertility, the hard one to risk measures demanding a sizable increase in mortality. As we shall see, both have been implemented.

The first indications of the change were at the People's Congress in Peiping in September, 1954. The earliest public statement in favor of birth control, as is usual in the announcement of many new policies in Communist countries, was made not by an important personage but by a veteran advocate of family planning and an only recent convert to the Party, Shao Li-tzu, who several months later wrote a widely publicized article on the same matter.[67] After this opening, statements followed by persons of unquestioned stature in the Party in, for example, the official organs of the All-China Federation of Democratic Women and the Communist Youth League, and finally, in October, 1955, in *Study,* the Party's principal ideological journal. The new line, as Taeuber aptly sums it up, was to retain Marx, repudiate Malthus, hurl invectives at Neo-Malthusians, and advocate the limitation of births. According to Yang Ssu-ying's article in *Study,* no "conceivable" rates of population growth could approach the increase in production envisioned in the First Five-Year Plan. The advocacy of family planning was not in the interest of society but of individual families:

> The fact that there are too many children in a family unduly increases the burden of the parents and affects adversely their work, their study of political doctrines, and their general livelihood. Similarly the children's education may be profoundly affected. In view of the above, in order to lessen the difficulties currently facing us, to protect the health of maternity womanhood and finally to ensure that the next generation may be brought up better, we are not at all opposed to birth control.[68]

A somewhat more direct support of family planning was made by Ma Yin-chu, an economist trained at Yale and Columbia and president of Peiping University. While he was subjected to a widespread and virulent attack, he was permitted to continue to voice his deviant position, perhaps because of his age (in 1960 he was almost 80), more likely because of the protection of someone high in the Party. His "New Principle of Popu-

---

[67] Both are cited in Irene B. Taeuber, "Population Policies in Communist China," *Population Index,* 22:4 (October, 1956), 261–274.
[68] Quoted in *ibid.*

lation," an essay of some 30 pages, has been summarized at length by Chandrasekhar.[69] Apart from advocating birth control and denouncing Malthus, Ma made the following points:

China's rate of natural increase is probably much higher than the assumed 2 per cent per year, and this large population growth impedes the economic development. Of her low national income, 79 per cent must be used for current consumption (compared with 75 in the Soviet Union). "Our population is too large; it drags down the speed of industrialisation." Moreover, in economic terms the large and rapidly growing numbers will become increasingly surplus, for a task that once needed 1,000 workers will be done by 50 once mechanization and automation are realized. "Then, may I ask, what are we going to do with the 950 persons?" There are shortages in grain, comestible oil, cloth; and if the efforts of the rural millions to raise their level of living should continue, "how dangerous would the outcome be?" "One of the reasons for the Polish and Hungarian incidents is precisely that the Government paid attention only to industrialisation and not to the needs of the people."

A no less direct connection between population increase and economic difficulties was made by Premier Chou En-lai. According to an official report he made to the National People's Congress in 1957, 10 to 15 per cent of China's population—that is, some 60 to 90 million persons— "are short of food and clothes and need aid from the state or the agricultural producers' cooperatives." He continued,

Ours is a country of 600 million people. If everyone's purchasing power increased by one *yuan* per year, that means an increase of 600 million *yuan* for the country, and the state must provide additional 600 million *yuan* worth of consumer goods. If people spend this money on food, that means supplying an additional 6,000 million caties of grain. If they spend it on clothes, that means supplying an additional 20 million bolts of cotton cloth—or increasing the production of cotton by 2 million piculs. . . . The living standard of our 600 million people can only be improved gradually on the basis of the increased production, and we must not demand too rapid an improvement.[70]

The traditional Chinese means of family limitation had been infanticide, and while this was not officially revived, all other methods were considered. The Minister of Health was reportedly collecting the sacred

[69] S. Chandrasekhar, "China's Population Problems: A Report," *Population Review* (Madras), 3:2 (July, 1959), 17–38. See also *Time,* February 15, 1960; Li, *op. cit.,* pp. 202–203, 218–219.

[70] Quoted in Subhash Chandra Sarker, "Population Planning in China," *Population Review* (Madras), 2:2 (July, 1958), 49–58.

formulas of herbalists as part of a search for contraceptives. One herbalist seriously offered the following prescription to a National People's Congress:

Fresh tadpoles coming out in the spring should be washed clean in cold well water, and swallowed whole three or four days after menstruation. If a woman swallows fourteen live tadpoles on the first day and ten more on the following day, she will not conceive for five years. If contraception is still required after that, she can repeat the formula twice, and be forever sterile. . . . This formula is good in that it is effective, safe, and not expensive. The defect is that it can be used only in the spring.[71]

Abortion specifically for medical reasons was legalized in 1954, and in the following years the conditions were liberalized. Similarly, the at first severe restrictions on sterilization were gradually eased. The main emphasis throughout the campaign, however, was on contraceptives. When he was in China at the end of 1958, Chandrasekhar was permitted to visit two contraceptive factories, a small one in Shanghai manufacturing 500,000 diaphragms and 5 million condoms annually, and a larger one in Canton, only two years old, with a productive capacity of 120 million condoms and an actual output in that year, after the propaganda for family planning had ceased, of only half that. Condoms cost 4 cents to produce and were sold in the villages for 2 cents.

During the height of the campaign, from 1955 to 1958, birth control was advertised in newspapers, magazines, and special pamphlets; with posters and billboards; at exhibitions and meetings, with lantern slides and lectures. The intent was both to instruct the audience on the importance of family planning and to explain techniques. Chandrasekhar writes,

The wife of an Indian embassy official in Peking told me that she visited the Birth Control Exhibition in Peking, but she was so embarrassed at the intimate exhibits being viewed jointly by men and women, that she promptly returned home! When I asked an Indian woman student at Peking University—a young mother—about the exhibition, she replied, . . . "An exhibition like that wouldn't last for a day in our country." . . . The authorities were not leaving anything to chance. Even the most illiterate peasant and the least intelligent worker went away from the exhibition knowing exactly what to do to prevent conception.[72]

[71] Quoted in Taeuber, "Population Policies," *op. cit.* As part of its effort to obliterate the notion that Western science is superior, the Party has fostered traditional Chinese medicine and pharmacology, which is based on a 52-volume work of the sixteenth century. In six-month cram courses, thousands of new practitioners are trained in, among other places, the former Peiping Union Medical College, American-founded and formerly American-supported, and once renowned throughout Asia. See Peggy Durdin, "Medicine in China: A Revealing Story," *New York Times Magazine,* February 28, 1960.

[72] Chandrasekhar, "China's Population Problems," *op. cit.*

Then, in the spring of 1958, the year of what is termed in Party writings "the great leap forward," the policy was suddenly reversed. Contraceptives and abortions were still legal, but the mass effort to encourage small families ended. In terms of the new tasks that the regime had set, Chandrasekhar was told, 650 million people were not enough. China "is really underpopulated and there is an acute labor shortage." [73]

In 1953, it will be recalled, the collectivization of agriculture was begun.[74] During the following years, peasants were both herded into collectives and organized into labor armies.

Official statistics show that in 1956, 17 million workers in five provinces were put to work on water projects; however, this labor force was still split up among small sites and thus in a sense belongs to another era. In 1957 another stage was reached when, at first, five to six hundred thousand peasants were mobilized in the depth of winter in one Manchurian province to work on canals and construction. From then on, the figures climb rapidly: in Kiangsi province a million peasants; in Shansi, 2,500,000; in Kansu, 3,400,000; in Hupei, 5,500,000; in Honan, 10,000,000; in Shantung, 15,000,000, etc. In August 1958, after ascertaining that the 1958 harvest results would top those of 1957 by a considerable margin, the new doctrine of the communes was officially adopted.[75]

Within two months most agricultural cooperatives throughout China had been merged into gigantic "people's communes."

What is a commune? How does it differ from an agricultural collective? [76]

1. A commune is large. The average in 1958 comprised 23,000 people, the largest 300,000. Collectives included a few dozen families, or at most several hundred.

2. A commune is totally state property. What remained of the peasant's private property in the collectives is absorbed, together with the peasant himself. He is no longer entitled to a share of the crop but is paid a wage, typically 100 yuan (or $40) per year, half in money and half in kind.[77]

---

[73] *Ibid.*

[74] The new policy was opposed by some of the country's leaders, and 1954 was devoted to a thorough purge of the Party, the army, and the state bureaucracy, removing all those who did not favor the "hard" line against the peasants. This corresponds to the purge of Bukharin, Rykov, and the Russian Party's "right" wing, which had also opposed enforced collectivization.

[75] David Rousset, "The New Tyranny in the Countryside," *Problems of Communism,* 8:1 (January–February, 1959), 5–13.

[76] See Stanley Rich, "The Communes—Mao's 'Big Family,' " *ibid.,* 1–5; H. F. Schurmann, "The Communes: A One-Year Balance Sheet," *ibid.,* 8:5 (September–October, 1959), 7–14.

[77] The figure is from an article by Finance Minister Li Hsien-nien, quoted in Rousset, "The New Tyranny," *op. cit.*

3. A commune is not merely agricultural but all-inclusive. Labor armies sow and harvest in the proper season, and during unproductive periods they are shuttled about the country "digging canals and wells, dragging rivers, draining swamps, building levees, carrying fertile soil onto naked rock, reforesting."

The Chinese press has. . . . indicated the required speed on the job: *"Two days' work in one,"* and *"Let us start in at dawn, and continue at night under the flood-lights,"* . . . the mobilization of a hundred million peasants, men and women, for hydraulic projects alone, . . . 200,000 wells dug in one month in one province, 95% of the peasants of another mobilized in the depth of winter, etc. . . .

In October 1958 the labor-army technique was officially introduced into industry, the mines, and public works. The transportation bottleneck was overcome by mobilizing armies of several million men for road construction, and by turning humans into beasts of burden on an unprecedented scale. Ore, coal, finished products, as well as earth and water—all were transported on men's backs, drawn or pushed by numberless coolies, from one frontier of China to the other.[78]

After a pause to consolidate the Party's gains, a new step forward was taken—communes in the cities. According to an official statement, by the spring of 1960 communal living had been imposed not only on 400 million Chinese peasants but also on 20 million town dwellers, a majority of those living in the three populous northern provinces of Heilungkiang, Honan, and Hopei.[79]

4. A commune is controlled by naked terror. Part of what Rousset terms China's "universalization of forced labor" was the creation, also in August 1958, of a new "people's militia." These are *armed* units of young activists, both male and female, who are organized as integral parts of the labor armies.

5. A commune is intended as a complete substitute for the home. In order to "emancipate" women from domestic chores so that they can also produce for the state, communes have established great messhalls, nurseries and kindergartens, and tailor shops. According to the description of one commune in a nationally distributed Party magazine, "The frames of individual families which had existed for thousands of years have been completely smashed."

In the more advanced communes, children see their parents twice a month. [During the day] wives see their husbands only at mealtimes, which are given only half to eating and half to participating in discussion in vast communal mess-halls. Unless, of course, their husbands are "camping out" at work projects from 60 to 100 miles away from their commune base. Grandparents are isolated in "Happiness

[78] *Ibid.;* italics in the original.
[79] *Time,* April 18, 1960.

Homes" where they will serve the "big family" by tilling communal vegetable plots, weaving communal baskets or feeding communal chickens. . . . A group of Young Pioneers (7- to 14-year olds) in Canton recently smelted their first heat of medium-carbon steel.[80]

How much this vast experiment in social engineering has cost in human life is not known. As in Russia the transformation of the country-side was carried out by young men anxious for a Party career. They insisted, undoubtedly following a decision at the highest level, that rice seedlings be planted two inches apart, rather than the traditional 14 to 18 inches; and the regime triumphantly announced an increase in the crop from 185 million tons in 1957 to 350 million in 1958. But this "harvest," estimated while the rice was still growing, proved to be a mirage. The stalks grew, but the heads were mostly empty.[81] This momentous error, when compounded by the drought and floods two years running, developed into what was finally called the worst famine in a century. But the Party was so thoroughly inculpated that it could not react quickly to the threat without undermining some of its authority. Still in 1959 more than U.S. $1 billion in exports, mostly agricultural products were shipped out; and even in 1961 the regime rejected the offer of help from the International Red Cross. Three emergency measures were taken: (a) "Bad elements" in the state bureaucracy, estimated at 10 per cent of the total, were blamed for the catastrophe and purged. (b) Members of communes were permitted to have small private plots and to work them two to four days a month. Since twice before the Party had sanctioned such a modest return to private ownership and then commandeered the produce, the peasants may well have been mistrustful. (c) Food, too little and too late, was purchased abroad. Australia made the largest sale of wheat since World War I, thus relieving her projected austerity program.[82]

THE FUTURE GROWTH OF THE WORLD'S POPULATION

The 1953 census-registration in China represents a significant addition to the estimated population not only of that country but also of the world.

[80] Rich, "The Communes," *op. cit.*

[81] Albert Ravenholt, "Red China's Food Crisis," American Universities Field Staff, *Reports Service,* January 1961.

[82] *New York Times,* January 21, February 5, 9, and 17, 1961. The Party organ, noting the recent experiments in Italy with laboratory-produced human embryos, looked forward hopefully to a new era. If children can be produced without being conceived, working mothers need not be affected by childbirth. This is happy news for women" (quoted in *ibid.,* March 19, 1961).

Because of it, the 1950 estimate was raised from 2.4 to 2.5 billion, or by more than 4 per cent. And since these newly discovered Chinese are assumed to be reproducing at a high rate, future projections have had to be revised even more.

There is no part of the world's population that is not increasing, but the rates vary greatly from one to another, as can be seen in Table 16-6. Note that the regions are listed in order, from the slowest to the fastest growing, and that most of the underdeveloped areas are at the latter end. In the future increase of the world's population, that is to say, the pro-

TABLE 16-6. Population of Major World Regions, 1955,
and Percentage Increase, 1950–1955

	Population, *1955* *(millions)*	*Population* *Increase,* *1950–1955* *(per cent)*
Northern and Western Europe	137	2.59
Southern Europe	138	4.75
Central Europe	134	4.79
Central South Asia	499	7.15
Japan area	89.9	7.54
East Asia (without Japan)	641	7.83
Middle Africa	153	7.99
Southeast Asia	186	8.56
Northern America [a]	183	8.84
USSR	197	8.84
Caribbean	17.8	9.05
Southern Africa	15.3	9.78
Temperate South America	30.0	10.33
Northern Africa	47.3	10.54
Pacific Islands	3.26	11.34
Tropical South America	94.6	12.15
Australia and New Zealand	11.5	12.27
Southwest Asia	71.6	12.96
Central America	40.0	15.35
The world	2,690	7.79

[a] That is, America north of Mexico.

Source: United Nations, Department of Economic and Social Affairs, *The Future Growth of World Population* (Population Studies, no. 28; New York, 1958), p. 2.

portion of persons of European stocks living in industrial countries will decline. This is even more evident from Table 16-7, which gives the population of continents projected to 2000, assuming a "medium" rate of growth. The percentage of the world's population living in Europe, the Soviet Union, the United States, Canada, and Oceania—which was 33 in 1900 and 30 in 1950—will be only 20.6 in the year 2000.

TABLE 16-7. Estimated Population of Continents and Population
Projections, 1900–2000

	1900		1925		1950		1975		2000	
	Mil-lions	*Per Cent*	*Mil-lions*	*Per Cent*	*Mil-lions*	*Per Cent*	*Mil-lions*	*Per Cent*	*Mil-lions*	*Per Cent*
Europe and USSR	423	27.3	505	26.5	574	23.0	751	19.6	947	15.1
Northern America [a]	81	5.2	126	6.6	168	6.7	240	6.3	312	5.0
Oceania	6	0.4	10	0.5	13	0.5	21	0.5	29	0.5
Latin America	63	4.1	99	5.2	163	6.5	303	7.9	592	9.4
Asia	857	55.3	1,020	53.5	1,380	55.2	2,210	57.7	3,870	61.8
Africa	120	7.7	147	7.7	199	8.0	303	7.9	517	8.2
World	1,550	100.0	1,907	100.0	2,497	100.0	3,828	100.0	6,267	100.0

[a] That is, America north of Mexico.

Source: United Nations, Department of Economic and Social Affairs, *The Future Growth of World Population* (Population Studies, no. 28; New York, 1958), pp. 23, 24.

The figure for the world's total at the end of the century, 6.3 billion, is so astronomical that the reader may try to evade its significance. As this is written, the year 2000 is only 40 years off, or well within the lifetime of many who are reading this book. "Barring either a catastrophe, or a deterioration of social conditions for progress in health, of global proportions, a world population of between 6,000 and 7,000 million by the end of the century should now be expected almost as a matter of certainty." [83] One can make this forecast with so much assurance in part because the rate of growth is still rising. There will have to be a considerable deceleration if the current increase—by about 1.25 billion per 25 years —is merely to be maintained during the coming century.

SUMMARY

The population explosion, the phrase that one often hears, is an apt metaphor. During the past 10 or 15 years insecticides and antibiotics have made possible enormous advances in the mass control of mortality in underdeveloped countries. A major portion of the cost of these measures is ordinarily borne by Western countries, acting through international agencies. The death rate can fall, thus, to around 10 per thousand population irrespective of the culture, the economy, or the government. Until fairly recently a people did not achieve a higher average life expectation until this was earned, as it were, through better food, more healthful living conditions, an economy able to carry more people, and the like.

[83] United Nations, *The Future Growth*, p. 20.

Now the very fact that people are kept alive so easily makes it more difficult to realize these other goals.

Fertility is at best falling very slowly, and in some underdeveloped countries it seems rather to be rising. A higher birth rate is the most likely initial consequence of a reduced incidence of various diseases—not only syphilis, which impairs fecundity directly, but also malaria and other endemic infections that tend to sap the virility of the affected population. There is some evidence that the mass of the world's peasantry would accept family planning, but they are not likely to find their own way to it fast enough to avoid a catastrophe. In an era when the state plans everything else, official intervention in support of birth control is imperative. In Japan, after government abortion clinics were established, the birth rate fell by half in ten years. In China, where the population of some 600 million is growing by about 2 per cent or more per year, the noisy birth-control campaign was called off after three or four years, and there is no way of determining what effect it had. Most promising beginnings have been made in India and Puerto Rico, but in both the population is still growing very fast.

SUGGESTIONS FOR FURTHER READING

Ragnar Nurkse, *Problems of Capital Formation in Underdeveloped Countries* (Oxford: Blackwell, 1953).

S. Herbert Frankel, *The Economic Impact of Under-Developed Societies: Essays on International Investment and Social Change* (Cambridge: Harvard University Press, 1955).

W. Arthur Lewis, *The Theory of Economic Growth* (Homewood, Ill.: Irwin, 1955).

Norman S. Buchanan and Howard S. Ellis, *Approaches to Economic Development* (New York: Twentieth Century Fund, 1955).

    Nurkse's rather short book is an excellent introduction to *economic* development narrowly conceived. Both Frankel and Lewis, and especially Buchanan and Ellis, include more of the whole social process in their analysis. All of these works can be read with profit by someone with no prior training in economics.

Bert F. Hoselitz, ed., *The Progress of Underdeveloped Areas* (Chicago: University of Chicago Press, 1952).

Bert F. Hoselitz, ed., "Agrarian Societies in Transition," *Annals of the American Academy of Political and Social Science,* vol. 305 (May, 1956).

Lyle W. Shannon, ed., *Underdeveloped Areas: A Book of Readings and Research* (New York: Harper, 1957).

Philip M. Hauser, ed., *Population and World Politics* (Glencoe, Ill.: Free Press, 1958).

Collections of articles that stress social, cultural, and political factors in development.

Kingsley Davis, *The Population of India and Pakistan* (Princeton: Princeton University Press, 1951).

Ansley J. Coale and Edgar M. Hoover, *Population Growth and Economic Development in Low-Income Countries: A Case Study of India's Prospects* (Princeton: Princeton University Press, 1958).

S. Chandrasekhar, *Population and Planned Parenthood in India* (London: Allen & Unwin, 1955).

Selig S. Harrison, *India: The Most Dangerous Decades* (Princeton: Princeton University Press, 1960).

J. Mayone Stycos, *Family and Fertility in Puerto Rico: A Study of the Lower Income Group* (New York: Columbia University Press, 1955).

A. J. Jaffe, *People, Jobs and Economic Development: A Case History of Puerto Rico Supplemented by Recent Mexican Experiences* (Glencoe, Ill.: Free Press, 1959).

George W. Roberts, *The Population of Jamaica* (Cambridge: Cambridge University Press, 1957).

Kingsley Davis, ed., "A Crowding Hemisphere: Population Change in the Americas," *Annals of the American Academy of Political and Social Science,* vol. 316 (March, 1958).

T. Lynn Smith, *Brazil: People and Institutions* (Rev. ed.; Baton Rouge: Louisiana State University Press, 1954).

Richard W. Stephens, *Population Pressures in Africa South of the Sahara* (Washington: George Washington University, 1959).

Some of the better case studies of population in underdeveloped areas. There is more of a range in approach than in geographical area, but many countries (e.g., Indonesia and modern China) still lack a good book-length demographic analysis.

Irene B. Taeuber, *The Population of Japan* (Princeton: Princeton University Press, 1958).

A work that traces the relation between Japan's population growth and her social-economic development in great detail.

PART III

The General Determinants
of Population

17. *MALTHUSIAN THEORY AND*
ITS DEVELOPMENT

As was suggested in Chapter 14, one reason that the early industrialization of England is of especial interest to demographers is that it was there and then, in the books of Malthus, that population theory in the modern sense began. Malthus had the faults of a pioneer, but his *Essay on the Principle of Population* has a more direct relevance today than the works of any of his predecessors, and even of many successors. He made his analysis within the framework of economic theory, which, with all its limitations, is still a powerful instrument. He saw the potential for the rapid growth that has taken place since he wrote, and for the deterioration in human welfare that this increase in numbers can effect (and threatens actually to effect in the underdeveloped areas of the world today). He saw also, though less clearly, how control over this multiplication could be established—by the gradual inculcation in each couple of a higher standard of life, which would induce them to forgo a numerous progeny in exchange for other values.

Malthus's work is important also for a significant line of development from it, the theory of population optimum. As in the case of Neo-Malthusianism, the father would not have recognized the child as legitimate, but the kinship is nonetheless patent.

MALTHUS

Thomas Robert Malthus was born in 1766, one of eight children of a country gentleman. He was educated privately and at Jesus College, Cambridge, where he read English and French literature as well as ancient history, and won prizes in Latin and English declamation. At the age of 22 he took orders and for a period became a curate. His main interest, however, lay in political economy. In 1804, the year of his marriage, he was appointed professor of history and political economy in the newly founded East India College in Hertford. This was the first professorship in the latter discipline established in Britain, and he filled the post with distinction until his death in 1834.[1]

Thomas Robert Malthus

Malthus was one of the founders of nineteenth-century economics. He was a good personal friend of David Ricardo, and their detailed discussions of many points of social policy and economic analysis have been

---

[1] John Maynard Keynes has written a delightful biographical sketch of Malthus, included in his *Essays in Biography* (New York: Harcourt, Brace, 1933). For a more detailed account, see James Bonar, *Malthus and his Work* (New York: Macmillan, 1924). G. F. McCleary, *The Malthusian Population Theory* (London: Faber & Faber, 1953), is an excellent analysis of Malthus's work, with a few chapters devoted to the man and his life.

preserved in a voluminous correspondence. Ricardo incorporated Malthus's principle of population virtually intact into economic theory and, indeed, carried it even farther than the author himself. In an important respect, however, Malthus stood outside the main line of development of classical theory. In the 1930's, when Keynes started a new trend in economics by emphasizing "effective demand," he based this concept in part on an insight of Malthus's that had been neglected for more than a century.

Malthus's most important work, however, the one for which he is most honored and maligned, is his *Essay on the Principle of Population*. It was first published anonymously in 1798, when the author was 32 years old. This first edition was written with an aggressive confidence, a dashing style that passed over exceptions, anomalies, and minor points, and swept on to the main conclusion with youthful confidence. It brought the author immediate fame and notoriety, but if he had been content to let his work rest with this version, his name would not be known today to every educated person. Malthus spent a good portion of the rest of his life collecting data on the relation between population and environment in various cultures, bringing his theory in accord with these facts and adjusting it to criticism. Since most countries of the Western world were just beginning to compile reliable demographic statistics, this empirical orientation required an extraordinary effort. The second edition of the *Essay*, published after five years of travel and study, was four times as long as the first. The style is much more sober; "I was willing," Malthus wrote in the Preface, "to sacrifice all pretensions to merit of composition to the chance of making an impression on a larger class of readers." There were seven editions of the *Essay* in all, the last published posthumously in 1872.

Background to the Theory

As his critics have often pointed out, Malthus's ideas were not wholly original with him. According to the author of the *Essay* himself, before he wrote the first edition he had read the works of only four writers on population—David Hume, Adam Smith, Robert Wallace, and Richard Price—and of these only Wallace is really relevant to Malthus's specific theory. For Hume and Smith population was a relatively subordinate subject, and Price was convinced that England's depopulation was proceeding apace. But in his later study, Malthus found a much longer list of men who had anticipated him. As Bonar pointed out, the *Essay* was

original in the same sense that Adam Smith's *Wealth of Nations* was:
"In both cases the author got most of his phrases, and even many of his
thoughts, from his predecessors; but he treated them as his predecessors
were unable to do; he saw them in their connection, perspective, and wide
bearings." [2] By putting these ideas that other men had expressed into a
larger framework and examining in detail the interrelation of population
growth with economic and political development, Malthus did more than
any of his predecessors or all of them together. He wrote a book that,
whether as guide or as target, all have had to recognize as the beginning
of modern population theory. And while in certain respects the *Essay*
was derivative, in more important ways it opposed two strong schools of
thought, mercantilism and revolutionary utopianism.

Mercantilism is, as Heckscher put it, "a phase in the history of economic policy," [3] a transition between the medieval and the modern
periods. The universalist elements of the Middle Ages, the Church and
the Empire, had lost their ability to hold society together, and their place
was taken by highly centralized national states. There was a close interaction of political and economic institutions. Very often state officials
planned, initiated, developed, and regulated economic enterprises; [4] and
the trading companies they formed had powers so broad that within their
territories they were equivalent to sovereign states. [5] According to a prime
tenet of mercantilist theory, any nation could benefit only at the cost of
others. The major aim of both political and economic policy was to pre-
pare for war, which came frequently. A wise state produced goods
cheaply—that is to say, with the lowest feasible wages—and exported
them in exchange for the maximum amount of gold.

And just as it hoarded bullion, so also the state hoarded people, and
for the same reason, to increase its economic, political, and military
power. During this period, "an almost fanatical desire to increase popula-

---

2 Bonar, *op. cit.*, pp. 32–33.

3 Eli F. Heckscher, *Mercantilism* (London: Allen & Unwin, 1935), 1, 19. (All rights
reserved, George Allen & Unwin Ltd.)

4 When the French East India Company was about to be formed, for example, Colbert had Louis XIV write a letter to various financiers "to the effect that he did not
doubt their willingness to take so favourable an opportunity of placing themselves at
the services of God, himself and the community by subscribing shares" (*ibid.*, 1, 346).

5 "The companies had the right to administer newly discovered or appropriated territories, set up law-courts there, make local laws, grant titles, build fortresses, mobilize
troops, wage war and conclude peace with non-christian princes and nations, ruthlessly
crush whatever threatened their privileges and arrest and deport anybody trading in
their territory without permission, in certain cases even the right to have coinage struck
for local currency. . . . [Disobedience was described] as an offense against 'God and
the company' " (*ibid.*, 1, 451).

tion prevailed in all countries." [6] France under Colbert in particular attempted to stimulate fertility and to proscribe emigration.[7] The asylum that Huguenots and Jews found in England and Holland was not merely a reflection of the greater tolerance in these Protestant countries, but also of a competition for foreign workers, particularly skilled craftsmen. The main emphasis in mercantilist demography, however, was on quantity, not quality. "As far as the mass of the working population was concerned, they were counted rather than weighed." [8] Their function was to produce for the greater power of the state, and to this end no child was too young to begin working.

Whereas from the beginning of the 19th century onwards, after tentative beginnings, stronger and stronger measures were taken to limit child labour by law, under mercantilism the power of the state was exerted in precisely the opposite direction. . . . In a decree of 1668 affecting the lace-making industry in Auxerre, . . . [Colbert] commanded . . . that all the inhabitants of the town should send their children into this industry at the age of six, on pain of a penalty of 30 *sous* per child.[9]

Wages should be at subsistence but never higher. A worker, in the words of Sir William Petty, should be able only to "live, labor, and generate," and "if you double wages, then he works but half so much as he could, or otherwise would." [10]

In spite of the axiom that a large population is good and a larger one better, mercantilist writers continually noted the "overcrowding" evidenced by a high incidence of vagrancy and crime. Anxious about both the insufficiency of people and their unemployment, they never reconciled these two positions. "At the most they believed that *other* countries must, for this reason, be careful about increases in their population." [11] The way to solve overcrowding in the mercantilist framework was to ship the surplus to colonies, where they could aggrandize the state's power in another quarter of the globe. And here the same cycle was started again, with renewed efforts to increase the overseas populations as rapidly as possible. Whole boatloads of women, usually corralled from houses

[6] *Ibid.*, 2, 158.
[7] For a detailed account, see D. V. Glass, *Population Policies and Movements in Europe* (Oxford: Clarendon, 1940), pp. 92 ff.
[8] Heckscher, *op. cit.*, 2, 44.
[9] *Ibid.*, 2, 155.
[10] Quoted in Eduard Heimann, *History of Economic Doctrines: An Introduction to Economic Theory* (New York: Oxford University Press, 1945), p. 36.
[11] Heckscher, *op. cit.*, 2, 163.

of correction but sometimes also young country girls, were sent to the French colonies, where soldiers who refused to marry them were punished. In the innumerable letters back and forth, these females were quite clearly seen simply as breeders. "In the same breath mention is made of shiploads of women, mares, and sheep, the methods of propagating human beings and cattle being regarded as roughly on the same plane." [12]

During the eighteenth century a new conception of humanity gradually evolved, particularly in the writings of the French political philosophers. With respect to demographic theory and policy, however, there was not a clear line of development, or a clean break with mercantilism. [13] Barnave was exceptional in his view that growth in numbers does not always benefit society. For Mirabeau, or for Brissot de Warville, a large population was symptomatic of a nation's happiness, but the state should foster it only indirectly by increasing the people's well-being. Saint-Just, later one of the instigators of the Jacobin Terror, adhered more closely to mercantilist ideas. In his view, misery could never be the effect of over-population, but only of social institutions. One can depend on nature "never to have more children than teats," but to keep the balance in the other direction nature needs the state's assistance. Saint-Just's ideas on marriage law, inspired by Rousseau, were "surprisingly harsh" in Fage's estimation. Not only should marriage be encouraged by state loans, but a couple still childless after seven years ought to be forcibly separated.

The Revolutionary Assembly, like the earlier philosophers, was in the main pronatalist. As defined in the new constitution itself, "No one can be a good citizen who is not a good son, a good father, a good brother, a good husband." [14] Membership in the *Conseil des Anciens* was constitutionally restricted to married persons. A national celebration to honor Husbands and Wives provoked a deluge of sentimental panegyrics. The principal instrument used by the republican government to stimulate population growth was the same as Colbert's, differential taxation; single persons 30 years old and over paid a surtax of 25 per cent. A campaign against celibates was reflected both in legislation and in crackpot ideas of fanatics—for example, that all celibates be required to wear clothing of a specific color, so that they might not escape the just ridicule of the

---

[12] *Ibid.,* 2, 300.

[13] The following discussion is based on Anita Fage, "La révolution française et la population," *Population,* 8:2 (April–June, 1953), 311–338.

[14] Quoted in Marcel Reinhard, "La révolution française et le problème de la population," *Population,* 1:3 (July–September, 1946), 419–427.

people; or the petition to the Convention that celibacy be made a capital offense.[15]

The population policy under Napoleon represented a compromise. Pronatalist decrees continued; in 1813, though the need for soldiers was great, married men were exempted from military service. Under the Civil Code, marriage remained a civil contract, divorce was possible, though difficult. The authority of the father was strengthened, both over his children and over his wife. As under the Republic, primogeniture was supplanted by a law requiring each owner of property to divide the bulk of it equally among all his children; and at one time some analysts believed that this clause had effected a decline in French fertility, particularly among the peasants, for whom a numerous progeny would mean a rapid subdivision of the farm into uneconomic plots. Actually, however, even before the Revolution equal division of property had not been the usual practice except among the nobility, so that the decline in family size cannot be ascribed to the law, and certainly not to its purpose.[16]

In the context of a discussion of Malthus, two revolutionary ideologues are especially relevant, Condorcet and Godwin. The first edition of Malthus's *Essay,* as its very title indicated, was intended to reply to "the speculations of Mr. Godwin, M. Condorcet, and other writers."

Marie-Jean-Antoine-Nicolas Caritat, Marquis de Condorcet, was an ardent revolutionary, a prominent member of the moderate Girondin faction. In 1793, after the more radical Jacobins gained full control, Condorcet was tried in absentia and sentenced to death. He remained in Paris, hiding in a students' boarding house, and over the next six months, while the tumbrils were rolling by almost under his window, he wrote his famous *Esquisse d'un tableau historique des progrès de l'esprit humain,* a history of human progress from its earliest beginnings to its imminent culmination in human perfection. According to Condorcet, all inequalities of wealth, of education, of opportunity, of sex, would soon disappear. Animosities between nations and races would be no more. All persons would speak the same language. The earth would be bountiful without stint. All diseases would be conquered, and if man did not become immortal, the span of his life would have no assignable upper limit. The question of whether production would always suffice to satisfy the peo-

---

[15] Fage, *op. cit.;* Glass, *op. cit.,* p. 146.

[16] J. G. C. Blacker, "Social Ambitions of the Bourgeoisie in 18th Century France, and their Relation to Family Limitation," *Population Studies,* 11:1 (July, 1957), 46–63. For an excellent discussion of French fertility generally, see Joseph J. Spengler, *France Faces Depopulation* (Durham, N.C.: Duke University Press, 1938).

ple's wants could not be answered, for the problem would not have to be faced for ages to come, by which time man would have acquired new types of now still unimagined knowledge. In this rational age to come, men would recognize their obligation to those not yet born and to the general well-being both of their society and of all humanity, and "not to the puerile idea of filling the earth with useless and unhappy beings." At that time a limit could be set to population other than by the premature death of a portion of those born. "Thus we find in Condorcet the entire genesis of the Malthusian population law, but in France these ideas remained unnoticed." [17]

In the same year in which Condorcet went into hiding, a book published across the channel by William Godwin, *Enquiry Concerning Political Justice,* looked forward to the early establishment of a similarly perfect society, in which a half hour's work a day would amply supply the wants of all.

> There will be no war, no crimes, no administration of justice, as it is called, and no government. Besides this, there will be neither disease, anguish, melancholy, nor resentment. Every man will seek, with ineffable ardour, the good of all.[18]

Malthus has often been characterized as a reactionary for his rejection of these effusions of Condorcet and Godwin, but by this measure there are few indeed who do not deserve the epithet.

The Principle of Population

"In an inquiry concerning the improvement of society," Malthus begins the final edition of the *Essay,* the natural procedure is to investigate past impediments to "the progress of mankind towards happiness" and the probability that these would be totally or partially removed in the future.[19] He does not pretend to be able to discuss so large a subject in its entirety, but "one great cause" is "the constant tendency in all animated life to increase beyond the nourishment prepared for it."

Population, "when unchecked," doubles once every generation. Among plants and "irrational animals," the potential increase is actual, and its

---

17 Fage, *op. cit.* See also McCleary, *op. cit.,* pp. 86–88.
18 Quoted in *ibid.,* p. 17.
19 This quotation and the following all come from T. R. Malthus, *An Essay on the Principle of Population* (7th ed.; London: Reeves and Turner, 1872), Book 1, Chs. 1–2.

"superabundant effects are repressed afterwards by want of room or nourishment." The matter is "more complicated" in the human species, for man, a rational being, can consider the effects of his potential fertility and curb his natural instinct. With man there are two types of controls of population growth, which Malthus terms the **preventive** and the **positive checks.** "In no state that we have yet known, has the power of population been left to exert itself with perfect freedom."

The principal preventive check is "moral restraint," or the postponement of marriage with no extramarital sexual gratification. Other types of preventive checks he terms "vice," namely, "promiscuous intercourse, unnatural passions, violations of the marriage bed, and improper arts to conceal the consequences of irregular connections"—or, in modern terminology, promiscuity, homosexuality, and birth control (or abortion) applied either within or outside marriage.

Positive checks include "wars, excesses, and many others which it would be in our power to avoid"; but in a country already fairly densely populated (Malthus used Great Britain as an example, and specifically excluded the America of his day), lack of food is the decisive factor. If the average produce from the land were doubled over one generation, or about 25 years, this would be "a greater increase than could with reason be expected." A second doubling in the following 25 years "would be contrary to all our knowledge of the properties of land." That is to say, the "tendency" or "power" of every species, including the human one, is to increase at a geometric rate, while under the most favorable circumstances usually to be found its subsistence increases at an arithmetic rate. Thus, "the human species would increase as the numbers, 1, 2, 4, 8, 16, 32, 64, 128, 256; and the subsistence as 1, 2, 3, 4, 5, 6, 7, 8, 9. In two centuries the population would be to the means of subsistence as 256 to 9; in three centuries as 4,096 to 13, and in two thousand years the difference would be almost incalculable." Lack of food, then, is the principal ultimate check to population growth but "never the immediate check, except in cases of actual famine."

Apart from migration, the population growth of any area depends on the preventive and positive checks taken together—or, in modern terminology, on practices affecting fertility and those affecting mortality. Moreover,

The preventive and the positive checks must vary inversely as each other; that is, in countries either naturally unhealthy, or subject to a great mortality, from whatever cause it may arise, the preventive check will prevail very little. In those countries, on the contrary, which are naturally healthy, and where the preventive check is found to prevail with considerable force, the positive check will prevail very little, or the mortality be very small.

Or, as we would say today, fertility and mortality, apart from transitional periods, are generally either both high or both low.

Population tends to oscillate around its means of subsistence. If a country with a population of 11 million, say, has food adequate for this number, then in most cases the population would increase sooner than the subsistence, which eventually would have to be divided among perhaps 11.5 million. Because of the consequent distress among the poor, more would put off getting married (the high negative correlation between the price of wheat and the marriage rate that Malthus noted has been repeatedly confirmed in subsequent studies). With a fall in the wage rate, farmers would be encouraged to hire more hands to "turn up fresh soil and to manure and improve more completely what is already in tillage," until the food supply was again on a par with the population— and the cycle began again. In primitive societies, where there is no market system, the same kind of oscillation takes place more directly. "When population has increased nearly to the utmost limits of the food, all the preventive and the positive checks will naturally operate with increased force. . . . till the population is sunk below the level of the food; and then the return to comparative plenty will again produce an increase, and, after a certain period, its further progress will again be checked by the same causes." [20]

The tension between population and subsistence, which Malthus saw as the major cause of misery and vice, could also have a beneficial effect. A man who postpones marriage until he is able to support his family is driven by his sexual urge to work hard. Malthus was therefore opposed to contraceptives, for their use permits sexual gratification free, as it were, and does not generate the same drive to work as would either a chaste postponement of marriage or children to care for. If a misunderstanding of Malthus's meaning was possible in the first edition, this should have been removed by a very specific denunciation of birth control that he made in the appendix to the 1817 edition, answering one James Grahame:

I should always particularly reprobate any artificial and unnatural modes of checking population, both on account of their immorality and their tendency to

[20] Cf. page 317.

remove a necessary stimulus to industry. If it were possible for each married couple to limit by a wish the number of their children, there is certainly reason to fear that the indolence of the human race would be very greatly increased, and that neither the population of individual countries nor of the whole earth would ever reach its natural and proper extent. But the restraints which I have recommended are quite of a different character. They are not only pointed out by reason and sanctioned by religion, but tend in the most marked manner to stimulate industry.[21]

A considerable difference in average family size was already discernible among social classes in Malthus's day, and the lower fertility of the upper classes was effected, at least in large part, by the postponement of marriage that he considered desirable. If prudence is exercised among the upper classes, "the obvious mode" of extending this practice to the lower classes is "to infuse into them a portion of that knowledge and foresight which so much facilitates the attainment of this object in the educated part of the community." [22] The way to do this, Malthus continued, would be to set up a universal educational system, as had been proposed by Adam Smith. Educating the mass would afford everyone the possibility of improving his situation, and this was, in Malthus's view, a strong counter force to the principle of population. "The desire of bettering our condition, and the fear of making it worse, has been constantly in action and has been constantly directing people into the right road." [23]

Once the people have been educated to regard prudential restraint as both feasible and good, this mode of checking the growth of population can be spread through society by raising the standard of living. This argument, which is merely suggested in the last chapters of the *Essay*, Malthus developed more fully in his *Principles of Political Economy*.[24] The lowest level to which wages can fall, in his theory as in the classical school generally, is the cost of bringing another generation of laborers into the world at the subsistence level. Malthus believed, however, that wages can be raised from this minimum by an increase in "the amount of those necessaries and conveniences without which [the workers] would not consent to keep up their numbers to the required point." Since Malthus has been so often associated with a contrary theory, if not actually

[21] Malthus, *op. cit.,* p. 512.

[22] *Ibid.,* p. 437.

[23] *Ibid.,* p. 477.

[24] T. R. Malthus, *Principles of Political Economy Considered with a View to their Practical Application* (2nd ed.; New York: Kelley, 1951). See also Joseph J. Spengler, "Malthus's Total Population Theory: A Restatement and Reappraisal," *Canadian Journal of Economics and Political Science,* 11:1 (February, 1945), 83–110; 11:2 (May, 1945), 234–264.

designated as the advocate of the vice and misery he discussed,[25] it may be well to amplify this quotation with a passage from Sidney and Beatrice Webb, who probably had a juster appreciation of his social philosophy than any other socialist writer.

> No argument could . . . be founded on the "principle of population" against Trade Union efforts to improve the conditions of sanitation and safety, or to protect the Normal Day. And the economists quickly found reason to doubt whether there was any greater cogency in the argument with regard to wages. . . . From the Malthusian point of view, the presumption was, as regards the artisans and factory operatives, always in favor of a rise in wages. For [as Malthus had written in the *Principles*] "in the vast majority of instances, before a rise of wages can be counteracted by the increased number of laborers it may be supposed to be the means of bringing into the market, time is afforded for the formation of . . . new and improved tastes and habits. . . . After the laborers have once acquired these tastes, population will advance in a slower ratio, as compared with capital, than formerly." . . . The ordinary middle-class view that the "principle of population" rendered nugatory all attempts to raise wages, otherwise than in the slow course of generations, was, in fact, based on sheer ignorance, not only of the facts of working-class life, but even of the opinions of the very economists from whom it was supposed to be derived.[26]

Criticism and Analysis

It is standard that important books are more often cited than read, but in the whole development of the social sciences, there has probably never been anyone attacked and defended with so little regard for what he had written as Malthus. The errors and misrepresentation have been so general and so persistent that an account of his theory cannot be considered complete until some attention has been paid them. Accounts in responsible works are sometimes mistaken even on matters of simple, easily ascertainable facts—where Malthus was educated, what his profession was,[27] how many editions there were of the *Essay*,[28] whether or not he was married,[29] and so on. Those most interested in Malthus,

---

25 McCleary cites a passage to this effect from an introductory text "emanating from a famous American seat of learning, Dartmouth College," and published in 1941 (*op. cit.*, p. 96).

26 Sidney and Beatrice Webb, *Industrial Democracy* (New ed.; London: Longmans, Green, 1902), pp. 632–635.

27 See McCleary, *op. cit.*, pp. 94–95.

28 We are told, for example, that there were five during his lifetime in H. L. Beales, "The Historical Context of the *Essay* on Population," in D. V. Glass, ed., *Introduction to Malthus* (New York: Wiley, 1953), pp. 1–24.

29 Marx was apparently responsible for spreading the legend that Malthus "had taken the monastic vow of celibacy" (Karl Marx, *Capital*, Chicago: Kerr, 1906, 1, 675–677, n. 1). Actually, he was married and had three children.

whether to praise or to damn him, have often started out with a misconception so fundamental that it enveloped the whole man. The "Malthusian" (later "Neo-Malthusian") Leagues sometimes took several generations to discover that the person whose name they used had been opposed in principle to the birth control they advocated. And the opponents of Malthus have often propagated the myth that he was a reactionary, that "the *Essay on Population* chimed with a growing tendency to repress—discussion, association, political organization were becoming less free, as the wars became more exacting and more intense." [30] A widely used text denounces Malthus as "an apologist for feudalism on a capitalist and utilitarian basis"—feudalism in England of 1800! Malthus, we are told, was "probably thinking in terms of a permanent social structure having the qualities of the transitional phase of the eighteenth century." [31]

These arguments, one might say, have a certain relevance to the highly simplified version of Malthus's theory that appeared in the first edition of the *Essay*, or that his avid supporters later bandied about in his name. Anyone in favor of absolute laissez faire found in Malthus's principle of population, as later in Darwin's principle of natural selection, a doctrine that seemed to give his political views scientific backing. The main impact on contemporary social and political events was not made by the *Essay* or the *Origin of Species*, but by vulgarized caricatures of these works, which generally had, it is true, a pernicious influence on British social policy. Malthus has been criticized for ignoring the many distortions of his theory that appeared during his lifetime; he might have answered that to refute all of them he would have had to devote full time to the task, and that in the prefaces to successive editions of the *Essay* he did try to correct the most important errors. Yet while subsequent generations have managed to distinguish Darwin from Social Darwinism,[32] Malthus is still usually pictured as a cartoon figure, Good or Evil incarnate, depending on one's politics.

Malthus was no revolutionary. His sensibilities were revolted by the Terror in Paris, and his solid English empiricism by such utopian extravagances as that man can become immortal by establishing a new form of

---

[30] Beales, "The Historical Context," *op. cit.*

[31] Erich Roll, *A History of Economic Thought* (Rev. ed.; London: Faber & Faber, 1954), pp. 211, 205.

[32] Even Jacques Barzun, who has written what is undoubtedly the least sympathetic recent account of Darwin, distinguishes "The Newton of Biology" from "The Uses of Darwinism"; see *Darwin, Marx, Wagner: Critique of a Heritage* (New York: Doubleday-Anchor, 1958), Chs. 4–5.

government. But neither was he a reactionary. He is vilified for having denounced the Speenhamland system, but he is less well known as the advocate of free universal education, free medical care for the poor, state assistance to emigrants, and even direct relief to casual laborers or families with more than six children; or as the opponent of child labor in factories, and of free trade when it benefited the traders but not the public.[33] More fundamentally, these policy recommendations derived from Malthus's underlying principles. That his sympathies lay with the upper classes is true, but these sympathies were weakened by the fact that they were divided between the gentry and the urban middle class. Brought up the son of a country gentleman, he ended his life as a staunch Whig. Appreciative of certain elements of country life ("feudalism"), he was for parliamentary reforms that would shift the political power to the cities. When he termed "most" men lazy, who would "sink to the level of brutes" if permitted to remain idle, he certainly had some basis for this judgment among the declassed peasants of his day. The key to his social philosophy is not his unflattering appraisal of the illiterate mass, but his conviction that their state was not ingrained, that social classes are *not,* as Edmund Burke later wrote, "as it were, different species of animals." Following the example of Adam Smith in *The Wealth of Nations,* Malthus proclaimed the right of each individual to seek happiness rather than serve the state, and to do this by following his own conscience rather than traditional usages. A full break with mercantilism—and with its paternalistic obverse, represented in Speenhamland—was a necessary prerequisite to the development of modern democracy. However, unlike some proponents of laissez-faire liberalism, who demanded of each man only that he seek his own interest, Malthus did not see the upper classes as automatically right by reason of their social position. If they failed to assist the lower classes in becoming self-reliant, they were thereby censurable.

To reject the frequent errors and misrepresentations in discussions of Malthus's work does not mean that we must accept it as gospel. He is still worth reading today because he forcefully posed a few very important questions, but his answers to them are inadequate by modern standards. These deficiencies derive in large part from three contradictions in his work that were never wholly resolved.

1. Moralist vs. Scientist.   To this day, social theorists find it difficult to separate an analysis of what is from what, in their opinion, ought to

---

[33] Cf. Bonar, *op. cit.,* p. 343, where citations are given to the passages in Malthus's work expressing these opinions.

be. Malthus wrote at a time when such subjects as population were ordinarily discussed in the context of "moral philosophy"; he himself, as mentioned above, was England's first professor of political economy. The pages of his books, reflecting this transition from a moralist to a scientific frame of reference, are sprinkled with allusions to "the Creator" and what He would prefer. The modern reader, even a pious one, finds such stylistic mannerisms inappropriate to a work in social science.

Sometimes the competition between the two analytical systems comes to the surface. Consider the proposition that "vice" leads to "misery." This might be the topic of a sermon, and Malthus the moralist would be pleased with the formulation. Malthus the scientist could hardly be. The main impetus to rapid population growth and thus, in his system, to misery, came from early marriage. While he strongly advocated "moral restraint," he never quite designated the failure to exercise it—getting married—as "vice." And, on the other hand, as he pointed out in an interesting footnote, some vice—for example, extramarital intercourse— may "have added to the happiness of both parties and have injured no one."

> These individual actions, therefore, cannot come under the head of misery. But they are still evidently vicious, because an action is so denominated which violates an express precept, founded upon its general tendency to produce misery, whatever may be its individual effect; and no person can doubt the general tendency of an illicit intercourse between the sexes to injure the happiness of society.[34]

Or, as a present-day sociologist would put it, no society can be viable if it lacks so fundamental an institution as the family, which, to persist, must be protected by a principle of legitimacy and moral injunctions against extramarital relations. In the *Essay* a hint of such a functional analysis is sometimes vaguely perceptible, intertwined with "moral philosophy."

As one other example, compare his opposition to birth control with that in Catholic dogma. When contraceptives are denounced as "unnatural," there is no way of translating this moral judgment into scientific language. Malthus disapproved of them "both on account of their immorality and their tendency to remove a necessary stimulus to industry," and of the two reasons he stressed the second. Birth control was what modern sociologists would term "dysfunctional." Malthus was wrong on this point, of course: man's ambition can be excited by many stimulants other than his sexuality. But the interesting point is that he was not

[34] Malthus, *Essay,* p. 9.

satisfied with labeling birth control as "immoral"; he tried to state his opposition also in an empirical context, in which he *could* be proved wrong.

Although he was for a period a curate of the Church of England, whom Marx and others referred to as "Parson Malthus," many clergymen found his interpretation of Providence not to their liking, and one went so far as to charge the author of the *Essay* with atheism.[35] The population theory appropriate to a "parson," they felt, was something along the lines of Luther's adage, *"Gott macht Kinder, der wird sie auch ernähren"*—God makes children, and He will also nourish them. The principle of population, on the contrary, brought man fully into nature, one species among others. As Darwin himself remarked, his casual reading of the *Essay,* "for amusement," furnished the first clue out of which the theory of evolution developed. Thus, in the dispute between evolutionists and traditional theologians, a momentous struggle that set the tone of intellectual life during the whole second half of the nineteenth century, the role of Malthus was not that of a theologian but rather a forerunner to scientific biology.

2. Biological Determinist vs. Sociologist. Sometimes Malthus's emphasis on the fact that man is an animal, with sexual passions and the need for food, has been taken as the sum of his theory, so that he is attacked (or defended) as a biological determinist. This is a reasonable interpretation of the first edition of the *Essay,* on which critics have usually concentrated, as the easier target. Malthus's life-long effort to improve the first statement of his theory has failed to impress many analysts, who note the later editions only to point out the inconsistencies.[36]

Malthus's emphasis on man's biological nature, which today often sounds like an insistence on the obvious, was not so pointless in his day. Many then believed that the fecundity of the human species was being reduced by its new urban setting or by food it was then eating. Sadler, for instance, was not the first to contend that "the fecundity of human beings under similar circumstances, varies inversely as their numbers on a given space";[37] or Doubleday, that abundant food destroys the physi-

35 Cf. Bonar, *op. cit.,* p. 365.

36 Bowen tells us, for example, that "the clear alternative" to Malthus's biological theory is "the hypothesis that economic as well as social conditions affect the growth and size of populations, and that sexual passions operate only within the restrictions or stimuli imposed by these conditions." And yet two pages earlier the reader was informed that Malthus had "emphasized the dependence of the actual level of population upon the laws, institutions and habits of each society." See Ian Bowen, *Population* (London: Nisbet, 1954), pp. 111, 109.

37 Michael Thomas Sadler, *Ireland, Its Evils and Their Remedies* (London: Murray, 1829), p. xxviii.

ological ability to reproduce, so that "in a nation highly and generally affluent and luxurious, population will [necessarily] decrease and decay." [38] And according to Godwin, if sexual intercourse were stripped of "all its attendant circumstances, . . . it would be generally despised." [39] Against such adversaries, it was relevant to stress man's physiological drives and needs.

In Malthus's final statement of his population theory (that is, the last edition of the *Essay* together with portions of the *Principles*), some remnants of his initial framework remained in an occasional turn of phrase. But basically he was less of a biological determinist than many other nineteenth-century economists. For most members of this school, the problem to be analyzed was production, and consumption was viewed rather mechanically in terms of a reified Economic Man. For Malthus, the standard of living was not a biological factor, but a cultural one. It is worth recalling again the debt Keynes acknowledged to Malthus on this point:

> The idea that we can safely neglect the aggregate demand function is fundamental to Ricardian economics, which underlie what we have been taught for more than a century. Malthus, indeed, had vehemently opposed Ricardo's doctrine that it was impossible for effective demand to be deficient; but . . . Ricardo conquered England as completely as the Holy Inquisition conquered Spain. . . . [Malthus was one of] the brave army of heretics, . . . who, following their intuitions, have preferred to see the truth obscurely and imperfectly rather than to maintain error, reached indeed with clearness and consistency and by easy logic, but on hypotheses inappropriate to the facts.[40]

3. Deductive vs. Inductive System.[41]

The principle of population, as enunciated in the first edition of the *Essay*, was wholly deductive. It started with axioms and proceeded to conclusions inferred from them. Subsequent editions, as we have seen, were based also on a mass of empirical data, gathered to check and support the original thesis. In its final statement, Malthus's theory is not clearly either deductive or inductive, but a sometimes confusing mixture of the two.

An indication of this confusion is the ambiguity of a number of key words. In the phrase, "the ultimate check to population appears to be a

[38] Thomas Doubleday, *The True Law of Population Shewn to Be Connected with the Food of the People* (London: Simpkin, Marshall, 1842), p. 7.

[39] Godwin, *Political Justice*, quoted in Malthus, *Essay*, p. 392.

[40] John Maynard Keynes, *The General Theory of Employment, Interest, and Money* (New York: Harcourt, Brace, 1935), pp. 32, 371. See below page 531.

[41] See Kingsley Davis, "Malthus and the Theory of Population," in Paul F. Lazarsfeld and Morris Rosenberg, *The Language of Social Research: A Reader in the Methodology of Social Research* (Glencoe, Ill.: Free Press, 1955), pp. 540–553.

want of food," what is the meaning of "ultimate"? Sometimes it seems to mean "in the long run" (if the potential population increase is realized, then ultimately the lack of food will become the most important check), but Malthus emphasized that the potential had never been fully realized, and if moral restraint became general, the population need never press on the means of subsistence. Sometimes "ultimate" seems to mean "fundamental, underlying all other checks" (for both vices and moral restraint were often the consequence of hunger, or of the fear of it); yet Malthus also emphasized that the standard of living could rise above the subsistence level, so that hunger would be completely irrelevant to actual population trends—as indeed it has become in the countries of the West since his day.

A more important symptom of the confusion between Malthus's deductive and inductive systems is the ambiguity of the word "tendency." [42] In the sentence—apart from "extreme cases, . . . population always increases where the means of subsistence increase"—the tendency seems to be a summary of empirical data. In other contexts, however, the "tendency" of population to increase up to the means of subsistence means its "power . . . when unchecked."

If we try to resolve these confusions, expressing Malthus's ideas in present-day terms, he seems to be making several assertions at once: Man's physiological ability to reproduce is great enough to permit any population to double each generation (true). Actual fertility has never been so high as this fecundity (probably true). In most cases, however, the checks on population growth imposed by reduced fertility were less important than those effected by heavy mortality (generally true of Malthus's day and of prior periods, though the postponement of marriage had also been a significant factor). The most important reason for late marriage, and for high death rates, was usually an actual or threatened shortage of food (the postponement of marriage had been enforced by institutionalized regulations; and, at least in Europe, disease was more significant than hunger as the cause of early death).

Malthus's population theory is neither wholly valid nor wholly defective. It suffers from inconsistencies and ambiguities. Yet Malthus's principle of population has been one element in almost every subsequent theory, and many of the later reformulations were no great improvement in either logical or empirical terms.

Malthus's results were not all new and were not all true; but his work has the merit of being the first thorough application of the inductive method to social

[42] See the interesting exchange between Malthus and Nassau Senior, reprinted in McCleary, *op. cit.,* pp. 114–128.

SACRED TO THE MEMORY

OF

The Rev. Thomas Robert Malthus

LONG KNOWN TO THE LETTERED WORLD
BY HIS ADMIRABLE WRITINGS ON THE SOCIAL BRANCHES OF
POLITICAL ECONOMY,
PARTICULARLY BY HIS 'ESSAY ON POPULATION'.

ONE OF THE BEST MEN AND TRUEST PHILOSOPHERS
OF ANY AGE OR COUNTRY,
RAISED BY NATIVE DIGNITY OF MIND
ABOVE THE MISREPRESENTATIONS OF THE IGNORANT
AND THE NEGLECT OF THE GREAT,
HE LIVED A SERENE AND HAPPY LIFE
DEVOTED TO THE PURSUIT AND COMMUNICATION
OF TRUTH,
SUPPORTED BY A CALM BUT FIRM CONVICTION OF THE
USEFULNESS OF HIS LABOURS,
CONTENT WITH THE APPROBATION OF THE WISE AND GOOD.

HIS WRITINGS WILL BE A LASTING MONUMENT
OF THE EXTENT AND CORRECTNESS OF HIS UNDERSTANDING.

THE SPOTLESS INTEGRITY OF HIS PRINCIPLES
THE EQUITY AND CANDOUR OF HIS NATURE,
HIS SWEETNESS OF TEMPER, URBANITY OF MANNERS,
AND TENDERNESS OF HEART,
HIS BENEVOLENCE AND HIS PIETY,
ARE THE STILL DEARER RECOLLECTIONS OF HIS FAMILY
AND FRIENDS

Born 14th Feb. 1766.   *Died 29 Dec. 1834.*

[*Inscription on the tablet in Bath Abbey*]

science. The chief workers therefore in the modern historical school of economics justly regard him as one of the founders of that school and his work as a solid possession for ever.[43]

[43] Alfred Marshall, *Principles of Economics*, quoted in McCleary, *op. cit.*, p. 50.

POPULATION OPTIMA

If the term "Neo-Malthusian" had not been appropriated by the advocates of birth control, it would be an apt designation for the economists who developed the concept of population optimum. In this sense, as in the usual one, "Neo-Malthusianism" would mean not merely a continuation of Malthus's ideas but their projection to a new level. The mathematical formulation of Malthus's principle could be called no more than a first approximation: population tends to increase by a geometrical ratio and food by an arithmetical ratio; therefore, population tends to press against the means of subsistence. These two progressions can be reformulated in terms of the **law of diminishing returns,** as follows: To produce food, two factors are required—land and labor. If to a fixed amount of land more and more labor is added, the result will generally be a declining per capita return. For while the two factors are interchangeable to some degree (as can be seen in the difference between extensive and intensive agriculture), eventually increasing the workers per acre by x per cent will result in a rise of production by less than x per cent. The first statement of population optimum was essentially a development from such a simple model.[44]

In his discussion of a newly settled area like America, Malthus sometimes half-intimated that population increase there was not only no problem but an actual benefit. If he meant to say this, he certainly did not say it clearly, and the first improvement on his theory is to posit **underpopulation** as well as **overpopulation** as a possible relation between people and land. Or, to continue with the same simple model, if to a fixed number of acres, more and more laborers are added, the first result may be a greater than proportionate increase in per capita production, then a proportionate increase, and only finally a decreasing return. As Cannan put it, "If we want to preserve the phrase 'diminishing returns' we must take the point of maximum return as the starting-point, and say that returns diminish in either direction, all commodities or industries being always and everywhere subject to this 'Law of diminishing returns.' "[45]

Cannan's second emendation of Malthus's theory is no less important

[44] For an excellent review of this development, see Lionel Robbins, "The Optimum Theory of Population," in T. E. Gregory and Hugh Dalton, eds., *London Essays in Economics in Honour of Edwin Cannan* (London: Routledge, 1927), pp. 103–134.

[45] Edwin Cannan, *Wealth: A Brief Explanation of the Causes of Economic Welfare* (3rd ed.; London: King, 1928), p. 59.

—the correction of his almost exclusive concern with food. Even the simplest list of economic factors includes land, labor, and also capital; and of the three the last is crucial in many circumstances. And if we analyze not only agriculture but also industry, then land is only one of the relevant natural resources that can be exhausted by growing numbers.[46]

The optimum population of any country, as defined in terms of these criticisms of Malthus, is the number of people that produces the highest per capita economic return. In the writings of various analysts, this "return" has been specified as total production per head, or real income per head, or the point at which the marginal and the average product per laborer are equal.[47] Which criterion is used is less important than the idea that it should be an exact measure of specifically economic welfare. Such a definition of a population optimum, however, has been challenged on a number of grounds.

Actual or Optimum Institutional Framework?

The issue between Godwin and Malthus, or between Malthusians and Marxists, is relevant also to the definition of optimum population. The famous dispute in the 1920's between Keynes and Beveridge about whether England was overpopulated, as another example, was largely terminological. As Warren Thompson later summarized it,

> If we are thinking of overpopulation as a condition which cannot arise so long as there are conceivable ways in which more people can be employed so as to produce larger real incomes, then apparently Sir William [Beveridge] was right, and there is no overpopulation in England or in Europe. . . . On the other hand, if we think of overpopulation as a condition in which there are too many people to be employed at good real wages under the conditions which actually exist and which appear likely to exist for some time to come, it would seem that Professor Keynes was fully justified in saying that England and Europe are overpopulated.[48]

In more recent years, the issue has often arisen with respect to the new nations of Asia and Africa, whose present population pressure is ascribed

[46] For an interesting discussion of the revival of Malthusianism in these terms, see Harold Wright, *Population* (New York: Harcourt, Brace, 1923), Ch. 5.

[47] The last formulation, which in theoretical terms is perhaps the best, is given in Julius Isaac, *Economics of Migration* (London: Kegan Paul, Trench, Trubner, 1947), p. 71. See also above, pages 323–325.

[48] Warren S. Thompson, *Population Problems* (2nd ed.; New York: McGraw-Hill, 1935), p. 426. See also Hugh Dalton, "The Theory of Population," *Economica*, 8:22 (March, 1928), 28–50.

to the imperial powers' maladministration during the earlier colonial period. By such an analysis, even Egypt is not overpopulated.[49] Soviet spokesmen have generalized this point in preposterously utopian terms. According to Alfred Sauvy, the French delegate to the United Nations Population Commission, at its very first session the Ukranian delegate, Rabishko, "violently opposed the theory of an optimum population, at least as he knew it, asserting more or less the following: 'I would consider it barbaric for the Commission to contemplate a limitation of marriages or of legitimate births, and this for any country whatsoever, at any period whatsoever. With an adequate social organization, it is possible to face any increase in population.' " [50]

In order to discuss the concept of optimum at all, one must first agree, then, (a) that population *is* a factor in economic welfare, no matter what the social organization, and (b) that it is the present institutions, with whatever changes may be reasonably expected, that are relevant— not those of the past ("imperialism") or the supposed future ("socialism").

Economic or General Welfare?

As the separate discipline of demography developed, population theorists began to wonder whether the economists had not delimited the optimum too narrowly. Attempts were made to restate it in terms of general welfare rather than income or production per head. Sometimes the new measure chosen was a demographic one, such as expectation of life,[51] but once a reasonably precise economic standard was abandoned as too narrow, the tendency was toward broader, vaguer criteria. By Penrose's definition, for example, the optimum population is "the numbers socially desirable." [52] The income and welfare concepts of optimum population are identical, in his view, "on the assumption that this income is spent in the consumption of the kinds and amounts of goods and services that make the maximum contribution to welfare." For example, all the money

[49] E. Nassif, "L'Égypte est-elle surpeuplée?" *Population,* 5:3 (July–September, 1950), 513–532. See also above, pages 478–479.

[50] Alfred Sauvy, *Théorie générale de la population,* 1: *Économie et population* (Paris: Presses Universitaires de France, 1952), 174. See also *ibid.,* vol. 2: *Biologie sociale* (1954), Ch. 22.

[51] Radha Kamal Mukerjee, "Optimum and Over-Population," *Indian Journal of Economics,* 10:3 (January, 1930), 407–421.

[52] E. F. Penrose, *Population Theories and Their Application with Special Reference to Japan* (Stanford, Calif.: Food Research Institute, 1934), p. 90.

for food should be spent in accord with a consensus among biochemists on the kind and amount needed for optimum physiological welfare, and similarly for other products.[53] There is, of course, no such consensus, even within any one culture. The concept of a general-welfare optimum, more broadly, "does not give sufficient weight to the influence of culture-patterns upon *how* given needs are satisfied, [and] it ignores the influence of the culture-pattern upon the *number* of needs that must be satisfied." [54]

One of the cultural elements that are relevant is the level of aspiration. Quite often, as the real income of a country (or of one social class) goes up, the people see their situation as deteriorating, for their expectations rise still faster. Thus, in the words of a League of Nations study committee, "Overpopulation may be said to exist, not so much in actual figures as in the consciousness of the country concerned." [55] With such a definition, *the* optimum is indeterminate. "A country is overpopulated in relation to another country when its standard of living is lower than in the latter. Thus country A, though underpopulated with reference to an absolute optimum, may consider itself overpopulated in relation to its neighbour B." [56]

An economic measure and a more general one are both indexes of the same variable, the first more reliable and the second more valid. But is the people's welfare the only objective that a nation seeks with its population policy? In particular, is the number of people that produces the maximum income per capita necessarily the same as the one best able to defend the country at war? Obviously not, yet these are only two out of several possible goals of policy. Sauvy has listed a number of such different national objectives, each of which would have a different optimum population associated with it. Rather than maximum wealth, a country may seek a maximum rate of increase in wealth; or the conservation of its natural resources for future generations; or power, whether military or other; or full employment; or the maximum distribution of knowledge and culture among its people; or general well-being, as measured by health or longevity or otherwise. He concludes,

[53] *Ibid.*, pp. 74–83.
[54] Spengler, *France Faces Depopulation*, pp. 274–275.
[55] Quoted in Fergus Chalmers Wright, *Population and Peace: A Survey of International Opinion on Claims for Relief from Population Pressure* (League of Nations, International Studies Conference; Paris: International Institute of Intellectual Cooperation, 1939), p. 80.
[56] Adolphe Landry, quoted in International Studies Conference, *Peaceful Change: Procedures, Population, Raw Materials, Colonies* (League of Nations; Paris: International Institute of Intellectual Co-operation, 1938), p. 122.

The optimum population is that which insures the realization of a given objective in the most satisfactory manner. . . . The concept is nothing more than a convenience at the present time. The demographer may use it as an intermediary tool in the same way that the mathematician uses imaginary numbers.[57]

Over two or three decades, thus, the concept of optimum population became so broad as to lose all real meaning. Perhaps the very word "optimum" was too moralistic to be apt for a scientific term. Originally it meant the number of people that would make best use of a given economy, but it gradually came to mean simply "the best population," with each analyst furnishing his own yardstick of what is "good." A nature enthusiast might call for more and larger national parks, with the optimum over large areas set at zero. A nationalist might be affronted at the very notion that there could be too many natives of Country X. A utopian, as we have noted, derides the proposition that population size has any economic or other effect at all in an optimum social environment. It cannot be the function of one definition to decide such questions, or even to take sides on them. The **optimum population** of any area is the number of people which, in the given natural, cultural, and social environment, produces the maximum economic return. The definition does not imply that this environment ought, or ought not, to be changed. Nor does it state that the maximum economic return is the only legitimate goal of a nation's population policy. These are different questions, and specifying the economic effects of population size is in itself a difficult enough problem.

The Economic Optimum

The *size* of a population, first of all, is a very gross measure of its economic relevance. Among purely demographic characteristics, the rate of growth and the age structure are of almost equal significance—not to mention health, literacy, skill, and so on. Moreover, the relation between population and resources in modified Malthusian terms, and that between population and economic growth in Keynesian terms, are quite different. Ultimately, the Malthusian model is still relevant even in wealthy countries. In the long run, maximum numbers are indeed set by the total resources available and the skill in exploiting them. However,

---

[57] Sauvy, *Théorie générale*, 1, 50–53. The various attempts to coalesce these diverse goals into a single definition of optimum cannot be regarded as very successful; see in particular Imre Ferenczi, *The Synthetic Optimum of Population: An Outline of an International Demographic Policy* (League of Nations; Paris: International Institute of Intellectual Co-operation, 1938).

in the long run, as Keynes once remarked, we are all dead. Within any one industrial country with a capitalist or mixed economy, over a period of, say, one generation, rapid growth not only uses up some of the resources but—and this is often the more important point—keeps the economy going.

In classical theory, just as every feasible demand elicits a supply, so supply creates its own demand; for in a free economy the production of goods in itself gives the eventual consumers the power to purchase them. True, the commodities produced may not wholly coincide in kind with those in demand; that is, local, specific crises are possible, but these are checked by the automatic adjustment between supply and demand. But a *general* economic crisis—a general fall of prices to below cost, general overproduction, general unemployment—is impossible by the very nature of the economic system. This doctrine—usually termed Say's Law, after Jean-Baptiste Say, who gave it its most precise formulation—had been challenged by Malthus and, in different terms, by Marx; but among orthodox economists it held its own until Keynes upset it by reviving the Malthusian concept of effective demand.

According to Keynes, the automatic circuit posited by classical theory is completed only in the special case when planned savings and planned investment are equal; in all other cases, a part of the potential purchasing power is siphoned off into idle savings, or "hoards." It is particularly in wealthy countries (that is, also those whose populations were presumed to be in "incipient decline") that investment tends to be inadequate, for two reasons—because a smaller share of the national income is consumed and thus a larger share is left to be invested, and because the larger capital stock means that new investment opportunities are more difficult to find. Thus, as the stock of capital grows in any one country, the possibilities for new investment are less; or, in Keynesian terms, other things being equal, the marginal efficiency of capital is lower, the greater the existing amount of capital. Why should this long-term decline in the marginal efficiency of capital not have been operative during the nineteenth century? Because, as Keynes put it, "the growth of population and of invention, the opening-up of new lands, the state of confidence and the frequency of war over the average of (say) each decade seem to have been sufficient." [58]

Keynes's primary concern was with another problem; but his few *obiter dicta* on population encouraged other economists to formulate a

[58] Keynes, *The General Theory,* p. 307.

tentative theory of demographic-economic development. "With increasing population, investment can go roaring ahead, even if invention is rather stupid; increasing population is therefore actually favourable to employment. It is actually easier to employ an expanding population than a contracting one, whatever arithmetic would suggest." [59] It may even be that the economic progress of the modern era had been based principally or largely on its population growth.

One is tempted to a "population interpretation" of modern capitalism. Professor Cannan sensed it. Professor J. R. Hicks now toys with it as he wonders in a footnote at the end of his *Value and Capital* whether the "whole industrial revolution of the last two centuries has been nothing else but a vast secular boom, largely induced by the unparalleled rise in population." Professor Schumpeter has little to say about population, yet perhaps the "first Schumpeter," as Dr. Innis in his review of Schumpeter's recent *Business Cycles* has playfully christened the long cycle (1787–1929), was mainly conditioned by population growth; and it may prove to be the only "Schumpeter." Modern capitalist free enterprise may prove to have been a boom system, and the modern trend to something like the old mercantilism may be a trend towards institutions appropriate to an era of stationary population.[60]

Thus, on the one hand, an increasing population requires larger investment in capital equipment; but, on the other hand, in a capitalist country with a developed economy this very demand keeps investment "roaring ahead" and the economy healthy. That is to say, if the number of a country's inhabitants is at its optimum point by one economic criterion, by another it may be too small—or, better, its rate of growth may be too low. There are at least two economic optima, a Malthusian one and a Keynesian one. The first is the population that, in terms of present or prospective technology and institutions, affords the highest per capita standard of living; the second is the population growing at the rate that, in terms of . . . etc. Though it is obvious that these are not the same concept, they are often treated as though they were. Thus, as one example out of many, the argument of the 1930's against immigration to Australia (that its empty land was largely uninhabitable desert [61])

[59] J. R. Hicks, "Mr. Keynes' Theory of Employment," *Economic Journal,* 46:182 (June, 1936), 238–253.

[60] V. W. Bladen, "Population Problems and Policies," in Chester Martin, ed., *Canada in Peace and War: Eight Studies in National Trends Since 1914* (Canadian Institute of International Affairs; Toronto: Oxford University Press, 1941), pp. 86–119.

[61] See, for example, W. D. Forsyth, *The Myth of Open Spaces: Australian, British and World Trend of Population and Migration* (Melbourne: Melbourne University Press, 1942).

has been answered by postwar proponents of immigration in part within the same Malthusian framework (by pointing out the potentialities of irrigation), but principally in Keynesian terms (a rapidly growing population makes for a healthy economy). A Keynesian analysis, however, is appropriate only when Malthusian pressure is not acute. On a true Sahara, more people bring no benefits.

The second element omitted from the concept of optimum population as this is ordinarily understood is age structure. Western Europe is too populous, let us suppose, in the sense that a smaller number of people would enjoy a higher average real income, and it is agreed that an attempt should therefore be made to reduce the rate of growth. This can be done in only three ways—by increasing mortality (which is, of course, ruled out as a policy in nontotalitarian countries), decreasing fertility, and increasing net emigration. But either a decline in births or a rise in emigration cuts down the proportion of young people, and thus aggravates Europe's other demographic problem—the large proportion of dependent aged. "These conditions pose a dilemma—grow or age—a conflict between population structure and population size." [62]

Dalton is certainly correct in his view that any conceivable test of the population optimum could not be "of very great precision." "We could hardly hope to determine the optimum, for any given area at any given time, more closely than within a range of, say, five per cent. on either side." [63] Even the restrained optimism of this "hope" is not warranted in many cases. For example, Spengler writes that France's population of 42 million (in 1938) ought to be cut down by a quarter to maximize the per capita income,[64] while Sauvy sets the optimum at somewhere between 50 and 75 million.[65] When two men so eminently qualified to discuss the population of France differ by this degree, others may wonder whether the concept has any utility. Myrdal, for instance, terms the theory of optimum population "one of the most sterile ideas" ever developed in economics. "Its elaboration has not increased its scientific significance or practical applicability. The theory stands mainly as an excuse for, and also as an actual inhibition of, the proper posing of the problem of the economic effects of population changes." [66]

[62] Alfred Sauvy, *L'Europe et sa population* (Paris: Editions Internationales, 1953), p. 119.
[63] Dalton, "The Theory," *op. cit.*
[64] Spengler, *France Faces Depopulation*, p. 273.
[65] Sauvy, *Théorie générale*, 1, 186.
[66] Gunnar Myrdal, *Population: A Problem for Democracy* (Cambridge: Harvard University Press, 1940), pp. 26–27. Cf. T. Lynn Smith, *Population Analysis* (New York: McGraw-Hill, 1948), pp. 388–389.

Yet the idea behind the concept, that national income can sometimes be increased by adjusting the population to the economy, should not be abandoned. It is the rationale behind many specific policies, including, for example, the pronatalist program in Sweden that Myrdal helped work out. If the theory of population optimum is to be at all useful, however, it is necessary first of all to dispense with both the heavy ideological luggage and the legitimate scientific questions to which we can as yet give no definite answers. Secondly, we must recognize that this measure, while a valid one if appropriately used, is extremely crude: to say that India is overpopulated is meaningful and correct, but with respect to France we should perhaps not even ask the question. While this is a much more modest achievement than the analysts who developed the concept of optimum envisioned, it is still something. So excellent a book as Coale and Hoover's on India [67] is a culmination of the type of analysis that began with Malthus and developed in part in the writings on the population optimum.

SUMMARY

Malthus's *Essay on the Principle of Population,* in spite of all its faults and limitations, marks the beginning of scientific demographic theory. It helped establish two valid theses: (a) Contrary to the beliefs of mercantilists, the population was growing rapidly. Wise social policy consisted in the opposite of pronatalist decrees—an effort to substitute the control of fertility for high death rates. (b) Contrary to utopian dogmas, man is not only a social being but also a biological one. The population of even a perfect society depends on births and deaths, and thus on the sexual drive and food.

The difficulty that Malthus had in separating scientific from ethical canons has persisted in various formulations of the optimum, a development from the population-resources dilemma that he analyzed. Some demographers believe that the very term is dispensable, but the idea behind it—the population that affords the highest economic return—is a necessary basis of any policy.

[67] Ansley J. Coale and Edgar M. Hoover, *Population Growth and Economic Development in Low-Income Countries: A Case Study of India's Prospects* (Princeton: Princeton University Press, 1958). See above, page 482.

SUGGESTIONS FOR FURTHER READING

T. R. Malthus, *An Essay on the Principle of Population* (7th ed.; London: Reeves and Turner, 1872).

G. F. McCleary, *The Malthusian Population Theory* (London: Faber & Faber, 1953).

D. V. Glass, ed., *Introduction to Malthus* (New York: Wiley, 1953).

Joseph J. Spengler, "Malthus's Total Population Theory: A Restatement and Reappraisal," *Canadian Journal of Economics and Political Science,* 11:1 (February, 1945), 83–110; 11:2 (May, 1945), 234–264.

> In order to know what Malthus said, it is necessary to read him. The three supplementary works are part of an enormous literature.

Lionel Robbins, "The Optimum Theory of Population," in T. E. Gregory and Hugh Dalton, eds., *London Essays in Economics in Honour of Edwin Cannan* (London: Routledge, 1927), pp. 103–134.

A. B. Wolfe, "The Optimum Size of Population," in Louis I. Dublin, ed., *Population Problems in the United States and Canada* (New York: Houghton Mifflin, 1926), pp. 63–76.

Roy G. Francis, ed., *The Population Ahead* (Minneapolis: University of Minnesota Press, 1958).

> Two of the best early discussions of population optimum, and a collection of interesting essays on Malthusian themes.

Harvey Leibenstein, *A Theory of Economic-Demographic Development* (Princeton: Princeton University Press, 1954).

> A good example of the kind of model that today's economists use. Not easy reading for one not trained in economics.

William Petersen, "Marx versus Malthus: The Men and the Symbols," *Population Review* (Madras), 1:2 (July, 1957), 21–32; "John Maynard Keynes's Theories of Population and the Concept of 'Optimum,'" *Population Studies,* 8:3 (March, 1955), 228–246.

> These articles overlap in part with this chapter.

18. *THE GENERAL DETERMINANTS*
OF FERTILITY

A "Malthusian" analysis is ordinarily taken to mean one that relates population to the natural resources on which it must subsist. This designation emphasizes only one portion of Malthus's own work, which included also some consideration of fertility and mortality, the two components of natural increase. It is true, of course, that it is not adequate to analyze either births or deaths separately. Whether in single families or in societies, the more that are born the more there are to die, and the fewer that die the more incentive there is to reduce the number born. It is also true, however, that some determinants of fertility and mortality, as well as of migration, operate independently of each other. Indeed, it is because of this fact that certain countries suffer from a population "problem," for an increase in the number of people does not adjust itself easily and automatically to a change in subsistence. In other words, there is not an inherent tendency in any population to move toward an optimum level.[1]

By the "general" determinants of fertility are meant those not specific to any particular culture. The ones most clearly general in this sense are the biological characteristics of the human species relevant to conception and childbearing, and these are discussed in the first section of the chapter. It is atypical behavior in almost any society, however, to realize the physiologically maximum family size. The actual number of children is reduced both by birth control and by various social usages that influence fertility even though this is not their purpose. Such value systems and institutional patterns can be universal culture traits in either of two senses: The nuclear family exists in all societies, and all of its varieties are similar

[1] The contrary was the view of A. M. Carr-Saunders, as given in *The Population Problem: A Study in Human Evolution* (Oxford: Clarendon, 1922), Ch. 9. See also above, page 492.

536

in a number of basic respects. The age at marriage, on the other hand, exemplifies a social pattern with a wide range from one society to another, a similarity "in classification, not in content." [2] Both types of universals are discussed in this chapter, as well as birth control, which is associated historically with the Western world but may become a universal in the future.

BIOLOGICAL DETERMINANTS OF FECUNDITY

The successful fertilization of a human egg, the beginning of a new life, is also the climax of a complex process. On the male side, healthy spermatazoa must have been formed in one of the testicles in sufficient number and safely stored in the epididymis, have passed through the vas deferens and mixed there with the proper amount of fluid from the seminal vesicles and the prostate, finally to be ejected into the vagina with sufficient force for some of the spermatazoa (only a few thousand out of the millions that started) to pass into the cervix and a still smaller number through the uterus, so that one finally reaches an ovum ready to be fertilized. On the female side, a healthy ovum must have been formed in one of the ovaries, have gone without mishap down the fallopian tube, to be fertilized there, and then passed into the uterus, where the fetus will develop. The male's role ends with conception, but a failure of the female may be either inability to conceive or inability to carry the child the full nine-month period and give successful birth.

Several times in the preceding chapters, the danger of confusing biological with cultural determinants of human behavior has been emphasized. The analysis of fertility trends, especially though not exclusively by nineteenth-century theorists, was an egregious example of this fault.[3] Did the smaller families in cities result from an impairment of the physiological ability to bear children, or from the desire for fewer children that the urban setting stimulated? The facts available to the earliest investigators, mainly that the urban middle classes were leading the trend toward lower fertility, could be used to support either theory, and indeed the two were often not sharply distinguished. Actually, the physiological ability to procreate has undoubtedly increased in industrial societies, to-

[2] George Peter Murdock, "The Common Denominator of Cultures," in Ralph Linton, ed., *The Science of Man in the World Crisis* (New York: Columbia University Press, 1945), pp. 123–142.

[3] See the summary of some of the important early studies in Edward Reynolds and Donald Macomber, *Fertility and Sterility in Human Marriages* (Philadelphia: Saunders, 1924), Ch. 2.

gether with the improvement in level of living, the conquest of venereal diseases, etc.

The terms *fecundity* and *fertility,* originally used synonymously, were differentiated from one another only gradually. In 1934 the Population Association of America officially endorsed the distinction between **fecundity,** the physiological ability to reproduce; and **fertility,** the realization of this potential, the actual birth performance as measured by the number of offspring.[4] Now that the distinction is made conceptually, it is still difficult to apply it in practice. For at the present level of medical knowledge, the only absolute evidence that a person is fecund is the production of an offspring, in which case fecundity and fertility are operationally identical. The available evidence suggests that the fecundity of each of the partners can be affected by several physical factors, of which the most important are discussed briefly in the following paragraphs.

Heredity

While the evidence is not clear-cut, it seems that one factor influencing the innate ability to reproduce is the relative fecundity of one's forebears. Such a physical determinant is often very difficult to estimate, of course, for whenever children remain in the same social and economic situation as their parents—which by and large is the typical case—a similar size in the two generations may be due merely to the continuous pressure of this unchanged environment. It is only at the two extremes of the fecundity range that hereditary influence is definitely perceptible. On the one hand, fecundity can be impaired by any one of a number of defects in the sexual organs; and a predisposition toward such constitutional impediments can be inherited. Certain of such hereditary defects block

---

[4] While this distinction is not always made in nonprofessional writings, it is now fairly consistently maintained in demographic works in English. "In many Latin languages, the etymological equivalents of fertility and fecundity are used in a sense diametrically opposite to that in English. Thus, the French *fécondité* or the Spanish *fecondidad* are properly translated by fertility, and *fertilité* or *fertilidad* by fecundity. It should also be noted that although the conventions outlined above are generally followed by demographers, the terms fertility and fecundity are used much more loosely in medical literature, where they are sometimes treated as being almost synonymous" (United Nations, Department of Economic and Social Affairs, *Multilingual Demographic Dictionary: English Section,* Population Studies, no. 29, New York, 1958, p. 38). The definitions in Norman L. Hoerr and Arthur Osol, eds., *Blackiston's New Gould Medical Dictionary* (2nd ed.; New York: McGraw-Hill, 1956), pp. 440, 443, agree with demographers' usage; but in *Stedman's Medical Dictionary* (17th rev. ed.; Baltimore: Williams & Wilkins, 1957), pp. 514, 517, the meanings are not distinguished.

reproduction altogether, and with others any offspring die before they in turn can procreate. The inheritance of a high level of fecundity, on the other hand, is suggested by the fact that the proportion of multiple births differs significantly both from one family line to another and from one race to another. In one notable case, when one of a set of quadruplets married one of a pair of twins, they had 32 children in eleven confinements. In the opinion of some analysts, such a tendency toward multiple births is one expression of high general fecundity, with which it seems to be correlated.[5]

Health

Like any other animal, a human being with a certain innate reproductive capacity has the highest possible fecundity when he or she is in a state of vigorous health. Certain infections, such as syphilis, gonorrhea, or tuberculosis of the genital tract, impede or prevent procreation directly. And if a person's health is impaired by any other causes—such as, among others, a nonvenereal disease,[6] food deficiency,[7] or psychoneurosis[8]— this also affects his reproductive capacity adversely.

This seemingly obvious statement, however, does not follow simply and directly from the empirical evidence. On the contrary, human misery and high fertility are very frequently associated, and some analysts have interpreted this correlation to mean that the relatively healthful and comfortable life of the middle class in Western countries has reduced the average fecundity. Thus, one has suggested that the decline in the average size of the Western family was due to factors like "the widespread habit of excessive washing";[9] another that it was due to the high-protein diet of well-to-do classes and nations.[10] Contrary to such interpretations, most

---

[5] Raymond Pearl, *The Natural History of Population* (New York: Oxford University Press, 1939), pp. 34–36, 58–65.

[6] John W. Ballew and William H. Masters, "Mumps: A Cause of Infertility," *Fertility and Sterility*, 5:6 (November–December, 1954), 536–543. The evidence in the case of this disease is still inconclusive.

[7] Harold B. Hulme, "Effect of Semistarvation on Human Semen," *ibid.*, 2:4 (July–August, 1951), 319–331.

[8] Among many other works, see Earle M. Marsh and Albert M. Vollmer, "Possible Psychogenic Aspects of Infertility," *ibid.*, 2:1 (January, 1951), 70–79; Carlo Bos and R. A. Gleghorn, "Psychogenic Sterility," *ibid.*, 9:2 (March–April, 1958), 84–98; John C. Flugel, *The Psycho-analytic Study of the Family* (8th ed.; London: Hogarth, 1950).

[9] Enid Charles, *The Menace of Under-Population: A Biological Study of the Decline of Population Growth* (London: Watts, 1936), pp. 182–183.

[10] Josué de Castro, *Geography of Hunger* (London: Gollancz, 1952); for a sharply critical appraisal of this work, see the review by Kingsley Davis in *American Sociological Review*, 17:4 (August, 1952), 500–501.

demographers today would agree that cleanliness and good food, together with all other conditions conducive to good health, increase reproductive capacity to the degree that they affect it at all, but that these physical factors have often been negated in industrial societies by the higher social valuation put on small families.

Age

Procreation is the normal function primarily of young adults. The capacity to reproduce, entirely lacking in childhood, begins to appear at the age of 13 to 16 years (puberty), develops gradually for a period of several years (adolescence), and reaches a high point at maturity. It then declines in middle age, relatively rapidly and completely in females, slowly and apparently sometimes only partially in males. Individual cases vary widely from this pattern,[11] and even the averages for social groups differ from it, though over a narrower range.

The normal level of human fecundity is not constant over the whole period during which it is present. In the female the first menstruation (menarche), which is usually taken to define puberty, is actually one step—the most clearly marked one—in a long process, and the regular development of healthy ova usually begins later. For several years, thus, the female is able to produce a child, but the probability that she will do so with a given amount of exposure is less than at maturity. Corresponding to this period of **adolescent subfecundity** [12] is one of **senescent subfecundity,** from about age 30 to the last menstruation (menopause).

Ovulation Cycle

The human female, like all other female mammals, produces ova periodically rather than continuously. In most subprimate species, the same hormone that controls this ovulation cycle also regulates the female's sexual desire. When the egg is ready to be fertilized, the female animal is "in heat" (estrus) and accepts, or seeks, the male's advances; and at

[11] Children have been born to a mother of 6.5 years, at one extreme, and to one of 59 or possibly even 63 years, at the other; see Pearl, *op. cit.,* pp. 57–58; Robert R. Kuczynski, *The Measurement of Population Growth: Methods and Results* (London: Sidgwick & Jackson, 1935), pp. 106–110.

[12] To term it "adolescent sterility" adds an unnecessary confusion; it is better to restrict the meaning of the word *sterility* to total physiological inability to procreate. See M. F. Ashley Montagu, *The Reproductive Development of the Female, with Especial Reference to the Period of Adolescent Sterility: A Study in the Comparative Physiology of the Infecundity of the Adolescent Organism* (New York: Julian, 1957).

all other times (during anestrus) she rejects them. Sexual union in such species is, in two senses, narrowly physiological: its timing is determined by the animal's glandular flow, and the union has the single function of physical reproduction.

In most primate species the female exhibits this estrus-anestrus cycle in a vestigial form. The vaginal skin of the female chimpanzee, for example, tightens and reddens at the time of ovulation, and this greater prominence of the sexual organ stimulates the male to more frequent copulation. In most respects, however, the sexual behavior of monkeys and apes resembles that of humans rather than that of mammals lower on the evolutionary scale. As with humans, there is a menstrual cycle, overlapping with the ovulation cycle. And, as with humans, the female is accessible to the male's advances at any time, not only when she is estrous. Among primates, that is to say, the sex drive serves two functions: to reproduce the species, and to induce a mating couple to form a permanent union.[13]

In the normal cycle of the human female, during the years of sexual maturity one or more ova are released from each ovary once every 28 days. Each month, while they are developing, the wall of the uterus swells, preparatory to receiving a fertilized ovum. Unless a successful copulation takes place during the several days (or, according to some authorities, the several hours) that fertilization is possible, the ova disintegrate. The female is then sterile until the following cycle. In that case the wall of the uterus also disintegrates, discharging blood through the vagina. There is thus also a menstrual cycle of 28 days, with each menstruation spaced about half-way between two ovulations. Human females, however, have no remnant of the estrus-anestrus cycle. On the contrary, if women experience a cyclical variation in sex drive, they are likely to feel the strongest desire just before and just after menstruation, when fertile copulation is normally impossible, and the weakest desire just at the time of ovulation.[14]

Lactation

After a woman has given birth to a child, if she does not breast-feed it, the menstrual cycle normally begins again in about two months and

[13] For an interesting elaboration of this thesis, see S. Zuckerman, *The Social Life of Monkeys and Apes* (London: Kegan Paul, Trench, Trubner, 1932).
[14] Katharine Bement Davis, *Factors in the Sex Life of Twenty-Two Hundred Women* (Publications of the Bureau of Social Hygiene; New York: Harper, 1929), Chs. 8–9; Pearl, *op. cit.*, pp. 32–34.

the ovulation cycle two months later still. The recurrence of regular ovulation, and thus the probability of another pregnancy, are usually impeded so long as the mammary glands remain active, though the evidence on this relation is not firmly established.[15]

Sex Drive

Sex drive, which may fall anywhere within a wide range, is markedly influenced by most of the physical factors already discussed, as well as by various cultural determinants. The dominance of the male in most cultures means that his sexuality is more likely than the female's to determine the incidence of marital coitus. According to nine American and European studies summarized by Pearl, the average frequency of coitus between married couples is very slightly more than ten times per month.[16] Kinsey gives a much lower over-all figure, 1.06 times per week.[17] If what anthropologists are told on this matter can be accepted, the frequency is considerably higher among nonindustrial peoples. "In most of the [primitive] societies on which information is available, every adult normally engages in heterosexual intercourse once daily or nightly during the periods when coitus is permitted." [18] In all cultures the range of individual differentiation is wide. And whether any of these data are trustworthy may be questioned, for they are distorted both by the inclination everywhere to preserve the privacy of the sexual act and the tendency, probably no less universal, of at least the male to exaggerate his prowess.

An Index of Fecundity

With the development of diagnostic skill, it should become possible to devise a reasonably accurate criterion of fecundity by combining measures of the various relevant physical characteristics of the two partners. Indeed, a pioneer attempt to construct such an index was made

[15] See Clellan S. Ford and Frank A. Beach, *Patterns of Sexual Behavior* (New York: Harper, 1951), pp. 217–220.

[16] Pearl, *op. cit.*, p. 69.

[17] Alfred C. Kinsey, Wardell B. Pomeroy, and Clyde E. Martin, *Sexual Behavior in the Human Male* (Philadelphia: Saunders, 1948), p. 568.

[18] Ford and Beach, *op. cit.*, p. 78. The comment of a physician in Central Africa may well be relevant generally: "We have interrogated a small proportion of our patients about the frequency of intercourse in young married couples, but do not wish to publish the results of the poll taken, because the answers, usually given rapidly, tend to cluster around two standards which are maybe in the mind of the people as much as in their practice; these two standards are three intercourses per week and three intercourses per day, the latter being much rarer" (A. Barlovatz, "Sterility in Central Africa," *Fertility and Sterility,* 6:4, July–August, 1955, 363–374).

in a recent study of a sample of subfecund couples.[19] They had all tried unsuccessfully to conceive for a year or more, and none had had any children. Males were divided into two fecundity classes, "good" and "poor," on the basis of the sperm count and several other measurable characteristics of the spermatozoa. Females were divided into two age-groups and, within each, into the same two classes according to such characteristics as the regularity of the menses and ovulation, the state of the fallopian tubes, etc. As can be seen from Table 18-1, on the basis of

TABLE 18-1. Percentage of Pregnancies Within One Year of Exposure, by Diagnosed Fecundity of the Marriage Partners and Age of Wife

Age of Wife:		*Under 30 Years*		*30 Years and Over*	
Fecundity of Wife:		*"Good"*	*"Poor"*	*"Good"*	*"Poor"*
Fecundity of husband	"Good"	40	23	18	8
	"Poor"	25	3	16	4

Source: John MacLeod *et al.*, "Correlation of the Male and Female Factors in Human Infertility," *Fertility and Sterility*, 6:2 (March–April, 1955), 112–143. Copyright, 1955, by the American Society for the Study of Sterility. ©.

this diagnostic differentiation in fecundity, the authors were able to predict to some degree the actual birth performance of various couples. That the age of the wife is a most important factor is evident from these data. When the wife was under 30, the rate of pregnancy was markedly low only when the fecundity of *both* partners was rated as "poor." But if a wife of 30 years or over had "poor" fecundity, the "good" fecundity of her husband did not much increase the probability of pregnancy. The highest figure, 40 per cent, would be low for normal couples, but for these it is an impressive performance. By such a test, the conceptual differentiation between fecundity and fertility is expressed in operational terms. That is, the potential ability to bear children can be measured, however imperfectly, by an index other than the actual bearing of children.

The Incidence of Fecundity

The biological potential of fecundity, properly speaking, is a characteristic of individuals (or, as we have seen, of couples). If it were possible

[19] John MacLeod *et al.*, "Correlation of the Male and Female Factors in Human Infertility," *Fertility and Sterility*, 6:2 (March–April, 1955), 112–143.

to designate it precisely for each couple, then for any population one could add up these figures and get a measure of the group's biological potential. While this has never been attempted, of course, we do have some data on the incidence of fecundity. As we have already pointed out in several contexts, the population structure is a major determinant of potential fertility and, moreover, this relation is continuous and sometimes cumulative from one generation to the next. Since the population pyramid of a people with large average families has a broad base, there is always a large number of potential parents for the coming years.[20] Apart from noting the proportion of women in childbearing ages and the sex ratio, analysts have seldom attempted to gauge the fecundity of a whole population.

According to a sample survey of wives aged 18 through 39,[21] the white population of the United States is divided as follows: (a) Approximately 10 per cent of all couples are completely sterile. This includes 9 per cent with one partner who has been sterilized, either for therapeutic or for contraceptive reasons. Such operations are especially prevalent among lower-class women in their late 30's. (b) Approximately 7 per cent of all couples are probably sterile, and 12 per cent are "semifecund." The incidence of subfecundity is greater among older women, among those who have borne more children, and possibly (though on this point the evidence is not clear) among lower-class women. (c) The fecundity of 5 per cent of the couples is indeterminate. (d) The remaining 66 per cent are fecund.[22]

How large would the average family be in a modern industrial society like the United States if fertility was not controlled? This is a difficult question to answer in empirical terms. Completed family size in a number of underdeveloped countries has ranged from 5.1 to 6.2 children per woman, 5.9 to 6.6 per wife, and 6.5 to 7.3 per mother.[23] These are minimum estimates of fecundity, since some control of fertility was practiced in these societies, the age of the women was generally under the outside limit of the childbearing period, and there was probably some underre-

---

[20] See Chapter 4, particularly pages 75–76.

[21] See pages 289–294.

[22] Ronald Freedman, Pascal K. Whelpton, and Arthur A. Campbell, *Family Planning, Sterility, and Population Growth* (New York: McGraw-Hill, 1959), Ch. 2. In the Indianapolis survey the respondents were classified into only two categories— 73 per cent "relatively fecund" and 27 per cent "relatively sterile" (*ibid.,* p. 407).

[23] *Ibid.,* p. 412. See also H. Hyrenius, "Fertility and Reproduction in a Swedish Population Group without Family Limitation," *Population Studies,* 12:2 (November, 1958), 121–130; Louis Henry, "Intervals Between Confinements in the Absence of Birth Control," *Eugenics Quarterly,* 5:4 (December, 1958), 200–211.

porting of births. Moreover, the lower level of health in these under-developed countries certainly reduced the fecundity to considerably under what it would be in a country with modern Western death control. The median time required by a large sample of American women to become

A Dutch couple and their children shortly before they emigrated to Canada. (Copyright Anpfoto, Amsterdam)

pregnant, according to one study, is only 2.3 months. About 30 per cent do so within a month, 60 per cent within three months, and more than 90 per cent by the end of a year.[24] The maximum family size feasible in the West is suggested by the fertility of the Hutterites, a fundamentalist sect whose members practice no birth control. They average 10.4 births per couple.[25] Even this rather frightening figure is not the maximum achievable. Guttmacher has deduced from a number of American and English studies that on the average a woman in these countries who nurses all her children can give birth each 24 months, and one who does not each 19 months. According to his "model timetable," if a girl married at age

[24] Christopher Tietze *et al.*, "Time Required for Conception in 1727 Planned Pregnancies," *Fertility and Sterility*, 1:4 (July, 1950), 338–346.

[25] Joseph W. Eaton and Albert J. Mayer, *Man's Capacity to Reproduce: The Demography of a Unique Population* (Glencoe, Ill.: Free Press, 1954), p. 20.

16, if the couple remained married and fecund for 30 years, if there were no fetal deaths, and if all babies were breast-fed, the average completed family size resulting from uncontrolled normal intercourse would be 15 children.[26]

BIRTH CONTROL AND ITS OPPONENTS

Our rather imprecise knowledge of how much fecundity varies from one population to another is not too serious a lack, for in most cases it is social rather than biological factors that determine differences in average family size. One important social factor is **birth control,** by which is meant the conscious use of any practice permitting sexual intercourse while reducing the likelihood of conception.[27]

The "total sexual outlet," to use Kinsey's term, includes intercourse with objects unlikely or unable to conceive—a prostitute, a person of the same sex, an animal, an imagined partner. While such relations absorb in the aggregate a large portion of the total sexual energy expended in any society, they generally have little effect on fertility. Some or all are everywhere defined as vice, and the moral pressure of the community induces most persons to conform most of the time. These deviant practices, then, are concentrated among "perverts," experimenting adolescents (masturbation, homosexuality in the United States [28]), and adults lacking a marital outlet (nocturnal emissions, intercourse with prostitutes) or seeking a romantic supplement to such an outlet (intercourse with prostitutes, homosexuality in the Levant). The usual pattern, thus, is that these practices represent a supplement to marital intercourse rather than a substitute for it, and thus do not affect fertility significantly.

[26] Alan F. Guttmacher, "Fertility of Man," *Fertility and Sterility,* 3:4 (July–August, 1952), 281–289.

[27] See United Nations, Department of Social Affairs, Population Division, *The Determinants and Consequences of Population Trends* (Population Studies, no. 17; New York, 1953), p. 74, n. 37. By the definition of birth control given there, the term also includes "not only the use of mechanical or chemical contraceptives, but also such other practices as 'withdrawal' and 'safe period.' " The emphasis, that is to say, is on how fertility is defined by the marriage partners: they see it in a rational rather than a traditional framework (as Weber used these words), and thus subject to their control.

[28] Kinsey, *op. cit.,* Ch. 21. Of Kinsey's male sample, 37 per cent had had some homosexual experience to the point of orgasm, usually during their adolescence, but only 4 per cent were exclusively homosexual throughout their lives. Probably no section of Kinsey's work has excited more adverse comment than the one on homosexuality; for a balanced criticism see William G. Cochran *et al., Statistical Problems of the Kinsey Report on Sexual Behavior in the Human Male* (Washington: American Statistical Association, 1954), pp. 142 ff. and *passim.*

Methods of Birth Control

The most common method of birth control throughout the world is the simplest, coitus interruptus, or withdrawal just before emission. This is, according to Himes, "the most popular, widely diffused method of contraception, . . . probably nearly as old as the group life of man." [29] It requires no preparations or appliances, costs nothing, is available at all times. It has, however, two important disadvantages: usually it ultimately fails to prevent impregnation, and it requires that the male be strongly motivated enough to frustrate his desire at the moment of highest excitation. We should expect to find, therefore, that coitus interruptus is less frequently practiced in societies where the economic and social responsibility for the child is borne in part by the broader kin group, rather than mainly or entirely by the father; but data to check this hypothesis are not available.

One important change in the determinants of Western fertility in the second half of the nineteenth century was that new and greatly improved contraceptive devices were developed. In the 1880's, the pessary was invented by Dr. W. P. J. Mensinga, later a professor of anatomy at Breslau, and in the following decades a considerable improvement in chemical spermicides took place. With a pessary and spermicidal jelly, the means now recommended by most clinics, it is possible to have virtually absolute assurance that there will be no conception. Mechanical and chemical contraceptives were novel in several senses. (a) With their use, the control is put at the beginning of the procreative process, so that the woman's health and life are not endangered by repeated unwanted pregnancies and Western ethical injunctions against abortion and infanticide can be obeyed. (b) On the other hand, in contrast to continence and coitus interruptus, contraceptives permit full expression to one of man's strongest natural drives. The link between the sexual instinct and reproduction, absolute in lower animals and mitigated in primates, is made subject to man's will. (c) Contraceptives have been more or less restricted to industrial societies, for primitive or peasant countries are generally unable or unwilling either to manufacture or even to import them in sufficient quantities. That Western means are expensive may be one reason that underdeveloped nations seldom try to inhibit their population growth, but it is never the decisive one.

[29] Norman E. Himes, *Medical History of Contraception* (Baltimore: Williams & Wilkins, 1936), pp. 183–184.

The use of surgery to prevent further births is atypical in most countries but apparently growing. Sterilization is very often hedged in by magical fears and legal restrictions, but in Puerto Rico it is the most popular method of birth control, and it is becoming more prevalent in a number of other countries.[30]

If an ovum *is* fertilized, this does not mean that a birth will necessarily take place, for the fetus may die before its full term. The analysis of fetal mortality is one of the most difficult areas in demography. Even in advanced countries the statistics are scanty and not based on random samples, and the meaning of basic terms is indefinite and in flux. The dictionary definition of *abort* is "to give birth prematurely" or "to cause to be delivered prematurely," while *abortionist* means "one who practices the producing of criminal abortions." The word *abortion* takes on both colorations: as used by physicians it refers to the physiological process, while as used by lawyers it refers to the law prohibiting persons from inducing premature birth. The usage in vital statistics recommended by the World Health Organization, finally, avoids the word altogether.[31]

While the evidence is inadequate, one can presume that the sharp reduction in infant mortality in modern Western societies was paralleled by a similar, if probably smaller, decline in fetal deaths. The contrast with respect to induced abortions is undoubtedly in the same direction, but also obscured by sparse data. Underdeveloped societies, since they are unable to develop effective contraceptive means, very often sanction birth control by some crude form of abortion. In industrial societies, with some exceptions (the Soviet Union for a period, Japan after World War II), the law generally permits induced abortions only when the mother's life is endangered or under other special circumstances. This does not mean, of course, that no other operations are performed. According to several different studies, the number of illegal abortions in various parts of the United States ranges between 0 and 23.8 per 100 pregnancies, and the number of spontaneous fetal deaths between 5.1 and 12.3 per 100 pregnancies.[32] While these figures represent a considerable wastage, this must be still higher in countries lacking both modern medicine and effective contraceptives.

Once a child has been born, it is still important to consider whether

[30] See pages 480–484.

[31] Cf. United Nations, Department of Social Affairs, Population Division, *Foetal, Infant and Early Childhood Mortality,* 1: *The Statistics* (Population Studies, no. 13; New York, 1954), 4.

[32] *Ibid.,* pp. 15, 20.

the fetus that passed through the travail of birth did so successfully, whether the child is viable. This depends in part on the social environment, but much less so than at one time. Two or three decades ago it was common in underdeveloped countries that a large fraction of the children born would die during the first year, but rates have declined greatly since then.

The postnatal mode of "birth control," **infanticide,** however barbarous it may be regarded by modern Western standards, has been a common practice in many nonindustrial societies. Moral considerations aside, infanticide has the disadvantage of exposing the mother to the pain and risk of pregnancy and childbirth to no purpose, but it is also the only method of birth control that permits a selection among offspring. Wherever infanticide is practiced, female infanticide is the rule, supplemented by the elimination of monsters, unhealthy offspring, and those undesirable by reason of some magical (e.g., multiple births) or social (e.g., illegitimate children) factor. Infanticide is thus associated with the higher evaluation of the male, as in hunting societies, where males play a dangerous but indispensable role (Eskimos); among certain polyandrous peoples (the Toda, a primitive people of southern India); and in many of the great agrarian civilizations (traditional China and India and even Japan well into the twentieth century, as well as medieval and early modern Europe [33]). In contemporary Western societies infanticide is a rarity not only because of strong moral and legal sanctions, but also because other methods of birth control reduce the number of unwanted children born, and when, in spite of contraceptives and abortions, these do arrive, they can be disposed of by offering them for adoption or placing them in a home.

The Neo-Malthusian Leagues

The very listing of these various methods of birth control suggests the fact that this practice is all but universal in one form or another. To find a "society" whose actual fertility probably approximates the physiological maximum, we must seek out such groups as the Hutterites. Even so, the small-family system that evolved in the modern Western world was in several respects a new phenomenon. The decline in fertility was usually (though not always) effected with more efficient means, and partly for this reason was probably greater than at any previous time. The control

[33] See pages 354–358.

of births, moreover, was incorporated into an ideology, propagated through a social movement. The battle to legitimize what Himes has termed the democratization of birth control is all but won in the West, and it constitutes one of the most interesting episodes in the history of ideas. Neo-Malthusianism was no less an invention of the nineteenth century than, say, the vulcanization of rubber, which made possible the development of more efficacious contraceptive devices. From one country or period to another, one can distinguish differences in doctrine; and occasionally the same country had several competing birth-control leagues, which opposed each other with all the vehemence of political or religious sects. Underlying this variation, however, a fundamental agreement on several key doctrines evolved from the works of the English and American pioneers:[34] (a) Control of family size is both physically possible and morally desirable. (b) The ultimate decision whether and when to have children should be made by parents, rather than by tradition, or fate, or church, or state. (c) A relatively small number of children is a social good, both because of favorable effects within the family and because too rapid population growth is a serious danger to social welfare.

The first book to recommend contraceptive measures as a substitute for Malthus's moral restraint appeared in England in 1822—*Illustrations and Proofs of the Principle of Population*, by Francis Place.[35] Though derivative from a number of predecessors (among them Benjamin Franklin), Place was original in the sense that he gave the birth-control movement its first systematic social theory and ethical rationale. The postponement of marriage that Malthus advocated, since it is too onerous a means of limiting population growth ever to be widely adopted, tends merely to generate vice and prostitution. (Most churches have recommended early marriage for the same reason, so that concupiscence may be relieved in sanctioned marital intercourse.) Marriages between young people, in Place's view, are generally happier ones, since older persons are less adaptable and cannot adjust to each other so readily. If one accepts Malthus's thesis that too rapid a population growth leads inevitably to social and economic distress, and Place repeated it in a simplified version, then "to avoid these miseries, the answer is short and

---

[34] The following account is based largely on Himes, *op. cit.*, Chs. 9–10. See also James Alfred Field, *Essays in Population and Other Papers* (Chicago: University of Chicago Press, 1931).

[35] See the edition that Himes edited—Boston: Houghton Mifflin, 1930.

plain"—the use of contraceptives. Place's *Diabolical Handbills* had a wide circulation among the working classes, especially in the North of England. His writings were soon supplemented by Richard Carlisle's handbook on birth control, which ran through several editions and was issued also in abridged form.

The next important development took place on the other side of the Atlantic. The first book published in America on birth control, *Moral Physiology* (1830) was written by Robert Dale Owen, the oldest son of Robert Owen; there were several printings the first year. In 1832 Charles Knowlton's *Fruits of Philosophy* appeared. Unlike Place and Owen, Knowlton was a physician, and in medical terms his pamphlet represented a substantial improvement over its predecessors. "Perhaps it is no exaggeration to say that Knowlton's treatment of contraceptive technique is the first really important account after those of Soranos and Aëtios" two millenia earlier.[36] Place and his associates had recommended a sponge, and Owen coitus interruptus; Knowlton's chief method was a douche with an astringent solution.

In England, Neo-Malthusianism was beginning to attract some of the best minds of the period—in particular, Jeremy Bentham and John Stuart Mill. The most important figure in the middle of the century was George Drysdale, author of *The Elements of Social Science* (1854), a book of some 600 finely printed pages. In medical terms, the author was less accurate than Knowlton or even Place. He believed that a condom could cause impotence. He was aware of a sterile period in the female's monthly cycle, but the 10 to 11 days he designated include the period of highest fecundity. The method he recommended was a sponge followed by a douche of tepid water. On the other hand, by Drysdale's extensive and sympathetic exposition of classical economic theory, he established a firmer link between it and Neo-Malthusian doctrine than had existed previously. Drysdale had an enormous influence: over the next 50 years *The Elements* appeared in 35 English editions and was translated into at least ten languages. In the 1860's he founded a Malthusian League and a journal, *The Malthusian*, but neither was very successful.

After 50 years of obscurity, in 1877 the birth-control movement was suddenly given wide publicity by the prosecution of two of its advocates, Charles Bradlaugh and Annie Besant. They had organized a firm for the express purpose of publishing and distributing Knowlton's *Fruits of Philosophy,* and thus testing a court decision banning it. Arrested and

[36] Himes, *op. cit.,* p. 227.

tried, for four days the defendants argued their case in social as well as legal terms: it was desirable that the poor should be informed on contraceptive means. The trial was reported in both the national and the local press, often with long verbatim passages from their testimony and even quotations from Knowlton's book itself. The sale of *Fruits of Philosophy*, which had been only 700 copies a year, jumped to some 125,000 in three months, not including a flood of imitations and pirated editions. The defendants were convicted and sentenced to six months' imprisonment and a fine of £200; they appealed and a year later were acquitted on a technicality. As a direct consequence of the publicity furnished by the Bradlaugh-Besant trial and a number of other prosecutions of birth-control proponents, a new Malthusian League was founded, with Charles R. Drysdale (brother of George) as president and Mrs. Besant as secretary. The League grew rapidly, receiving a sympathetic reception from a portion of the population not only in large cities but in "places as unlike as the Isle of Wight, Merthyr, and Aberdare, and Staffordshire." [37] Reverberations from the trial contributed to successful movements not only in Britain but in Holland (1881), Germany (1889), and France (1896).

The United States went through a similar cycle a generation later. In 1913 Mrs. Margaret Sanger, then a visiting nurse in New York's East Side slums, went to England, Holland, and France seeking information on reliable contraceptive methods. On her return she opened a clinic and served 30 days in prison for maintaining a "public nuisance." She started *The Birth Control Review*, a propaganda organization, another clinic, a research bureau, the National Committee on Maternal Health. As early as 1922, she helped set up birth-control movements in Hawaii, Japan, and China. That contraceptives are legal today in most of the United States is due in considerable degree to the courage and perseverance of this one woman. [38]

In all countries the birth-control movement has been shaped to a considerable degree by the opposition to it. The more principled adversaries can be classified into four types—Traditional, Catholic, Socialist, and Nationalist.

---

[37] D. V. Glass, *Population Policies and Movements in Europe* (Oxford: Clarendon, 1940), p. 38. See also Himes, *op. cit.*, Ch. 10; J. A. Banks and Olive Banks, "The Bradlaugh-Besant Trial and the English Newspapers," *Population Studies*, 8:1 (July, 1954), 22–34.

[38] See Margaret Sanger, *My Fight for Birth Control* (New York: Farrar & Rinehart, 1931); *Margaret Sanger—An Autobiography* (New York: Norton, 1938).

Margaret Sanger
(Floyd C. Wheat—Creative Photographers)

Traditional Opposition

In the traditional view children come as gifts of God, and should be accepted gratefully, unquestioningly. To subject the process of reproduction to man's will is "unnatural." The difficulty with this view is that it makes no allowance for the no less unnatural death control that has been achieved in the modern world. An inefficient check to fertility, combined with modern medicine, public sanitation, insecticides, and so on, results in a population growth so great that, indeed, the balance with nature is endangered. If they were consistent, the principled opponents of birth control would have to advocate restoring this balance by a higher death rate. Gandhi once remarked in a discussion of how to cope with India's

Brownsville district of Brooklyn in 1916, where Mrs. Sanger established the first birth-control clinic in the United States. (Planned Parenthood Federation)

population pressure that "perhaps we need some good epidemics." [39] He laughed as he said this, for one cannot offer such a proposal seriously;

[39] Louis Fischer, *A Week with Gandhi* (New York: Duell, 1942), p. 89. For a compilation of his various writings on the subject, see M. K. Gandhi, *Birth-Control: The Right Way and the Wrong Way* (Ahmedabad: Navajivan, 1959).

but he was serious in holding to his absolute opposition to contraceptives, no matter what the demographic consequences.

The notion that parents should be permitted to determine the size of their family began everywhere as the point of view of an embattled minority, the sort of people who held and expressed unpopular opinions. Bradlaugh, for instance, was a militant atheist; Mrs. Besant was an ardent feminist, later a theosophist. More generally, the advocacy of birth control tended to overlap with support of other sectarian views—pacifism, temperance, vegetarianism, and the like; and when the link did not exist in substance, it was often created in form by the libertarians who defended anyone whose freedom of speech had been infringed. Like any other social reform, then, Neo-Malthusianism was opposed first of all because of its novelty, its affront to the solid respectability of run-of-the-mill conventionality. And in this case the automatic rejection was strengthened by the specific proposal, particularly in so prurient a nation as Victorian England. One of the worst offences of Bradlaugh and Besant was their plain speaking, their threat to what *The Times* termed "certain reserves and proprieties surrounding the first law of Nature and the domestic hearth." [40]

Wherever the use of contraceptives became general, this conventional opposition was dissipated, partly also because of a frequent change in the character of the movement itself. In Britain, for instance, the early emphasis on the economic effects of population growth gave way to a narrower concentration on family budgets or the health of the mother. Political economists tended to be supplanted by social workers or physicians. In 1927 the Malthusian League disbanded at a celebration dinner, considering its work to be done; and its place was taken by the Society for Constructive Birth Control, headed for many years by Dr. Marie Stopes. A similar shift of emphasis, even if not accompanied by a change in organization, took place also in other countries.

As the idea of birth control achieved a certain degree of respectability, there was a gradual change in the position of Christian churches, which in the West are the main formal defenders of ethical tradition. Religious opposition to birth control, all but universal in the nineteenth century, has gradually diminished. In the United States, for example, the Federal Council of the Churches of Christ in America published a report in 1931 approving it in principle; and more recently a number of Protestant denominations have taken the stand that it is their moral duty to propa-

[40] Quoted in Banks and Banks, "The Bradlaugh-Besant Trial," *op. cit.*

gate planned parenthood. In 1961 the National Council of Churches officially approved "artificial" birth control. Roman Catholicism is the one important Christian denomination that still upholds, at least to some degree, the earlier view.

The Catholic Position on Birth Control

The rhythm method of birth control, the only one sanctioned by the Roman Catholic Church, is based on the ovulation cycle. If continence is practiced during the short period each month that mature ova are in place, in theory conception can be completely avoided. However, the usual way of determining any woman's ovulation cycle is to relate it to the overlapping menstruation cycle, and in fact this is more difficult than it might seem in the abstract. The couples must be completely continent for a number of months while a trained worker determines how regular the two cycles are, and then periodic abstention must be regularly practiced not only during the assumed ovulation phase but also for several days before and after it. Under such circumstances, the method "offers a satisfactory degree of protection against unwanted pregnancy to rigorously selected and carefully instructed wives who, with their husbands, are intelligent and strongly motivated. For others and for those to whom pregnancy would be dangerous, the effectiveness of the method in preventing conception is not considered adequate." [41] Many American Catholics begin with rhythm and then, after the birth of several children, shift to more efficient means. According to a survey of a nationwide sample, 30 per cent of all couples of which the wife is Catholic use methods condemned by the Church, and among fully fecund couples married ten years or more the proportion is half.[42]

The Church's present stand on birth control is related to its historical position toward sexuality. In the Near East, during the centuries that Christian doctrine was evolving, asceticism was seen as the prime virtue. The Neo-Platonist opposition between spirit and flesh suggested a negative stance toward all sexual relations,[43] and one line of development in Church doctrine was to stress the supreme value of chastity, and thus to excuse sex relations within marriage only because they are necessary for pro-

---

[41] Christopher Tietze *et al.*, "Clinical Effectiveness of the Rhythm Method of Contraception," *Fertility and Sterility*, 2:5 (September–October, 1951), 444–450.

[42] Freedman, Whelpton, and Campbell, *op. cit.*, pp. 182–183.

[43] When the citizens of Corinth asked Paul whether Christian norms permitted marriage (the question itself suggests the temper of the times), he replied that "it is good for a man not to touch a woman. . . . I would that all men were even as I myself," a celibate. But it is not possible for all men to restrain their natural drives completely; and "if they cannot contain, let them marry: for it is better to marry than to burn" (I Corinthians 7).

creation. The evolution of priestly celibacy and the cult of virginity both reflected and reinforced this point of view.[44] On the other hand, the Church has also stressed the sanctity of the marriage sacrament and endorsed family life as morally good. Some of the difficulties in developing a policy toward birth control suited to the modern world derive from this fundamental ambivalence concerning sexuality.

In present-day Catholic doctrine, as expressed in the Code of Canon Law, "The primary end of marriage is the procreation and education of offspring; the secondary end, mutual aid and the remedying of concupiscence." [45] As we have noted, sexuality does indeed serve two biological functions among primates, rather than the single one of procreation, as in lower animals. The nuclear family of man, wife, and children—the fundamental unit of human society—has a natural basis in the fact that the sexual attraction between man and woman is not cyclical but permanent. Under some circumstances, Catholic doctrine defines it as licit to serve the secondary ends (mitigating the sex drive and increasing the bond of marital affection) even when conception is impossible. For example, persons known to be sterile may enjoy marital relations without sin. It would seem that intercourse during a wife's sterile period is free from sin in the same way, and indeed Catholic publications since 1930 have placed a new emphasis on the secondary functions of marriage.[46]

On the other hand, birth control by periodic abstinence is not sanctioned unless there is a "serious motive" for avoiding childbearing, and the crucial question is how this "serious motive" is defined. In what is probably the earliest official statement on rhythm (1853), "legitimate reasons" are mentioned but not discussed. In 1880 the Sacred Penitentiary reported that couples using periodic continence as a substitute for coitus interruptus should not be dissuaded from following the practice; and "a confessor may suggest, but cautiously, the opinion under discussion to those spouses whom he had vainly tried by another method to lead away from the detestable crime of onan." [47] The culmination of modern Catholic doctrine on the family is *Casti Connubii*, the encyclical pub-

[44] For a fascinating account of early Christian doctrine on sex, see Geoffrey May, *Social Control of Sex Expression* (New York: Morrow, 1931).

[45] C. 1013, par. 1, quoted in William J. Gibbons, S.J., "Fertility Control in the Light of Some Recent Catholic Statements," *Eugenics Quarterly*, 3:1 (March, 1956), 9–15; 3:2 (June, 1956), 82–87. This is an excellent statement of the Church's position. See also the exchange between Father Gibbons and Kingsley Davis in George F. Mair, ed., *Studies in Population* (Princeton: Princeton University Press, 1949), pp. 108–139.

[46] See Alvah W. Sulloway, *Birth Control and Catholic Doctrine* (Boston: Beacon, 1959), Ch. 7.

[47] Both statements are quoted in Freedman, Whelpton, and Campbell, *op. cit.*, pp. 416–417.

lished in 1930, by which time many Catholics had learned to use contraceptives. As Pius XI stated in its introductory paragraphs, these "false principles of a new and utterly perverse morality . . . have begun to spread even among the faithful and are gradually gaining ground." In one somewhat ambiguous sentence the encyclical seemed to permit the use of periodic abstinence to prevent conception, but it did not state under what conditions. At the same time, the *intention* to control births was very specifically prohibited:

> Every attempt on the part of the married couple during the conjugal act or during the development of its natural consequences, to deprive it of its inherent power and to hinder the procreation of a new life is immoral. No "indication" or need can change an action that is intrinsically immoral into an action that is moral and lawful.[48]

The latest position of the Church has been given in several official statements of Pius XII, in particular an address to the Italian Catholic Union of Midwives in 1951.[49] This repeats the usual stringent prohibition of sterilization and of mechanical or chemical contraceptives but sanctions the use of the rhythm method under a wide variety of loosely specified conditions. According to Pius XII, it is legitimate for a Catholic couple to restrict intercourse to the sterile period "always and deliberately" if there is a "serious reason" for avoiding marriage's primary end of procreation while satisfying the secondary one.

> There are serious motives, such as those often mentioned in the so-called medical, eugenic, economic, and social "indications," that can exempt for a long time, perhaps even the whole duration of the marriage, from the positive and obligatory carrying out of the act [of procreation]. From this it follows that observing the nonfertile periods alone can be lawful only under a moral aspect. Under the conditions mentioned it really is so.[50]

To a non-Catholic, as Father Gibbons puts it, "this may appear as metaphysical hair-splitting." Unlike most moral injunctions, whether of the Catholic or of other Christian churches, the emphasis here is neither on the motive of the person nor on the effect of his behavior, but simply on the means used to bring about a desired end.

48 Alvin Werth, O.F.M. Cap., and Clement S. Mihanovich, *Papal Pronouncements on Marriage and the Family: From Leo XIII to Pius XII (1878–1954)* (Milwaukee: Bruce, 1955), pp. 67–68.

49 For an English translation, see Edgar Schmiedeler, O.S.B., ed., *Moral Questions Affecting Married Life* (Washington: National Catholic Welfare Conference [1952]), pp. 3–23.

50 *Ibid.*, p. 14.

It seems that Catholic dogma on this matter is in the process of change, and that the present position is transitional. From "every attempt to hinder procreation is immoral" (1930) to the "so-called medical, eugenic, economic, and social" exceptions to this dictum (1951), a considerable distance has been covered. Pius XII called periodic abstinence a "method of birth regulation that can be reconciled with God's law" and he expressed the hope that medical science would give this permissible method "a sufficiently safe basis." [51] Catholic dissatisfaction with the current position of the Church is expressed not only in the large number of persons who use contraceptives but also in Catholic opinion on the moral issues involved.[52] In the meantime, however, the Catholic Church remains the strongest adversary of planned-parenthood movements in the West, as well as in international bodies like the World Health Organization.

Socialist Ambivalence

Socialist antagonism to the birth-control movement is more complex and less well known than traditional or Catholic opposition. Since both socialism and Neo-Malthusianism contradicted the conventional values of middle-class society of the nineteenth century, they have often appealed to the same rebellious spirits, so that a number of individuals—Annie Besant among others—wrote pamphlets in support of both. However, the usual pattern, and the all but invariable one for organizations rather than individuals, was contravention. Members of the German Social Democratic Party, the largest and most influential unit of the pre-1914 Second International, were against the birth-control movement "almost without exception." [53] In Britain Drysdale complained that Neo-Malthusianism, "the especial *bête noire* of the Socialists," was in part as a consequence "disliked by the labouring classes which it was especially intended to help." [54] Similar attitudes were common in France and Holland.

---

[51] *Osservatore Romano*, October 29–30 and November 29, 1951, quoted in G. H. L. Zeegers, "Introduction to the International Contest on the Population Problem of Underdeveloped Areas," *Social Compass*, 2:5/6 (January–April, 1955), 217–233.

[52] *Ibid.* This article announces a contest sponsored by the Catholic Institute for Social-Ecclesiastical Research (the Dutch branch of the International Catholic Institute for Social Research); prizes totaling $5,000 were to be paid by a Dutch Catholic daily for the best proposals on means of limiting population increase in underdeveloped areas that are both in accord with Catholic moral principles and scientifically effective.

[53] Richard Lewinsohn, "Die Stellung der deutschen Sozialdemokratie zur Bevölkerungsfrage," *Schmollers Jahrbuch*, 46:3 (1922), 813–859 (191–237).

[54] C. V. Drysdale, *The Malthusian Doctrine and Its Modern Aspects* (London: Malthusian League [1917]), p. 4.

Why should socialists, whose first principle is a planned society, have objected to family planning? This dispute was in part a continuation of the one that Malthus had started in his attack on utopians like Condorcet and Godwin. In Marx's writings "the contemptible Malthus" is rejected as a "plagiarist," "a shameless sycophant of the ruling classes," who perpetrated a "sin against science," "this libel on the human race." Apart from such vituperations, Marx's main objection to the principle of population can be stated in a single sentence: "Every special historic mode of production has its own special laws of population, historically valid within its limits alone." [55] Marx himself, however, had nothing to say about what governed growth of numbers in primitive, feudal, or socialist societies, and what he termed his law of population for capitalist society was markedly incomplete. The inevitable accumulation of capital, according to his analysis, necessarily increases the size and the misery of the "industrial reserve army" of technologically unemployed, and this trend operates "independently of the limits of the actual increase of population." [56] Marx in fact took the rapid growth of nineteenth-century Europe as a permanent feature and built his system around it, without even so imperfect a theory as Malthus's principle to account for the continuing increase in numbers. If the population declined at the same rate at which machines displaced workers (a contingency that many demographers of the 1930's considered not only possible but even likely), then there would be no industrial reserve army, no "immiseration," no Marxian model altogether. Marx could reject Malthus only by taking the essence of Malthusianism for granted.

In the nineteenth century socialists and Neo-Malthusians were competitive dealers in utopias. Malthus's caution in the final statement of his theory disappeared altogether in the subsequent "Malthusian" pamphlets. Even so sympathetic a commentator as Himes believes that the "peroration on the Utopian effects" of birth control of Mrs. Besant, for instance, "over-stated and therefore weakened her case," though he excuses the excess as a "natural enthusiasm and self-defence" against "hot and irresponsible calumniation." [57] An orthodox Marxist, on the contrary, believed that when the capitalist system was supplanted by a planned economy, population pressure would disappear, but that before that fundamental transformation took place, the limitation of family size could not improve matters substantially. In the words of Kautsky, for "at least

[55] Karl Marx, *Capital*, 1: *The Process of Capitalist Production* (Chicago: Kerr, 1906), 693.
[56] *Ibid.*
[57] Himes, *op. cit.*, p. 247.

a century" after it broke the capitalist dams to technological progress, socialist society would be able to expand food production "much faster than any possible population growth." True, mortality would decline "enormously," since many of its specific causes would be eliminated together with the profit system; but fertility would also decline as the new woman took an interest in "the possibility of enjoyment and creativity in nature, art, and science." In fact, one might suppose that with so many distractions from family life, depopulation rather than overpopulation would ensue. This fear, however, is also groundless, for the anxieties that inhibit childbearing in a capitalist era would also have been removed. In short, socialist society will be perfect, as defined; for whenever population growth varies from the optimum, "public opinion and the conscience of individuals. . . . will make women's duty clear." [58]

Nationalist Pronatalist Policies

Nationalist opposition to birth limitation is based on two propositions —that any state is stronger, the more people it has, and that it must therefore foster the maximum possible rate of reproduction of its military and industrial manpower. This was the population doctrine of the mercantilist period, and echoes of it have often been heard since then. Particularly in totalitarian countries, the usual reaction to birth control has been to prohibit it. In order that Fascist Italy, for example, might attain its "place in the sun," Mussolini insisted that its population had to grow from 40 million in 1927 to 60 million in 1950. "With a falling population, one does not create an empire but becomes a colony." [59]

Such a view, even if one accepts the values on which it is based, is still oversimplified. Great national power must indeed be based on populous nations, but it does not at all follow that the more people there are, the more power their nation wields. A society encumbered with economically surplus population is militarily weaker by that fact, not stronger. [60] And the attempts of various governments to induce a more rapid population

---

[58] Karl Kautsky, *Vermehrung und Entwicklung in Natur und Gesellschaft* (3rd ed.; Stuttgart: Dietz, 1921), Chs. 15–16. As a young man, Kautsky had been one of the few socialist leaders who tried to come to grips with the population problem (see his *Der Einfluss der Volksvermehrung auf den Fortschritt der Gesellschaft,* Vienna: Bloch und Hasbach, 1880), but this utopian statement was his final word on the subject.

[59] Mussolini's Ascension Day speech, May 26, 1927, quoted in Glass, *op. cit.,* p. 220.

[60] See Kingsley Davis, "The Demographic Foundations of National Power," in Morroe Berger *et al.,* eds., *Freedom and Control in Modern Society* (New York: Van Nostrand, 1954), pp. 206–242.

increase, whether by family subsidies or by the prohibition of contraceptives, have generally failed to achieve their full purpose. Nazi Germany's pronatalist policy is perhaps the one exception to this statement,
but it is very difficult even in this case to separate analytically the several
factors that in combination raised Germany's birth rate in the 1930's.

SOCIAL DETERMINANTS OF FERTILITY

In the two previous sections of this chapter, we have discussed human
fecundity and birth control. Fertility is often perceived as the resultant
of these two factors: biology sets a maximum number of offspring per
family, and man contrives with one means or another to reduce the
actual number of children. That the secular decline in Western birth
rates took place largely because of a change in parents' attitudes, however,
is both a hypothesis to explain this trend and the statement of another
question—what brought about such a new view of parental responsi-
bilities? More generally, in every society there are policies, laws, institutions, styles of living, and so on, all with no intended and sometimes no
easily perceptible effect on fertility, but as important as purposive action
in setting the average number of children per family.

A **fertility determinant** is any behavior pattern that influences average
family size, whether or not this is its conscious purpose or generally
known effect. A number of analysts have suggested, for instance, that one
reason for the lower fertility in cities is the decline in coital frequency
within marriage consequent from the competitive diversions of urban
life. In this case, the persons involved may be completely unaware of the
cause-effect relation. Another example would be the factors, whatever
they may be, that determine the "proper" age at which to marry. In this
case, while the effect on fertility is patent, this is not necessarily the purpose of the behavior pattern.

While the sex drive is sufficient to induce copulation and thus reproduction, this biological link between man and woman is everywhere
reinforced by cultural norms. If a society is to persist, physically and culturally, it can be only because the physical care, socialization, and social
placement of its young are not left to the sometimes haphazard dictates
of the sex drive. The family, in short, is not merely a biological group but
one held together also by complementary economic needs, moral codes,
and the integrative force of the whole social structure. In particular, the
bond between father and offspring, which in physiological terms is the
weakest one in the nuclear family, is culturally reinforced by what Mal-

inowski termed "the principle of legitimacy," which designates one man (usually though not necessarily the biological father) as responsible for each infant born into the society.

The conjugal family is the basic social unit in all cultures, but the wider structures built from this base vary considerably. Incest taboos, universal within the nuclear family, are extended to include cousins and other relatives of second and higher degree according to a number of different patterns; and these various limitations on the choice of a marriage partner reinforce the societal type from which they derive.[61] Family types and the kind of social structure with which they are generally associated, moreover, tend together to encourage different levels of fertility.[62] This complex interrelation can be expressed through social usages governing (a) the conditions of marriage and (b) family behavior patterns that can affect the relative frequency of conception and childbearing.

The age at which couples typically marry in any culture depends primarily on two factors, the amount of preparation they need to take over adult roles, and how much assistance they can get from others. These points can be illustrated by two countries noted for their very low and very high age at marriage, India and Ireland.

Child marriage is traditional in India.[63] The Sarda Act of 1929, which prohibited marriage for males under 18 and females under 14, has not been very rigorously enforced. According to the 1951 census, there were then 2,833,000 husbands plus 66,000 widowers and 6,180,000 wives plus 134,000 widows, all between the ages of 5 and 14. Only 6.4 per cent of females aged 15 and over were unmarried, and only one in 1,000 still remained a spinster at age 44. This pattern of early and virtually universal marriage developed as a feature of the traditional Hindu joint family, which was similar in its essential features to that in China.[64] The existence of the joint household made it possible for persons not yet old enough to care for themselves to get married, and the dominant motive in arranging a marriage was to perpetuate the family line. Societies based on a joint-family system, thus, typically have an early age at marriage and, to the extent that this affects family size, therefore also a high level of fertility.

---

[61] Cf. George Peter Murdock, *Social Structure* (New York: Macmillan, 1949).

[62] See Kingsley Davis and Judith Blake, "Social Structure and Fertility: An Analytical Framework," *Economic Development and Cultural Change*, 4:3 (April, 1956), 211–235.

[63] For a recent survey, see S. Chandrasekhar, "The Family in India," *Marriage and Family Living*, 16:4 (November, 1954), 336–342.

[64] See pages 353–355.

The example of Ireland is especially interesting because it illustrates how a particular family structure functions under radically changing economic conditions. In common with most of Western Europe, Ireland in the eighteenth century had the tradition that a young man ought not to marry until he had a patch of land to cultivate, and this meant that in general he had to wait for his inheritance. Around 1780 several factors operated together to increase the amount of free land available: under the impetus of mercantilist encouragements to the cultivation of grain, pastureland was converted to agriculture; by a new law, Catholics were permitted to purchase land; much swampland was drained. A boy in his teens with his own small holding could now build a hut and grow enough potatoes to raise a family. Girls were typically married and mothers at 16, sometimes at 14 or 15, and in a country with no birth control this decrease in the age at marriage had a decisive effect. In 60 years the population of Ireland more than doubled, increasing from 4.0 million in 1781 to 8.2 million in 1841.[65] This growth stimulated a large emigration, which became a mass exodus after the failure of the potato crop and the great famine of the 1840's. A new law was passed inhibiting the division of land, and the tradition was re-established that a man could not get married until he had received his inheritance. The age at marriage, therefore, increased markedly; in 1946 it was 33.1 years for males and 28.0 years for females.[66] By 1951 the population had fallen to 4.2 million, or only slightly more than it was in 1781, at the start of the tremendous increase. Throughout this period, thus, the principle of "no holding, no marriage" remained constant, but while new land was available it was interpreted as "holding, therefore marriage."

The contrast between the family types of India and Ireland is relevant also with respect to the proportion of the population that marries, for the same factors that encourage or inhibit early marriage operate also in later years. As has been noted, virtually all Indian women marry before the end of the fecund period. In Ireland in 1951, on the other hand, 24.7 per cent of females aged 45 and over were still single and 28.8 per cent of the corresponding male age-group.[67]

---

[65] The first census was in 1821; the estimate for the earlier period is that of K. H. Connell, *The Population of Ireland, 1750–1845* (Oxford: Clarendon, 1950).

[66] John A. O'Brien, ed., *The Vanishing Irish: The Enigma of the Modern World* (New York: McGraw-Hill, 1953), p. 28. The question concerning age at marriage was not asked in the 1951 census.

[67] This remarkably high proportion had been even higher a decade earlier: unmarried females between 25 and 34 years declined from 54.8 per cent of that age-group in 1936 to 45.6 per cent in 1951, and for the corresponding male group from 73.8 to 67.4 per cent. See Ireland Central Statistics Office, *Statistical Abstract of Ireland, 1953* (Dublin: Stationery Office, 1954), pp. 13, 24.

These examples suggest a relation between one element of the social structure, the family, and two factors influencing fertility—age at marriage and proportion married. The moral code by which this relation is maintained—for example, the prescription of absolute filial obedience in China or India—is also important, of course, though its effect is more difficult to analyze. The hypothesis that the fertility of a society derives from its values is sometimes "validated" by a circular argument, for the only secure proof that such values exist and are really effective is the level of fertility. The ambivalent effect of a normative system on the birth rate can be illustrated by Ireland. While this country has been predominantly Roman Catholic throughout the modern period, this constant faith operated, paradoxically, to increase the difference in age at marriage before and after the famine. While land was available, the Church encouraged its members to marry young as a deterrent to premarital dalliance. It is true that Church spokesmen still urge early marriage at the present time, but the principal reason that Irishmen put off taking a wife is that otherwise, with the Catholic ban on contraceptives, they would have to accept responsibility for a probably very large family.

When a marriage is dissolved by the death of one of its partners or by divorce, the period of celibacy until a new union may be formed varies from one culture to another. Among some primitive peoples, at one extreme, a widow is expected to wed the brother (or other close kin) of her deceased husband. "If she still is fecund, the lineage feels it would be losing potential children if she did not remarry . . . within the clan." [68] In India, at the other extreme, the remarriage of widows is banned by Hindu norms. Here the dominant social unit is not the clan but the joint family, which is generally too small to reabsorb the widow and too intent on getting its own females married to take responsibility for widowed in-laws. This ban, by canceling a portion of the fertility implicit in the normal early marriage, acts as a functional substitute for birth control. Modern Western societies fall between the two extremes: remarriage is neither universal nor banned.[69]

Virtually all societies, including our own, impose periods of sexual abstinence within marriage. Many of these are set by female physiology: intercourse is typically banned during menstruation, during the gestation

[68] Davis and Blake, "Social Structure," *op. cit.* On the levirate among the ancient Hebrews, vestiges of which survived to modern times, see Willystine Goodsell, *A History of Marriage and the Family* (Rev. ed.; New York: Macmillan, 1934), pp. 57–58.

[69] According to one study, widowers in the United States remarry at twice the rate that widows do; the reasons seem to be the larger number of widows, because of women's greater longevity and their earlier marriage, and the greater difficulty that older women have in finding a spouse, whether or not they were married previously.

period or at least the last portion of it, and for some time after the birth of a child. These taboos are not intended as means of birth control and generally have little effect on fertility, except sometimes indirectly through promoting the health of the woman or increasing the incidence of intercourse when conception is possible. Other prescriptions of periodic abstinence are difficult to classify. They may represent a denial of pleasurable experience, analogous to fasting, during a time when solemnity or mourning is appropriate. Or they may be determined by occasions when the man's virility is particularly important (thus, among many primitives during a war, and in our own culture during the training period of a professional pugilist). Since many of these miscellaneous bans are enforced by a religious sanction, they tend to be more important in nonindustrial societies. On the other hand, industrial societies generally offer at least urban residents a wide variety of diversions, which may, as we have noted, reduce the frequency of marital intercourse.

SUMMARY

Fecundity, the physiological ability to procreate, varies with a number of physical characteristics, of which the most important are heredity, health, age, the ovulation cycle, lactation, and sex drive. The distribution of these characteristics, particularly age, in any population determines its relative ability to reproduce itself.

The age at marriage and the proportion married depend principally on how important the family is in the social structure: the marital state is the norm everywhere, but the pressure to follow this is less in industrial countries. In a traditional agrarian society many social wants can be satisfied only through the family, and persons are thereby induced to form one early, while in the institutional complex of an industrial urban society, on the contrary, the family is relatively less important, and there may be thus less pressure on any individual to marry, or to marry early. Occasionally, as in Ireland, putting off one's marriage is a conscious means of birth control, but generally the means-end relation is not so close to the surface. The "suitable" age at marriage is not ordinarily set in terms of its known effect on fertility.

In modern Western societies fertility has depended in large part on the practice of birth control. While the deliberate limitation of family size was not novel, the ideology of Neo-Malthusianism was. In this movement the use of contraceptives has been taught as a social good, leading to happier family life and improved general welfare. Neo-Malthusianism started with the writings and activities of Francis Place in the 1820's. From England the ideology was carried first to the United States and then, at the end of the nineteenth century, to the European Continent. Efforts were made beginning in this century to establish birth-control leagues and clinics in a number of other countries, but participation has usually been limited to a small minority of westernized urban residents. It is often assumed that the future worldwide success of the movement is only a matter of time, since it is implicitly fostered by the urbanization and industrialization under way everywhere, but this view is perhaps too sanguine. Opposition to birth control, particularly of the composite socialist-nationalist type represented in Communist writings and policies, is still strong; and in such countries as India, where principled antagonism would seem to be weaker, population growth is outdistancing the best efforts to control it.

So far effective control has been established only in one country outside the Western world—namely, Japan. But both Europe and Japan were atypical in that fertility was held in check to a marked degree also before an industrial culture was established.[70] At least so far in modern history, that is to say, the only societies where family limitation became general have been those in which procreation up to the physiological limit was never a traditional value. If we are to judge the future of underdeveloped areas by these two cases, it will mean that the rational control of family size, other things being equal, will take longer than in the West to become established as an accepted norm. Other factors are not equal, of course, but the probable effect of the many differences is not clear. In any case, there is little reason for optimism.

In Table 18-2 fertility determinants have been divided into four broad types according to the point in the physiology of reproduction they affect —continence, contraception, fetal mortality, and infant mortality. For each type the relative importance of deliberate and nondeliberate regulation is indicated. The overriding differentiation that this table suggests is that between industrial and nonindustrial societies. An industrial society, first of all, is one with more knowledge of the natural world and better techniques to control it. Infant mortality and, to a smaller degree, fetal mortality are reduced, and effective contraceptives obviate the need for clumsier, more dangerous methods of birth control later in the physiological process. This improved control of both fertility and mortality means that institutional patterns have a less significant influence on fertility.

[70] See pages 355, 358–360.

TABLE 18-2. Types of Fertility Determinants

	Conscious Means of Birth Control	Significant Effect on Fertility
Continence		
Permanent celibacy	No	Generally not; possibly in Tibet
Premarital	Generally not; yes in Ireland	Yes in some societies
Intermarital	Generally not	Often
Intermittent	No, except "rhythm"	No, except "rhythm"
Contraception		
Vices	No	Generally not
Coitus interruptus	Yes	Yes
Chemical, mechanical	Yes	Yes in industrial societies
Sterilization	Generally yes	Not usually; yes in Puerto Rico, portions of India, etc.
Fetal mortality		
Spontaneous miscarriage	No	Yes
Induced abortions	Yes	Yes, especially in nonindustrial countries, France, and Japan
Infant mortality		
Unintended	No	Yes in nonindustrial societies, though less than before 1945
Infanticide	Yes	Yes in nonindustrial societies

Industrialization loosens the social structure of an agrarian society: the sharp increase in both geographical and social mobility means that more and more persons are removed from the influence and control of the extended kin group to the relatively anonymous life of the large city. The normative system of the agrarian society (religious values, family sentiments, etc.), also weakened by this loss of its institutional base, is challenged as well by the higher valuation of rationality in an industrial urban setting. Fertility level, in brief, tends to be associated with social structure, technological standards, and specific prescriptions or taboos; and all three of these determinants have been markedly changed by industrialization. We cannot be sure, however, that this association will hold in countries presently undergoing modernization, for the traditional norms governing family life there usually favor procreation more than did those of the preindustrial West or Japan.

SUGGESTIONS FOR FURTHER READING

Robert L. Dickinson, *Human Sex Anatomy: A Topographical Hand Atlas* (Baltimore: Williams & Wilkins, 1949).
    One of many good books on the subject.

John MacLeod, "The Present Status of Human Male Infertility," *American Journal of Obstetrics and Gynecology,* 69:6 (June, 1955), 1256–1267.

M. James Whitelaw, "What Is Normal Female Fertility," *Fertility and Sterility,* 6:2 (March–April, 1955), 103–111.

I. C. Rubin, "Thirty Years of Progress in Treating Infertility," *ibid.,* 1:5 (September, 1950), 389–406.

Good reviews of an area of human knowledge that is expanding rapidly.

Raymond Pearl, *The Natural History of Population* (New York: Oxford University Press, 1939).

Richard L. Meier, *Modern Science and the Human Fertility Problem* (New York: Wiley, 1959).

Pearl is out of date in some respects but still worth reading. Meier is both a natural and a social scientist, and in this work the two disciplines are joined.

Norman E. Himes, *Medical History of Contraception* (Baltimore: Williams & Wilkins, 1936).

D. V. Glass, *Population Policies and Movements in Europe* (Oxford: Clarendon, 1940).

Standard works on, respectively, the rise of birth-control movements and pronatalist policies in Europe.

William J. Gibbons, S.J., "Fertility Control in the Light of Some Recent Catholic Statements," *Eugenics Quarterly,* 3:1 (March, 1956), 9–15; 3:2 (June, 1956), 82–87.

Alvah W. Sulloway, *Birth Control and Catholic Doctrine* (Boston: Beacon, 1959).

Authoritative statements, pro and con, on Catholic doctrine.

Kingsley Davis and Judith Blake, "Social Structure and Fertility: An Analytic Framework," *Economic Development and Cultural Change,* 4:3 (April, 1956), 211–235.

Christopher Tietze, "Statistical Contributions to the Study of Human Fertility," *Fertility and Sterility,* 7:1 (January–February, 1956), 88–94.

Julia S. Brown, "A Comparative Study of Deviations from Sexual Mores," *American Sociological Review,* 17:2 (April, 1952), 135–146.

Three excellent contributions to an underdeveloped subject, the general analysis of social-population interrelations.

19. *THE GENERAL DETERMINANTS*
OF MORTALITY

How much has life expectation increased since the time of the first available records? As indicated by the approximate figures in Table 19-1, progress has been great. The average length of life about doubled from prehistoric times to the Middle Ages, and then it remained more or less static until the nineteenth century. During the last 150 years it has

TABLE 19-1. Expectation of Life at Birth through History

Period	*Area*	*Average Length of Life (years)*
I. Bronze Age	Greece	18
Beginning of		
Christian era	Rome	22
II. Middle Ages	England	33
1687–1691	Breslau, Germany	33.5
Before 1789	Massachusetts and	
	New Hampshire	35.5
III. 1838–1854	England and Wales	40.9
1900–1902	United States	49.2
1958	United States	
	White males	67.2
	White females	73.7

Source: Various authors, compiled by Louis I. Dublin, Alfred J. Lotka, and Mortimer Spiegelman, *Length of Life: A Study of the Life Table* (Rev. ed.; New York: Ronald, 1949), p. 42. Copyright 1949 The Ronald Press Company.

doubled again. The increase from roughly 18 to roughly 35 years, which took place before the development of industrial society, was due in the main to social innovations—in particular, the consolidation of large areas over which a powerful state maintained social order. The second

570

doubling, from about 35 to about 70 years, can be ascribed in large part to technological improvements in agriculture, medicine, and public health. The successful application in underdeveloped countries of the most recent innovations in death control is almost completely independent, as we have seen in Chapter 16, of whether or not these nations are able to effect concomitant rises in social welfare. The efficacy of modern scientific means of death control is so great, in fact, that they tend to obscure other relevant factors. It is hardly an exaggeration to say that the social determinants of mortality have been reduced more and more to the single decisive one, whether the fruits of modern Western science are available. However plausible, this view is still somewhat limited. Among the scientific advances of recent years are weapons far more destructive than any ever used in past wars. How man will use his increasing control over his natural environment, that is to say, will depend on the social order—and in this sense it is still correct to maintain that the social determinants of mortality are decisive.

In another sense, the ultimate factor is biology. The average span of life has been extended, but man is still mortal. How much can we anticipate, on the basis of present knowledge, that expectation of life will be increased? Is medical science close to the impassable barrier, or is another major breakthrough likely? These questions cannot be answered precisely, but some relevant information is available.

BIOLOGICAL DETERMINANTS OF MORTALITY

Like all other forms of life, human beings must have a regular supply of food, and they have a better chance of surviving when living in an environment relatively free of their natural enemies, especially the microscopic organisms that cause various diseases. Each of these truisms, on closer examination, turns out to be less simple than this first statement would indicate. Man's ability to resist infection, or to remain healthy with less than the optimum amount of food, differs greatly from one individual to another; and a part of this variation depends on biological factors.

Food Requirements

Food nourishes man in two ways: by providing the material with which the body is built, maintained, and regulated, and by supplying fuel for energy and warmth. Food requirements, thus, include both a certain amount and a certain balance among various types of nutrients. Either a deficiency in quantity or an imbalance has as its successive consequences a less than optimum well-being, sickness, and ultimately death. Man has always known something of the general conditions and effects of starvation, and the etiology of most of the food-deficiency maladies (pellagra, scurvy, goiter, beriberi, and others) was established in the nineteenth century. If we direct our attention, however, from such instances of the marked lack of food to the question of the precise needs for optimum body functioning, we find that experts are still often in doubt.

Even whether malnutrition short of starvation contributes substantially to mortality is a matter of dispute. We are told in a standard population text, for example, that "underfeeding weakens the individual and renders him less resistant to disease," so that "a great many people who die of a specific disease would not have died at that time if they had not been suffering from chronic undernourishment." [1] According to a prominent nutritionist, however, "there is no aspect of undernutrition about which there is a more fixed common belief—and less objective evidence—than the question of the effect on resistance to infection." [2] Keys points out that in Nazi-occupied Holland and Greece, where the mass starvation was not accompanied by general social disorganization, the typical association of famine and epidemic did not take place. On the other hand, the 1946 diphtheria epidemic in Germany seemed to affect the American occupation troops as severely as the underfed German population. Thus, apart from certain specific ailments, the most important of which is tuberculosis, whether the susceptibility to disease is *directly* affected by malnutrition remains an open question.

The energy requirements of an individual depend on a large number of variables—among others, his age, sex, basal metabolism rate, body type, occupation and avocation, the climate he lives in, and the type of clothing he wears. In a sizable population, of course, most of these factors balance out. The average amount of energy food that a moderately active, mature person requires in a temperate climate, according to the Food and Nutrition Board of the National Research Council, is 3,000 calories per day for a 154-pound man and 2,400 per day for a 123-pound woman.[3] These "recommended allowances" (*not* "standards") would

[1] Warren S. Thompson, *Population Problems* (4th ed.; New York: McGraw-Hill, 1953), pp. 48–49.

[2] Ancel Keys, "Caloric Undernutrition and Starvation, With Notes on Protein Deficiency," in American Medical Association, Council on Foods and Nutrition, *Handbook on Nutrition* (2nd ed.; New York: Blakiston, 1951), pp. 409–444.

[3] Cf. Grace MacLeod and Henry C. Sherman, "Recommended Dietary Allowances," *ibid.*, pp. 233–257.

vary considerably according to temperature or other circumstances, and one can hardly extend them to other countries without adjustment.

Whether the National Research Council's recommendations should be accepted even for the United States, moreover, is disputed. According to Keys, "The orienting philosophy behind them has been to emphasize the frequency and danger of undernutrition and to promote an abundance of food supplies." [4] Actually, caloric inadequacy has all but disappeared from the American scene, even in times of economic depression, while overeating and obesity have become important causes of ill health. Various surveys indicate that eating less than the recommended allowance is not only not detrimental but, within limits, beneficial to health.

The determination of the optimum intake of other nutrients is even more difficult than in the case of energy-foods. With some of them—for example, calcium and vitamins A and C—the consumption of larger amounts than the minimum required seems to confer corresponding increases in well-being, while with others this apparently is not the case. Moreover, the interaction among food elements means that the correct amount of any one varies also according to the amounts of others consumed.

Diseases, Communicable and Other

That infectious diseases are the consequence of an invasion of the body by microorganisms has been a secure datum of medical science for less than a century, only since the epoch-making experiments of Louis Pasteur. Once the cause of these ailments was known, much more effective ways were devised to control their transmission. Simply the rigorous segregation of sewage from drinking water, for example, broke the usual path of infection of such waterborne plagues as cholera; and the spraying of DDT brought under control malaria and other insect-transmitted diseases. The Western pharmacopoeia now includes not only specific medicaments against a large number of germs but also antibiotics and other general anti-infection preparations. These advances in scientific knowledge made possible an almost total conquest of early mortality.

However, if a germ is not prevented from entering the body by public-health measures, and if it is not destroyed in the body by medicaments, whether the germ will cause an infection, and if so how virulent it will be, are difficult questions.

[4] Ancel Keys, "Energy Requirements of Adults," *ibid.,* pp. 259–274.

Every infectious disease is the result of a struggle between two variables—the pathogenic powers of the bacteria on the one hand, and the resistance of the subject on the other—each of these again modified by variations in the conditions under which the struggle takes place. . . . The conceptions "resistance," "immunity," and "susceptibility" are relative terms which can never be properly discussed without consideration of all modifying conditions.[5]

These modifying conditions may include an inherited resistance to the particular disease, whether on the part of the race or of the particular individual. They may include an acquired immunity, the consequence of either an inoculation or an earlier case of the same disease. In some instances the will to live may be relevant.[6] Variations in the environment, as in the temperature, may reduce the body's resistance. The virulence of the germ itself may be markedly increased or weakened by, say, passage through the body of an animal of a different species.

These changes in the relation between germs and their human hosts have resulted occasionally in the disappearance of diseases, and in the appearance of new ones. Bubonic plague, which devastated Europe in the fourteenth century and struck again in the seventeenth, has not occurred in epidemic proportions anywhere in the Western world for more than 100 years. Leprosy, similarly, was all but unknown in Europe by the seventeenth century. On the other hand, the first reliable evidence of infantile paralysis in epidemic form dates from 1840, and there are other examples of new maladies. Sometimes a terrifying plague appears briefly and then completely and inexplicably vanishes. The most remarkable example is the so-called English sweating disease, of which there is no mention either before 1485 or after 1552, but which during that short period disorganized English society.[7]

In spite of such remaining puzzles, it has been possible to eliminate many communicable diseases almost totally as causes of death. The frontiers of medical science, as was indicated in Chapter 10, seem to be moving beyond infections, into the difficult terrain of "morbid conditions," psychosomatic ailments, allergies, and "positive health."

[5] Hans Zinsser, John F. Enders, and LeRoy D. Fothergill, *Immunity: Principles and Application in Medicine and Public Health* (5th ed.; New York: Macmillan, 1940), p. 106.

[6] "Some of the most eminent phthisiologists believe that tuberculosis is often quite clearly a form of unconscious suicide on the part of a patient who has conflicting wishes both to live and to die" (Karl A. Menninger, *The Human Mind,* 3rd ed., New York: Knopf, 1957, p. 125).

[7] Hans Zinsser, *Rats, Lice and History: . . . The Life History of Typhus Fever* (Boston: Little, Brown, 1935), Ch. 5.

Genetic Factors

The probability of dying seems to depend to some degree on the inherited capacity to maintain life, but it is not easy to distinguish this influence. Whenever children remain in essentially the same social and economic situation as their parents, a similar average length of life in the two generations may be due either to a genetic proclivity or to the continued influence of the unchanged environment, or to both. What is inherited, moreover, is not a trait but a predisposition to react in certain ways to various environments, so that if these change, the significance of the inheritance may change with them. These methodological difficulties notwithstanding, the genetic factor in mortality can be indicated in a number of ways.

TABLE 19-2. Percentage Distribution of Longevous and Random Samples by Parents' Age at Death

Respondents' Parents that Lived to 70 Years	*Sample of Persons Aged*	
	10–89 Years	*90 Years and Over*
Neither parent	57.4	13.4
One parent only	30.8	40.8
Both parents	11.9	45.8
Total	100.1	100.0

Source: Raymond and Ruth DeWitt Pearl, *The Ancestry of the Long-Lived* (Baltimore: Johns Hopkins Press, 1934), p. 150.

Several investigators have studied the average length of life in successive generations of various families in order to see whether a trend is discernible. According to the combined results of a number of such studies, in the United States today a favorable ancestry would add two to four years to one's expectation of life at age 25, as compared with the general increase in this country of 6.7 years between 1900 and 1946.[8] The relative insignificance of the hereditary element, however, is due to quite recent advances in medicine. In 1915, according to evidence cited by Pearl, having long-lived parents added seven more years to one's expectation of life than the utmost that medical science could then achieve.[9] A later monograph by him and his wife, although it is now out of date, is still worth reviewing in its own terms. Its data, as summarized in Table 19-2,

[8] Louis I. Dublin, Alfred J. Lotka, and Mortimer Spiegelman, *Length of Life: A Study of the Life Table* (Rev. ed.; New York: Ronald, 1949), p. 117.
[9] Raymond Pearl, *The Biology of Death* (Philadelphia: Lippincott, 1922), p. 165.

certainly showed a significant relation.[10] However, the study hardly attempted to differentiate between biological and cultural influences: in the four-page questionnaire that was circulated only two questions related to social variables.

It is known that the incidence of some diseases varies markedly from one race to another. While this datum suggests that susceptibility to them may be inherited, here again the evidence is muddied by the difficulty of distinguishing biological from environmental factors. As we have noted in previous chapters, the first meeting of two peoples previously isolated from one another frequently marks in a dramatic way the effect of such race differences. For example, when the whites took measles with them to the South Seas, this was transformed from a relatively minor illness to a raging epidemic; and when Columbus's men brought syphilis to Europe from the West Indies, its virulence was also much greater among this fresh population. Such events may indicate a genetic factor: if the constitutional immunity to any disease originally varies in a population, an epidemic kills off the more susceptible, and the survivors pass on to their progeny their greater inherent resistance. It may be, however, that the relative immunity to an endemic disease is acquired not genetically but by a mild, perhaps unrecognized, case of it in infancy or childhood.

A more specific racial comparison, that between whites and Negroes in the United States, shows wide differences in both the incidence of various diseases and mortality from them. Some of this contrast is due to the generally lower economic level of Negroes, but not all. The clearest example of a disease that is genetic in origin, sickle-cell anemia, is virtually confined to Negroes, perhaps wholly so. Kroeber, after compiling the list of such race-related diseases given here in Table 19-3, warns the reader that care is necessary in interpreting these data. "While it is as good as certain that races differ genetically in their pathology, as in other traits, the problem is beset by so many contingencies and pitfalls that exact proof can be brought only rarely, and in general we are lucky if reasonable probabilities can be determined." [11] As with the inheritance of longevity, the data concerning racial differences indicate that genetic influences are operative but not precisely how important they are.

---

[10] This was true also when the analysis was carried back another generation. The average age at death of the two parents and four grandparents of the respondents, which for the whole sample ranged between 42 and 100 years, was 16 years higher for the forebears of nonagenarians and centenarians than for those of the random sample.

[11] A. L. Kroeber, *Anthropology* (Rev. ed.; New York: Harcourt, Brace, 1948), pp. 188–190.

TABLE 19-3. Comparative Pathology of Negroes and Whites
in the United States

	Diseases with Higher Incidence	
	Among Negroes	Among Whites
Difference definite and marked, almost certainly racial	Sickle-cell anemia Whooping cough Fibroids in womb Keloid tumors Nephritis	Diphtheria Yellow fever Hemophilia Peptic ulcer Psoriasis Lupus Trachoma Surgical suppuration

Difference perceptible, possibly racial	Lobar pneumonia
	Hypertension
	Cerebral hemorrhage
	Syphilitic heart
	   disease
	Cancer of female
	   genitalia
		Scarlet fever
		Measles
		Infantile paralysis
		Angina pectoris
		Arteriosclerosis
		Coronary occlusion
		Gallstones
		Urinary stones
		Most cancers

Fact or cause of difference in dispute	Tuberculosis Syphilis Typhoid fever Malaria	Pernicious anemia Diabetes

Source: From *Anthropology,* New Edition, Revised, by A. L. Kroeber, copyright, 1923, 1948, by Harcourt, Brace and Company, Inc.; renewed, 1951, by A. L. Kroeber. Reprinted by permission of the publishers.

Sex Differences

Except during their childbearing years, females generally have lower age-specific death rates than males; and in modern Western societies the rule holds without this exception. It is apparently true of all human cultures and even of other animal species. The higher the age-group, therefore, the higher the proportion of females usually is. For example, in the United States in 1950 the sex ratio ranged from 1,037 for those aged 14 and under to 896 for those 65 and over. This contrast, moreover, has been increasing over the past half-century: among the white population, the female expectation of life at birth was 2.9 years greater in 1900, 3.6 in 1930, and 6.5 in 1958. One reason for this differentiation, as we have noted,[12] is that recent improvements in death control have been greater for female than for male ailments.

[12] See pages 263–266.

Some of the sex difference in mortality, however, is almost certainly innate. The much larger proportion of males who die in infancy (and presumably also in the uterus, though here the evidence is uncertain) cannot be explained by any systematic variation in the environment. While for adults it is difficult to distinguish biological from environmental influences, such a differentiation was made in a recent ingenious study, which compared the mortality of Catholic monks and nuns engaged principally in teaching. The life patterns of these two groups were very similar, especially in the absence of sex-linked activities most relevant to mortality—namely, childbearing for females and dangerous occupations and strains for males. In these culturally standardized groups the divergence in expectation of life by sex was greater than in the population as a whole, and it had also been increasing over the past decades. The author concludes that biological factors are more important than sociocultural ones in effecting the differentiation in death rates by sex. He suggests as a hypothesis:

> *Under conditions of equal stress* women may be no more resistant to the *infectious* and *contagious* diseases than men—perhaps even less so—and . . . the gains which women have been making over men in this century may be chiefly bound up with a greater constitutional resistance to the *degenerative* diseases. . . . The growing advantage of American women over men is a function of the transition from conditions when infectious and contagious diseases were the main causes of death to conditions wherein the degenerative diseases play this role.[13]

Senescence

The most important characteristic related to innate susceptibility to death is age. The power of self-renewal and the ability to reproduce the species, the principal features that distinguish living beings from inert matter, both decline with advancing age. We tend to think that "aging" begins some time after full adulthood, and in some contexts this is a useful interpretation of the term. Actually, physiological senescence begins before birth and continues throughout life. One index of this process is the rate at which body lesions heal. If persons of various ages sustain a wound of 20 square centimeters, under otherwise identical conditions this will heal in 20 days on the body of a child of 10, in 31 with a man of 20, in 41 with one aged 30, in 78 with one aged 50, and in 100 with

---

[13] Francis C. Madigan, S.J., "Are Sex Mortality Differentials Biologically Caused?" *Milbank Memorial Fund Quarterly*, 35:2 (April, 1957), 202–223; italics in the original.

one aged 60.[14] A child of 10 thus typically cicatrizes a wound at five times the rate of a man of 60.

However, the rate at which one ages, whether by this or any other index, varies widely according to life conditions. A person of any particular age combines the effects of physiological senescence, which we may take as the same for the whole of the species, with those of his particular life experience. It would be useful to separate these two elements into what has been termed "chronologic age," or the number of years lived, and "biologic age," or the person's relative functioning capacity as determined by the sum of genetic and environmental factors, including his chronologic age.[15] While this distinction cannot yet be finely drawn, an approximation is sometimes attempted. Whether or not a life insurance company grants a policy to any applicant, for instance, depends not only on the probability that someone of his chronologic age will die but also on such rough indications of his biologic age as his parents' longevity, his personal and medical history, his present state of health, and his occupation.

It is now possible to retard senescence to some degree, and this control may improve during the coming decades. In that case, as the proportion of aged in the population increases, the physiological and psychological characteristics typical of elderly persons might also change. We still know rather little about how much the biological process of senescence can be altered by a favorable medical, social, and psychological environment.

A priori, it is often assumed that aging is accompanied by measurable and meaningful mental deterioration, and this negative assumption is the starting point for much of the research in gerontology. An examination of the literature reveals that most information has been obtained from senile inmates of mental institutions and homes for the aged and that the findings from such studies have been generalized to the aged at large. . . . [There has been a general] failure to control pertinent variables which may have far more influence on the experimental findings than age per se.[16]

How far can this conquest of nature go? Must not the remarkable advances in medical science at one point reach an impassable barrier? Contrary to what one might suppose, death is not the inevitable con-

---

[14] Pierre Lecomte du Noüy, *Biological Time* (London: Methuen, 1936), pp. 154–155.

[15] Harry Benjamin, "Biologic versus Chronologic Age," *Journal of Gerontology*, 2:3 (July, 1947), 217–227. Cf. also Read Bain, "The Ages of Man," *American Sociological Review*, 10:3 (June, 1945), 337–343; E. V. Cowdry, "We Grow Old," *Scientific Monthly*, 50:1 (January, 1940), 51–58.

[16] Franklyn N. Arnhoff, "Research Problems in Gerontology," *Journal of Gerontology*, 10:4 (October, 1955), 452–456.

comitant of life, but only of specialized forms of life. In a favorable environment unicellular bodies have been observed to live for millions of generations with no diminution of vitality; and to the degree that the word has any empirical meaning, they can be called "immortal." In the laboratory a portion of a chicken's heart has been kept alive much longer than the natural span of the species. The question arises, then, whether the link between specialization and death is inevitable, or whether a suitable change in environment might alter it.

The utopian vision of Condorcet and his contemporaries—an era free from disease, in which old age and death could be postponed indefinitely —has attained a certain scientific respectability from the actual achievements in this century. In the words of M. G. Candau, Director General of the World Health Organization,

> If the great advances gained in science and technology are put at the service of all the people of the world, our children will live in an age from which most of the diseases our grandparents and parents took for granted will be banished. It may no longer be Utopian to envisage a new chapter in the history of medicine.[17]

Opposed to this rosy perspective is one that emphasizes the rise of new ailments associated, actually or supposedly, with modern Western civilization—cancers from smoking or x-rays, allergies from detergents and synthetics, alcoholism, and so on.

At the same time responsible physicians have begun to express concern about what one of them called "medicated survival."

> More of us, healthy or infirm, are living to be old. More handicapped survive at all ages. More people live to have more mental illness. More people live to become socially and financially dependent. More people live to acquire chronic illness of all kinds. More suffering and helpless people are kept alive whom it would be kinder to allow to die. . . .
>
> We hear much of the vast amount of brilliant research being carried on to find measures of prevention and cure for heart disease and cancer. All very well and I hope we find them (although I, personally, am not too sanguine about that for the near future). But just suppose we *did* find these cures tomorrow and could apply them easily and cheaply to everybody. What then? That thought should chill you. Are we prepared to care for the thousands who would survive still more years? Where would we put them? Where are the people to care for them? How would we even support them? Suppose instead of 15,000,000 people over 65 we suddenly had 30,000,000? The problems would make the shock of Sputnik and the costs of the defense program look like peanuts indeed. . . .

[17] Quoted in René J. Dubos, "Medical Utopias," *Daedalus,* Summer, 1959, pp. 410–424.

Not long ago I heard a minister talk on the various freedoms he would like to see available to all mankind. After reviewing the more familiar ones, he added a new one: Freedom to die.[18]

SOCIAL DETERMINANTS OF MORTALITY

As has been noted in earlier chapters, the conquest of death in modern times has consisted largely in the greatly improved control of early death. This can be illustrated by the example of Sweden, which has both the longest historical series of accurate statistics and, at the present time, one of the world's best records for effective control. From 1750 to about 1810 infant mortality in Sweden fluctuated around 200 per 1,000 live births; that is, at that time one child out of every five born died before its first birthday. During the rest of the nineteenth century the rate fell slowly but consistently, reaching 100 by 1900. From that date on, the decline was much faster, down to about 20 in 1950. The reduction in infant mortality over the last 150 years, thus, was by about 90 per cent. For the most recent decades, death rates are available by shorter periods than the whole of the first year, and these are suggestive. From 1915 to 1945 the proportion of deaths under the age of one week remained essentially constant at about 16 per 1,000 live births, while deaths from age one week to one year fell off by about 70 per cent.[19]

In his work on the population of Europe Kirk found a way of dramatizing the superior death control practiced in Holland, whose recent record is even better than Sweden's. He compared the number of deaths in each country with the number there would have been if Holland's age-specific rates in 1939 had obtained; and then he calculated the difference as a percentage of the total and labeled this "excess deaths." On this basis, excess mortality for Europe as a whole amounted to 35 per cent; and for Northwestern and Central Europe alone it was 23 per cent.[20] This rather significant contrast is not based on a difference in medical techniques, which are more or less identical all over Western Europe. The reasons for it must rather be sought in the country's social history.

The rise of Dutch industry and the development of social-welfare

[18] Dean A. Clark, "Where Does the Nation's Health Stand Today?" in Milbank Memorial Fund, *Selected Studies of Migration Since World War II* (New York, 1958), pp. 233–242.

[19] United Nations, Department of Social Affairs, Population Division, *Foetal, Infant and Early Childhood Mortality, 1: The Statistics* (Population Studies, no. 13; New York, 1954), 29–35.

[20] Dudley Kirk, *Europe's Population in the Interwar Years* (League of Nations; Princeton: Princeton University Press, 1946), pp. 180–182.

legislation in Holland were almost simultaneous. There were only 30 years of uncontrolled urbanization—from about 1870, when industrialization really got under way, to 1900, when the Housing Act was passed. The evils associated with the factory system of England, to take the classic example, existed in the Netherlands, but on a proportionately much smaller scale and for a much shorter period. The impetus to develop this social-welfare program, moreover, came in large part from such traditionalist institutions as the churches, which thus established for themselves a significant function in relation to the new society. As one consequence, the best of modern medical science is now made available to the people through institutions connected with religious or other groups to which they are bound by strong sentiments. The Dutch equivalent of the Red Cross, for example, is three "Cross Societies," associated, respectively, with the Catholic, the Protestant, and the secularist sectors of the population. Similarly, the Dutch medical profession itself established a health-insurance plan, which has remained private in the sense that the physicians and the member-patients control it; but health insurance is now compulsory for all wage and salary earners, with half of the premiums paid by the employers.[21]

While the entire population of all Western nations has benefited from some technical advances in death control, the unequal distribution of others is reflected in class differences in mortality. In the United States in 1950, for instance, the age-standardized death rate of unskilled laborers was almost double that of professionals;[22] and this contrast represents at least in part differential access to medical treatment. Innovations in medical practice like prepayment and physicians groups, which were radically new proposals in the 1930's, have spread rapidly in the postwar years, with important benefits to the health of the nation. But the social organization of medical care in the United States is still very much less efficient than the technical.[23]

Important class and national differences still remain in Western age-specific death rates, but these have tended everywhere to converge. It may be realistic to extrapolate this trend to the virtual elimination of malnutrition and infectious diseases *as causes of death,* not only in the West but also in the rest of the world. If indeed such an advance is

[21] For a more extended discussion of Holland's mortality, see William Petersen, *Planned Migration: The Social Determinants of the Dutch-Canadian Movement* (Berkeley: University of California Press, 1955), pp. 15–32.

[22] See pages 267–268.

[23] For a balanced discussion by an eminent physician, see Clark, "Where Does the Nation's Health Stand Today?" *op. cit.*

technically possible, whether it will take place will depend in large part on social developments. Unless the fertility of underdeveloped areas falls almost as rapidly as their mortality, the consequent increase in numbers may overwhelm modern science. In some totalitarian countries, as we have seen in Chapter 15, the "normal" death rate is as low as anywhere else, but millions die as a side-effect of the Party's attempt to control the whole society absolutely. Whether a small-family system is established, whether totalitarian governments are avoided, whether there is a third world war —these are contingencies that go beyond both the techniques of death control and the efficacy of the institutions through which they are applied. In particular, the effect of war on mortality is a subject that demands further comment.

War

Over the centuries the deadliness of weapons has increased considerably, and to the extent that this is the decisive factor, the number of casualties should have gone up proportionately. According to Sorokin's reckoning, thus, the proportion of the armed forces of four major European powers that were killed or wounded increased from less than 5 per cent in the thirteenth and fourteenth centuries to more than 16 per cent in the nineteenth century.[24] By Wright's estimate, on the contrary, military casualties decreased from about 30–50 per cent of the armed forces in the Middle Ages to about 6 per cent in World War I.[25] That is to say, the data are too poor to make such comparisons over the past several centuries.

Nevertheless, it is almost certain that there has been a downward trend in the human cost of war if we include in this class also deaths from disease. Before the development of modern surgery, a serious wound was more or less equivalent to death; and in many wars of the past epidemics were more deadly than battles. Zinsser has summarized some of the more striking examples of this point in a chapter entitled "On the influence of epidemic diseases on political and military history, and on the relative unimportance of generals." Disease was the decisive factor in many of the wars of the preindustrial world—in the Crusades, in the struggle

[24] Pitirim A. Sorokin, *Social and Cultural Dynamics, 3: Fluctuations of Social Relationships, War, and Revolution* (New York: American Book Company, 1937), 337. Since all data on military casualties are inadequate, Sorokin concentrated his analysis on the four major European powers that had the best statistics—England, France, Austria-Hungary, and Russia.

[25] Quincy Wright, *A Study of War* (Chicago: University of Chicago Press, 1942), 1, 242.

between Catholics and Protestants during the Reformation, in the wars of the Napoleonic period (particularly the disastrous retreat from Moscow), in colonial wars (independent Haiti was established mainly because 22,000 of the 25,000 invading French troops died of yellow fever). In short, "typhus, with its brothers and sisters—plague, cholera, typhoid, dysentery—has decided more campaigns than Caesar, Hannibal, Napoleon, and all the inspector generals of history. The epidemics get the blame for defeat, the generals the credit for victory. It ought to be the other way around." [26]

Sorokin's main thesis, that war is especially characteristic of modern, rationalized, so-called "sensate" societies, is even more questionable. Industrialism spread from England during the nineteenth century, and its rise coincided with a phenomenon unheard of in the annals of Western civilization—a century of peace in Europe. From 1815, the end of the Napoleonic wars, to 1914, the beginning of World War I, "apart from the Crimean war—a more or less colonial event—England, France, Prussia, Austria, Italy, and Russia were engaged in war among each other for altogether only eighteen months. A computation of comparable figures for the two preceding centuries gives an average of sixty to seventy years of major wars in each." [27] To equate industrialism with belligerence is obviously inadequate.

Speier has distinguished three types of war, which he terms absolute war, instrumental war, and agonistic fighting.[28] Absolute war, whose purpose is to annihilate the enemy, is conducted without rules. Each belligerent perceives the other not as an opposed force, but as animals. Instrumental war is waged in order to gain access to values that the enemy controls, with the cost calculated against the possible gain; it is typically regulated by religious or social norms. If what is coveted is considered to be very important, it may verge on the absolute type; or it may approximate the third type, agonistic fighting, which is very closely regulated by strict observance of rules. Such a social definition of the purpose of a war—annihilation of the enemy, relative advantage (economic or other), or glory—has a much greater effect on mortality than the efficacy of the weapons used.

Absolute war is waged at all levels of society—among certain primitive peoples, for whom this is a way of life; [29] among advanced civilizations, particularly against enemies defined as "savages" or "infidels"; and

---

[26] Zinsser, *Rats, Lice and History,* p. 153.

[27] Karl Polanyi, *The Great Transformation* (New York: Rinehart, 1944), p. 5.

[28] Hans Speier, *Social Order and the Risks of War* (New York: Stewart, 1952), pp. 223–229.

[29] See Wright, *op. cit.,* vol. 1, Appendixes 9, 10, and 13.

among present-day totalitarian powers. By the twelfth century, when Sorokin's figures begin, the social controls of feudal society had been established in Europe; fighting was for limited aims and, when Christians opposed other Christians, according to the code of chivalry. With the breakdown of feudalism, this chivalric norm disappeared, and the religious and civil conflict of the following centuries took a much greater toll. In the nineteenth century, with bourgeois industrial society well established in Europe, a new code—the balance-of-power system—effectively limited warfare and mortality from it.

The military conflicts since 1914 have been more devastating principally because the international structure of the nineteenth century has broken down. In the two world wars, regulations of various kinds have successively been abrogated—concerning places (open cities, etc.), concerning weapons (tanks, poison gas, atomic bombs), concerning forms (declaration of war, treatment of prisoners), and concerning values (setting limits to the spoliation of property or of persons, etc.).

Comparing the total (military and civilian) casualties in the two world wars, we find that the estimated number of dead increased from 9.7 to 54.8 million and of wounded from 21.1 to 35.0 million.[30] This greater mortality, however, was concentrated among the nationals of only a few countries, particularly Germany, Poland, and the Soviet Union, while for the other belligerents World War II proved to be considerably less deadly than World War I. In the case of France, for example, military casualties amounted to about 200,000, or about one-seventh of those in 1914–1918.[31] France's total loss of life due to World War II, including both direct and indirect mortality, amounted to about 1,130,000, which was made up in a few years by the unusually high postwar fertility. This decline in casualties was due in part to the improvement in military technology, with which the Nazi armies were really able to conduct a "lightning war."

In Germany, from one world war to the next, the number of military dead increased by about half (from 2,037,000 to 3,050,000) but the number of civilian dead by more than four times (from 500,000 to 2,050,000). Of the approximately 25 million adults killed in the Soviet Union during the war of 1941–1945, more were civilians (some 15 million) than soldiers.[32] These figures illustrate what is perhaps the most

[30] German Federal Government, Press and Information Office, *Germany Reports* (Wiesbaden, 1953), pp. 101–103.
[31] Paul Vincent, "Conséquences de six années de guerre sur la population française," *Population*, 1:3 (July–September, 1946), 429–440.
[32] See pages 446–448.

One of the main squares of Rotterdam, before and after the Germans bombed it in 1940. This was not a military action but rather a punishment of the Dutch for having resisted the Nazis' invasion of their country. (Royal Dutch Airlines—KLM)

important change that total war has effected with respect to mortality—the all but complete disappearance of the prior distinction between military and civilians as legitimate targets. The millions who were killed as the direct consequence of political conflict also suggest that a classification of "causes of death" restricted in the main to biological factors is markedly incomplete.

THE CAUSE OF DEATH: A SECOND LOOK

One of the sections of Chapter 10, entitled "Causes of Death," is concerned with how these are ascribed in medical practice and vital statistics. "The" cause of death, so conceived, is what the physician writes on the certificate he signs. It has been generally recognized that this classification is quite inadequate in a number of ways, and "it is expected that the Eighth Revision of the International Lists of Diseases and Causes of Death in 1965 will provide an opportunity for a sweeping revision." [33] Several kinds of improvements are anticipated. It is estimated that as many as a quarter of the death certificates signed in the United States do not clearly state the physician's opinion of the cause of death. There is much regional variation, some of which could possibly be eliminated. But a more important change will be the shift from single diseases to disease-complexes (for example, coronary disease with diabetes rather than either one separately). Such a practice would be an extension of the present one, by which the certifying physician is instructed to report "other significant conditions contributing to the death but not related to the disease or condition causing it." How far this directive could lead can be suggested by a few examples.

Perhaps the difficulty can be put most cogently in a hypothetical case. Let us suppose that a number of persons were in an accident and sustained identical injuries. Two-thirds recovered after being treated. In most types of analysis this fact alone would make us hesitate in describing the accident as the cause of the death of the others. Of those that died, let us suppose, one was an elderly man, whose lesions healed too slowly; one had a chronically weak heart; one had had an appendectomy, the scar of which released a thrombus; one, a Negro, was denied admission to the nearest hospital. For all these persons the accident would be listed as "the" cause of death; and of the other circumstances and those like them some might be included as contributory factors, but many

[33] Mortimer Spiegelman *et al.,* "Problems in the Medical Certification of Causes of Death," *American Journal of Public Health,* 48:1 (January, 1958), 71–80.

would not be mentioned or even known to the person compiling the statistics.

In 1958 a British doctor issued a death certificate listing as the cause "carcinoma [cancer] of bronchus due to excessive smoking." The registrar refused to accept so unorthodox a juncture of "natural" and social causes, and there had to be an inquest. The coroner, an unrepentant smoker, declared that the physician had been attempting "to judge the habits of [his] fellow men. That must be the province of the coroner." His verdict was death from natural causes.[34]

When an inhabitant of Los Angeles with a weak heart strained it trying to get enough air during one of the city's recurrent bouts of smog and died, the physician denoted the smog as "a significant condition contributing to death." Once again the coroner refused to accept the certification. "Los Angeles smog is not a disease," he declared, with no great show of logic. He added, more relevantly: "We would be opening the gates to litigation against the Board of Supervisors if we accepted such a certificate." [35]

A child had died of diphtheria. At the clinical pathological conference, the pathologist demonstrated the organs, showed the culture of diphtheria bacilli isolated from the lesions and expressed regret at the relatively uninstructive program of the morning. The case was so straightforward, the cause of death so evident. An elderly physician in the audience then rose to say that he did not believe the real cause of death had been brought out at all; that he had other information. The birth of the child had never been reported to the responsible authority. As a consequence the family was not visited at the child's first birthday, as was the practice of the Health Department, to present to the father and mother the advantages of immunization against diphtheria and the means to obtain that service. The child was not immunized. The cause of death was social, and biological.[36]

Such examples could be multiplied, but these should suffice to indicate the range of difficulties that would ensue if a serious attempt were made to list the main cause, the ancillary causes, and the significant contributing factors leading to each death. It is as though it were required to enter on each birth certificate not merely the "natural cause" of coitus but also all the personal, social, and accidental factors that to a significant degree had resulted in two persons meeting, marrying, and having this child.

The conceptual differentiation between fecundity and fertility, as was pointed out in the last chapter, contributed greatly to improving the

[34] *Time,* November 17, 1958.
[35] *Ibid.*
[36] John E. Gordon, "Discussion," in Milbank Memorial Fund, *Trends and Differentials in Mortality* (New York, 1956), pp. 43–47.

empirical analysis of both. It would be no less useful, supposedly, to divide mortality into two analogous types—constitutional and environmental, or intrinsic and extrinsic, or natural and accidental, or some other pair of terms separating the inevitable from the controllable. This is more difficult, however, in the case of mortality than with fertility-fecundity. The fact that a birth is always the effect of a single event, fertilization of an ovum, simplifies the problem of distinguishing natural from environmental; for operationally "sterility" is simply a residual term, encompassing all cases of continued exposure that do not result in pregnancy. Since death is typically the effect of a number of factors, both intrinsic and extrinsic, whether to assign one or another as *the* cause is to some degree an arbitrary decision.[37]

The analytic problem can perhaps be clarified by recalling the several types of causation that Aristotle and the medieval schoolmen used. The proximate factor, the **efficient cause** of death, is what physicians have generally concentrated on. Their job is to keep their patient alive, not to understand the whole social context of dying.

Lawyers, on the other hand, are concerned with the **formal cause** of death. From their point of view, all deaths are divided into "violent" and "natural," depending on whether they do or do not involve the law. For some types of death this differentiation is of such practical importance that it is included in the physicians' International Classification.

The **material cause** is the particular susceptibility of the organic system affected. In the same sense that one can say a house burned down because it was built of combustible material, so one can say that a person died of enteritis only because his intestinal tract was too weak to withstand an attack of the germs.[38] If the building had been made of

---

[37] See also a discussion by a physician on the same subject—Alan E. Treloar, "The Enigma of Cause of Death," *Journal of the American Medical Association,* 162:15 (December 8, 1956), 1376–1379.

[38] Pearl classified mortality according to the organic system of the body affected—that is, deaths "caused" by the breakdown, respectively, of the skeletal and muscular, circulatory, respiratory, alimentary, excretory, nervous, and endocrinal systems, the sex organs, and the skin, and deaths from all other causes. He then grouped the mortality in the U.S. Registration Area in 1910 and found that a very high proportion of all deaths were associated with the failure of only three of these ten organic systems. About half of all infant deaths were the consequence of malfunctioning of the alimentary tract; during childhood and adulthood almost as high a proportion were related to the respiratory system; and above the age of 60 between a quarter and a third of all deaths followed from a breakdown of the circulatory system. In such an analysis, that a person dies of pneumonia, for example, is incidental to the main point —that man's lungs (unlike his skin, say) cannot withstand pneumonia germs. While Pearl's data were specific to a particular time and place, he believed that they would not be very different for any other group of *Homo sapiens.* See *The Biology of Death,* Ch. 4.

concrete, or if man's intestines were as resistant to this disease as his bones, then neither the arsonist nor the germ could have caused any damage.

The **first cause** of death, on the other hand, is that ultimate beginning of a chain of occurrences that eventually led to the one being analyzed. In such a view, any death takes place only because unicellular animals began to evolve into more complex beings.

The **final cause** of anything is its plan or design. A building has two stories, for example, because it was so drawn in the architect's blueprint. While it is difficult, except in a religious context, to discuss such a teleological principle with respect to natural phenomena, one can say that death does have a function in nature. It makes possible the evolution of the species by removing one generation and replacing it with its slightly different successor. Natural selection can operate only because living beings are not immortal.

SUMMARY

While it would be useful to divide mortality into two types analogous to fecundity and fertility, such a division is, in practical terms, extremely difficult, for in most deaths biological and environmental influences are interlinked. What is known about the biological causes of death can be summed up under the following headings: nutrition, infectious diseases, hereditary factors, sex differences, and senescence. Generally several of these factors are relevant, and what is ascribed as "the" cause of death depends on the degree of knowledge concerning its circumstances and on the purpose of the ascription.

The most important reason for the great decline in mortality in recent times has been the marked improvement in the production, preservation, and transportation of food, and in the prevention and the cure of infectious diseases. There still remain social differentials in death rates—for example, by nation, by race, by occupation, by educational level, and so on; but these have generally diminished, sometimes almost disappeared, in the over-all decline since 1945. One might conclude that once modern techniques of death control have become available, social determinants of mortality are largely irrelevant; and this is so if we postulate a non-totalitarian society at peace.

However, if the world should engage in another all-out war, fought with weapons of unique destructive power, the devastation could be greater than at any time in all history. This must be noted as a possibility in spite of the fact that up to the war of 1939–1945 improved military technology generally was associated with a proportionate decline in the casualties. The reversal of this trend in World War II was not the consequence of new weapons, but rather of a new social system, represented in Nazi Germany and the Soviet Union. More generally, the principal social determinant of mortality in the modern world is the type of political control exercised. Extraordinary mortality in totalitarian countries, particularly but not exclusively during a total war, may mount up to tens of millions of persons.

SUGGESTIONS FOR FURTHER READING

Raymond Pearl, *The Biology of Death* (Philadelphia: Lippincott, 1922).
> Out of date in some respects, but still a stimulating discussion of its subject.

Louis I. Dublin, Alfred J. Lotka, and Mortimer Spiegelman, *Length of Life: A Study of the Life Table* (Rev. ed.; New York: Ronald, 1949).
> The best general discussion of that indispensable tool, the life table, and of the factors that have determined the average length of life in the United States.

Ralph W. Gerard, ed., *Food for Life* (Chicago: University of Chicago Press, 1952).

Henry C. Sherman and Caroline Sherman Lanford, *Essentials of Nutrition* (4th ed.; New York: Macmillan, 1957).

American Medical Association, Council on Foods and Nutrition, *Handbook of Nutrition* (2nd ed.; New York: Blakiston, 1951).
> Good discussions of the principles of nutrition at three levels of difficulty—a widely read popularization, an elementary text, and an authoritative professional handbook.

C.-E. A. Winslow, *Man and Epidemics* (Princeton: Princeton University Press, 1952).

Hans Zinsser, *Rats, Lice and History: . . . The Life History of Typhus Fever* (Boston: Little, Brown, 1935).
> Works for the general reader by two of the foremost experts in their field.

Milbank Memorial Fund, *Trends and Differentials in Mortality* (New York, 1956).
> A survey consisting of a number of excellent articles.

20. *THE GENERAL DETERMINANTS*
OF MIGRATION

There are no biological determinants of migration in the same sense as of fertility and mortality. Strong incentives to move sometimes are present, and these may be related to physiological needs. For example, the inhabitants of a famine-stricken region may leave it—but famine has sometimes resulted merely in apathy and eventually in death by starvation. Even the strongest motivation, that is, results in migration only when it has been translated into action by human will. On the other hand, migration often takes place even though there is a complete absence of such biological incentives.

Migration, thus, is not usually universal in the sense that fertility and mortality are. We are all born and we all die, but in most cases only some of us migrate, and those who do generally are not a random sample of the populations they leave and enter. Young adults, for example, are much more likely to respond to an impetus to move than either children or old persons. A migration means, therefore, not merely a shift of a certain number of undifferentiated persons from one place to another, but also a change in the occupational and population structure of both countries or regions.

MIGRATORY SELECTION

Given a sedentary population and an inducement to leave home, typically some persons go and some stay behind. The process of differentiation of migrants from nonmigrants by the fact that those who leave are not randomly distributed with respect to various social characteristics is termed **migratory selection.**[1] Whether the decision is made by the

[1] Sometimes the phrase "selective migration" is used to convey the same meaning.

592

migrants themselves is not a crucial distinction in a demographic context. A century ago a slave-trader raiding the African coast would have chosen only young, healthy Negroes; or, more recently, various governments have established quotas by which the immigration of some classes is fostered and that of others is impeded or prohibited. Such regulations by an outside force, while quite dissimilar in some respects from a process of self-selection, are also examples of what we term migratory selection.

In the following survey, as we pass from the age of migrants to other physical and then psychological characteristics, we will pass also to less certain and more polemical data.

Age

With respect to age differentiation, all migration is one: in both internal and international movements, adolescents and young adults usually predominate. This is one of the most firmly established generalizations in demography. Between two-thirds and four-fifths of the immigrants to the United States in the nineteenth century were aged between 15 and 40 years.[2] The proportion in internal migration is typically just as large: for example, the median ages of persons who had moved within the United States during the year 1949/1950 ranged, according to their color and the size of their 1949 place of residence, from 19.8 to 30.5 years.[3] One reason for the high proportion of young adults in any migration would seem to be that this generally involves a certain amount of adjustment at the destination, and young people are usually better able to adapt to new conditions. A second reason, relevant when geographical mobility is a concomitant of job changes, is that these are more frequent among persons who have only recently started to work.

Since this age-group is also distinguished from the rest of a population by many other characteristics, both physiological and social, a comparison

[2] Imre Ferenczi, *International Migrations,* 1: *Statistics* (Publication 14; New York: National Bureau of Economic Research, 1929), 212–213.

[3] Otis Dudley Duncan and Albert J. Reiss, Jr., *Social Characteristics of Urban and Rural Communities, 1950* (New York: Wiley, 1956), pp. 83–87. Even Sorokin and Zimmerman, who doubt whether rural-urban migration is selective by other characteristics, hold that it is so with respect to age and, to a lesser degree, sex; see Pitirim A. Sorokin and Carle C. Zimmerman, *Principles of Rural-Urban Sociology* (New York: Holt, 1929), p. 582. That young adults predominate does not mean, of course, that other persons never migrate. Families that move about may include young children or, less frequently, elderly parents; and in recent years a certain proportion of the migration within the United States has consisted of the movement of retired persons.

between migrants and nonmigrants is misleading unless age is held constant. In the years before World War I, it was often pointed out, for example, that immigrants had a much higher birth rate than the native population; and today some of the new suburbs appear to be hardly more than mass nurseries. In both cases the real difference in fertility has been exaggerated by the atypical age structure. For the same reason, migrants generally enter the labor force in proportionately larger numbers than a sedentary population.

Sex

Selection by sex is also usual, but whether males or females predominate depends on the circumstances. One of Ravenstein's famous "laws" was that "females are more migratory than males," but even he noted that this was more true for short distances than for longer ones.[4] The even greater differences between internal and international migration can be illustrated by two extreme examples.

The nineteenth-century movement into European towns from the surrounding countryside, the short-distance movement that Ravenstein alluded to, was made up in large part of young farm girls who found work as domestic servants in the homes of the urban middle class. An international migration that does not involve great distances or the crossing of an important cultural boundary may also show a predominance of females, and for the same reason. Thus, for example, most of those who left Germany for the Netherlands in the interwar years were also domestic servants, and the sex ratio of this international immigration was therefore very low.[5] Another example is the settlement of Irish servants in England or even the United States. A nineteenth-century farm boy, on the other hand, acquired no skills useful to him in getting established in the city; if he left the farm, he would be more likely to go to a place where his youthful energy and physical strength were at a premium.

The characteristic features of any frontier town—say, in the American West a century ago or in New Guinea today—derive in part from its very high sex ratio and the consequent almost total lack of family life.

---

[4] E. G. Ravenstein, "The Laws of Migration," *Journal of the Royal Statistical Society,* 48:2 (June, 1885), 167–235; 52:2 (June, 1889), 241–305. These two articles, the first important empirical investigation of migratory selection, are still worth reading.

[5] Cf. Dudley Kirk, *Europe's Population in the Interwar Years* (League of Nations; Princeton: Princeton University Press, 1946), p. 117, n. 21.

In Colorado in 1860, for example, only 3.2 per cent of the total population consisted of women in the reproductive age-group.[6] Similarly, males are likely to predominate during the first stages of emigration from any country, no matter what the destination. Thus, for example, among pre-1914 migrants to the United States, the sex ratio of those from Southern and Eastern Europe was very much higher than of those from Northwestern Europe, even though in these decades most newcomers, of whatever nationality, settled in cities. These were certainly not a frontier in the usual sense, but until a sizable Polish or Italian community, for example, was built up in America, there were more males among the immigrants from those countries.

Characteristically, then, internal migrants are predominantly female and international ones predominantly male, but this generalization cannot aptly be designated as a "law." In both cases the reason for the sex ratio is that the social conditions at the destinations favor one or the other sex. In India, as an example of another pattern, most who left the country were contract laborers, and thus male; and only somewhat later did the more successful of overseas Indians have females brought over as brides. Those who move within India from village to town, however, have also been predominantly male. In the only four large cities with adequate statistics, the average sex ratio of in-migrants was 1,540.[7] Single girls have generally been too closely bound to traditional village roles to be able to leave independently, and when husbands have gone to the city, they very often have left their families at home and returned to them as soon as they could. The sex ratio of a city in underdeveloped areas, that is to say, is generally high, and it thus has some of the social characteristics of a frontier town.

How significant an effect international migration can have on sex ratios is indicated in Table 20-1. The great degree of consistency is particularly striking, since there is no reason to suppose that other factors influencing the ratio of males to females varied with this one. In West European countries, where emigration was at its peak around the middle of the nineteenth century, the sex ratio was well under 1,000 by 1900, while in the countries of East Europe and in Japan, where the high point came later, it declined from 1,000 in 1900 to about 900–950 in 1950. The one

---

[6] Kuczynski used this skewed population to illustrate how deceptive crude birth rates can be; see Robert R. Kuczynski, *The Measurement of Population Growth: Methods and Results* (London: Sidgwick & Jackson, 1935), p. 111.

[7] Kingsley Davis, *The Population of India and Pakistan* (Princeton: Princeton University Press, 1951), p. 135.

596 *The General Determinants of Population*

TABLE 20-1. Males per 1,000 Females in Various Countries,
c. 1900 and c. 1950

	c. 1900	c. 1950
Emigration countries		
England and Wales	936	934
Ireland	974	1,024
Norway	924	975
Sweden	953	992
Denmark	950	984
Germany	969	837
Netherlands	976	994
Belgium	987	970
France	968	929
Spain	954	922
Portugal	915	942
Switzerland	964	950
Italy	990	952
Austria	967	876
Hungary	991	959 [a]
Rumania	1,033	935
Greece	1,014	980
Bulgaria	1,041	1,005
Poland } U.S.S.R. }	989	{ 912 { 920 [b]
Japan	1,018	962
Immigration countries		
United States	1,044	986
Canada	1,050	1,035
Australia	1,101	1,006
New Zealand	1,107	1,009
Union of South Africa (Europeans)	1,319	1,014
Argentina	1,119	1,051
Brazil	1,040	1,000 [c]
Chile	987	983

[a] 1941.
[b] 1939.
[c] 1940.
Source: Metropolitan Life Insurance Company, *Statistical Bulletin,* February, 1953, p. 9.

important exception to this pattern is Ireland, the emigration country par excellence, where the ratio actually increased; the reason presumably is the already noted sizable number of *female* domestic servants who left. In receiving countries, on the contrary, with the influx of males to frontier areas, the sex ratio tended to be high in 1900 and to approach parity over the next half-century, as the size of the immigration decreased in many cases and the frontier was pushed back.

Family Status

Whenever their sex ratio varies markedly from 1,000, this means of course that many of the migrants are not married; and the usual theory is that they generally are *single* young adults. This is true of the two characteristic types already discussed, male pioneers and female domestic servants. It may be, however, that the contrast between unmarried transients and relatively fixed families now fits the facts less than it used to.

Urbanization was at one time predominantly a movement of single persons, but as cities grew larger and older a tendency developed to move out of the crowded centers to the suburbs. The continuing in-migration of unmarried persons was then matched by an out-migration of families.[8] In the United States today not only do married seem to move about as much as single persons, but they are often motivated to do so precisely because of their family life—in order to have a larger house for an increasing number of children, in order to live in a "nicer" neighborhood or close to a better school, and so on.[9]

It is possible that there has been a shift in the marital status also of international migrants. In the nineteenth century the typical European who went overseas was a young unmarried adult trying to establish himself economically. The exodus of Jews from Eastern Europe during the decades before World War I, however, did not fit into this pattern. Since they were induced to leave not merely for economic reasons but because of the threat of persecution or actual pogroms, Jewish migrants included a much larger proportion of females and children than other nationalities.[10] With the rise of totalitarian states and the consequent shift from economic to political motivations, the proportion of family migration probably would have risen, but this tendency has been blocked by the same social forces that initiated it. "Among refugees it is *usual* to be separated, husband from wife, children from parents; it is *unusual* for a whole family to be together.

---

[8] One of the earliest and most careful analyses of this dual movement was made in Amsterdam; see T. van den Brink, "Vestiging en vertrek," *Statistische Mededeelingen van het Bureau van Statistiek der Gemeente Amsterdam,* no. 103 (1936), pp. 153–188; summarized in English in Dorothy Swaine Thomas, *Research Memorandum on Migration Differentials* (Bulletin 43; New York: Social Science Research Council, 1938), pp. 70–92.

[9] Cf. Peter H. Rossi, *Why Families Move: A Study in the Social Psychology of Urban Residential Mobility* (Glencoe, Ill.: Free Press, 1955).

[10] Cf. Liebmann Hersch, "International Migration of the Jews," in Walter F. Willcox, ed., *International Migrations, 2: Interpretations* (Publication 18; New York: National Bureau of Economic Research, 1931), 471–520.

Never before in history have war and persecution led to family separation on so vast a scale." [11]

Occupation

The effect of international migration on the labor force of the two countries is complex. In the Liberal economic theory of the nineteenth century, free movement was justified on the ground that those in an over-crowded occupation tended to go wherever their skill was in short supply, so that this natural functioning of the international labor market benefited everyone concerned, both the migrants and the two nations. The principle has a certain validity—or would have, if there were still such a phenomenon as free movement of laborers; but in any case it must certainly be qualified. First of all, it does not hold for migration that is not wholly economically motivated; and the persecution of minorities, the fear of another war, and other political considerations play a large if indeterminate role. Secondly, even economic competition is weighted in favor of the area with the higher standard of living. Thus, for example, immediately after World War II, when Europe needed all its building workers for reconstruction, many of them left nevertheless; for they were wanted also for the developmental programs of overseas countries, which often could offer more attractive prospects. Thirdly, and most fundamentally, the assumption in the Liberal principle that skills are fixed is not warranted. In many cases, selection by occupation is less significant than the *change* of occupation that takes place as a concomitant of migration. Only a very small proportion of the villagers who flocked to the United States in the decades before 1914 became farmers; and the work that they and their sons did generally had nothing to do with what they had done in Europe. Four-fifths of the immigrants had had no previous experience in manufacturing or mining, the sectors of American industry in which most of them found jobs as unskilled laborers.[12] That America was a "land of opportunity" meant precisely that it was a country whose economy was expanding rapidly enough to enable a man to earn his living with aptitudes never used before.

This does not mean, of course, that selection by occupation never takes place in international migration. According to several careful studies, if conditions in the home country are such as to build up a general desire

[11] Maurice R. Davie, *Refugees in America: Report of the Committee for the Study of Recent Immigration from Europe* (New York: Harper, 1947), p. 145.
[12] Maurice R. Davie, *World Immigration, with Special Reference to the United States* (New York: Macmillan, 1949), p. 238. See above, pages 134–136.

to leave, the volume, direction, and timing of the movement are set largely by business conditions in the receiving country. The correlation between the business cycle and emigration is not negative, as might be expected, but "positive and moderately high"; for it is the pull of opportunities overseas that determines the migration rate, and in their broad trends business cycles tend to be international.[13] It is a reasonable development from this generalization to suppose that those attracted most to good jobs are those with skills to fill them; that is, if migrants do the same work in the new country, it can be assumed that they came in part for that purpose.

The tendency to remain in the same type of work has been greater among those not primarily economically motivated, as indicated in Table 20-2. These figures mask important differences among separate occupations; for example, the percentages among the professionals ranged from

TABLE 20-2. Percentage of Interwar Refugees Employed in the Same Occupational Group in the United States as in Europe

	Male	*Female*
Professionals	66.9	51.7
Proprietors, managers, officials	38.9	18.0
Clerks and kindred workers	46.7	36.7
Skilled workers	66.9	52.8
Semiskilled workers	62.8	58.4
Unskilled workers	38.7	38.8
Housewives	—	59.3
Students	47.9	33.5
Unemployed and retired	60.0	13.1

Source: Maurice R. Davie, *Refugees in America: Report of the Committee for the Study of Recent Immigration from Europe* (New York: Harper, 1947), pp. 132, 135. Copyright, 1947, by Harper & Brothers.

76.7 for chemists to only 5.8 for lawyers. Moreover, the size of the groups varied considerably; in particular, more than half of the women had been housewives in Europe. Nevertheless, the figures clearly indicate that among urban emigrants, particularly professionals and skilled workers, the usual shift is smaller.

Selection by occupation among internal migrants certainly takes place to some degree, but it is difficult with the data ordinarily available to pin

[13] Dorothy Swaine Thomas, *Social Aspects of the Business Cycle* (New York: Dutton, 1925), p. 148. Cf. also Thomas, *Social and Economic Aspects of Swedish Population Movements, 1750–1933* (New York: Macmillan, 1941); Harry Jerome, *Migration and Business Cycles* (New York: National Bureau of Economic Research, 1926).

down motives for what has become, at least in the United States, so casual
an act as moving to another home and job. In 1940 Stouffer presented
his well known **theory of intervening opportunities:** "The number of
persons going a given distance is directly proportional to the number of
opportunities at that distance and inversely proportional to the number
of intervening opportunities." [14] In both Stouffer's original study and the
several replications, "opportunities" are defined operationally as, in effect,
the number of persons who have moved into various areas. The hypothesis
leaves out not only all noneconomic factors but also some of the specific
influences on job-hunting migrants as such. Even so, there has been what
one writer termed an "encouraging" degree of confirmation.

Psychical Factors

The study of psychical factors differs from that of the usual demographic variables in several respects. (a) In the definition of the characteristic: When a person tells us that he is 27 years old and married, this
is information on a different level from, for instance, the results of intelligence tests. (b) In the amount of data available: Questions on age,
sex, and marital status are included in all censuses and in virtually all
special studies of migratory selection. Census data are lacking on factors
like intelligence; and of the smaller number of specific studies that include
such variables, many are based on inadequate methodology.

Even if the relevance of a psychical factor is established, the time of
its first appearance is often uncertain. A statement that a person was
single when he left and that he got married after he reached his destination is unambiguous. But if a migrant turns out to be a criminal or
psychopathic, it is usually impossible to choose among three possible
causes: (a) It may be that the home country or area has a higher incidence than the destination. This is perhaps the most common popular
explanation of observed differences: thus, Italians are "prone to be

---

[14] Samuel A. Stouffer, "Intervening Opportunities: A Theory Relating Mobility
and Distance," *American Sociological Review,* 5:6 (December, 1940), 845–867. The
hypothesis has been tested by a number of other persons; see in particular Margaret
L. Bright and Dorothy S. Thomas, "Interstate Migration and Intervening Opportunities," *ibid.,* 6:6 (December, 1941), 773–783; Eleanor Collins Isbell, "Internal
Migration in Sweden and Intervening Opportunities," *ibid.,* 9:6 (December, 1944),
627–639; Fred L. Strodtbeck, "Equal Opportunity Intervals: A Contribution to the
Method of Intervening Opportunity Analysis," *ibid.,* 14:4 (August, 1949), 490–497.
See also Theodore R. Anderson, "Intermetropolitan Migration: A Comparison of the
Hypotheses of Zipf and Stouffer," *ibid.,* 20:3 (June, 1955), 287–291, with comment
by Fred Charles Ikle and rejoinder in *ibid.,* 20:6 (December, 1955), 713–715; C. T.
Pihlblad and C. L. Gregory, "Occupation and Patterns of Migration," *Social Forces,*
36:1 (October, 1957), 56–64.

criminals"; villagers are "dim-witted." (b) It may be that migratory selection takes place—that is, that persons with a predisposition to "criminality" or mental illness or whatever tend to leave in larger proportion. Or (c) it may be that the newcomers fail to adapt successfully to the strange conditions and therefore exhibit one or another form of social pathology.

A priori one can argue that either the less or the more intelligent tend to leave any particular area: (a) In the competition to achieve satisfactory living conditions, by and large the more intelligent will succeed more often, and the less so will thus be forced to seek their fortunes elsewhere. Or (b) in any population it will be the more adaptable—that is to say, the more intelligent—who will respond first to an impetus to emigrate, and the duller who will remain behind.

Whether selection by intelligence takes place in international migrations is still an open question. Indeed, many I.Q. tests have been made of the foreign stock, particularly in the United States; but it is difficult to say what these prove. Immigrants generally score lower, but one reason is certainly their less adequate knowledge of English and of the American culture generally. If this deficiency could be removed, probably the group differences would disappear with it; but the various attempts to devise a so-called culture-free intelligence test have not been very successful. In any case, the testing of newcomers to the United States, whatever importance it may have for other reasons, is irrelevant to a study of migratory selection, for it is made at the wrong end of the journey. The question is not how German immigrants, for example, compare with native Americans, but rather how those Germans who leave compare with those who remain in Germany. This is a matter, however, that has never been studied systematically with respect to international migrants.

A large number of analyses of selectivity by intelligence has been made in internal migration, on the other hand. Many of the older studies attempted to prove, sometimes with inadequate methodology, that urbanization selected the more intelligent in the rural population; but more recently this conclusion has often been challenged. For example, in an especially careful and important analysis of the migration of southern Negroes to the northern cities of the United States, Klineberg showed that there had been no selection, and that the higher intelligence ratings of Negro children in northern schools was therefore due to the more favorable social environment rather than to innate qualities.[15]

---

[15] Otto Klineberg, *Negro Intelligence and Selective Migration* (New York: Columbia University Press, 1935); summarized in Thomas, *Migration Differentials*, pp. 111–121.

It is difficult, in view of the small number of good studies and their contradictory results, to come to general conclusions. Thomas does not believe that any generalization at all can be made: "Migration may, under given circumstances, select the intelligent; under other circumstances, the less intelligent; and under still other circumstances, be quite unselective with regard to intelligence."[16] The tentative conclusion offered by Sorokin and Zimmerman is that "cities attract the extremes while the farms attract the mean strata in society."[17]

An essay by the Dutch sociologist Hofstee[18] has helped to dispel some of the confusion concerning this question. Most of the previous discussion had centered on so-called *push* factors—that is, conditions at home that induce some persons to leave. Hofstee shifted the argument to *pull* factors —that is, conditions abroad that attract migrants. Everything that we know about selectivity by more easily defined characteristics, such as sex, indicates the greater importance of pull factors: the dominance of males or of females is generally determined less by the conditions at home than by the opportunities for one or the other at the destination. In the same way, selection by intelligence depends mainly on the level of opportunities available. Since many urban occupations both require a greater mental capacity and offer more income and status, there is a tendency for the more intelligent in a rural population, particularly if they are well educated, to migrate to the towns. On the other hand, the Negroes that Klineberg studied were moving into unskilled jobs, which did not induce any such selection. A migration from one portion of the rural area to another, similarly, is typically not selective. Thus, what has been analyzed as selection by intelligence is mainly one by actual or potential vocational skill.

Several recent studies on the relation between urbanization and the incidence of mental disease indicate both the possibilities of improving on the methodology of earlier analyses and the difficulties, even so, in reaching a firm conclusion. According to one monograph,[19] based on an analysis of first admissions to New York State mental institutions, immigrants were represented in much higher proportion than those born in the state. The difference was in part due to age structure, but it held

16 Thomas, *Migration Differentials,* p. 125.
17 Sorokin and Zimmerman, *op. cit.,* p. 571.
18 E. W. Hofstee, *Some Remarks on Selective Migration* (Research Group for European Migration Problems, Publication 7; The Hague: Nijhoff, 1952).
19 Benjamin Malzberg and Everett S. Lee, *Migration and Mental Disease: A Study of First Admissions to Hospitals for Mental Disease, New York, 1939–1941* (New York: Social Science Research Council, 1956). See also above, page 247.

also when migrants and nonmigrants of the same age were compared. The contrast in age-standardized rates between those undergoing the initial adjustment to a new environment and the static population was especially unequivocal; among whites the rate was twice, among non-whites about three times that of the native-born. The admission rate of in-migrants who had lived in the state for more than five years was higher, but only slightly higher, than that of native New Yorkers.

These data suggest that all three of the causes noted above are relevant: (a) Since the standards of institutional care are relatively good in New York State, the incidence of mentally ill *outside* hospitals is certainly higher in the population of many other states, particularly in the South and among Negroes. (b) In many cases admission to a mental hospital took place so soon after arrival in the state that the disease must have been well advanced prior to the migration. This suggests (though only an investigation at the point of origin could prove this) that the mentally ill tend to migrate in greater proportion; and in that case some of those originally resident in New York presumably would have left, and this may explain part of the observed differences in rates. (c) The sharp contrast between recent migrants and those in the state more than five years is a clear indication that the strains of adjustment to a new environment are etiologically significant.

The process of migratory selection that has been reviewed in this chapter is obviously of great practical importance: to a large degree it defines the meaning of any movement for the two areas concerned. Unfortunately, as this discussion has indicated, it is a subject about which we know rather little. We have seen that migrants are in most respects not a random sample of the populations they leave and enter. In virtually all cases adolescents and young adults predominate. With respect to other characteristics—sex and occupation, possibly intelligence and mental health—selection usually seems to depend more on conditions at the destination than on those at the origin.

MIGRATION AND POPULATION GROWTH

Common sense tells us that if 1,000 persons migrate from Country A to Country B, then the population of Country A is decreased by 1,000 and that of Country B is increased by 1,000. However, in all probability the shift will bring about changes in the population structure, economy, and social conditions of both countries, and these changes in turn will influence the number of inhabitants of each. If we take these indirect effects into account, the relation between migration and population growth is a good deal more complex than it would seem at first sight.

The most obvious reason why the full consequence of migration cannot be calculated by mere subtraction and addition is its effect on population structure. Since migrants are characteristically young adults, their departure typically means a rise in the average age in the emigration country or area and thus an increase in its death rate. And since they take with them, as it were, their future progeny, the birth rate typically falls. If these changes in their mortality and fertility are also included, therefore, the movement of 1,000 persons generally means a total change in the populations of the two areas by many more than this figure. Moreover, if the migrants are peasants moving to a city, their rural family-building habits will raise the urban birth rate of their new home by a still greater proportion.

The effect on growth is not, however, always larger than the number who actually move. Indeed, under some circumstances it may be nil. As we have seen in Chapter 17, Malthus's principal thesis was that the population of any area generally tends to increase up to the maximum that the economy can support. Wherever this is indeed the case, the effect of migration on the size of the population of either of the areas involved cannot be very great. Emigrants will eventually be replaced through a higher natural increase, and immigrants will merely take the place of natives who would otherwise have been born (or, if born, would have stayed alive). Thus, under such conditions migration really effects a shift in population only when those who move have special skills, so that there is a concomitant shift of what Benjamin Franklin termed "the state of the arts." In general, emigration was for Malthus "a slight palliative," "a partial and temporary expedient" with "no permanent effect on population." [20]

Thus, the full effect of migration on the population growth of the two areas will vary greatly from one time to another and from one country to another, depending on various factors.

Let us take first the possible **effects of migration on the home country**

---

[20] T. R. Malthus, *An Essay on the Principle of Population* (7th ed.; London: Reeves and Turner, 1872), Book 3, Ch. 4. It must be noted, however, that with respect to policy Malthus's usual emphasis was not on this presumed absence of long-term effects but on the more immediate, temporary consequences. He considered emigration "well worthy the attention of the government, both as a matter of humanity and policy" (*ibid.*). The evidence that he gave before the Second Select Committee on Emigration in 1827 was based on these considerations rather than on the hypothesis that emigration would have no permanent effect on the size of the Irish population.

or area. If the emigration is the consequence of population pressure, this pressure will have influenced the life of the country also in other ways. A very great disparity between the number of people and the land they live off, as in the densely settled countries of Asia, can result in a very high death rate, as from intermittent famines. A more moderate population pressure, as in some European countries in the nineteenth century, often results in the widespread postponement of marriage or the limitation of family size by other means. To the degree that emigration effects a real relief from the population pressure, it can bring about a change in any of these other determinants of growth. People leaving a country like India or China, thus, have practically no effect on the eventual number remaining, for those who depart will probably be replaced through a small decrease in infant mortality resulting from the slight improvement in material conditions. In nineteenth-century West European countries, on the other hand, since mortality was under much better control than in the peasant countries of Asia (at least until very recently), it is debatable whether the mass exodus brought about a significant decrease in death rates. There, however, it may well have influenced the birth rate, especially by making earlier marriage possible for many couples. Young people always find it onerous to have to forgo the satisfactions of family life until they can afford to have children, and when late marriage is the typical mode of family limitation, any reduction in the economic pressure is likely to bring about a very rapid change (although, as we have seen, Ireland has been both a prime instance and, in modern times, an outstanding exception to this rule).

That is, if the release from population pressure that emigration effects brings about any change in either mortality or fertility, the change in growth of the area of origin will be negated to some degree. If, however, the death rate was already low and the small-family system generally established, then the decrease in numbers from emigration can be very great, because, as we have noted, those who leave will be principally potential parents with low age-specific death rates.

The **effect of migration on the area of destination** also depends on circumstances. Whether, for example, the immigration to the United States has increased its population and, if so, by how much, have been the subject of a dispute going back for many decades. In the 1890's Malthus's theory concerning the effect of migration was revived in the United States by Francis A. Walker, a former superintendent of the census.[21] Immigration, he held, had "amounted not to a re-enforcement

[21] See page 92.

of our population, but to a replacement of native by foreign stock,"
because the competition of immigrant laborers caused a proportionate
decline in the native birth rate. "That if the foreigners had not come, the
native element would long have filled the places the foreigners usurped,
I entertain not a doubt." [22]

While Walker's argument was exceedingly weak, it had the value of
questioning the common-sense view. This does not mean that immigration indeed had no effect on the American growth. An influx to such a
country as the United States in the nineteenth century, with much free
land and a declining birth rate, generally increases the population, though
not necessarily by the same amount as the number of immigrants. The
increase may be greater—because the fertility of foreign-born (at least in
the American case) was generally higher, due to their favorable age
structure and their old-country, rural family-building habits; or it may
be smaller—because the rate of industrialization and urbanization, and
thus the native birth rate, may be affected by the influx.

In summary, the relation between migration and population growth
can be divided into three parts: (a) the direct movement of the migrants
themselves; (b) the effect of the movement on the population structure
of the two areas, which ordinarily increases the size of the transfer; and
(c) the effect on social-economic conditions in the two areas, which may
reduce or negate the results of the transfer. In the abstract, one can say
that all three of these factors are always relevant. In the concrete, their
total impact is discernible only in such extreme cases as, for example,
emigration from a very densely settled country like India or immigration
to a relatively empty country like nineteenth-century United States. In
general, the effect of migration on the population growth of the two
areas concerned is so complex as to be indeterminate.

A GENERAL TYPOLOGY OF MIGRATION

If we try to develop further these observations on migratory selection
and the relation between migration and population growth, we cannot

[22] Francis A. Walker, "Immigration and Degradation," *Forum,* 11 (August, 1891),
634–644. In 1873, when the immigration to the United States was still predominantly
from Northwest Europe, Walker had imputed the decline in native fertility to the
change in the mode of living; and in his view at that time, immigration did not cause
the fall in natality but rather temporarily disguised its effects: "The change [in the
birth rate] came; came later even than it had been reasonable to expect. It began
when the people of the United States began to leave agricultural for manufacturing
pursuits; to turn from the country to the town; to live in up-and-down houses, and
to follow closely the fashion of foreign life. The first effects of it were covered from
the common sight by a flood of immigration unprecedented in history" (Walker, "Our
Population in 1900," *Atlantic Monthly,* 32:192, October, 1873, 487–495).

formulate valid "laws," for the empirical regularities do not always hold. The ultimate generalization in this case is a typology, in which the various conditions under which migration takes place are related to its probable effects.

A crude first step in this direction is the contrast frequently made between "push" and "pull" factors—that is, between circumstances at home that repel and those abroad that attract. This conceptualization is inadequate, first of all, because it implies that man is everywhere sedentary, remaining fixed until he is induced to move by some force. Like most psychological universals, this can be matched by its opposite: man migrates because of wanderlust. And, like all such universals, these cannot explain differential behavior: if all men are sedentary (or migratory) "by nature," why do some migrate and some not? If a simplistic metaphor is used, it should be at least as complex as its mechanical analogue, which includes not only the concept of forces but also that of inertia.

Thus, one might better say that a social group at rest, or a social group in motion (e.g., nomads), tends to remain so unless impelled to change; for with any viable pattern of life a social structure and a value system are developed to support that pattern. To analyze the migration of Gypsies, for example, in terms of push and pull is no better than to explain modern Western migration, as Herbert Spencer did, in terms of "the restlessness inherited from ancestral nomads." [23] If the principle of inertia is accepted as valid, then the difference between gathering and nomadic peoples, on the one hand, and agricultural and industrial peoples, on the other hand, is fundamental with respect to migration. For once a people has a permanent place of residence, the relevance of push and pull factors is presumably much greater.

If wanderlust and what might be termed *sitzlust* are not useful as psychological universals, they do suggest a criterion for a significant distinction. If persons leave as a means of achieving the new, let us term such migration **innovating.** If, on the contrary, they respond to a change in conditions by trying to retain what they have had, moving geographically in order to remain where they are in all other respects, let us term such migration **conservative.** When the migrants themselves play a passive role, as in the case of African slaves being transported to the New World, the movement is termed innovating or conservative depending on how it is defined by the activating agent, in this case the slave-traders.

The fact that the familiar push-pull polarity implies a universal sedentary quality, however, is only one of its faults. The push factors alleged

[23] Herbert Spencer, *The Principles of Sociology* (3rd rev. ed.; New York: Appleton, 1892), 1, 566.

to "cause" emigration ordinarily comprise a heterogeneous array, ranging from agricultural crises to the spirit of adventure, from the development of shipping to overpopulation. No attempt is generally made to
distinguish among underlying causes, facilitative environment, precipi-
tants, and motives. In particular, if we fail to distinguish between personal
motives and social causes—that is, if we do not take the emigrants' level
of aspiration into account—our analysis must lack logical clarity.

No principled difference is usually made between what is sometimes
termed "absolute overpopulation," which results in hunger and starvation, and milder degrees of "overpopulation," which reflect not physiological but cultural standards.[24] In the first case the aspiration of emigrants
can be ignored, for it is a bare physiological minimum that can be taken
as universal; but in the second case it is the level of aspiration itself that
defines the "overpopulation" and sets the impetus to emigrate. Similarly,
economic hardships can appropriately be termed a "cause" of emigration only if there is a positive correlation between hardship, however
defined, and the propensity to leave. The mass exodus from Europe in
modern times, it must be recalled, developed together with a marked *rise*
in European levels of living; and this inverse relation is not exceptional.
In short, it is probably true that most transatlantic migrants were economically motivated, but not that the propensity to leave was directly associated with economic conditions in the home country. As has already
been noted, the correlation was rather with the business cycle in the
receiving country, and even this explains fluctuations in the migration
rate more than its absolute level.

Nor can the class differential in the rate of emigration be ascribed
simply to economic differences. While the European bourgeoisie lived
in more comfortable circumstances than workers, for many a move to
America would also have meant a definite material improvement. During
the period of mass exodus, however, this was stereotyped as lower-class
behavior, a bit unpatriotic for the well-to-do. For a son of a businessman
to emigrate meant a break with the established group pattern; and from
this class, thus, only marginal types like idealists or black sheep tended
to leave the country, and these for relevant *personal* reasons. Once a
migration has reached the stage of a social movement, however, such
individual motivations are generally of little interest.

This kind of confusion is not limited to economic factors. Religious
oppression or the infringement of political liberty was often a *motive*

24 See pages 529–530.

for leaving Europe, but before the rise of modern totalitarianism emigrants were predominantly from those countries least marked by such stigmata. An increasing propensity to emigrate spread east and south from Northwest Europe, together with democratic institutions and religious tolerance. Again, we are faced with the anomaly that those who departed "because" of the persecution tended to come from countries where there was less than elsewhere. And sometimes the real problem is not why people leave but rather why they do not. The vast majority of American Negroes, as we have seen in an earlier chapter, remained in the South until World War I, in spite of the Jim Crow pattern and lynch law that developed there from the 1870's on, and, as an equally powerful pull, the many opportunities available in the West or the burgeoning northern cities.[25]

When the push-pull polarity has been refined in these two senses, by distinguishing innovating from conservative migration and by including in the analysis the migrants' level of aspiration, it can form the basis of a typology of migration. Five broad classes are defined, which are designated as primitive, forced, impelled, free, and mass. It should be noted that while these words are terms in common usage rather than neologisms, since they are here more precisely defined than in most contexts, they denote a narrower range of meaning. Free migration, thus, is *not* all migration that is not forced, for it is one of five rather than two classes.

Primitive Migration

The first class is that consequent from an ecological push, which is termed **primitive migration.** In this context, then, this does not define the wandering of primitive peoples as such, but rather a movement related to man's inability to cope with natural forces. However, since the reaction to a deterioration in the physical environment can be either remedial action or emigration, depending on the technology available to the people concerned, there is a tendency for primitive migration in this narrower sense to be associated with primitive peoples.

Many of the treks of preindustrial folk, it would seem, have been conservative as we have defined this term here. "There is often a strong

[25] See pages, 167–169. For an international example, see William Petersen, *Planned Migration: The Social Determinants of the Dutch-Canadian Movement* (Berkeley: University of California Press, 1955), Ch. 3, which discusses the several factors in prewar Holland that seemingly should have induced a large emigration, but did not.

tendency for [such] a migrating group to hold conservatively to the same type of environment; pastoral peoples, for example, attempt to remain on grasslands, where their accustomed life may be continued." [26] The impetus to leave, the route, and the destination are set not by push and pull, but by the interplay of push and *control*. If they are indifferent about precisely where they are going, men migrate as liquids flow, along the lines of least resistance. Their way is shaped by barriers, both natural and man-made—both mountains, rivers, or rainfall or the lack of it, and the Great Wall of China or other, less monumental evidences of hostility toward aliens. Conservative migrants seek only a place where they can resume the old way of life, and when this is possible, they are content. Sometimes it is not possible, and any migration, therefore, may be associated with a fundamental change in culture.

The usual designation for treks of prehistoric primitives used to be "wandering of peoples," a translation from the German that, however inelegant, is nevertheless appropriate, for it denotes two of the characteristics that define it. It is usually a people as a whole that moves about and not merely certain families or groups, and they leave without a definite destination, as "wander" implies in English. Let us, then, term such migrations as those induced by ecological pressure **wandering of peoples.** Unintended movements over the ocean—an analogous type of primitive migrations, which can be termed **marine wanderings**—have occurred more frequently than was once supposed.

There are countless . . . examples . . . [of] more or less accidental wanderings from island to island over oceanic expanses of water, brought about by winds and currents. The space of time and the extent of these voyages seem to play a subordinate part. Journeys covering 3,000 miles are not unusual. They may last six weeks or several months. Even without provisions the natives can get along, as they fish for their food and collect rain-water to drink.[27]

As we have seen in Chapter 12, contemporary primitives also often move about in a way directly related to the low level of their material culture. A food-gathering or hunting people cannot ordinarily subsist from what is available in one vicinity; it must range over a wider area, moving either haphazardly or back and forth over its traditional territory. Such movements are called **gathering.** The analogous migrations

[26] Roland B. Dixon, "Migrations, Primitive," *Encyclopedia of the Social Sciences,* 10 (New York: Macmillan, 1933), 420–425.
[27] Ragnar Numelin, *The Wandering Spirit: A Study of Human Migration* (London: Macmillan, 1937), pp. 180–181.

of cattle-owning peoples are called **nomadism,** from the Greek word for *graze.* Gatherers and nomads together are termed **rangers.**

The way of life of rangers is to be on the move, and their culture is adapted to this state. Their home is temporary or portable; some Australian peoples have no word for "home" in their language. Their value system adjudges the specific hardships of their life to be good; the contempt that the desert Arab feels for the more comfortable city Arab is traditional. Although they are ordinarily restricted to a particular area, bounded by either physical barriers or peoples able to defend their territories, rangers are presumably more likely to migrate over longer distances (apart from differences in the means of transportation) simply because they are already in motion. Whether any particular nomad people settles down and becomes agricultural does not depend merely on geography. Geography determines only whether such a shift in their way of life is possible—it is barely feasible on the steppe, for example. But even when physical circumstances permit a change, the social pattern of ranging may be too strong to be broken down. Thus, the Soviet program of settling the Kirghiz and other nomad peoples on collective farms succeeded only because it was implemented by sufficient terror to overcome their opposition.[28] That is to say, ranging, like wandering, is typically conservative.

A primitive migration of an agrarian population takes place when there is a disparity between the produce of the land and the number of people subsisting from it. This can come about either suddenly, as by drought or an attack of locusts, or by the steady Malthusian pressure of growing numbers on land of limited area and fertility. Persons induced to migrate by such population pressure can seek another agricultural site elsewhere, but in the modern era the more usual destination has been a town. That is to say, the migration has ordinarily been innovating rather than conservative. The Irish immigrants to the United States in the decades after the Great Famine, for example, resolutely ignored the Homestead Act and other inducements to settle on the land; in overwhelming proportion, they moved to the cities and stayed there. Let us term such an innovating movement **flight from the land** (again an inelegant but useful translation from the German).

To recapitulate, primitive migration has been divided as shown in Table 20-3. These are the types set by a physical push and geographical or social controls.

[28] See pages 434–438.

TABLE 20-3. Types of Primitive Migration

Primitive	Wandering	Wandering of peoples
		Marine wandering
	Ranging	Gathering
		Nomadism
	Flight from the land	

Impelled and Forced Migrations

The activating agent in migration is often not ecological pressure, but rather the state or some equivalent social institution. It is useful to distinguish **impelled migration,** when the persons involved retain some power to decide whether or not to leave, from **forced migration,** when they do not have this power. Often the boundary between the two, the point at which the choice becomes nominal, may be difficult to set. Analytically, however, the distinction is clear-cut, and historically it is often so. The difference is real, for example, between the Nazis' policy (roughly 1933–1938) of encouraging Jewish emigration by various anti-Semitic acts and laws, and the later policy (roughly 1938–1945) of herding Jews into cattle trains and transporting them to camps.

A second criterion by which we can delineate types of forced or impelled migration is its function, as defined by the activating agent. If persons are induced to move simply to be gotten rid of, since this does not ordinarily bring about a change in the migrants' way of life, it is analogous to conservative migration and can be subsumed under it. Others are moved in order that their labor power can be used elsewhere; and such a migration, which constitutes a shift in behavior patterns as well as in locale, is designated as innovating. Four types are thus defined, as shown in Table 20-4. Each of these will be discussed briefly.

In all of human history **flight** has been an important form of migration.

TABLE 20-4. Types of Impelled and Forced Migrations

	Impelled	*Forced*
To be rid of migrants (conservative)	Flight	Displacement
To use migrants' labor (innovating)	Coolie trade	Slave trade

Whenever a stronger people moves into a new territory, it may drive before it the weaker former occupants. The invasion of Europe during the early centuries of the Christian era, thus, was induced not only by the power vacuum consequent from the disintegration of the Roman Empire, but also by a series of successive pushes, originating from either the desiccation of the Central Asian steppes (Huntington) or the expansion of the Chinese empire still farther east (Teggart).[29]

Many more recent migrations have also been primarily a flight before invading armies.[30] In modern times, however, those induced to flee have often been only certain groups among the population, rather than everyone occupying a particular territory. Indeed, political dissidents had always been ousted when they became a danger to state security; but with the growth of nationalism, ethnic as well as political homogeneity has been sought. The right of national self-determination proclaimed by the Treaty of Versailles, thus, included no provision for the minorities scattered through Central Europe; and in the interwar period the League of Nations negotiated a series of population transfers designed to eliminate national minorities from adjacent countries or, more usually, to legitimate expulsions already effected.[31] The separation of Pakistan from India, as another example, was accompanied by one of the largest migrations in human history, in part induced by terrorist groups on both sides and in part arranged under official auspices.

It is useful to distinguish between two classes of those who have fled their homeland—**émigrés,** who regard their exile as temporary and live for the day when they may return, and **refugees,** who intend rather to settle permanently in the new country. Under otherwise similar circumstances, the acculturation of the latter would presumably be much more rapid than that of persons still living spiritually in their fatherland.

A forced movement intended merely to remove a dissident population is here called **displacement.**[32] One purpose of the forced migrations

[29] Ellsworth Huntington, *Civilization and Climate* (3rd rev. ed.; New Haven: Yale University Press, 1924); Frederick J. Teggart, *Rome and China: A Study of Correlations in Historical Events* (Berkeley: University of California Press, 1939).

[30] See, for example, Eugene M. Kulischer, *Europe on the Move: War and Population Changes, 1917–47* (New York: Columbia University Press, 1948).

[31] Cf. Stephen P. Ladas, *The Exchange of Minorities: Bulgaria, Greece and Turkey* (New York: Macmillan, 1932), p. 721: "Both conventions [of Neuilly and Lausanne], and especially that of Lausanne, proved to be agreements confirming accomplished facts," and the Greek-Turkish exchange, while "voluntary in theory, . . . became, in fact, to a great extent compulsory."

[32] The word is suggested by "displaced persons," the designation in the jargon of the official bureaus for those who had been forcibly removed from their homeland. Note, however, that many of the DP's were former forced laborers, a group not here included in this class.

After the partition of British India, an "exchange of populations" took place. Caravans of desperate refugees crawled along the poor roads—Hindus and Sikhs south to India, Muslims north to Pakistan. They were all but defenceless against terrorists and robbers, famine and disease. Thousands upon thousands died on the way. (Margaret Bourke-White—courtesy LIFE, © 1947 Time, Inc.)

under both Nazi and Soviet auspices has typically been to remove a hostile or potentially hostile group from its home. For example, after Poland was divided between Nazi Germany and Communist Russia in 1939, the more than a million Poles deported to Asiatic Russia were chosen not merely on the basis of actual or alleged opposition to their country's invasion, but more often as members of a large variety of occupational groups, which were defined as potentially oppositionist.

Regarded as "anti-Soviet elements," and so treated, were administrative officials, police, judges, lawyers, members of Parliament, prominent members of political parties, non-communist non-political societies, clubs, and the Red Cross; civil servants not included above, retired military officers, officers in the reserve, priests, tradesmen, landowners, hotel and restaurant owners, clerks of the local Chambers of Commerce, and any class of persons engaged in trade or correspondence with foreign countries—the latter definition extending even to stamp collectors and Esperantists—were also deported. Many artisans, peasants, and laborers (both agricultural and industrial) were banished too, so that, in effect, no Polish element was spared.[33]

A second purpose of forced migrations has often been to furnish an unskilled labor force. During the war, for example, Nazi Germany imported workers from all occupied countries to keep its economy going. While this modern variant of the **slave trade** differs in some respects from the overseas shipment of Africans during the mercantile age, the two criteria that define the type are the same—the use of force and the supply of manpower.

The analogous form of impelled migration is termed **coolie trade.** This includes not only the movement of Asians to plantations, the most typical form, but also, for example, that of white indentured servants to the British colonies in the eighteenth century. Such migrants, while formally bound only for the period of a definite contract, very often are forced to go into debt and thus to extend their service almost indefinitely.[34] Many coolies eventually return to their homeland: the total Indian emigration from 1834 to 1937, for example, was estimated at slightly more than 30 million, but of these almost 24 million returned, leaving a net outward movement over the century of only 6 million.[35]

[33] Edward J. Rozek, *Allied Wartime Diplomacy: A Pattern in Poland* (New York: Wiley, 1958), p. 39.

[34] See, for example, Victor Purcell, *The Chinese in Southeast Asia* (London: Oxford University Press, 1951), p. 348.

[35] Davis, *op. cit.,* p. 99.

Free Migration

In the types discussed so far, the will of the migrants has been a relatively unimportant factor. A primitive migration results from the lack of means to satisfy basic physiological needs, and in the forced (or impelled) type the persons involved are also wholly (or partially) passive. We now consider the type in which the will of the migrants is the decisive element—or what is termed **free migration.**

Overseas movements from Europe during the nineteenth century, which in large part illustrate this class of migration, can be discussed most conveniently in terms of one illustrative example; and because of the excellence of its formal analysis, Lindberg's monograph on emigration from Sweden [36] has been chosen for this purpose. Lindberg begins by distinguishing three periods, each with a characteristic type of emigrants. During the first stage, beginning around 1840, they came principally from the two university towns of Upsala and Lund, "men with a good cultural and social background, mostly young and of a romantic disposition" (p. 3). Since the risks overseas were great and impossible to calculate in a rational manner, those who left tended to be adventurers or intellectuals motivated by their ideals, especially by their alienation from European society during a period of political reaction. The significance of this **pioneer migration** was not in its size, which was never large, but in the example it set: "It was this emigration that helped to break the ice and clear the way for the later emigration, which included quite different classes" (p. 7). These pioneers wrote letters home; their adventures in the New World were recounted in Swedish newspapers. Once settled, they helped finance the passage of their families or friends.

Imperceptibly, this first stage developed into the second, the period of **group migration**—the departure, for example, of Pietist communities under the leadership of their pastor or another person of recognized authority. Even when not associated through their adherence to a dissident sect, emigrants banded together for mutual protection during the hazardous journey and against the wilderness and the often hostile Indians at its end. The significance of this group movement also lay not in its size but in the further impulse it gave. Those leaving during the decade

---

[36] John S. Lindberg, *The Background of Swedish Emigration to the United States: An Economic and Sociological Study in the Dynamics of Migration* (Minneapolis: University of Minnesota Press, 1930).

beginning in 1841 averaged only 400 persons annually, and during the following ten years still only 1,500.

Mass Migration

Free migration is always rather small, for individuals strongly motivated to seek novelty or improvement are not commonplace. The most significant attribute of pioneers, as in other areas of life, is that they blaze trails that others follow, and sometimes the number who do so grows into a broad stream. Migration becomes a style, an established pattern, an example of collective behavior. Once it is well begun, the growth of such a movement is semi-automatic: the principal cause of emigration is prior emigration. Other circumstances operate as deterrents or incentives, but within the attitudinal framework as already defined; all factors except population growth are important principally in terms of the established behavior.

As we have already noted, when emigration has been set as a *social* pattern, it is no longer relevant to inquire concerning *individual* motivations. For the individual is, in Lindberg's phrase, in an "unstable state of equilibrium," in which only a small impulse in either direction decides his course; thus, the motives he ascribes to his emigration are either trivial or, more likely, the generalities that he thinks are expected. Hansen has pointed out that the migrants' stated motivation was likely to be pruned to suit the person asking for it. The official in the home country was told of material difficulties, but to cite these in America would confirm the natives' belief that the foreigner was a dangerous economic competitor. The village clergyman, should he attempt to dissuade a prospective emigrant, was told that his sons were growing up without a future and becoming lazy and shiftless; but in America these moral motives would give point to the argument that immigrants were depraved. Hence, to the American "the newcomer said, 'I came to the United States to enjoy the blessings of your marvelous government and laws.' " [37]

Migration as collective behavior can be aptly illustrated, again, by the Swedish case. The decade 1861–1870, when the average number of emigrants jumped to 9,300 per year, began the transition to the third stage of **mass migration.** Transportation facilities improved. Railroads connected the interior with the port cities, and the sailing ship began to

[37] Marcus Lee Hansen, *The Immigrant in American History* (Cambridge: Harvard University Press, 1948), pp. 77–78.

be replaced by the much faster and safer steamer. Not only was the geographical distance cut down, but also what Lindberg terms the social distance: as communities in the new country grew in size and importance, the shift from Sweden to America required less and less of a personal adjustment. Before someone left to go to a Swedish-American settlement, he started his acculturation in an American-Swedish milieu, made up of New World letters, photographs, mementoes, knick-knacks. There developed what the peasants called "America fever." In some districts there was not a farm without relatives in America, and from many all the young people had gone overseas. According to a government report that Lindberg quotes, children were "educated to emigrate," and he continues,

When they finally arrived at a decision, they merely followed a tradition which made emigration the natural thing in a certain situation. In fact, after the imagination and fantasy had, so to speak, become "charged with America," a positive decision *not* to emigrate may have been necessary if difficulties arose (pp. 56–57).

The Swedes who migrated to Minnesota became farmers or small-town craftsmen or merchants. In a more general analysis, it is useful to distinguish two types of mass movement according to the nature of the destination—**settlement,** such as Lindberg described, and **urbanization,** or mass migration to a larger town or city. No principled distinction is made here between internal and international migration; for the fundamentals of the rural-urban shift so characteristic of the modern era are usually the same whether or not the new city dwellers cross a national border.

SUMMARY

Migration differs from fertility and mortality in that it cannot be analyzed, even preliminarily, in terms of supracultural, physiological factors but must be differentiated even at the most abstract level with respect to the social conditions obtaining. This means that the most general statement that one can make concerning migration must be in the form of a typology, rather than a law. Classifications of modern migrations tend to be set simply by the statistics that are collected, whether or not these have any relevance to theoretical questions. It is as though those interested in the *causes* of divorce studied this matter exclusively with the data classified according to *grounds* on which divorces happen to be granted. Even the principal statistical differentiation, that between internal and international migration, is not necessarily of theoretical significance. Similarly, when the species *migrant* is set off from the genus *traveler* by arbitrarily defining removal for a year or more as "permanent" migration, such a distinction obviously has little or no theoretical basis, and it is not even certain that it is the most convenient one that could be made.[38]

The typology developed in this chapter is summarized in Table 20-5 These are so-called ideal types, analytical constructs derived from historical examples but stripped of accidental, specific features in order to make them as general as seems to be useful. That such abstract concepts can indeed be of some use is indicated by the contrasts we examined in earlier chapters between *fertility* and *fecundity,* and between *urbanization* and *urbanism,* both of which helped clarify long scholarly debates.

TABLE 20-5. General Typology of Migration

Type of Interaction	Migratory Force	Class of Migration	Type of Migration	
			Conservative	Innovating
Nature and man	Ecological push	Primitive	Wandering	Flight from the land
			Ranging	
State (or equivalent) and man	Migration policy	Impelled	Flight	Coolie trade
		Forced	Displacement	Slave trade
Man and his norms	Higher aspirations	Free	Group	Pioneer
Collective behavior	Social momentum	Mass	Settlement	Urbanization

Several of the distinctions made in this typology are related to currently moot issues. The most general clarification concerns migratory selection. While few today would follow Ravenstein's example and designate their statements "laws," most discussions of this topic still imply an almost equal degree of universality. Actually, selection ranges along a continuum, from total migration to total nonmigration, and the intermediate cases vary not only in the proportion that leave but also in the typical characteristics of those that do. The predominance of females in rural-urban migration that Ravenstein noted for England must be contrasted with male predominance in, for example, India's urbanization. In Table 20-6 a principle of selection is suggested for

[38] See pages 53–54.

each type of migration. How accurate this is in each instance is an empirical question, and further research may make a number of revisions necessary. But we know enough now to assert that migratory selection does vary considerably, and that a search for universal generalizations would be fruitless.

TABLE 20-6. Migratory Selection by Type of Migration

Types		Destination of Migrants	Migratory Selection	Comments; Examples
Wandering	Wandering of peoples	None	Survival of the fittest?	Prehistoric migrations
	Marine wandering			
Ranging	Gathering	Greener pastures; commutation	None	Migratory way of life
	Nomadism			
	Flight from the land	More fertile land (or towns)	?	Malthusian pressure
	Flight	Place of safety	None; or minority groups	Emigrés and refugees
	Coolie trade	Site of work, usually plantations	Young males	Large remigration
	Displacement	Any	None; or minority groups	Population exchanges
	Slave trade	Site of work	Young adults	Mercantile or industrial
	Pioneers	Frontier lands	Young males	Individually motivated
	Group migration	New lands	Dissident groups	
	Settlement	Rural areas	Young males predominate	Social momentum
	Urbanization	Towns	Young females predominate (in the West)	

The most useful distinction in the typology, perhaps, is that between mass migration and all other kinds, for this emphasizes the fact that the movement of Europeans to the New World during the nineteenth century, the instance with which we are most familiar, does not constitute the whole of the phenomenon. After World War I, largely because of new political limitations imposed by both sending and receiving countries, there was a change to a different type, and this was very often interpreted as the end of significant human migration altogether. A world in which hardly anyone dies in the place where he was born, however, cannot be termed sedentary.

SUGGESTIONS FOR FURTHER READING

Dorothy Swaine Thomas, *Research Memorandum on Migration Differentials* (Bulletin 43; New York: Social Science Research Council, 1938).

E. W. Hofstee, *Some Remarks on Selective Migration* (Research Group for European Migration Problems, Publication 7; The Hague: Nijhoff, 1952).

    Two of the best of many works on migratory selection.

Rudolf Heberle, "Types of Migration," in Research Group for European Migration Problems, *Bulletin*, 4:1 (January–March, 1956), 1–5.

Henry Pratt Fairchild, *Immigration: A World Movement and Its American Significance* (Rev. ed.; New York: Macmillan, 1925), Ch. 1.

William Petersen, "A General Typology of Migration," *American Sociological Review*, 23:3 (June, 1958), 256–266.

    Two alternative migration typologies; that by Heberle is well conceived, that by Fairchild is better known. The typology in this chapter was abridged from the cited article.

See also the recommendations following Chapters 6 and 7, particularly the volume by Everett S. Lee *et al.* cited on pages 176–177.

APPENDIX

SOME NOTES ON THE TECHNIQUES OF POPULATION ANALYSIS

The modest purpose of this appendix is to bring together a few elementary concepts and techniques, including some that were presented in a different context in earlier chapters.[1] No more than in the main body of the text is it the intention here to furnish a training manual in formal demography.

The calculations to be made in analyzing population data depend on the information available and the analyst's purpose. Sometimes a gross figure is more appropriate than any alternative. The datum that the Chinese are increasing by 12 to 15 million a year, or that over a particular holiday weekend there were 325 deaths in automobile accidents, cannot be put more forcibly than as these simple statements. Usually, however, a ratio or proportion or rate tells us more.

A **ratio** is of the form $\frac{a}{b} k,$ where a and b denote sectors of the population and k any convenient constant. Examples are the sex ratio (males per 1,000 females) and the fertility ratio (children under five per 1,000 women in the childbearing ages). In both these cases the value assigned to k is 1,000. More generally, in both ratios and other types of calculations, k is conventionally fixed according to the relative frequency of the phenomenon, in order to avoid cumbersome decimals. Thus, occupational rates are ordinarily expressed as percentages (Latin for "per 100") rather than per 1,000, while suicide rates are usually given as so-and-so many per 100,000.

A **proportion** is of the form $\frac{a}{a + b} k$—that is, a relation between a total and one of its parts. For example, a sex ratio of 1,000 can also be expressed as the statement that 50 per cent of the population is male.

A **crude rate** is of the form $\frac{m}{P} k,$ where P is the total midyear population and m the number of births, or deaths, or marriages, or other demographic events during that year. Note that m and P are not from the same set of statistical

---

[1] For a more extended discussion at an elementary level, one of the best works is George W. Barclay, *Techniques of Population Analysis* (New York: Wiley, 1958). See also the list of suggested readings appended to Chapter 3, pages 67–68.

622

records, or universe; [2] in the birth rate, for example, the numerator comes from vital statistics, and the denominator from the census. For this reason, among others, this rate is indeed "crude." The two universes do not refer to quite the same population: that enumerated in the census, or estimated from successive censuses, is fixed at one particular time, while that included in the vital registration fluctuates throughout the year. The variation in the numerator, moreover, may also (as by births or deaths) change the size of the denominator.

A more serious question is whether the total population is the most apposite base. Ideally, one might say, a rate should express the relation between the actual and the potential; but when it is convenient to ignore this logic or difficult to define the "potential" precisely, we may use a crude rate. Suppose we want to compare the military forces of two countries. A direct comparison—Country A has 1 million men under arms as against 2 million in Country B—is for some purposes the most relevant. But if we want to judge the relative drain on the population, and thus the relative possibility of expanding the size of the armed forces, the 1 or 2 million can be compared with the respective total populations. And a further step is to relate the number of persons who are in the armed forces to the number that can be. In that case the denominator of the fraction would not be the whole population, but rather the number of men of military age (or men and women, if the latter are to be drafted; or healthy men only, for a further refinement; and so on). Such a rate, together with the crude one, indicates the importance of such factors as the population structure in determining the number of soldiers.

Analogous clarifications are made in demographic rates. One important method of refinement, thus, is to use a sector of the population, rather than the whole, as the denominator. This principle can be exemplified by several measures of fertility used to supplement, or to replace, the crude birth rate. The simplest of these is the **general fertility rate,** or the number of births per 1,000 women in the childbearing ages. Here we have, it would seem, a direct relation of actual procreation to potential procreators, but the difficulty of defining the "potential" has not been overcome entirely. As we have noted,[3] female fecundity develops gradually during adolescence and declines gradually from age 30 or 35 on; and the distribution of births over the whole of this period is also affected by age at marriage, the use of contraceptives, and other social patterns. Demographers are not agreed on a conventional definition of the "childbearing ages." In the United Nations *Demographic Yearbooks,* which include data from all societies for which figures are available, the fecund period is taken to begin at age 10, which makes no sense for many populations. In the West a significant but relatively small proportion of all births—say, about 5 per cent—are to women aged 45 to 49, who typically constitute much more than this percentage of the total fecund age-group. Whether or not these cohorts are included, a decision difficult to make on principle,[4] effects

[2] By **universe** is meant the aggregate of the individuals being analyzed, as compiled in one statistical record. In the language of statistics, the usual word for this concept is *population,* but in a demographic work we must use a substitute term. See *ibid.,* pp. 19–20.

[3] See page 540.

[4] Cf. Robert R. Kuczynski, *The Balance of Births and Deaths* (Brookings Institution; New York: Macmillan, 1928), 1, 102–103.

a considerable difference in the rate. For example, for the United States in 1950 it was 91.7 if the childbearing ages are defined as 15 to 49 years; if as 15 to 44 years, it was 103.9, or 7.5 per cent higher.

The basic pattern of relating births to women in the fecund period can be varied as widely as the data permit and the analyst's purpose demands. For example, *legitimate* births per 1,000 *married* women aged 15 to 44 define the **marital fertility rate.** Children ever born to women aged 45 or over define the **completed family size.** If no vital statistics are available for the country or period being analyzed, data wholly from the census can be substituted to calculate the **fertility ratio,** or the number of children under five years per 1,000 women in the fecund period.

Since even within the childbearing age-group the fecundity of females varies according to age, a more precise measure is to calculate a special rate for each cohort. An **age-specific fertility rate** is defined as the number of births to a specified age-group per 1,000 women in that age-group. Usually the division is made by five-year periods, as in Table A-1. The figures in the last column of this table,

TABLE A-1. **Age-Specific Fertility Rates, United States, 1950**

Age-group *(1)*	*Number of Females* *(2)*	*Births to Women of Specified Age-group* *(3)*	*Age-specific Fertility Rates* $(4) = \dfrac{(3)}{(2)} \times 1,000$
15–19	5,305,256	424,556 [a]	80.0
20–24	5,875,535	1,131,234	192.5
25–29	6,270,182	1,021,902	163.0
30–34	5,892,284	597,821	101.5
35–39	5,728,842	293,440	51.2
40–44	5,133,704	74,804	14.6
45–49	4,544,099	4,830 [a]	1.1
			603.9

[a] Births to mothers aged under 15 and over 49 are included, respectively, in the first and last rows.

Source: U.S. National Office of Vital Statistics, *Vital Statistics of the United States, 1950* (Washington: U.S. Government Printing Office, 1954), 2, 198.

for greater convenience of presentation, can be added up to one figure, which is multiplied by five in order to relate it to the age of mothers by single years. The resultant figure, called the **total fertility rate,** is in this case 603.9 × 5, or 3,019.5. It tells us how many children on the average each 1,000 women have while passing through their childbearing period.

Sometimes this rate is calculated as in Table A-2, to show rather how many daughters—that is, future mothers—they would have. Since in 1950 the sex ratio at birth was 1,054, it is necessary to reduce the total fertility rate by slightly more than half (multiplying by .487); and it is the convention to give the resultant figure, called the **gross reproduction rate,** per woman rather than per 1,000 women. In this case, it is 1.47. In order to include also the effect of mortality, each age-specific fertility rate is reduced by the proportion that would not survive, on the

TABLE A-2. The Calculation of Reproduction Rates from
Age-Specific Fertility Rates and Life-Table Survival Rates,
White Females, United States, 1950

Age-group (1)	Age-specific Fertility Rates (2)	Proportion Surviving from Birth to Mid-point of Age-group (3)	Columns (2) × (3) (4)
15–19	80.0	.96683	77.3
20–24	192.5	.96338	185.4
25–29	163.0	.95915	156.3
30–34	101.5	.95387	96.8
35–39	51.2	.94658	48.5
40–44	14.6	.93569	13.7
45–49	1.1	.91912	1.0
	603.9		579.0

Gross Reproduction Rate $= 603.9 \times 5 \times .487 \times 0.001 = 1.47$
Net Reproduction Rate $= 579.0 \times 5 \times .487 \times 0.001 = 1.41$

basis of current age-specific death rates, from birth to the midpoint of each age-group (Column 3). The sum of Column 4 is then multiplied by the same series of figures, for the same reasons, to get the **net reproduction rate.**[5] This rate, in this case 1.41, is of course always smaller than the gross reproduction rate, although when female mortality is as low as in the United States today, the difference is not very great.

If the age-specific fertility and death rates of a self-contained population remained constant for a century or more, then the population structure would also eventually become fixed. Such a population, in which the proportion in each age-group remains constant, is called **stable.** It must be emphasized that this is not necessarily one of constant size, but one whose growth is at a constant rate (which can be negative or zero as well as positive). The vital rates of a stable population, called its "true" or **intrinsic birth** and **death rates,** reflect the fertility and mortality apart from the effect of the population structure on them. The difference between them, the "true" or **intrinsic rate of natural increase,** thus, is similar to the net reproduction rate, except that it is calculated on an annual rather than a generational basis.[6]

How useful are these more elaborate measures of fertility? They are a significant improvement over the crude rate, obviously, only when the proportion of fecund women in the total population varies greatly, and in any particular society during a

[5] For a more detailed discussion of how to compute these rates, see Robert R. Kuczynski, *Fertility and Reproduction: Methods of Measuring the Balance of Births and Deaths* (New York: Falcon, 1932).

[6] For a more detailed discussion of these rates, see Louis I. Dublin, Alfred J. Lotka, and Mortimer Spiegelman, *Length of Life: A Study of the Life Table* (Rev. ed.; New York: Ronald, 1949), Ch. 12; Dublin and Lotka, "On the True Rate of Natural Increase As Exemplified by the Population of the United States, 1920," *Journal of the American Statistical Association,* 20:150 (September, 1925), 305–339.

period of uniform demographic change, this is likely to be more or less fixed. Even Kuczynski, who did more than any other individual to popularize reproduction rates, pointed out that the proportion of women of childbearing ages was virtually constant between 1860 and 1910 in the countries of Northwest Europe. It rose by several percentage points after World War I, when fertility and therefore the relative number of minors declined faster.[7] The issue that this datum suggests was developed by Stolnitz in an interesting paper.[8] He compiled all the reproduction rates available for the period up to the late 1940's, and in each case matched the gross reproduction rate with the birth rate (the obvious analogue among crude vital measures) and the net reproduction rate with the crude rate of natural increase. For example, for France the gross reproduction rate fell from 1.31 in 1904–1907 to 1.23 in 1908–1913, or by 6.1 per cent, while over the same period the birth rate fell from 20.4 to 19.3, or by 5.4 per cent. As in this example, the trend of the reproduction rate was in general not markedly different from that of the crude birth rate.

> Among the eleven countries with 20 or more values on record, the coefficient of linear correlation between the two measures was .93 in one instance, .98 to .99 in four cases, and .99 or over in the remaining six. The implications of these results for purposes of estimation are obvious. Perhaps equally interesting is their bearing on traditional methodology. Judging from the past, at least, our substantive knowledge of movements in the gross reproduction rate would have been very nearly the same, had it been necessary to rely on the birth rate alone. It is slight exaggeration to say that the theory underlying the gross rate has been less important as a source of new empirical findings than as a basis for reinterpreting the trend of the birth rate.

The correlation, though not quite so high, was also sizable between net reproduction rates and crude rates of natural increase. Some of these divergences, moreover, were due to the lesser precision of the reproduction rates, when these had been computed on the basis of life tables some years out of date.

These comparisons do not condemn the reproduction rates altogether, of course, but they do challenge the widespread notion that the more work that goes into a computation, the more precisely its end product reflects reality. The limitations of a crude rate must be pointed out, but the current feeling among demographers seems to be that they have perhaps been stressed too much.

When the total population is used as the base in calculating a crude birth rate, the "potential" parents include some who can never become actual. The crude death rate is not illogical in the same sense: all persons are mortal. But the probability of dying varies greatly according to age and sex, and in practice the two crude rates have the same virtues and limitations. They are simple to calculate from data often available, and if the effect of the population structure on fertility or mortality is not great, they give a good indication of what is happening. When a Western and

[7] Kuczynski, *The Balance*, 1, 17–19.

[8] George J. Stolnitz, "Uses of Crude Vital Rates in the Analysis of Reproductivity," *Journal of the American Statistical Association*, 50:272 (December, 1955), 1215–1234.

a non-Western country are compared, however, or a recent period with the past, then the difference in age structure is likely to be so large that a measure of mortality that takes it into account may be preferable. Apart from infant and other age-specific rates, and life expectation from various ages as derived in life tables, the principal tool in refining measures of mortality is **standardization.** This means, simply, holding the age structure (or other variable) constant while comparing the differential effect of other factors.

Suppose, for example, that in order to compare the relative efficiency of social welfare in the various states, we use as one index their crude death rates. Some of the differences among them, however, will be due to the extraneous fact that there are proportionately more elderly people, or more infants, in some states than in others. The usual way to remove this effect is to calculate the specific death rates of convenient age-groups for each of the states, multiply these by the number of persons in the same age-groups of the United States (the so-called standard population), thus deriving the number of deaths in each age-group that would have obtained if the age structure had been uniform throughout the country. For each state the total of such deaths per thousand population is its **standardized death rate.**[9]

The value of standardization is merely suggested by this example. It can be used to hold constant any variable while comparing the effect of any other, so long as these are expressed in figures and the data are available. Suppose, as another example, that we wanted to study the effect of occupations on marital status. It would be appropriate to standardize not only for age but also sex ratio, ethnic and religious homogeneity, and any other possibly relevant demographic characteristic.

The stable population, which was introduced together with intrinsic rates, is a concept of much wider application. For instance, we can distinguish three broad types of stable population—that is, three fixed patterns of interaction between population structure and fertility and mortality. They are: (a) **expansive,** with a broad base to the population pyramid, indicating a high proportion of children and a rapid rate of population growth; (b) **stationary,** with a narrower base to the population pyramid, indicating a moderate proportion of children and a slow or zero rate of growth; and (c) **constrictive,** with a base narrower than the middle of the pyramid, indicating a proportion of children insufficient to maintain the population.

In Figure A-1 three stylized pyramids are compared with three actual population structures that approximate their shape. The expansive type could have been exemplified as well by the structure of almost any other Asian or Latin American population. By 1947 Switzerland had already experienced a considerable increase in fertility, so that the bottom bar is longer than it ought to be to represent exactly the stationary type. Any one of several West European countries in the mid-1930's—

---

[9] This is the so-called direct method of standardization. If the data needed for it are not available, it is possible to achieve a similar result by multiplying the age-specific rates of the standard population by each age-group for the various states (the so-called indirect method). A more detailed discussion of standardization is included in almost any work on statistics. See, for example, Barclay, *op. cit.,* pp. 161–166, 175–177; A. J. Jaffe, *Handbook of Statistical Methods for Demographers: Selected Problems in the Analysis of Census Data* (U.S. Bureau of the Census; Washington: U.S. Government Printing Office, 1951), Ch. 3; Margaret J. Hagood, *Statistics for Sociologists* (New York: Reynal and Hitchcock, 1941), pp. 836 ff.

France, Germany, or England, for example, as well as Sweden—approximate the constrictive type fairly closely. The postwar revival of fertility in all of these countries has changed the shape of their population pyramids radically.

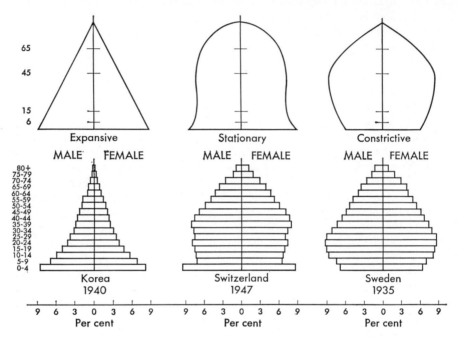

Figure A-1. Three Stylized Population Pyramids and Comparable Population Structures

The three types of population structure also approximate the three stages in the demographic transition of Western countries, corresponding to periods of actual or potential rapid growth, little or no growth, and actual or potential decline in numbers. One reason that demographers in the 1930's generally spoke of an "incipient decline" even of those Western countries—like the United States—whose population was still growing, was that they knew that this increase was more the consequence of the population structure than of the average family size. Once the large proportion of young adults—the temporary heritage of the high birth rates several decades earlier—was reduced, then the "true" vital rates would become actual. The analysis represented a considerable improvement in method; it failed only because the assumption that fertility would remain constant, or continue to decline, proved to be quite unrealistic.

INDEX

abortion. *See* birth control.
acculturation, Chap. 6
  defined, 147–148
  differential, 70
    by intermarriage, 144–147
    by language, 138–139
    by naturalization, 139–140
    by occupation, 126–127, 134–137,
      145–146
    by race, 338–340
    by religion, 100, 115, 120–121, 146–
      147, 368
    by universals, 138–142
    by voting record, 140–141
  facilitative factors in, 148–149, 158,
    613
  indexes of, 132–147
  melting pot, 114–115, 137, 144
  Old and New immigrants compared,
    93, 96–99, 129
  in Rome, 367–368, 371–372
  self-identification a factor in, 130–131
  social mobility and, 134–137, 367–368
  Soviet, 434
  success of, in U.S., 38, 114–115, 125,
    134, 148.
  See also individual ethnic groups; na-
    tivism.
Adams, Henry, 21–25
Adams, John, 88
Adams, Romanzo C., 146, 151
Adams, William F., 151
Aëtios, 551
Africa(ns), 86, 95, 141–142, 149, 328,
    334, 461–463, 465, 469–474, 500–
    501, 542n. *See also* Algeria, Egypt.
age:
  biologic vs. chronologic, 579
  classification of, 41–43, 78
  errors in reporting, 61, 71, 361n
  fertility and, 71, 75–76, 79, 164, 236–
    239, 251, 292, 294, 399, 533, 540,
    543, 594

age *(Cont.)*:
  groups, 76–83
  illiteracy by, 82
  index numbers of, 84
  labor force by, 43, 76, 78–79
  at marriage, 79, 83, 190, 212, 232–235,
    239, 292, 294, 354, 357–359, 398–
    400, 550, 562–565
  median, in U.S., 20–21, 25, 116–117,
    190–191
  migration and, 75, 77, 79, 82, 116–117,
    168, 169, 533, 593–594
  mortality and, 71, 75, 164, 250–263,
    366, 579–581
  sex ratio by, 82–83, 264–265, 565n,
    577.
  See also population structure.
aged:
  dependent, 80–83, 580–581
  health of, 82, 579–581
  in China, 81, 499
  migration of, 82
  number of, U.S., 80
  proportion of, 77, 80–81, 579–581
  retirement of, 78–79, 82, 117
  by sex, 82–83, 264–265, 565n, 577
  by social class, 82
aging:
  cause of, 80–81
  index of, 77, 81, 578–579
  in U.S., 77, 80–83
Aging, 85
Aging, Committee on, 85
Aging, Federal Council on, 85
agriculture:
  British, 382–385, 393
  Chinese, 372–373, 497–499
  hoe culture, 318–319
  origins of, 318–319, 323
  rain vs. irrigation, 320–321, 350–351,
    364, 460
  Soviet, 408, 410, 413–423, 434–435,
    448–452, 490

629